The Privacy Law Sourcebook 2001

United States Law, International Law, and Recent Developments

MARC ROTENBERG

Electronic Privacy Information Center

WASHINGTON DC

EPIC Publications
1718 Connecticut Ave. NW
Suite 200
Washington, DC 20009

Visit the EPIC Bookstore
http://www.epic.org/bookstore/

First edition 2001
Printed in the United States of America
All Rights Reserved

ISBN: 1-893044-12-2

Preface to 2001 Edition

The new edition of the *Privacy Law Sourcebook* is updated and expanded for 2001 with information about the EU Standard Contract Clauses for Transfers of Personal Data, recent privacy legislation in Eastern Europe, and the ILO Guidelines for the Protection of Worker's Personal Data. Also included are the final documents from the Safe Harbor agreement between the United States and Europe, the sections from the Financial Modernization Services Act concerning the protection of privacy, and several of the recent reports from the Article 29 Working Group, and other related materials. We have added new summaries and references for primary statutory materials and updated the listing of privacy organizations and online resources. The section on Recent Developments is entirely new for 2001.

In a continuing effort to keep the *Privacy Law Sourcebook* to one volume, we did not reprint certain materials that can be found in earlier editions. These include (from the *Privacy Law Sourcebook 2000*) the Italian Data Protection Act, the Council of Europe Guidelines for Internet Privacy, the Privacy Law of Chile, the Personal Information Protection Act of Canada, the UK Regulation of Investigative Powers Act and (from the *Privacy Law Sourcebook 1999*) the Freedom of Information and Protection of Privacy Act for British Columbia, the German Law for Information and Communication, and the Hong Kong Personal Data (Privacy) Ordinance. Readers are encouraged to consult the 2000 and 1999 editions for these materials.

The 2001 edition was prepared with the assistance of Sarah Andrews and the law students who participated in the Internet Public Interest Opportunities Program (IPIOP) during the past year. Please send comments, corrections, and suggestions to pls@epic.org.

Marc Rotenberg
Washington, DC
August 2001

Preface to First Edition

This collection provides a basic set of privacy materials for the United States and the international sphere. The materials are current as of the time of publication. Application of U.S. statutes and international instruments, such as the Council of Europe Convention, are subject to judicial interpretation and case decisions that are not included in this volume. Certain U.S. privacy laws, such as the Privacy Act of 1974, are qualified by federal regulations, which are also not included. The section on privacy resources provides information about how to locate additional legal material on privacy.

Several points should be made about the development of privacy laws. In the United States, privacy statutes have typically resulted from an effort by the legislative branch to address a matter left unresolved by the judicial branch or they have resulted from an attempt to codify a legal standard for privacy for commercial transactions in new technological services.

In the first category are such laws as the Right to Financial Privacy Act of 1978, the Privacy Protection Act of 1980, and to some extent, the Electronic Communication Privacy Act of 1986. These laws came about in response to decisions of the United States Supreme Court where the Court chose not establish a privacy right. Part of the development of privacy law in the United States is, therefore, the dialogue between the courts and the legislature on the proper scope of privacy as a legal claim.

In the second category are such laws as the Privacy Act of 1974, the Video Privacy Protection Act of 1988, the Employee Polygraph Protection Act of 1988, and the Telephone Consumer Protection Act of 1991. These statutes came about in direct response to new technologies that raised public concern and called for the establishment of legal standards to protect privacy.

The Electronic Communications Privacy Act is, in many respects, the most complex of US privacy laws. Its roots can be found in the dissent of Justice Brandeis in *Olmstead v. United States,* the first case in which the United States Supreme Court considered the Constitutionality of electronic surveillance. Title III of the Omnibus Crime Control Act of 1968, the precursor to ECPA, codified two decisions of the Supreme Court from the 1967 term and established the legislative framework for regulating electronic surveillance. In 1986 Title III was amended to include stored electronic mail and data in transit, and the name was changed to the "Electronic Communications Privacy Act." Then in 1994, the Act was once again amended to provide law enforcement access to electronic communications.

The Privacy Act of 1974 and the Freedom of Information Act, first enacted in 1966 and then significantly expanded in 1974, are a special case. These two laws were passed to give citizens rights of privacy and rights of access, two complimentary legal claims, in government record-keeping systems. They fall into a hybrid of the two categories described above: an attempt by Congress to establish legal rights in the absence of judicial decision-making and a response to new developments in technology.

The privacy materials provided here from the international sphere are of a different origin. In the first instance, they reflect a fundamental concern with human rights. This can be seen, for example, in Article 12 of the Universal Declaration of Human Rights that established privacy as a fundamental human right shortly after the end of World War II. Language similar to that found in Article 12 will be found in other international instruments on human rights, not included in this volume, such as the International Covenant on Civil and Political Rights (Article 17), the European Convention on Human Rights (Article 8), and the American Convention on Human Rights (Article 11). Many of these documents can be found at the web site of Privacy International.

In the second instance, international privacy law attempts to address the problem of privacy protection across national borders, what is sometimes called "transborder data flows."

The Council of Europe Convention, for example, and the European Data Directive set out privacy standards so that personal information is protected when it moves between nations. Commentators on international privacy law have often noted that the paradox of privacy is found in this need to protect data so that it may be exchanged more freely.

The guidelines of the Organization for Economic Cooperation and Development do not of themselves have the force of law. However, OECD principles have played an important role in directing the development of national law and helping to establish international legal norms. By way of example, the subscriber privacy provisions of the Cable Communications Policy Act adopted in the United States in 1984 follow closely the OECD Privacy Guidelines of 1980.

The Data Protection Directive of the European Union is the most significant development in privacy law in many years. It draws together several of the traditions in privacy law. Based on the precept that privacy is a fundamental human right, it establishes a common standard for privacy protection for the benefit of European citizens among the member states of the European Union. It also seeks to extend privacy standards to the new, rapidly evolving commercial environment. The critical question of how the European Commission will determine whether data may be transferred to countries that lack similar privacy standards is taken up in the Recent Developments section in a short piece prepared by a working group of the European Commission on the problem of "adequacy."

The Recent Developments section also looks at several attempts to extend privacy principles in the age of the Internet. The German Telecommunications law is the first privacy law specifically tailored to recent on-line developments. It is noteworthy in that it both applies traditional Fair Information Practices to new commercial services and also encourages the use of anonymous payment techniques.

The OECD Cryptography Guidelines cover one of the most interesting and rapidly developing areas in privacy law and policy. The technique to encode digital data offers the possibility that technology could protect privacy, a belief that runs contrary to the premise supporting most privacy law to date. An appropriate role for public policy may be to encourage its adoption. Cryptography also raises some new privacy issues. Both dimensions were considered in the development of the OECD Cryptography Guidelines.

Also included in this section is the pledge of database firms concerning the protection of personal privacy. This might not generally be considered appropriate for a volume of legal materials. It is included here to show one approach to privacy protection.

The Freedom of Information and Protection of Privacy Act for British Columbia is one of the most recent privacy laws adopted in North America. Its structure and scope provides a helpful example of the role of privacy and access law in our modern society. Recent developments include the growing presence of the US Federal Trade Commission in the enforcement of privacy policies. Excerpts from the Federal Trade Commission Act are included.

I am grateful to the Georgetown University Law Center for the opportunity to develop my course on information privacy law over the last several years and to the

Washington College of Law. Shauna Van Dongen, Lisa Harrinanan, and Dan Lin helped with the production of this volume. Privacy International and the Electronic Privacy Information Center provided excellent resources for privacy materials.

Marc Rotenberg
Washington, DC
August 1998

TABLE OF CONTENTS

UNITED STATES LAW   **1**

FAIR CREDIT REPORTING ACT (1970)   1
PRIVACY ACT (1974)   39
FREEDOM OF INFORMATION ACT (1974)   60
FAMILY EDUCATIONAL RIGHTS AND PRIVACY ACT (1974)   72
RIGHT TO FINANCIAL PRIVACY ACT (1978)   79
PRIVACY PROTECTION ACT (1980)   101
CABLE COMMUNICATIONS POLICY ACT (1984)   107
ELECTRONIC COMMUNICATIONS PRIVACY ACT (1986)   111
VIDEO PRIVACY PROTECTION ACT (1988)   165
EMPLOYEE POLYGRAPH PROTECTION ACT (1988)   168
TELEPHONE CONSUMER PROTECTION ACT (1991)   178
DRIVER'S PRIVACY PROTECTION ACT (1994)   188
TELECOMMUNICATIONS ACT (1996) [EXCERPT]   192
CHILDREN'S ONLINE PRIVACY PROTECTION ACT (1998)   196
FINANCIAL MODERNIZATION SERVICES ACT (1999) [EXCERPTS]   205
FEDERAL TRADE COMMISSION ACT (US)   222

INTERNATIONAL PRIVACY LAW   **256**

UNIVERSAL DECLARATION OF HUMAN RIGHTS (1948)   256
COUNCIIL OF EUROPE CONVENTION ON HUMAN RIGHTS (1950)   262
OECD PRIVACY GUIDELINES (1980)   268
COUNCIL OF EUROPE CONVENTION ON PRIVACY (1981)   297
UN GUIDELINES FOR PERSONAL DATA FILES (1990)   307
EU DATA PROTECTION DIRECTIVE (1995)   311
EU TELECOMMUNICATIONS PRIVACY DIRECTIVE (1997)   339
OECD CRYPTOGRAPHY GUIDELINES (1997)   351
GENERAL AGREEMENT ON TRADE IN SERVICES   362
PROTECTION OF WORKERS' PERSONAL DATA (1996)   364
PERSONAL DATA PROTECTION LAW (LATVIA 2000)   371
PROTECTION OF THE PERSONAL DATA (CZECH REPUBLIC 2000)   382

RECENT DEVELOPMENTS   **403**

OPINION 4/2001 ON DRAFT CONVENTION ON CYBER-CRIME   403
OPINION 3/2001 ON THE AUSTRALIAN PRIVACY ACT 2000   413
OPINION 2/2001 ON THE CANADIAN PERSONAL INFORMATION ACT   419
OPINION 7/2000 ON THE COMMUNICATIONA PRIVACY DIRECTIVE   432
STANDARD CONTRACTUAL CLAUSES FOR THE TRANSFER OF DATA   445
MATERIALS ON SAFE HARBOR ARRANGEMENT (2000)   461
ARTICLE 29 WORKING GROUP - FOURTH ANNUAL REPORT   536

SELECTED BIBLIOGRAPHY   **595**

PRIVACY RESOURCES   **598**

AGENCIES   598
NATIONAL LEGISLATION   601
ORGANIZATIONS   606
PUBLICATIONS   613
WEB SITES   615
INDEX OF PRIVACY RESOURCES   624

DETAILED TABLE OF CONTENTS

UNITED STATES LAW   1

FAIR CREDIT REPORTING ACT (1970)   1
Summary   *1*
References   *1*
§ 601. Short title   *2*
§ 602. Congressional findings and statement of purpose [15 U.S.C. § 1681]   *2*
§ 603. Definitions; rules of construction [15 U.S.C. § 1681a]   *2*
§ 604. Permissible purposes of consumer reports [15 U.S.C. § 1681b]   *7*
§ 605. Requirements relating to information contained in consumer reports
[15 U.S.C. § 1681c]   *11*
§ 606. Disclosure of investigative consumer reports [15 U.S.C. § 1681d]   *12*
§ 607. Compliance procedures [15 U.S.C. § 1681e]   *14*
§ 608. Disclosures to governmental agencies [15 U.S.C. § 1681f]   *15*
§ 609. Disclosures to consumers [15 U.S.C. § 1681g]   *15*
§ 610. Conditions and form of disclosure to consumers [15 U.S.C. § 1681h]   *17*
§ 611. Procedure in case of disputed accuracy [15 U.S.C. § 1681i]   *18*
§ 612. Charges for certain disclosures [15 U.S.C. § 1681j]   *22*
§ 613. Public record information for employment purposes [15 U.S.C. § 1681k]23
§ 614. Restrictions on investigative consumer reports [15 U.S.C. § 1681l]   *24*
§ 615. Requirements on users of consumer reports [15 U.S.C. § 1681m]   *24*
§ 616. Civil liability for willful noncompliance [15 U.S.C. § 1681n]   *27*
§ 617. Civil liability for negligent noncompliance [15 U.S.C. § 1681o]   *27*
§ 618. Jurisdiction of courts; limitation of actions [15 U.S.C. § 1681p]   *28*
§ 619. Obtaining information under false pretenses [15 U.S.C. § 1681q]   *28*
§ 620. Unauthorized disclosures by officers or employees [15 U.S.C. § 1681r]28
§ 621. Administrative enforcement [15 U.S.C. § 1681s]   *28*
§ 622. Information on overdue child support obligations [15 U.S.C. § 1681s-1]32
§ 623. Responsibilities of furnishers of information to consumer reporting
agencies [15 U.S.C. § 1681s-2]   *32*
§ 624. Relation to State laws [15 U.S.C. § 1681t]   *34*
§ 625. Disclosures to FBI for counterintelligence purposes [15 U.S.C. § 1681u]36
PRIVACY ACT (1974)   39
Summary   *39*
References   *40*
Congressional findings and statement of purpose   *40*
5 U.S.C. § 552a Public information; agency rules, opinions, orders, records, and
proceedings   *41*
    (a) Definitions   41
    (b) Conditions of Disclosure   43
    (c) Accounting of Certain Disclosures   44
    (d) Access to Records   45
    (e) Agency Requirements   46
    (f) Agency Rules   47
    (g) Civil Remedies   48
    (h) Rights of Legal Guardians   49
    (i) Criminal Penalties.   50
    (j) General Exemptions   50
    (k) Specific Exemptions   51

(l) Archival Records 52
(m) Government Contractors 52
(n) Mailing Lists 52
(o) Matching Agreements 53
(p) Verification and Opportunity to Contest Findings 54
(q) Sanctions 55
(r) Report on New Systems and Matching Programs 55
(s) Biennial Report 55
(t) Effect of Other Laws 56
(u) Data Integrity Boards 56
(v) Office of Management and Budget Responsibilities 58
Section 7 Disclosure of Social Security Number 58

FREEDOM OF INFORMATION ACT (1974) 60
Summary 60
References 60
§ 552. Public information; agency rules, opinions, orders, records, and
proceedings 61

FAMILY EDUCATIONAL RIGHTS AND PRIVACY ACT (1974) 72
Summary 72
20 U.S.C. § 1232g. Family educational and privacy rights 73
(a) Conditions for availability of funds to educational agencies or institutions; 73
(b) Release of education records; 75
(c) Surveys or data-gathering activities; regulations. 77
(d) Students' rather than parents' permission or consent. 78
(e) Informing parents or students of rights under this section. 78
(f) Enforcement; termination of assistance. 78
(g) Office and review board; creation; functions. 78

RIGHT TO FINANCIAL PRIVACY ACT (1978) 79
Summary 79
References 80
12 USC § 3401. Definitions 80
Sec. 3402. Access to financial records by Government authorities prohibited;
exceptions 81
Sec. 3403. Confidentiality of financial records 81
Sec. 3404. Customer authorizations 82
Sec. 3405. Administrative subpoena and summons 83
Sec. 3406. Search warrants 84
Sec. 3407. Judicial subpoena 85
Sec. 3408. Formal written request 85
Sec. 3409. Delayed notice 87
Sec. 3410. Customer challenges 88
Sec. 3411. Duty of financial institutions 90
Sec. 3412. Use of information 90
Sec. 3413. Exceptions 92
Sec. 3414. Special procedures 96
Sec. 3415. Cost reimbursement 98
Sec. 3416. Jurisdiction 98
Sec. 3417. Civil penalties 98
Sec. 3418. Injunctive relief 99
Sec. 3419. Suspension of limitations 99
Sec. 3420. Grand jury information; notification of certain persons prohibited 99
Sec. 3421. [Repealed] 100
Sec. 3422. Applicability to Securities and Exchange Commission 100

PRIVACY PROTECTION ACT (1980)   101
  Summary   101
  References   101
  42 U.S.C. 2000aa. Searches and seizures by government officers and employees
    in connection with investigation or prosecution of criminal offenses   101
  Sec. 2000aa-5. Border and customs searches   103
  Sec. 2000aa-6. Civil actions by aggrieved persons   103
  Sec. 2000aa-7. Definitions   104
  Sec. 2000aa-11. Guidelines for Federal officers and employees   105
  Sec. 2000aa-12. Binding nature of guidelines; disciplinary actions for
    violations; legal proceedings for non-compliance prohibited   106
CABLE COMMUNICATIONS POLICY ACT (1984)   107
  Summary   107
  References   107
  47 U.S.C. § 551. Protection of subscriber privacy   107
ELECTRONIC COMMUNICATIONS PRIVACY ACT (1986)   111
  Summary   111
  References   111
  Congressional Findings (1968)   112
  18 U.S.C. § 2510. Definitions   112
  Sec. 2511. Interception and disclosure of wire, oral, or electronic
    communications prohibited   115
  Sec. 2512. Manufacture, distribution, possession, and advertising of wire,
    oral, or electronic communication intercepting devices prohibited 121
  Sec. 2513. Confiscation of wire, oral, or electronic communication
    intercepting devices   122
  Sec. 2514. [Repealed]   122
  Sec. 2515. Prohibition of use as evidence of intercepted wire or oral
    communications   122
  Sec. 2516. Authorization for interception of wire, oral, or electronic
    communications   122
  Sec. 2517. Authorization for disclosure and use of intercepted wire, oral,
    or electronic communications   126
  Sec. 2518. Procedure for interception of wire, oral, or electronic
    communications   126
  Sec. 2519. Reports concerning intercepted wire, oral, or electronic
    communications   133
  Sec. 2520. Recovery of civil damages authorized   134
  Sec. 2521. Injunction against illegal interception   135
  Sec. 2522. Enforcement of the Communications Assistance for Law
    Enforcement Act   135
  Sec. 2701. Unlawful access to stored communications   136
  Sec. 2702. Disclosure of contents   137
  Sec. 2703. Requirements for governmental access   138
  Sec. 2704. Backup preservation   140
  Sec. 2705. Delayed notice   142
  Sec. 2706. Cost reimbursement   144
  Sec. 2707. Civil action   144
  Sec. 2708. Exclusivity of remedies   145
  Sec. 2709. Counterintelligence access to telephone toll and transactional
    records   145
  Sec. 2711. Definitions for chapter   147

Sec. 3121. General prohibition on pen register and trap and trace device use; exception 147

Sec. 3122. Application for an order for a pen register or a trap and trace device 147

Sec. 3123. Issuance of an order for a pen register or a trap and trace device ... 148

Sec. 3124. Assistance in installation and use of a pen register or a trap and trace device 149

Sec. 3125. Emergency pen register and trap and trace device installation ... 150

Sec. 3126. Reports concerning pen registers and trap and trace devices ... 151

Sec. 3127. Definitions for chapter 151

47 USC Sec. 1001. Definitions 152

Sec. 1002. Assistance capability requirements 153

Sec. 1003. Notices of capacity requirements 155

Sec. 1004. Systems security and integrity 156

Sec. 1005. Cooperation of equipment manufacturers and providers of telecommunications support services 157

Sec. 1006. Technical requirements and standards; extension of compliance date 157

Sec. 1007. Enforcement orders 159

Sec. 1008. Payment of costs of telecommunications carriers to comply with capability requirements 160

Sec. 1009. Authorization of appropriations 162

Sec. 1010. Reports 162

Sec. 1021. Department of Justice Telecommunications Carrier Compliance Fund 163

VIDEO PRIVACY PROTECTION ACT (1988) 165

Summary 165

References 165

18 U.S.C. § 2710. Wrongful disclosure of video tape rental or sale records ... 165

EMPLOYEE POLYGRAPH PROTECTION ACT (1988) 168

Summary 168

References 168

29 USC Sec. 2001. Definitions 168

Sec. 2002. Prohibitions on lie detector use 169

Sec. 2003. Notice of protection 170

Sec. 2004. Authority of Secretary 170

Sec. 2005. Enforcement provisions 170

Sec. 2006. Exemptions 171

Sec. 2007. Restrictions on use of exemptions 174

Sec. 2008. Disclosure of information 176

Sec. 2009. Effect on other law and agreements 177

TELEPHONE CONSUMER PROTECTION ACT (1991) 178

Summary 178

References 178

Congressional Statement of Findings 179

47 U.S.C. Sec. 227. Restrictions on use of telephone equipment 180

DRIVER'S PRIVACY PROTECTION ACT (1994) 188

Summary 188

References 188

18 U.S.C. § 2721. Prohibition on release and use of certain personal information from State motor vehicle records 189

Sec. 2722. Additional unlawful acts	*191*
Sec. 2723. Penalties	*191*
Sec. 2724. Civil action	*191*
Sec. 2725. Definitions	*191*
TELECOMMUNICATIONS ACT (1996) [EXCERPT]	192
Summary	*192*
References	*192*
Sec. 222. Privacy of customer information	*193*
CHILDREN'S ONLINE PRIVACY PROTECTION ACT (1998)	196
Summary	*196*
References	*196*
15 USC § 6501. Definitions	*196*
§ 6502. Regulation of unfair and deceptive acts and practices in connection with the collection and use of personal information from and about children on the Internet	*198*
§ 6503. Safe harbors	*201*
§ 6504. Actions by States	*201*
§ 6505. Administration and applicability of Act	*203*
FINANCIAL MODERNIZATION SERVICES ACT (1999) [EXCERPTS]	205
Summary	*205*
References	*206*
§ 501. Protection of non-public personal information.	*206*
§ 502. Obligations with respect to disclosures of personal information.	*207*
§ 503. Disclosure of institution privacy	*209*
§ 504. Rulemaking.	*210*
§ 505. Enforcement.	*210*
§ 506. Protection of fair credit reporting act	*212*
§ 507. Relation to state law	*212*
§ 508. Study of information sharing among financial affiliates.	*213*
§ 509. Definitions	*213*
§ 510. Effective date	*216*
§ 521. Privacy protection for customer information of financial institutions	*216*
§ 522. Administrative enforcement	*217*
§ 523. Criminal penalty	*218*
§ 524. Relation to state laws	*219*
§ 525. Agency guidance	*219*
§ 526. Reports	*219*
§ 527. Definitions	*220*
FEDERAL TRADE COMMISSION ACT (US)	222
Summary	*222*
References	*222*
§ 45. Unfair methods of competition unlawful; prevention by Commission	*222*
(a) Declaration of unlawfulness; power to prohibit unfair practices; inapplicability to foreign trade	222
(b) Proceeding by Commission; modifying and setting aside orders	223
(c) Review of order; rehearing	224
(d) Jurisdiction of court	225
(e) Exemption from liability	225
(f) Service of complaints, orders and other processes; return	225
(g) Finality of order	225
(h) Modification or setting aside of order by Supreme Court	227
(i) Modification or setting aside of order by Court of Appeals	227
(j) Rehearing upon order or remand	227

(k) "Mandate" defined 227

(l) Penalty for violation of order; injunctions and other appropriate equitable relief227

(m) Civil actions for recovery of penalties for knowing violations of rules and cease and desist orders respecting unfair or deceptive acts or practices; jurisdiction; maximum amount of penalties; continuing violations; de novo determinations; compromise or settlement procedure 228

(n) Standard of proof; public policy consideration 229

§ 46. *Additional powers of Commission* 229

(a) Investigation of persons, partnerships, or corporations 229

(b) Reports of persons, partnerships, and corporations 229

(c) Investigation of compliance with antitrust decrees. 230

(d) Investigations of violations of antitrust statutes 230

(e) Readjustment of business of corporations violating antitrust statutes. 230

(f) Publication of information; reports 230

(g) Classification of corporations; regulations 231

(h) Investigations of foreign trade conditions; reports 231

(i) Investigations of foreign antitrust law violations 231

§ 57a. *Unfair or deceptive acts or practices rulemaking proceedings.* 232

§ 57b. *Civil actions for violations of rules and cease and desist orders respecting unfair or deceptive acts or practices.* 240

§ 57b-1. *Civil investigative demands.* 242

§ 57b-2. *Confidentiality* 249

§ 57b-3. *Rulemaking process* 253

INTERNATIONAL PRIVACY LAW 256

UNIVERSAL DECLARATION OF HUMAN RIGHTS (1948) 256
Summary 256
References 256

COUNCIIL OF EUROPE CONVENTION FOR THE PROTECTION OF
HUMAN RIGHTS AND FUNDAMENTAL FREEDOMS (1950) 262
Summary 262
References 262
Article 1 – Obligation to respect human rights 263
Article 2 – Right to life 263
Article 3 – Prohibition of torture 263
Article 4 – Prohibition of slavery and forced labour 263
Article 5 – Right to liberty and security 263
Article 6 – Right to a fair trial 264
Article 7 – No punishment without law 265
Article 8 – Right to respect for private and family life 265
Article 9 – Freedom of thought, conscience and religion 265
Article 10 – Freedom of expression 265
Article 11 – Freedom of assembly and association 266
Article 12 – Right to marry 266
Article 13 – Right to an effective remedy 266
Article 14 – Prohibition of discrimination 266
Article 15 – Derogation in time of emergency 266
Article 16 – Restrictions on political activity of aliens 267
Article 17 – Prohibition of abuse of rights 267
Article 18 – Limitation on use of restrictions on rights 267

OECD PRIVACY GUIDELINES (1980) 268
Summary 268
References 268

GENERAL 270
  Definitions 270
  Scope of Guidelines 270
BASIC PRINCIPLES OF NATIONAL APPLICATION 271
  Collection Limitation Principle 271
  Data Quality Principle 271
  Purpose Specification Principle 271
  Use Limitation Principle 271
  Security Safeguards Principle 271
  Openness Principle 271
  Individual Participation Principle 272
  Accountability Principle 272
BASIC PRINCIPLES OF INTERNATIONAL APPLICATION: FREE FLOW
AND LEGITIMATE RESTRICTIONS 272
NATIONAL IMPLEMENTATION 273
INTERNATIONAL CO-OPERATION 273
APPENDIX 273
  Introduction 273
  I GENERAL BACKGROUND 274
    The Problems 274
    Activities at national level 275
    International aspects of privacy and data banks 276
    Relevant international activities 277
    Activities of the OECD 278
  II. THE GUIDELINES 280
    A. Purpose and Scope 280
    General 280
    Objectives 281
    Level of detail 281
    Non-Member countries 282
    The broader regulatory perspective 282
    Legal persons, groups and similar entities 282
    Automated and non-automated data 283
    General 284
COUNCIL OF EUROPE CONVENTION ON PRIVACY (1981) ... 297
  Summary 297
  References 297
  CHAPTER I – GENERAL PROVISIONS 298
    Article 1: Object and purpose 298
    Article 2: Definitions 298
    Article 3: Scope 298
  CHAPTER II - BASIC PRINCIPLES FOR DATA PROTECTION 299
    Article 4: Duties of the Parties 299
    Article 5: Quality of data 299
    Article 6: Special categories of data 300
    Article 7: Data security 300
    Article 8: Additional safeguards for the data subject . 300
    Article 9: Exceptions and restrictions 300
    Article 10: Sanctions and remedies 301
    Article 11: Extended protection 301
  CHAPTER III – TRANSBORDER DATA FLOWS 301
    Article 12: Transborder flows of personal data and domestic law . 301
  CHAPTER IV – MUTUAL ASSISTANCE 301
    Article 13: Co-operation between Parties 301
    Article 14: Assistance to data subjects resident abroad . 302

Article 15: Safeguards concerning assistance rendered by designated authorities 302
Article 16: Refusal of requests for assistance 302
Article 17: Costs and procedures of assistance 303
CHAPTER V – CONSULTATIVE COMMITTEE 303
Article 18: Composition of the committee 303
Article 19: Functions of the committee 303
Article 20: Procedure 303
CHAPTER VI – AMENDMENTS 304
Article 21: Amendments 304
CHAPTER VII – FINAL CLAUSES 304
Article 22: Entry into force 304
Article 23: Accession by non-member States 305
Article 24: Territorial clause 305
Article 25: Reservations 305
Article 26: Denunciation 305
Article 27: Notifications 305
UN GUIDELINES FOR THE REGULATION OF COMPUTERIZED
PERSONAL FILES (1990) 307
Summary 307
A. PRINCIPLES CONCERNING THE MINIMUM GUARANTEES THAT
SHOULD BE PROVIDED IN NATIONAL LEGISLATIONS 307
1. Principle of lawfulness and fairness 307
2. Principle of accuracy 308
3. Principle of the purpose-specification 308
4. Principle of interested-person access 308
5. Principle of non-discrimination 308
6. Power to make exceptions 308
7. Principle of security 309
8. Supervision and sanctions 309
9. Transborder data flows 309
10. Field of application 309
B. APPLICATION OF THE GUIDELINES TO PERSONAL DATA FILES
KEPT BY GOVERNMENTAL INTERNATIONAL ORGANIZATIONS 309
EUROPEAN UNION DATA PROTECTION DIRECTIVE (1995) 311
Summary 311
References 311
CHAPTER I: GENERAL PROVISIONS 322
Article 1 Object of the Directive 322
Article 2 Definitions 322
Article 3 Scope 323
Article 4 National law applicable 323
CHAPTER II: GENERAL RULES ON THE LAWFULNESS OF THE
PROCESSING OF PERSONAL DATA 323
SECTION 1: PRINCIPLES RELATING TO DATA QUALITY 324
Article 6 324
SECTION II PRINCIPLES RELATING TO THE REASONS FOR MAKING
DATA PROCESSING LEGITIMATE 324
Article 7 324
SECTION III SPECIAL CATEGORIES OF PROCESSING 325
Article 8 The processing of special categories of data 325
Article 9 Processing of personal data and freedom of expression 326
SECTION IV INFORMATION TO BE GIVEN TO THE DATA SUBJECT 326
Article 10 Information in cases of collection of data from the data subject 326
Article 11 Information where the data have not been obtained from the
data subject 326

SECTION V THE DATA SUBJECT'S RIGHT OF ACCESS TO DATA 327
    Article 12 Right of access 327
SECTION VI: EXEMPTIONS AND RESTRICTIONS 327
    Article 13: Exemptions and restrictions 327
SECTION VII: THE DATA SUBJECT'S RIGHT TO OBJECT 328
    Article 14 The data subject's right to object 328
    Article 15: Automated individual decisions 328
SECTION VIII: CONFIDENTIALITY AND SECURITY OF PROCESSING 329
    Article 16 Confidentiality of processing 329
    Article 17 Security of processing 329
SECTION IX: NOTIFICATION 330
    Article 18 Obligation to notify the supervisory authority 330
    Article 19 Contents of notification 330
    Article 20 Prior checking 331
    Article 21 Publicizing of processing operations 331
CHAPTER III JUDICIAL REMEDIES, LIABILITY AND PENALTIES *331*
    Article 22 Remedies 331
    Article 23 Liability 332
    Article 24 Sanctions 332
CHAPTER IV TRANSFER OF PERSONAL DATA TO THIRD COUNTRIES *332*
    Article 25 Principles 332
    Article 26 Derogations 333
CHAPTER V CODES OF CONDUCT *334*
    Article 27 334
CHAPTER VI SUPERVISORY AUTHORITY AND WORKING PARTY ON THE
PROTECTION OF INDIVIDUALS WITH REGARD TO THE PROCESSING OF
PERSONAL DATA *334*
    Article 28 Supervisory authority 334
    Article 29 Working Party on the Protection of Individuals with regard to
    the Processing of Personal Data 335
    Article 30 336
CHAPTER VII COMMUNITY IMPLEMENTING MEASURES *337*
    Article 31 The Committee 337
FINAL PROVISIONS *337*
    Article 32 337
    Article 33 338
    Article 34 338
EUROPEAN UNION DIRECTIVE FOR THE PROTECTION OF PRIVACY
IN THE TELECOMMUNICATIONS SECTOR (1997) 339
    References *339*
    Article 1 - Object and scope *344*
    Article 2 - Definitions *344*
    Article 3 - Services concerned *344*
    Article 4 - Security *345*
    Article 5 - Confidentiality of the communications *345*
    Article 6 - Traffic and billing data *345*
    Article 7 - Itemized billing *346*
    Article 8 - Presentation and restriction of calling and connected line
     identification *346*
    Article 9 - Exceptions *347*
    Article 10 - Automatic call forwarding *347*
    Article 11 - Directories of subscribers *347*
    Article 12 - Unsolicited calls *348*
    Article 13 - Technical features and standardisation *348*

Article 14 - Extension of the scope of application of certain provisions of Directive 95/46/EC   *348*
Article 15 - Implementation of the Directive   *349*
Article 16 - Addressees   *349*
ANNEX - List of data   *350*
OECD CRYPTOGRAPHY GUIDELINES (1997)   351
Summary   *351*
References   *352*
I. AIMS   *355*
II. SCOPE   *355*
III. DEFINITIONS   *355*
IV. INTEGRATION   *357*
V. PRINCIPLES   *357*
    1. TRUST IN CRYPTOGRAPHIC METHODS   357
    2. CHOICE OF CRYPTOGRAPHIC METHODS   357
    3. MARKET DRIVEN DEVELOPMENT OF CRYPTOGRAPHIC METHODS   358
    4. STANDARDS FOR CRYPTOGRAPHIC METHODS   358
    5. PROTECTION OF PRIVACY AND PERSONAL DATA   359
    6. LAWFUL ACCESS   359
    7. LIABILITY   360
    8. INTERNATIONAL CO-OPERATION   360

GENERAL AGREEMENT ON TRADE IN SERVICES (1994) [EXCERPT]   **362**

Reference   *362*
Article XIV General Exceptions   *362*
PROTECTION OF WORKERS' PERSONAL DATA (1996)   364
    1. Preamble   *364*
    2. Purpose   *364*
    3. Definitions   *364*
    4. Scope of application   *365*
    5. General principles   *365*
    6. Collection of personal data   *365*
    7. Security of personal data   *367*
    8. Storage of personal data   *367*
    9. Use of personal data   *368*
    10. Communication of personal data   *368*
    11. Individual rights   *369*
    12. Collective rights   *370*
    13. Employment agencies   *370*
PERSONAL DATA PROTECTION LAW   371
    CHAPTER I-GENERAL PROVISIONS   *371*
      Section 1   371
      Section 2   371
      Section 3   372
      Section 4   372
      Section 5   372
    CHAPTER II - GENERAL PRINCIPLES FOR PERSONAL DATA PROCESSING   *372*
      Section 6   372
      Section 7   372
      Section 8   373
      Section 9   373

Section 10	373
Section 11	374
Section 12	374
Section 13	374
Section 14	375
CHAPTER III - RIGHTS OF A DATA SUBJECT	375
Section 15	375
Section 16	376
Section 17	376
Section 18	376
Section 19	376
Section 20	376
CHAPTER IV - REGISTRATION AND PROTECTION OF A PERSONAL DATA PROCESSING SYSTEM	377
Section 21	377
Section 22	377
Section 23	378
Section 24	378
Section 25	378
Section 26	378
Section 27	379
Section 28	379
Section 29	379
Section 30	380
Section 31	381
Section 32	381
PROTECTION OF THE PERSONAL DATA (2000)	382
PART ONE	382
PERSONAL DATA PROTECTION	382
Article 1 - Purpose of the Act	382
Article 2	382
Article 3 - Scope of the Act	382
Article 4 - Definition of Terms	383
Article 5	384
Article 6	386
Article 7	386
Article 8	386
Article 9 - Sensitive Data	387
Article 10	387
Article 11	387
Article 12	388
Article 13 - Obligations of Persons when Securing the Personal Data	389
Article 14	389
Article 15	389
Article 16 - Notification Obligation	389
Article 17	390
Article 18	391
Article 19	391
Article 20 - Liquidation of the Personal Data	391
Article 21 - Protection of the Data Subjects' Rights	391
Article 22	392
Article 23 - Remedy of Non-material Detriment	392
Article 24	392
Article 25 - Indemnity	392
Article 26	393
Article 27	393

Article 28   394
Article 29   394
Article 30   395
Article 31   395
Article 32 - Chairman of the Office   395
Article 33 - The Office's Inspectors   396
Article 34   396
Article 35   397
Article 36 - Annual Report   397
Article 37 - Authorities of the Supervisors   397
Article 38 - Obligations of the Supervisors   398
Article 39   399
Article 40 - Remedial Measures   399
Article 41   400
Article 42   400
Article 43 - Authorities and Responsibilities in the Course of Inspection   400
Article 44 - Offences   400
Article 45 - Disciplinary Penalty   400
Article 46 - Penalties to Controllers and Processors   400
Article 47 - Measures for a Transitional Period   401
Article 48 - Repealing Provision   401
PART TWO   401
Article 49 - Amendment to the Criminal Code   401
PART THREE   402
Article 50 - Amendment of the Act on Free Access to Information   402
PART FOUR   402
Article 51 - Effectiveness   402

RECENT DEVELOPMENTS   **403**

OPINION 4/2001 ON THE COUNCIL OF EUROPE'S DRAFT CONVENTION ON
CYBER-CRIME   403
    Introduction   403
    The Draft Convention   404
    Human Rights, Privacy and Data Protection   405
    Traffic data   408
    Conclusions   410
OPINION 3/2001 ON THE LEVEL OF PROTECTION OF THE AUSTRALIAN PRIVACY
AMENDMENT (PRIVATE SECTOR) ACT 2000   413
    Introduction   413
    Privacy Amendment (Private Sector) Act 2000   414
    Sectors and activities excluded   414
    Employee data: 415
    Exceptions: 415
    Publicly available data: 416
    Transparency to data subjects: 416
    Collection and use of data in particular with regard to direct marketing 416
    Sensitive data   417
    Lack of correction rights for EU citizens   417
    Onward transfers from Australia to other third countries   417
    Conclusions   418
OPINION 2/2001 ON THE ADEQUACY OF THE CANADIAN PERSONAL
INFORMATION AND ELECTRONIC DOCUMENTS ACT   419
    Introduction   419
    Scope of the Act   420
    Sensitive Data: 421
    Employment data   422

Interaction with Provincial legislation and Onward transfers   423
Conclusions   424
Annex 1 Provincial and Territorial Information Protection Legislation   *425*
OPINION 7/2000 ON THE EUROPEAN COMMISSION PROPOSAL FOR A DIRECTIVE
OF THE EUROPEAN PARLIAMENT AND OF THE COUNCIL CONCERNING THE
PROCESSING OF PERSONAL DATA AND THE PROTECTION OF PRIVACY IN THE
ELECTRONIC COMMUNICATIONS SECTOR OF 12 JULY 2000 COM (2000) 385   432
Reference   *432*
1. Introduction   *432*
2. Analysis of the draft directive   *433*
Article 1 - Objective and Scope and Article 3 - Services concerned   433
Article 2 - Definitions   434
Article 4 - Security   436
Article 5 - Confidentiality of Communications   437
Article 6 - Traffic data and billing data   437
Article 7 - Itemised billing   438
Article 9 - Location data   438
Article 10 - Exceptions   439
Article 12-Directories of Subscribers   440
Article 13 - Unsolicited Communications   441
Article 14 - Technical features and standardisation (and recital 22)   442
Transparency   *443*
3. Conclusions   *443*
COMMISSION DECISION ON STANDARD CONTRACTUAL CLAUSES FOR THE
TRANSFER OF PERSONAL DATA TO THIRD COUNTRIES UNDER DIRECTIVE 95/46/EC445
Reference   *445*
Article 1   448
Article 2   449
Article 3   449
Article 5   450
Article 6   450
Article 7   450
ANNEX   450
Standard contractual clauses   450
Clause 1 - Definitions   451
Clause 2 - Details of the Transfer   451
Clause 3 - Third-party beneficiary clause   452
Clause 4 - Obligations of the Data Exporter   452
Clause 5 - Obligations of the Data Importer   452
Clause 6 - Liability   453
Clause 7 - Mediation and Jurisdiction   453
Clause 8 - Cooperation with Supervisory Authorities   454
Clause 9 - Termination of the Clauses   454
Clause 10 - Governing Law   454
Clause 11 - Variation of the contract   454
MATERIALS ON SAFE HARBOR ARRANGEMENT (2000)   461
Reference   *461*
SAFE HARBOR PRIVACY PRINCIPLES ISSUED BY THE U.S.
DEPARTMENT OF COMMERCE ON JULY 21, 2000   *461*
Frequently Asked Questions   *465*
FAQ 1 - Sensitive Data   465
FAQ 2 - Journalistic Exceptions   465
FAQ 3 - Secondary Liability   465
FAQ 4 - Investment banking and audits   465
FAQ 5 - The Role of the Data Protection Authorities   466

FAQ 6 - Self-Certification   468
FAQ 7 - Verification   469
FAQ 8 - Access   470
FAQ 9 - Human Resources   474
FAQ 10 - Article 17 contracts   476
FAQ 11 - Dispute Resolution and Enforcement   476
FAQ 12 - Choice - Timing of Opt Out   479
FAQ 13 - Travel Information   479
FAQ 14 - Pharmaceutical and Medical Products   480
FAQ 15- Public Record and Publicly Available Information   481

*Letter from U.S. Department of Commerce to Commission Services
transmitting the Safe Harbor Privacy Principles and FAQs, etc.*   *482*
Safe Harbor Enforcement Overview   *484*
*Department of Commerce Memorandum on Damages for Breaches of Privacy,
Legal Authorizations and Mergers and Takeovers in U.S. Law*   *492*
*Letter from the Federal Trade Commission concerning its jurisdiction over
consumer privacy issues*   *504*
*Letter from the Department of Transportation concerning its authority in
protecting the privacy of consumers with respect to information*   *513*
*Letter from Commission Services transmitting the European Commission's
Adequacy Finding*   *515*
*European Commission's decision C(2000) 2441 finding the safe harbor to
provide adequate protection*   *520*
    Article 1   522
    Article 2   523
    Article 3   523
    Article 4   524
    Article 5   524
    Article 6   524
    Annex VII   525
*Text on Non-Discrimination adopted by the Article 31 Committee on
May 31, 2000*   *526*
*Text on Non-Discrimination adopted by the Article 29 Working Party on
February 3, 2000*   *528*
*European Parliament resolution on the Draft Commission Decision on the
adequacy of the protection provided by the Safe Harbour Privacy Principles
and related Frequently Asked Questions issued by the US Department of
Commerce*   *529*
    The meaning of data protection in the framework of the competences of
    the Union   529
    The data protection system used in the United States   532
    The nature and scope of the enforceability of the safe harbour   532
ARTICLE 29 WORKING GROUP - FOURTH ANNUAL REPORT   536
1. INTRODUCTION   *536*
2. DEVELOPMENTS IN EU ON PRIVACY AND DATA PROTECTION   *538*
2.1 Directive 95/46/EC   *538*
    2.1.1 Implementation into national law   538
    Austria   538
    Belgium   538
    Denmark   539
    Finland   539
    France   539
    Germany   539
    Italy   539

Ireland 541
Luxembourg 541
Portugal 541
Spain 541
Sweden 541
The Netherlands 541
The United Kingdom 541
2.1.2 Infringement proceedings 542
2.2 *Directive 97/66/EC* 542
2.2.1 Implementation into national law 542
Austria 542
Belgium 542
Denmark 543
Finland 543
France 543
Germany 543
Italy 543
Ireland 543
Luxembourg 543
Portugal 543
Spain 544
Sweden 544
The Netherlands 544
The United Kingdom 544
2.2.2 Infringement proceedings 544
2.3 *Issues addressed by the Article 29 Data Protection Working Party* 544
2.3.1 Transfer of data to third countries 545
2.3.1.1 United States of America: Safe Harbor Principles 546
January 1999 546
April-May 547
June 547
July 1999 547
December 1999 548
2.3.1.2 Switzerland 549
2.3.1.3 Hungary
2.3.1.4 The Working Party entered into preliminary discussions on the level
of protection in Hong Kong, Norway and Iceland. 550
2.3.2 Working documents about the ICC and CBI model contractual clauses 550
2.3.3 Internet and Telecommunications 551
2.3.3.1 Working document on processing of personal data on the Internet 551
2.3.3.2 Recommendation on Invisible and Automated Processing on the Internet 552
2.3.3.3 Recommendation 2/99 on privacy in interceptions 553
2.3.3.4 Recommendation 3/99 on the preservation of traffic data by the
Internet Service Providers for law enforcement purposes 554
2.3.4 P3P seminar 555
2.3.5 Public sector information 556
2.3.6 Codes of conduct 557
FEDMA 557
IATA 558
2.3.7 EU Charta on Fundamental Rights 558
2.4 *Main developments in Member States* 558
AUSTRIA 559
A. Legislative measures adopted in Austria under the first pillar (this is
excluding Directive 95/46/EC and 97/66/EC) 559
B. Changes made in Austria under the second and third pillar 560
BELGIUM 560

A. Legislative measures adopted in Belgium under the first pillar (excluding Directive 95/46/EC and 97/66/EC)   560
B. Changes made in Belgium under the second and third pillar   560
C. Major case law   561
D. Specific issues   561
E. Website   562
DENMARK   562
A. Legislative measures adopted in Denmark under the first pillar (excluding Directives 95/46/EC and Directive 97/66/EC)   562
B. Changes made in Denmark under the second and third pillar of the EU None562
C. Major case law   562
D. Specific issues   562
E. Website   563
FINLAND   563
A. Legislative measures adopted in Finland under the first pillar (excluding Directives 95/46/EC and 97/66/EC)   563
B. Changes made in Finland under the second and third pillar   563
C. Major case law   563
D. Specific issues   563
E. Website   564
FRANCE   564
A. Legislative measures adopted in France under the first pillar (excluding Directives 95/46/EC and 97/66/EC)   564
B. Changes made in France under the second and third pillar   565
C. Major case law   565
D. Specific issues   566
E. Website   567
GERMANY   567
A. Legislative measures adopted in Germany under the first pillar (excluding Directives 95/46/EC and 97/66/EC)   567
B. Changes made in Germany under the second and third pillar   567
C. Major case law   567
D. Specific issues   567
E. Website   568
GREECE   568
Conditions for the lawful processing of personal data as regards the purposes of direct marketing/advertising and the ascertainment of credibility   568
Non-inclusion of religion beliefs and other personal data in identity cards   569
Decision on fingerprints   570
IRELAND   571
A. Legislative measures adopted in Ireland under the first pillar of the EU (excluding Directives 95/46/EC and 97/66/EC)   571
B. Changes made in Ireland under the second and third pillar of the EU   571
C. Major case law   571
D. Specific issues   571
E. Website   572
ITALY   572
A. Legislative measures adopted in Italy under the first pillar (excluding Directives 95/46/EC and 97/66/EC)   572
B. Changes made in Italy under the second and third pillar of the EU   572
C. Major case law   572
D. Specific issues   573
E. Website   574
PORTUGAL   574
B. Changes made in Portugal under the second and third pillar   574
C. Major case law   574
4. Website   574

SPAIN   574
A. Legislative measures adopted in Spain under the first pillar of the EU
(excluding Directives 95/46/EC and 97/66/EC)   574
B. Changes made in Spain under the second and third pillar of the EU   575
C. Major case law   575
D. Specific issues   576
E. Website   580
SWEDEN   580
A. Legislative measures in Sweden under the first pillar of the EU (excluding
Directives 95/46/EC and Directive 97/66/EC)   580
B. Changes made in Sweden under the second and third pillar of the EU   580
C. Major case law   580
D. Specific issues   581
E. Website   581
THE NETHERLANDS   582
A. Legislative measures adopted in the Netherlands under the first pillar of
the EU (excluding Directives 95/46/EC and 97/66/EC)   582
B. Changes made in the Netherlands under the second and third pillar of the EU 582
C. Major case law   582
D. Specific issues   582
Most important publications   583
E. Websites   583
THE UNITED KINGDOM   584
A. Legislative measures adopted in the United Kingdom under the first pillar
of the EU (excluding Directives 95/46/EC and 97/66/EC)   584
B. Changes made in the United Kingdom under the second and third pillar of
the EU   584
C. Major case law   584
D. Specific issues   584
E. Website   584
2.5 Community activities   584
2.5.1 Draft Regulation on Data Protection in Community Institutions and bodies 584
2.5.2 Electronic Signatures Directive   585
2.5.3 Electronic Commerce Directive   586
2.5.4 Transparency Directive 98/34/EC   587
2.5.5 Telecom review 1999   587
2.5.6 Standardisation   588
2.5.7 Privacy Enhancing Technologies   588
2.5.8 Europol   588
3. THE COUNCIL OF EUROPE   588
4. PRINCIPAL DEVELOPMENTS IN THIRD COUNTRIES   589
4.1 European Economic Area   589
4.1.1 Iceland   589
A. Legislative measures adopted in 1999 in your country under the first
pillar of the EU   589
B. Changes made in Iceland under the second and third pillar of the EU   590
C. Major case law (national courts) /jurisprudence   590
D. Specific issues   590
E. Website   590
4.1.2 Norway   590
A. Legislative measures adopted in 1999 in your country under the first
pillar of the EU   590
B. Changes made in Iceland under the second and third pillar of the EU   590
C. Major case law (national courts) /jurisprudence   591
D. Specific issues   591
E. Website   591

    4.2 Acceding Countries   *591*

    4.3 United States of America   *592*

    4.4 Other third countries   *592*

        4.4.1 Australia   *592*

        4.4.2 Canada   *592*

        4.4.3 Japan   *593*

        4.4.4 Hungary   *593*

        4.4.5 Switzerland   *593*

    5. OTHER DEVELOPMENTS AT INTERNATIONAL LEVEL   *593*

    5.1 Organisation for Economic Co-operation and Development (OECD)

    Conference on electronic commerce   *593*

    5.2 World Trade Organisation (WTO)   *594*

    5.3 Word Intellectual Property Organisation (WIPO)   *594*

    6. ANNEXES   *594*

SELECTED BIBLIOGRAPHY   **595**

        Books   595

        Law Review Symposia   597

PRIVACY RESOURCES   **598**

AGENCIES   598

   Australia   *598*

   Austria   *598*

   Belgium   *598*

   Canada   *598*

   Czech Republic   *598*

   Denmark   *598*

   Estonia   *598*

   Finland   *599*

   France   *599*

   Germany   *599*

   Greece   *599*

   Hong Kong   *599*

   Hungary   *599*

   Iceland   *599*

   Ireland   *599*

   Israel   *600*

   Italy   *600*

   Japan   *600*

   Luxembourg   *600*

   Lithuania   *600*

   Netherlands   *600*

   New Zealand   *600*

   Norway   *600*

   Poland   *601*

   Portugal   *601*

   Slovak Republic   *601*

   Spain   *601*

   Sweden   *601*

   Switzerlandd   *601*

   Taiwan   *601*

   United Kingdom   *601*

NATIONAL LEGISLATION 601
    References 602
ORGANIZATIONS 606
    US Organizations 606
    International Organizations 611
PUBLICATIONS 613
    US Publications 614
    International Publications 614
    Reports 615
WEB SITES 615
    General Interest 615
    Government 619
    Legal 620
    Organizations 621
INDEX OF PRIVACY RESOURCES 624

United States Law

FAIR CREDIT REPORTING ACT (1970)

Summary

Congress passed the Fair Credit Reporting Act of 1970 to protect individuals from the misuse of personal information by Credit Reporting Agencies, or CRAs. Under the Act, CRAs may only disclose personal information to persons whom they have reason to believe intend to use the information to evaluate an application for credit, employment, insurance, license, or governmental benefit. Notice must be given to an individual when the CRA is asked to procure extensive information on the individual's character and habits, if this information is being procured to evaluate initial eligibility for a benefit. Individuals are entitled to a copy of their credit report, and if errors or discrepancies are found, the CRA must investigate and correct them.

The Act also provides guidelines for the information that can be gathered, and how long it may be maintained within a credit report. For example, bankruptcy can only be reported for ten years, whereas information about criminal convictions may be reported indefinitely. A private action may be brought for any violation of the act, regardless of damages. The Federal Trade Commission is charged with enforcement of the Act.

By the 1990s, many commentators believed the FCRA needed to be updated to bring it into line with new developments in banking and in technology. In 1996, Congress amended the FCRA, in the Consumer Credit Reporting Reform Act. The CCRRA allows for greater sharing of information between affiliate-entities without their becoming CRAs within the meaning of the Act. The CCRRA also tightens some loopholes in the pre-existing FCRA, imposes new obligations on businesses to ensure the accuracy of reports, and increases civil and criminal penalties. The CCRRA also provides for extensive preemption of state laws dealing with credit reporting, where the CCRRA also deals with the issue.

References

Public Law 91-508, as amended by Public Law 104-208 (Sept. 30, 1996)
[http://www.ftc.gov/os/statutes/fcra.htm]

FTC, Summary of Consumer Rights under the FCRA
[http://www.ftc.gov/bcp/conline/edcams/fcra/summary.htm]

FTC, Consumer's Brochure on the FCRA
[http://www.ftc.gov/bcp/conline/pubs/credit/fcra.htm]

United States
Fair Credit Reporting Act

§ 601. Short title

This title may be cited as the Fair Credit Reporting Act.

§ 602. Congressional findings and statement of purpose [15 U.S.C. § 1681]

(a) Accuracy and fairness of credit reporting. The Congress makes the following findings:

(1) The banking system is dependent upon fair and accurate credit reporting. Inaccurate credit reports directly impair the efficiency of the banking system, and unfair credit reporting methods undermine the public confidence which is essential to the continued functioning of the banking system.

(2) An elaborate mechanism has been developed for investigating and evaluating the credit worthiness, credit standing, credit capacity, character, and general reputation of consumers.

(3) Consumer reporting agencies have assumed a vital role in assembling and evaluating consumer credit and other information on consumers.

(4) There is a need to insure that consumer reporting agencies exercise their grave responsibilities with fairness, impartiality, and a respect for the consumer's right to privacy.

(b) Reasonable procedures. It is the purpose of this title to require that consumer reporting agencies adopt reasonable procedures for meeting the needs of commerce for consumer credit, personnel, insurance, and other information in a manner which is fair and equitable to the consumer, with regard to the confidentiality, accuracy, relevancy, and proper utilization of such information in accordance with the requirements of this title.

§ 603. Definitions; rules of construction [15 U.S.C. § 1681a]

(a) Definitions and rules of construction set forth in this section are applicable for the purposes of this title.

(b) The term "person" means any individual, partnership, corporation, trust, estate, cooperative, association, government or governmental subdivision or agency, or other entity.

(c) The term "consumer" means an individual.

(d) Consumer report.

(1) In general. The term "consumer report" means any written, oral, or other communication of any information by a consumer reporting agency bearing on a consumer's credit worthiness, credit standing, credit capacity, character, general reputation, personal characteristics, or mode of living which is used or expected to be used or collected in whole or in part for the purpose of serving as a factor in establishing the consumer's eligibility for

(A) credit or insurance to be used primarily for personal, family, or household purposes;

(B) employment purposes; or

(C) any other purpose authorized under section 604 [§ 1681b].

(2) Exclusions. The term "consumer report" does not include

(A) any

    (i) report containing information solely as to transactions or experiences between the consumer and the person making the report;

    (ii) communication of that information among persons related by common ownership or affiliated by corporate control; or

    (iii) any communication of other information among persons related by common ownership or affiliated by corporate control if it is clearly and conspicuously disclosed to the consumer that the information may be communicated among such persons and the consumer is given the opportunity, before the time that the information is initially communicated, to direct that such information not be communicated among such persons;

(B) any authorization or approval of a specific extension of credit directly or indirectly by the issuer of a credit card or similar device;

(C) any report in which a person who has been requested by a third party to make a specific extension of credit directly or indirectly to a consumer conveys his or her decision with respect to such request, if the third party advises the consumer of the name and address of the person to whom the request was made, and such person makes the disclosures to the consumer required under section 615 [§ 1681m]; or

(D) a communication described in subsection (o).

(e) The term "investigative consumer report" means a consumer report or portion thereof in which information on a consumer's character, general reputation, personal characteristics, or mode of living is obtained through personal interviews with neighbors, friends, or associates of the consumer reported on or with others with whom he is acquainted or who may have knowledge concerning any such items of information. However, such information shall not include specific factual information on a consumer's credit record obtained directly from a creditor of the consumer or from a consumer reporting agency when such information was obtained directly from a creditor of the consumer or from the consumer.

(f) The term "consumer reporting agency" means any person which, for monetary fees, dues, or on a cooperative nonprofit basis, regularly engages in whole or in part in the practice of assembling or evaluating consumer credit information or other information on consumers for the purpose of furnishing consumer reports to third parties, and which uses any means or facility of interstate commerce for the purpose of preparing or furnishing consumer reports.

(g) The term "file," when used in connection with information on any consumer, means all of the information on that consumer recorded and retained by a consumer reporting agency regardless of how the information is stored.

(h) The term "employment purposes" when used in connection with a consumer report means a report used for the purpose of evaluating a consumer for employment, promotion, reassignment or retention as an employee.

(i) The term "medical information" means information or records obtained, with the consent of the individual to whom it relates, from licensed physicians or medical practitioners, hospitals, clinics, or other medical or medically related facilities.

(j) Definitions relating to child support obligations.

(1) Overdue support. The term "overdue support" has the meaning given to such term in section 666(e) of title 42 [Social Security Act, 42 U.S.C. § 666(e)].

(2) State or local child support enforcement agency. The term "State or local child support enforcement agency" means a State or local agency which administers a State or local program for establishing and enforcing child support obligations.

(k) Adverse action.

(1) Actions included. The term "adverse action"

(A) has the same meaning as in section 701(d)(6) of the Equal Credit Opportunity Act; and

(B) means

(i) a denial or cancellation of, an increase in any charge for, or a reduction or other adverse or unfavorable change in the terms of coverage or amount of, any insurance, existing or applied for, in connection with the underwriting of insurance;

(ii) a denial of employment or any other decision for employment purposes that adversely affects any current or prospective employee;

(iii) a denial or cancellation of, an increase in any charge for, or any other adverse or unfavorable change in the terms of, any license or benefit described in section 604(a)(3)(D) [§ 1681b]; and

(iv) an action taken or determination that is

(I) made in connection with an application that was made by, or a transaction that was initiated by, any consumer, or in connection with a review of an account under section 604(a)(3)(F)(ii)[§ 1681b]; and

(II) adverse to the interests of the consumer.

(2) Applicable findings, decisions, commentary, and orders. For purposes of any determination of whether an action is an adverse action under paragraph (1)(A), all appropriate final findings, decisions, commentary, and orders issued under section 701(d)(6) of the Equal Credit Opportunity Act by the Board of Governors of the Federal Reserve System or any court shall apply.

(l) Firm offer of credit or insurance. The term "firm offer of credit or insurance" means any offer of credit or insurance to a consumer that will be honored if the consumer is determined, based on information in a consumer report on the consumer, to meet the specific criteria used to select the consumer for the offer, except that the offer may be further conditioned on one or more of the following:

(1) The consumer being determined, based on information in the consumer's application for the credit or insurance, to meet specific criteria bearing on credit worthiness or insurability, as applicable, that are established

(A) before selection of the consumer for the offer; and

(B) for the purpose of determining whether to extend credit or insurance pursuant to the offer.

(2) Verification

(A) that the consumer continues to meet the specific criteria used to select the consumer for the offer, by using information in a consumer report on the consumer, information in the consumer's application for the credit or insurance, or other information bearing on the credit worthiness or insurability of the consumer; or

(B) of the information in the consumer's application for the credit or insurance, to determine that the consumer meets the specific criteria bearing on credit worthiness or insurability.

(3) The consumer furnishing any collateral that is a requirement for the extension of the credit or insurance that was

(A) established before selection of the consumer for the offer of credit or insurance; and

(B) disclosed to the consumer in the offer of credit or insurance.

(m) Credit or insurance transaction that is not initiated by the consumer. The term "credit or insurance transaction that is not initiated by the consumer" does not include the use of a consumer report by a person with which the consumer has an account or insurance policy, for purposes of

(1) reviewing the account or insurance policy; or

(2) collecting the account.

(n) State. The term "State" means any State, the Commonwealth of Puerto Rico, the District of Columbia, and any territory or possession of the United States.

(o) Excluded communications. A communication is described in this subsection if it is a communication

(1) that, but for subsection (d)(2)(E),(1) would be an investigative consumer report;

(2) that is made to a prospective employer for the purpose of

(A) procuring an employee for the employer; or

(B) procuring an opportunity for a natural person to work for the employer;

(3) that is made by a person who regularly performs such procurement;

(4) that is not used by any person for any purpose other than a purpose described in subparagraph (A) or (B) of paragraph (2); or

(5) with respect to which

(A) the consumer who is the subject of the communication

(i) consents orally or in writing to the nature and scope of the communication, before the collection of any information for the purpose of making the communication;

(ii) consents orally or in writing to the making of the communication to a prospective employer, before the making of the communication; and

(iii) in the case of consent under clause (i) or (ii) given orally, is provided written confirmation of that consent by the person making the communication, not later than 3 business days after the receipt of the consent by that person;

(B) the person who makes the communication does not, for the purpose of making the communication, make any inquiry that if made by a prospective employer of the consumer who is the subject of the communication would violate any applicable Federal or State equal employment opportunity law or regulation; and

(C) the person who makes the communication

(i) discloses in writing to the consumer who is the subject of the communication, not later than 5 business days after receiving any request from the consumer for such disclosure, the nature and substance of all information in the consumer's file at the time of the request, except that the sources of any information that is acquired solely for use in making the communication and is actually used for no other purpose, need not be disclosed other than under appropriate discovery procedures in any court of competent jurisdiction in which an action is brought; and

(ii) notifies the consumer who is the subject of the communication, in writing, of the consumer's right to request the information described in clause (i).

(p) Consumer reporting agency that compiles and maintains files on consumers on a nationwide basis. The term "consumer reporting agency that compiles and maintains files on consumers on a nationwide basis" means a consumer reporting agency that regularly engages in the practice of assembling or evaluating, and maintaining, for the purpose of furnishing consumer reports to third parties bearing on a consumer's credit worthiness, credit standing, or credit capacity, each of the following regarding consumers residing nationwide:

(1) Public record information.

(2) Credit account information from persons who furnish that information regularly and in the ordinary course of business.

§ 604. Permissible purposes of consumer reports [15 U.S.C. § 1681b]

(a) In general. Subject to subsection (c), any consumer reporting agency may furnish a consumer report under the following circumstances and no other:

(1) In response to the order of a court having jurisdiction to issue such an order, or a subpoena issued in connection with proceedings before a Federal grand jury.

(2) In accordance with the written instructions of the consumer to whom it relates.

(3) To a person which it has reason to believe

(A) intends to use the information in connection with a credit transaction involving the consumer on whom the information is to be furnished and involving the extension of credit to, or review or collection of an account of, the consumer; or

(B) intends to use the information for employment purposes; or

(C) intends to use the information in connection with the underwriting of insurance involving the consumer; or

(D) intends to use the information in connection with a determination of the consumer's eligibility for a license or other benefit granted by a governmental instrumentality required by law to consider an applicant's financial responsibility or status; or

(E) intends to use the information, as a potential investor or servicer, or current insurer, in connection with a valuation of, or an assessment of the credit or prepayment risks associated with, an existing credit obligation; or

(F) otherwise has a legitimate business need for the information

(i) in connection with a business transaction that is initiated by the consumer; or

(ii) to review an account to determine whether the consumer continues to meet the terms of the account.

(4) In response to a request by the head of a State or local child support enforcement agency (or a State or local government official authorized by the head of such an agency), if the person making the request certifies to the consumer reporting agency that

(A) the consumer report is needed for the purpose of establishing an individual's capacity to make child support payments or determining the appropriate level of such payments;

(B) the paternity of the consumer for the child to which the obligation relates has been established or acknowledged by the consumer in accordance with State laws under which the obligation arises (if required by those laws);

(C) the person has provided at least 10 days' prior notice to the consumer whose report is requested, by certified or registered mail to the last known address of the consumer, that the report will be requested; and

(D) the consumer report will be kept confidential, will be used solely for a purpose described in subparagraph (A), and will not be used in connection with any other civil, administrative, or criminal proceeding, or for any other purpose.

(5) To an agency administering a State plan under Section 454 of the Social Security Act (42 U.S.C. § 654) for use to set an initial or modified child support award.

(b) Conditions for furnishing and using consumer reports for employment purposes.

(1) Certification from user. A consumer reporting agency may furnish a consumer report for employment purposes only if

(A) the person who obtains such report from the agency certifies to the agency that

(i) the person has complied with paragraph (2) with respect to the consumer report, and the person will comply with paragraph (3) with respect to the consumer report if paragraph (3) becomes applicable; and

(ii) information from the consumer report will not be used in violation of any applicable Federal or State equal employment opportunity law or regulation; and

(B) the consumer reporting agency provides with the report a summary of the consumer's rights under this title, as prescribed by the Federal Trade Commission under section 609(c)(3) [§ 1681g].

(2) Disclosure to consumer. A person may not procure a consumer report, or cause a consumer report to be procured, for employment purposes with respect to any consumer, unless

(A) a clear and conspicuous disclosure has been made in writing to the consumer at any time before the report is procured or caused to be procured, in a document that consists solely of the disclosure, that a consumer report may be obtained for employment purposes; and

(B) the consumer has authorized in writing the procurement of the report by that person.

(3) Conditions on use for adverse actions. In using a consumer report for employment purposes, before taking any adverse action based in whole or in part on the report, the person intending to take such adverse action shall provide to the consumer to whom the report relates

(A) a copy of the report; and

(B) a description in writing of the rights of the consumer under this title, as prescribed by the Federal Trade Commission under section 609(c)(3) [§ 1681g].

(c) Furnishing reports in connection with credit or insurance transactions that are not initiated by the consumer.

(1) In general. A consumer reporting agency may furnish a consumer report relating to any consumer pursuant to subparagraph (A) or (C) of subsection

(a)(3) in connection with any credit or insurance transaction that is not initiated by the consumer only if

(A) the consumer authorizes the agency to provide such report to such person; or

(B) (i) the transaction consists of a firm offer of credit or insurance;

(ii) the consumer reporting agency has complied with subsection (e); and

(iii) there is not in effect an election by the consumer, made in accordance with subsection (e), to have the consumer's name and address excluded from lists of names provided by the agency pursuant to this paragraph.

(2) Limits on information received under paragraph (1)(B). A person may receive pursuant to paragraph (1)(B) only

(A) the name and address of a consumer;

(B) an identifier that is not unique to the consumer and that is used by the person solely for the purpose of verifying the identity of the consumer; and

(C) other information pertaining to a consumer that does not identify the relationship or experience of the consumer with respect to a particular creditor or other entity.

(3) Information regarding inquiries. Except as provided in section 609(a)(5) [§ 1681g], a consumer reporting agency shall not furnish to any person a record of inquiries in connection with a credit or insurance transaction that is not initiated by a consumer.

(d) Reserved.

(e) Election of consumer to be excluded from lists.

(1) In general. A consumer may elect to have the consumer's name and address excluded from any list provided by a consumer reporting agency under subsection (c)(1)(B) in connection with a credit or insurance transaction that is not initiated by the consumer, by notifying the agency in accordance with paragraph (2) that the consumer does not consent to any use of a consumer report relating to the consumer in connection with any credit or insurance transaction that is not initiated by the consumer.

(2) Manner of notification. A consumer shall notify a consumer reporting agency under paragraph (1)

(A) through the notification system maintained by the agency under paragraph (5); or

(B) by submitting to the agency a signed notice of election form issued by the agency for purposes of this subparagraph.

(3) Response of agency after notification through system. Upon receipt of notification of the election of a consumer under paragraph (1) through the notification system maintained by the agency under paragraph (5), a consumer reporting agency shall

(A) inform the consumer that the election is effective only for the 2-year period following the election if the consumer does not submit to the agency a signed notice of election form issued by the agency for purposes of paragraph (2)(B); and

(B) provide to the consumer a notice of election form, if requested by the consumer, not later than 5 business days after receipt of the notification of the election through the system established under paragraph (5), in the case of a request made at the time the consumer provides notification through the system.

(4) Effectiveness of election. An election of a consumer under paragraph (1)

(A) shall be effective with respect to a consumer reporting agency beginning 5 business days after the date on which the consumer notifies the agency in accordance with paragraph (2);

(B) shall be effective with respect to a consumer reporting agency

(i) subject to subparagraph (C), during the 2-year period beginning 5 business days after the date on which the consumer notifies the agency of the election, in the case of an election for which a consumer notifies the agency only in accordance with paragraph (2)(A); or

(ii) until the consumer notifies the agency under subparagraph (C), in the case of an election for which a consumer notifies the agency in accordance with paragraph (2)(B);

(C) shall not be effective after the date on which the consumer notifies the agency, through the notification system established by the agency under paragraph (5), that the election is no longer effective; and

(D) shall be effective with respect to each affiliate of the agency.

(5) Notification system.

(A) In general. Each consumer reporting agency that, under subsection (c)(1)(B), furnishes a consumer report in connection with a credit or insurance transaction that is not initiated by a consumer, shall

(i) establish and maintain a notification system, including a toll-free telephone number, which permits any consumer whose consumer report is maintained by the agency to notify the agency, with appropriate identification, of the consumer's election to have the consumer's name and address excluded from any such list of names and addresses provided by the agency for such a transaction; and

(ii) publish by not later than 365 days after the date of enactment of the Consumer Credit Reporting Reform Act of 1996, and not less than annually thereafter, in a publication of general circulation in the area served by the agency

(I) a notification that information in consumer files maintained by the agency may be used in connection with such transactions; and

(II) the address and toll-free telephone number for consumers to use to notify the agency of the consumer's election under clause (i).

(B) Establishment and maintenance as compliance. Establishment and maintenance of a notification system (including a toll-free telephone number) and publication by a consumer reporting agency on the agency's own behalf and on behalf of any of its affiliates in accordance with this paragraph is deemed to be compliance with this paragraph by each of those affiliates.

(6) Notification system by agencies that operate nationwide. Each consumer reporting agency that compiles and maintains files on consumers on a nationwide basis shall establish and maintain a notification system for purposes of paragraph (5) jointly with other such consumer reporting agencies.

(f) Certain use or obtaining of information prohibited. A person shall not use or obtain a consumer report for any purpose unless

(1) the consumer report is obtained for a purpose for which the consumer report is authorized to be furnished under this section; and

(2) the purpose is certified in accordance with section 607 [§ 1681e] by a prospective user of the report through a general or specific certification.

(g) Furnishing reports containing medical information. A consumer reporting agency shall not furnish for employment purposes, or in connection with a credit or insurance transaction or a direct marketing transaction, a consumer report that contains medical information about a consumer, unless the consumer consents to the furnishing of the report.

§ 605. Requirements relating to information contained in consumer reports [15 U.S.C. § 1681c]

(a) Information excluded from consumer reports. Except as authorized under subsection (b) of this section, no consumer reporting agency may make any consumer report containing any of the following items of information:

(1) Cases under title 11 [United States Code] or under the Bankruptcy Act that, from the date of entry of the order for relief or the date of adjudication, as the case may be, antedate the report by more than 10 years.

(2) Suits and judgments which, from date of entry, antedate the report by more than seven years or until the governing statute of limitations has expired, whichever is the longer period.

(3) Paid tax liens which, from date of payment, antedate the report by more than seven years.

(4) Accounts placed for collection or charged to profit and loss which antedate the report by more than seven years.

(5) Records of arrest, indictment, or conviction of crime which, from date of disposition, release, or parole, antedate the report by more than seven years.

(6) Any other adverse item of information which antedates the report by more than seven years.

(b) Exempted cases. The provisions of subsection (a) of this section are not applicable in the case of any consumer credit report to be used in connection with

(1) a credit transaction involving, or which may reasonably be expected to involve, a principal amount of $150,000 or more;

(2) the underwriting of life insurance involving, or which may reasonably be expected to involve, a face amount of $150,000 or more; or

(3) the employment of any individual at an annual salary which equals, or which may reasonably be expected to equal $75,000, or more.

(c) Running of reporting period.

(1) In general. The 7-year period referred to in paragraphs (4) and (6) of subsection (a) shall begin, with respect to any delinquent account that is placed for collection (internally or by referral to a third party, whichever is earlier), charged to profit and loss, or subjected to any similar action, upon the expiration of the 180-day period beginning on the date of the commencement of the delinquency which immediately preceded the collection activity, charge to profit and loss, or similar action.

(2) Effective date. Paragraph (1) shall apply only to items of information added to the file of a consumer on or after the date that is 455 days after the date of enactment of the Consumer Credit Reporting Reform Act of 1996.

(d) Information required to be disclosed. Any consumer reporting agency that furnishes a consumer report that contains information regarding any case involving the consumer that arises under title 11, United States Code, shall include in the report an identification of the chapter of such title 11 under which such case arises if provided by the source of the information. If any case arising or filed under title 11, United States Code, is withdrawn by the consumer before a final judgment, the consumer reporting agency shall include in the report that such case or filing was withdrawn upon receipt of documentation certifying such withdrawal.

(e) Indication of closure of account by consumer. If a consumer reporting agency is notified pursuant to section 623(a)(4) [§ 1681s-2] that a credit account of a consumer was voluntarily closed by the consumer, the agency shall indicate that fact in any consumer report that includes information related to the account.

(f) Indication of dispute by consumer. If a consumer reporting agency is notified pursuant to section 623(a)(3) [§ 1681s-2] that information regarding a consumer who was furnished to the agency is disputed by the consumer, the agency shall indicate that fact in each consumer report that includes the disputed information.

§ 606. Disclosure of investigative consumer reports [15 U.S.C. § 1681d]

(a) Disclosure of fact of preparation. A person may not procure or cause to be prepared an investigative consumer report on any consumer unless

(1) it is clearly and accurately disclosed to the consumer that an investigative consumer report including information as to his character, general reputation, personal characteristics and mode of living, whichever are applicable, may be made, and such disclosure

(A) is made in a writing mailed, or otherwise delivered, to the consumer, not later than three days after the date on which the report was first requested, and

(B) includes a statement informing the consumer of his right to request the additional disclosures provided for under subsection (b) of this section and the written summary of the rights of the consumer prepared pursuant to section 609(c) [§ 1681g]; and

(2) the person certifies or has certified to the consumer reporting agency that

(A) the person has made the disclosures to the consumer required by paragraph (1); and

(B) the person will comply with subsection (b).

(b) Disclosure on request of nature and scope of investigation. Any person who procures or causes to be prepared an investigative consumer report on any consumer shall, upon written request made by the consumer within a reasonable period of time after the receipt by him of the disclosure required by subsection (a) (1) of this section, shall(3) make a complete and accurate disclosure of the nature and scope of the investigation requested. This disclosure shall be made in a writing mailed, or otherwise delivered, to the consumer not later than five days after the date on which the request for such disclosure was received from the consumer or such report was first requested, whichever is the later.

(c) Limitation on liability upon showing of reasonable procedures for compliance with provisions. No person may be held liable for any violation of subsection (a) or (b) of this section if he shows by a preponderance of the evidence that at the time of the violation he maintained reasonable procedures to assure compliance with subsection (a) or (b) of this section.

(d) Prohibitions.

(1) Certification. A consumer reporting agency shall not prepare or furnish investigative consumer report unless the agency has received a certification under subsection (a)(2) from the person who requested the report.

(2) Inquiries. A consumer reporting agency shall not make an inquiry for the purpose of preparing an investigative consumer report on a consumer for employment purposes if the making of the inquiry by an employer or prospective employer of the consumer would violate any applicable Federal or State equal employment opportunity law or regulation.

(3) Certain public record information. Except as otherwise provided in section 613 [§ 1681k], a consumer reporting agency shall not furnish an investigative consumer report that includes information that is a matter of public record and that relates to an arrest, indictment, conviction, civil judicial action, tax lien, or

outstanding judgment, unless the agency has verified the accuracy of the information during the 30-day period ending on the date on which the report is furnished.

(4) Certain adverse information. A consumer reporting agency shall not prepare or furnish an investigative consumer report on a consumer that contains information that is adverse to the interest of the consumer and that is obtained through a personal interview with a neighbor, friend, or associate of the consumer or with another person with whom the consumer is acquainted or who has knowledge of such item of information, unless

(A) the agency has followed reasonable procedures to obtain confirmation of the information, from an additional source that has independent and direct knowledge of the information; or

(B) the person interviewed is the best possible source of the information.

§ 607. Compliance procedures [15 U.S.C. § 1681e]

(a) Identity and purposes of credit users. Every consumer reporting agency shall maintain reasonable procedures designed to avoid violations of section 605 [§ 1681c] and to limit the furnishing of consumer reports to the purposes listed under section 604 [§ 1681b] of this title. These procedures shall require that prospective users of the information identify themselves, certify the purposes for which the information is sought, and certify that the information will be used for no other purpose. Every consumer reporting agency shall make a reasonable effort to verify the identity of a new prospective user and the uses certified by such prospective user prior to furnishing such user a consumer report. No consumer reporting agency may furnish a consumer report to any person if it has reasonable grounds for believing that the consumer report will not be used for a purpose listed in section 604 [§ 1681b] of this title.

(b) Accuracy of report. Whenever a consumer reporting agency prepares a consumer report it shall follow reasonable procedures to assure maximum possible accuracy of the information concerning the individual about whom the report relates.

(c) Disclosure of consumer reports by users allowed. A consumer reporting agency may not prohibit a user of a consumer report furnished by the agency on a consumer from disclosing the contents of the report to the consumer, if adverse action against the consumer has been taken by the user based in whole or in part on the report.

(d) Notice to users and furnishers of information.

(1) Notice requirement. A consumer reporting agency shall provide to any person

(A) who regularly and in the ordinary course of business furnishes information to the agency with respect to any consumer; or

(B) to whom a consumer report is provided by the agency; a notice of such person's responsibilities under this title.

(2) Content of notice. The Federal Trade Commission shall prescribe the content of notices under paragraph (1), and a consumer reporting agency shall be in compliance with this subsection if it provides a notice under paragraph (1) that is substantially similar to the Federal Trade Commission prescription under this paragraph.

(e) Procurement of consumer report for resale.

(1) Disclosure. A person may not procure a consumer report for purposes of reselling the report (or any information in the report) unless the person discloses to the consumer reporting agency that originally furnishes the report

(A) the identity of the end-user of the report (or information); and

(B) each permissible purpose under section 604 [§ 1681b] for which the report is furnished to the end-user of the report (or information).

(2) Responsibilities of procurers for resale. A person who procures a consumer report for purposes of reselling the report (or any information in the report) shall

(A) establish and comply with reasonable procedures designed to ensure that the report (or information) is resold by the person only for a purpose for which the report may be furnished under section 604 [§ 1681b], including by requiring that each person to which the report (or information) is resold and that resells or provides the report (or information) to any other person

(i) identifies each end user of the resold report (or information);

(ii) certifies each purpose for which the report (or information) will be used; and

(iii) certifies that the report (or information) will be used for no other purpose; and

(B) before reselling the report, make reasonable efforts to verify the identifications and certifications made under subparagraph (A).

§ 608. Disclosures to governmental agencies [15 U.S.C. § 1681f]

Notwithstanding the provisions of section 604 [§ 1681b] of this title, a consumer reporting agency may furnish identifying information respecting any consumer, limited to his name, address, former addresses, places of employment, or former places of employment, to a governmental agency.

§ 609. Disclosures to consumers [15 U.S.C. § 1681g]

(a) Information on file; sources; report recipients. Every consumer reporting agency shall, upon request, and subject to 610(a)(1) [§ 1681h], clearly and accurately disclose to the consumer:

(1) All information in the consumer's file at the time of the request, except that nothing in this paragraph shall be construed to require a consumer reporting agency

to disclose to a consumer any information concerning credit scores or any other risk scores or predictors relating to the consumer.

(2) The sources of the information; except that the sources of information acquired solely for use in preparing an investigative consumer report and actually used for no other purpose need not be disclosed: Provided, That in the event an action is brought under this title, such sources shall be available to the plaintiff under appropriate discovery procedures in the court in which the action is brought.

(3)

    (A) Identification of each person (including each end-user identified under section 607(e)(1) [§ 1681e]) that procured a consumer report

        (i) for employment purposes, during the 2-year period preceding the date on which the request is made; or

        (ii) for any other purpose, during the 1-year period preceding the date on which the request is made.

    (B) An identification of a person under subparagraph (A) shall include

        (i) the name of the person or, if applicable, the trade name (written in full) under which such person conducts business; and

        (ii) upon request of the consumer, the address and telephone number of the person.

(4) The dates, original payees, and amounts of any checks upon which is based any adverse characterization of the consumer, included in the file at the time of the disclosure.

(5) A record of all inquiries received by the agency during the 1-year period preceding the request that identified the consumer in connection with a credit or insurance transaction that was not initiated by the consumer.

(b) Exempt information. The requirements of subsection (a) of this section respecting the disclosure of sources of information and the recipients of consumer reports do not apply to information received or consumer reports furnished prior to the effective date of this title except to the extent that the matter involved is contained in the files of the consumer reporting agency on that date.

(c) Summary of rights required to be included with disclosure.

    (1) Summary of rights. A consumer reporting agency shall provide to a consumer, with each written disclosure by the agency to the consumer under this section

        (A) a written summary of all of the rights that the consumer has under this title; and

        (B) in the case of a consumer reporting agency that compiles and maintains files on consumers on a nationwide basis, a toll-free telephone number established by the agency, at which personnel are accessible to consumers during normal business hours.

    (2) Specific items required to be included. The summary of rights required under paragraph (1) shall include

(A) a brief description of this title and all rights of consumers under this title;

(B) an explanation of how the consumer may exercise the rights of the consumer under this title;

(C) a list of all Federal agencies responsible for enforcing any provision of this title and the address and any appropriate phone number of each such agency, in a form that will assist the consumer in selecting the appropriate agency;

(D) a statement that the consumer may have additional rights under State law and that the consumer may wish to contact a State or local consumer protection agency or a State attorney general to learn of those rights; and

(E) a statement that a consumer reporting agency is not required to remove accurate derogatory information from a consumer's file, unless the information is outdated under section 605 [§ 1681c] or cannot be verified.

(3) Form of summary of rights. For purposes of this subsection and any disclosure by a consumer reporting agency required under this title with respect to consumers' rights, the Federal Trade Commission (after consultation with each Federal agency referred to in section 621(b) [§ 1681s]) shall prescribe the form and content of any such disclosure of the rights of consumers required under this title. A consumer reporting agency shall be in compliance with this subsection if it provides disclosures under paragraph (1) that are substantially similar to the Federal Trade Commission prescription under this paragraph.

(4) Effectiveness. No disclosures shall be required under this subsection until the date on which the Federal Trade Commission prescribes the form and content of such disclosures under paragraph (3).

§ 610. Conditions and form of disclosure to consumers [15 U.S.C. § 1681h]

(a) In general.

(1) Proper identification. A consumer reporting agency shall require, as a condition of making the disclosures required under section 609 [§ 1681g], that the consumer furnish proper identification.

(2) Disclosure in writing. Except as provided in subsection (b), the disclosures required to be made under section 609 [§ 1681g] shall be provided under that section in writing.

(b) Other forms of disclosure.

(1) In general. If authorized by a consumer, a consumer reporting agency may make the disclosures required under 609 [§ 1681g]

(A) other than in writing; and

(B) in such form as may be

(i) specified by the consumer in accordance with paragraph (2); and

(ii) available from the agency.

(2) Form. A consumer may specify pursuant to paragraph (1) that disclosures under section 609 [§ 1681g] shall be made

(A) in person, upon the appearance of the consumer at the place of business of the consumer reporting agency where disclosures are regularly provided, during normal business hours, and on reasonable notice;

(B) by telephone, if the consumer has made a written request for disclosure by telephone;

(C) by electronic means, if available from the agency; or

(D) by any other reasonable means that is available from the agency.

(c) Trained personnel. Any consumer reporting agency shall provide trained personnel to explain to the consumer any information furnished to him pursuant to section 609 [§ 1681g] of this title.

(d) Persons accompanying consumer. The consumer shall be permitted to be accompanied by one other person of his choosing, who shall furnish reasonable identification. A consumer reporting agency may require the consumer to furnish a written statement granting permission to the consumer reporting agency to discuss the consumer's file in such person's presence.

(e) Limitation of liability. Except as provided in sections 616 and 617 [§§ 1681n and 1681o] of this title, no consumer may bring any action or proceeding in the nature of defamation, invasion of privacy, or negligence with respect to the reporting of information against any consumer reporting agency, any user of information, or any person who furnishes information to a consumer reporting agency, based on information disclosed pursuant to section 609, 610, or 615 [§§ 1681g, 1681h, or 1681m] of this title or based on information disclosed by a user of a consumer report to or for a consumer against whom the user has taken adverse action, based in whole or in part on the report, except as to false information furnished with malice or willful intent to injure such consumer.

§ 611. Procedure in case of disputed accuracy [15 U.S.C. § 1681i]

(a) Reinvestigations of disputed information.

(1) Reinvestigation required.

(A) In general. If the completeness or accuracy of any item of information contained in a consumer's file at a consumer reporting agency is disputed by the consumer and the consumer notifies the agency directly of such dispute, the agency shall reinvestigate free of charge and record the current status of the disputed information, or delete the item from the file in accordance with paragraph (5), before the end of the 30-day period beginning on the date on which the agency receives the notice of the dispute from the consumer.

(B) Extension of period to reinvestigate. Except as provided in subparagraph (C), the 30-day period described in subparagraph (A) may be extended for not more than 15 additional days if the consumer reporting agency receives information from the consumer during that 30-day period that is relevant to the reinvestigation.

(C) Limitations on extension of period to reinvestigate. Subparagraph (B) shall not apply to any reinvestigation in which, during the 30-day period described in subparagraph (A), the information that is the subject of the reinvestigation is found to be inaccurate or incomplete or the consumer reporting agency determines that the information cannot be verified.

(2) Prompt notice of dispute to furnisher of information.

(A) In general. Before the expiration of the 5-business-day period beginning on the date on which a consumer reporting agency receives notice of a dispute from any consumer in accordance with paragraph (1), the agency shall provide notification of the dispute to any person who provided any item of information in dispute, at the address and in the manner established with the person. The notice shall include all relevant information regarding the dispute that the agency has received from the consumer.

(B) Provision of other information from consumer. The consumer reporting agency shall promptly provide to the person who provided the information in dispute all relevant information regarding the dispute that is received by the agency from the consumer after the period referred to in subparagraph (A) and before the end of the period referred to in paragraph (1)(A).

(3) Determination that dispute is frivolous or irrelevant.

(A) In general. Notwithstanding paragraph (1), a consumer reporting agency may terminate a reinvestigation of information disputed by a consumer under that paragraph if the agency reasonably determines that the dispute by the consumer is frivolous or irrelevant, including by reason of a failure by a consumer to provide sufficient information to investigate the disputed information.

(B) Notice of determination. Upon making any determination in accordance with subparagraph (A) that a dispute is frivolous or irrelevant, a consumer reporting agency shall notify the consumer of such determination not later than 5 business days after making such determination, by mail or, if authorized by the consumer for that purpose, by any other means available to the agency.

(C) Contents of notice. A notice under subparagraph (B) shall include

(i) the reasons for the determination under subparagraph (A); and

(ii) identification of any information required to investigate the disputed information, which may consist of a standardized form describing the general nature of such information.

(4) Consideration of consumer information. In conducting any reinvestigation under paragraph (1) with respect to disputed information in the file of any consumer, the consumer reporting agency shall review and consider all relevant

United States
Fair Credit Reporting Act

information submitted by the consumer in the period described in paragraph (1)(A) with respect to such disputed information.

(5) Treatment of inaccurate or unverifiable information.

   (A) In general. If, after any reinvestigation under paragraph (1) of any information disputed by a consumer, an item of the information is found to be inaccurate or incomplete or cannot be verified, the consumer reporting agency shall promptly delete that item of information from the consumer's file or modify that item of information, as appropriate, based on the results of the reinvestigation.

   (B) Requirements relating to reinsertion of previously deleted material.

   (i) Certification of accuracy of information. If any information is deleted from a consumer's file pursuant to subparagraph (A), the information may not be reinserted in the file by the consumer reporting agency unless the person who furnishes the information certifies that the information is complete and accurate.

   (ii) Notice to consumer. If any information that has been deleted from a consumer's file pursuant to subparagraph (A) is reinserted in the file, the consumer reporting agency shall notify the consumer of the reinsertion in writing not later than 5 business days after the reinsertion or, if authorized by the consumer for that purpose, by any other means available to the agency.

   (iii) Additional information. As part of, or in addition to, the notice under clause (ii), a consumer reporting agency shall provide to a consumer in writing not later than 5 business days after the date of the reinsertion

      (I) a statement that the disputed information has been reinserted;

      (II) the business name and address of any furnisher of information contacted and the telephone number of such furnisher, if reasonably available, or of any furnisher of information that contacted the consumer reporting agency, in connection with the reinsertion of such information; and

      (III) a notice that the consumer has the right to add a statement to the consumer's file disputing the accuracy or completeness of the disputed information.

   (C) Procedures to prevent reappearance. A consumer reporting agency shall maintain reasonable procedures designed to prevent the reappearance in a consumer's file, and in consumer reports on the consumer, of information that is deleted pursuant to this paragraph (other than information that is reinserted in accordance with subparagraph (B)(i)).

   (D) Automated reinvestigation system. Any consumer reporting agency that compiles and maintains files on consumers on a nationwide basis shall implement an automated system through which furnishers of information to

The Privacy Law Sourcebook 2001   20

that consumer reporting agency may report the results of a reinvestigation that finds incomplete or inaccurate information in a consumer's file to other such consumer reporting agencies.

(6) Notice of results of reinvestigation.

(A) In general. A consumer reporting agency shall provide written notice to a consumer of the results of a reinvestigation under this subsection not later than 5 business days after the completion of the reinvestigation, by mail or, if authorized by the consumer for that purpose, by other means available to the agency.

(B) Contents. As part of, or in addition to, the notice under subparagraph (A), a consumer reporting agency shall provide to a consumer in writing before the expiration of the 5-day period referred to in subparagraph (A)

(i) a statement that the reinvestigation is completed;

(ii) a consumer report that is based upon the consumer's file as that file is revised as a result of the reinvestigation;

(iii) a notice that, if requested by the consumer, a description of the procedure used to determine the accuracy and completeness of the information shall be provided to the consumer by the agency, including the business name and address of any furnisher of information contacted in connection with such information and the telephone number of such furnisher, if reasonably available;

(iv) a notice that the consumer has the right to add a statement to the consumer's file disputing the accuracy or completeness of the information; and

(v) a notice that the consumer has the right to request under subsection (d) that the consumer reporting agency furnish notifications under that subsection.

(7) Description of reinvestigation procedure. A consumer reporting agency shall provide to a consumer a description referred to in paragraph (6)(B)(iv) by not later than 15 days after receiving a request from the consumer for that description.

(8) Expedited dispute resolution. If a dispute regarding an item of information in a consumer's file at a consumer reporting agency is resolved in accordance with paragraph (5)(A) by the deletion of the disputed information by not later than 3 business days after the date on which the agency receives notice of the dispute from the consumer in accordance with paragraph (1)(A), then the agency shall not be required to comply with paragraphs (2), (6), and (7) with respect to that dispute if the agency

(A) provides prompt notice of the deletion to the consumer by telephone;

(B) includes in that notice, or in a written notice that accompanies a confirmation and consumer report provided in accordance with subparagraph (C), a statement of the consumer's right to request under subsection (d) that the agency furnish notifications under that subsection; and

(C) provides written confirmation of the deletion and a copy of a consumer report on the consumer that is based on the consumer's file after the deletion, not later than 5 business days after making the deletion.

(b) Statement of dispute. If the reinvestigation does not resolve the dispute, the consumer may file a brief statement setting forth the nature of the dispute. The consumer reporting agency may limit such statements to not more than one hundred words if it provides the consumer with assistance in writing a clear summary of the dispute.

(c) Notification of consumer dispute in subsequent consumer reports. Whenever a statement of a dispute is filed, unless there is reasonable grounds to believe that it is frivolous or irrelevant, the consumer reporting agency shall, in any subsequent consumer report containing the information in question, clearly note that it is disputed by the consumer and provide either the consumer's statement or a clear and accurate codification or summary thereof.

(d) Notification of deletion of disputed information. Following any deletion of information which is found to be inaccurate or whose accuracy can no longer be verified or any notation as to disputed information, the consumer reporting agency shall, at the request of the consumer, furnish notification that the item has been deleted or the statement, codification or summary pursuant to subsection (b) or (c) of this section to any person specifically designated by the consumer who has within two years prior thereto received a consumer report for employment purposes, or within six months prior thereto received a consumer report for any other purpose, which contained the deleted or disputed information.

§ 612. Charges for certain disclosures [15 U.S.C. § 1681j]

(a) Reasonable charges allowed for certain disclosures.

(1) In general. Except as provided in subsections (b), (c), and (d), a consumer reporting agency may impose a reasonable charge on a consumer

(A) for making a disclosure to the consumer pursuant to section 609 [§ 1681g], which charge

(i) shall not exceed $8; and

(ii) shall be indicated to the consumer before making the disclosure; and

(B) for furnishing, pursuant to 611(d) [§ 1681i], following a reinvestigation under section 611(a) [§ 1681i], a statement, codification, or summary to a person designated by the consumer under that section after the 30-day period beginning on the date of notification of the consumer under paragraph (6) or (8) of section 611(a) [§ 1681i] with respect to the reinvestigation, which charge

(i) shall not exceed the charge that the agency would impose on each designated recipient for a consumer report; and

(ii) shall be indicated to the consumer before furnishing such information.

(2) Modification of amount. The Federal Trade Commission shall increase the amount referred to in paragraph (1)(A)(i) on January 1 of each year, based proportionally on changes in the Consumer Price Index, with fractional changes rounded to the nearest fifty cents.

(b) Free disclosure after adverse notice to consumer. Each consumer reporting agency that maintains a file on a consumer shall make all disclosures pursuant to section 609 [§ 1681g] without charge to the consumer if, not later than 60 days after receipt by such consumer of a notification pursuant to section 615 [§ 1681m], or of a notification from a debt collection agency affiliated with that consumer reporting agency stating that the consumer's credit rating may be or has been adversely affected, the consumer makes a request under section 609 [§ 1681g].

(c) Free disclosure under certain other circumstances. Upon the request of the consumer, a consumer reporting agency shall make all disclosures pursuant to section 609 [§ 1681g] once during any 12-month period without charge to that consumer if the consumer certifies in writing that the consumer

(1) is unemployed and intends to apply for employment in the 60-day period beginning on the date on which the certification is made;

(2) is a recipient of public welfare assistance; or

(3) has reason to believe that the file on the consumer at the agency contains inaccurate information due to fraud.

(d) Other charges prohibited. A consumer reporting agency shall not impose any charge on a consumer for providing any notification required by this title or making any disclosure required by this title, except as authorized by subsection (a).

§ 613. Public record information for employment purposes [15 U.S.C. § 1681k]

A consumer reporting agency which furnishes a consumer report for employment purposes and which for that purpose compiles and reports items of information on consumers which are matters of public record and are likely to have an adverse effect upon a consumer's ability to obtain employment shall

(1) at the time such public record information is reported to the user of such consumer report, notify the consumer of the fact that public record information is being reported by the consumer reporting agency, together with the name and address of the person to whom such information is being reported; or

(2) maintain strict procedures designed to insure that whenever public record information which is likely to have an adverse effect on a consumer's ability to obtain employment is reported it is complete and up to date. For purposes of this paragraph, items of public record relating to arrests, indictments, convictions,

suits, tax liens, and outstanding judgments shall be considered up to date if the current public record status of the item at the time of the report is reported.

§ 614. Restrictions on investigative consumer reports [15 U.S.C. § 1681l]

Whenever a consumer reporting agency prepares an investigative consumer report, no adverse information in the consumer report (other than information which is a matter of public record) may be included in a subsequent consumer report unless such adverse information has been verified in the process of making such subsequent consumer report, or the adverse information was received within the three-month period preceding the date the subsequent report is furnished.

§ 615. Requirements on users of consumer reports [15 U.S.C. § 1681m]

(a) Duties of users taking adverse actions on the basis of information contained in consumer reports. If any person takes any adverse action with respect to any consumer that is based in whole or in part on any information contained in a consumer report, the person shall

(1) provide oral, written, or electronic notice of the adverse action to the consumer;

(2) provide to the consumer orally, in writing, or electronically

(A) the name, address, and telephone number of the consumer reporting agency (including a toll-free telephone number established by the agency if the agency compiles and maintains files on consumers on a nationwide basis) that furnished the report to the person; and

(B) a statement that the consumer reporting agency did not make the decision to take the adverse action and is unable to provide the consumer the specific reasons why the adverse action was taken; and

(3) provide to the consumer an oral, written, or electronic notice of the consumer's right

(A) to obtain, under section 612 [§ 1681j], a free copy of a consumer report on the consumer from the consumer reporting agency referred to in paragraph (2), which notice shall include an indication of the 60-day period under that section for obtaining such a copy; and

(B) to dispute, under section 611 [§ 1681i], with a consumer reporting agency the accuracy or completeness of any information in a consumer report furnished by the agency.

(b) Adverse action based on information obtained from third parties other than consumer reporting agencies.

(1) In general. Whenever credit for personal, family, or household purposes involving a consumer is denied or the charge for such credit is increased either wholly or partly because of information obtained from a person other than a consumer reporting agency bearing upon the consumer's credit worthiness, credit

standing, credit capacity, character, general reputation, personal characteristics, or mode of living, the user of such information shall, within a reasonable period of time, upon the consumer's written request for the reasons for such adverse action received within sixty days after learning of such adverse action, disclose the nature of the information to the consumer. The user of such information shall clearly and accurately disclose to the consumer his right to make such written request at the time such adverse action is communicated to the consumer.

(2) Duties of person taking certain actions based on information provided by affiliate.

(A) Duties, generally. If a person takes an action described in subparagraph (B) with respect to a consumer, based in whole or in part on information described in subparagraph (C), the person shall

(i) notify the consumer of the action, including a statement that the consumer may obtain the information in accordance with clause (ii); and

(ii) upon a written request from the consumer received within 60 days after transmittal of the notice required by clause (i), disclose to the consumer the nature of the information upon which the action is based by not later than 30 days after receipt of the request.

(B) Action described. An action referred to in subparagraph (A) is an adverse action described in section 603(k)(1)(A) [§ 1681a], taken in connection with a transaction initiated by the consumer, or any adverse action described in clause (i) or (ii) of section 603(k)(1)(B) [§ 1681a].

(C) Information described. Information referred to in subparagraph (A)

(i) except as provided in clause (ii), is information that

(I) is furnished to the person taking the action by a person related by common ownership or affiliated by common corporate control to the person taking the action; and

(II) bears on the credit worthiness, credit standing, credit capacity, character, general reputation, personal characteristics, or mode of living of the consumer; and

(ii) does not include

(I) information solely as to transactions or experiences between the consumer and the person furnishing the information; or

(II) information in a consumer report.

(c) Reasonable procedures to assure compliance. No person shall be held liable for any violation of this section if he shows by a preponderance of the evidence that at the time of the alleged violation he maintained reasonable procedures to assure compliance with the provisions of this section.

(d) Duties of users making written credit or insurance solicitations on the basis of information contained in consumer files.

(1) In general. Any person who uses a consumer report on any consumer in connection with any credit or insurance transaction that is not initiated by the consumer, that is provided to that person under section 604(c)(1)(B) [§ 1681b], shall provide with each written solicitation made to the consumer regarding the transaction a clear and conspicuous statement that

(A) information contained in the consumer's consumer report was used in connection with the transaction;

(B) the consumer received the offer of credit or insurance because the consumer satisfied the criteria for credit worthiness or insurability under which the consumer was selected for the offer;

(C) if applicable, the credit or insurance may not be extended if, after the consumer responds to the offer, the consumer does not meet the criteria used to select the consumer for the offer or any applicable criteria bearing on credit worthiness or insurability or does not furnish any required collateral;

(D) the consumer has a right to prohibit information contained in the consumer's file with any consumer reporting agency from being used in connection with any credit or insurance transaction that is not initiated by the consumer; and

(E) the consumer may exercise the right referred to in subparagraph (D) by notifying a notification system established under section 604(e) [§ 1681b].

(2) Disclosure of address and telephone number. A statement under paragraph (1) shall include the address and toll-free telephone number of the appropriate notification system established under section 604(e) [§ 1681b].

(3) Maintaining criteria on file. A person who makes an offer of credit or insurance to a consumer under a credit or insurance transaction described in paragraph (1) shall maintain on file the criteria used to select the consumer to receive the offer, all criteria bearing on credit worthiness or insurability, as applicable, that are the basis for determining whether or not to extend credit or insurance pursuant to the offer, and any requirement for the furnishing of collateral as a condition of the extension of credit or insurance, until the expiration of the 3-year period beginning on the date on which the offer is made to the consumer.

(4) Authority of federal agencies regarding unfair or deceptive acts or practices not affected. This section is not intended to affect the authority of any Federal or State agency to enforce a prohibition against unfair or deceptive acts or practices, including the making of false or misleading statements in connection with a credit or insurance transaction that is not initiated by the consumer.

§ 616. Civil liability for willful noncompliance [15 U.S.C. § 1681n]

(a) In general. Any person who willfully fails to comply with any requirement imposed under this title with respect to any consumer is liable to that consumer in an amount equal to the sum of

(1)

(A) any actual damages sustained by the consumer as a result of the failure or damages of not less than $100 and not more than $1,000; or

(B) in the case of liability of a natural person for obtaining a consumer report under false pretenses or knowingly without a permissible purpose, actual damages sustained by the consumer as a result of the failure or $1,000, whichever is greater;

(2) such amount of punitive damages as the court may allow; and

(3) in the case of any successful action to enforce any liability under this section, the costs of the action together with reasonable attorney's fees as determined by the court.

(b) Civil liability for knowing noncompliance. Any person who obtains a consumer report from a consumer reporting agency under false pretenses or knowingly without a permissible purpose shall be liable to the consumer reporting agency for actual damages sustained by the consumer reporting agency or $1,000, whichever is greater.

(c) Attorney's fees. Upon a finding by the court that an unsuccessful pleading, motion, or other paper filed in connection with an action under this section was filed in bad faith or for purposes of harassment, the court shall award to the prevailing party attorney's fees reasonable in relation to the work expended in responding to the pleading, motion, or other paper.

§ 617. Civil liability for negligent noncompliance [15 U.S.C. § 1681o]

(a) In general. Any person who is negligent in failing to comply with any requirement imposed under this title with respect to any consumer is liable to that consumer in an amount equal to the sum of

(1) any actual damages sustained by the consumer as a result of the failure;

(2) in the case of any successful action to enforce any liability under this section, the costs of the action together with reasonable attorney's fees as determined by the court.

(b) Attorney's fees. On a finding by the court that an unsuccessful pleading, motion, or other paper filed in connection with an action under this section was filed in bad faith or for purposes of harassment, the court shall award to the prevailing party attorney's fees reasonable in relation to the work expended in responding to the pleading, motion, or other paper.

United States
Fair Credit Reporting Act

§ 618. Jurisdiction of courts; limitation of actions [15 U.S.C. § 1681p]

An action to enforce any liability created under this title may be brought in any appropriate United States district court without regard to the amount in controversy, or in any other court of competent jurisdiction, within two years from the date on which the liability arises, except that where a defendant has materially and willfully misrepresented any information required under this title to be disclosed to an individual and the information so misrepresented is material to the establishment of the defendant's liability to that individual under this title, the action may be brought at any time within two years after discovery by the individual of the misrepresentation.

§ 619. Obtaining information under false pretenses [15 U.S.C. § 1681q]

Any person who knowingly and willfully obtains information on a consumer from a consumer reporting agency under false pretenses shall be fined under title 18, United States Code, imprisoned for not more than 2 years, or both.

§ 620. Unauthorized disclosures by officers or employees [15 U.S.C. § 1681r]

Any officer or employee of a consumer reporting agency who knowingly and willfully provides information concerning an individual from the agency's files to a person not authorized to receive that information shall be fined under title 18, United States Code, imprisoned for not more than 2 years, or both.

§ 621. Administrative enforcement [15 U.S.C. § 1681s]

   (a)

      (1) Enforcement by Federal Trade Commission. Compliance with the requirements imposed under this title shall be enforced under the Federal Trade Commission Act [15 U.S.C. §§ 41 et seq.] by the Federal Trade Commission with respect to consumer reporting agencies and all other persons subject thereto, except to the extent that enforcement of the requirements imposed under this title is specifically committed to some other government agency under subsection (b) hereof. For the purpose of the exercise by the Federal Trade Commission of its functions and powers under the Federal Trade Commission Act, a violation of any requirement or prohibition imposed under this title shall constitute an unfair or deceptive act or practice in commerce in violation of section 5(a) of the Federal Trade Commission Act [15 U.S.C. § 45(a)] and shall be subject to enforcement by the Federal Trade Commission under section 5(b) thereof [15 U.S.C. § 45(b)] with respect to any consumer reporting agency or person subject to enforcement by the Federal Trade Commission pursuant to this subsection, irrespective of whether that person is engaged in commerce or meets any other jurisdictional tests in the Federal Trade Commission Act. The Federal Trade Commission shall have such procedural,

investigative, and enforcement powers, including the power to issue procedural rules in enforcing compliance with the requirements imposed under this title and to require the filing of reports, the production of documents, and the appearance of witnesses as though the applicable terms and conditions of the Federal Trade Commission Act were part of this title. Any person violating any of the provisions of this title shall be subject to the penalties and entitled to the privileges and immunities provided in the Federal Trade Commission Act as though the applicable terms and provisions thereof were part of this title.

(2)

(A) In the event of a knowing violation, which constitutes a pattern or practice of violations of this title, the Commission may commence a civil action to recover a civil penalty in a district court of the United States against any person that violates this title. In such action, such person shall be liable for a civil penalty of not more than $2,500 per violation.

(B) In determining the amount of a civil penalty under subparagraph (A), the court shall take into account the degree of culpability, any history of prior such conduct, ability to pay, effect on ability to continue to do business, and such other matters as justice may require.

(3) Notwithstanding paragraph (2), a court may not impose any civil penalty on a person for a violation of section 623(a)(1) [§ 1681s-2] unless the person has been enjoined from committing the violation, or ordered not to commit the violation, in an action or proceeding brought by or on behalf of the Federal Trade Commission, and has violated the injunction or order, and the court may not impose any civil penalty for any violation occurring before the date of the violation of the injunction or order.

(4) Neither the Commission nor any other agency referred to in subsection (b) may prescribe trade regulation rules or other regulations with respect to this title.

(b) Enforcement by other agencies. Compliance with the requirements imposed under this title with respect to consumer reporting agencies, persons who use consumer reports from such agencies, persons who furnish information to such agencies, and users of information that are subject to subsection (d) or (e) of section 615 [§ 1681m] shall be enforced under

(1) section 8 of the Federal Deposit Insurance Act [12 U.S.C. § 1818], in the case of

(A) national banks, and Federal branches and Federal agencies of foreign banks, by the Office of the Comptroller of the Currency;

(B) member banks of the Federal Reserve System (other than national banks), branches and agencies of foreign banks (other than Federal branches, Federal agencies, and insured State branches of foreign banks), commercial lending companies owned or controlled by foreign banks, and organizations operating under section 25 or 25(a) [25A] of the Federal Reserve Act [12 U.S.C. §§ 601 et seq., §§ 611 et seq], by the Board of Governors of the Federal Reserve System; and

(C) banks insured by the Federal Deposit Insurance Corporation (other than members of the Federal Reserve System) and insured State branches of foreign banks, by the Board of Directors of the Federal Deposit Insurance Corporation;

(2) section 8 of the Federal Deposit Insurance Act [12 U.S.C. § 1818], by the Director of the Office of Thrift Supervision, in the case of a savings association the deposits of which are insured by the Federal Deposit Insurance Corporation;

(3) the Federal Credit Union Act [12 U.S.C. §§ 1751 et seq.], by the Administrator of the National Credit Union Administration [National Credit Union Administration Board] with respect to any Federal credit union;

(4) subtitle IV of title 49 [49 U.S.C. §§ 10101 et seq.], by the Secretary of Transportation, with respect to all carriers subject to the jurisdiction of the Surface Transportation Board;

(5) the Federal Aviation Act of 1958 [49 U.S.C. Appx §§ 1301 et seq.], by the Secretary of Transportation with respect to any air carrier or foreign air carrier subject to that Act [49 U.S.C. Appx §§ 1301 et seq.]; and

(6) the Packers and Stockyards Act, 1921 [7 U.S.C. §§ 181 et seq.] (except as provided in section 406 of that Act [7 U.S.C. §§ 226 and 227]), by the Secretary of Agriculture with respect to any activities subject to that Act.

The terms used in paragraph (1) that are not defined in this title or otherwise defined in section 3(s) of the Federal Deposit Insurance Act (12 U.S.C. § 1813(s)) shall have the meaning given to them in section 1(b) of the International Banking Act of 1978 (12 U.S.C. § 3101).

(c) State action for violations.

(1) Authority of states. In addition to such other remedies as are provided under State law, if the chief law enforcement officer of a State, or an official or agency designated by a State, has reason to believe that any person has violated or is violating this title, the State

(A) may bring an action to enjoin such violation in any appropriate United States district court or in any other court of competent jurisdiction;

(B) subject to paragraph (5), may bring an action on behalf of the residents of the State to recover

(i) damages for which the person is liable to such residents under sections 616 and 617 [§§ 1681n and 1681o] as a result of the violation;

(ii) in the case of a violation of section 623(a) [§ 1681s-2], damages for which the person would, but for section 623(c) [§ 1681s-2], be liable to such residents as a result of the violation; or

(iii) damages of not more than $1,000 for each willful or negligent violation; and

(C) in the case of any successful action under subparagraph (A) or (B), shall be awarded the costs of the action and reasonable attorney fees as determined by the court.

(2) Rights of federal regulators. The State shall serve prior written notice of any action under paragraph (1) upon the Federal Trade Commission or the appropriate Federal regulator determined under subsection (b) and provide the Commission or appropriate Federal regulator with a copy of its complaint, except in any case in which such prior notice is not feasible, in which case the State shall serve such notice immediately upon instituting such action. The Federal Trade Commission or appropriate Federal regulator shall have the right

(A) to intervene in the action;

(B) upon so intervening, to be heard on all matters arising therein;

(C) to remove the action to the appropriate United States district court; and

(D) to file petitions for appeal.

(3) Investigatory powers. For purposes of bringing any action under this subsection, nothing in this subsection shall prevent the chief law enforcement officer, or an official or agency designated by a State, from exercising the powers conferred on the chief law enforcement officer or such official by the laws of such State to conduct investigations or to administer oaths or affirmations or to compel the attendance of witnesses or the production of documentary and other evidence.

(4) Limitation on state action while federal action pending. If the Federal Trade Commission or the appropriate Federal regulator has instituted a civil action or an administrative action under section 8 of the Federal Deposit Insurance Act for a violation of this title, no State may, during the pendency of such action, bring an action under this section against any defendant named in the complaint of the Commission or the appropriate Federal regulator for any violation of this title that is alleged in that complaint.

(5) Limitations on state actions for violation of section 623(a)(1) [§ 1681s-2].

(A) Violation of injunction required. A State may not bring an action against a person under paragraph (1)(B) for a violation of section 623(a)(1) [§ 1681s-2], unless

(i) the person has been enjoined from committing the violation, in an action brought by the State under paragraph (1)(A); and

(ii) the person has violated the injunction.

(B) Limitation on damages recoverable. In an action against a person under paragraph (1)(B) for a violation of section 623(a)(1) [§ 1681s-2], a State may not recover any damages incurred before the date of the violation of an injunction on which the action is based.

(d) Enforcement under other authority. For the purpose of the exercise by any agency referred to in subsection (b) of this section of its powers under any Act referred to in that subsection, a violation of any requirement imposed under this title shall be deemed to be a violation of a requirement imposed under that Act. In addition to its powers under any provision of law specifically referred to in subsection (b) of this section, each of the agencies referred to in that subsection may exercise, for the purpose of enforcing compliance with any requirement imposed under this title any other authority conferred on it by law. Notwithstanding the preceding, no agency referred to in subsection (b) may conduct an examination of a bank, savings association, or credit union regarding compliance with the provisions of this title, except in response to a complaint (or if the agency otherwise has knowledge) that the bank, savings association, or credit union has violated a provision of this title, in which case, the agency may conduct an examination as necessary to investigate the complaint. If an agency determines during an investigation in response to a complaint that a violation of this title has occurred, the agency may, during its next 2 regularly scheduled examinations of the bank, savings association, or credit union, examine for compliance with this title.

(e) Interpretive authority. The Board of Governors of the Federal Reserve System may issue interpretations of any provision of this title as such provision may apply to any persons identified under paragraph (1), (2), and (3) of subsection (b), or to the holding companies and affiliates of such persons, in consultation with Federal agencies identified in paragraphs (1), (2), and (3) of subsection (b).

§ 622. Information on overdue child support obligations [15 U.S.C. § 1681s-1]

Notwithstanding any other provision of this title, a consumer reporting agency shall include in any consumer report furnished by the agency in accordance with section 604 [§ 1681b] of this title, any information on the failure of the consumer to pay overdue support which

    (1) is provided

        (A) to the consumer reporting agency by a State or local child support enforcement agency; or

        (B) to the consumer reporting agency and verified by any local, State, or Federal government agency; and

    (2) antedates the report by 7 years or less.

§ 623. Responsibilities of furnishers of information to consumer reporting agencies [15 U.S.C. § 1681s-2]

    (a) Duty of furnishers of information to provide accurate information.

        (1) Prohibition.

            (A) Reporting information with actual knowledge of errors. A person shall not furnish any information relating to a consumer to any consumer reporting agency if the person knows or consciously avoids knowing that the information is inaccurate.

(B) Reporting information after notice and confirmation of errors. A person shall not furnish information relating to a consumer to any consumer reporting agency if

(i) the person has been notified by the consumer, at the address specified by the person for such notices, that specific information is inaccurate; and

(ii) the information is, in fact, inaccurate.

(C) No address requirement. A person who clearly and conspicuously specifies to the consumer an address for notices referred to in subparagraph (B) shall not be subject to subparagraph (A); however, nothing in subparagraph (B) shall require a person to specify such an address.

(2) Duty to correct and update information. A person who

(A) regularly and in the ordinary course of business furnishes information to one or more consumer reporting agencies about the person's transactions or experiences with any consumer; and

(B) has furnished to a consumer reporting agency information that the person determines is not complete or accurate, shall promptly notify the consumer reporting agency of that determination and provide to the agency any corrections to that information, or any additional information, that is necessary to make the information provided by the person to the agency complete and accurate, and shall not thereafter furnish to the agency any of the information that remains not complete or accurate.

(3) Duty to provide notice of dispute. If the completeness or accuracy of any information furnished by any person to any consumer reporting agency is disputed to such person by a consumer, the person may not furnish the information to any consumer reporting agency without notice that such information is disputed by the consumer.

(4) Duty to provide notice of closed accounts. A person who regularly and in the ordinary course of business furnishes information to a consumer reporting agency regarding a consumer who has a credit account with that person shall notify the agency of the voluntary closure of the account by the consumer, in information regularly furnished for the period in which the account is closed.

(5) Duty to provide notice of delinquency of accounts. A person who furnishes information to a consumer reporting agency regarding a delinquent account being placed for collection, charged to profit or loss, or subjected to any similar action shall, not later than 90 days after furnishing the information, notify the agency of the month and year of the commencement of the delinquency that immediately preceded the action.

(b) Duties of furnishers of information upon notice of dispute.

(1) In general. After receiving notice pursuant to section 611(a)(2) [§ 1681i] of a dispute with regard to the completeness or accuracy of any information provided by a person to a consumer reporting agency, the person shall

(A) conduct an investigation with respect to the disputed information;

(B) review all relevant information provided by the consumer reporting agency pursuant to section 611(a)(2) [§ 1681i];

(C) report the results of the investigation to the consumer reporting agency; and

(D) if the investigation finds that the information is incomplete or inaccurate, report those results to all other consumer reporting agencies to which the person furnished the information and that compile and maintain files on consumers on a nationwide basis.

(2) Deadline. A person shall complete all investigations, reviews, and reports required under paragraph (1) regarding information provided by the person to a consumer reporting agency, before the expiration of the period under section 611(a)(1) [§ 1681i] within which the consumer reporting agency is required to complete actions required by that section regarding that information.

(c) Limitation on liability. Sections 616 and 617 [§§ 1681n and 1681o] do not apply to any failure to comply with subsection (a), except as provided in section 621(c)(1)(B) [§ 1681s].

(d) Limitation on enforcement. Subsection (a) shall be enforced exclusively under section 621 [§ 1681s] by the Federal agencies and officials and the State officials identified in that section.

§ 624. Relation to State laws [15 U.S.C. § 1681t]

(a) In general. Except as provided in subsections (b) and (c), this title does not annul, alter, affect, or exempt any person subject to the provisions of this title from complying with the laws of any State with respect to the collection, distribution, or use of any information on consumers, except to the extent that those laws are inconsistent with any provision of this title, and then only to the extent of the inconsistency.

(b) General exceptions. No requirement or prohibition may be imposed under the laws of any State

(1) with respect to any subject matter regulated under

(A) subsection (c) or (e) of section 604 [§ 1681b], relating to the prescreening of consumer reports;

(B) section 611 [§ 1681i], relating to the time by which a consumer reporting agency must take any action, including the provision of notification to a consumer or other person, in any procedure related to the disputed accuracy of information in a consumer's file, except that this subparagraph shall not apply to any State law in effect on the date of enactment of the Consumer Credit Reporting Reform Act of 1996;

(C) subsections (a) and (b) of section 615 [§ 1681m], relating to the duties of a person who takes any adverse action with respect to a consumer;

(D) section 615(d) [§ 1681m], relating to the duties of persons who use a consumer report of a consumer in connection with any credit or insurance transaction that is not initiated by the consumer and that consists of a firm offer of credit or insurance;

(E) section 605 [§ 1681c], relating to information contained in consumer reports, except that this subparagraph shall not apply to any State law in effect on the date of enactment of the Consumer Credit Reporting Reform Act of 1996; or

(F) section 623 [§ 1681s-2], relating to the responsibilities of persons who furnish information to consumer reporting agencies, except that this paragraph shall not apply

> (i) with respect to section 54A(a) of chapter 93 of the Massachusetts Annotated Laws (as in effect on the date of enactment of the Consumer Credit Reporting Reform Act of 1996); or

> (ii) with respect to section 1785.25(a) of the California Civil Code (as in effect on the date of enactment of the Consumer Credit Reporting Reform Act of 1996);

(2) with respect to the exchange of information among persons affiliated by common ownership or common corporate control, except that this paragraph shall not apply with respect to subsection (a) or (c)(1) of section 2480e of title 9, Vermont Statutes Annotated (as in effect on the date of enactment of the Consumer Credit Reporting Reform Act of 1996); or

(3) with respect to the form and content of any disclosure required to be made under section 609(c) [§ 1681g].

(c) Definition of firm offer of credit or insurance. Notwithstanding any definition of the term "firm offer of credit or insurance" (or any equivalent term) under the laws of any State, the definition of that term contained in section 603(l) [§ 1681a] shall be construed to apply in the enforcement and interpretation of the laws of any State governing consumer reports.

(d) Limitations. Subsections (b) and (c)

(1) do not affect any settlement, agreement, or consent judgment between any State Attorney General and any consumer reporting agency in effect on the date of enactment of the Consumer Credit Reporting Reform Act of 1996; and

(2) do not apply to any provision of State law (including any provision of a State constitution) that

> (A) is enacted after January 1, 2004;

> (B) states explicitly that the provision is intended to supplement this title; and

> (C) gives greater protection to consumers than is provided under this title.

United States
Fair Credit Reporting Act

§ 625. Disclosures to FBI for counterintelligence purposes [15 U.S.C. § 1681u]

(a) Identity of financial institutions. Notwithstanding section 604 [§ 1681b] or any other provision of this title, a consumer reporting agency shall furnish to the Federal Bureau of Investigation the names and addresses of all financial institutions (as that term is defined in section 1101 of the Right to Financial Privacy Act of 1978 [12 U.S.C. § 3401]) at which a consumer maintains or has maintained an account, to the extent that information is in the files of the agency, when presented with a written request for that information, signed by the Director of the Federal Bureau of Investigation, or the Director's designee, which certifies compliance with this section. The Director or the Director's designee may make such a certification only if the Director or the Director's designee has determined in writing that

(1) such information is necessary for the conduct of an authorized foreign counterintelligence investigation; and

(2) there are specific and articulable facts giving reason to believe that the consumer

(A) is a foreign power (as defined in section 101 of the Foreign Intelligence Surveillance Act of 1978 [50 U.S.C. § 1801]) or a person who is not a United States person (as defined in such section 101) and is an official of a foreign power; or

(B) is an agent of a foreign power and is engaging or has engaged in an act of international terrorism (as that term is defined in section 101(c) of the Foreign Intelligence Surveillance Act of 1978 [50 U.S.C. § 1801(c)]) or clandestine intelligence activities that involve or may involve a violation of criminal statutes of the United States.

(b) Identifying information. Notwithstanding the provisions of section 604 [§ 1681b] or any other provision of this title, a consumer reporting agency shall furnish identifying information respecting a consumer, limited to name, address, former addresses, places of employment, or former places of employment, to the Federal Bureau of Investigation when presented with a written request, signed by the Director or the Director's designee, which certifies compliance with this subsection. The Director or the Director's designee may make such a certification only if the Director or the Director's designee has determined in writing that

(1) such information is necessary to the conduct of an authorized counterintelligence investigation; and

(2) there is information giving reason to believe that the consumer has been, or is about to be, in contact with a foreign power or an agent of a foreign power (as defined in section 101 of the Foreign Intelligence Surveillance Act of 1978 [50 U.S.C. § 1801]).

(c) Court order for disclosure of consumer reports. Notwithstanding section 604 [§ 1681b] or any other provision of this title, if requested in writing by the Director of the Federal Bureau of Investigation, or a designee of the Director, a court may issue an order ex parte directing a consumer reporting agency to furnish a consumer report to the Federal Bureau of Investigation, upon a showing in camera that

(1) the consumer report is necessary for the conduct of an authorized foreign counterintelligence investigation; and

(2) there are specific and articulable facts giving reason to believe that the consumer whose consumer report is sought

(A) is an agent of a foreign power, and

(B) is engaging or has engaged in an act of international terrorism (as that term is defined in section 101(c) of the Foreign Intelligence Surveillance Act of 1978 [50 U.S.C. § 1801(c)]) or clandestine intelligence activities that involve or may involve a violation of criminal statutes of the United States.

The terms of an order issued under this subsection shall not disclose that the order is issued for purposes of a counterintelligence investigation.

(d) Confidentiality. No consumer reporting agency or officer, employee, or agent of a consumer reporting agency shall disclose to any person, other than those officers, employees, or agents of a consumer reporting agency necessary to fulfill the requirement to disclose information to the Federal Bureau of Investigation under this section, that the Federal Bureau of Investigation has sought or obtained the identity of financial institutions or a consumer report respecting any consumer under subsection (a), (b), or (c), and no consumer reporting agency or officer, employee, or agent of a consumer reporting agency shall include in any consumer report any information that would indicate that the Federal Bureau of Investigation has sought or obtained such information or a consumer report.

(e) Payment of fees. The Federal Bureau of Investigation shall, subject to the availability of appropriations, pay to the consumer reporting agency assembling or providing report or information in accordance with procedures established under this section a fee for reimbursement for such costs as are reasonably necessary and which have been directly incurred in searching, reproducing, or transporting books, papers, records, or other data required or requested to be produced under this section.

(f) Limit on dissemination. The Federal Bureau of Investigation may not disseminate information obtained pursuant to this section outside of the Federal Bureau of Investigation, except to other Federal agencies as may be necessary for the approval or conduct of a foreign counterintelligence investigation, or, where the information concerns a person subject to the Uniform Code of Military Justice, to appropriate investigative authorities within the military department concerned as may be necessary for the conduct of a joint foreign counterintelligence investigation.

(g) Rules of construction. Nothing in this section shall be construed to prohibit information from being furnished by the Federal Bureau of Investigation pursuant to a subpoena or court order, in connection with a judicial or administrative proceeding to enforce the provisions of this Act. Nothing in this section shall be construed to authorize or permit the withholding of information from the Congress.

(h) Reports to Congress. On a semiannual basis, the Attorney General shall fully inform the Permanent Select Committee on Intelligence and the Committee on Banking, Finance and Urban Affairs of the House of Representatives, and the Select Committee on Intelligence and the Committee on Banking, Housing, and Urban Affairs of the Senate concerning all requests made pursuant to subsections (a), (b), and (c).

(i) Damages. Any agency or department of the United States obtaining or disclosing any consumer reports, records, or information contained therein in violation of this section is liable to the consumer to whom such consumer reports, records, or information relate in an amount equal to the sum of

(1) $100, without regard to the volume of consumer reports, records, or information involved;

(2) any actual damages sustained by the consumer as a result of the disclosure;

(3) if the violation is found to have been willful or intentional, such punitive damages as a court may allow; and

(4) in the case of any successful action to enforce liability under this subsection, the costs of the action, together with reasonable attorney fees, as determined by the court.

(j) Disciplinary actions for violations. If a court determines that any agency or department of the United States has violated any provision of this section and the court finds that the circumstances surrounding the violation raise questions of whether or not an officer or employee of the agency or department acted willfully or intentionally with respect to the violation, the agency or department shall promptly initiate a proceeding to determine whether or not disciplinary action is warranted against the officer or employee who was responsible for the violation.

(k) Good-faith exception. Notwithstanding any other provision of this title, any consumer reporting agency or agent or employee thereof making disclosure of consumer reports or identifying information pursuant to this subsection in good-faith reliance upon a certification of the Federal Bureau of Investigation pursuant to provisions of this section shall not be liable to any person for such disclosure under this title, the constitution of any State, or any law or regulation of any State or any political subdivision of any State.

(l) Limitation of remedies. Notwithstanding any other provision of this title, the remedies and sanctions set forth in this section shall be the only judicial remedies and sanctions for violation of this section.

(m) Injunctive relief. In addition to any other remedy contained in this section, injunctive relief shall be available to require compliance with the procedures of this section. In the event of any successful action under this subsection, costs together with reasonable attorney fees, as determined by the court, may be recovered

(handwritten margin notes: "limited to maintain, collect, use or disseminate NOT create, destroy or alter")

(handwritten, right margin: "purpose")

United States Privacy Act

PRIVACY ACT (1974)

Summary

In passing the Privacy Act of 1974 into law, Congress's stated purpose was to promote governmental respect for citizens' privacy by requiring federal agencies to observe certain guidelines in the use and disclosure of citizens' personal information. The Act was to promote accountability and legislative oversight with respect to the use of computer databases and other information systems in managing personal data files. The Act was also meant to strengthen review within agencies of criteria for the collection and retention of personal data.

The Act implements a set of privacy principles known as 'Fair Information Practices'. The Code of Fair Information Practices was first articulated by the Department of Health, Education and Welfare Special Advisory Commission in its 1973 report on "Records, Computers and the Rights of Citizens." It includes five core principles: that there should be no secret record keeping systems; that information collected for one purpose should not be used for another purpose without the consent of the individual; that individuals should be given access to information held about them and the opportunity to correct or amend that information; that information is kept relevant, accurate, and up to date; and that information is protected against unauthorized loss, alteration or disclosure.

Accordingly, the Act requires each Federal agency to publish a description of each system of records maintained by that agency. It requires that surrender of personal information is made with informed consent or with some guarantees of the uses and confidentiality of the information. It grants individuals the right of access including the right to review, copy and amend the record. It requires that information is maintained with "accuracy, relevance, timeliness and completeness." Finally, it requires agencies to protect against any security breaches which could result in "substantial harm, embarrassment, inconvenience, or unfairness to any individual on whom information is maintained." To aid in the enforcement of these legislative restraints, the Act provides administrative and judicial machinery for oversight and for civil remedy of violations. The Act also provides a private cause of action to individuals denied access to their information.

As originally drafted, the Privacy Act would have created a Federal Privacy Board to act as an oversight and enforcement mechanism. The final Act, however, created a far more limited body, the Privacy Protection Study Commission which issued a report in 1977 examining the problems with both private and public sector record keeping systems and making numerous recommendations for change. The Commission was dissolved following the release of its report.

United States
Privacy Act

References

Public Law 93-579, codified at 5 USC §552
http://www4.law.cornell.edu/uscode/5/552.html

Senate Report No. 93-1183, September 26, 1974.

U.S. Department of Health, Education & Welfare, Report of the Secretary's Advisory Committee on Automated Personal Data Systems, *Records Computers and the Rights of Citizens* (MIT 1973)

Congressional findings and statement of purpose

(a) The Congress finds that--

(1) the privacy of an individual is directly affected by the collection, maintenance, use, and dissemination of personal information by Federal agencies;

(2) the increasing use of computers and sophisticated information technology, while essential to the efficient operations of the Government, has greatly magnified the harm to individual privacy that can occur from any collection, maintenance, use, or dissemination of personal information;

(3) the opportunities for an individual to secure employment, insurance, and credit, and his right to due process, and other legal protections are endangered by the misuse of certain information systems;

(4) the right to privacy is a personal and fundamental right protected by the Constitution of the United States; and

(5) in order to protect the privacy of individuals identified in information systems maintained by Federal agencies, it is necessary and proper for the Congress to regulate the collection, maintenance, use, and dissemination of information by such agencies.

(b) The purpose of this Act is to provide certain safeguards for an individual against an invasion of personal privacy by requiring Federal agencies, except as otherwise provided by law, to--

(1) permit an individual to determine what records pertaining to him are collected, maintained, used, or disseminated by such agencies;

(2) permit an individual to prevent records pertaining to him obtained by such agencies for a particular purpose from being used or made available for another purpose without his consent;

(3) permit an individual to gain access to information pertaining to him in Federal agency records, to have a copy made of all or any portion thereof, and to correct or amend such records;

(4) collect, maintain, use, or disseminate any record of identifiable personal information in a manner that assures that such action is for a necessary and lawful

civil suit damages

purpose, that the information is current and accurate for its intended use, and that adequate safeguards are provided to prevent misuse of such information;

(5) permit exemptions from the requirements with respect to records provided in this Act only in those cases where there is an important public policy need for such exemption as has been determined by specific statutory authority, and

(6) be subject to civil suit for any damages which occur as a result of willful or intentional action which violates any individual's rights under this Act.

5 U.S.C. § 552a Public information; agency rules, opinions, orders, records, and proceedings

(a) Definitions

For purposes of this section–

(1) the term ``agency'' means agency as defined in section 552(e) \1\ of this title;

(2) the term ``individual'' means a citizen of the United States or an alien lawfully admitted for permanent residence;

(3) the term ``maintain'' includes maintain, collect, use, or disseminate;

(4) the term ``record'' means any item, collection, or grouping of information about an individual that is maintained by an agency, including, but not limited to, his education, financial transactions, medical history, and criminal or employment history and that contains his name, or the identifying number, symbol, or other identifying particular assigned to the individual, such as a finger or voice print or a photograph;

only for individuals

(5) the term ``system of records'' means a group of any records under the control of any agency from which information is retrieved by the name of the individual or by some identifying number, symbol, or other identifying particular assigned to the individual;

(6) the term ``statistical record'' means a record in a system of records maintained for statistical research or reporting purposes only and not used in whole or in part in making any determination about an identifiable individual, except as provided by section 8 of title 13;

(7) the term ``routine use'' means, with respect to the disclosure of a record, the use of such record for a purpose which is compatible with the purpose for which it was collected;

(8) the term ``matching program''–

(A) means any computerized comparison of–

(i) two or more automated systems of records or a system of records with non-Federal records for the purpose of–

(I) establishing or verifying the eligibility of, or continuing compliance with statutory and regulatory requirements by, applicants for, recipients *[handwritten annotations: "Matt w/ criminal databases", "Federal work", "B)", various marks]*

or beneficiaries of, participants in, or providers of services with respect to, cash or in-kind assistance or payments under Federal benefit programs, or

(II) recouping payments or delinquent debts under such Federal benefit programs, or

(ii) two or more automated Federal personnel or payroll systems of records or a system of Federal personnel or payroll records with non-Federal records,

(B) but does not include—

(i) matches performed to produce aggregate statistical data without any personal identifiers;

(ii) matches performed to support any research or statistical project, the specific data of which may not be used to make decisions concerning the rights, benefits, or privileges of specific individuals;

(iii) matches performed, by an agency (or component thereof) which performs as its principal function any activity pertaining to the enforcement of criminal laws, subsequent to the initiation of a specific criminal or civil law enforcement investigation of a named person or persons for the purpose of gathering evidence against such person or persons;

(iv) matches of tax information (I) pursuant to section 6103(d) of the Internal Revenue Code of 1986, (II) for purposes of tax administration as defined in section 6103(b)(4) of such Code, (III) for the purpose of intercepting a tax refund due an individual under authority granted by section 464 or 1137 of the Social Security Act; or (IV) for the purpose of intercepting a tax refund due an individual under any other tax refund intercept program authorized by statute which has been determined by the Director of the Office of Management and Budget to contain verification, notice, and hearing requirements that are substantially similar to the procedures in section 1137 of the Social Security Act;

(v) matches—

(I) using records predominantly relating to Federal personnel, that are performed for routine administrative purposes (subject to guidance provided by the Director of the Office of Management and Budget pursuant to subsection (v)); or

(II) conducted by an agency using only records from systems of records maintained by that agency; if the purpose of the match is not to take any adverse financial, personnel, disciplinary, or other adverse action against Federal personnel;

(vi) matches performed for foreign counterintelligence purposes, or to produce background checks for security clearances of Federal personnel or Federal contractor personnel; or

(vii) matches performed pursuant to section 6103(l)(12) of the Internal Revenue Code of 1986, and section 1144 of the Social Security Act;

(9) the term ``recipient agency'' means any agency, or contractor thereof, receiving records contained in a system of records from a source agency for use in a matching program;

(10) the term ``non-Federal agency'' means any State or local government, or agency thereof, which receives records contained in a system of records from a source agency for use in a matching program;

(11) the term ``source agency'' means any agency which discloses records contained in a system of records to be used in a matching program, or any State or local government, or agency thereof, which discloses records to be used in a matching program;

(12) the term ``Federal benefit program'' means any program administered or funded by the Federal Government, or by any agent or State on behalf of the Federal Government, providing cash or in-kind assistance in the form of payments, grants, loans, or loan guarantees to individuals; and

(13) the term ``Federal personnel'' means officers and employees of the Government of the United States, members of the uniformed services (including members of the Reserve Components), individuals entitled to receive immediate or deferred retirement benefits under any retirement program of the Government of the United States (including survivor benefits).

exceptions to the written request rule

(b) Conditions of Disclosure

No agency shall disclose any record which is contained in a system of records by any means of communication to any person, or to another agency, except pursuant to a written request by, or with the prior written consent of, the individual to whom the record pertains, unless disclosure of the record would be—

(1) to those officers and employees of the agency which maintains the record who have a need for the record in the performance of their duties;

(2) required under section 552 of this title; → FOIA → *means it was closed to for use*

(3) for a routine use as defined in subsection (a)(7) of this section and described under subsection (e)(4)(D) of this section; *which was compatible w/ the use i.e. reason it was collected*

(4) to the Bureau of the Census for purposes of planning or carrying out a census or survey or related activity pursuant to the provisions of title 13;

(5) to a recipient who has provided the agency with advance adequate written assurance that the record will be used solely as a statistical research or reporting record, and the record is to be transferred in a form that is not individually identifiable;

not necessarily the exact use it was intended for.

(6) to the National Archives and Records Administration as a record which has sufficient historical or other value to warrant its continued preservation by the United States Government, or for evaluation by the Archivist of the United States or the designee of the Archivist to determine whether the record has such value;

(7) to another agency or to an instrumentality of any governmental jurisdiction within or under the control of the United States for a civil or criminal law enforcement activity if the activity is authorized by law, and if the head of the agency or instrumentality has made a written request to the agency which maintains the record specifying the particular portion desired and the law enforcement activity for which the record is sought;

(8) to a person pursuant to a showing of compelling circumstances affecting the health or safety of an individual if upon such disclosure notification is transmitted to the last known address of such individual;

(9) to either House of Congress, or, to the extent of matter within its jurisdiction, any committee or subcommittee thereof, any joint committee of Congress or subcommittee of any such joint committee;

(10) to the Comptroller General, or any of his authorized representatives, in the course of the performance of the duties of the General Accounting Office;

(11) pursuant to the order of a court of competent jurisdiction; or

(12) to a consumer reporting agency in accordance with section 3711(f) of title 31.

(c) Accounting of Certain Disclosures

Each agency, with respect to each system of records under its control, shall–

(1) except for disclosures made under subsections (b)(1) or (b)(2) of this section, keep an accurate accounting of–

    (A) the date, nature, and purpose of each disclosure of a record to any person or to another agency made under subsection (b) of this section; and

    (B) the name and address of the person or agency to whom the disclosure is made;

(2) retain the accounting made under paragraph (1) of this subsection for at least five years or the life of the record, whichever is longer, after the disclosure for which the accounting is made;

(3) except for disclosures made under subsection (b)(7) of this section, make the accounting made under paragraph (1) of this subsection available to the individual named in the record at his request; and

(4) inform any person or other agency about any correction or notation of dispute made by the agency in accordance with subsection (d) of this section of any record that has been disclosed to the person or agency if an accounting of the disclosure was made.

(d) Access to Records

Each agency that maintains a system of records shall–

(1) upon request by any individual to gain access to his record or to any information pertaining to him which is contained in the system, permit him and upon his request, a person of his own choosing to accompany him, to review the record and have a copy made of all or any portion thereof in a form comprehensible to him, except that the agency may require the individual to furnish a written statement authorizing discussion of that individual's record in the accompanying person's presence;

(2) permit the individual to request amendment of a record pertaining to him and–

(A) not later than 10 days (excluding Saturdays, Sundays, and legal public holidays) after the date of receipt of such request, acknowledge in writing such receipt; and

(B) promptly, either–

(i) make any correction of any portion thereof which the individual believes is not accurate, relevant, timely, or complete; or

(ii) inform the individual of its refusal to amend the record in accordance with his request, the reason for the refusal, the procedures established by the agency for the individual to request a review of that refusal by the head of the agency or an officer designated by the head of the agency, and the name and business address of that official;

(3) permit the individual who disagrees with the refusal of the agency to amend his record to request a review of such refusal, and not later than 30 days (excluding Saturdays, Sundays, and legal public holidays) from the date on which the individual requests such review, complete such review and make a final determination unless, for good cause shown, the head of the agency extends such 30-day period; and if, after his review, the reviewing official also refuses to amend the record in accordance with the request, permit the individual to file with the agency a concise statement setting forth the reasons for his disagreement with the refusal of the agency, and notify the individual of the provisions for judicial review of the reviewing official's determination under subsection (g)(1)(A) of this section;

(4) in any disclosure, containing information about which the individual has filed a statement of disagreement, occurring after the filing of the statement under paragraph (3) of this subsection, clearly note any portion of the record which is disputed and provide copies of the statement and, if the agency deems it appropriate, copies of a concise statement of the reasons of the agency for not making the amendments requested, to persons or other agencies to whom the disputed record has been disclosed; and

(5) nothing in this section shall allow an individual access to any information compiled in reasonable anticipation of a civil action or proceeding.

United States
Privacy Act

(e) Agency Requirements

Each agency that maintains a system of records shall–

(1) maintain in its records only such information about an individual as is relevant and necessary to accomplish a purpose of the agency required to be accomplished by statute or by executive order of the President;

(2) collect information to the greatest extent practicable directly from the subject individual when the information may result in adverse determinations about an individual's rights, benefits, and privileges under Federal programs;

(3) inform each individual whom it asks to supply information, on the form which it uses to collect the information or on a separate form that can be retained by the individual–

(A) the authority (whether granted by statute, or by executive order of the President) which authorizes the solicitation of the information and whether disclosure of such information is mandatory or voluntary;

(B) the principal purpose or purposes for which the information is intended to be used;

(C) the routine uses which may be made of the information, as published pursuant to paragraph (4)(D) of this subsection; and

(D) the effects on him, if any, of not providing all or any part of the requested information;

(4) subject to the provisions of paragraph (11) of this subsection, publish in the Federal Register upon establishment or revision a notice of the existence and character of the system of records, which notice shall include–

(A) the name and location of the system;

(B) the categories of individuals on whom records are maintained in the system;

(C) the categories of records maintained in the system;

(D) each routine use of the records contained in the system, including the categories of users and the purpose of such use;

(E) the policies and practices of the agency regarding storage, retrievability, access controls, retention, and disposal of the records;

(F) the title and business address of the agency official who is responsible for the system of records;

(G) the agency procedures whereby an individual can be notified at his request if the system of records contains a record pertaining to him;

(H) the agency procedures whereby an individual can be notified at his request how he can gain access to any record pertaining to him contained in the system of records, and how he can contest its content; and

(I) the categories of sources of records in the system;

(5) maintain all records which are used by the agency in making any determination about any individual with such accuracy, relevance, timeliness, and completeness as is reasonably necessary to assure fairness to the individual in the determination;

(6) prior to disseminating any record about an individual to any person other than an agency, unless the dissemination is made pursuant to subsection (b)(2) of this section, make reasonable efforts to assure that such records are accurate, complete, timely, and relevant for agency purposes;

(7) maintain no record describing how any individual exercises rights guaranteed by the First Amendment unless expressly authorized by statute or by the individual about whom the record is maintained or unless pertinent to and within the scope of an authorized law enforcement activity;

(8) make reasonable efforts to serve notice on an individual when any record on such individual is made available to any person under compulsory legal process when such process becomes a matter of public record;

(9) establish rules of conduct for persons involved in the design, development, operation, or maintenance of any system of records, or in maintaining any record, and instruct each such person with respect to such rules and the requirements of this section, including any other rules and procedures adopted pursuant to this section and the penalties for noncompliance;

(10) establish appropriate administrative, technical, and physical safeguards to insure the security and confidentiality of records and to protect against any anticipated threats or hazards to their security or integrity which could result in substantial harm, embarrassment, inconvenience, or unfairness to any individual on whom information is maintained;

(11) at least 30 days prior to publication of information under paragraph (4)(D) of this subsection, publish in the Federal Register notice of any new use or intended use of the information in the system, and provide an opportunity for interested persons to submit written data, views, or arguments to the agency; and

(12) if such agency is a recipient agency or a source agency in a matching program with a non-Federal agency, with respect to any establishment or revision of a matching program, at least 30 days prior to conducting such program, publish in the Federal Register notice of such establishment or revision.

(f) Agency Rules

In order to carry out the provisions of this section, each agency that maintains a system of records shall promulgate rules, in accordance with the requirements (including general notice) of section 553 of this title, which shall–

(1) establish procedures whereby an individual can be notified in response to his request if any system of records named by the individual contains a record pertaining to him;

(2) define reasonable times, places, and requirements for identifying an individual who requests his record or information pertaining to him before the agency shall make the record or information available to the individual;

(3) establish procedures for the disclosure to an individual upon his request of his record or information pertaining to him, including special procedure, if deemed necessary, for the disclosure to an individual of medical records, including psychological records, pertaining to him;

(4) establish procedures for reviewing a request from an individual concerning the amendment of any record or information pertaining to the individual, for making a determination on the request, for an appeal within the agency of an initial adverse agency determination, and for whatever additional means may be necessary for each individual to be able to exercise fully his rights under this section; and

(5) establish fees to be charged, if any, to any individual for making copies of his record, excluding the cost of any search for and review of the record.

The Office of the Federal Register shall biennially compile and publish the rules promulgated under this subsection and agency notices published under subsection (e)(4) of this section in a form available to the public at low cost.

(g) Civil Remedies

(1) Whenever any agency

(A) makes a determination under subsection (d)(3) of this section not to amend an individual's record in accordance with his request, or fails to make such review in conformity with that subsection;

(B) refuses to comply with an individual request under subsection (d)(1) of this section;

(C) fails to maintain any record concerning any individual with such accuracy, relevance, timeliness, and completeness as is necessary to assure fairness in any determination relating to the qualifications, character, rights, or opportunities of, or benefits to the individual that may be made on the basis of such record, and consequently a determination is made which is adverse to the individual; or

(D) fails to comply with any other provision of this section, or any rule promulgated thereunder, in such a way as to have an adverse effect on an individual, the individual may bring a civil action against the agency, and the district courts of the United States shall have jurisdiction in the matters under the provisions of this subsection.

(2)(A) In any suit brought under the provisions of subsection (g)(1)(A) of this section, the court may order the agency to amend the individual's record in accordance with his request or in such other way as the court may direct. In such a case the court shall determine the matter de novo.

(B) The court may assess against the United States reasonable attorney fees and other litigation costs reasonably incurred in any case under this paragraph in which the complainant has substantially prevailed.

(3)(A) In any suit brought under the provisions of subsection (g)(1)(B) of this section, the court may enjoin the agency from withholding the records and order the production to the complainant of any agency records improperly withheld from him. In such a case the court shall determine the matter de novo, and may examine the contents of any agency records in camera to determine whether the records or any portion thereof may be withheld under any of the exemptions set forth in subsection (k) of this section, and the burden is on the agency to sustain its action.

(B) The court may assess against the United States reasonable attorney fees and other litigation costs reasonably incurred in any case under this paragraph in which the complainant has substantially prevailed.

(4) In any suit brought under the provisions of subsection (g)(1)(C) or (D) of this section in which the court determines that the agency acted in a manner which was intentional or willful, the United States shall be liable to the individual in an amount equal to the sum of–

(A) actual damages sustained by the individual as a result of the refusal or failure, but in no case shall a person entitled to recovery receive less than the sum of $1,000; and

(B) the costs of the action together with reasonable attorney fees as determined by the court.

(5) An action to enforce any liability created under this section may be brought in the district court of the United States in the district in which the complainant resides, or has his principal place of business, or in which the agency records are situated, or in the District of Columbia, without regard to the amount in controversy, within two years from the date on which the cause of action arises, except that where an agency has materially and willfully misrepresented any information required under this section to be disclosed to an individual and the information so misrepresented is material to establishment of the liability of the agency to the individual under this section, the action may be brought at any time within two years after discovery by the individual of the misrepresentation. Nothing in this section shall be construed to authorize any civil action by reason of any injury sustained as the result of a disclosure of a record prior to September 27, 1975.

(h) Rights of Legal Guardians

For the purposes of this section, the parent of any minor, or the legal guardian of any individual who has been declared to be incompetent due to physical or mental incapacity or age by a court of competent jurisdiction, may act on behalf of the individual.

United States
Privacy Act

(i) Criminal Penalties.

(1) Any officer or employee of an agency, who by virtue of his employment or official position, has possession of, or access to, agency records which contain individually identifiable information the disclosure of which is prohibited by this section or by rules or regulations established thereunder, and who knowing that disclosure of the specific material is so prohibited, willfully discloses the material in any manner to any person or agency not entitled to receive it, shall be guilty of a misdemeanor and fined not more than $5,000.

(2) Any officer or employee of any agency who willfully maintains a system of records without meeting the notice requirements of subsection (e)(4) of this section shall be guilty of a misdemeanor and fined not more than $5,000.

(3) Any person who knowingly and willfully requests or obtains any record concerning an individual from an agency under false pretenses shall be guilty of a misdemeanor and fined not more than $5,000.

(j) General Exemptions

The head of any agency may promulgate rules, in accordance with the requirements (including general notice) of sections 553(b)(1), (2), and (3), (c), and (e) of this title, to exempt any system of records within the agency from any part of this section except subsections (b), (c)(1) and (2), (e)(4)(A) through (F), (e)(6), (7), (9), (10), and (11), and (i) if the system of records is–

(1) maintained by the Central Intelligence Agency; or

(2) maintained by an agency or component thereof which performs as its principal function any activity pertaining to the enforcement of criminal laws, including police efforts to prevent, control, or reduce crime or to apprehend criminals, and the activities of prosecutors, courts, correctional, probation, pardon, or parole authorities, and which consists of (A) information compiled for the purpose of identifying individual criminal offenders and alleged offenders and consisting only of identifying data and notations of arrests, the nature and disposition of criminal charges, sentencing, confinement, release, and parole and probation status; (B) information compiled for the purpose of a criminal investigation, including reports of informants and investigators, and associated with an identifiable individual; or (C) reports identifiable to an individual compiled at any stage of the process of enforcement of the criminal laws from arrest or indictment through release from supervision.

At the time rules are adopted under this subsection, the agency shall include in the statement required under section 553(c) of this title, the reasons why the system of records is to be exempted from a provision of this section.

(k) Specific Exemptions

The head of any agency may promulgate rules, in accordance with the requirements (including general notice) of sections 553(b)(1), (2), and (3), (c), and (e) of this title, to exempt any system of records within the agency from subsections (c)(3), (d), (e)(1), (e)(4)(G), (H), and (I) and (f) of this section if the system of records is–

(1) subject to the provisions of section 552(b)(1) of this title;

(2) investigatory material compiled for law enforcement purposes, other than material within the scope of subsection (j)(2) of this section: Provided, however, That if any individual is denied any right, privilege, or benefit that he would otherwise be entitled by Federal law, or for which he would otherwise be eligible, as a result of the maintenance of such material, such material shall be provided to such individual, except to the extent that the disclosure of such material would reveal the identity of a source who furnished information to the Government under an express promise that the identity of the source would be held in confidence, or, prior to the effective date of this section, under an implied promise that the identity of the source would be held in confidence;

(3) maintained in connection with providing protective services to the President of the United States or other individuals pursuant to section 3056 of title 18;

(4) required by statute to be maintained and used solely as statistical records;

(5) investigatory material compiled solely for the purpose of determining suitability, eligibility, or qualifications for Federal civilian employment, military service, Federal contracts, or access to classified information, but only to the extent that the disclosure of such material would reveal the identity of a source who furnished information to the Government under an express promise that the identity of the source would be held in confidence, or, prior to the effective date of this section, under an implied promise that the identity of the source would be held in confidence;

(6) testing or examination material used solely to determine individual qualifications for appointment or promotion in the Federal service the disclosure of which would compromise the objectivity or fairness of the testing or examination process; or

(7) evaluation material used to determine potential for promotion in the armed services, but only to the extent that the disclosure of such material would reveal the identity of a source who furnished information to the Government under an express promise that the identity of the source would be held in confidence, or, prior to the effective date of this section, under an implied promise that the identity of the source would be held in confidence.

At the time rules are adopted under this subsection, the agency shall include in the statement required under section 553(c) of this title, the reasons why the system of records is to be exempted from a provision of this section.

(l) Archival Records

Each agency record which is accepted by the Archivist of the United States for storage, processing, and servicing in accordance with section 3103 of title 44 shall, for the purposes of this section, be considered to be maintained by the agency which deposited the record and shall be subject to the provisions of this section. The Archivist of the United States shall not disclose the record except to the agency which maintains the record, or under rules established by that agency which are not inconsistent with the provisions of this section.

(2) Each agency record pertaining to an identifiable individual which was transferred to the National Archives of the United States as a record which has sufficient historical or other value to warrant its continued preservation by the United States Government, prior to the effective date of this section, shall, for the purposes of this section, be considered to be maintained by the National Archives and shall not be subject to the provisions of this section, except that a statement generally describing such records (modeled after the requirements relating to records subject to subsections (e)(4)(A) through (G) of this section) shall be published in the Federal Register.

(3) Each agency record pertaining to an identifiable individual which is transferred to the National Archives of the United States as a record which has sufficient historical or other value to warrant its continued preservation by the United States Government, on or after the effective date of this section, shall, for the purposes of this section, be considered to be maintained by the National Archives and shall be exempt from the requirements of this section except subsections (e)(4)(A) through (G) and (e)(9) of this section.

(m) Government Contractors

(1) When an agency provides by a contract for the operation by or on behalf of the agency of a system of records to accomplish an agency function, the agency shall, consistent with its authority, cause the requirements of this section to be applied to such system. For purposes of subsection (i) of this section any such contractor and any employee of such contractor, if such contract is agreed to on or after the effective date of this section, shall be considered to be an employee of an agency.

(2) A consumer reporting agency to which a record is disclosed under section 3711(f) of title 31 shall not be considered a contractor for the purposes of this section.

(n) Mailing Lists

 An individual's name and address may not be sold or rented by an agency unless such action is specifically authorized by law. This provision shall not be construed to require the withholding of names and addresses otherwise permitted to be made public.

(o) Matching Agreements

(1) No record which is contained in a system of records may be disclosed to a recipient agency or non-Federal agency for use in a computer matching program except pursuant to a written agreement between the source agency and the recipient agency or non-Federal agency specifying—

[handwritten marginalia: Notice date — subject isn't involved here.]

(A) the purpose and legal authority for conducting the program;

(B) the justification for the program and the anticipated results, including a specific estimate of any savings;

(C) a description of the records that will be matched, including each data element that will be used, the approximate number of records that will be matched, and the projected starting and completion dates of the matching program;

(D) procedures for providing individualized notice at the time of application, and notice periodically thereafter as directed by the Data Integrity Board of such agency (subject to guidance provided by the Director of the Office of Management and Budget pursuant to subsection (v)), to–

(i) applicants for and recipients of financial assistance or payments under Federal benefit programs, and

(ii) applicants for and holders of positions as Federal personnel, that any information provided by such applicants, recipients, holders, and individuals may be subject to verification through matching programs;

(E) procedures for verifying information produced in such matching program as required by subsection (p);

(F) procedures for the retention and timely destruction of identifiable records created by a recipient agency or non-Federal agency in such matching program;

(G) procedures for ensuring the administrative, technical, and physical security of the records matched and the results of such programs;

(H) prohibitions on duplication and redisclosure of records provided by the source agency within or outside the recipient agency or the non-Federal agency, except where required by law or essential to the conduct of the matching program;

(I) procedures governing the use by a recipient agency or non-Federal agency of records provided in a matching program by a source agency, including procedures governing return of the records to the source agency or destruction of records used in such program;

(J) information on assessments that have been made on the accuracy of the records that will be used in such matching program; and

(K) that the Comptroller General may have access to all records of a recipient agency or a non-Federal agency that the Comptroller General deems necessary in order to monitor or verify compliance with the agreement.

(2)(A) A copy of each agreement entered into pursuant to paragraph (1) shall–

> (i) be transmitted to the Committee on Governmental Affairs of the Senate and the Committee on Government Operations of the House of Representatives; and

> (ii) be available upon request to the public.

(B) No such agreement shall be effective until 30 days after the date on which such a copy is transmitted pursuant to subparagraph (A)(i).

(C) Such an agreement shall remain in effect only for such period, not to exceed 18 months, as the Data Integrity Board of the agency determines is appropriate in light of the purposes, and length of time necessary for the conduct, of the matching program.

(D) Within 3 months prior to the expiration of such an agreement pursuant to subparagraph (C), the Data Integrity Board of the agency may, without additional review, renew the matching agreement for a current, ongoing matching program for not more than one additional year if–

> (i) such program will be conducted without any change; and

> (ii) each party to the agreement certifies to the Board in writing that the program has been conducted in compliance with the agreement.

(p) Verification and Opportunity to Contest Findings

(1) In order to protect any individual whose records are used in a matching program, no recipient agency, non-Federal agency, or source agency may suspend, terminate, reduce, or make a final denial of any financial assistance or payment under a Federal benefit program to such individual, or take other adverse action against such individual, as a result of information produced by such matching program, until–

(A)(i) the agency has independently verified the information; or

> (ii) the Data Integrity Board of the agency, or in the case of a non-Federal agency the Data Integrity Board of the source agency, determines in accordance with guidance issued by the Director of the Office of Management and Budget that–

> > (I) the information is limited to identification and amount of benefits paid by the source agency under a Federal benefit program; and

> > (II) there is a high degree of confidence that the information provided to the recipient agency is accurate;

(B) the individual receives a notice from the agency containing a statement of its findings and informing the individual of the opportunity to contest such findings; and

(C)(i) the expiration of any time period established for the program by statute or regulation for the individual to respond to that notice; or

(ii) in the case of a program for which no such period is established, the end of the 30-day period beginning on the date on which notice under subparagraph (B) is mailed or otherwise provided to the individual.

(2) Independent verification referred to in paragraph (1) requires investigation and confirmation of specific information relating to an individual that is used as a basis for an adverse action against the individual, including where applicable investigation and confirmation of–

(A) the amount of any asset or income involved;

(B) whether such individual actually has or had access to such asset or income for such individual's own use; and

(C) the period or periods when the individual actually had such asset or income.

(3) Notwithstanding paragraph (1), an agency may take any appropriate action otherwise prohibited by such paragraph if the agency determines that the public health or public safety may be adversely affected or significantly threatened during any notice period required by such paragraph.

(q) Sanctions

(1) Notwithstanding any other provision of law, no source agency may disclose any record which is contained in a system of records to a recipient agency or non-Federal agency for a matching program if such source agency has reason to believe that the requirements of subsection (p), or any matching agreement entered into pursuant to subsection (o), or both, are not being met by such recipient agency.

(2) No source agency may renew a matching agreement unless–

(A) the recipient agency or non-Federal agency has certified that it has complied with the provisions of that agreement; and

(B) the source agency has no reason to believe that the certification is inaccurate.

(r) Report on New Systems and Matching Programs

Each agency that proposes to establish or make a significant change in a system of records or a matching program shall provide adequate advance notice of any such proposal (in duplicate) to the Committee on Government Operations of the House of Representatives, the Committee on Governmental Affairs of the Senate, and the Office of Management and Budget in order to permit an evaluation of the probable or potential effect of such proposal on the privacy or other rights of individuals.

(s) Biennial Report

The President shall biennially submit to the Speaker of the House of Representatives and the President pro tempore of the Senate a report–

(1) describing the actions of the Director of the Office of Management and Budget pursuant to section 6 of the Privacy Act of 1974 during the preceding 2 years;

(2) describing the exercise of individual rights of access and amendment under this section during such years;

(3) identifying changes in or additions to systems of records;

(4) containing such other information concerning administration of this section as may be necessary or useful to the Congress in reviewing the effectiveness of this section in carrying out the purposes of the Privacy Act of 1974.

(t) Effect of Other Laws

(1) No agency shall rely on any exemption contained in section 552 of this title to withhold from an individual any record which is otherwise accessible to such individual under the provisions of this section.

(2) No agency shall rely on any exemption in this section to withhold from an individual any record which is otherwise accessible to such individual under the provisions of section 552 of this title.

(u) Data Integrity Boards

(1) Every agency conducting or participating in a matching program shall establish a Data Integrity Board to oversee and coordinate among the various components of such agency the agency's implementation of this section.

(2) Each Data Integrity Board shall consist of senior officials designated by the head of the agency, and shall include any senior official designated by the head of the agency as responsible for implementation of this section, and the inspector general of the agency, if any. The inspector general shall not serve as chairman of the Data Integrity Board.

(3) Each Data Integrity Board–

(A) shall review, approve, and maintain all written agreements for receipt or disclosure of agency records for matching programs to ensure compliance with subsection (o), and all relevant statutes, regulations, and guidelines;

(B) shall review all matching programs in which the agency has participated during the year, either as a source agency or recipient agency, determine compliance with applicable laws, regulations, guidelines, and agency agreements, and assess the costs and benefits of such programs;

(C) shall review all recurring matching programs in which the agency has participated during the year, either as a source agency or recipient agency, for continued justification for such disclosures;

(D) shall compile an annual report, which shall be submitted to the head of the agency and the Office of Management and Budget and made available to the public on request, describing the matching activities of the agency, including–

(i) matching programs in which the agency has participated as a source agency or recipient agency;

(ii) matching agreements proposed under subsection (o) that were disapproved by the Board;

(iii) any changes in membership or structure of the Board in the preceding year;

(iv) the reasons for any waiver of the requirement in paragraph (4) of this section for completion and submission of a cost-benefit analysis prior to the approval of a matching program;

(v) any violations of matching agreements that have been alleged or identified and any corrective action taken; and

(vi) any other information required by the Director of the Office of Management and Budget to be included in such report;

(E) shall serve as a clearinghouse for receiving and providing information on the accuracy, completeness, and reliability of records used in matching programs;

(F) shall provide interpretation and guidance to agency components and personnel on the requirements of this section for matching programs;

(G) shall review agency recordkeeping and disposal policies and practices for matching programs to assure compliance with this section; and

(H) may review and report on any agency matching activities that

are not matching programs.

(4)(A) Except as provided in subparagraphs (B) and (C), a Data Integrity Board shall not approve any written agreement for a matching program unless the agency has completed and submitted to such Board a cost-benefit analysis of the proposed program and such analysis demonstrates that the program is likely to be cost effective.

(B) The Board may waive the requirements of subparagraph (A) of this paragraph if it determines in writing, in accordance with guidelines prescribed by the Director of the Office of Management and Budget, that a cost-benefit analysis is not required.

(C) A cost-benefit analysis shall not be required under subparagraph (A) prior to the initial approval of a written agreement for a matching program that is specifically required by statute. Any subsequent written agreement for such a program shall not be approved by the Data Integrity Board unless the agency has submitted a cost-benefit analysis of the program as conducted under the preceding approval of such agreement.

(5)(A) If a matching agreement is disapproved by a Data Integrity Board, any party to such agreement may appeal the disapproval to the Director of the Office of Management and Budget. Timely notice of the filing of such an appeal shall be provided by the Director of the Office of Management and Budget to the

Committee on Governmental Affairs of the Senate and the Committee on Government Operations of the House of Representatives.

(B) The Director of the Office of Management and Budget may approve a matching agreement notwithstanding the disapproval of a Data Integrity Board if the Director determines that–

(i) the matching program will be consistent with all applicable legal, regulatory, and policy requirements;

(ii) there is adequate evidence that the matching agreement will be cost-effective; and

(iii) the matching program is in the public interest.

(C) The decision of the Director to approve a matching agreement shall not take effect until 30 days after it is reported to committees described in subparagraph (A).

(D) If the Data Integrity Board and the Director of the Office of Management and Budget disapprove a matching program proposed by the inspector general of an agency, the inspector general may report the disapproval to the head of the agency and to the Congress.

(6) In the reports required by paragraphs (3)(D), agency matching activities that are not matching programs may be reported on an aggregate basis, if and to the extent necessary to protect ongoing law enforcement or counterintelligence investigations.

(v) *Office of Management and Budget Responsibilities*

The Director of the Office of Management and Budget shall–

(1) develop and, after notice and opportunity for public comment, prescribe guidelines and regulations for the use of agencies in implementing the provisions of this section; and

(2) provide continuing assistance to and oversight of the implementation of this section by agencies.

Section 7 Disclosure of Social Security Number

(a)(1) It shall be unlawful for any Federal, State or local government agency to deny to any individual any right, benefit, or privilege provided by law because of such individual's refusal to disclose his social security account number.

(2) the provisions of paragraph (1) of this subsection shall not apply with respect to--

(A) any disclosure which is required by Federal statute, or

(B) the disclosure of a social security number to any Federal, State, or local agency maintaining a system of records in existence and operating before January 1, 1975, if such disclosure was required under statute or regulation adopted prior to such date to verify the identity of an individual.

(b) Any Federal, State, or local government agency which requests an individual to disclose his social security account number shall inform that individual whether that disclosure is mandatory or voluntary, by what statutory or other authority such number is solicited, and what uses will be made of it.

United States
Freedom of Information Act

FREEDOM OF INFORMATION ACT
(1974)

Summary

Whereas the Privacy Act of 1974 grants citizens access to their own personal files kept by the government, the Freedom of Information Act (FOIA) allows citizens to access all federal agency records. FOIA requires federal agencies to make information available to any person making an appropriate request. Any conflicts between the Privacy Act and FOIA (for example when personal records of some sort are requested under FOIA) are reconciled by Section 552a(b)(2) of the Privacy Act, which exempts information requested under FOIA from the scope of the Privacy Act.

Once material has been requested under FOIA, an agency has twenty days to reply. The agency may comply with the request, ask for clarification, or deny the request under one of the Act's nine enumerated exceptions. Two of these exceptions relate to the protection of personal data held by government agencies. Section 552(b)(6) exempts agencies from providing personnel and medical files, and other files "the disclosures of which would constitute a clearly unwarranted invasion of personal privacy." Section 552(b)(7) exempts information compiled for law enforcement purposes where release of that information would jeopardize the right to a fair trial, unreasonably intrude on privacy, or disclose the identity of confidential sources. The FOIA favors disclosure and where agencies invoke exemptions such decisions are subject to judicial review.

In 1996, the Senate and the House of Representatives completed action on the Electronic Freedom of Information Act Amendments. The President signed this legislation into law on October 2, 1996. The EFIOA expands the Freedom of Information Act to include access to electronic records and databases in electronic format, if such format is requested. The amendments also require agencies to expedite the processing of certain FOIA requests.

References

Public Law 89-554 as amended. Codified at 5 USC § 552.
[http://www.usdoj.gov/04foia/foiastat.htm]

Department of Justice, *Freedom of Information Act Guide & Privacy Act Overview* (May 2000)
[http://www.usdoj.gov/oip/foi-act.htm]

Department of Justice, *Freedom of Information Act Reference Guide* (August 2000)
[http://www.usdoj.gov/04foia/04_3.html]

Department of Justice and the General Services Administration, *Your Right to Federal Records Questions and Answers on the Freedom of Information Act and Privacy Act* (October 2000)

[http://www.pueblo.gsa.gov/cic_text/fed_prog/foia/foia.htm]

§ 552. Public information; agency rules, opinions, orders, records, and proceedings

(a) Each agency shall make available to the public information as follows:

(1) Each agency shall separately state and currently publish in the Federal Register for the guidance of the public -

(A) descriptions of its central and field organization and the established places at which, the employees (and in the case of a uniformed service, the members) from whom, and the methods whereby, the public may obtain information, make submittals or requests, or obtain decisions;

(B) statements of the general course and method by which its functions are channeled and determined, including the nature and requirements of all formal and informal procedures available;

(C) rules of procedure, descriptions of forms available or the places at which forms may be obtained, and instructions as to the scope and contents of all papers, reports, or examinations;

(D) substantive rules of general applicability adopted as authorized by law, and statements of general policy or interpretations of general applicability formulated and adopted by the agency; and

(E) each amendment, revision, or repeal of the foregoing. Except to the extent that a person has actual and timely notice of the terms thereof, a person may not in any manner be required to resort to, or be adversely affected by, a matter required to be published in the Federal Register and not so published. For the purpose of this paragraph, matter reasonably available to the class of persons affected thereby is deemed published in the Federal Register when incorporated by reference therein with the approval of the Director of the Federal Register.

(2) Each agency, in accordance with published rules, shall make available for public inspection and copying -

(A) final opinions, including concurring and dissenting opinions, as well as orders, made in the adjudication of cases;

(B) those statements of policy and interpretations which have been adopted by the agency and are not published in the Federal Register;

(C) administrative staff manuals and instructions to staff that affect a member of the public;

(D) copies of all records, regardless of form or format, which have been released to any person under paragraph (3) and which, because of the nature of their subject matter, the agency determines have become or are likely to become the subject of subsequent requests for substantially the same records; and

(E) a general index of the records referred to under subparagraph (D); unless the materials are promptly published and copies offered for sale. For records created on or after November 1, 1996, within one year after such date, each agency shall make such records available, including by computer telecommunications or, if computer telecommunications means have not been established by the agency, by other electronic means. To the extent required to prevent a clearly unwarranted invasion of personal privacy, an agency may delete identifying details when it makes available or publishes an opinion, statement of policy, interpretation, staff manual, instruction, or copies of records referred to in subparagraph (D). However, in each case the justification for the deletion shall be explained fully in writing, and the extent of such deletion shall be indicated on the portion of the record which is made available or published, unless including that indication would harm an interest protected by the exemption in subsection (b) under which the deletion is made. If technically feasible, the extent of the deletion shall be indicated at the place in the record where the deletion was made. Each agency shall also maintain and make available for public inspection and copying current indexes providing identifying information for the public as to any matter issued, adopted, or promulgated after July 4, 1967, and required by this paragraph to be made available or published. Each agency shall promptly publish, quarterly or more frequently, and distribute (by sale or otherwise) copies of each index or supplements thereto unless it determines by order published in the Federal Register that the publication would be unnecessary and impracticable, in which case the agency shall nonetheless provide copies of such index on request at a cost not to exceed the direct cost of duplication. Each agency shall make the index referred to in subparagraph (E) available by computer telecommunications by December 31, 1999. A final order, opinion, statement of policy, interpretation, or staff manual or instruction that affects a member of the public may be relied on, used, or cited as precedent by an agency against a party other than an agency only if -

> (i) it has been indexed and either made available or published as provided by this paragraph; or
>
> (ii) the party has actual and timely notice of the terms thereof.

(3)

> (A) Except with respect to the records made available under paragraphs (1) and (2) of this subsection, each agency, upon any request for records which (i) reasonably describes such records and (ii) is made in accordance with published

rules stating the time, place, fees (if any), and procedures to be followed, shall make the records promptly available to any person.

(B) In making any record available to a person under this paragraph, an agency shall provide the record in any form or format requested by the person if the record is readily reproducible by the agency in that form or format. Each agency shall make reasonable efforts to maintain its records in forms or formats that are reproducible for purposes of this section.

(C) In responding under this paragraph to a request for records, an agency shall make reasonable efforts to search for the records in electronic form or format, except when such efforts would significantly interfere with the operation of the agency's automated information system.

(D) For purposes of this paragraph, the term "search" means to review, manually or by automated means, agency records for the purpose of locating those records which are responsive to a request.

(4)

  (A)

    (i) In order to carry out the provisions of this section, each agency shall promulgate regulations, pursuant to notice and receipt of public comment, specifying the schedule of fees applicable to the processing of requests under this section and establishing procedures and guidelines for determining when such fees should be waived or reduced. Such schedule shall conform to the guidelines which shall be promulgated, pursuant to notice and receipt of public comment, by the Director of the Office of Management and Budget and which shall provide for a uniform schedule of fees for all agencies.

    (ii) Such agency regulations shall provide that -

      (I) fees shall be limited to reasonable standard charges for document search, duplication, and review, when records are requested for commercial use;

      (II) fees shall be limited to reasonable standard charges for document duplication when records are not sought for commercial use and the request is made by an educational or noncommercial scientific institution, whose purpose is scholarly or scientific research; or a representative of the news media; and

      (III) for any request not described in (I) or (II), fees shall be limited to reasonable standard charges for document search and duplication.

    (iii) Documents shall be furnished without any charge or at a charge reduced below the fees established under clause (ii) if disclosure of the information is in the public interest because it is likely to contribute significantly to public understanding of the operations or activities of the government and is not primarily in the commercial interest of the requester.

(iv) Fee schedules shall provide for the recovery of only the direct costs of search, duplication, or review. Review costs shall include only the direct costs incurred during the initial examination of a document for the purposes of determining whether the documents must be disclosed under this section and for the purposes of withholding any portions exempt from disclosure under this section. Review costs may not include any costs incurred in resolving issues of law or policy that may be raised in the course of processing a request under this section. No fee may be charged by any agency under this section -

(I) if the costs of routine collection and processing of the fee are likely to equal or exceed the amount of the fee; or

(II) for any request described in clause (ii) (II) or (III) of this subparagraph for the first two hours of search time or for the first one hundred pages of duplication.

(v) No agency may require advance payment of any fee unless the requester has previously failed to pay fees in a timely fashion, or the agency has determined that the fee will exceed $250.

(vi) Nothing in this subparagraph shall supersede fees chargeable under a statute specifically providing for setting the level of fees for particular types of records.

(vii) In any action by a requester regarding the waiver of fees under this section, the court shall determine the matter de novo: Provided, That the court's review of the matter shall be limited to the record before the agency.

(B) On complaint, the district court of the United States in the district in which the complainant resides, or has his principal place of business, or in which the agency records are situated, or in the District of Columbia, has jurisdiction to enjoin the agency from withholding agency records and to order the production of any agency records improperly withheld from the complainant. In such a case the court shall determine the matter de novo, and may examine the contents of such agency records in camera to determine whether such records or any part thereof shall be withheld under any of the exemptions set forth in subsection (b) of this section, and the burden is on the agency to sustain its action. In addition to any other matters to which a court accords substantial weight, a court shall accord substantial weight to an affidavit of an agency concerning the agency's determination as to technical feasibility under paragraph (2)(C) and subsection (b) and reproducibility under paragraph (3)(B).

(C) Notwithstanding any other provision of law, the defendant shall serve an answer or otherwise plead to any complaint made under this subsection within thirty days after service upon the defendant of the pleading in which such complaint is made, unless the court otherwise directs for good cause shown.

(D) Repealed. Pub. L. 98-620, title IV, Sec. 402(2), Nov. 8, 1984, 98 Stat. 3357.)

(E) The court may assess against the United States reasonable attorney fees and other litigation costs reasonably incurred in any case under this section in which the complainant has substantially prevailed.

(F) Whenever the court orders the production of any agency records improperly withheld from the complainant and assesses against the United States reasonable attorney fees and other litigation costs, and the court additionally issues a written finding that the circumstances surrounding the withholding raise questions whether agency personnel acted arbitrarily or capriciously with respect to the withholding, the Special Counsel shall promptly initiate a proceeding to determine whether disciplinary action is warranted against the officer or employee who was primarily responsible for the withholding. The Special Counsel, after investigation and consideration of the evidence submitted, shall submit his findings and recommendations to the administrative authority of the agency concerned and shall send copies of the findings and recommendations to the officer or employee or his representative. The administrative authority shall take the corrective action that the Special Counsel recommends.

(G) In the event of noncompliance with the order of the court, the district court may punish for contempt the responsible employee, and in the case of a uniformed service, the responsible member.

(5) Each agency having more than one member shall maintain and make available for public inspection a record of the final votes of each member in every agency proceeding.

(6)

(A) Each agency, upon any request for records made under paragraph (1), (2), or (3) of this subsection, shall -

(i) determine within 20 days (excepting Saturdays, Sundays, and legal public holidays) after the receipt of any such request whether to comply with such request and shall immediately notify the person making such request of such determination and the reasons therefor, and of the right of such person to appeal to the head of the agency any adverse determination; and

(ii) make a determination with respect to any appeal within twenty days (excepting Saturdays, Sundays, and legal public holidays) after the receipt of such appeal. If on appeal the denial of the request for records is in whole or in part upheld, the agency shall notify the person making such request of the provisions for judicial review of that determination under paragraph (4) of this subsection.

(B)

(i) In unusual circumstances as specified in this subparagraph, the time limits prescribed in either clause (i) or clause (ii) of subparagraph (A) may be extended by written notice to the person making such request setting forth the unusual circumstances for such extension and the date on which a determination is expected to be dispatched. No such notice shall specify a date that would result in an extension for more than ten working days, except as provided in clause (ii) of this subparagraph.

(ii) With respect to a request for which a written notice under clause (i) extends the time limits prescribed under clause (i) of subparagraph (A), the agency shall notify the person making the request if the request cannot be processed within the time limit specified in that clause and shall provide the person an opportunity to limit the scope of the request so that it may be processed within that time limit or an opportunity to arrange with the agency an alternative time frame for processing the request or a modified request. Refusal by the person to reasonably modify the request or arrange such an alternative time frame shall be considered as a factor in determining whether exceptional circumstances exist for purposes of subparagraph (C).

(iii) As used in this subparagraph, "unusual circumstances" means, but only to the extent reasonably necessary to the proper processing of the particular requests -

(I) the need to search for and collect the requested records from field facilities or other establishments that are separate from the office processing the request;

(II) the need to search for, collect, and appropriately examine a voluminous amount of separate and distinct records which are demanded in a single request; or

(III) the need for consultation, which shall be conducted with all practicable speed, with another agency having a substantial interest in the determination of the request or among two or more components of the agency having substantial subject-matter interest therein.

(iv) Each agency may promulgate regulations, pursuant to notice and receipt of public comment, providing for the aggregation of certain requests by the same requestor, or by a group of requestors acting in concert, if the agency reasonably believes that such requests actually constitute a single request, which would otherwise satisfy the unusual circumstances specified in this subparagraph, and the requests involve clearly related matters. Multiple requests involving unrelated matters shall not be aggregated.

(C)

(i) Any person making a request to any agency for records under paragraph (1), (2), or (3) of this subsection shall be deemed to have exhausted his administrative remedies with respect to such request if the agency fails to comply with the applicable time limit provisions of this paragraph. If the Government can show exceptional circumstances exist and that the agency is exercising due diligence in responding to the request, the court may retain jurisdiction and allow the agency additional time to complete its review of the records. Upon any determination by an agency to comply with a request for records, the records shall be made promptly available to such person making such request. Any notification of denial of any request for records under this subsection shall set forth the names and titles or positions of each person responsible for the denial of such request.

(ii) For purposes of this subparagraph, the term "exceptional circumstances" does not include a delay that results from a predictable agency workload of requests under this section, unless the agency demonstrates reasonable progress in reducing its backlog of pending requests.

(iii) Refusal by a person to reasonably modify the scope of a request or arrange an alternative time frame for processing a request (or a modified request) under clause (ii) after being given an opportunity to do so by the agency to whom the person made the request shall be considered as a factor in determining whether exceptional circumstances exist for purposes of this subparagraph.

(D)

(i) Each agency may promulgate regulations, pursuant to notice and receipt of public comment, providing for multitrack processing of requests for records based on the amount of work or time (or both) involved in processing requests.

(ii) Regulations under this subparagraph may provide a person making a request that does not qualify for the fastest multitrack processing an opportunity to limit the scope of the request in order to qualify for faster processing.

(iii) This subparagraph shall not be considered to affect the requirement under subparagraph (C) to exercise due diligence.

(E)

(i) Each agency shall promulgate regulations, pursuant to notice and receipt of public comment, providing for expedited processing of requests for records -

(I) in cases in which the person requesting the records demonstrates a compelling need; and

(II) in other cases determined by the agency.

(ii) Notwithstanding clause (i), regulations under this subparagraph must ensure -

United States
Freedom of Information Act

(I) that a determination of whether to provide expedited processing shall be made, and notice of the determination shall be provided to the person making the request, within 10 days after the date of the request; and

(II) expeditious consideration of administrative appeals of such determinations of whether to provide expedited processing.

(iii) An agency shall process as soon as practicable any request for records to which the agency has granted expedited processing under this subparagraph. Agency action to deny or affirm denial of a request for expedited processing pursuant to this subparagraph, and failure by an agency to respond in a timely manner to such a request shall be subject to judicial review under paragraph (4), except that the judicial review shall be based on the record before the agency at the time of the determination.

(iv) A district court of the United States shall not have jurisdiction to review an agency denial of expedited processing of a request for records after the agency has provided a complete response to the request.

(v) For purposes of this subparagraph, the term "compelling need" means -

(I) that a failure to obtain requested records on an expedited basis under this paragraph could reasonably be expected to pose an imminent threat to the life or physical safety of an individual; or

(II) with respect to a request made by a person primarily engaged in disseminating information, urgency to inform the public concerning actual or alleged Federal Government activity.

(vi) A demonstration of a compelling need by a person making a request for expedited processing shall be made by a statement certified by such person to be true and correct to the best of such person's knowledge and belief.

(F) In denying a request for records, in whole or in part, an agency shall make a reasonable effort to estimate the volume of any requested matter the provision of which is denied, and shall provide any such estimate to the person making the request, unless providing such estimate would harm an interest protected by the exemption in subsection (b) pursuant to which the denial is made.

(b) This section does not apply to matters that are -

(1) (A) specifically authorized under criteria established by an Executive order to be kept secret in the interest of national defense or foreign policy and (B) are in fact properly classified pursuant to such Executive order;

(2) related solely to the internal personnel rules and practices of an agency;

(3) specifically exempted from disclosure by statute (other than section 552b of this title), provided that such statute (A) requires that the matters be withheld from the public in such a manner as to leave no discretion on the issue, or (B) establishes particular criteria for withholding or refers to particular types of matters to be withheld;

(4) trade secrets and commercial or financial information obtained from a person and privileged or confidential;

(5) inter-agency or intra-agency memorandums or letters which would not be available by law to a party other than an agency in litigation with the agency;

(6) personnel and medical files and similar files the disclosure of which would constitute a clearly unwarranted invasion of personal privacy;

(7) records or information compiled for law enforcement purposes, but only to the extent that the production of such law enforcement records or information (A) could reasonably be expected to interfere with enforcement proceedings, (B) would deprive a person of a right to a fair trial or an impartial adjudication, (C) could reasonably be expected to constitute an unwarranted invasion of personal privacy, (D) could reasonably be expected to disclose the identity of a confidential source, including a State, local, or foreign agency or authority or any private institution which furnished information on a confidential basis, and, in the case of a record or information compiled by criminal law enforcement authority in the course of a criminal investigation or by an agency conducting a lawful national security intelligence investigation, information furnished by a confidential source, (E) would disclose techniques and procedures for law enforcement investigations or prosecutions, or would disclose guidelines for law enforcement investigations or prosecutions if such disclosure could reasonably be expected to risk circumvention of the law, or (F) could reasonably be expected to endanger the life or physical safety of any individual;

(8) contained in or related to examination, operating, or condition reports prepared by, on behalf of, or for the use of an agency responsible for the regulation or supervision of financial institutions; or

(9) geological and geophysical information and data, including maps, concerning wells. Any reasonably segregable portion of a record shall be provided to any person requesting such record after deletion of the portions which are exempt under this subsection. The amount of information deleted shall be indicated on the released portion of the record, unless including that indication would harm an interest protected by the exemption in this subsection under which the deletion is made. If technically feasible, the amount of the information deleted shall be indicated at the place in the record where such deletion is made.

(c) (1) Whenever a request is made which involves access to records described in subsection (b)(7)(A) and -

(A) the investigation or proceeding involves a possible violation of criminal law; and

(B) there is reason to believe that (i) the subject of the investigation or proceeding is not aware of its pendency, and (ii) disclosure of the existence of the records could reasonably be expected to interfere with enforcement

proceedings, the agency may, during only such time as that circumstance continues, treat the records as not subject to the requirements of this section.

(2) Whenever informant records maintained by a criminal law enforcement agency under an informant's name or personal identifier are requested by a third party according to the informant's name or personal identifier, the agency may treat the records as not subject to the requirements of this section unless the informant's status as an informant has been officially confirmed.

(3) Whenever a request is made which involves access to records maintained by the Federal Bureau of Investigation pertaining to foreign intelligence or counterintelligence, or international terrorism, and the existence of the records is classified information as provided in subsection (b)(1), the Bureau may, as long as the existence of the records remains classified information, treat the records as not subject to the requirements of this section.

(d) This section does not authorize withholding of information or limit the availability of records to the public, except as specifically stated in this section. This section is not authority to withhold information from Congress.

(e) (1) On or before February 1 of each year, each agency shall submit to the Attorney General of the United States a report which shall cover the preceding fiscal year and which shall include -

(A) the number of determinations made by the agency not to comply with requests for records made to such agency under subsection (a) and the reasons for each such determination;

(B) (i) the number of appeals made by persons under subsection (a)(6), the result of such appeals, and the reason for the action upon each appeal that results in a denial of information; and (ii) a complete list of all statutes that the agency relies upon to authorize the agency to withhold information under subsection (b)(3), a description of whether a court has upheld the decision of the agency to withhold information under each such statute, and a concise description of the scope of any information withheld;

(C) the number of requests for records pending before the agency as of September 30 of the preceding year, and the median number of days that such requests had been pending before the agency as of that date;

(D) the number of requests for records received by the agency and the number of requests which the agency processed;

(E) the median number of days taken by the agency to process different types of requests;

(F) the total amount of fees collected by the agency for processing requests; and

(G) the number of full-time staff of the agency devoted to processing requests for records under this section, and the total amount expended by the agency for processing such requests.

(2) Each agency shall make each such report available to the public including by computer telecommunications, or if computer telecommunications means have not been established by the agency, by other electronic means.

(3) The Attorney General of the United States shall make each report which has been made available by electronic means available at a single electronic access point. The Attorney General of the United States shall notify the Chairman and ranking minority member of the Committee on Government Reform and Oversight of the House of Representatives and the Chairman and ranking minority member of the Committees on Governmental Affairs and the Judiciary of the Senate, no later than April 1 of the year in which each such report is issued, that such reports are available by electronic means.

(4) The Attorney General of the United States, in consultation with the Director of the Office of Management and Budget, shall develop reporting and performance guidelines in connection with reports required by this subsection by October 1, 1997, and may establish additional requirements for such reports as the Attorney General determines may be useful.

(5) The Attorney General of the United States shall submit an annual report on or before April 1 of each calendar year which shall include for the prior calendar year a listing of the number of cases arising under this section, the exemption involved in each case, the disposition of such case, and the cost, fees, and penalties assessed under subparagraphs (E), (F), and (G) of subsection (a)(4). Such report shall also include a description of the efforts undertaken by the Department of Justice to encourage agency compliance with this section.

(f) For purposes of this section, the term -

(1) "agency" as defined in section 551(1) of this title includes any executive department, military department, Government corporation, Government controlled corporation, or other establishment in the executive branch of the Government (including the Executive Office of the President), or any independent regulatory agency; and

(2) "record" and any other term used in this section in reference to information includes any information that would be an agency record subject to the requirements of this section when maintained by an agency in any format, including an electronic format.

(g) The head of each agency shall prepare and make publicly available upon request, reference material or a guide for requesting records or information from the agency, subject to the exemptions in subsection (b), including -

(1) an index of all major information systems of the agency;

(2) a description of major information and record locator systems maintained by the agency; and

(3) a handbook for obtaining various types and categories of public information from the agency pursuant to chapter 35 of title 44, and under this section.

United States
Family Educational Rights and Privacy Act

FAMILY EDUCATIONAL RIGHTS AND PRIVACY ACT (1974)

Summary

The Family Educational Rights and Privacy Act (FERPA) protects the confidentiality of student educational records. It states that educational institutions shall not disclose any information from those records without the written consent of the student, or, if the student is a minor, without the written consent of his or her parents. Under the Act, students have the right to inspect and review their own educational records, request corrections, stop the release of personally identifiable information, and obtain a copy of the institutional policy concerning access to educational records. The Act applies to primary, secondary, and post-secondary educational institutions.

Federal funding will be denied to any institution that discloses information without the student's prior written consent, or without his or her parent's consent if the student is under eighteen years of age. There are exceptions to allow certain personnel within the institution to see the records and to allow certain information to be disclosed to the public and to the parents. There are also certain exceptions allowing disclosure to aid in development, validation, and administration of standardized tests, to administer student aid programs, and to improve instruction. However, such information may be released only when it protects the personal identification of students. Written consent is needed for any disclosure of personally identifiable information.

Individuals who have grievances under the Act must petition the head of the educational institution for redress. If unsatisfied, they may petition the Secretary of Education, who is the only person authorized to limit federal funding for non-complying institutions. In 2001 the Supreme Court agreed to review a case in which an appeals court found that the practice of "peer grading" violated the FERPA and granted relief under section 1983 of title 42 which allows a private suit for damages to brought against any person who "under color of any statute" denies "rights, privileges, or immunities secured by the Constitution."

References

Public Law 90-247 as amended. Codified at 20 USC § 1232g et seq.
[http://www4.law.cornell.edu/uscode/20/1232g.html]

Owasso Independent School District v. Falvo (U.S. June 25, 2001) No 00-1073.
[http:// www.supremecourtus.gov/orders/courtorders/062501pzor.pdf]

20 U.S.C. § 1232g. Family educational and privacy rights

(a) *Conditions for availability of funds to educational agencies or institutions;*

inspection and review of education records; specific information to be made available; procedure for access to education records; reasonableness of time for such access; hearings; written explanations by parents; definitions.

(1) (A) No funds shall be made available under any applicable program to any educational agency or institution which has a policy of denying, or which effectively prevents, the parents of students who are or have been in attendance at a school of such agency or at such institution, as the case may be, the right to inspect and review the education records of their children. If any material or document in the education record of a student includes information on more than one student, the parents of one of such students shall have the right to inspect and review only such part of such material or document as relates to such student or to be informed of the specific information contained in such part of such material. Each educational agency or institution shall establish appropriate procedures for the granting of a request by parents for access to the education records of their children within a reasonable period of time, but in no case more than forty-five days after the request has been made.

(B) The first sentence of subparagraph (A) shall not operate to make available to students in institutions of postsecondary education the following materials:

(i) financial records of the parents of the student or any information contained therein;

(ii) confidential letters and statements of recommendation, which were placed in the education records prior to January 1, 1975, if such letters or statements are not used for purposes other than those for which they were specifically intended;

(iii) if the student has signed a waiver of the student's right of access under this subsection in accordance with subparagraph (C), confidential recommendations–

(I) respecting admission to any educational agency or institution,

(II) respecting an application for employment, and

(III) respecting the receipt of an honor or honorary recognition.

(C) A student or a person applying for admission may waive his right of access to confidential statements described in clause (iii) of subparagraph (B), except that such waiver shall apply to recommendations only if

(i) the student is, upon request, notified of the names of all persons making confidential recommendations and

(ii) such recommendations are used solely for the purpose for which they were specifically intended. Such waivers may not be required as a condition for admission to, receipt of financial aid from, or receipt of any other services or benefits from such agency or institution.

(2) No funds shall be made available under any applicable program to any educational agency or institution unless the parents of students who are or have been in attendance at a school of such agency or at such institution are provided an opportunity for a hearing by such agency or institution, in accordance with regulations of the Secretary, to challenge the content of such student's education records, in order to insure that the records are not inaccurate, misleading, or otherwise in violation of the privacy or other rights of students, and to provide an opportunity for the correction or deletion of any such inaccurate, misleading, or otherwise inappropriate data contained therein and to insert into such records a written explanation of the parents respecting the content of such records.

(3) For the purposes of this section the term "educational agency or institution" means any public or private agency or institution which is the recipient of funds under any applicable program.

(4) (A) For the purposes of this section, the term "education records" means, except as may be provided otherwise in subparagraph (B), those records, files, documents, and other materials which–

(i) contain information directly related to a student; and

(ii) are maintained by an educational agency or institution or by a person acting for such agency or institution.

(B) The term "education records" does not include–

(i) records of instructional, supervisory, and administrative personnel and educational personnel ancillary thereto which are in the sole possession of the maker thereof and which are not accessible or revealed to any other person except a substitute;

(ii) records maintained by a law enforcement unit of the educational agency or institution that were created by that law enforcement unit for the purpose of law enforcement.

(iii) in the case of persons who are employed by an educational agency or institution but who are not in attendance at such agency or institution, records made and maintained in the normal course of business which relate exclusively to such person in that person's capacity as an employee and are not available for use for any other purpose; or

(iv) records on a student who is eighteen years of age or older, or is attending an institution of postsecondary education, which are made or maintained by a physician, psychiatrist, psychologist, or other recognized professional or paraprofessional acting in his professional or paraprofessional capacity, or assisting in that capacity, and which are made, maintained, or used only in connection with the provision of treatment to the student, and are not available to anyone other than persons providing such treatment, except that such records can be personally reviewed by a physician or other appropriate professional of the student's choice.

(5) (A) For the purposes of this section the term "directory information" relating to a student includes the following: the student's name, address, telephone listing, date and place of birth, major field of study, participation in officially recognized activities and sports, weight and height of members of athletic teams, dates of attendance, degrees and awards received, and the most recent previous educational agency or institution attended by the student.

(B) Any educational agency or institution making public directory information shall give public notice of the categories of information which it has designated as such information with respect to each student attending the institution or agency and shall allow a reasonable period of time after such notice has been given for a parent to inform the institution or agency that any or all of the information designated should not be released without the parent's prior consent.

(6) For the purposes of this section, the term "student" includes any person with respect to whom an educational agency or institution maintains education records or personally identifiable information, but does not include a person who has not been in attendance at such agency or institution.

(b) *Release of education records;*

parental consent requirement; exceptions; compliance with judicial orders and subpoenas; audit and evaluation of Federally-supported education programs; recordkeeping.

(1) No funds shall be made available under any applicable program to any educational agency or institution which has a policy or practice of permitting the release of educational records (or personally identifiable information contained therein other than directory information, as defined in paragraph (5) of subsection (a)) of students without the written consent of their parents to any individual, agency, or organization, other than to the following–

(A) other school officials, including teachers within the educational institution or local educational agency, who have been determined by such agency or institution to have legitimate educational interests;

(B) officials of other schools or school systems in which the student seeks or intends to enroll, upon condition that the student's parents be notified of the transfer, receive a copy of the record if desired, and have an opportunity for a hearing to challenge the content of the record;

(C) authorized representatives of

(i) the Comptroller General of the United States,

(ii) the Secretary,

(iii) an administrative head of an educational agency (as defined in section 408(c) , or

(iv) State educational authorities, under the conditions set forth in paragraph (3) of this subsection;

(D) in connection with a student's application for, or receipt of, financial aid;

(E) State and local officials or authorities to whom such information is specifically required to be reported or disclosed pursuant to State statute adopted prior to November 19, 1974;

(F) organizations conducting studies for, or on behalf of, educational agencies or institutions for the purpose of developing, validating, or administering predictive tests, administering student aid programs, and improving instruction, if such studies are conducted in such a manner as will not permit the personal identification of students and their parents by persons other than representatives of such organizations and such information will be destroyed when no longer needed for the purpose for which it is conducted;

(G) accrediting organizations in order to carry out their accrediting functions;

(H) parents of a dependent student of such parents, as defined in section 152 of the Internal Revenue Code of 1954; and

(I) subject to regulations of the Secretary, in connection with an emergency, appropriate persons if the knowledge of such information is necessary to protect the health or safety of the student or other persons.

Nothing in clause (E) of this paragraph shall prevent a State from further limiting the number or type of State or local officials who will continue to have access thereunder.

(2) No funds shall be made available under any applicable program to any educational agency or institution which has a policy or practice of releasing, or providing access to, any personally identifiable information in education records other than directory information, or as is permitted under paragraph (1) of this subsection unless–

(A) there is written consent from the student's parents specifying records to be released, the reasons for such release, and to whom, and with a copy of the records to be released to the student's parents and the student if desired by the parents, or

(B) such information is furnished in compliance with judicial order, or pursuant to any lawfully issued subpoena, upon condition that parents and the students are notified of all such orders or subpoenas in advance of the compliance therewith by the educational institution or agency.

(3) Nothing contained in this section shall preclude authorized representatives of

(A) the Comptroller General of the United States,

(B) the Secretary,

(C) an administrative head of an education agency or

(D) State educational authorities from having access to student or other records which may be necessary in connection with the audit and evaluation of Federally-supported education program, or in connection with the enforcement of the Federal legal requirements which relate to such programs: Provided, That except when collection of personally identifiable information is specifically authorized by Federal law, any data collected by such officials shall be protected in a manner which will not permit the personal identification of students and their parents by other than those officials, and such personally identifiable data shall be destroyed when no longer needed for such audit, evaluation, and enforcement of Federal legal requirements.

(4) (A) Each educational agency or institution shall maintain a record, kept with the education records of each student, which will indicate all individuals (other than those specified in paragraph (1)(A) of this subsection), agencies, or organizations which have requested or obtained access to a student's education records maintained by such educational agency or institution, and which will indicate specifically the legitimate interest that each such person, agency, or organization has in obtaining this information. Such record of access shall be available only to parents, to the school official and his assistants who are responsible for the custody of such records, and to persons or organizations authorized in, and under the conditions of, clauses (A) and (C) of paragraph (1) as a means of auditing the operation of the system.

(B) With respect to this subsection, personal information shall only be transferred to a third party on the condition that such party will not permit any other party to have access to such information without the written consent of the parents of the student.

(5) Nothing in this section shall be construed to prohibit State and local educational officials from having access to student or other records which may be necessary in connection with the audit and evaluation of any federally or State supported education program or in connection with the enforcement of the Federal legal requirements which relate to any such program, subject to the conditions specified in the proviso in paragraph (3).

(6) Nothing in this section shall be construed to prohibit an institution of postsecondary education from disclosing, to an alleged victim of any crime of violence (as that term is defined in section 16 of title 18, United States Code), the results of any disciplinary proceeding conducted by such institution against the alleged perpetrator of such crime with respect to such crime.

(c) Surveys or data-gathering activities; regulations.

The Secretary shall adopt appropriate regulations to protect the rights of privacy of students and their families in connection with any surveys or data-gathering activities conducted, assisted, or authorized by the Secretary or an administrative head of an education agency. Regulations established under this subsection shall include provisions controlling the use, dissemination, and protection of such data. No survey or data-gathering activities shall be conducted by the Secretary, or an administrative head of an education agency under an applicable program, unless such activities are authorized by law.

(d) Students' rather than parents' permission or consent.

For the purposes of this section, whenever a student has attained eighteen years of age, or is attending an institution of postsecondary education the permission or consent required of and the rights accorded to the parents of the student shall thereafter only be required of and accorded to the student.

(e) Informing parents or students of rights under this section.

No funds shall be made available under any applicable program to any educational agency or institution unless such agency or institution informs the parents of students, or the students, if they are eighteen years of age or older, or are attending an institution of postsecondary education, of the rights accorded them by this section.

(f) Enforcement; termination of assistance.

The Secretary, or an administrative head of an education agency, shall take appropriate actions to enforce provisions of this section and to deal with violations of this section, according to the provisions of this Act, except that action to terminate assistance may be taken only if the Secretary finds there has been a failure to comply with the provisions of this section, and he has determined that compliance cannot be secured by voluntary means.

(g) Office and review board; creation; functions.

The Secretary shall establish or designate an office and review board within the Department of Health, Education, and Welfare for the purpose of investigating, processing, reviewing, and adjudicating violations of the provisions of this section and complaints which may be filed concerning alleged violations of this section. Except for the conduct of hearings, none of the functions of the Secretary under this section shall be carried out in any of the regional offices of such Department.

RIGHT TO FINANCIAL PRIVACY ACT
(1978)

Summary

The Right to Financial Privacy Act was precipitated by the Supreme Court's decision in United States v Miller, 425 U.S. 435 (1976) in which a customer challenged the disclosure of his personal financial information by his bank. The Court held that the records were the property of the bank and, therefore, that the customer did not have standing under the Fourth Amendment to challenge the disclosure. Furthermore, the Court ruled that the customer did not have a reasonable expectation of privacy regarding records of his checking account because in writing a check, the customer knew that the bank employees would see the information on it.

The Right to Financial Privacy Act sought to regulate disclosure of personal financial information to federal agencies, to recognize individuals' privacy interest in their bank records, and to give them rights regarding the disclosure of those records. The Act does not prohibit the disclosure of financial information to federal agencies. Instead it puts strict guidelines into place regarding such disclosures, and mandates a procedure for notice and challenge. The Act only applies to the federal government; it does not regulate disclosure of financial information to private parties or businesses.

The Right to Financial Privacy Act prohibits any Government authority from obtaining copies of, access to, or the information contained in, the financial records of any customer from a financial institution unless such records are reasonably described and: (1) such customer has authorized such disclosure in accordance with this Act; (2) such records are disclosed in response to an administrative subpoena or summons; (3) such records are disclosed in response to a court order; (4) such records are disclosed in response to a judicial subpoena; or (5) such financial records are disclosed in response to a formal written request meeting specified requirements. Requires in all cases that the customer be notified of the agency seeking such records, the purpose for which such records are sought, and the rights of customers under this Act.

The Act establishes specific conditions and procedures for the delay of notice to a customer. It states that no financial institution may provide to a Government authority copies of or the information contained in the financial records of any customer except in accordance with the requirements of this Act. It sets forth provisions governing customer authorization, administrative subpoenas and summons, judicial subpoenas, and search warrants. It establishes procedures for a customer to challenge the disclosure of financial records. It provides exceptions to the provisions of this Act and special procedures for the disclosure of records to the Secret Service and government authorities acting in the field of foreign intelligence.

United States
Right to Financial Privacy Act

The Act establishes civil penalties and the right to injunctive relief without regard to the amount in controversy for violation of the provisions of this Title. Actions may be brought within three years of a customer's discovery of violation. Injunctive relief and compensatory and punitive damages are available under the Act.

References

Public Law 95-630 as amended. Codified at 12 USC § 3401 et seq.
[http://www4.law.cornell.edu/uscode/12/3401.html
L. Richard Fischer, *The Law of Financial Privacy* (A.S. Pratt & Sons 2000)

12 USC § 3401. Definitions

For the purpose of this chapter, the term -

(1) "financial institution" means any office of a bank, savings bank, card issuer as defined in section 1602(n) of title 15, industrial loan company, trust company, savings association, building and loan, or homestead association (including cooperative banks), credit union, or consumer finance institution, located in any State or territory of the United States, the District of Columbia, Puerto Rico, Guam, American Samoa, or the Virgin Islands;

(2) "financial record" means an original of, a copy of, or information known to have been derived from, any record held by a financial institution pertaining to a customer's relationship with the financial institution;

(3) "Government authority" means any agency or department of the United States, or any officer, employee, or agent thereof;

(4) "person" means an individual or a partnership of five or fewer individuals;

(5) "customer" means any person or authorized representative of that person who utilized or is utilizing any service of a financial institution, or for whom a financial institution is acting or has acted as a fiduciary, in relation to an account maintained in the person's name;

(6) "holding company" means -

(A) any bank holding company (as defined in section 1841 of this title);

(B) any company described in section 1843(f)(1) of this title; and

(C) any savings and loan holding company (as defined in the Home Owners' Loan Act (12 U.S.C. 1461 et seq.));

(7) "supervisory agency" means with respect to any particular financial institution, holding company, or any subsidiary of a financial institution or holding company, any of the following which has statutory authority to examine the financial condition, business operations, or records or transactions of that institution, holding company, or subsidiary -

(A) the Federal Deposit Insurance Corporation;

(B) Director, Office of Thrift Supervision;

(C) the National Credit Union Administration;

(D) the Board of Governors of the Federal Reserve System;

(E) the Comptroller of the Currency;

(F) the Securities and Exchange Commission;

(G) the Secretary of the Treasury, with respect to the Bank Secrecy Act (Public Law 91-508, title I) (12 U.S.C. 1951 et seq.) and subchapter II of chapter 53 of title 31; or

(H) any State banking or securities department or agency; and

(8) "law enforcement inquiry" means a lawful investigation or official proceeding inquiring into a violation of, or failure to comply with, any criminal or civil statute or any regulation, rule, or order issued pursuant thereto.

Sec. 3402. Access to financial records by Government authorities prohibited; exceptions

Except as provided by section 3403(c) or (d), 3413, or 3414 of this title, no Government authority may have access to or obtain copies of, or the information contained in the financial records of any customer from a financial institution unless the financial are reasonably described and -

(1) such customer has authorized such disclosure in accordance with section 3404 of this title;

(2) such financial records are disclosed in response to an administrative subpena or summons which meets the requirements of section 3405 of this title;

(3) such financial records are disclosed in response to a search warrant which meets the requirements of section 3406 of this title;

(4) such financial records are disclosed in response to a judicial subpoena which meets the requirements of section 3407 of this title; or

(5) such financial records are disclosed in response to a formal written request which meets the requirements of section 3408 of this title.

Sec. 3403. Confidentiality of financial records

(a) Release of records by financial institutions prohibited

No financial institution, or officer, employees, or agent of a financial institution, may provide to any Government authority access to or copies of, or the information contained in, the financial records of any customer except in accordance with the provisions of this chapter.

(b) Release of records upon certification of compliance with chapter

A financial institution shall not release the financial records of a customer until the Government authority seeking such records certifies in writing to the financial institution that it has complied with the applicable provisions of this chapter.

(c) Notification to Government authority of existence of relevant information in records

Nothing in this chapter shall preclude any financial institution, or any officer, employee, or agent of a financial institution, from notifying a Government authority that such institution, or officer, employee, or agent has information which may be relevant to a possible violation of any statute or regulation. Such information may include only the name or other identifying information concerning any individual, corporation, or account involved in and the nature of any suspected illegal activity. Such information may be disclosed notwithstanding any constitution, law, or regulation of any State or political subdivision thereof to the contrary. Any financial institution, or officer, employee, or agent thereof, making a disclosure of information pursuant to this subsection, shall not be liable to the customer under any law or regulation of the United States or any constitution, law, or regulation of any State or political subdivision thereof, for such disclosure or for any failure to notify the customer of such disclosure.

(d) Release of records as incident to perfection of security interest, proving a claim in bankruptcy, collecting a debt, or processing an application with regard to a Government loan, loan guarantee, etc.

(1) Nothing in this chapter shall preclude a financial institution, as an incident to perfecting a security interest, proving a claim in bankruptcy, or otherwise collecting on a debt owing either to the financial institution itself or in its role as a fiduciary, from providing copies of any financial record to any court or Government authority.

(2) Nothing in this chapter shall preclude a financial institution, as an incident to processing an application for assistance to a customer in the form of a Government loan, loan guaranty, or loan insurance agreement, or as an incident to processing a default on, or administering, a Government guaranteed or insured loan, from initiating contact with an appropriate Government authority for the purpose of providing any financial record necessary to permit such authority to carry out its responsibilities under a loan, loan guaranty, or loan insurance agreement.

Sec. 3404. Customer authorizations

(a) Statement furnished by customer to financial institution and Government authority; contents

A customer may authorize disclosure under section 3402(1) of this title if he furnishes to the financial institution and to the Government authority seeking to obtain such disclosure a signed and dated statement which -

(1) authorizes such disclosure for a period not in excess of three months;

(2) states that the customer may revoke such authorization at any time before the financial records are disclosed;

(3) identifies the financial records which are authorized to be disclosed;

(4) specifies the purposes for which, and the Government authority to which, such records may be disclosed; and

(5) states the customer's rights under this chapter.

(b) Authorization as condition of doing business prohibited

No such authorization shall be required as a condition of doing business with any financial institution.

(c) Right of customer to access to financial institution's record of disclosures

The customer has the right, unless the Government authority obtains a court order as provided in section 3409 of this title, to obtain a copy of the record which the financial institution shall keep of all instances in which the customer's record is disclosed to a Government authority pursuant to this section, including the identity of the Government authority to which such disclosure is made.

Sec. 3405. Administrative subpoena and summons

A Government authority may obtain financial records under section 3402(2) of this title pursuant to an administrative subpoena or summons otherwise authorized by law only if -

(1) there is reason to believe that the records sought are relevant to a legitimate law enforcement inquiry;

(2) a copy of the subpoena or summons has been served upon the customer or mailed to his last known address on or before the date on which the subpoena or summons was served on the financial institution together with the following notice which shall state with reasonable specificity the nature of the law enforcement inquiry:

"Records or information concerning your transactions held by the financial institution named in the attached subpoena or summons are being sought by this (agency or department) in accordance with the Right to Financial Privacy Act of 1978 (12 U.S.C. 3401 et seq.) for the following purpose: If you desire that such records or information not be made available, you must:

"1. Fill out the accompanying motion paper and sworn statement or write one of your own, stating that you are the customer whose records are being requested by the Government and either giving the reasons you believe that the records are not relevant to the legitimate law enforcement inquiry stated in this notice or any other legal basis for objecting to the release of the records.

"2. File the motion and statement by mailing or delivering them to the clerk of any one of the following United States district courts:

"3. Serve the Government authority requesting the records by mailing or delivering a copy of your motion and statement to .

"4. Be prepared to come to court and present your position in further detail.

"5. You do not need to have a lawyer, although you may wish to employ one to represent you and protect your rights.

If you do not follow the above procedures, upon the expiration of ten days from the date of service or fourteen days from the date of mailing of this notice, the records or information requested therein will be made available. These records may be transferred to other Government authorities for legitimate law enforcement inquiries, in which event you will be notified after the transfer."; and

(3) ten days have expired from the date of service of the notice or fourteen days have expired from the date of mailing the notice to the customer and within such time period the customer has not filed a sworn statement and motion to quash in an appropriate court, or the customer challenge provisions of section 3410 of this title have been complied with.

Sec. 3406. Search warrants

(a) Applicability of Federal Rules of Criminal Procedure

A Government authority may obtain financial records under section 3402(3) of this title only if it obtains a search warrant pursuant to the Federal Rules of Criminal Procedure.

(b) Mailing of copy and notice to customer

No later than ninety days after the Government authority serves the search warrant, it shall mail to the customer's last known address a copy of the search warrant together with the following notice:

"Records or information concerning your transactions held by the financial institution named in the attached search warrant were obtained by this (agency or department) on (date) for the following purpose: . You may have rights under the Right to Financial Privacy Act of 1978 (12 U.S.C. 3401 et seq.).".

(c) Court-ordered delays in mailing

Upon application of the Government authority, a court may grant a delay in the mailing of the notice required in subsection (b) of this section, which delay shall not exceed one hundred and eighty days following the service of the warrant, if the court makes the findings required in section 3409(a) of this title. If the court so finds, it shall enter an ex parte order granting the requested delay and an order prohibiting the financial institution from disclosing that records have been obtained or that a search warrant for such records has been executed. Additional delays of up to ninety days may be granted by the court upon application, but only in accordance with this subsection. Upon expiration of the period of delay of notification of the customer, the following notice shall be mailed to the customer along with a copy of the search warrant:

"Records or information concerning your transactions held by the financial institution named in the attached search warrant were obtained by this (agency or department) on (date). Notification was delayed beyond the statutory ninety-day delay period pursuant to a determination by the court that such notice would seriously jeopardize an investigation concerning . You may have rights under the Right to Financial Privacy Act of 1978 (12 U.S.C. 3401 et seq.).".

Sec. 3407. Judicial subpoena

A Government authority may obtain financial records under section 3402(4) of this title pursuant to judicial subpoena only if -

(1) such subpoena is authorized by law and there is reason to believe that the records sought are relevant to a legitimate law enforcement inquiry;

(2) a copy of the subpoena has been served upon the customer or mailed to his last known address on or before the date on which the subpoena was served on the financial institution together with the following notice which shall state with reasonable specificity the nature of the law enforcement inquiry:

"Records or information concerning your transactions which are held by the financial institution named in the attached subpoena are being sought by this (agency or department or authority) in accordance with the Right to Financial Privacy Act of 1978 (12 U.S.C. 3401 et seq.) for the following purpose: If you desire that such records or information not be made available, you must:

"1. Fill out the accompanying motion paper and sworn statement or write one of your own, stating that you are the customer whose records are being requested by the Government and either giving the reasons you believe that the records are not relevant to the legitimate law enforcement inquiry stated in this notice or any other legal basis for objecting to the release of the records.

"2. File the motion and statement by mailing or delivering them to the clerk of the Court.

"3. Serve the Government authority requesting the records by mailing or delivering a copy of your motion and statement to .

"4. Be prepared to come to court and present your position in further detail.

"5. You do not need to have a lawyer, although you may wish to employ one to represent you and protect your rights. If you do not follow the above procedures, upon the expiration of ten days from the date of service or fourteen days from the date of mailing of this notice, the records or information requested therein will be made available. These records may be transferred to other government authorities for legitimate law enforcement inquiries, in which event you will be notified after the transfer;" and

(3) ten days have expired from the date of service or fourteen days from the date of mailing of the notice to the customer and within such time period the customer has not filed a sworn statement and motion to quash in an appropriate court, or the customer challenge provisions of section 3410 of this title have been complied with.

Sec. 3408. Formal written request

A Government authority may request financial records under section 3402(5) of this title pursuant to a formal written request only if -

United States
Right to Financial Privacy Act

(1) no administrative summons or subpoena authority reasonably appears to be available to that Government authority to obtain financial records for the purpose for which such records are sought;

(2) the request is authorized by regulations promulgated by the head of the agency or department;

(3) there is reason to believe that the records sought are relevant to a legitimate law enforcement inquiry; and

(4)(A) a copy of the request has been served upon the customer or mailed to his last known address on or before the date on which the request was made to the financial institution together with the following notice which shall state with reasonable specificity the nature of the law enforcement inquiry:

"Records or information concerning your transactions held by the financial institution named in the attached request are being sought by this (agency or department) in accordance with the Right to Financial Privacy Act of 1978 (12 U.S.C. 3401 et seq.) for the following purpose:

"If you desire that such records or information not be made available, you must:

"1. Fill out the accompanying motion paper and sworn statement or write one of your own, stating that you are the customer whose records are being requested by the Government and either giving the reasons you believe that the records are not relevant to the legitimate law enforcement inquiry stated in this notice or any other legal basis for objecting to the release of the records.

"2. File the motion and statement by mailing or delivering them to the clerk of any one of the following United States District Courts:

"3. Serve the Government authority requesting the records by mailing or delivering a copy of your motion and statement to .

"4. Be prepared to come to court and present your position in further detail.

"5. You do not need to have a lawyer, although you may wish to employ one to represent you and protect your rights. If you do not follow the above procedures, upon the expiration of ten days from the date of service or fourteen days from the date of mailing of this notice, the records or information requested therein may be made available. These records may be transferred to other Government authorities for legitimate law enforcement inquiries, in which event you will be notified after the transfer;" and

(B) ten days have expired from the date of service or fourteen days from the date of mailing of the notice by the customer and within such time period the customer has not filed a sworn statement and an application to enjoin the Government authority in an appropriate court, or the customer challenge provisions of section 3410 of this title have been complied with.

Sec. 3409. Delayed notice

(a) Application by Government authority; findings

Upon application of the Government authority, the customer notice required under section 3404(c), 3405(2), 3406(c), 3407(2), 3408(4), or 3412(b) of this title may be delayed by order of an appropriate court if the presiding judge or magistrate judge finds that -

(1) the investigation being conducted is within the lawful jurisdiction of the Government authority seeking the financial records;

(2) there is reason to believe that the records being sought are relevant to a legitimate law enforcement inquiry; and

(3) there is reason to believe that such notice will result in

(A) endangering life or physical safety of any person;

(B) flight from prosecution;

(C) destruction of or tampering with evidence;

(D) intimidation of potential witnesses; or

(E) otherwise seriously jeopardizing an investigation or official proceeding or unduly delaying a trial or ongoing official proceeding to the same extent as the circumstances in the preceding subparagraphs.

An application for delay must be made with reasonable specificity.

(b) Grant of delay order; duration and specifications; extensions; copy of request and notice to customer

(1) If the court makes the findings required in paragraphs (1), (2), and (3) of subsection (a) of this section, it shall enter an ex parte order granting the requested delay for a period not to exceed ninety days and an order prohibiting the financial institution from disclosing that records have been obtained or that a request for records has been made, except that, if the records have been sought by a Government authority exercising financial controls over foreign accounts in the United States under section 5(b) of the Trading with the Enemy Act (12 U.S.C. 95a, 50 App. U.S.C. 5(b)), the International Emergency Economic Powers Act (title II, Public Law 95-223) (50 U.S.C. 1701 et seq.), or section 287c of title 22, and the court finds that there is reason to believe that such notice may endanger the lives or physical safety of a customer or group of customers, or any person or group of persons associated with a customer, the court may specify that the delay be indefinite.

(2) Extensions of the delay of notice provided in paragraph (1) of up to ninety days each may be granted by the court upon application, but only in accordance with this subsection.

(3) Upon expiration of the period of delay of notification under paragraph (1) or (2), the customer shall be served with or mailed a copy of the process or request

together with the following notice which shall state with reasonable specificity the nature of the law enforcement inquiry:

> "Records or information concerning your transactions which are held by the financial institution named in the attached process or request were supplied to or requested by the Government authority named in the process or request on (date). Notification was withheld pursuant to a determination by the (title of court so ordering) under the Right to Financial Privacy Act of 1978 (12 U.S.C. 3401 et seq.) that such notice might (state reason). The purpose of the investigation or official proceeding was .".

(c) Notice requirement respecting emergency access to financial records

When access to financial records is obtained pursuant to section 3414(b) of this title (emergency access), the Government authority shall, unless a court has authorized delay of notice pursuant to subsections (a) and (b) of this section, as soon as practicable after such records are obtained serve upon the customer, or mail by registered or certified mail to his last known address, a copy of the request to the financial institution together with the following notice which shall state with reasonable specificity the nature of the law enforcement inquiry:

> "Records concerning your transactions held by the financial institution named in the attached request were obtained by (agency or department) under the Right to Financial Privacy Act of 1978 (12 U.S.C. 3401 et seq.) on (date) for the following purpose: Emergency access to such records was obtained on the grounds that (state grounds).".

(d) Preservation of memorandums, affidavits, or other papers

Any memorandum, affidavit, or other paper filed in connection with a request for delay in notification shall be preserved by the court. Upon petition by the customer to whom such records pertain, the court may order disclosure of such papers to the petitioner unless the court makes the findings required in subsection (a) of this section.

Sec. 3410. Customer challenges

(a) Filing of motion to quash or application to enjoin; proper court; contents

Within ten days of service or within fourteen days of mailing of a subpoena, summons, or formal written request, a customer may file a motion to quash an administrative summons or judicial subpoena, or an application to enjoin a Government authority from obtaining financial records pursuant to a formal written request, with copies served upon the Government authority. A motion to quash a judicial subpoena shall be filed in the court which issued the subpoena. A motion to quash an administrative summons or an application to enjoin a Government authority from obtaining records pursuant to a formal written request shall be filed in the appropriate United States district court. Such motion or application shall contain an affidavit or sworn statement -

(1) stating that the applicant is a customer of the financial institution from which financial records pertaining to him have been sought; and

(2) stating the applicant's reasons for believing that the financial records sought are not relevant to the legitimate law enforcement inquiry stated by the Government authority in its notice, or that there has not been substantial compliance with the provisions of this chapter.

Service shall be made under this section upon a Government authority by delivering or mailing by registered or certified mail a copy of the papers to the person, office, or department specified in the notice which the customer has received pursuant to this chapter. For the purposes of this section, "delivery" has the meaning stated in rule 5(b) of the Federal Rules of Civil Procedure.

(b) Filing of response; additional proceedings

If the court finds that the customer has complied with subsection (a) of this section, it shall order the Government authority to file a sworn response, which may be filed in camera if the Government includes in its response the reasons which make in camera review appropriate. If the court is unable to determine the motion or application on the basis of the parties' initial allegations and response, the court may conduct such additional proceedings as it deems appropriate. All such proceedings shall be completed and the motion or application decided within seven calendar days of the filing of the Government's response.

(c) Decision of court

If the court finds that the applicant is not the customer to whom the financial records sought by the Government authority pertain, or that there is a demonstrable reason to believe that the law enforcement inquiry is legitimate and a reasonable belief that the records sought are relevant to that inquiry, it shall deny the motion or application, and, in the case of an administrative summons or court order other than a search warrant, order such process enforced. If the court finds that the applicant is the customer to whom the records sought by the Government authority pertain, and that there is not a demonstrable reason to believe that the law enforcement inquiry is legitimate and a reasonable belief that the records sought are relevant to that inquiry, or that there has not been substantial compliance with the provisions of this chapter, it shall order the process quashed or shall enjoin the Government authority's formal written request.

(d) Appeals

A court ruling denying a motion or application under this section shall not be deemed a final order and no interlocutory appeal may be taken therefrom by the customer. An appeal of a ruling denying a motion or application under this section may be taken by the customer

(1) within such period of time as provided by law as part of any appeal from a final order in any legal proceeding initiated against him arising out of or based upon the financial records, or

(2) within thirty days after a notification that no legal proceeding is contemplated against him. The Government authority obtaining the financial records shall promptly notify a customer when a determination has been made that no legal proceeding against him is contemplated. After one hundred and eighty days from the denial of the motion or application, if the Government authority obtaining the records has not initiated such a proceeding, a supervisory official of the Government authority shall certify to the appropriate court that no such determination has been made. The court may require that such certifications be made, at reasonable intervals thereafter, until either notification to the customer has occurred or a legal proceeding is initiated as described in clause (A).

(e) Sole judicial remedy available to customer

The challenge procedures of this chapter constitute the sole judicial remedy available to a customer to oppose disclosure of financial records pursuant to this chapter.

(f) Affect on challenges by financial institutions

Nothing in this chapter shall enlarge or restrict any rights of a financial institution to challenge requests for records made by a Government authority under existing law. Nothing in this chapter shall entitle a customer to assert the rights of a financial institution.

Sec. 3411. Duty of financial institutions

Upon receipt of a request for financial records made by a Government authority under section 3405 or 3407 of this title, the financial institution shall, unless otherwise provided by law, proceed to assemble the records requested and must be prepared to deliver the records to the Government authority upon receipt of the certificate required under section 3403(b) of this title.

Sec. 3412. Use of information

(a) Transfer of financial records to other agencies or departments; certification

Financial records originally obtained pursuant to this chapter shall not be transferred to another agency or department unless the transferring agency or department certifies in writing that there is reason to believe that the records are relevant to a legitimate law enforcement inquiry within the jurisdiction of the receiving agency or department.

(b) Mailing of copy of certification and notice to customer

When financial records subject to this chapter are transferred pursuant to subsection (a) of this section, the transferring agency or department shall, within fourteen days, send to the customer a copy of the certification made pursuant to subsection (a) of this section and the following notice, which shall state the nature of the law enforcement inquiry with reasonable specificity:

"Copies of, or information contained in, your financial records lawfully in possession of have been furnished to pursuant to the Right of Financial Privacy

Act of 1978 (12 U.S.C. 3401 et seq.) for the following purpose: . If you believe that this transfer has not been made to further a legitimate law enforcement inquiry, you may have legal rights under the Financial Privacy Act of 1978 or the Privacy Act of 1974 (5 U.S.C. 552a)."

(c) Court-ordered delays in mailing

Notwithstanding subsection (b) of this section, notice to the customer may be delayed if the transferring agency or department has obtained a court order delaying notice pursuant to section 3409(a) and (b) of this title and that order is still in effect, or if the receiving agency or department obtains a court order authorizing a delay in notice pursuant to section 3409(a) and (b) of this title. Upon the expiration of any such period of delay, the transferring agency or department shall serve to the customer the notice specified in subsection (b) of this section and the agency or department that obtained the court order authorizing a delay in notice pursuant to section 3409(a) and (b) of this title shall serve to the customer the notice specified in section 3409(b) of this title.

(d) Exchanges of examination reports by supervisory agencies; transfer of financial records to defend customer action; withholding of information

Nothing in this chapter prohibits any supervisory agency from exchanging examination reports or other information with another supervisory agency. Nothing in this chapter prohibits the transfer of a customer's financial records needed by counsel for a Government authority to defend an action brought by the customer. Nothing in this chapter shall authorize the withholding of information by any officer or employee of a supervisory agency from a duly authorized committee or subcommittee of the Congress.

(e) Federal Financial Institutions Examination Council supervisory agencies; Securities and Exchange Commission; authorization of exchange of financial records or other information

Notwithstanding section 3401(6) of this title or any other provision of this chapter, the exchange of financial records or other information with respect to a financial institution, holding company, or any subsidiary of a depository institution or holding company, among and between the five member supervisory agencies of the Federal Financial Institutions Examination Council and the Securities and Exchange Commission is permitted.

(f) Transfer to Attorney General or Secretary of the Treasury

(1) In general

Nothing in this chapter shall apply when financial records obtained by an agency or department of the United States are disclosed or transferred to the Attorney General or the Secretary of the Treasury upon the certification by a supervisory level official of the transferring agency or department that -

(A) there is reason to believe that the records may be relevant to a violation of Federal criminal law; and

(B) the records were obtained in the exercise of the agency's or department's supervisory or regulatory functions.

(2) Limitation on use

Records so transferred shall be used only for criminal investigative or prosecutive purposes, for civil actions under section 1833a of this title, or for forfeiture under sections 981 or 982 of title 18 by the Department of Justice and only for criminal investigative purposes relating to money laundering and other financial crimes by the Department of the Treasury and shall, upon completion of the investigation or prosecution (including any appeal), be returned only to the transferring agency or department. No agency or department so transferring such records shall be deemed to have waived any privilege applicable to those records under law.

Sec. 3413. Exceptions

(a) Disclosure of financial records not identified with particular customers

Nothing in this chapter prohibits the disclosure of any financial records or information which is not identified with or identifiable as being derived from the financial records of a particular customer.

(b) Disclosure to, or examination by, supervisory agency pursuant to exercise of supervisory, regulatory, or monetary functions with respect to financial institutions holding companies, subsidiaries, institution-affiliated parties, or other persons

This chapter shall not apply to the examination by or disclosure to any supervisory agency of financial records or information in the exercise of its supervisory, regulatory, or monetary functions, including conservatorship or receivership functions, with respect to any financial institution, holding company, subsidiary of a financial institution or holding company, institution-affiliated party (within the meaning of section 1813(u) of this title) with respect to a financial institution, holding company, or subsidiary, or other person participating in the conduct of the affairs thereof.

(c) Disclosure pursuant to title 26

Nothing in this chapter prohibits the disclosure of financial records in accordance with procedures authorized by title 26.

(d) Disclosure pursuant to Federal statute or rule promulgated thereunder

Nothing in this chapter shall authorize the withholding of financial records or information required to be reported in accordance with any Federal statute or rule promulgated thereunder.

(e) Disclosure pursuant to Federal Rules of Criminal Procedure or comparable rules of other courts

Nothing in this chapter shall apply when financial records are sought by a Government authority under the Federal Rules of Civil or Criminal Procedure or comparable rules of other courts in connection with litigation to which the Government authority and the customer are parties.

(f) Disclosure pursuant to administrative subpoena issued by administrative law judge

Nothing in this chapter shall apply when financial records are sought by a Government authority pursuant to an administrative subpoena issued by an administrative law judge in an adjudicatory proceeding subject to section 554 of title 5 and to which the Government authority and the customer are parties.

(g) Disclosure pursuant to legitimate law enforcement inquiry respecting name, address, account number, and type of account of particular customers

The notice requirements of this chapter and sections 3410 and 3412 of this title shall not apply when a Government authority by a means described in section 3402 of this title and for a legitimate law enforcement inquiry is seeking only the name, address, account number, and type of account of any customer or ascertainable group of customers associated

(1) with a financial transaction or class of financial transactions, or

(2) with a foreign country or subdivision thereof in the case of a Government authority exercising financial controls over foreign accounts in the United States under section 5(b) of the Trading with the Enemy Act (12 U.S.C. 95a, 50 App. U.S.C. 5(b)); the International Emergency Economic Powers Act (title II, Public Law 95-223) (50 U.S.C. 1701 et seq.); or section 287c of title 22.

(h) Disclosure pursuant to lawful proceeding, investigation, etc., directed at financial institution or legal entity or consideration or administration respecting Government loans, loan guarantees, etc.

(1) Nothing in this chapter (except sections 3403, 3417 and 3418 of this title) shall apply when financial records are sought by a Government authority -

(A) in connection with a lawful proceeding, investigation, examination, or inspection directed at a financial institution (whether or not such proceeding, investigation, examination, or inspection is also directed at a customer) or at a legal entity which is not a customer; or

(B) in connection with the authority's consideration or administration of assistance to the customer in the form of a Government loan, loan guaranty, or loan insurance program.

(2) When financial records are sought pursuant to this subsection, the Government authority shall submit to the financial institution the certificate required by section 3403(b) of this title. For access pursuant to paragraph (1)(B), no further certification shall be required for subsequent access by the certifying Government authority during the term of the loan, loan guaranty, or loan insurance agreement.

(3) After the effective date of this chapter, whenever a customer applies for participation in a Government loan, loan guaranty, or loan insurance program, the Government authority administering such program shall give the customer written notice of the authority's access rights under this subsection. No further notification shall be required for subsequent access by that authority during the term of the loan, loan guaranty, or loan insurance agreement.

(4) Financial records obtained pursuant to this subsection may be used only for the purpose for which they were originally obtained, and may be transferred to another agency or department only when the transfer is to facilitate a lawful proceeding, investigation, examination, or inspection directed at a financial institution (whether or not such proceeding, investigation, examination, or inspection is also directed at a customer), or at a legal entity which is not a customer, except that -

(A) nothing in this paragraph prohibits the use or transfer of a customer's financial records needed by counsel representing a Government authority in a civil action arising from a Government loan, loan guaranty, or loan insurance agreement; and

(B) nothing in this paragraph prohibits a Government authority providing assistance to a customer in the form of a loan, loan guaranty, or loan insurance agreement from using or transferring financial records necessary to process, service or foreclose a loan, or to collect on an indebtedness to the Government resulting from a customer's default.

(5) Notification that financial records obtained pursuant to this subsection may relate to a potential civil, criminal, or regulatory violation by a customer may be given to an agency or department with jurisdiction over that violation, and such agency or department may then seek access to the records pursuant to the provisions of this chapter.

(6) Each financial institution shall keep a notation of each disclosure made pursuant to paragraph (1)(B) of this subsection, including the date of such disclosure and the Government authority to which it was made. The customer shall be entitled to inspect this information.

(i) Disclosure pursuant to issuance of subpoena or court order respecting grand jury proceeding

Nothing in this chapter (except sections 3415 and 3420 of this title) shall apply to any subpoena or court order issued in connection with proceedings before a grand jury, except that a court shall have authority to order a financial institution, on which a grand jury subpoena for customer records has been served, not to notify the customer of the existence of the subpoena or information that has been furnished to the grand jury, under the circumstances and for the period specified and pursuant to the procedures established in section 3409 of this title.

(j) Disclosure pursuant to proceeding, investigation, etc., instituted by General Accounting Office and directed at a government authority

This chapter shall not apply when financial records are sought by the General Accounting Office pursuant to an authorized proceeding, investigation, examination or audit directed at a government authority.

(k) Disclosure necessary for proper administration of programs of withholding taxes on nonresident aliens, Federal Old-Age, Survivors, and Disability Insurance Benefits, and Railroad Retirement Act Benefits

(1) Nothing in this chapter shall apply to the disclosure by the financial institution of the name and address of any customer to the Department of the Treasury, the Social Security Administration, or the Railroad Retirement Board, where the disclosure of such information is necessary to, and such information is used solely for the purpose of, the proper administration of section 1441 of title 26, title II of the Social Security Act (42 U.S.C. 401 et seq.), or the Railroad Retirement Act of 1974 (45 U.S.C. 231 et seq.).

(2) Notwithstanding any other provision of law, any request authorized by paragraph (1) (and the information contained therein) may be used by the financial institution or its agents solely for the purpose of providing the customer's name and address to the Department of the Treasury, the Social Security Administration, or the Railroad Retirement Board and shall be barred from redisclosure by the financial institution or its agents.

(l) Crimes against financial institutions by insiders

Nothing in this chapter shall apply when any financial institution or supervisory agency provides any financial record of any officer, director, employee, or controlling shareholder (within the meaning of subparagraph (A) or (B) of section 1841(a)(2) of this title or subparagraph (A) or (B) of section 1730a(a)(2) of this title) of such institution, or of any major borrower from such institution who there is reason to believe may be acting in concert with any such officer, director, employee, or controlling shareholder, to the Attorney General of the United States, to a State law enforcement agency, or, in the case of a possible violation of subchapter II of chapter 53 of title 31, to the Secretary of the Treasury if there is reason to believe that such record is relevant to a possible violation by such person of -

(1) any law relating to crimes against financial institutions or supervisory agencies by directors, officers, employees, or controlling shareholders of, or by borrowers from, financial institutions; or

(2) any provision of subchapter II of chapter 53 of title 31 or of section 1956 or 1957 of title 18.

No supervisory agency which transfers any such record under this subsection shall be deemed to have waived any privilege applicable to that record under law.

(m) Disclosure to, or examination by, employees or agents of Board of Governors of Federal Reserve System or Federal Reserve Bank

This chapter shall not apply to the examination by or disclosure to employees or agents of the Board of Governors of the Federal Reserve System or any Federal Reserve Bank of financial records or information in the exercise of the Federal Reserve System's authority to extend credit to the financial institutions or others.

(n) Disclosure to, or examination by, Resolution Trust Corporation or its employees or agents

This chapter shall not apply to the examination by or disclosure to the Resolution Trust Corporation or its employees or agents of financial records or information in the exercise of its conservatorship, receivership, or liquidation functions with respect to a financial institution.

(o) Disclosure to, or examination by, Federal Housing Finance Board or Federal home loan banks

This chapter shall not apply to the examination by or disclosure to the Federal Housing Finance Board or any of the Federal home loan banks of financial records or information in the exercise of the Federal Housing Finance Board's authority to extend credit (either directly or through a Federal home loan bank) to financial institutions or others.

(p) Access to information necessary for administration of certain veteran benefits laws

(1) Nothing in this chapter shall apply to the disclosure by the financial institution of the name and address of any customer to the Department of Veterans Affairs where the disclosure of such information is necessary to, and such information is used solely for the purposes of, the proper administration of benefits programs under laws administered by the Secretary.

(2) Notwithstanding any other provision of law, any request authorized by paragraph (1) (and the information contained therein) may be used by the financial institution or its agents solely for the purpose of providing the customer's name and address to the Department of Veterans Affairs and shall be barred from redisclosure by the financial institution or its agents.

Sec. 3414. Special procedures

(a)(1) Nothing in this chapter (except sections 3415, 3417, 3418, and 3421 shall apply to the production and disclosure of financial records pursuant to requests from -

(A) a Government authority authorized to conduct foreign counter- or foreign positive-intelligence activities for purposes of conducting such activities; or

(B) the Secret Service for the purpose of conducting its protective functions (18 U.S.C. 3056; 3 U.S.C. 202, Public Law 90-331, as amended).

(2) In the instances specified in paragraph (1), the Government authority shall submit to the financial institution the certificate required in section 3403(b) of this title signed by a supervisory official of a rank designated by the head of the Government authority.

(3) No financial institution, or officer, employee, or agent of such institution, shall disclose to any person that a Government authority described in paragraph (1) has sought or obtained access to a customer's financial records.

(4) The Government authority specified in paragraph (1) shall compile an annual tabulation of the occasions in which this section was used.

(5)

(A) Financial institutions, and officers, employees, and agents thereof, shall comply with a request for a customer's or entity's financial records made pursuant to this subsection by the Federal Bureau of Investigation when the

Director of the Federal Bureau of Investigation (or the Director's designee) certifies in writing to the financial institution that such records are sought for foreign counterintelligence purposes and that there are specific and articulable facts giving reason to believe that the customer or entity whose records are sought is a foreign power or an agent of a foreign power as defined in section 1801 of title 50.

(B) The Federal Bureau of Investigation may disseminate information obtained pursuant to this paragraph only as provided in guidelines approved by the Attorney General for foreign intelligence collection and foreign counterintelligence investigations conducted by the Federal Bureau of Investigation, and, with respect to dissemination to an agency of the United States, only if such information is clearly relevant to the authorized responsibilities of such agency.

(C) On a semiannual basis the Attorney General shall fully inform the Permanent Select Committee on Intelligence of the House of Representatives and the Select Committee on Intelligence of the Senate concerning all requests made pursuant to this paragraph.

(D) No financial institution, or officer, employee, or agent of such institution, shall disclose to any person that the Federal Bureau of Investigation has sought or obtained access to a customer's or entity's financial records under this paragraph.

(b)

(1) Nothing in this chapter shall prohibit a Government authority from obtaining financial records from a financial institution if the Government authority determines that delay in obtaining access to such records would create imminent danger of -

(A) physical injury to any person;

(B) serious property damage; or

(C) flight to avoid prosecution.

(2) In the instances specified in paragraph (1), the Government shall submit to the financial institution the certificate required in section 3403(b) of this title signed by a supervisory official of a rank designated by the head of the Government authority.

(3) Within five days of obtaining access to financial records under this subsection, the Government authority shall file with the appropriate court a signed, sworn statement of a supervisory official of a rank designated by the head of the Government authority setting forth the grounds for the emergency access. The Government authority shall thereafter comply with the notice provisions of section 3409(c) of this title.

(4) The Government authority specified in paragraph (1) shall compile an annual tabulation of the occasions in which this section was used.

United States
Right to Financial Privacy Act

Sec. 3415. Cost reimbursement

Except for records obtained pursuant to section 3403(d) or 3413(a) through (h) of this title, or as otherwise provided by law, a Government authority shall pay to the financial institution assembling or providing financial records pertaining to a customer and in accordance with procedures established by this chapter a fee for reimbursement for such costs as are reasonably necessary and which have been directly incurred in searching for, reproducing, or transporting books, papers, records, or other data required or requested to be produced. The Board of Governors of the Federal Reserve System shall, by regulation, establish the rates and conditions under which such payment may be made.

Sec. 3416. Jurisdiction

An action to enforce any provision of this chapter may be brought in any appropriate United States district court without regard to the amount in controversy within three years from the date on which the violation occurs or the date of discovery of such violation, whichever is later.

Sec. 3417. Civil penalties

(a) Liability of agencies or departments of United States or financial institutions
Any agency or department of the United States or financial institution obtaining or disclosing financial records or information contained therein in violation of this chapter is liable to the customer to whom such records relate in an amount equal to the sum of
-

   (1) $100 without regard to the volume of records involved;

   (2) any actual damages sustained by the customer as a result of the disclosure;

   (3) such punitive damages as the court may allow, where the violation is found to have been willful or intentional; and

   (4) in the case of any successful action to enforce liability under this section, the costs of the action together with reasonable attorney's fees as determined by the court.

(b) Disciplinary action for willful or intentional violation of chapter by agents or employees of department or agency
Whenever the court determines that any agency or department of the United States has violated any provision of this chapter and the court finds that the circumstances surrounding the violation raise questions of whether an officer or employee of the department or agency acted willfully or intentionally with respect to the violation, the Director of the Office of Personnel Management shall promptly initiate a proceeding to determine whether disciplinary action is warranted against the agent or employee who was primarily responsible for the violation. The Director after investigation and consideration of the evidence submitted, shall submit his findings and recommendations to the administrative authority of the agency concerned and shall send copies of the

findings and recommendations to the officer or employee or his representative. The administrative authority shall take the corrective action that the Director recommends.

(c) Good faith defense

Any financial institution or agent or employee thereof making a disclosure of financial records pursuant to this chapter in good-faith reliance upon a certificate by any Government authority or pursuant to the provisions of section 3413(l) of this title shall not be liable to the customer for such disclosure under this chapter, the constitution of any State, or any law or regulation of any State or any political subdivision of any State.

(d) Exclusive judicial remedies and sanctions

The remedies and sanctions described in this chapter shall be the only authorized judicial remedies and sanctions for violations of this chapter.

Sec. 3418. Injunctive relief

In addition to any other remedy contained in this chapter, injunctive relief shall be available to require that the procedures of this chapter are complied with. In the event of any successful action, costs together with reasonable attorney's fees as determined by the court may be recovered.

Sec. 3419. Suspension of limitations

If any individual files a motion or application under this chapter which has the effect of delaying the access of a Government authority to financial records pertaining to such individual, any applicable statute of limitations shall be deemed to be tolled for the period extending from the date such motion or application was filed until the date upon which the motion or application is decided.

Sec. 3420. Grand jury information; notification of certain persons prohibited

(a) Financial records about a customer obtained from a financial institution pursuant to a subpoena issued under the authority of a Federal grand jury -

(1) shall be returned and actually presented to the grand jury unless the volume of such records makes such return and actual presentation impractical in which case the grand jury shall be provided with a description of the contents of the records.;

(2) shall be used only for the purpose of considering whether to issue an indictment or presentment by that grand jury, or of prosecuting a crime for which that indictment or presentment is issued, or for a purpose authorized by rule 6(e) of the Federal Rules of Criminal Procedure;

(3) shall be destroyed or returned to the financial institution if not used for one of the purposes specified in paragraph (2); and

(4) shall not be maintained, or a description of the contents of such records shall not be maintained by any Government authority other than in the sealed records of the grand jury, unless such record has been used in the prosecution of a crime for which the grand jury issued an indictment or presentment or for a purpose authorized by rule 6(e) of the Federal Rules of Criminal Procedure.

(b)

(1) No officer, director, partner, employee, or shareholder of, or agent or attorney for, a financial institution shall, directly or indirectly, notify any person named in a grand jury subpoena served on such institution in connection with an investigation relating to a possible -

(A) crime against any financial institution or supervisory agency or crime involving a violation of the Controlled Substance Act (21 U.S.C. 801 et seq.), the Controlled Substances Import and Export Act (21 U.S.C. 951 et seq.), section 1956 or 1957 of title 18, sections 5313, 5316 and 5324 of title 31, or section 6050I of title 26; or

(B) conspiracy to commit such a crime, about the existence or contents of such subpoena, or information that has been furnished to the grand jury in response to such subpoena.

(2) Section 1818 of this title and section 1786(k)(2) of this title shall apply to any violation of this subsection.

Sec. 3421. [Repealed]

Sec. 3422. Applicability to Securities and Exchange Commission

Except as provided in the Securities Exchange Act of 1934 (15 U.S.C. 78a et seq.), this chapter shall apply with respect to the Securities and Exchange Commission.

PRIVACY PROTECTION ACT (1980)

Summary

The Privacy Protection Act of 1980 was passed in response to Zurcher v. Stanford Daily, 436 U.S. 547 (1978), which upheld broad law enforcement access to a newspaper's files. The Act establishes procedures for law enforcement seeking access to records and other information from the offices and employees of a media organization. In general, the Act prohibits both federal and state officers and employees from searching or seizing journalists' "work product" or the "documentary materials" in their possession. Under the Act, in order to gain access to journalists' information, law enforcement must obtain a court subpoena, rather than a simple search warrant.

The Act provides limited exceptions that allow the government to use a warrant, rather than a subpoena, to search for certain types of national security information, child pornography, evidence that the journalists themselves have committed a crime, or materials that must be immediately seized to prevent death or serious bodily injury. "Documentary materials" may also be seized if there is reason to believe that they would be destroyed in the time it took to obtain them using a subpoena, or if a court has ordered disclosure, the news organization has refused to release the materials, and all other remedies have been exhausted.

A search may be conducted only when there is probable cause to believe that an individual is involved in a crime. Also, only those who are involved with a particular investigation can do the searching. Although the statute specifically provides that its violation is not grounds to suppress evidence, it does provide a civil remedy in Federal court against either the government entity or individual officers involved in the search where a search warrant, rather than a subpoena, is used contrary to the Act's provisions.

References

Public 96-440 as amended 104-208. Codified at 42 USC § 2000aa et seq.
[http://www4.law.cornell.edu/uscode/42/2000aa.html]

42 U.S.C. 2000aa. Searches and seizures by government officers and employees in connection with investigation or prosecution of criminal offenses

(a) Work product materials

Notwithstanding any other law, it shall be unlawful for a government officer or employee, in connection with the investigation or prosecution of a criminal offense, to search for or seize any work product materials possessed by a person reasonably believed to have a purpose to disseminate to the public a newspaper, book, broadcast, or other similar form of public communication, in or affecting interstate or foreign commerce; but this provision shall not impair or affect the ability of any government officer or employee, pursuant to otherwise applicable law, to search for or seize such materials, if -

(1) there is probable cause to believe that the person possessing such materials has committed or is committing the criminal offense to which the materials relate: Provided, however, That a government officer or employee may not search for or seize such materials under the provisions of this paragraph if the offense to which the materials relate consists of the receipt, possession, communication, or withholding of such materials or the information contained therein (but such a search or seizure may be conducted under the provisions of this paragraph if the offense consists of the receipt, possession, or communication of information relating to the national defense, classified information, or restricted data under the provisions of section 793, 794, 797, or 798 of title 18, or section 2274, 2275, or 2277 of this title, or section 783 of title 50; or if the offense involves the production, possession, receipt, mailing, sale, distribution, shipment, or transportation of child pornography, the sexual exploitation of children, or the sale or purchase of children under section 2251, 2251A, 2252, or 2252A of title 18); or

(2) there is reason to believe that the immediate seizure of such materials is necessary to prevent the death of, or serious bodily injury to, a human being.

(b) Other documents

Notwithstanding any other law, it shall be unlawful for a government officer or employee, in connection with the investigation or prosecution of a criminal offense, to search for or seize documentary materials, other than work product materials, possessed by a person in connection with a purpose to disseminate to the public a newspaper, book, broadcast, or other similar form of public communication, in or affecting interstate or foreign commerce; but this provision shall not impair or affect the ability of any government officer or employee, pursuant to otherwise applicable law, to search for or seize such materials, if -

(1) there is probable cause to believe that the person possessing such materials has committed or is committing the criminal offense to which the materials relate: Provided, however, That a government officer or employee may not search for or seize such materials under the provisions of this paragraph if the offense to which the materials relate consists of the receipt, possession, communication, or withholding of such materials or the information contained therein (but such a search or seizure may be conducted under the provisions of this paragraph if the offense consists of the receipt, possession, or communication of information relating to the national defense, classified information, or restricted data under the provisions of section 793, 794, 797, or 798 of title 18, or section 2274, 2275, or 2277 of this title, or section 783 of title 50, or if the offense involves the production, possession, receipt, mailing, sale, distribution, shipment, or

transportation of child pornography, the sexual exploitation of children, or the sale or purchase of children under section 2251, 2251A, 2252, or 2252A of title 18);

(2) there is reason to believe that the immediate seizure of such materials is necessary to prevent the death of, or serious bodily injury to, a human being;

(3) there is reason to believe that the giving of notice pursuant to a subpoena duces tecum would result in the destruction, alteration, or concealment of such materials; or

(4) such materials have not been produced in response to a court order directing compliance with a subpoena duces tecum, and-

>   (A) all appellate remedies have been exhausted; or

>   (B) there is reason to believe that the delay in an investigation or trial occasioned by further proceedings relating to the subpoena would threaten the interests of justice.

(c) Objections to court ordered subpoenas; affidavits

In the event a search warrant is sought pursuant to paragraph (4)(B) of subsection (b) of this section, the person possessing the materials shall be afforded adequate opportunity to submit an affidavit setting forth the basis for any contention that the materials sought are not subject to seizure.

Sec. 2000aa-5. Border and customs searches

This chapter shall not impair or affect the ability of a government officer or employee, pursuant to otherwise applicable law, to conduct searches and seizures at the borders of, or at international points of entry into the United States in order to enforce the customs laws of the United States.

Sec. 2000aa-6. Civil actions by aggrieved persons

(a) Right of action

A person aggrieved by a search for or seizure of materials in violation of this chapter shall have a civil cause of action for damages for such search or seizure -

>   (1) against the United States, against a State which has waived its sovereign immunity under the Constitution to a claim for damages resulting from a violation of this chapter, or against any other governmental unit, all of which shall be liable for violations of this chapter by their officers or employees while acting within the scope or under color of their office or employment; and

>   (2) against an officer or employee of a State who has violated this chapter while acting within the scope or under color of his office or employment, if such State has not waived its sovereign immunity as provided in paragraph (1).

(b) Good faith defense

It shall be a complete defense to a civil action brought under paragraph (2) of subsection (a) of this section that the officer or employee had a reasonable good faith belief in the lawfulness of his conduct.

(c) Official immunity

The United States, a State, or any other governmental unit liable for violations of this chapter under subsection (a)(1) of this section, may not assert as a defense to a claim arising under this chapter the immunity of the officer or employee whose violation is complained of or his reasonable good faith belief in the lawfulness of his conduct, except that such a defense may be asserted if the violation complained of is that of a judicial officer.

(d) Exclusive nature of remedy

The remedy provided by subsection (a)(1) of this section against the United States, a State, or any other governmental unit is exclusive of any other civil action or proceeding for conduct constituting a violation of this chapter, against the officer or employee whose violation gave rise to the claim, or against the estate of such officer or employee.

(e) Admissibility of evidence

Evidence otherwise admissible in a proceeding shall not be excluded on the basis of a violation of this chapter.

(f) Damages; costs and attorneys' fees

A person having a cause of action under this section shall be entitled to recover actual damages but not less than liquidated damages of $1,000, and such reasonable attorneys' fees and other litigation costs reasonably incurred as the court, in its discretion, may award: Provided, however, That the United States, a State, or any other governmental unit shall not be liable for interest prior to judgment.

(g) Attorney General; claims settlement; regulations

The Attorney General may settle a claim for damages brought against the United States under this section, and shall promulgate regulations to provide for the commencement of an administrative inquiry following a determination of a violation of this chapter by an officer or employee of the United States and for the imposition of administrative sanctions against such officer or employee, if warranted.

(h) Jurisdiction

The district courts shall have original jurisdiction of all civil actions arising under this section.

Sec. 2000aa-7. Definitions

(a) "Documentary materials", as used in this chapter, means materials upon which information is recorded, and includes, but is not limited to, written or printed materials, photographs, motion picture films, negatives, video tapes, audio tapes, and other mechanically, magnetically or electronically recorded cards, tapes, or discs, but does not include contraband or the fruits of a crime or things otherwise criminally possessed, or property designed or intended for use, or which is or has been used as, the means of committing a criminal offense.

(b) "Work product materials", as used in this chapter, means materials, other than contraband or the fruits of a crime or things otherwise criminally possessed, or property designed or intended for use, or which is or has been used, as the means of committing a criminal offense, and -

> (1) in anticipation of communicating such materials to the public, are prepared, produced, authored, or created, whether by the person in possession of the materials or by any other person;

> (2) are possessed for the purposes of communicating such materials to the public; and

> (3) include mental impressions, conclusions, opinions, or theories of the person who prepared, produced, authored, or created such material.

(c) "Any other governmental unit", as used in this chapter, includes the District of Columbia, the Commonwealth of Puerto Rico, any territory or possession of the United States, and any local government, unit of local government, or any unit of State government.

Sec. 2000aa-11. Guidelines for Federal officers and employees

(a) Procedures to obtain documentary evidence; protection of certain privacy interests

The Attorney General shall, within six months of October 13, 1980, issue guidelines for the procedures to be employed by any Federal officer or employee, in connection with the investigation or prosecution of an offense, to obtain documentary materials in the private possession of a person when the person is not reasonably believed to be a suspect in such offense or related by blood or marriage to such a suspect, and when the materials sought are not contraband or the fruits or instrumentalities of an offense. The Attorney General shall incorporate in such guidelines

> (1) a recognition of the personal privacy interests of the person in possession of such documentary materials;

> (2) a requirement that the least intrusive method or means of obtaining such materials be used which do not substantially jeopardize the availability or usefulness of the materials sought to be obtained;

> (3) a recognition of special concern for privacy interests in cases in which a search or seizure for such documents would intrude upon a known confidential relationship such as that which may exist between clergyman and parishioner; lawyer and client; or doctor and patient; and

> (4) a requirement that an application for a warrant to conduct a search governed by this subchapter be approved by an attorney for the government, except that in an emergency situation the application may be approved by another appropriate

supervisory official if within 24 hours of such emergency the appropriate United States Attorney is notified.

(b) Use of search warrants; reports to Congress

The Attorney General shall collect and compile information on, and report annually to the Committees on the Judiciary of the Senate and the House of Representatives on the use of search warrants by Federal officers and employees for documentary materials described in subsection (a)(3) of this section.

Sec. 2000aa-12. Binding nature of guidelines; disciplinary actions for violations; legal proceedings for non-compliance prohibited

Guidelines issued by the Attorney General under this subchapter shall have the full force and effect of Department of Justice regulations and any violation of these guidelines shall make the employee or officer involved subject to appropriate administrative disciplinary action. However, an issue relating to the compliance, or the failure to comply, with guidelines issued pursuant to this subchapter may not be litigated, and a court may not entertain such an issue as the basis for the suppression or exclusion of evidence.

CABLE COMMUNICATIONS POLICY ACT (1984)

Summary

The Cable Communications Policy Act of 1984 provides a strong statutory framework for the protection of cable subscribers' personal information and incorporates the privacy principles set out in the OECD Privacy Guidelines of 1980.

Under the Act, cable providers must provide written notice to subscribers of their privacy rights at the time they first subscribe to the cable service and, thereafter, at least once a year. These notices must specify the kind of information that may be collected, how it will be used, to whom and how often it may be disclosed, how long it will be stored, how a subscriber may access this information and the liability imposed by the Act on providers.

Subject to limited exceptions, the Act requires providers to obtain the prior written or electronic consent of the cable subscriber before collecting or disclosing personally identifiable information. Cable providers do not need consent to collect personally identifiable information needed to offer or render cable service to a subscriber, or to detect cable piracy. Furthermore, they do not need consent to disclose subscriber information where disclosure is necessary to rendering a legitimate business activity related to a cable service or pursuant to a court order.

The Act grants cable subscribers the right to access the data collected about them and to correct any errors. It also provides for the destruction of personally identifiable information if that information is no longer necessary. Finally, it sets out a private right of action including actual and punitive damages, attorney's fees and litigation costs for violations of any of its provisions. State and local cable privacy laws are not preempted by the Act.

References

Public Law 98-549 as codified at 47 USC § 551 et seq.
[http://www4.law.cornell.edu/uscode/47/551.html]

Notice to customer

David H. Flaherty, *Protecting Privacy in Two-Way Electronic Services (1985)*

47 U.S.C. § 551. Protection of subscriber privacy

(a) Notice to subscriber regarding personally identifiable information; definitions

(1) At the time of entering into an agreement to provide any cable service or other service to a subscriber and at least once a year thereafter, a cable operator shall provide notice in the form of a separate, written statement to such subscriber which clearly and conspicuously informs the subscriber of -

United States
Cable Communication Policy Act

(A) the nature of personally identifiable information collected or to be collected with respect to the subscriber and the nature of the use of such information;

(B) the nature, frequency, and purpose of any disclosure which may be made of such information, including an identification of the types of persons to whom the disclosure may be made;

(C) the period during which such information will be maintained by the cable operator;

(D) the times and place at which the subscriber may have access to such information in accordance with subsection (d) of this section; and

(E) the limitations provided by this section with respect to the collection and disclosure of information by a cable operator and the right of the subscriber under subsections (f) and (h) of this section to enforce such limitations.

In the case of subscribers who have entered into such an agreement before the effective date of this section, such notice shall be provided within 180 days of such date and at least once a year thereafter.

(2) For purposes of this section, other than subsection (h) of this section -

(A) the term "personally identifiable information" does not include any record of aggregate data which does not identify particular persons;

B) the term "other service" includes any wire or radio communications service provided using any of the facilities of a cable operator that are used in the provision of cable service; and

(C) the term "cable operator" includes, in addition to persons within the definition of cable operator in section 522 of this title, any person who

(i) is owned or controlled by, or under common ownership or control with, a cable operator, and

(ii) provides any wire or radio communications service.

(b) Collection of personally identifiable information using cable system

(1) Except as provided in paragraph (2), a cable operator shall not use the cable system to collect personally identifiable information concerning any subscriber without the prior written or electronic consent of the subscriber concerned.

(2) A cable operator may use the cable system to collect such information in order to -

(A) obtain information necessary to render a cable service or other service provided by the cable operator to the subscriber; or

(B) detect unauthorized reception of cable communications.

(c) Disclosure of personally identifiable information

(1) Except as provided in paragraph (2), a cable operator shall not disclose personally identifiable information concerning any subscriber without the prior written or electronic consent of the subscriber concerned and shall take such actions as are necessary to prevent unauthorized access to such information by a person other than the subscriber or cable operator.

Exceptions to General Disclosure Rule [handwritten annotation]

(2) A cable operator may disclose such information if the disclosure is -

(A) necessary to render, or conduct a legitimate business activity related to, a cable service or other service provided by the cable operator to the subscriber;

(B) subject to subsection (h) of this section, made pursuant to a court order authorizing such disclosure, if the subscriber is notified of such order by the person to whom the order is directed; or

(C) a disclosure of the names and addresses of subscribers to any cable service or other service, if -

(i) the cable operator has provided the subscriber the opportunity to prohibit or limit such disclosure, and

Opt-out [handwritten annotation]

(ii) the disclosure does not reveal, directly or indirectly, the -

(I) extent of any viewing or other use by the subscriber of a cable service or other service provided by the cable operator, or

(II) the nature of any transaction made by the subscriber over the cable system of the cable operator.

(d) Subscriber access to information A cable subscriber shall be provided access to all personally identifiable information regarding that subscriber which is collected and maintained by a cable operator. Such information shall be made available to the subscriber at reasonable times and at a convenient place designated by such cable operator. A cable subscriber shall be provided reasonable opportunity to correct any error in such information.

(e) Destruction of information A cable operator shall destroy personally identifiable information if the information is no longer necessary for the purpose for which it was collected and there are no pending requests or orders for access to such information under subsection (d) of this section or pursuant to a court order.

mandatory destruction [handwritten annotation]

(f) Civil action in United States district court; damages; attorney's fees and costs; nonexclusive nature of remedy

(1) Any person aggrieved by any act of a cable operator in violation of this section may bring a civil action in a United States district court.

always [handwritten annotation]

(2) The court may award -

(A) actual damages but not less than liquidated damages computed at the rate of $100 a day for each day of violation or $1,000, whichever is higher;

(B) punitive damages; and

(C) reasonable attorneys' fees and other litigation costs reasonably incurred.

(3) The remedy provided by this section shall be in addition to any other lawful remedy available to a cable subscriber.

(g) Regulation by States or franchising authorities Nothing in this subchapter shall be construed to prohibit any State or any franchising authority from enacting or enforcing laws consistent with this section for the protection of subscriber privacy.

(h) Disclosure of information to governmental entity pursuant to court order A governmental entity may obtain personally identifiable information concerning a cable subscriber pursuant to a court order only if, in the court proceeding relevant to such court order -

(1) such entity offers clear and convincing evidence that the subject of the information is reasonably suspected of engaging in criminal activity and that the information sought would be material evidence in the case; and

(2) the subject of the information is afforded the opportunity to appear and contest such entity's claim.

ELECTRONIC COMMUNICATIONS PRIVACY ACT (1986)

Summary

The Electronic Communications Privacy Act (ECPA) was enacted in 1986, as an amendment to the Omnibus Crime Control Act of 1968, to address technological advancements in communication networks and to bring "electronic communication" within the purview of federal law regarding wiretapping and bugging. ECPA covers wireless communication, email, and digitally transmitted conversations. ECPA criminalizes the interception of such communication, and provides civil remedies for violations. It also prevents government entities from requiring disclosure of electronic communications from a provider without proper procedure.

Title I of the Act protects electronic communications from unauthorized interception during transmission. In this way it mirrors the wiretap statute under the Omnibus Crime Control Act. Title II protects electronic data and messages in storage from unauthorized access and disclosure. Title II protects two kinds of data. First, it protects email and similar substantive electronic communications. Second, it protects data transfers between businesses and customers, such as fund transfers and computerized transfer of medical records.

It is useful to note that while the ECPA prohibits operators of electronic communications services from disclosing the content of messages in storage, this does not apply to purely internal email systems.

Both Title I and Title II mirror the principle of one-party consent found in the Omnibus Crime Control Act. Anyone may access electronic information if authorized by the user. Anyone may divulge such information with the consent of either the sender or recipient of the information. Sanctions under Title I include criminal penalties, a special injunction procedure, and a civil right of action. Penalties for Title II violations vary, but can include fines of up to $250,000 and prison sentences of no more than two years.

References

Public Law 90-351 (Omnibus Crime Control and Safe Streets Act of 1968)
[http://www4.law.cornell.edu/uscode/18/2510.html]

Public Law 99-508 (Electronic Communications Privacy Act of 1986)
[http://www4.law.cornell.edu/uscode/18/2701.html]

Public Law 103-414 (Communications Assistance for Law Enforcement
Act of 1994)
[http://www4.law.cornell.edu/uscode/47/1001.html]

United States
Electronic Communications Privacy Act

James G. Carr, *The Law of Electronic Surveillance* (Clark, Boardman & Callaghan 2001)

Clifford S. Fishman & Anne T. McKenna, *Wiretapping and Eavesdropping* (Clark, Boardman & Callaghan 1995)

Congressional Findings (1968)

Section 801 of Pub. L. 90-351 provided that: "On the basis of its own investigations and of published studies, the Congress makes the following findings:

"(a) Wire communications are normally conducted through the use of facilities which form part of an interstate network. The same facilities are used for interstate and intrastate communications. There has been extensive wiretapping carried on without legal sanctions, and without the consent of any of the parties to the conversation. Electronic, mechanical, and other intercepting devices are being used to overhear oral conversations made in private, without the consent of any of the parties to such communications. The contents of these communications and evidence derived therefrom are being used by public and private parties as evidence in court and administrative proceedings, and by persons whose activities affect interstate commerce. The possession, manufacture, distribution, advertising, and use of these devices are facilitated by interstate commerce.

"(b) In order to protect effectively the privacy of wire and oral communications, to protect the integrity of court and administrative proceedings, and to prevent the obstruction of interstate commerce, it is necessary for Congress to define on a uniform basis the circumstances and conditions under which the interception of wire and oral communications may be authorized, to prohibit any unauthorized interception of such communications, and the use of the contents thereof in evidence in courts and administrative proceedings.

"(c) Organized criminals make extensive use of wire and oral communications in their criminal activities. The interception of such communications to obtain evidence of the commission of crimes or to prevent their commission is an indispensable aid to law enforcement and the administration of justice.

"(d) To safeguard the privacy of innocent persons, the interception of wire or oral communications where none of the parties to the communication has consented to the interception should be allowed only when authorized by a court of competent jurisdiction and should remain under the control and supervision of the authorizing court. Interception of wire and oral communications should further be limited to certain major types of offenses and specific categories of crime with assurances that the interception is justified and that the information obtained thereby will not be misused."

18 U.S.C. § 2510. Definitions

As used in this chapter -

(1) "wire communication" means any aural transfer made in whole or in part through the use of facilities for the transmission of communications by the aid of wire, cable, or other like connection between the point of origin and the point of reception (including the use of such connection in a switching station) furnished or operated by any person engaged in providing or operating such facilities for the transmission of interstate or foreign communications or communications affecting interstate or foreign commerce and such term includes any electronic storage of such communication;

(2) "oral communication" means any oral communication uttered by a person exhibiting an expectation that such communication is not subject to interception under circumstances justifying such expectation, but such term does not include any electronic communication;

(3) "State" means any State of the United States, the District of Columbia, the Commonwealth of Puerto Rico, and any territory or possession of the United States;

(4) "intercept" means the aural or other acquisition of the contents of any wire, electronic, or oral communication through the use of any electronic, mechanical, or other device.

(5) "electronic, mechanical, or other device" means any device or apparatus which can be used to intercept a wire, oral, or electronic communication other than -

> (a) any telephone or telegraph instrument, equipment or facility, or any component thereof,

> > (i) furnished to the subscriber or user by a provider of wire or electronic communication service in the ordinary course of its business and being used by the subscriber or user in the ordinary course of its business or furnished by such subscriber or user for connection to the facilities of such service and used in the ordinary course of its business; or

> > (ii) being used by a provider of wire or electronic communication service in the ordinary course of its business, or by an investigative or law enforcement officer in the ordinary course of his duties;

> (b) a hearing aid or similar device being used to correct subnormal hearing to not better than normal;

(6) "person" means any employee, or agent of the United States or any State or political subdivision thereof, and any individual, partnership, association, joint stock company, trust, or corporation;

(7) "Investigative or law enforcement officer" means any officer of the United States or of a State or political subdivision thereof, who is empowered by law to conduct investigations of or to make arrests for offenses enumerated in this chapter, and any attorney authorized by law to prosecute or participate in the prosecution of such offenses;

(8) "contents", when used with respect to any wire, oral, or electronic communication, includes any information concerning the substance, purport, or meaning of that communication;

(9) "Judge of competent jurisdiction" means -

(a) a judge of a United States district court or a United States court of appeals; and

(b) a judge of any court of general criminal jurisdiction of a State who is authorized by a statute of that State to enter orders authorizing interceptions of wire, oral, or electronic communications;

(10) "communication common carrier" shall have the same meaning which is given the term "common carrier" by section 153(h) of title 47 of the United States Code;

(11) "aggrieved person" means a person who was a party to any intercepted wire, oral, or electronic communication or a person against whom the interception was directed;

(12) "electronic communication" means any transfer of signs, signals, writing, images, sounds, data, or intelligence of any nature transmitted in whole or in part by a wire, radio, electromagnetic, photoelectronic or photooptical system that affects interstate or foreign commerce, but does not include -

(A) any wire or oral communication;

(B) any communication made through a tone-only paging device; or

(C) any communication from a tracking device (as defined in section 3117 of this title);

(13) "user" means any person or entity who -

(A) uses an electronic communication service; and

(B) is duly authorized by the provider of such service to engage in such use;

(14) "electronic communications system" means any wire, radio, electromagnetic, photooptical or photoelectronic facilities for the transmission of electronic communications, and any computer facilities or related electronic equipment for the electronic storage of such communications;

(15) "electronic communication service" means any service which provides to users thereof the ability to send or receive wire or electronic communications;

(16) "readily accessible to the general public" means, with respect to a radio communication, that such communication is not

(A) scrambled or encrypted;

(B) transmitted using modulation techniques whose essential parameters have been withheld from the public with the intention of preserving the privacy of such communication;

(C) carried on a subcarrier or other signal subsidiary to a radio transmission;

(D) transmitted over a communication system provided by a common carrier, unless the communication is a tone only paging system communication;

(E) transmitted on frequencies allocated under part 25, subpart D, E, or F of part 74, or part 94 of the Rules of the Federal Communications Commission, unless, in the case of a communication transmitted on a frequency allocated under part 74 that is not exclusively allocated to broadcast auxiliary services, the communication is a two-way voice communication by radio; or

(F) an electronic communication;

(17) "electronic storage" means -

    (A) any temporary, intermediate storage of a wire or electronic communication incidental to the electronic transmission thereof; and

    (B) any storage of such communication by an electronic communication service for purposes of backup protection of such communication; and

(18) "aural transfer" means a transfer containing the human voice at any point between and including the point of origin and the point of reception.

Sec. 2511. Interception and disclosure of wire, oral, or electronic communications prohibited

(1) Except as otherwise specifically provided in this chapter any person who -

    (a) intentionally intercepts, endeavors to intercept, or procures any other person to intercept or endeavor to intercept, any wire, oral, or electronic communication;

    (b) intentionally uses, endeavors to use, or procures any other person to use or endeavor to use any electronic, mechanical, or other device to intercept any oral communication when -

        (i) such device is affixed to, or otherwise transmits a signal through, a wire, cable, or other like connection used in wire communication; or

        (ii) such device transmits communications by radio, or interferes with the transmission of such communication; or

        (iii) such person knows, or has reason to know, that such device or any component thereof has been sent through the mail or transported in interstate or foreign commerce; or

        (iv) such use or endeavor to use (A) takes place on the premises of any business or other commercial establishment the operations of which affect interstate or foreign commerce; or (B) obtains or is for the purpose of obtaining information relating to the operations of any business or other commercial establishment the operations of which affect interstate or foreign commerce; or

        (v) such person acts in the District of Columbia, the Commonwealth of Puerto Rico, or any territory or possession of the United States;

    (c) intentionally discloses, or endeavors to disclose, to any other person the contents of any wire, oral, or electronic communication, knowing or having reason to know that the information was obtained through the interception of a wire, oral, or electronic communication in violation of this subsection;

    (d) intentionally uses, or endeavors to use, the contents of any wire, oral, or electronic communication, knowing or having reason to know that the information was obtained through the interception of a wire, oral, or electronic communication in violation of this subsection; or

    (e)

        (i) intentionally discloses, or endeavors to disclose, to any other person the contents of any wire, oral, or electronic communication, intercepted by means authorized by sections 2511(2)(A)(ii), 2511(b)-(c), 2511(e), 2516, and 2518 of this subchapter,

(ii) knowing or having reason to know that the information was obtained through the interception of such a communication in connection with a criminal investigation,

(iii) having obtained or received the information in connection with a criminal investigation, and

(iv) with intent to improperly obstruct, impede, or interfere with a duly authorized criminal investigation, shall be punished as provided in subsection (4) or shall be subject to suit as provided in subsection (5).

(2)

(a)

(i) It shall not be unlawful under this chapter for an operator of a switchboard, or an officer, employee, or agent of a provider of wire or electronic communication service, whose facilities are used in the transmission of a wire or electronic communication, to intercept, disclose, or use that communication in the normal course of his employment while engaged in any activity which is a necessary incident to the rendition of his service or to the protection of the rights or property of the provider of that service, except that a provider of wire communication service to the public shall not utilize service observing or random monitoring except for mechanical or service quality control checks.

(ii) Notwithstanding any other law, providers of wire or electronic communication service, their officers, employees, and agents, landlords, custodians, or other persons, are authorized to provide information, facilities, or technical assistance to persons authorized by law to intercept wire, oral, or electronic communications or to conduct electronic surveillance, as defined in section 101 of the Foreign Intelligence Surveillance Act of 1978, if such provider, its officers, employees, or agents, landlord, custodian, or other specified person, has been provided with -

(A) a court order directing such assistance signed by the authorizing judge, or

(B) a certification in writing by a person specified in section 2518(7) of this title or the Attorney General of the United States that no warrant or court order is required by law, that all statutory requirements have been met, and that the specified assistance is required, setting forth the period of time during which the provision of the information, facilities, or technical assistance is authorized and specifying the information, facilities, or technical assistance required. No provider of wire or electronic communication service, officer, employee, or agent thereof, or landlord, custodian, or other specified person shall disclose the existence of any interception or surveillance or the device used to accomplish the interception or surveillance with respect to which the person has been furnished a court order or certification under this chapter, except as may otherwise be required by legal process and then only after prior notification to the Attorney General or to the principal prosecuting attorney of a State or any political subdivision of a State, as may be appropriate. Any such disclosure, shall render such person liable for the civil damages provided for in section 2520. No cause of action shall lie in any court against any provider of wire or electronic communication service, its officers, employees, or agents, landlord, custodian, or other specified person for providing information, facilities, or assistance in accordance with the terms of a court order or certification under this chapter.

(b) It shall not be unlawful under this chapter for an officer, employee, or agent of the Federal Communications Commission, in the normal course of his employment and in discharge of the monitoring responsibilities exercised by the Commission in the enforcement of chapter 5 of title 47 of the United States Code, to intercept a wire or electronic communication, or oral communication transmitted by radio, or to disclose or use the information thereby obtained.

(c) It shall not be unlawful under this chapter for a person acting under color of law to intercept a wire, oral, or electronic communication, where such person is a party to the communication or one of the parties to the communication has given prior consent to such interception.

(d) It shall not be unlawful under this chapter for a person not acting under color of law to intercept a wire, oral, or electronic communication where such person is a party to the communication or where one of the parties to the communication has given prior consent to such interception unless such communication is intercepted for the purpose of committing any criminal or tortious act in violation of the Constitution or laws of the United States or of any State.

(e) Notwithstanding any other provision of this title or section 705 or 706 of the Communications Act of 1934, it shall not be unlawful for an officer, employee, or agent of the United States in the normal course of his official duty to conduct electronic surveillance, as defined in section 101 of the Foreign Intelligence Surveillance Act of 1978, as authorized by that Act.

(f) Nothing contained in this chapter or chapter 121, or section 705 of the Communications Act of 1934, shall be deemed to affect the acquisition by the United States Government of foreign intelligence information from international or foreign communications, or foreign intelligence activities conducted in accordance with otherwise applicable Federal law involving a foreign electronic communications system, utilizing a means other than electronic surveillance as defined in section 101 of the Foreign Intelligence Surveillance Act of 1978, and procedures in this chapter or chapter 121 and the Foreign Intelligence Surveillance Act of 1978 shall be the exclusive means by which electronic surveillance, as

United States
Electronic Communications Privacy Act

defined in section 101 of such Act, and the interception of domestic wire and oral communications may be conducted.

(g) It shall not be unlawful under this chapter or chapter 121 of this title for any person

(i) to intercept or access an electronic communication made through an electronic communication system that is configured so that such electronic communication is readily accessible to the general public;

(ii) to intercept any radio communication which is transmitted

(I) by any station for the use of the general public, or that relates to ships, aircraft, vehicles, or persons in distress;

(II) by any governmental, law enforcement, civil defense, private land mobile, or public safety communications system, including police and fire, readily accessible to the general public;

(III) by a station operating on an authorized frequency within the bands allocated to the amateur, citizens band, or general mobile radio services; or

(IV) by any marine or aeronautical communications system;

(iii) to engage in any conduct which -

(I) is prohibited by section 633 of the Communications Act of 1934; or

(II) is excepted from the application of section 705(a) of the Communications Act of 1934 by section 705(b) of that Act;

(iv) to intercept any wire or electronic communication the transmission of which is causing harmful interference to any lawfully operating station or consumer electronic equipment, to the extent necessary to identify the source of such interference; or

(v) for other users of the same frequency to intercept any radio communication made through a system that utilizes frequencies monitored by individuals engaged in the provision or

the use of such system, if such communication is not scrambled or encrypted.

(h) It shall not be unlawful under this chapter -

(i) to use a pen register or a trap and trace device (as those terms are defined for the purposes of chapter 206 (relating to pen registers and trap and trace devices) of this title); or

(ii) for a provider of electronic communication service to record the fact that a wire or electronic communication was initiated or completed in order to protect such provider, another provider furnishing service toward the completion of the wire or electronic communication, or a user of that service, from fraudulent, unlawful or abusive use of such service.

(3)

(a) Except as provided in paragraph (b) of this subsection, a person or entity providing an electronic communication service to the public shall not intentionally divulge the contents of any communication (other than one to such person or entity, or an agent thereof) while in transmission on that service to any person or entity other than an addressee or intended recipient of such communication or an agent of such addressee or intended recipient.

(b) A person or entity providing electronic communication service to the public may divulge the contents of any such communication -

   (i) as otherwise authorized in section 2511(2)(a) or 2517 of this title;

   (ii) with the lawful consent of the originator or any addressee or intended recipient of such communication;

   (iii) to a person employed or authorized, or whose facilities are used, to forward such communication to its destination; or

   (iv) which were inadvertently obtained by the service provider and which appear to pertain to the commission of a crime, if such divulgence is made to a law enforcement agency.

(4)

(a) Except as provided in paragraph (b) of this subsection or in subsection (5), whoever violates subsection (1) of this section shall be fined under this title or imprisoned not more than five

years, or both.

(b) If the offense is a first offense under paragraph (a) of this subsection and is not for a tortious or illegal purpose or for purposes of direct or indirect commercial advantage or private commercial gain, and the wire or electronic communication with respect to which the offense under paragraph (a) is a radio communication that is not scrambled, encrypted, or transmitted using modulation techniques the essential parameters of which have been withheld from the public with the intention of preserving the privacy of such communication, then -

   (i) if the communication is not the radio portion of a cellular telephone communication, a cordless telephone communication that is transmitted between the cordless telephone handset and the base unit, a public land mobile radio service communication or a paging service communication, and the conduct is not that described in subsection (5), the offender shall be fined under this title or imprisoned not more than one year, or both; and

   (ii) if the communication is the radio portion of a cellular telephone communication, a cordless telephone communication that is transmitted between the cordless telephone handset and the base unit, a public land mobile radio service communication or a paging service communication, the offender shall be fined under this title.

(c) Conduct otherwise an offense under this subsection that consists of or relates to the interception of a satellite transmission that is not encrypted or scrambled and that is

transmitted -

(i) to a broadcasting station for purposes of retransmission to the general public; or

(ii) as an audio subcarrier intended for redistribution to facilities open to the public, but not including data transmissions or telephone calls,

is not an offense under this subsection unless the conduct is for the purposes of direct or indirect commercial advantage or private financial gain.

(5)

   (a)

(i) If the communication is -

(A) a private satellite video communication that is not scrambled or encrypted and the conduct in violation of this chapter is the private viewing of that communication and is not for a tortious or illegal purpose or for purposes of direct or indirect commercial advantage or private commercial gain; or

(B) a radio communication that is transmitted on frequencies allocated under subpart D of part 74 of the rules of the Federal Communications Commission that is not scrambled or encrypted and the conduct in violation of this chapter is not for a tortious or illegal purpose or for purposes of direct or indirect commercial advantage or private commercial gain, then the person who engages in such conduct shall be subject to suit by the Federal Government in a court of competent jurisdiction.

(ii) In an action under this subsection -

(A) if the violation of this chapter is a first offense for the person under paragraph (a) of subsection (4) and such person has not been found liable in a civil action under section 2520 of this title, the Federal Government shall be entitled to appropriate injunctive relief; and

(B) if the violation of this chapter is a second or subsequent offense under paragraph (a) of subsection (4) or such person has been found liable in any prior civil action under section 2520, the person shall be subject to a mandatory $500 civil fine.

(b) The court may use any means within its authority to enforce an injunction issued under paragraph (ii)(A), and shall impose a civil fine of not less than $500 for each violation of such an injunction.

Sec. 2512. Manufacture, distribution, possession, and advertising of wire, oral, or electronic communication intercepting devices prohibited

(1) Except as otherwise specifically provided in this chapter, any person who intentionally

(a) sends through the mail, or sends or carries in interstate or foreign commerce, any electronic, mechanical, or other device, knowing or having reason to know that the design of such device renders it primarily useful for the purpose of the surreptitious interception of wire, oral, or electronic communications;

(b) manufactures, assembles, possesses, or sells any electronic, mechanical, or other device, knowing or having reason to know that the design of such device renders it primarily useful for the purpose of the surreptitious interception of wire, oral, or electronic communications, and that such device or any component thereof has been or will be sent through the mail or transported in interstate or foreign commerce; or

(c) places in any newspaper, magazine, handbill, or other publication any advertisement of

(i) any electronic, mechanical, or other device knowing or having reason to know that the design of such device renders it primarily useful for the purpose of the surreptitious interception of wire, oral, or electronic communications; or

(ii) any other electronic, mechanical, or other device, where such advertisement promotes the use of such device for the purpose of the surreptitious interception of wire, oral, or electronic communications, knowing or having reason to know that such advertisement will be sent through the mail or transported in interstate or foreign commerce, shall be fined under this title or imprisoned not more than five years, or both.

(2) It shall not be unlawful under this section for

(a) a provider of wire or electronic communication service or an officer, agent, or employee of, or a person under contract with, such a provider, in the normal course of the business of providing that wire or electronic communication service, or

(b) an officer, agent, or employee of, or a person under contract with, the United States, a State, or a political subdivision thereof, in the normal course of the activities of the United States, a State, or a political subdivision thereof, to send through the mail, send or carry in interstate or foreign commerce, or manufacture, assemble, possess, or sell any electronic, mechanical, or other device knowing or having reason to know that the design of such device renders it primarily useful for the purpose of the surreptitious interception of wire, oral, or electronic communications.

(3) It shall not be unlawful under this section to advertise for sale a device described in subsection (1) of this section if the advertisement is mailed, sent, or carried in interstate or foreign commerce solely to a domestic provider of wire or electronic communication

service or to an agency of the United States, a State, or a political subdivision thereof which is duly authorized to use such device.

Sec. 2513. Confiscation of wire, oral, or electronic communication intercepting devices

Any electronic, mechanical, or other device used, sent, carried, manufactured, assembled, possessed, sold, or advertised in violation of section 2511 or section 2512 of this chapter may be seized and forfeited to the United States. All provisions of law relating to (1) the seizure, summary and judicial forfeiture, and condemnation of vessels, vehicles, merchandise, and baggage for violations of the customs laws contained in title 19 of the United States Code, (2) the disposition of such vessels, vehicles, merchandise, and baggage or the proceeds from the sale thereof, (3) the remission or mitigation of such forfeiture, (4) the compromise of claims, and (5) the award of compensation to informers in respect of such forfeitures, shall apply to seizures and forfeitures incurred, or alleged to have been incurred, under the provisions of this section, insofar as applicable and not inconsistent with the provisions of this section; except that such duties as are imposed upon the collector of customs or any other person with respect to the seizure and forfeiture of vessels, vehicles, merchandise, and baggage under the provisions of the customs laws contained in title 19 of the United States Code shall be performed with respect to seizure and forfeiture of electronic, mechanical, or other intercepting devices under this section by such officers, agents, or other persons as may be authorized or designated for that purpose by the Attorney General.

Sec. 2514. [Repealed]

Sec. 2515. Prohibition of use as evidence of intercepted wire or oral communications

Whenever any wire or oral communication has been intercepted, no part of the contents of such communication and no evidence derived therefrom may be received in evidence in any trial, hearing, or other proceeding in or before any court, grand jury, department, officer, agency, regulatory body, legislative committee, or other authority of the United States, a State, or a political subdivision thereof if the disclosure of that information would be in violation of this chapter.

Sec. 2516. Authorization for interception of wire, oral, or electronic communications

(1) The Attorney General, Deputy Attorney General, Associate Attorney General, (FOOTNOTE 1) or any Assistant Attorney General, any acting Assistant Attorney General, or any Deputy Assistant Attorney General or acting Deputy Assistant Attorney General in the Criminal Division specially designated by the Attorney General, may authorize an application to a Federal judge of competent jurisdiction for,

and such judge may grant in conformity with section 2518 of this chapter an order authorizing or approving the interception of wire or oral communications by the Federal Bureau of Investigation, or a Federal agency having responsibility for the investigation of the offense as to which the application is made, when such interception may provide or has provided evidence of - (FOOTNOTE 1) See 1984 Amendment note below.

(a) any offense punishable by death or by imprisonment for more than one year under sections 2274 through 2277 of title 42 of the United States Code (relating to the enforcement of the Atomic Energy Act of 1954), section 2284 of title 42 of the United States Code (relating to sabotage of nuclear facilities or fuel), or under the following chapters of this title: chapter 37 (relating to espionage), chapter 105 (relating to sabotage), chapter 115 (relating to treason), chapter 102 (relating to riots), chapter 65 (relating to malicious mischief), chapter 111(relating to destruction of vessels), or chapter 81 (relating to piracy);

(b) a violation of section 186 or section 501(c) of title 29, United States Code (dealing with restrictions on payments and loans to labor organizations), or any offense which involves murder, kidnapping, robbery, or extortion, and which is punishable under this title;

(c) any offense which is punishable under the following sections of this title: section 201 (bribery of public officials and witnesses), section 215 (relating to bribery of bank officials), section 224 (bribery in sporting contests), subsection (d), (e), (f), (g), (h), or (i) of section 844 (unlawful use of explosives), section 1032 (relating to concealment of assets), section 1084 (transmission of wagering information), section 751 (relating to escape), section 1014 (relating to loans and credit applications generally; renewals and discounts), sections 1503, 1512, and 1513 (influencing or injuring an officer, juror, or witness generally), section 1510 (obstruction of criminal investigations), section 1511 (obstruction of State or local law enforcement), section 1751(Presidential and Presidential staff assassination, kidnapping, and assault), section 1951 (interference with commerce by threats or violence), section 1952 (interstate and foreign travel or transportation in aid of racketeering enterprises), section 1958 (relating to use of interstate commerce facilities in the commission of murder for hire), section 1959 (relating to violent crimes in aid of racketeering activity), section 1954 (offer, acceptance, or solicitation to influence operations of employee benefit plan), section 1955 (prohibition of business enterprises of gambling), section 1956 (laundering of monetary instruments),section 1957 (relating to engaging in monetary transactions in property derived from specified unlawful activity), section 659 (theft from interstate shipment), section 664 (embezzlement from pension and welfare funds), section 1343 (fraud by wire, radio, or television), section 1344 (relating to bank fraud), sections 2251 and 2252 (sexual exploitation of children), sections 2312,2313, 2314, and 2315 (interstate transportation of stolen property), section

2321 (relating to trafficking in certain motor vehicles or motor vehicle parts), section 1203 (relating to hostage taking), section 1029 (relating to fraud and related activity in connection with access devices), section 3146 (relating to penalty for failure to appear), section 3521(b)(3)(relating to witness relocation and assistance), section 32 (relating to destruction of aircraft or aircraft facilities), section 1963 (violations with respect to racketeer influenced and corrupt organizations), section 115 (relating to threatening or retaliating against a Federal official), and section 1341 (relating to mail fraud), section 351 (violations with respect to congressional, Cabinet, or Supreme Court assassinations, kidnapping, and assault), section 831 (relating to prohibited transactions involving nuclear materials), section 33 (relating to destruction of motor vehicles or motor vehicle facilities), section 175 (relating to biological weapons), or section 1992 (relating to wrecking trains); a felony violation of section 1028 (relating to production of false identification documentation), section 1425 (relating to the procurement of citizenship or nationalization unlawfully), section 1426 (relating to the reproduction of naturalization or citizenship papers), section 1427 (relating to the sale of naturalization or citizenship papers), section 1541 (relating to passport issuance without authority), section 1542 (relating to false statements in passport applications), section 1543 (relating to forgery or false use of passports), section 1544 (relating to misuse of passports), or section 1546 (relating to fraud and misuse of visas, permits, and other documents);

(d) any offense involving counterfeiting punishable under section 471, 472, or 473 of this title;

(e) any offense involving fraud connected with a case under title 11 or the manufacture, importation, receiving, concealment, buying, selling, or otherwise dealing in narcotic drugs, marihuana, or other dangerous drugs, punishable under any law of the United States;

(f) any offense including extortionate credit transactions under sections 892, 893, or 894 of this title;

(g) a violation of section 5322 of title 31, United States Code (dealing with the reporting of currency transactions);

(h) any felony violation of sections 2511 and 2512 (relating to interception and disclosure of certain communications and to certain intercepting devices) of this title;

(i) any felony violation of chapter 71 (relating to obscenity) of this title;

(j) any violation of section 60123(b) (relating to destruction of a natural gas pipeline) or 46502 (relating to aircraft piracy) of title 49;

(k) any criminal violation of section 2778 of title 22 (relating to the Arms Export Control Act);

(l) the location of any fugitive from justice from an offense described in this section;

(m) a violation of section 274, 277, or 278 of the Immigration

and Nationality Act (8 U.S.C. 1324, 1327, or 1328) (relating to the smuggling of aliens);

(n) any felony violation of sections 922 and 924 of title 18, United States Code (relating to firearms);

(o) any violation of section 5861 of the Internal Revenue Code of 1986 (relating to firearms);

(p) [2] a felony violation of section 1028 (relating to production of false identification documents), section 1542 (relating to false statements in passport applications), section 1546 (relating to fraud and misuse of visas, permits, and other documents) of this title or a violation of section 274, 277, or 278 of the Immigration and Nationality Act (relating to the

smuggling of aliens); or

(p) [2] any conspiracy to commit any offense described

in any subparagraph of this paragraph

([2] So in original. Two subpars. (p) have been enacted.)

(2) The principal prosecuting attorney of any State, or the principal prosecuting attorney of any political subdivision thereof, if such attorney is authorized by a statute of that State to make application to a State court judge of competent jurisdiction for an order authorizing or approving the interception of wire, oral, or electronic communications, may apply to such judge for, and such judge may grant in conformity with section 2518 of this chapter and with the applicable State statute an order authorizing, or approving the interception of wire, oral, or electronic communications by investigative or law enforcement officers having responsibility for the investigation of the offense as to which the application is made, when such interception may provide or has provided evidence of the commission of the offense of murder, kidnapping, gambling, robbery, bribery, extortion, or dealing in narcotic drugs, marihuana or other dangerous drugs, or other crime dangerous to life, limb, or property, and punishable by imprisonment for more than one year, designated in any applicable State statute authorizing such interception, or any conspiracy to commit any of the foregoing offenses.

(3) Any attorney for the Government (as such term is defined for the purposes of the Federal Rules of Criminal Procedure) may authorize an application to a Federal judge of competent jurisdiction for, and such judge may grant, in conformity with section 2518 of this title, an order authorizing or approving the interception of electronic communications by an investigative or law enforcement officer having responsibility for the investigation of the offense as to which the application is made, when such interception may provide or has provided evidence of any Federal felony.

United States
Electronic Communications Privacy Act

Sec. 2517. Authorization for disclosure and use of intercepted wire, oral, or electronic communications

(1) Any investigative or law enforcement officer who, by any means authorized by this chapter, has obtained knowledge of the contents of any wire, oral, or electronic communication, or evidence derived therefrom, may disclose such contents to another investigative or law enforcement officer to the extent that such disclosure is appropriate to the proper performance of the official duties of the officer making or receiving the disclosure.

(2) Any investigative or law enforcement officer who, by any means authorized by this chapter, has obtained knowledge of the contents of any wire, oral, or electronic communication or evidence derived therefrom may use such contents to the extent such use is appropriate to the proper performance of his official duties.

(3) Any person who has received, by any means authorized by this chapter, any information concerning a wire, oral, or electronic communication, or evidence derived therefrom intercepted in accordance with the provisions of this chapter may disclose the contents of that communication or such derivative evidence while giving testimony under oath or affirmation in any proceeding held under the authority of the United States or of any State or political subdivision thereof.

(4) No otherwise privileged wire, oral, or electronic communication intercepted in accordance with, or in violation of, the provisions of this chapter shall lose its privileged character.

(5) When an investigative or law enforcement officer, while engaged in intercepting wire, oral, or electronic communications in the manner authorized herein, intercepts wire, oral, or electronic communications relating to offenses other than those specified in the order of authorization or approval, the contents thereof, and evidence derived therefrom, may be disclosed or used as provided in subsections (1) and (2) of this section. Such contents and any evidence derived therefrom may be used under subsection (3) of this section when authorized or approved by a judge of competent jurisdiction where such judge finds on subsequent application that the contents were otherwise intercepted in accordance with the provisions of this chapter. Such application shall be made as soon as practicable.

Sec. 2518. Procedure for interception of wire, oral, or electronic communications

(1) Each application for an order authorizing or approving the interception of a wire, oral, or electronic communication under this chapter shall be made in writing upon oath or affirmation to a judge of competent jurisdiction and shall state the applicant's authority to make such application. Each application shall include the following information:

(a) the identity of the investigative or law enforcement officer making the application, and the officer authorizing the application;

(b) a full and complete statement of the facts and circumstances relied upon by the applicant, to justify his belief that an order should be issued, including

(i) details as to the particular offense that has been, is being, or is about to be committed,

(ii) except as provided in subsection (11), a particular description of the nature and location of the facilities from which or the place where the communication is to be intercepted,

(iii) a particular description of the type of communications sought to be intercepted,

(iv) the identity of the person, if known, committing the offense and whose communications are to be intercepted;

(c) a full and complete statement as to whether or not other investigative procedures have been tried and failed or why they reasonably appear to be unlikely to succeed if tried or to be too dangerous;

(d) a statement of the period of time for which the interception is required to be maintained. If the nature of the investigation is such that the authorization for interception should not automatically terminate when the described type of communication has been first obtained, a particular description of facts establishing probable cause to believe that additional communications of the same type will occur thereafter;

(e) a full and complete statement of the facts concerning all previous applications known to the individual authorizing and making the application, made to any judge for authorization to intercept, or for approval of interceptions of, wire, oral, or electronic communications involving any of the same persons, facilities or places specified in the application, and the action taken by the judge on each such application; and

(f) where the application is for the extension of an order, a statement setting forth the results thus far obtained from the interception, or a reasonable explanation of the failure to obtain such results.

(2) The judge may require the applicant to furnish additional testimony or documentary evidence in support of the application.

(3) Upon such application the judge may enter an ex parte order, as requested or as modified, authorizing or approving interception of wire, oral, or electronic communications within the territorial jurisdiction of the court in which the judge is sitting (and outside that jurisdiction but within the United States in the case of a mobile interception device authorized by a Federal court within such jurisdiction), if the judge determines on the basis of the facts submitted by the applicant that -

(a) there is probable cause for belief that an individual is committing, has committed, or is about to commit a particular offense enumerated in section 2516 of this chapter;

(b) there is probable cause for belief that particular communications concerning that offense will be obtained through such interception;

(c) normal investigative procedures have been tried and have failed or reasonably appear to be unlikely to succeed if tried or to be too dangerous;

(d) except as provided in subsection (11), there is probable cause for belief that the facilities from which, or the place where, the wire, oral, or electronic communications are to be intercepted are being used, or are about to be used, in connection with the commission of such offense, or are leased to, listed in the name of, or commonly used by such person.

(4) Each order authorizing or approving the interception of any wire, oral, or electronic communication under this chapter shall specify -

(a) the identity of the person, if known, whose communications are to be intercepted;

(b) the nature and location of the communications facilities as to which, or the place where, authority to intercept is granted;

(c) a particular description of the type of communication sought to be intercepted, and a statement of the particular offense to which it relates;

(d) the identity of the agency authorized to intercept the communications, and of the person authorizing the application; and

(e) the period of time during which such interception is authorized, including a statement as to whether or not the interception shall automatically terminate when the described communication has been first obtained.

An order authorizing the interception of a wire, oral, or electronic communication under this chapter shall, upon request of the applicant, direct that a provider of wire or electronic communication service, landlord, custodian or other person shall furnish the applicant forthwith all information, facilities, and technical assistance necessary to accomplish the interception unobtrusively and with a minimum of interference with the services that such service provider, landlord, custodian, or person is according the person whose communications are to be intercepted. Any provider of wire or electronic communication service, landlord, custodian or other person furnishing such facilities or technical assistance shall be compensated therefor by the applicant for reasonable expenses incurred in providing such facilities or assistance. Pursuant to section 2522 of this chapter, an order may also be issued to enforce the assistance capability and capacity requirements under the Communications Assistance for Law Enforcement Act.

(5) No order entered under this section may authorize or approve the interception of any wire, oral, or electronic communication for any period longer than is necessary to achieve the objective of the authorization, nor in any event longer than thirty days. Such thirty-day period begins on the earlier of the day on which the investigative or law

enforcement officer first begins to conduct an interception under the order or ten days after the order is entered. Extensions of an order may be granted, but only upon application for an extension made in accordance with subsection (1) of this section and the court making the findings required by subsection (3) of this section. The period of extension shall be no longer than the authorizing judge deems necessary to achieve the purposes for which it was granted and in no event for longer than thirty days. Every order and extension thereof shall contain a provision that the authorization to intercept shall be executed as soon as practicable, shall be conducted in such a way as to minimize the interception of communications not otherwise subject to interception under this chapter, and must terminate upon attainment of the authorized objective, or in any event in thirty days. In the event the intercepted communication is in a code or foreign language, and an expert in that foreign language or code is not reasonably available during the interception period, minimization may be accomplished as soon as practicable after such interception. An interception under this chapter may be conducted in whole or in part by Government personnel, or by an individual operating under a contract with the Government, acting under the supervision of an investigative or law enforcement officer authorized to conduct the interception.

(6) Whenever an order authorizing interception is entered pursuant to this chapter, the order may require reports to be made to the judge who issued the order showing what progress has been made toward achievement of the authorized objective and the need for continued interception. Such reports shall be made at such intervals as the judge may require.

(7) Notwithstanding any other provision of this chapter, any investigative or law enforcement officer, specially designated by the Attorney General, the Deputy Attorney General, the Associate Attorney General, or by the principal prosecuting attorney of any State or subdivision thereof acting pursuant to a statute of that State, who reasonably determines that -

(a) an emergency situation exists that involves -

(i) immediate danger of death or serious physical injury to any person,

(ii) conspiratorial activities threatening the national security interest, or

(iii) conspiratorial activities characteristic of organized crime, that requires a wire, oral, or electronic communication to be intercepted before an order authorizing such interception can, with due diligence, be obtained, and

(b) there are grounds upon which an order could be entered under this chapter to authorize such interception, may intercept such wire, oral, or electronic communication if an application for an order approving the interception is made in accordance with this section within forty-eight hours after the interception has occurred, or begins to occur. In the absence of an order, such interception shall immediately terminate when the communication sought is obtained or when the application for the order is denied, whichever is earlier. In the event such application for approval is denied, or in any other case where the interception is terminated without an order having been issued, the contents of any wire, oral, or electronic communication intercepted shall be treated as having been obtained in violation of this chapter, and an inventory shall be served as provided for in subsection (d) of this section on the person named in the application.

(8)

(a) The contents of any wire, oral, or electronic communication intercepted by any means authorized by this chapter shall, if possible, be recorded on tape or wire or other comparable device. The recording of the contents of any wire, oral, or electronic communication under this subsection shall be done in such a way as will protect the recording from editing or other alterations. Immediately upon the expiration of the period of the order, or extensions thereof, such recordings shall be made available to the judge issuing such order and sealed under his directions. Custody of the recordings shall be wherever the judge orders. They shall not be destroyed except upon an order of the issuing or denying judge and in any event shall be kept for ten years. Duplicate recordings may be made for use or disclosure pursuant to the provisions of subsections (1) and (2) of section 2517 of this chapter for investigations. The presence of the seal provided for by this subsection, or a satisfactory explanation for the absence thereof, shall be a prerequisite for the use or disclosure of the contents of any wire, oral, or electronic communication or evidence derived therefrom under subsection (3) of section 2517.

(b) Applications made and orders granted under this chapter shall be sealed by the judge. Custody of the applications and orders shall be wherever the judge directs. Such applications and orders shall be disclosed only upon a showing of good cause before a judge of competent jurisdiction and shall not be destroyed except on order of the issuing or denying judge, and in any event shall be kept for ten years.

(c) Any violation of the provisions of this subsection may be punished as contempt of the issuing or denying judge.

(d) Within a reasonable time but not later than ninety days after the filing of an application for an order of approval under section 2518(7)(b) which is denied or the termination of the period of an order or extensions thereof, the issuing or denying judge shall cause to be served, on the persons named in the order or the application, and such other parties to intercepted communications as the judge may determine in his discretion that is in the interest of justice, an inventory which shall include notice of -

(1) the fact of the entry of the order or the application;

(2) the date of the entry and the period of authorized, approved or disapproved interception, or the denial of the application; and

(3) the fact that during the period wire, oral, or electronic communications were or were not intercepted.

The judge, upon the filing of a motion, may in his discretion make available to such person or his counsel for inspection such portions of the intercepted communications, applications and orders as the judge determines to be in the interest of justice. On an ex parte showing of good cause to a judge of competent jurisdiction the serving of the inventory required by this subsection may be postponed.

(9) The contents of any wire, oral, or electronic communication intercepted pursuant to this chapter or evidence derived therefrom shall not be received in evidence or otherwise disclosed in any trial, hearing, or other proceeding in a Federal or State court unless each party, not less than ten days before the trial, hearing, or proceeding, has been furnished with a copy of the court order, and accompanying application, under which the interception was authorized or approved. This ten-day period may be waived by the judge if he finds that it was not possible to furnish the party with the above information ten days before the trial, hearing, or proceeding and that the party will not be prejudiced by the delay in receiving such information.

(10)

(a) Any aggrieved person in any trial, hearing, or proceeding in or before any court, department, officer, agency, regulatory body, or other authority of the United States, a State, or a political subdivision thereof, may move to suppress the contents of any wire or oral communication intercepted pursuant to this chapter, or evidence derived therefrom, on the grounds that -

(i) the communication was unlawfully intercepted;

(ii) the order of authorization or approval under which it was intercepted is insufficient on its face; or

(iii) the interception was not made in conformity with the order of authorization or approval.

Such motion shall be made before the trial, hearing, or proceeding unless there was no opportunity to make such motion or the person was not aware of the grounds of the motion. If the motion is granted, the contents of the intercepted wire or oral communication, or evidence derived therefrom, shall be treated as having been obtained in violation of this chapter. The judge, upon the filing of such motion by the aggrieved person, may in his discretion make available to the aggrieved person or his counsel for inspection such portions of the intercepted communication or evidence derived therefrom as the judge determines to be in the interests of justice.

(b) In addition to any other right to appeal, the United States shall have the right to appeal from an order granting a motion to suppress made under paragraph (a) of this subsection, or the denial of an application for an order of approval, if the United States attorney shall certify to the judge or other official granting such motion or denying such application that the appeal is not taken for purposes of delay. Such appeal shall be taken within thirty days after the date the order was entered and shall be diligently prosecuted.

(c) The remedies and sanctions described in this chapter with respect to the interception of electronic communications are the only judicial remedies and sanctions for nonconstitutional violations of this chapter involving such communications.

(11) The requirements of subsections (1)(b)(ii) and (3)(d) of this section relating to the specification of the facilities from which, or the place where, the communication is to be intercepted do not apply if -

(a) in the case of an application with respect to the interception of an oral communication -

(i) the application is by a Federal investigative or law enforcement officer and is approved by the Attorney General, the Deputy Attorney General, the Associate Attorney General, an Assistant Attorney General, or an acting Assistant Attorney General;

(ii) the application contains a full and complete statement as to why such specification is not practical and identifies the person committing the offense and whose communications are to be intercepted; and

(iii) the judge finds that such specification is not practical; and

(b) in the case of an application with respect to a wire or electronic communication -

(i) the application is by a Federal investigative or law enforcement officer and is approved by the Attorney General, the Deputy Attorney General, the Associate Attorney General, an Assistant Attorney General, or an acting Assistant Attorney General;

(ii) the application identifies the person believed to be committing the offense and whose communications are to be intercepted and the applicant makes a showing of a purpose, on the part of that person, to thwart interception by changing facilities;

(iii) the judge finds that such purpose has been adequately shown; and

(iv) the order authorizing or approving the interception is limited to interception only for such time as it is reasonable to presume that the person identified in the application is or was reasonably proximate to the instrument through which such communication will be or was transmitted.

(12) An interception of a communication under an order with respect to which the requirements of subsections (1)(b)(ii) and (3)(d) of this section do not apply by reason of subsection (11) shall not begin until the facilities from which, or the place where, the communication is to be intercepted is ascertained by the person implementing the interception order. A provider of wire or electronic communications service that has received an order as provided for in subsection (11)(b) may move the court to modify or quash the order on the ground that its assistance with respect to the interception cannot be performed in a timely or reasonable fashion. The court, upon notice to the government, shall decide such a motion expeditiously.

Sec. 2519. Reports concerning intercepted wire, oral, or electronic communications

(1) Within thirty days after the expiration of an order (or each extension thereof) entered under section 2518, or the denial of an order approving an interception, the issuing or denying judge shall report to the Administrative Office of the United States Courts -

(a) the fact that an order or extension was applied for;

(b) the kind of order or extension applied for (including whether or not the order was an order with respect to which the requirements of sections 2518(1)(b)(ii) and 2518(3)(d) of this title did not apply by reason of section 2518(11) of this title);

(c) the fact that the order or extension was granted as applied for, was modified, or was denied;

(d) the period of interceptions authorized by the order, and the number and duration of any extensions of the order;

(e) the offense specified in the order or application, or extension of an order;

(f) the identity of the applying investigative or law enforcement officer and agency making the application and the person authorizing the application; and

(g) the nature of the facilities from which or the place where communications were to be intercepted.

(2) In January of each year the Attorney General, an Assistant Attorney General specially designated by the Attorney General, or the principal prosecuting attorney of a State, or the principal prosecuting attorney for any political subdivision of a State, shall report to the Administrative Office of the United States Courts -

(a) the information required by paragraphs (a) through (g) of subsection (1) of this section with respect to each application for an order or extension made during the preceding calendar year;

(b) a general description of the interceptions made under such order or extension, including

(i) the approximate nature and frequency of incriminating communications intercepted,

(ii) the approximate nature and frequency of other communications intercepted,

(iii) the approximate number of persons whose communications were intercepted, and

(iv) the approximate nature, amount, and cost of the manpower and other resources used in the interceptions;

(c) the number of arrests resulting from interceptions made under such order or extension, and the offenses for which arrests were made;

(d) the number of trials resulting from such interceptions;

(e) the number of motions to suppress made with respect to such interceptions, and the number granted or denied;

(f) the number of convictions resulting from such interceptions and the offenses for which the convictions were obtained and a general assessment of the importance of the interceptions; and

(g) the information required by paragraphs (b) through (f) of this subsection with respect to orders or extensions obtained in a preceding calendar year.

(3) In April of each year the Director of the Administrative Office of the United States Courts shall transmit to the Congress a full and complete report concerning the number of applications for orders authorizing or approving the interception of wire, oral, or electronic communications pursuant to this chapter and the number of orders and extensions granted or denied pursuant to this chapter during the preceding calendar year. Such report shall include a summary and analysis of the data required to be filed with the Administrative Office by subsections (1) and (2) of this section. The Director of the Administrative Office of the United States Courts is authorized to issue binding regulations dealing with the content and form of the reports required to be filed by subsections (1) and (2) of this section.

Sec. 2520. Recovery of civil damages authorized

(a) In General. - Except as provided in section 2511(2)(a)(ii), any person whose wire, oral, or electronic communication is intercepted, disclosed, or intentionally used in violation of this chapter may in a civil action recover from the person or entity which engaged in that violation such relief as may be appropriate.

(b) Relief. - In an action under this section, appropriate relief includes -

(1) such preliminary and other equitable or declaratory relief as may be appropriate;

(2) damages under subsection (c) and punitive damages in appropriate cases; and

(3) a reasonable attorney's fee and other litigation costs reasonably incurred.

(c) Computation of Damages. -

(1) In an action under this section, if the conduct in violation of this chapter is the private viewing of a private satellite video communication that is not scrambled or encrypted or if the communication is a radio communication that is transmitted on frequencies allocated under subpart D of part 74 of the rules of the Federal Communications Commission that is not scrambled or encrypted and the conduct is not for a tortious or illegal purpose or for purposes of direct or indirect commercial advantage or private commercial gain, then the court shall assess damages as follows:

(A) If the person who engaged in that conduct has not previously been enjoined under section 2511(5) and has not been found liable in a prior civil action under this section, the court shall assess the greater of the sum of actual damages suffered by the plaintiff, or statutory damages of not less than $50 and not more than $500.

(B) If, on one prior occasion, the person who engaged in that conduct has been enjoined under section 2511(5) or has been found liable in a civil action under this section, the court shall assess the greater of the sum of actual damages suffered by the plaintiff, or statutory damages of not less than $100 and not more than $1000.

(2) In any other action under this section, the court may assess as damages whichever is the greater of -

(A) the sum of the actual damages suffered by the plaintiff and any profits made by the violator as a result of the violation; or

(B) statutory damages of whichever is the greater of $100 a day for each day of violation or $10,000.

(d) Defense. - A good faith reliance on -

(1) a court warrant or order, a grand jury subpoena, a legislative authorization, or a statutory authorization;

(2) a request of an investigative or law enforcement officer under section 2518(7) of this title; or

(3) a good faith determination that section 2511(3) of this title permitted the conduct complained of;

is a complete defense against any civil or criminal action brought under this chapter or any other law.

(e) Limitation. - A civil action under this section may not be commenced later than two years after the date upon which the claimant first has a reasonable opportunity to discover the violation.

Sec. 2521. Injunction against illegal interception

Whenever it shall appear that any person is engaged or is about to engage in any act which constitutes or will constitute a felony violation of this chapter, the Attorney General may initiate a civil action in a district court of the United States to enjoin such violation. The court shall proceed as soon as practicable to the hearing and determination of such an action, and may, at any time before final determination, enter such a restraining order or prohibition, or take such other action, as is warranted to prevent a continuing and substantial injury to the United States or to any person or class of persons for whose protection the action is brought. A proceeding under this section is governed by the Federal Rules of Civil Procedure, except that, if an indictment has been returned against the respondent, discovery is governed by the Federal Rules of Criminal Procedure.

Sec. 2522. Enforcement of the Communications Assistance for Law Enforcement Act

(a) Enforcement by Court Issuing Surveillance Order. - If a court authorizing an interception under this chapter, a State statute, or the Foreign Intelligence Surveillance

United States
Electronic Communications Privacy Act

Act of 1978 (50 U.S.C. 1801 et seq.) or authorizing use of a pen register or a trap and trace device under chapter 206 or a State statute finds that a telecommunications carrier has failed to comply with the requirements of the Communications Assistance for Law Enforcement Act, the court may, in accordance with section 108 of such Act, direct that the carrier comply forthwith and may direct that a provider of support services to the carrier or the manufacturer of the carrier's transmission or switching equipment furnish forthwith modifications necessary for the carrier to comply.

(b) Enforcement Upon Application by Attorney General. - The Attorney General may, in a civil action in the appropriate United States district court, obtain an order, in accordance with section 108 of the Communications Assistance for Law Enforcement Act, directing that a telecommunications carrier, a manufacturer of telecommunications transmission or switching equipment, or a provider of telecommunications support services comply with such Act.

(c) Civil Penalty. -

(1) In general. - A court issuing an order under this section against a telecommunications carrier, a manufacturer of telecommunications transmission or switching equipment, or a provider of telecommunications support services may impose a civil penalty of up to $10,000 per day for each day in violation after the issuance of the order or after such future date as the court may specify.

(2) Considerations. - In determining whether to impose a civil penalty and in determining its amount, the court shall take into account -

(A) the nature, circumstances, and extent of the violation;

(B) the violator's ability to pay, the violator's good faith efforts to comply in a timely manner, any effect on the violator's ability to continue to do business, the degree of culpability, and the length of any delay in undertaking efforts to comply; and

(C) such other matters as justice may require.

(d) Definitions. - As used in this section, the terms defined in section 102 of the Communications Assistance for Law Enforcement Act have the meanings provided, respectively, in such section.

Sec. 2701. Unlawful access to stored communications

(a) Offense. - Except as provided in subsection (c) of this section whoever -

(1) intentionally accesses without authorization a facility through which an electronic communication service is provided; or

(2) intentionally exceeds an authorization to access that facility; and thereby obtains, alters, or prevents authorized access to a wire or electronic communication while it is in electronic storage in such system shall be punished as provided in subsection (b) of this section.

(b) Punishment. - The punishment for an offense under subsection (a) of this section is -

    (1) if the offense is committed for purposes of commercial advantage, malicious destruction or damage, or private commercial gain -

        (A) a fine of under this title or imprisonment for not more than one year, or both, in the case of a first offense under this subparagraph; and

        (B) a fine under this title or imprisonment for not more than two years, or both, for any subsequent offense under this subparagraph; and

    (2) a fine of under this title or imprisonment for not more than six months, or both, in any other case.

(c) Exceptions. - Subsection (a) of this section does not apply with respect to conduct authorized

    (1) by the person or entity providing a wire or electronic communications service;

    (2) by a user of that service with respect to a communication of or intended for that user; or

    (3) in section 2703, 2704 or 2518 of this title.

Sec. 2702. Disclosure of contents

(a) Prohibitions. - Except as provided in subsection (b) -

    (1) a person or entity providing an electronic communication service to the public shall not knowingly divulge to any person or entity the contents of a communication while in electronic storage by that service; and

    (2) a person or entity providing remote computing service to the public shall not knowingly divulge to any person or entity the contents of any communication which is carried or maintained on that service -

        (A) on behalf of, and received by means of electronic transmission from (or created by means of computer processing of communications received by means of electronic transmission from), a subscriber or customer of such service; and

        (B) solely for the purpose of providing storage or computer processing services to such subscriber or customer, if the provider is not authorized to access the contents of any such communications for purposes of providing any services other than storage or computer processing.

(b) Exceptions. - A person or entity may divulge the contents of a communication -

    (1) to an addressee or intended recipient of such communication or an agent of such addressee or intended recipient;

    (2) as otherwise authorized in section 2517, 2511(2)(a), or 2703 of this title;

    (3) with the lawful consent of the originator or an addressee or intended recipient of such communication, or the subscriber in the case of remote computing service;

    (4) to a person employed or authorized or whose facilities are used to forward such communication to its destination;

United States
Electronic Communications Privacy Act

(5) as may be necessarily incident to the rendition of the service or to the protection of the rights or property of the provider of that service; or

(6) to a law enforcement agency, if such contents -

(A) were inadvertently obtained by the service provider; and

(B) appear to pertain to the commission of a crime.

6) to a law enforcement agency -

(A) if the contents -

(i) were inadvertently obtained by the service provider; and

(ii) appear to pertain to the commission of a crime; or

(B) if required by section 227 of the Crime Control Act of 1990.

Sec. 2703. Requirements for governmental access

(a) Contents of Electronic Communications in Electronic Storage.

A governmental entity may require the disclosure by a provider of electronic communication service of the contents of an electronic communication, that is in electronic storage in an electronic communications system for one hundred and eighty days or less, only pursuant to a warrant issued under the Federal Rules of Criminal Procedure or equivalent State warrant. A governmental entity may require the disclosure by a provider of electronic communications services of the contents of an electronic communication that has been in electronic storage in an electronic communications system for more than one hundred and eighty days by the means available under subsection (b) of this section.

(b) Contents of Electronic Communications in a Remote Computing Service.

(1) A governmental entity may require a provider of remote computing service to disclose the contents of any electronic communication to which this paragraph is made applicable by paragraph (2) of this subsection -

(A) without required notice to the subscriber or customer, if the governmental entity obtains a warrant issued under the Federal Rules of Criminal Procedure or equivalent State warrant; or

(B) with prior notice from the governmental entity to the subscriber or customer if the governmental entity -

(i) uses an administrative subpoena authorized by a Federal or State statute or a Federal or State grand jury or trial subpoena; or

(ii) obtains a court order for such disclosure under subsection (d) of this section; except that delayed notice may be given pursuant to section 2705 of this title.

(2) Paragraph (1) is applicable with respect to any electronic communication that is held or maintained on that service -

(A) on behalf of, and received by means of electronic transmission from (or created by means of computer processing of communications received by means of electronic transmission from), a subscriber or customer of such remote computing service; and

(B) solely for the purpose of providing storage or computer processing services to such subscriber or customer, if the provider is not authorized to access the contents of any such communications for purposes of providing any services other than storage or computer processing.

(c) Records Concerning Electronic Communication Service or Remote Computing Service. -

(1)(A) Except as provided in subparagraph (B), a provider of electronic communication service or remote computing service may disclose a record or other information pertaining to a subscriber to or customer of such service (not including the contents of communications covered by subsection (a) or (b) of this section) to any person other than a governmental entity.

(B) A provider of electronic communication service or remote computing service shall disclose a record or other information pertaining to a subscriber to or customer of such service (not including the contents of communications covered by subsection (a) or (b) of this section) to a governmental entity only when the governmental entity -

(i) obtains a warrant issued under the Federal Rules of Criminal Procedure or equivalent State warrant;

(ii) obtains a court order for such disclosure under subsection

(d) of this section;

(iii) has the consent of the subscriber or customer to such disclosure; or

(iv) submits a formal written request relevant to a law enforcement investigation concerning telemarketing fraud for the name, address, and place of business of a subscriber or customer of such provider, which subscriber or customer is engaged in telemarketing (as such term is defined in section 2325 of this title).

(C) A provider of electronic communication service or remote computing service shall disclose to a governmental entity the name, address, telephone toll billing records, telephone number or other subscriber number or identity, and length of service of a subscriber to or customer of such service and the types of services the subscriber or customer utilized, when the governmental entity uses an administrative subpoena authorized by a Federal or State statute or a Federal or State grand jury or trial subpoena or any means available under subparagraph (B).

(2) A governmental entity receiving records or information under this subsection is not required to provide notice to a subscriber or customer.

(d) Requirements for Court Order.

A court order for disclosure under subsection (b) or (c) may be issued by any court that is a court of competent jurisdiction described in section 3126(2)(A) and shall issue only if the governmental entity offers specific and articulable facts showing that there are reasonable grounds to believe that the contents of a wire or electronic communication, or the records or other information sought, are relevant and material to an ongoing criminal investigation. In the case of a State governmental authority, such a court order shall not issue if prohibited by the law of such State. A court issuing an order pursuant to this section, on a motion made promptly by the service provider, may quash or modify such order, if the information or records requested are unusually voluminous in nature or compliance with such order otherwise would cause an undue burden on such provider.

(e) No Cause of Action Against a Provider Disclosing Information Under This Chapter. -

No cause of action shall lie in any court against any provider of wire or electronic communication service, its officers, employees, agents, or other specified persons for providing information, facilities, or assistance in accordance with the terms of a court order, warrant, subpoena, or certification under this chapter.

(f) Requirement To Preserve Evidence. -

(1) In general. - A provider of wire or electronic communication services or a remote computing service, upon the request of a governmental entity, shall take all necessary steps to preserve records and other evidence in its possession pending the issuance of a court order or other process.

(2) Period of retention. - Records referred to in paragraph (1) shall be retained for a period of 90 days, which shall be extended for an additional 90-day period upon a renewed request by the governmental entity.

Sec. 2704. Backup preservation

(a) Backup Preservation. -

(1) A governmental entity acting under section 2703(b)(2) may include in its subpoena or court order a requirement that the service provider to whom the request is directed create a backup copy of the contents of the electronic communications sought in order to preserve those communications. Without notifying the subscriber or customer of such subpoena or court order, such service provider shall create such backup copy as soon as practicable consistent with its regular business practices and shall confirm to the governmental entity that such backup copy has been made. Such backup copy shall be created within two business days after receipt by the service provider of the subpoena or court order.

(2) Notice to the subscriber or customer shall be made by the governmental entity within three days after receipt of such confirmation, unless such notice is delayed pursuant to section 2705(a).

(3) The service provider shall not destroy such backup copy until the later of -

(A) the delivery of the information; or

(B) the resolution of any proceedings (including appeals of any proceeding) concerning the government's subpoena or court order.

(4) The service provider shall release such backup copy to the requesting governmental entity no sooner than fourteen days after the governmental entity's notice to the subscriber or customer if such service provider -

(A) has not received notice from the subscriber or customer that the subscriber or customer has challenged the governmental entity's request; and

(B) has not initiated proceedings to challenge the request of the governmental entity.

(5) A governmental entity may seek to require the creation of a backup copy under subsection (a)(1) of this section if in its sole discretion such entity determines that there is reason to believe that notification under section 2703 of this title of the existence of the subpoena or court order may result in destruction of or tampering with evidence. This determination is not subject to challenge by the subscriber or customer or service provider.

(b) Customer Challenges. -

(1) Within fourteen days after notice by the governmental entity to the subscriber or customer under subsection (a)(2) of this section, such subscriber or customer may file a motion to quash such subpoena or vacate such court order, with copies served upon the governmental entity and with written notice of such challenge to the service provider. A motion to vacate a court order shall be filed in the court which issued such order. A motion to quash a subpoena shall be filed in the appropriate United States district court or State court. Such motion or application shall contain an affidavit or sworn statement-

(A) stating that the applicant is a customer or subscriber to the service from which the contents of electronic communications maintained for him have been sought; and

(B) stating the applicant's reasons for believing that the records sought are not relevant to a legitimate law enforcement inquiry or that there has not been substantial compliance with the provisions of this chapter in some other respect.

(2) Service shall be made under this section upon a governmental entity by delivering or mailing by registered or certified mail a copy of the papers to the person, office, or department specified in the notice which the customer has received pursuant to this chapter. For the purposes of this section, the term "delivery" has the meaning given that term in the Federal Rules of Civil Procedure.

(3) If the court finds that the customer has complied with paragraphs (1) and (2) of this subsection, the court shall order the governmental entity to file a sworn response, which may be filed in camera if the governmental entity includes in its response the reasons which make in camera review appropriate. If the court is unable to determine the motion or application on the basis of the parties' initial

allegations and response, the court may conduct such additional proceedings as it deems appropriate. All such proceedings shall be completed and the motion or application decided as soon as practicable after the filing of the governmental entity's response.

(4) If the court finds that the applicant is not the subscriber or customer for whom the communications sought by the governmental entity are maintained, or that there is a reason to believe that the law enforcement inquiry is legitimate and that the communications sought are relevant to that inquiry, it shall deny the motion or application and order such process enforced. If the court finds that the applicant is the subscriber or customer for whom the communications sought by the governmental entity are maintained, and that there is not a reason to believe that the communications sought are relevant to a legitimate law enforcement inquiry, or that there has not been substantial compliance with the provisions of this chapter, it shall order the process quashed.

(5) A court order denying a motion or application under this section shall not be deemed a final order and no interlocutory appeal may be taken therefrom by the customer.

Sec. 2705. Delayed notice

(a) Delay of Notification. -

(1) A governmental entity acting under section 2703(b) of this title may -

(A) where a court order is sought, include in the application a request, which the court shall grant, for an order delaying the notification required under section 2703(b) of this title for a period not to exceed ninety days, if the court determines that there is reason to believe that notification of the existence of the court order may have an adverse result described in paragraph (2) of this subsection; or

(B) where an administrative subpoena authorized by a Federal or State statute or a Federal or State grand jury subpoena is obtained, delay the notification required under section 2703(b) of this title for a period not to exceed ninety days upon the execution of a written certification of a supervisory official that there is reason to believe that notification of the existence of the subpoena may have an adverse result described in paragraph (2) of this subsection.

(2) An adverse result for the purposes of paragraph (1) of this subsection is -

(A) endangering the life or physical safety of an individual;

(B) flight from prosecution;

(C) destruction of or tampering with evidence;

(D) intimidation of potential witnesses; or

(E) otherwise seriously jeopardizing an investigation or unduly delaying a trial.

(3) The governmental entity shall maintain a true copy of certification under paragraph (1)(B).

(4) Extensions of the delay of notification provided in section 2703 of up to ninety days each may be granted by the court upon application, or by certification by a governmental entity, but only in accordance with subsection (b) of this section.

(5) Upon expiration of the period of delay of notification under paragraph (1) or (4) of this subsection, the governmental entity shall serve upon, or deliver by registered or first-class mail to, the customer or subscriber a copy of the process or request together with notice that -

(A) states with reasonable specificity the nature of the law enforcement inquiry; and

(B) informs such customer or subscriber -

(i) that information maintained for such customer or subscriber by the service provider named in such process or request was supplied to or requested by that governmental authority and the date on which the supplying or request took place;

(ii) that notification of such customer or subscriber was delayed;

(iii) what governmental entity or court made the certification or determination pursuant to which that delay was made; and

(iv) which provision of this chapter allowed such delay.

(6) As used in this subsection, the term "supervisory official" means the investigative agent in charge or assistant investigative agent in charge or an equivalent of an investigating agency's headquarters or regional office, or the chief prosecuting attorney or the first assistant prosecuting attorney or an equivalent of a prosecuting attorney's headquarters or regional office.

(b) Preclusion of Notice to Subject of Governmental Access. -

A governmental entity acting under section 2703, when it is not required to notify the subscriber or customer under section 2703(b)(1), or to the extent that it may delay such notice pursuant to subsection (a) of this section, may apply to a court for an order commanding a provider of electronic communications service or remote computing service to whom a warrant, subpoena, or court order is directed, for such period as the court deems appropriate, not to notify any other person of the existence of the warrant, subpoena, or court order. The court shall enter such an order if it determines that there is reason to believe that notification of the existence of the warrant, subpoena, or court order will result in -

(1) endangering the life or physical safety of an individual;

(2) flight from prosecution;

(3) destruction of or tampering with evidence;

(4) intimidation of potential witnesses; or

(5) otherwise seriously jeopardizing an investigation or unduly delaying a trial.

United States
Electronic Communications Privacy Act

Sec. 2706. Cost reimbursement

(a) Payment. -

Except as otherwise provided in subsection (c), a governmental entity obtaining the contents of communications, records, or other information under section 2702, 2703, or 2704 of this title shall pay to the person or entity assembling or providing such information a fee for reimbursement for such costs as are reasonably necessary and which have been directly incurred in searching for, assembling, reproducing, or otherwise providing such information. Such reimbursable costs shall include any costs due to necessary disruption of normal operations of any electronic communication service or remote computing service in which such information may be stored.

(b) Amount. -

The amount of the fee provided by subsection (a) shall be as mutually agreed by the governmental entity and the person or entity providing the information, or, in the absence of agreement, shall be as determined by the court which issued the order for production of such information (or the court before which a criminal prosecution relating to such information would be brought, if no court order was issued for production of the information).

(c) Exception. -

The requirement of subsection (a) of this section does not apply with respect to records or other information maintained by a communications common carrier that relate to telephone toll records and telephone listings obtained under section 2703 of this title. The court may, however, order a payment as described in subsection (a) if the court determines the information required is unusually voluminous in nature or otherwise caused an undue burden on the provider.

Sec. 2707. Civil action

(a) Cause of Action. -

Except as provided in section 2703(e), any provider of electronic communication service, subscriber, or customer aggrieved by any violation of this chapter in which the conduct constituting the violation is engaged in with a knowing or intentional state of mind may, in a civil action, recover from the person or entity which engaged in that violation such relief as may be appropriate.

(b) Relief. - In a civil action under this section, appropriate relief includes -

(1) such preliminary and other equitable or declaratory relief as may be appropriate;

(2) damages under subsection (c); and

(3) a reasonable attorney's fee and other litigation costs reasonably incurred.

(c) Damages. -

The court may assess as damages in a civil action under this section the sum of the actual damages suffered by the plaintiff and any profits made by the violator as a result of the violation, but in no case shall a person entitled to recover receive less than the sum of $1,000.

(d) Disciplinary Actions for Violations. - If a court determines that any agency or department of the United States has violated this chapter and the court finds that the circumstances surrounding the violation raise the question whether or not an officer or employee of the agency or department acte willfully or intentionally with respect to the violation, the agency or department concerned shall promptly initiate a proceeding to determine whether or not disciplinary action is warranted against the officer or employee.

(e) Defense. - A good faith reliance on -

(1) a court warrant or order, a grand jury subpoena, a legislative authorization, or a statutory authorization;

(2) a request of an investigative or law enforcement officer under section 2518(7) of this title; or

(3) a good faith determination that section 2511(3) of this title permitted the conduct complained of; is a complete defense to any civil or criminal action brought under this chapter or any other law.

(f) Limitation. - A civil action under this section may not be commenced later than two years after the date upon which the claimant first discovered or had a reasonable opportunity to discover the violation.

Sec. 2708. Exclusivity of remedies

The remedies and sanctions described in this chapter are the only judicial remedies and sanctions for nonconstitutional violations of this chapter.

Sec. 2709. Counterintelligence access to telephone toll and transactional records

(a) Duty to Provide. -

A wire or electronic communication service provider shall comply with a request for subscriber information and toll billing records information, or electronic communication transactional records in its custody or possession made by the Director of the Federal Bureau of Investigation under subsection (b) of this section.

(b) Required Certification. -

The Director of the Federal Bureau of Investigation, or his designee in a position not lower than Deputy Assistant Director, may -

(1) request the name, address, length of service, and toll billing records of a person or entity if the Director (or his designee in a position not lower than Deputy Assistant Director) certifies in writing to the wire or electronic communication service provider to which the request is made that -

(A) the name, address, length of service, and toll billing records sought are relevant to an authorized foreign counterintelligence investigation; and

(B) there are specific and articulable facts giving reason to believe that the person or entity to whom the information sought pertains is a foreign power or an agent of a foreign power as defined in section 101 of the Foreign Intelligence Surveillance Act of 1978 (50 U.S.C. 1801); and

(2) request the name, address, and length of service of a person or entity if the Director (or his designee in a position not lower than Deputy Assistant Director) certifies in writing to the wire or electronic communication service provider to which the request is made that -

(A) the information sought is relevant to an authorized foreign counterintelligence investigation; and

(B) there are specific and articulable facts giving reason to believe that communication facilities registered in the name of the person or entity have been used, through the services of such provider, in communication with -

(i) an individual who is engaging or has engaged in international terrorism as defined in section 101(c) of the Foreign Intelligence Surveillance Act or clandestine intelligence activities that involve or may involve a violation of the criminal statutes of the United States; or

(ii) a foreign power or an agent of a foreign power under circumstances giving reason to believe that the communication concerned international terrorism as defined in section 101(c) of the Foreign Intelligence Surveillance Act or clandestine intelligence activities that involve or may involve a violation of the criminal statutes of the United States.

(c) Prohibition of Certain Disclosure. -

No wire or electronic communication service provider, or officer, employee, or agent thereof, shall disclose to any person that the Federal Bureau of Investigation has sought or obtained access to information or records under this section.

(d) Dissemination by Bureau. -

The Federal Bureau of Investigation may disseminate information and records obtained under this section only as provided in guidelines approved by the Attorney General for foreign intelligence collection and foreign counterintelligence investigations conducted by the Federal Bureau of Investigation, and, with respect to dissemination to an agency of the United States, only if such information is clearly relevant to the authorized responsibilities of such agency.

(e) Requirement That Certain Congressional Bodies Be Informed. -

On a semiannual basis the Director of the Federal Bureau of Investigation shall fully inform the Permanent Select Committee on Intelligence of the House of Representatives and the Select Committee on Intelligence of the Senate, and the Committee on the Judiciary of the House of Representatives and the Committee on the

Judiciary of the Senate, concerning all requests made under subsection (b) of this section.

Sec. 2711. Definitions for chapter

As used in this chapter -

(1) the terms defined in section 2510 of this title have, respectively, the definitions given such terms in that section; and

(2) the term "remote computing service" means the provision to the public of computer storage or processing services by means of an electronic communications system.

Sec. 3121. General prohibition on pen register and trap and trace device use; exception

(a) In General. - Except as provided in this section, no person may install or use a pen register or a trap and trace device without first obtaining a court order under section 3123 of this title or under the Foreign Intelligence Surveillance Act of 1978 (50 U.S.C. 1801 et seq.).

(b) Exception. - The prohibition of subsection (a) does not apply with respect to the use of a pen register or a trap and trace device by a provider of electronic or wire communication service -

(1) relating to the operation, maintenance, and testing of a wire or electronic communication service or to the protection of the rights or property of such provider, or to the protection of users of that service from abuse of service or unlawful use of service; or

(2) to record the fact that a wire or electronic communication was initiated or completed in order to protect such provider, another provider furnishing service toward the completion of the wire communication, or a user of that service, from fraudulent, unlawful or abusive use of service; or (3) where the consent of the user of that service has been obtained.

(c) Limitation. - A government agency authorized to install and use a pen register under this chapter or under State law shall use technology reasonably available to it that restricts the recording or decoding of electronic or other impulses to the dialing and signaling information utilized in call processing.

(d) Penalty. - Whoever knowingly violates subsection (a) shall be fined under this title or imprisoned not more than one year, or both.

Sec. 3122. Application for an order for a pen register or a trap and trace device

(a) Application. -

(1) An attorney for the Government may make application for an order or an extension of an order under section 3123 of this title authorizing or approving the installation and use of a pen register or a trap and trace device under this chapter, in writing under oath or equivalent affirmation, to a court of competent jurisdiction.

(2) Unless prohibited by State law, a State investigative or law enforcement officer may make application for an order or an extension of an order under section 3123 of this title authorizing or approving the installation and use of a pen register or a trap and trace device under this chapter, in writing under oath or equivalent affirmation, to a court of competent jurisdiction of such State.

(b) Contents of Application. - An application under subsection (a) of this section shall include -

(1) the identity of the attorney for the Government or the State law enforcement or investigative officer making the application and the identity of the law enforcement agency conducting the investigation; and

(2) a certification by the applicant that the information likely to be obtained is relevant to an ongoing criminal investigation being conducted by that agency.

Sec. 3123. Issuance of an order for a pen register or a trap and trace device

(a) In General. - Upon an application made under section 3122 of this title, the court shall enter an ex parte order authorizing the installation and use of a pen register or a trap and trace device within the jurisdiction of the court if the court finds that the attorney for the Government or the State law enforcement or investigative officer has certified to the court that the information likely to be obtained by such installation and use is relevant to an ongoing criminal investigation.

(b) Contents of Order. - An order issued under this section -

(1) shall specify -

(A) the identity, if known, of the person to whom is leased or in whose name is listed the telephone line to which the pen register or trap and trace device is to be attached;

(B) the identity, if known, of the person who is the subject of the criminal investigation;

(C) the number and, if known, physical location of the telephone line to which the pen register or trap and trace device is to be attached and, in the case of a trap and trace device, the geographic limits of the trap and trace order; and

(D) a statement of the offense to which the information likely to be obtained by the pen register or trap and trace device relates; and

(2) shall direct, upon the request of the applicant, the furnishing of information, facilities, and technical assistance necessary to accomplish the installation of the pen register or trap and trace device under section 3124 of this title.

(c) Time Period and Extensions. –

(1) An order issued under this section shall authorize the installation and use of a pen register or a trap and trace device for a period not to exceed sixty days.

(2) Extensions of such an order may be granted, but only upon an application for an order under section 3122 of this title and upon the judicial finding required by subsection (a) of this section. The period of extension shall be for a period not to exceed sixty days.

(d) Nondisclosure of Existence of Pen Register or a Trap and Trace Device. - An order authorizing or approving the installation and use of a pen register or a trap and trace device shall direct that -

(1) the order be sealed until otherwise ordered by the court; and

(2) the person owning or leasing the line to which the pen register or a trap and trace device is attached, or who has been ordered by the court to provide assistance to the applicant, not disclose the existence of the pen register or trap and trace device or the existence of the investigation to the listed subscriber, or to any other person, unless or until otherwise ordered by the court.

Sec. 3124. Assistance in installation and use of a pen register or a trap and trace device

(a) Pen Registers. - Upon the request of an attorney for the Government or an officer of a law enforcement agency authorized to install and use a pen register under this chapter, a provider of wire or electronic communication service, landlord, custodian, or other person shall furnish such investigative or law enforcement officer forthwith all information, facilities, and technical assistance necessary to accomplish the installation of the pen register unobtrusively and with a minimum of interference with the services that the person so ordered by the court accords the party with respect to whom the installation and use is to take place, if such assistance is directed by a court order as provided in section 3123(b)(2) of this title.

(b) Trap and Trace Device. - Upon the request of an attorney for the Government or an officer of a law enforcement agency authorized to receive the results of a trap and trace device under this chapter, a provider of a wire or electronic communication service, landlord, custodian, or other person shall install such device forthwith on the appropriate line and shall furnish such investigative or law enforcement officer all additional information, facilities and technical assistance including installation and operation of the device unobtrusively and with a minimum of interference with the services that the person so ordered by the court accords the party with respect to whom the installation and use is to take place, if such installation and assistance is directed by a court order as provided in section 3123(b)(2) of this title. Unless otherwise ordered by the court, the results of the trap and trace device shall be furnished, pursuant to section 3123(b) or section 3125 of this title, to the officer of a law enforcement agency, designated in the court order, at reasonable intervals during regular business hours for the duration of the order.

(c) Compensation. - A provider of a wire or electronic communication service, landlord, custodian, or other person who furnishes facilities or technical assistance pursuant to this section shall be reasonably compensated for such reasonable expenses incurred in providing such facilities and assistance.

(d) No Cause of Action Against a Provider Disclosing Information Under This Chapter. - No cause of action shall lie in any court against any provider of a wire or electronic communication service, its officers, employees, agents, or other specified persons for providing information, facilities, or assistance in accordance with the terms of a court order under this chapter or request pursuant to section 3125 of this title.

(e) Defense. - A good faith reliance on a court order under this chapter, a request pursuant to section 3125 of this title, a legislative authorization, or a statutory authorization is a complete defense against any civil or criminal action brought under this chapter or any other law.

(f) Communications Assistance Enforcement Orders. - Pursuant to section 2522, an order may be issued to enforce the assistance capability and capacity requirements under the Communications Assistance for Law Enforcement Act.

Sec. 3125. Emergency pen register and trap and trace device installation

(a) Notwithstanding any other provision of this chapter, any investigative or law enforcement officer, specially designated by the Attorney General, the Deputy Attorney General, the Associate Attorney General, any Assistant Attorney General, any acting Assistant Attorney General, or any Deputy Assistant Attorney General, or by the principal prosecuting attorney of any State or subdivision thereof acting pursuant to a statute of that State, who reasonably determines that -

(1) an emergency situation exists that involves -

(A) immediate danger of death or serious bodily injury to any person; or

(B) conspiratorial activities characteristic of organized crime, that requires the installation and use of a pen register or a trap and trace device before an order authorizing such installation and use can, with due diligence, be obtained, and

(2) there are grounds upon which an order could be entered under this chapter to authorize such installation and use; may have installed and use a pen register or trap and trace device if, within forty-eight hours after the installation has occurred, or begins to occur, an order approving the installation or use is issued in accordance with section 3123 of this title.

(b) In the absence of an authorizing order, such use shall immediately terminate when the information sought is obtained, when the application for the order is denied or when forty-eight hours have lapsed since the installation of the pen register or trap and trace device, whichever is earlier.

(c) The knowing installation or use by any investigative or law enforcement officer of a pen register or trap and trace device pursuant to subsection (a) without application for the authorizing order within forty-eight hours of the installation shall constitute a violation of this chapter.

(d) A provider of a wire or electronic service, landlord, custodian, or other person who furnished facilities or technical assistance pursuant to this section shall be reasonably compensated for such reasonable expenses incurred in providing such facilities and assistance.

Sec. 3126. Reports concerning pen registers and trap and trace devices

The Attorney General shall annually report to Congress on the number of pen register orders and orders for trap and trace devices applied for by law enforcement agencies of the Department of Justice.

Sec. 3127. Definitions for chapter

As used in this chapter -

(1) the terms "wire communication", "electronic communication", and "electronic communication service" have the meanings set forth for such terms in section 2510 of this title;

(2) the term "court of competent jurisdiction" means -

(A) a district court of the United States (including a magistrate of such a court) or a United States Court of Appeals; or

(B) a court of general criminal jurisdiction of a State authorized by the law of that State to enter orders authorizing the use of a pen register or a trap and trace device;

(3) the term "pen register" means a device which records or decodes electronic or other impulses which identify the numbers dialed or otherwise transmitted on the telephone line to which such device is attached, but such term does not include any device used by a provider or customer of a wire or electronic communication service for billing, or recording as an incident to billing, for communications services provided by such provider or any device used by a provider or customer of a wire communication service for cost accounting or other like purposes in the ordinary course of its business;

(4) the term "trap and trace device" means a device which captures the incoming electronic or other impulses which identify the originating number of an instrument or device from which a wire or electronic communication was transmitted;

(5) the term "attorney for the Government" has the meaning given such term for the purposes of the Federal Rules of Criminal Procedure; and

(6) the term "State" means a State, the District of Columbia, Puerto Rico, and any other possession or territory of the United States.

United States
Electronic Communications Privacy Act

47 USC Sec. 1001. Definitions

For purposes of this subchapter -

(1) The terms defined in section 2510 of title 18 have, respectively, the meanings stated in that section.

(2) The term "call-identifying information" means dialing or signaling information that identifies the origin, direction, destination, or termination of each communication generated or received by a subscriber by means of any equipment, facility, or service of a telecommunications carrier.

(3) The term "Commission" means the Federal Communications Commission.

(4) The term "electronic messaging services" means software-based services that enable the sharing of data, images, sound, writing, or other information among computing devices controlled by the senders or recipients of the messages.

(5) The term "government" means the government of the United States and any agency or instrumentality thereof, the District of Columbia, any commonwealth, territory, or possession of the United States, and any State or political subdivision thereof authorized by law to conduct electronic surveillance.

(6) The term "information services" –

(A) means the offering of a capability for generating, acquiring, storing, transforming, processing, retrieving, utilizing, or making available information via telecommunications; and (B) includes -

(i) a service that permits a customer to retrieve stored information from, or file information for storage in, information storage facilities;

(ii) electronic publishing; and

(iii) electronic messaging services; but

(C) does not include any capability for a telecommunications carrier's internal management, control, or operation of its telecommunications network.

(7) The term "telecommunications support services" means a product, software, or service used by a telecommunications carrier for the internal signaling or switching functions of its telecommunications network.

(8) The term "telecommunications carrier" -

(A) means a person or entity engaged in the transmission or switching of wire or electronic communications as a common carrier for hire; and

(B) includes -

(i) a person or entity engaged in providing commercial mobile service (as defined in section 332(d) of this title); or

(ii) a person or entity engaged in providing wire or electronic communication switching or transmission service to the extent that the Commission finds that such service is a replacement for a substantial portion of the local telephone exchange service and that it is in the public interest to deem such a person or entity to be a telecommunications carrier for purposes of this subchapter; but

(C) does not include -

(i) persons or entities insofar as they are engaged in providing information services; and

(ii) any class or category of telecommunications carriers that the Commission exempts by rule after consultation with the Attorney General.

Sec. 1002. Assistance capability requirements

(a) Capability requirements

Except as provided in subsections (b), (c), and (d) of this section and sections 1007(a) and 1008(b) and (d) of this title, a telecommunications carrier shall ensure that its equipment, facilities, or services that provide a customer or subscriber with the ability to originate, terminate, or direct communications are capable of -

(1) expeditiously isolating and enabling the government, pursuant to a court order or other lawful authorization, to intercept, to the exclusion of any other communications, all wire and electronic communications carried by the carrier within a service area to or from equipment, facilities, or services of a subscriber of such carrier concurrently with their transmission to or from the subscriber's equipment, facility, or service, or at such later time as may be acceptable to the government;

(2) expeditiously isolating and enabling the government, pursuant to a court order or other lawful authorization, to access call-identifying information that is reasonably available to the carrier -

(A) before, during, or immediately after the transmission of a wire or electronic communication (or at such later time as may be acceptable to the government); and

(B) in a manner that allows it to be associated with the communication to which it pertains, except that, with regard to information acquired solely pursuant to the authority for pen registers and trap and trace devices (as defined in section 3127 of title 18), such call-identifying information shall not include any information that may disclose the physical location of the subscriber (except to the extent that the location may be determined from the telephone number);

(3) delivering intercepted communications and call-identifying information to the government, pursuant to a court order or other lawful authorization, in a format such that they may be transmitted by means of equipment, facilities, or services procured by the government to a location other than the premises of the carrier; and

(4) facilitating authorized communications interceptions and access to call-identifying information unobtrusively and with a minimum of interference with any subscriber's telecommunications service and in a manner that protects -

United States
Electronic Communications Privacy Act

(A) the privacy and security of communications and call-identifying information not authorized to be intercepted; and

(B) information regarding the government's interception of communications and access to call-identifying information.

(b) Limitations

(1) Design of features and systems configurations

This subchapter does not authorize any law enforcement agency or officer -

(A) to require any specific design of equipment, facilities, services, features, or system configurations to be adopted by any provider of a wire or electronic communication service, any manufacturer of telecommunications equipment, or any provider of telecommunications support services; or

(B) to prohibit the adoption of any equipment, facility, service, or feature by any provider of a wire or electronic communication service, any manufacturer of telecommunications equipment, or any provider of telecommunications support services.

(2) Information services; private networks and interconnection services and facilities The requirements of subsection (a) of this section do not apply to -

(A) information services; or

(B) equipment, facilities, or services that support the transport or switching of communications for private networks or for the sole purpose of interconnecting telecommunications carriers.

(3) Encryption

A telecommunications carrier shall not be responsible for decrypting, or ensuring the government's ability to decrypt, any communication encrypted by a subscriber or customer, unless the encryption was provided by the carrier and the carrier possesses the information necessary to decrypt the communication.

(c) Emergency or exigent circumstances

In emergency or exigent circumstances (including those described in sections 2518(7) or (11)(b) and 3125 of title 18 and section 1805(e) of title 50), a carrier at its discretion may comply with subsection (a)(3) of this section by allowing monitoring at its premises if that is the only means of accomplishing the interception or access.

(d) Mobile service assistance requirements

A telecommunications carrier that is a provider of commercial mobile service (as defined in section 332(d) of this title) offering a feature or service that allows subscribers to redirect, hand off, or assign their wire or electronic communications to another service area or another service provider or to utilize facilities in another service area or of another service provider shall ensure that, when the carrier that had been providing assistance for the interception of wire or electronic communications or access to call-identifying information pursuant to a court order or lawful authorization no longer has access to the content of such communications or call-identifying information within the service area in which interception has been occurring as a result of the subscriber's use of such a feature or service, information is made available to the government (before, during, or immediately after the transfer of such communications) identifying the provider of a wire or electronic communication service that has acquired access to the communications.

Sec. 1003. Notices of capacity requirements

(a) Notices of maximum and actual capacity requirements

(1) In general

Not later than 1 year after October 25, 1994, after consulting with State and local law enforcement agencies, telecommunications carriers, providers of telecommunications support services, and manufacturers of telecommunications equipment, and after notice and comment, the Attorney General shall publish in the Federal Register and provide to appropriate telecommunications industry associations and standard-setting organizations -

(A) notice of the actual number of communication interceptions, pen registers, and trap and trace devices, representing a portion of the maximum capacity set forth under subparagraph (B), that the Attorney General estimates that government agencies authorized to conduct electronic surveillance may conduct and use simultaneously by the date that is 4 years after October 25, 1994; and

(B) notice of the maximum capacity required to accommodate all of the communication interceptions, pen registers, and trap and trace devices that the Attorney General estimates that government agencies authorized to conduct electronic surveillance may conduct and use simultaneously after the date that is 4 years after October 25, 1994.

(2) Basis of notices

The notices issued under paragraph (1) -

(A) may be based upon the type of equipment, type of service, number of subscribers, type or size or carrier, nature of service area, or any other measure; and

(1) Initial capacity

Within 3 years after the publication by the Attorney General of a notice of capacity requirements or within 4 years after October 25, 1994, whichever is longer, a telecommunications carrier shall, subject to subsection (e) of this section, ensure that its systems are capable of -

(A) accommodating simultaneously the number of interceptions, pen registers, and trap and trace devices set forth in the notice under subsection (a)(1)(A) of this section; and

(B) expanding to the maximum capacity set forth in the notice under subsection (a)(1)(B) of this section.

(2) Expansion to maximum capacity

After the date described in paragraph (1), a telecommunications carrier shall, subject to subsection (e) of this section, ensure that it can accommodate expeditiously any increase in the actual number of communication interceptions, pen registers, and trap and trace devices that authorized agencies may seek to conduct and use, up to the maximum capacity requirement set forth in the notice under subsection (a)(1)(B) of this section.

(c) Notices of increased maximum capacity requirements

(1) Notice

The Attorney General shall periodically publish in the Federal Register, after notice and comment, notice of any necessary increases in the maximum capacity requirement set forth in the notice under subsection (a)(1)(B) of this section.

(2) Compliance

Within 3 years after notice of increased maximum capacity requirements is published under paragraph (1), or within such longer time period as the Attorney General may specify, a telecommunications carrier shall, subject to subsection (e) of this section, ensure that its systems are capable of expanding to the increased maximum capacity set forth in the notice.

(d) Carrier statement

Within 180 days after the publication by the Attorney General of a notice of capacity requirements pursuant to subsection (a) or (c) of this section, a telecommunications carrier shall submit to the Attorney General a statement identifying any of its systems or services that do not have the capacity to accommodate simultaneously the number of interceptions, pen registers, and trap and trace devices set forth in the notice under such subsection.

(e) Reimbursement required for compliance

The Attorney General shall review the statements submitted under subsection (d) of this section and may, subject to the availability of appropriations, agree to reimburse a telecommunications carrier for costs directly associated with modifications to attain such capacity requirement that are determined to be reasonable in accordance with section 1008(e) of this title. Until the Attorney General agrees to reimburse such carrier for such modification, such carrier shall be considered to be in compliance with the capacity notices under subsection (a) or (c) of this section.

Sec. 1004. Systems security and integrity

A telecommunications carrier shall ensure that any interception of communications or access to call-identifying information effected within its switching premises can be activated only in accordance with a court order or other lawful authorization and with the affirmative intervention of an individual officer or employee of the carrier acting in accordance with regulations prescribed by the Commission.

Sec. 1005. Cooperation of equipment manufacturers and providers of telecommunications support services

(a) Consultation

A telecommunications carrier shall consult, as necessary, in a timely fashion with manufacturers of its telecommunications transmission and switching equipment and its providers of telecommunications support services for the purpose of ensuring that current and planned equipment, facilities, and services comply with the capability requirements of section 1002 of this title and the capacity requirements identified by the Attorney General under section 1003 of this title.

(b) Cooperation

Subject to sections 1003(e), 1007(a), and 1008(b) and (d) of this title, a manufacturer of telecommunications transmission or switching equipment and a provider of telecommunications support services shall, on a reasonably timely basis and at a reasonable charge, make available to the telecommunications carriers using its equipment, facilities, or services such features or modifications as are necessary to permit such carriers to comply with the capability requirements of section 1002 of this title and the capacity requirements identified by the Attorney General under section 1003 of this title.

Sec. 1006. Technical requirements and standards; extension of compliance date

(a) Safe harbor

(1) Consultation

To ensure the efficient and industry-wide implementation of the assistance capability requirements under section 1002 of this title, the Attorney General, in coordination with other Federal, State, and local law enforcement agencies, shall consult with appropriate associations and standard-setting organizations of the telecommunications industry, with representatives of users of telecommunications equipment, facilities, and services, and with State utility commissions.

(2) Compliance under accepted standards

A telecommunications carrier shall be found to be in compliance with the assistance capability requirements under section 1002 of this title, and a manufacturer of telecommunications transmission or switching equipment or a provider of telecommunications support services shall be found to be in compliance with section 1005 of this title, if the carrier, manufacturer, or support service provider is in compliance with publicly available technical requirements or standards adopted by an industry association or standard-setting organization, or by the Commission under subsection (b) of this section, to meet the requirements of section 1002 of this title.

(3) Absence of standards

The absence of technical requirements or standards for implementing the assistance capability requirements of section 1002 of this title shall not -

(A) preclude a telecommunications carrier, manufacturer, or telecommunications support services provider from deploying a technology or service; or

(B) relieve a carrier, manufacturer, or telecommunications support services provider of the obligations imposed by section 1002 or 1005 of this title, as applicable.

(b) Commission authority

If industry associations or standard-setting organizations fail to issue technical requirements or standards or if a Government agency or any other person believes that such requirements or standards are deficient, the agency or person may petition the Commission to establish, by rule, technical requirements or standards that - (1) meet the assistance capability requirements of section 1002 of this title by cost-effective methods;

(2) protect the privacy and security of communications not authorized to be intercepted;

(3) minimize the cost of such compliance on residential ratepayers;

(4) serve the policy of the United States to encourage the provision of new technologies and services to the public; and

(5) provide a reasonable time and conditions for compliance with and the transition to any new standard, including defining the obligations of telecommunications carriers under section 1002 of this title during any transition period.

(c) Extension of compliance date for equipment, facilities, and services

(1) Petition

A telecommunications carrier proposing to install or deploy, or having installed or deployed, any equipment, facility, or service prior to the effective date of section 1002 of this title may petition the Commission for 1 or more extensions of the deadline for complying with the assistance capability requirements under section 1002 of this title.

(2) Grounds for extension

The Commission may, after consultation with the Attorney General, grant an extension under this subsection, if the Commission determines that compliance with the assistance capability requirements under section 1002 of this title is not reasonably achievable through application of technology available within the compliance period.

(3) Length of extension

An extension under this subsection shall extend for no longer than the earlier of -

(A) the date determined by the Commission as necessary for the carrier to comply with the assistance capability requirements under section 1002 of this title; or

(B) the date that is 2 years after the date on which the extension is granted.

(4) Applicability of extension

An extension under this subsection shall apply to only that part of the carrier's business on which the new equipment, facility, or service is used.

Sec. 1007. Enforcement orders

(a) Grounds for issuance

A court shall issue an order enforcing this subchapter under section 2522 of title 18 only if the court finds that -

> (1) alternative technologies or capabilities or the facilities of another carrier are not reasonably available to law enforcement for implementing the interception of communications or access to call-identifying information; and
>
> (2) compliance with the requirements of this subchapter is reasonably achievable through the application of available technology to the equipment, facility, or service at issue or would have been reasonably achievable if timely action had been taken.

(b) Time for compliance

Upon issuing an order enforcing this subchapter, the court shall specify a reasonable time and conditions for complying with its order, considering the good faith efforts to comply in a timely manner, any effect on the carrier's, manufacturer's, or service provider's ability to continue to do business, the degree of culpability or delay in undertaking efforts to comply, and such other matters as justice may require.

(c) Limitations

An order enforcing this subchapter may not -

> (1) require a telecommunications carrier to meet the Government's [1] demand for interception of communications and acquisition of call-identifying information to any extent in excess of the capacity for which the Attorney General has agreed to reimburse such carrier;
>
> (2) require any telecommunications carrier to comply with assistance capability requirement [2] of section 1002 of this title if the Commission has determined (pursuant to section 1008(b)(1) of this title) that compliance is not reasonably achievable, unless the Attorney General has agreed (pursuant to section 1008(b)(2) of this title) to pay the costs described in section 1008(b)(2)(A) of this title; or
>
> (3) require a telecommunications carrier to modify, for the purpose of complying with the assistance capability requirements of section 1002 of this title, any equipment, facility, or service deployed on or before January 1, 1995, unless -
>
>> (A) the Attorney General has agreed to pay the telecommunications carrier for all reasonable costs directly associated with modifications necessary to bring the equipment, facility, or service into compliance with those requirements; or
>>
>> (B) the equipment, facility, or service has been replaced or significantly upgraded or otherwise undergoes major modification.

United States
Electronic Communications Privacy Act

Sec. 1008. Payment of costs of telecommunications carriers to comply with capability requirements

(a) Equipment, facilities, and services deployed on or before January 1, 1995 The Attorney General may, subject to the availability of appropriations, agree to pay telecommunications carriers for all reasonable costs directly associated with the modifications performed by carriers in connection with equipment, facilities, and services installed or deployed on or before January 1, 1995, to establish the capabilities necessary to comply with section 1002 of this title.

(b) Equipment, facilities, and services deployed after January 1, 1995

(1) Determinations of reasonably achievable

The Commission, on petition from a telecommunications carrier or any other interested person, and after notice to the Attorney General, shall determine whether compliance with the assistance capability requirements of section 1002 of this title is reasonably achievable with respect to any equipment, facility, or service installed or deployed after January 1, 1995. The Commission shall make such determination within 1 year after the date such petition is filed. In making such determination, the Commission shall determine whether compliance would impose significant difficulty or expense on the carrier or on the users of the carrier's systems and shall consider the following factors:

(A) The effect on public safety and national security.

(B) The effect on rates for basic residential telephone service.

(C) The need to protect the privacy and security of communications not authorized to be intercepted.

(D) The need to achieve the capability assistance requirements of section 1002 of this title by cost-effective methods.

(E) The effect on the nature and cost of the equipment, facility, or service at issue.

(F) The effect on the operation of the equipment, facility, or service at issue.

(G) The policy of the United States to encourage the provision of new technologies and services to the public. (H) The financial resources of the telecommunications carrier.

(I) The effect on competition in the provision of telecommunications services.

(J) The extent to which the design and development of the equipment, facility, or service was initiated before January 1, 1995.

(K) Such other factors as the Commission determines are appropriate.

(2) Compensation

If compliance with the assistance capability requirements of section 1002 of this title is not reasonably achievable with respect to equipment, facilities, or services deployed after January 1, 1995 -

(A) the Attorney General, on application of a telecommunications carrier, may agree, subject to the availability of appropriations, to pay the telecommunications carrier for the additional reasonable costs of making compliance with such assistance capability requirements reasonably achievable; and

(B) if the Attorney General does not agree to pay such costs, the telecommunications carrier shall be deemed to be in compliance with such capability requirements.

(c) Allocation of funds for payment

The Attorney General shall allocate funds appropriated to carry out this subchapter in accordance with law enforcement priorities determined by the Attorney General.

(d) Failure to make payment with respect to equipment, facilities, and services deployed on or before January 1, 1995 If a carrier has requested payment in accordance with procedures promulgated pursuant to subsection (e) of this section, and the Attorney General has not agreed to pay the telecommunications carrier for all reasonable costs directly associated with modifications necessary to bring any equipment, facility, or service deployed on or before January 1, 1995, into compliance with the assistance capability requirements of section 1002 of this title, such equipment, facility, or service shall be considered to be in compliance with the assistance capability requirements of section 1002 of this title until the equipment, facility, or service is replaced or significantly upgraded or otherwise undergoes major modification.

(e) Cost control regulations

(1) In general

The Attorney General shall, after notice and comment, establish regulations necessary to effectuate timely and cost-efficient payment to telecommunications carriers under this subchapter, under chapters 119 and 121 of title 18, and under the Foreign Intelligence Surveillance Act of 1978 (50 U.S.C. 1801 et seq.).

(2) Contents of regulations

The Attorney General, after consultation with the Commission, shall prescribe regulations for purposes of determining reasonable costs under this subchapter. Such regulations shall seek to minimize the cost to the Federal Government and shall -

(A) permit recovery from the Federal Government of -

(i) the direct costs of developing the modifications described in subsection (a) of this section, of providing the capabilities requested under subsection (b)(2) of this section, or of providing the capacities requested under section 1003(e) of this title, but only to the extent that such costs have not been recovered from any other governmental or nongovernmental entity;

(ii) the costs of training personnel in the use of such capabilities or capacities; and

(iii) the direct costs of deploying or installing such capabilities or capacities;

(B) in the case of any modification that may be used for any purpose other than lawfully authorized electronic surveillance by a law enforcement agency of a government, permit recovery of only the incremental cost of making the modification suitable for such law enforcement purposes; and

(C) maintain the confidentiality of trade secrets.

(3) Submission of claims

Such regulations shall require any telecommunications carrier that the Attorney General has agreed to pay for modifications pursuant to this section and that has installed or deployed such modification to submit to the Attorney General a claim for payment that contains or is accompanied by such information as the Attorney General may require.

Sec. 1009. Authorization of appropriations

There are authorized to be appropriated to carry out this subchapter a total of $500,000,000 for fiscal years 1995, 1996, 1997, and 1998. Such sums are authorized to remain available until expended.

Sec. 1010. Reports

(a) Reports by Attorney General

(1) In general

On or before November 30, 1995, and on or before November 30 of each year thereafter, the Attorney General shall submit to Congress and make available to the public a report on the amounts paid during the preceding fiscal year to telecommunications carriers under sections 1003(e) and 1008 of this title.

(2) Contents

A report under paragraph (1) shall include -

(A) a detailed accounting of the amounts paid to each carrier and the equipment, facility, or service for which the amounts were paid; and

(B) projections of the amounts expected to be paid in the current fiscal year, the carriers to which payment is expected to be made, and the equipment, facilities, or services for which payment is expected to be made.

(b) Reports by Comptroller General and Inspector General

(1) On or before April 1, 1996, the Comptroller General of the United States, and every two years thereafter, the Inspector General of the Department of Justice, shall submit to the Congress a report, after consultation with the Attorney General and the telecommunications industry -

(A) describing the type of equipment, facilities, and services that have been brought into compliance under this subchapter; and

(B) reflecting its analysis of the reasonableness and cost-effectiveness of the payments made by the Attorney General to telecommunications carriers for modifications necessary to ensure compliance with this subchapter.

(2) Compliance cost estimates. - A report under paragraph (1) shall include findings and conclusions on the costs to be incurred by telecommunications carriers to comply with the assistance capability requirements of section 1002 of this title after the effective date of such section 1002 of this title, including projections of the amounts expected to be incurred and a description of the equipment, facilities, or services for which they are expected to be incurred.

Sec. 1021. Department of Justice Telecommunications Carrier Compliance Fund

(a) Establishment of Fund

There is hereby established in the United States Treasury a fund to be known as the Department of Justice Telecommunications Carrier Compliance Fund (hereafter referred to as "the Fund"), which shall be available without fiscal year limitation to the Attorney General for making payments to telecommunications carriers, equipment manufacturers, and providers of telecommunications support services pursuant to section 1008 of this title.

(b) Deposits to Fund

Notwithstanding any other provision of law, any agency of the United States with law enforcement or intelligence responsibilities may deposit as offsetting collections to the Fund any unobligated balances that are available until expended, upon compliance with any Congressional notification requirements for reprogrammings of funds applicable to the appropriation from which the deposit is to be made.

(c) Termination

(1) The Attorney General may terminate the Fund at such time as the Attorney General determines that the Fund is no longer necessary.

(2) Any balance in the Fund at the time of its termination shall be deposited in the General Fund of the Treasury.

(3) A decision of the Attorney General to terminate the Fund shall not be subject to judicial review.

(d) Availability of funds for expenditure

Funds shall not be available for obligation unless an implementation plan as set forth in subsection (e) of this section is submitted to each member of the Committees on the Judiciary and Appropriations of both the House of Representatives and the Senate and the Congress does not by law block or prevent the obligation of such funds. Such funds shall be treated as a reprogramming of funds under section 605 of the Department of Commerce, Justice, and State, the Judiciary, and Related Agencies Appropriations Act, 1997, and shall not be available for obligation or expenditure except in compliance with the procedures set forth in that section and this section.

(e) Implementation plan

The implementation plan shall include:

(1) the law enforcement assistance capability requirements and an explanation of law enforcement's recommended interface;

(2) the proposed actual and maximum capacity requirements for the number of simultaneous law enforcement communications intercepts, pen registers, and trap and trace devices that authorized law enforcement agencies may seek to conduct, set forth on a county-by-county basis for wireline services and on a market service area basis for wireless services, and the historical baseline of electronic surveillance activity upon which such capacity requirements are based;

(3) a prioritized list of carrier equipment, facilities, and services deployed on or before January 1, 1995, to be modified by carriers at the request of law enforcement based on its investigative needs;

(4) a projected reimbursement plan that estimates the cost for the coming fiscal year and for each fiscal year thereafter, based on the prioritization of law enforcement needs as outlined in () a projected reimbursement plan that estimates the cost for facilities and services, installed on or before January 1, 1995.

(f) Annual report to Congress

The Attorney General shall submit to the Congress each year a report specifically detailing all deposits and expenditures made pursuant to subchapter I of this chapter in each fiscal year. This report shall be submitted to each member of the Committees on the Judiciary and Appropriations of both the House of Representatives and the Senate, and to the Speaker and minority leader of the House of Representatives and to the majority and minority leaders of the Senate, no later than 60 days after the end of each fiscal year.

VIDEO PRIVACY PROTECTION ACT
(1988)

Summary

The Video Privacy Protection Act of 1988 amends the Federal criminal code to prohibit the disclosure of video rental records containing personally identifiable information. The Act permits the disclosure of such information: (1) to the consumer; (2) with the written consent of the consumer (3) pursuant to a Federal criminal warrant, an equivalent State warrant, a grand jury subpoena, or a court order under specified guidelines; (4) to any person if such disclosure is solely the names and addresses of consumers and the consumer has had the opportunity to prohibit such disclosure; (5) to any person if such disclosure is incident to the ordinary course of business of the video tape service provider; or (6) pursuant to a civil court order.

The Act permits any person who is aggrieved by a violation of this Act to bring a civil action for damages. It establishes a two-year statute of limitations for such actions. It states that any such information unlawfully obtained may not be used in any court proceeding. It further requires the destruction of personally identifiable records within a specified period of time.

References

> Public Law 100-618 codified at 18 USC § 2710
> [http://www4.law.cornell.edu/uscode/18/2710.html]

18 U.S.C. § 2710. Wrongful disclosure of video tape rental or sale records

(a) Definitions. - For purposes of this section -

(1) the term "consumer" means any renter, purchaser, or subscriber of goods or services from a video tape service provider;

(2) the term "ordinary course of business" means only debt collection activities, order fulfillment, request processing, and the transfer of ownership;

(3) the term "personally identifiable information" includes information which identifies a person as having requested or obtained specific video materials or services from a video tape service provider; and

(4) the term "video tape service provider" means any person, engaged in the business, in or affecting interstate or foreign commerce, of rental, sale, or delivery of prerecorded video cassette tapes or similar audio visual materials, or any person or other entity to whom a disclosure is made under subparagraph (D) or (E) of subsection (b)(2), but only with respect to the information contained in the disclosure.

(b) Video Tape Rental and Sale Records. -

United States
Video Privacy Protection Act

(1) A video tape service provider who knowingly discloses, to any person, personally identifiable information concerning any consumer of such provider shall be liable to the aggrieved person for the relief provided in subsection (d).

(2) A video tape service provider may disclose personally identifiable information concerning any consumer -

(A) to the consumer;

(B) to any person with the informed, written consent of the consumer given at the time the disclosure is sought;

(C) to a law enforcement agency pursuant to a warrant issued under the Federal Rules of Criminal Procedure, an equivalent State warrant, a grand jury subpoena, or a court order;

(D) to any person if the disclosure is solely of the names and addresses of consumers and if -

(i) the video tape service provider has provided the consumer with the opportunity, in a clear and conspicuous manner, to prohibit such disclosure; and

(ii) the disclosure does not identify the title, description, or subject matter of any video tapes or other audio visual material; however, the subject matter of such materials may be disclosed if the disclosure is for the exclusive use of marketing goods and services directly to the consumer;

(E) to any person if the disclosure is incident to the ordinary course of business of the video tape service provider; or

(F) pursuant to a court order, in a civil proceeding upon a showing of compelling need for the information that cannot be accommodated by any other means, if -

(i) the consumer is given reasonable notice, by the person seeking the disclosure, of the court proceeding relevant to the issuance of the court order; and

(ii) the consumer is afforded the opportunity to appear and contest the claim of the person seeking the disclosure.

If an order is granted pursuant to subparagraph (C) or (F), the court shall impose appropriate safeguards against unauthorized disclosure.

(3) Court orders authorizing disclosure under subparagraph (C) shall issue only with prior notice to the consumer and only if the law enforcement agency shows that there is probable cause to believe that the records or other information sought are relevant to a legitimate law enforcement inquiry. In the case of a State government authority, such a court order shall not issue if prohibited by the law of such State. A court issuing an order pursuant to this section, on a motion made promptly by the video tape service provider, may quash or modify such order if the information or records requested are unreasonably voluminous in nature or if

compliance with such order otherwise would cause an unreasonable burden on such provider.

(c) Civil Action. -

(1) Any person aggrieved by any act of a person in violation of this section may bring a civil action in a United States district court.

(2) The court may award -

(A) actual damages but not less than liquidated damages in an amount of $2,500;

(B) punitive damages;

(C) reasonable attorneys' fees and other litigation costs reasonably incurred; and

(D) such other preliminary and equitable relief as the court determines to be appropriate.

(3) No action may be brought under this subsection unless such action is begun within 2 years from the date of the act complained of or the date of discovery.

(4) No liability shall result from lawful disclosure permitted by this section.

(d) Personally Identifiable Information. - Personally identifiable information obtained in any manner other than as provided in this section shall not be received in evidence in any trial, hearing, arbitration, or other proceeding in or before any court, grand jury, department, officer, agency, regulatory body, legislative committee, or other authority of the United States, a State, or a political subdivision of a State.

(e) Destruction of Old Records. - A person subject to this section shall destroy personally identifiable information as soon as practicable, but no later than one year from the date the information is no longer necessary for the purpose for which it was collected and there are no pending requests or orders for access to such information under subsection (b)(2) or (c)(2) or pursuant to a court order.

(f) Preemption - The provisions of this section preempt only the provisions of State or local law that require disclosure prohibited by this section.

United States
Employee Polygraph Protection Act

EMPLOYEE POLYGRAPH PROTECTION
ACT (1988)

Summary

The Employee Polygraph Protection Act of 1988 prohibits any employer from: (1) requiring or suggesting that an employee or prospective employee take a lie detector test; (2) using lie detector test results; or (3) taking employment action against an employee or prospective employee who refuses to take a lie detector test or institutes or testifies in a proceeding under or related to this Act. The Act requires the Secretary to Labor (the Secretary) to prepare notices setting forth such prohibitions, and requires employers to post such notices. The Act provides civil penalties for violations of this Act, and grants the Secretary authority to restrain violations of the Act. It allows employees and prospective employees to bring civil actions against any employer who violates its provisions.

The Act exempts from coverage under this Act: (1) Federal, State, and local governments; (2) certain Federal contractors; (3) tests conducted pursuant to the performance of intelligence or counterintelligence functions or Federal security clearances; (4) certain security personnel and other security services; and (5) employers who are authorized to manufacture, distribute, or dispense controlled substances. It provides a limited exemption under which an employer may request certain employees to submit to a polygraph test if the test is administered in connection with an ongoing investigation involving economic loss or injury to the employer's business, including theft, embezzlement, misappropriation, or an act of unlawful industrial espionage or sabotage. The Act specifies reporting requirements of the employer under such circumstances. It further declares that such limited exemption does not apply if an employee is discharged, dismissed, disciplined, or discriminated against in any manner on the basis of the results of one or more polygraph tests or the refusal to take a polygraph test, without additional supporting evidence.

The Act sets forth the rights of an examinee during a pretest phase, the actual testing phase, and the post-test phase. It specifies the qualification of an examiner. It prohibits the disclosure of information obtained from a polygraph test, except as provided by the Act.

References

Public Law 100-347 codified at 29 USC § 2001 et seq.
[http://www4.law.cornell.edu/uscode/29/2001.html]

Conference report, House Report 100-659 (May 26, 1988)

29 USC Sec. 2001. Definitions

As used in this chapter:

    (1) Commerce

The term "commerce" has the meaning provided by section 203(b) of this title.

(2) Employer

The term "employer" includes any person acting directly or indirectly in the interest of an employer in relation to an employee or prospective employee.

(3) Lie detector

The term "lie detector" includes a polygraph, deceptograph, voice stress analyzer, psychological stress evaluator, or any other similar device (whether mechanical or electrical) that is used, or the results of which are used, for the purpose of rendering a diagnostic opinion regarding the honesty or dishonesty of an individual.

(4) Polygraph

The term "polygraph" means an instrument that -

(A) records continuously, visually, permanently, and simultaneously changes in cardiovascular, respiratory, and electrodermal patterns as minimum instrumentation standards; and

(B) is used, or the results of which are used, for the

purpose of rendering a diagnostic opinion regarding the honesty or dishonesty of an individual.

(5) Secretary

The term "Secretary" means the Secretary of Labor.

Sec. 2002. Prohibitions on lie detector use

Except as provided in sections 2006 and 2007 of this title, it shall be unlawful for any employer engaged in or affecting commerce or in the production of goods for commerce -

(1) directly or indirectly, to require, request, suggest, or cause any employee or prospective employee to take or submit to any lie detector test;

(2) to use, accept, refer to, or inquire concerning the results of any lie detector test of any employee or prospective employee;

(3) to discharge, discipline, discriminate against in any manner, or deny employment or promotion to, or threaten to take any such action against -

(A) any employee or prospective employee who refuses, declines, or fails to take or submit to any lie detector test, or

(B) any employee or prospective employee on the basis of the results of any lie detector test; or

(4) to discharge, discipline, discriminate against in any manner, or deny employment or promotion to, or threaten to take any such action against, any employee or prospective employee because -

(A) such employee or prospective employee has filed any complaint or instituted or caused to be instituted any proceeding under or related to this chapter,

(B) such employee or prospective employee has testified or is about to testify in any such proceeding, or

(C) of the exercise by such employee or prospective employee, on behalf of such employee or another person, of any right afforded by this chapter.

Sec. 2003. Notice of protection

The Secretary shall prepare, have printed, and distribute a notice setting forth excerpts from, or summaries of, the pertinent provisions of this chapter. Each employer shall post and maintain such notice in conspicuous places on its premises where notices to employees and applicants to employment are customarily posted.

Sec. 2004. Authority of Secretary

(a) In general

The Secretary shall -

(1) issue such rules and regulations as may be necessary or appropriate to carry out this chapter;

(2) cooperate with regional, State, local, and other agencies, and cooperate with and furnish technical assistance to employers, labor organizations, and employment agencies to aid in effectuating the purposes of this chapter; and

(3) make investigations and inspections and require the keeping of records necessary or appropriate for the administration of this chapter.

(b) Subpoena authority

For the purpose of any hearing or investigation under this chapter, the Secretary shall have the authority contained in sections 49 and 50 of title 15.

Sec. 2005. Enforcement provisions

(a) Civil penalties

(1) In general

Subject to paragraph (2), any employer who violates any provision of this chapter may be assessed a civil penalty of not more than $10,000.

(2) Determination of amount

In determining the amount of any penalty under paragraph (1), the Secretary shall take into account the previous record of the person in terms of compliance with this chapter and the gravity of the violation.

(3) Collection

Any civil penalty assessed under this subsection shall be collected in the same manner as is required by subsections (b) through (e) of section 1853 of this title with respect to civil penalties assessed under subsection (a) of such section.

(b) Injunctive actions by Secretary

The Secretary may bring an action under this section to restrain violations of this chapter. The Solicitor of Labor may appear for and represent the Secretary in any litigation brought under this chapter. In any action brought under this section, the district courts of the United States shall have jurisdiction, for cause shown, to issue temporary or permanent restraining orders and injunctions to require compliance with this chapter, including such legal or equitable relief incident thereto as may be appropriate, including, but not limited to, employment, reinstatement, promotion, and the payment of lost wages and benefits.

(c) Private civil actions

(1) Liability

An employer who violates this chapter shall be liable to the employee or prospective employee affected by such violation. Such employer shall be liable for such legal or equitable relief as may be appropriate, including, but not limited to, employment, reinstatement, promotion, and the payment of lost wages and benefits.

(2) Court

An action to recover the liability prescribed in paragraph (1) may be maintained against the employer in any Federal or State court of competent jurisdiction by an employee or prospective employee for or on behalf of such employee, prospective employee, and other employees or prospective employees similarly situated. No such action may be commenced more than 3 years after the date of the alleged violation.

(3) Costs

The court, in its discretion, may allow the prevailing party (other than the United States) reasonable costs, including attorney's fees.

(d) Waiver of rights prohibited

The rights and procedures provided by this chapter may not be waived by contract or otherwise, unless such waiver is part of a written settlement agreed to and signed by the parties to the pending action or complaint under this chapter.

Sec. 2006. Exemptions

(a) No application to governmental employers

This chapter shall not apply with respect to the United States Government, any State or local government, or any political subdivision of a State or local government.

(b) National defense and security exemption

(1) National defense

Nothing in this chapter shall be construed to prohibit the administration, by the Federal Government, in the performance of any counterintelligence function, of any lie detector test to -

(A) any expert or consultant under contract to the Department of Defense or any employee of any contractor of such Department; or

(B) any expert or consultant under contract with the Department of Energy in connection with the atomic energy defense activities of such Department or any employee of any contractor of such Department in connection with such activities.

United States
Employee Polygraph Protection Act

(2) Security

Nothing in this chapter shall be construed to prohibit the administration, by the Federal Government, in the performance of any intelligence or counterintelligence function, of any lie detector test to -

    (A)

        (i) any individual employed by, assigned to, or detailed to, the National Security Agency, the Defense Intelligence Agency, the Central Imagery Office, or the Central Intelligence Agency,

        (ii) any expert or consultant under contract to any such agency,

        (iii) any employee of a contractor to any such agency,

        (iv) any individual applying for a position in any such agency, or

        (v) any individual assigned to a space where sensitive cryptologic information is produced, processed, or stored for any such agency; or

    (B) any expert, or consultant (or employee of such expert or consultant) under contract with any Federal Government department, agency, or program whose duties involve access to information that has been classified at the level of top secret or designated as being within a special access program under section 4.2(a) of Executive Order 12356 (or a successor Executive order).

(c) FBI contractors exemption

Nothing in this chapter shall be construed to prohibit the administration, by the Federal Government, in the performance of any counterintelligence function, of any lie detector test to an employee of a contractor of the Federal Bureau of Investigation of the Department of Justice who is engaged in the performance of any work under the contract with such Bureau.

(d) Limited exemption for ongoing investigations

Subject to sections 2007 and 2009 of this title, this chapter shall not prohibit an employer from requesting an employee to submit to a polygraph test if -

    (1) the test is administered in connection with an ongoing investigation involving economic loss or injury to the employer's business, such as theft, embezzlement, misappropriation, or an act of unlawful industrial espionage or sabotage;

    (2) the employee had access to the property that is the subject of the investigation;

    (3) the employer has a reasonable suspicion that the employee was involved in the incident or activity under investigation; and

    (4) the employer executes a statement, provided to the examinee before the test, that -

        (A) sets forth with particularity the specific incident or activity being investigated and the basis for testing particular employees,

        (B) is signed by a person (other than a polygraph examiner) authorized to legally bind the employer,

        (C) is retained by the employer for at least 3 years, and

        (D) contains at a minimum -

(i) an identification of the specific economic loss or injury to the business of the employer,

(ii) a statement indicating that the employee had access to the property that is the subject of the investigation, and

(iii) a statement describing the basis of the employer's reasonable suspicion that the employee was involved in the incident or activity under investigation.

(e) Exemption for security services

(1) In general

Subject to paragraph (2) and sections 2007 and 2009 of this title, this chapter shall not prohibit the use of polygraph tests on prospective employees by any private employer whose primary business purpose consists of providing armored car personnel, personnel engaged in the design, installation, and maintenance of security alarm systems, or other uniformed or plainclothes security personnel and whose function includes protection of -

(A) facilities, materials, or operations having a significant impact on the health or safety of any State or political subdivision thereof, or the national security of the United States, as determined under rules and regulations issued by the Secretary within 90 days after June 27, 1988, including -

(i) facilities engaged in the production, transmission, or distribution of electric or nuclear power,

(ii) public water supply facilities,

(iii) shipments or storage of radioactive or other toxic waste materials, and

(iv) public transportation, or

(B) currency, negotiable securities, precious commodities or instruments, or proprietary information.

(2) Access

The exemption provided under this subsection shall not apply if the test is administered to a prospective employee who would not be employed to protect facilities, materials, operations, or assets referred to in paragraph (1).

(f) Exemption for drug security, drug theft, or drug diversion investigations

(1) In general

Subject to paragraph (2) and sections 2007 and 2009 of this title, this chapter shall not prohibit the use of a polygraph test by any employer authorized to manufacture, distribute, or dispense a controlled substance listed in schedule I, II, III, or IV of section 812 of title 21.

(2) Access

The exemption provided under this subsection shall apply -

(A) if the test is administered to a prospective employee who would have direct access to the manufacture, storage, distribution, or sale of any such controlled substance; or

United States
Employee Polygraph Protection Act

(B) in the case of a test administered to a current employee,

if -

(i) the test is administered in connection with an ongoing investigation of criminal or other misconduct involving, or potentially involving, loss or injury to the manufacture, distribution, or dispensing of any such controlled substance by such employer, and

(ii) the employee had access to the person or property that is the subject of the investigation.

Sec. 2007. Restrictions on use of exemptions

(a) Test as basis for adverse employment action

(1) Under ongoing investigations exemption

Except as provided in paragraph (2), the exemption under subsection (d) of section 2006 of this title shall not apply if an employee is discharged, disciplined, denied employment or promotion, or otherwise discriminated against in any manner on the basis of the analysis of a polygraph test chart or the refusal to take a polygraph test, without additional supporting evidence. The evidence required by such subsection may serve as additional supporting evidence.

(2) Under other exemptions

In the case of an exemption described in subsection (e) or (f) of such section, the exemption shall not apply if the results of an analysis of a polygraph test chart are used, or the refusal to take a polygraph test is used, as the sole basis upon which an adverse employment action described in paragraph (1) is taken against an employee or prospective employee.

(b) Rights of examinee

The exemptions provided under subsections (d), (e), and (f) of section 2006 of this title shall not apply unless the requirements described in the following paragraphs are met:

(1) All phases

Throughout all phases of the test -

(A) the examinee shall be permitted to terminate the test at any time;

(B) the examinee is not asked questions in a manner designed to degrade, or needlessly intrude on, such examinee;

(C) the examinee is not asked any question concerning -

(i) religious beliefs or affiliations,

(ii) beliefs or opinions regarding racial matters,

(iii) political beliefs or affiliations,

(iv) any matter relating to sexual behavior; and

(v) beliefs, affiliations, opinions, or lawful activities regarding unions or labor organizations; and

(D) the examiner does not conduct the test if there is sufficient written evidence by a physician that the examinee is suffering from a medical or psychological condition or undergoing treatment that might cause abnormal responses during the actual testing phase.

(2) Pretest phase

During the pretest phase, the prospective examinee -

(A) is provided with reasonable written notice of the date, time, and location of the test, and of such examinee's right to obtain and consult with legal counsel or an employee representative before each phase of the test;

(B) is informed in writing of the nature and characteristics of the tests and of the instruments involved;

(C) is informed, in writing -

(i) whether the testing area contains a two-way mirror, a camera, or any other device through which the test can be observed,

(ii) whether any other device, including any device for recording or monitoring the test, will be used, or

(iii) that the employer or the examinee may (with mutual knowledge) make a recording of the test;

(D) is read and signs a written notice informing such examinee -

(i) that the examinee cannot be required to take the test as a condition of employment,

(ii) that any statement made during the test may constitute additional supporting evidence for the purposes of an adverse employment action described in subsection (a) of this section,

(iii) of the limitations imposed under this section,

(iv) of the legal rights and remedies available to the examinee if the polygraph test is not conducted in accordance with this chapter, and

(v) of the legal rights and remedies of the employer under this chapter (including the rights of the employer under section 2008(c)(2) of this title); and

(E) is provided an opportunity to review all questions to be asked during the test and is informed of the right to terminate the test at any time.

(3) Actual testing phase

During the actual testing phase, the examiner does not ask such examinee any question relevant during the test that was not presented in writing for review to such examinee before the test.

(4) Post-test phase

Before any adverse employment action, the employer shall -

(A) further interview the examinee on the basis of the results of the test; and

(B) provide the examinee with -

(i) a written copy of any opinion or conclusion rendered as a result of the test, and

(ii) a copy of the questions asked during the test along with the corresponding charted responses.

(5) Maximum number and minimum duration of tests The examiner shall not conduct and complete more than five polygraph tests on a calendar day on which the test is given, and shall not conduct any such test for less than a 90-minute duration.

(c) Qualifications and requirements of examiners

The exemptions provided under subsections (d), (e), and (f) of section 2006 of this title shall not apply unless the individual who conducts the polygraph test satisfies the requirements under the following paragraphs:

(1) Qualifications

The examiner -

(A) has a valid and current license granted by licensing and regulatory authorities in the State in which the test is to be conducted, if so required by the State; and

(B) maintains a minimum of a $50,000 bond or an equivalent amount of professional liability coverage.

(2) Requirements

The examiner -

(A) renders any opinion or conclusion regarding the test -

(i) in writing and solely on the basis of an analysis of polygraph test charts,

(ii) that does not contain information other than admissions, information, case facts, and interpretation of the charts relevant to the purpose and stated objectives of the test, and

(iii) that does not include any recommendation concerning the employment of the examinee; and

(B) maintains all opinions, reports, charts, written questions, lists, and other records relating to the test for a minimum period of 3 years after administration of the test.

Sec. 2008. Disclosure of information

(a) In general

A person, other than the examinee, may not disclose information obtained during a polygraph test, except as provided in this section.

(b) Permitted disclosures

A polygraph examiner may disclose information acquired from a polygraph test only to -

(1) the examinee or any other person specifically designated in writing by the examinee;

(2) the employer that requested the test; or

(3) any court, governmental agency, arbitrator, or mediator, in accordance with due process of law, pursuant to an order from a court of competent jurisdiction.

(c) Disclosure by employer

An employer (other than an employer described in subsection (a), (b), or (c) of section 2006 of this title) for whom a polygraph test is conducted may disclose information from the test only to -

(1) a person in accordance with subsection (b) of this section; or

(2) a governmental agency, but only insofar as the disclosed information is an admission of criminal conduct.

Sec. 2009. Effect on other law and agreements

Except as provided in subsections (a), (b), and (c) of section 2006 of this title, this chapter shall not preempt any provision of any State or local law or of any negotiated collective bargaining agreement that prohibits lie detector tests or is more restrictive with respect to lie detector tests than any provision of this chapter.

United States
Telephone Consumer Protection Act

TELEPHONE CONSUMER PROTECTION
ACT (1991)

Summary

The Telephone Consumer Protection Act of 1991 amended the Communications Act of 1934 to prohibit any person within the United States from using an automatic telephone dialing system to make a call to any emergency telephone line or to any telephone number for which the called party is charged for the call without the consent of the called party, with specified exceptions. The Act also prohibited the use of a telephone facsimile machine, computer, or other device to send an unsolicited advertisement to a FAX machine. The Act also directs the Federal Communications Commission (FCC) to issue regulations to implement these requirements, and authorizes private actions and the recovery of damages with respect to violations of such requirements.

The Act further directs the FCC to initiate a rulemaking proceeding concerning the need to protect residential telephone subscribers' privacy rights to avoid receiving telephone solicitations to which they object and issue regulations to implement methods and procedures for protecting such privacy rights without the imposition of any additional charge to telephone subscribers. It states that such regulations may require the establishment and operation of a single national database to compile a list of telephone numbers of residential subscribers who object to receiving such solicitations, or to receiving certain classes or categories of solicitations, and to make the compiled list available for purchase. The Act authorizes private actions and the recovery of damages with respect to violations of such privacy rights.

The Act makes it unlawful for any person within the United States to initiate any communication using a FAX or ATDS that does not comply with certain technical and procedural standards or to use a computer or other electronic device to send any message via FAX unless such person clearly marks on the document the date and time it is sent and identifies the entity sending the message and the telephone number of the sending machine or entity.

The Act permits States to bring civil actions to enjoin calls to residents in violation of the Act and to recover monetary damages. It grants U.S. district courts exclusive jurisdiction over such actions. It prohibits a State, whenever the FCC has instituted a civil action for violation of this Act, from bringing an action against any defendant named in the FCC's complaint.

References

Public Law 102-243 codified at 47 USC § 227
http://www4.law.cornell.edu/uscode/47/227.html

Congressional Statement of Findings

Section 2 of Pub. L. 102-243 provided that: "The Congress finds that:

"(1) The use of the telephone to market goods and services to the home and other businesses is now pervasive due to the increased use of cost-effective telemarketing techniques.

"(2) Over 30,000 businesses actively telemarket goods and services to business and residential customers.

"(3) More than 300,000 solicitors call more than 18,000,000 Americans every day.

"(4) Total United States sales generated through telemarketing amounted to $435,000,000,000 in 1990, a more than four-fold increase since 1984.

"(5) Unrestricted telemarketing, however, can be an intrusive invasion of privacy and, when an emergency or medical assistance telephone line is seized, a risk to public safety.

"(6) Many consumers are outraged over the proliferation of intrusive, nuisance calls to their homes from telemarketers.

"(7) Over half the States now have statutes restricting various uses of the telephone for marketing, but telemarketers can evade their prohibitions through interstate operations; therefore, Federal law is needed to control residential telemarketing practices.

"(8) The Constitution does not prohibit restrictions on commercial telemarketing solicitations.

"(9) Individuals' privacy rights, public safety interests, and commercial freedoms of speech and trade must be balanced in a way that protects the privacy of individuals and permits legitimate telemarketing practices.

"(10) Evidence compiled by the Congress indicates that residential telephone subscribers consider automated or prerecorded telephone calls, regardless of the content or the initiator of the message, to be a nuisance and an invasion of privacy.

"(11) Technologies that might allow consumers to avoid receiving such calls are not universally available, are costly, are unlikely to be enforced, or place an inordinate burden on the consumer.

"(12) Banning such automated or prerecorded telephone calls to the home, except when the receiving party consents to receiving the call or when such calls are necessary in an emergency situation affecting the health and safety of the consumer, is the only effective means of protecting telephone consumers from this nuisance and privacy invasion.

"(13) While the evidence presented to the Congress indicates that automated or prerecorded calls are a nuisance and an invasion of privacy, regardless of the type of call, the Federal Communications Commission should have the flexibility to design different rules for those types of automated or prerecorded calls that it finds are not considered a nuisance or invasion of privacy, or for noncommercial calls, consistent with the free speech protections embodied in the First Amendment of the Constitution.

United States
Telephone Consumer Protection Act

"(14) Businesses also have complained to the Congress and the Federal Communications Commission that automated or prerecorded telephone calls are a nuisance, are an invasion of privacy, and interfere with interstate commerce.

"(15) The Federal Communications Commission should consider adopting reasonable restrictions on automated or prerecorded calls to businesses as well as to the home, consistent with the constitutional protections of free speech."

47 U.S.C. Sec. 227. Restrictions on use of telephone equipment

(a) Definitions As used in this section -

(1) The term "automatic telephone dialing system" means equipment which has the capacity -

(A) to store or produce telephone numbers to be called, using a random or sequential number generator; and

(B) to dial such numbers.

(2) The term "telephone facsimile machine" means equipment which has the capacity (A) to transcribe text or images, or both, from paper into an electronic signal and to transmit that signal over a regular telephone line, or (B) to transcribe text or images (or both) from an electronic signal received over a regular telephone line onto paper.

(3) The term "telephone solicitation" means the initiation of a telephone call or message for the purpose of encouraging the purchase or rental of, or investment in, property, goods, or services, which is transmitted to any person, but such term does not include a call or message

(A) to any person with that person's prior express invitation or permission,

(B) to any person with whom the caller has an established business relationship, or

(C) by a tax exempt nonprofit organization.

(4) The term "unsolicited advertisement" means any material advertising the commercial availability or quality of any property, goods, or services which is transmitted to any person without that person's prior express invitation or permission.

(b) Restrictions on use of automated telephone equipment

(1) Prohibitions It shall be unlawful for any person within the United States -

(A) to make any call (other than a call made for emergency purposes or made with the prior express consent of the called party) using any automatic telephone dialing system or an artificial or prerecorded voice -

(i) to any emergency telephone line (including any "911" line and any emergency line of a hospital, medical physician or service office, health care facility, poison control center, or fire protection or law enforcement agency);

(ii) to the telephone line of any guest room or patient room of a hospital, health care facility, elderly home, or similar establishment; or

(iii) to any telephone number assigned to a paging service, cellular telephone service, specialized mobile radio service, or other radio common carrier service, or any service for which the called party is charged for the call;

(B) to initiate any telephone call to any residential telephone line using an artificial or prerecorded voice to deliver a message without the prior express consent of the called party, unless the call is initiated for emergency purposes or is exempted by rule or order by the Commission under paragraph (2)(B);

(C) to use any telephone facsimile machine, computer, or other device to send an unsolicited advertisement to a telephone facsimile machine; or

(D) to use an automatic telephone dialing system in such a way that two or more telephone lines of a multi-line business are engaged simultaneously.

(2) Regulations; exemptions and other provisions The Commission shall prescribe regulations to implement the requirements of this subsection. In implementing the requirements of this subsection, the Commission -

(A) shall consider prescribing regulations to allow businesses to avoid receiving calls made using an artificial or prerecorded voice to which they have not given their prior express consent;

(B) may, by rule or order, exempt from the requirements of paragraph (1)(B) of this subsection, subject to such conditions as the Commission may prescribe -

(i) calls that are not made for a commercial purpose; and

(ii) such classes or categories of calls made for commercial purposes as the Commission determines -

(I) will not adversely affect the privacy rights that this section is intended to protect; and

(II) do not include the transmission of any unsolicited advertisement; and

(C) may, by rule or order, exempt from the requirements of paragraph (1)(A)(iii) of this subsection calls to a telephone number assigned to a cellular telephone service that are not charged to the called party, subject to such conditions as the Commission may prescribe as necessary in the interest of the privacy rights this section is intended to protect.

(3) Private right of action A person or entity may, if otherwise permitted by the laws or rules of court of a State, bring in an appropriate court of that State -

(A) an action based on a violation of this subsection or the regulations prescribed under this subsection to enjoin such violation,

(B) an action to recover for actual monetary loss from such a violation, or to receive $500 in damages for each such violation, whichever is greater, or

(C) both such actions.

If the court finds that the defendant willfully or knowingly violated this subsection or the regulations prescribed under this subsection, the court may, in its discretion, increase the amount of the award to an amount equal to not more than 3 times the amount available under subparagraph (B) of this paragraph.

(c) Protection of subscriber privacy rights

(1) Rulemaking proceeding required Within 120 days after December 20, 1991, the Commission shall initiate a rulemaking proceeding concerning the need to protect residential telephone subscribers' privacy rights to avoid receiving telephone solicitations to which they object. The proceeding shall -

(A) compare and evaluate alternative methods and procedures (including the use of electronic databases, telephone network technologies, special directory markings, industry-based or company-specific "do not call" systems, and any other alternatives, individually or in combination) for their effectiveness in protecting such privacy rights, and in terms of their cost and other advantages and disadvantages;

(B) evaluate the categories of public and private entities that would have the capacity to establish and administer such methods and procedures;

(C) consider whether different methods and procedures may apply for local telephone solicitations, such as local telephone solicitations of small businesses or holders of second class mail permits;

(D) consider whether there is a need for additional Commission authority to further restrict telephone solicitations, including those calls exempted under subsection (a)(3) of this section, and, if such a finding is made and supported by the record, propose specific restrictions to the Congress; and

(E) develop proposed regulations to implement the methods and procedures that the Commission determines are most effective and efficient to accomplish the purposes of this section.

(2) Regulations Not later than 9 months after December 20, 1991, the Commission shall conclude the rulemaking proceeding initiated under paragraph (1) and shall prescribe regulations to implement methods and procedures for protecting the privacy rights described in such paragraph in an efficient, effective, and economic manner and without the imposition of any additional charge to telephone subscribers.

(3) Use of database permitted The regulations required by paragraph (2) may require the establishment and operation of a single national database to compile a list of telephone numbers of residential subscribers who object to receiving telephone solicitations, and to make that compiled list and parts thereof available for purchase. If the Commission determines to require such a database, such regulations shall -

(A) specify a method by which the Commission will select an entity to administer such database;

(B) require each common carrier providing telephone exchange service, in accordance with regulations prescribed by the Commission, to inform subscribers for telephone exchange service of the opportunity to provide notification, in accordance with regulations established under this paragraph, that such subscriber objects to receiving telephone solicitations;

(C) specify the methods by which each telephone subscriber shall be informed, by the common carrier that provides local exchange service to that subscriber, of

> (i) the subscriber's right to give or revoke a notification of an objection under subparagraph (A), and
>
> (ii) the methods by which such right may be exercised by the subscriber;

(D) specify the methods by which such objections shall be collected and added to the database;

(E) prohibit any residential subscriber from being charged for giving or revoking such notification or for being included in a database compiled under this section;

(F) prohibit any person from making or transmitting a telephone solicitation to the telephone number of any subscriber included in such database;

(G) specify

> (i) the methods by which any person desiring to make or transmit telephone solicitations will obtain access to the database, by area code or local exchange prefix, as required to avoid calling the telephone numbers of subscribers included in such database; and
>
> (ii) the costs to be recovered from such persons;

(H) specify the methods for recovering, from persons accessing such database, the costs involved in identifying, collecting, updating, disseminating, and selling, and other activities relating to, the operations of the database that are incurred by the entities carrying out those activities;

(I) specify the frequency with which such database will be updated and specify the method by which such updating will take effect for purposes of compliance with the regulations prescribed under this subsection;

(J) be designed to enable States to use the database mechanism selected by the Commission for purposes of administering or enforcing State law;

(K) prohibit the use of such database for any purpose other than compliance with the requirements of this section and any such State law and specify methods for protection of the privacy rights of persons whose numbers are included in such database; and

(L) require each common carrier providing services to any person for the purpose of making telephone solicitations to notify such person of the requirements of this section and the regulations thereunder.

(4) Considerations required for use of database method If the Commission determines to require the database mechanism described in paragraph (3), the Commission shall -

(A) in developing procedures for gaining access to the database, consider the different needs of telemarketers conducting business on a national, regional, State, or local level;

(B) develop a fee schedule or price structure for recouping the cost of such database that recognizes such differences and -

(i) reflect the relative costs of providing a national, regional, State, or local list of phone numbers of subscribers who object to receiving telephone solicitations;

(ii) reflect the relative costs of providing such lists on paper or electronic media; and

(iii) not place an unreasonable financial burden on small businesses; and

(C) consider

(i) whether the needs of telemarketers operating on a local basis could be met through special markings of area white pages directories, and

(ii) if such directories are needed as an adjunct to database lists prepared by area code and local exchange prefix.

(5) Private right of action A person who has received more than one telephone call within any 12-month period by or on behalf of the same entity in violation of the regulations prescribed under this subsection may, if otherwise permitted by the laws or rules of court of a State bring in an appropriate court of that State -

(A) an action based on a violation of the regulations prescribed under this subsection to enjoin such violation,

(B) an action to recover for actual monetary loss from such a violation, or to receive up to $500 in damages for each such violation, whichever is greater, or

(C) both such actions.

It shall be an affirmative defense in any action brought under this paragraph that the defendant has established and implemented, with due care, reasonable practices and procedures to effectively prevent telephone solicitations in violation of the regulations prescribed under this subsection. If the court finds that the defendant willfully or knowingly violated the regulations prescribed under this subsection, the court may, in its discretion, increase the amount of the award to an amount equal to not more than 3 times the amount available under subparagraph (B) of this paragraph.

(6) Relation to subsection (b) The provisions of this subsection shall not be construed to permit a communication prohibited by subsection (b) of this section.

(d) Technical and procedural standards

(1) Prohibition It shall be unlawful for any person within the United States -

(A) to initiate any communication using a telephone facsimile machine, or to make any telephone call using any automatic telephone dialing system, that does not comply with the technical and procedural standards prescribed under this subsection, or to use any telephone facsimile machine or automatic telephone dialing system in a manner that does not

(B) to use a computer or other electronic device to send any message via a telephone facsimile machine unless such person clearly marks, in a margin at the top or bottom of each transmitted page of the message or on the first page of the transmission, the date and time it is sent and an identification of the business, other entity, or individual sending the message and the telephone number of the sending machine or of such business, other entity, or individual.

(2) Telephone facsimile machines The Commission shall revise the regulations setting technical and procedural standards for telephone facsimile machines to require that any such machine which is manufactured after one year after December 20, 1991, clearly marks, in a margin at the top or bottom of each transmitted page or on the first page of each transmission, the date and time sent, an identification of the business, other entity, or individual sending the message, and the telephone number of the sending machine or of such business, other entity, or individual.

(3) Artificial or prerecorded voice systems The Commission shall prescribe technical and procedural standards for systems that are used to transmit any artificial or prerecorded voice message via telephone. Such standards shall require that -

(A) all artificial or prerecorded telephone messages

(i) shall, at the beginning of the message, state clearly the identity of the business, individual, or other entity initiating the call, and

(ii) shall, during or after the message, state clearly the telephone number or address of such business, other entity, or individual; and

(B) any such system will automatically release the called party's line within 5 seconds of the time notification is transmitted to the system that the called party has hung up, to allow the called party's line to be used to make or receive other calls.

(e) Effect on State law

(1) State law not preempted Except for the standards prescribed under subsection (d) of this section and subject to paragraph (2) of this subsection, nothing in this section or in the regulations prescribed under this section shall preempt any State law that imposes more restrictive intrastate requirements or regulations on, or which prohibits -

(A) the use of telephone facsimile machines or other electronic devices to send unsolicited advertisements;

(B) the use of automatic telephone dialing systems;

(C) the use of artificial or prerecorded voice messages; or

(D) the making of telephone solicitations.

(2) State use of databases If, pursuant to subsection (c)(3) of this section, the Commission requires the establishment of a single national database of telephone numbers of subscribers who object to receiving telephone solicitations, a State or local authority may not, in its regulation of telephone solicitations, require the use of any database, list, or listing system that does not include the part of such single national database that relates to such State.

(f) Actions by States

(1) Authority of States Whenever the attorney general of a State, or an official or agency designated by a State, has reason to believe that any person has engaged or is engaging in a pattern or practice of telephone calls or other transmissions to residents of that State in violation of this section or the regulations prescribed under this section, the State may bring a civil action on behalf of its residents to enjoin such calls, an action to recover for actual monetary loss or receive $500 in damages for each violation, or both such actions. If the court finds the defendant willfully or knowingly violated such regulations, the court may, in its discretion, increase the amount of the award to an amount equal to not more than 3 times the amount available under the preceding sentence.

(2) Exclusive jurisdiction of Federal courts The district courts of the United States, the United States courts of any territory, and the District Court of the United States for the District of Columbia shall have exclusive jurisdiction over all civil actions brought under this subsection. Upon proper application, such courts shall also have jurisdiction to issue writs of mandamus, or orders affording like relief, commanding the defendant to comply with the provisions of this section or regulations prescribed under this section, including the requirement that the defendant take such action as is necessary to remove the danger of such violation. Upon a proper showing, a permanent or temporary injunction or restraining order shall be granted without bond.

(3) Rights of Commission The State shall serve prior written notice of any such civil action upon the Commission and provide the Commission with a copy of its complaint, except in any case where such prior notice is not feasible, in which case the State shall serve such notice immediately upon instituting such action. The Commission shall have the right

(A) to intervene in the action,

(B) upon so intervening, to be heard on all matters arising therein, and

(C) to file petitions for appeal.

(4) Venue; service of process Any civil action brought under this subsection in a district court of the United States may be brought in the district wherein the defendant is found or is an inhabitant or transacts business or wherein the violation occurred or is occurring, and process in such cases may be served in any district in which the defendant is an inhabitant or where the defendant may be found.

(5) Investigatory powers For purposes of bringing any civil action under this subsection, nothing in this section shall prevent the attorney general of a State, or an official or agency designated by a State, from exercising the powers conferred on the attorney general or such official by the laws of such State to conduct investigations or to administer oaths or affirmations or to compel the attendance of witnesses or the production of documentary and other evidence.

(6) Effect on State court proceedings Nothing contained in this subsection shall be construed to prohibit an authorized State official from proceeding in State court on the basis of an alleged violation of any general civil or criminal statute of such State.

(7) Limitation Whenever the Commission has instituted a civil action for violation of regulations prescribed under this section, no State may, during the pendency of such action instituted by the Commission, subsequently institute a civil action against any defendant named in the Commission's complaint for any violation as alleged in the Commission's complaint.

(8) "Attorney general" defined As used in this subsection, the term "attorney general" means the chief legal officer of a State.

United States
Driver's Privacy Protection Act

DRIVER'S PRIVACY PROTECTION ACT
(1994)

Summary

The Driver's Privacy Protection Act requires all States to protect the privacy of personal information contained in an individual's motor vehicle record. This information includes the driver's name, address, phone number, Social Security Number, driver identification number, photograph, height, weight, gender, age, certain medical or disability information, and in some states, fingerprints. It does not include information concerning a driver's traffic violations, license status, or accidents.

The Act has a number of exceptions. A driver's personal information may be obtained from the department of motor vehicles for any federal, state or local agency use in carrying out its functions; for any federal, state or local legal proceeding if the proceeding involves a motor vehicle; for automobile and driver safety purposes, such as conducting recall of motor vehicles; and for use in marketing activities if the individual has been given an opportunity to "opt-out."

The Act imposes criminal fines for non-compliance and grants individuals a private right of action including actual and punitive damages as well as attorney's fees and litigation costs.

In 1999 Congress amended the law to give drivers additional privacy protections. The amendment requires State DMVs to obtain a driver's express consent before releasing any personal information, regardless of whether the request is made for a particular individual's information or in bulk for marketing purposes. Previously, such information would be released if the individual had failed to opt out of the disclosure.

In 2000 the Supreme Court upheld the constitutionality of the Drivers Privacy Protection Act following a challenge by the state of South Carolina which alleged that the Act violated principles of federalism. The Court held that the Act is a proper exercise of Congress' authority to regulate interstate commerce under the Commerce Clause.

References

Public Law 103-322 as amended by Public Law 106-69. Codified at 18 USC § 2721.
[http://www4.law.cornell.edu/uscode/18/2721.html]

Condon v. Reno, 528 U.S. ____ (2000).
[http://www.supremecourtus.gov/opinions/99pdf/98-1464.pdf]

United States
Driver's Privacy Protection Act

18 U.S.C. § 2721. Prohibition on release and use of certain personal information from State motor vehicle records

(a) In General. - Except as provided in subsection (b), a State department of motor vehicles, and any officer, employee, or contractor, thereof, shall not knowingly disclose or otherwise make available to any person or entity personal information about any individual obtained by the department in connection with a motor vehicle record.

(b) Permissible Uses. - Personal information referred to in subsection (a) shall be disclosed for use in connection with matters of motor vehicle or driver safety and theft, motor vehicle emissions, motor vehicle product alterations, recalls, or advisories, performance monitoring of motor vehicles and dealers by motor vehicle manufacturers, and removal of non-owner records from the original owner records of motor vehicle manufacturers to carry out the purposes of the Automobile Information Disclosure Act, the Motor Vehicle Information and Cost Saving Act, the National Traffic and Motor Vehicle Safety Act of 1966, the Anti-Car Theft Act of 1992, and the Clean Air Act, and may be disclosed as follows:

(1) For use by any government agency, including any court or law enforcement agency, in carrying out its functions, or any private person or entity acting on behalf of a Federal, State, or local agency in carrying out its functions.

(2) For use in connection with matters of motor vehicle or driver safety and theft; motor vehicle emissions; motor vehicle product alterations, recalls, or advisories; performance monitoring of motor vehicles, motor vehicle parts and dealers; motor vehicle market research activities, including survey research; and removal of non-owner records from the original owner records of motor vehicle manufacturers.

(3) For use in the normal course of business by a legitimate business or its agents, employees, or contractors, but only -

    (A) to verify the accuracy of personal information submitted by the individual to the business or its agents, employees, or contractors; and

    (B) if such information as so submitted is not correct or is no longer correct, to obtain the correct information, but only for the purposes of preventing fraud by, pursuing legal remedies against, or recovering on a debt or security interest against, the individual.

(4) For use in connection with any civil, criminal, administrative, or arbitral proceeding in any Federal, State, or local court or agency or before any self-regulatory body, including the service of process, investigation in anticipation of litigation, and the execution or enforcement of judgments and orders, or pursuant to an order of a Federal, State, or local court.

(5) For use in research activities, and for use in producing statistical reports, so long as the personal information is not published, redisclosed, or used to contact individuals.

(6) For use by any insurer or insurance support organization, or by a self-insured entity, or its agents, employees, or contractors, in connection with claims investigation activities, antifraud activities, rating or underwriting.

(7) For use in providing notice to the owners of towed or impounded vehicles.

(8) For use by any licensed private investigative agency or licensed security service for any purpose permitted under this subsection.

(9) For use by an employer or its agent or insurer to obtain or verify information relating to a holder of a commercial driver's license that is required under the Commercial Motor Vehicle Safety Act of 1986 (49 U.S.C. App. 2710 et seq.)

(10) For use in connection with the operation of private toll transportation facilities.

(11) For any other use in response to requests for individual motor vehicle records if the State has obtained the express consent of the person to whom such personal information pertains.

(12) For bulk distribution for surveys, marketing or solicitations if the State has obtained the express consent of the person to whom such personal information pertains.

(13) For use by any requester, if the requester demonstrates it has obtained the written consent of the individual to whom the information pertains.

(14) For any other use specifically authorized under the law of the State that holds the record, if such use is related to the operation of a motor vehicle or public safety.

(c) Resale or Redisclosure. - An authorized recipient of personal information (except a recipient under subsection (b)(11) or (12)) may resell or redisclose the information only for a use permitted under subsection (b) (but not for uses under subsection (b)(11) or (12)). An authorized recipient under subsection (b)(11) may resell or redisclose personal information for any purpose. An authorized recipient under subsection (b)(12) may resell or redisclose personal information pursuant to subsection (b)(12). Any authorized recipient (except a recipient under subsection (b)(11)) that resells or rediscloses personal information covered by this title must keep for a period of 5 years records identifying each person or entity that receives information and the permitted purpose for which the information will be used and must make such records available to the motor vehicle department upon request.

(d) Waiver Procedures. - A State motor vehicle department may establish and carry out procedures under which the department or its agents, upon receiving a request for personal information that does not fall within one of the exceptions in subsection (b), may mail a copy of the request to the individual about whom the information was requested, informing such individual of the request, together with a statement to the effect that the information will not be released unless the individual waives such individual's right to privacy under this section.

Sec. 2722. Additional unlawful acts

(a) Procurement for Unlawful Purpose. - It shall be unlawful for any person knowingly to obtain or disclose personal information, from a motor vehicle record, for any use not permitted under section 2721(b) of this title.

(b) False Representation. - It shall be unlawful for any person to make false representation to obtain any personal information from an individual's motor vehicle record.

Sec. 2723. Penalties

(a) Criminal Fine. - A person who knowingly violates this chapter shall be fined under this title.

(b) Violations by State Department of Motor Vehicles. - Any State department of motor vehicles that has a policy or practice of substantial noncompliance with this chapter shall be subject to a civil penalty imposed by the Attorney General of not more than $5,000 a day for each day of substantial noncompliance.

Sec. 2724. Civil action

(a) Cause of Action. - A person who knowingly obtains, discloses or uses personal information, from a motor vehicle record, for a purpose not permitted under this chapter shall be liable to the individual to whom the information pertains, who may bring a civil action in a United States district court.

(b) Remedies. - The court may award - (1) actual damages, but not less than liquidated damages in the amount of $2,500; (2) punitive damages upon proof of willful or reckless disregard of the law; (3) reasonable attorneys' fees and other litigation costs reasonably incurred; and (4) such other preliminary and equitable relief as the court determines to be appropriate.

Sec. 2725. Definitions

In this chapter -

(1) "motor vehicle record" means any record that pertains to a motor vehicle operator's permit, motor vehicle title, motor vehicle registration, or identification card issued by a department of motor vehicles;

(2) "person" means an individual, organization or entity, but does not include a State or agency thereof; and

(3) "personal information" means information that identifies an individual, including an individual's photograph, social security number, driver identification number, name, address (but not the 5-digit zip code), telephone number, and medical or disability information, but does not include information on vehicular accidents, driving violations, and driver's status.

United States
Telecommunications Act

TELECOMMUNICATIONS ACT (1996)
[EXCERPT]

Summary

The Telecommunications Act of 1996 amends the 1934 Communications Act. Section 222 of the Act provides that telecommunications carriers must protect the confidentiality of Consumer Proprietary Network Information (CPNI). CPNI includes calling patterns, billing records, unlisted telephone numbers and home addresses of service subscribers. The Act further provides that carriers receiving CPNI in connection with providing services can use the information only for that purpose and not for their own marketing purposes. Moreover, the Act allows carriers to use, disclose, and permit access to individually identifiable CPNI only when directed by the consumer or in connection with providing services for the consumer.

In 1998 the Federal Communications Commission issued a Second Report and Order and Further Notice of Proposed Rulemaking, which interpreted and implemented Section 222 of the Telecommunications Act of 1996. The FCC's Order adopted an opt-in approach, requiring carriers to obtain express approval before disclosing a customer's CPNI. However, in 1999 a federal appeals court vacated the FCC's Order, holding that the regulations of the FCC violated the First Amendment.

In 1999 the Congress enacted the Wireless Communications and Public Safety Act which promoted the use of 9-1-1, the universal emergency assistance number, and established certain privacy safeguards to limit the use of call location information to the delivery of emergency services and to further limit the use of wireless location information to those circumstances where the customer has provided "express prior authorization."

References

Public Law 104-104 ad amended by Public Law 106-81. Codified at 47 USC §222. [http://www4.law.cornell.edu/uscode/47/222.html]

"In the Matter of Implementation of the Telecommunications Act of 1996: Telecommunications Carriers' Use of Customer Proprietary Network Information and Other Customer Information," adopted May 21, 1998.
Order: http://www.fcc.gov/Bureaus/Common_Carrier/Orders/1998/da980971.pdf

US West v. FCC, No. 98-9518 (10th Cir. 1999)
[http://www.kscourts.org/ca10/cases/1999/08/98-9518.htm]

Sec. 222. Privacy of customer information

(a) In general Every telecommunications carrier has a duty to protect the confidentiality of proprietary information of, and relating to, other telecommunication carriers, equipment manufacturers, and customers, including telecommunication carriers reselling telecommunications services provided by a telecommunications carrier.

(b) Confidentiality of carrier information A telecommunications carrier that receives or obtains proprietary information from another carrier for purposes of providing any telecommunications service shall use such information only for such purpose, and shall not use such information for its own marketing efforts.

(c) Confidentiality of customer proprietary network information

(1) Privacy requirements for telecommunications carriers Except as required by law or with the approval of the customer, a telecommunications carrier that receives or obtains customer proprietary network information by virtue of its provision of a telecommunications service shall only use, disclose, or permit access to individually identifiable customer proprietary network information in its provision of (A) the telecommunications service from which such information is derived, or (B) services necessary to, or used in, the provision of such telecommunications service, including the publishing of directories.

(2) Disclosure on request by customers A telecommunications carrier shall disclose customer proprietary network information, upon affirmative written request by the customer, to any person designated by the customer.

(3) Aggregate customer information A telecommunications carrier that receives or obtains customer proprietary network information by virtue of its provision of a telecommunications service may use, disclose, or permit access to aggregate customer information other than for the purposes described in paragraph (1). A local exchange carrier may use, disclose, or permit access to aggregate customer information other than for purposes described in paragraph (1) only if it provides such aggregate information to other carriers or persons on reasonable and nondiscriminatory terms and conditions upon reasonable request therefor.

(d) Exceptions Nothing in this section prohibits a telecommunications carrier from using, disclosing, or permitting access to customer proprietary network information obtained from its customers, either directly or indirectly through its agents -

(1) to initiate, render, bill, and collect for telecommunications services;

(2) to protect the rights or property of the carrier, or to protect users of those services and other carriers from fraudulent, abusive, or unlawful use of, or subscription to, such services;

(3) to provide any inbound telemarketing, referral, or administrative services to the customer for the duration of the call, if such call was initiated by the customer and the customer approves of the use of such information to provide such service; and

(4) to provide call location information concerning the user of a commercial mobile service (as such term is defined in section 332(d) of this title) -

(A) to a public safety answering point, emergency medical service provider or emergency dispatch provider, public safety, fire service, or law enforcement official, or hospital emergency or trauma care facility, in order to respond to the user's call for emergency services;

(B) to inform the user's legal guardian or members of the user's immediate family of the user's location in an emergency situation that involves the risk of death or serious physical harm; or

(C) to providers of information or database management services solely for purposes of assisting in the delivery of emergency services in response to an emergency.

(e) Subscriber list information Notwithstanding subsections (b), (c), and (d) of this section, a telecommunications carrier that provides telephone exchange service shall provide subscriber list information gathered in its capacity as a provider of such service on a timely and unbundled basis, under nondiscriminatory and reasonable rates, terms, and conditions, to any person upon request for the purpose of publishing directories in any format.

(f) Authority to use wireless location information For purposes of subsection (c)(1) of this section, without the express prior authorization of the customer, a customer shall not be considered to have approved the use or disclosure of or access to -

(1) call location information concerning the user of a commercial mobile service (as such term is defined in section 332(d) of this title), other than in accordance with subsection (d)(4) of this section; or

(2) automatic crash notification information to any person other than for use in the operation of an automatic crash notification system.

(g) Subscriber listed and unlisted information for emergency services Notwithstanding subsections (b), (c), and (d) of this section, a telecommunications carrier that provides telephone exchange service shall provide information described in subsection (i)(3)(A) [1] of this section (including information pertaining to subscribers whose information is unlisted or unpublished) that is in its possession or control (including information pertaining to subscribers of other carriers) on a timely and unbundled basis, under nondiscriminatory and reasonable rates, terms, and conditions to providers of emergency services, and providers of emergency support services, solely for purposes of delivering or assisting in the delivery of emergency services.

(h) Definitions As used in this section:

(1) Customer proprietary network information The term "customer proprietary network information" means -

(A) information that relates to the quantity, technical configuration, type, destination, location, and amount of use of a telecommunications service subscribed to by any customer of a telecommunications carrier, and that is made available to the carrier by the customer solely by virtue of the carrier-customer relationship; and

(B) information contained in the bills pertaining to telephone exchange service or telephone toll service received by a customer of a carrier; except that such term does not include subscriber list information.

(2) Aggregate information The term "aggregate customer information" means collective data that relates to a group or category of services or customers, from which individual customer identities and characteristics have been removed.

(3) Subscriber list information The term "subscriber list information" means any information -

(A) identifying the listed names of subscribers of a carrier and such subscribers' telephone numbers, addresses, or primary advertising classifications (as such classifications are assigned at the time of the establishment of such service), or any combination of such listed names, numbers, addresses, or classifications; and

(B) that the carrier or an affiliate has published, caused to be published, or accepted for publication in any directory format.

(4) Public safety answering point The term "public safety answering point" means a facility that has been designated to receive emergency calls and route them to emergency service personnel.

(5) Emergency services The term "emergency services" means 9-1-1 emergency services and emergency notification services.

(6) Emergency notification services The term "emergency notification services" means services that notify the public of an emergency.

(7) Emergency support services The term "emergency support services" means information or data base management services used in support of emergency services.

United States
Children's Online Privacy Protection Act

CHILDREN'S ONLINE PRIVACY
PROTECTION ACT (1998)

Summary

The Children's Online Privacy Protection Act of 1998 prohibits an operator of a website or online service directed to children, or any operator having actual knowledge that it is doing so, from collecting personal information from a child in a manner that violates regulations required under this title which are designed to protect such children from unlawful and deceptive practices in the collection of personal information. Provides an exception for information disclosed to a child's parent.

The Act directs the Federal Trade Commission (FTC) to prescribe regulations requiring such operators to follow specified procedures in connection with the collection and use of personal information from children, including: (1) obtaining verifiable parental consent for the collection, use, or disclosure of such information; and (2) requiring such operators to establish and maintain procedures to protect the confidentiality, security, and integrity of collected information. It provides exceptions to the parental consent requirement. The Act allows an operator to satisfy such regulatory requirements by following a set of FTC-approved self-regulatory guidelines established by appropriate online representatives. The Act directs the FTC to provide incentives for such self-regulation.

The Act authorizes the States to enforce such regulations by bringing actions on behalf of its residents, requiring the appropriate attorney general to first notify the FTC of such action. It authorizes the FTC to intervene in any such action, and it provides for enforcement through the Federal Trade Commission Act. It also directs the FTC to review and report to the Congress on implementation.

References

Public Law 105-277 codified at 16 USC § 6501
[http://www4.law.cornell.edu/uscode/15/6501.html]

15 USC § 6501. Definitions

In this title:

(1) Child. The term "child" means an individual under the age of 13.

(2) Operator. The term "operator"–

(A) means any person who operates a website located on the Internet or an online service and who collects or maintains personal information from or about the users of or visitors to such website or online service, or on whose behalf such information is collected or maintained, where such website or online service is operated for commercial purposes, including any person offering products or services for sale through that website or online service, involving commerce–

(i) among the several States or with 1 or more foreign nations;

(ii) in any territory of the United States or in the District of Columbia, or between any such territory and–

(I) another such territory; or

(II) any State or foreign nation; or

(iii) between the District of Columbia and any State, territory, or foreign nation; but

(B) does not include any nonprofit entity that would otherwise be exempt from coverage under section 5 of the Federal Trade Commission Act.

(3) Commission. The term "Commission" means the Federal Trade Commission.

(4) Disclosure. The term "disclosure" means, with respect to personal information–

(A) the release of personal information collected from a child in identifiable form by an operator for any purpose, except where such information is provided to a person other than the operator who provides support for the internal operations of the website and does not disclose or use that information for any other purpose; and

(B) making personal information collected from a child by a website or online service directed to children or with actual knowledge that such information was collected from a child, publicly available in identifiable form, by any means including by a public posting, through the Internet, or through–

(i) a home page of a website;

(ii) a pen pal service;

(iii) an electronic mail service;

(iv) a message board; or

(v) a chat room.

(5) Federal agency. The term "Federal agency" means an agency, as that term is defined in section 551(1) of title 5, United States Code.

(6) Internet. The term "Internet" means collectively the myriad of computer and telecommunications facilities, including equipment and operating software, which comprise the interconnected world-wide network of networks that employ the Transmission Control Protocol/Internet Protocol, or any predecessor or successor protocols to such protocol, to communicate information of all kinds by wire or radio.

(7) Parent. The term "parent" includes a legal guardian.

(8) Personal information. The term "personal information" means individually identifiable information about an individual collected online, including–

(A) a first and last name;

(B) a home or other physical address including street name and name of a city or town;

(C) an e-mail address;

(D) a telephone number;

(E) a Social Security number;

(F) any other identifier that the Commission determines permits the physical or online contacting of a specific individual; or

(G) information concerning the child or the parents of that child that the website collects online from the child and combines with an identifier described in this paragraph.

(9) Verifiable parental consent. The term "verifiable parental consent" means any reasonable effort (taking into consideration available technology), including a request for authorization for future collection, use, and disclosure described in the notice, to ensure that a parent of a child receives notice of the operator's personal information collection, use, and disclosure practices, and authorizes the collection, use, and disclosure, as applicable, of personal information and the subsequent use of that information before that information is collected from that child.

(10) Website or online service directed to children.

(A) In general. The term "website or online service directed to children" means–

(i) a commercial website or online service that is targeted to children; or

(ii) that portion of a commercial website or online service that is targeted to children.

(B) Limitation. A commercial website or online service, or a portion of a commercial website or online service, shall not be deemed directed to children solely for referring or linking to a commercial website or online service directed to children by using information location tools, including a directory, index, reference, pointer, or hypertext link.

(11) Person. The term "person" means any individual, partnership, corporation, trust, estate, cooperative, association, or other entity.

(12) Online contact information. The term "online contact information" means an e-mail address or another substantially similar identifier that permits direct contact with a person online.

§ 6502. Regulation of unfair and deceptive acts and practices in connection with the collection and use of personal information from and about children on the Internet

(a) Acts prohibited

(1) In general. It is unlawful for an operator of a website or online service directed to children, or any operator that has actual knowledge that it is collecting personal information from a child, to collect personal information from a child in a manner that violates the regulations prescribed under subsection (b).

(2) Disclosure to parent protected. Notwithstanding paragraph (1), neither an operator of such a website or online service nor the operator's agent shall be held to

be liable under any Federal or State law for any disclosure made in good faith and following reasonable procedures in responding to a request for disclosure of personal information under subsection (b)(1)(B)(iii) to the parent of a child.

(b) Regulations.

(1) In general. Not later than 1 year after the date of the enactment of this Act [enacted Oct. 21, 1998], the Commission shall promulgate under section 553 of title 5, United States Code, regulations that–

(A) require the operator of any website or online service directed to children that collects personal information from children or the operator of a website or online service that has actual knowledge that it is collecting personal information from a child–

(i) to provide notice on the website of what information is collected from children by the operator, how the operator uses such information, and the operator's disclosure practices for such information; and

(ii) to obtain verifiable parental consent for the collection, use, or disclosure of personal information from children;

(B) require the operator to provide, upon request of a parent under this subparagraph whose child has provided personal information to that website or online service, upon proper identification of that parent, to such parent–

(i) a description of the specific types of personal information collected from the child by that operator;

(ii) the opportunity at any time to refuse to permit the operator's further use or maintenance in retrievable form, or future online collection, of personal information from that child; and

(iii) notwithstanding any other provision of law, a means that is reasonable under the circumstances for the parent to obtain any personal information collected from that child;

(C) prohibit conditioning a child's participation in a game, the offering of a prize, or another activity on the child disclosing more personal information than is reasonably necessary to participate in such activity; and

(D) require the operator of such a website or online service to establish and maintain reasonable procedures to protect the confidentiality, security, and integrity of personal information collected from children.

(2) When consent not required. The regulations shall provide that verifiable parental consent under paragraph (1)(A)(ii) is not required in the case of–

(A) online contact information collected from a child that is used only to respond directly on a one-time basis to a specific request from the child and is not used to recontact the child and is not maintained in retrievable form by the operator;

(B) a request for the name or online contact information of a parent or child that is used for the sole purpose of obtaining parental consent or providing notice under this section and where such information is not maintained in retrievable form by the operator if parental consent is not obtained after a reasonable time;

(C) online contact information collected from a child that is used only to respond more than once directly to a specific request from the child and is not used to recontact the child beyond the scope of that request–

(i) if, before any additional response after the initial response to the child, the operator uses reasonable efforts to provide a parent notice of the online contact information collected from the child, the purposes for which it is to be used, and an opportunity for the parent to request that the operator make no further use of the information and that it not be maintained in retrievable form; or

(ii) without notice to the parent in such circumstances as the Commission may determine are appropriate, taking into consideration the benefits to the child of access to information and services, and risks to the security and privacy of the child, in regulations promulgated under this subsection;

(D) the name of the child and online contact information (to the extent reasonably necessary to protect the safety of a child participant on the site)–

(i) used only for the purpose of protecting such safety;

(ii) not used to recontact the child or for any other purpose; and

(iii) not disclosed on the site,

if the operator uses reasonable efforts to provide a parent notice of the name and online contact information collected from the child, the purposes for which it is to be used, and an opportunity for the parent to request that the operator make no further use of the information and that it not be maintained in retrievable form; or

(E) the collection, use, or dissemination of such information by the operator of such a website or online service necessary–

(i) to protect the security or integrity of its website;

(ii) to take precautions against liability;

(iii) to respond to judicial process; or

(iv) to the extent permitted under other provisions of law, to provide information to law enforcement agencies or for an investigation on a matter related to public safety.

(3) Termination of service. The regulations shall permit the operator of a website or an online service to terminate service provided to a child whose parent has refused, under the regulations prescribed under paragraph (1)(B)(ii), to permit the operator's further use or maintenance in retrievable form, or future online collection, of personal information from that child.

(c) Enforcement. Subject to sections 1304 and 1306 [15 USCS § § 6503 and 6505], a violation of a regulation prescribed under subsection (a) shall be treated as a violation of a rule defining an unfair or deceptive act or practice prescribed under section 18(a)(1)(B) of the Federal Trade Commission Act *(15 U.S.C. 57a*(a)(1)(B)).

(d) Inconsistent State law. No State or local government may impose any liability for commercial activities or actions by operators in interstate or foreign commerce in connection with an activity or action described in this title that is inconsistent with the treatment of those activities or actions under this section.

§ 6503. Safe harbors

(a) Guidelines. An operator may satisfy the requirements of regulations issued under section 1303(b) *[15 USCS § 6502*(b)] by following a set of self-regulatory guidelines, issued by representatives of the marketing or online industries, or by other persons, approved under subsection (b).

(b) Incentives.

(1) Self-regulatory incentives. In prescribing regulations under section 1303 *[15 USCS § 6502]*, the Commission shall provide incentives for self-regulation by operators to implement the protections afforded children under the regulatory requirements described in subsection (b) of that section.

(2) Deemed compliance. Such incentives shall include provisions for ensuring that a person will be deemed to be in compliance with the requirements of the regulations under section 1303 *[15 USCS § 6502]* if that person complies with guidelines that, after notice and comment, are approved by the Commission upon making a determination that the guidelines meet the requirements of the regulations issued under section 1303 *[15 USCS § 6502]*.

(3) Expedited response to requests. The Commission shall act upon requests for safe harbor treatment within 180 days of the filing of the request, and shall set forth in writing its conclusions with regard to such requests.

(c) Appeals. Final action by the Commission on a request for approval of guidelines, or the failure to act within 180 days on a request for approval of guidelines, submitted under subsection (b) may be appealed to a district court of the United States of appropriate jurisdiction as provided for in section 706 of title 5, United States Code.

§ 6504. Actions by States

(a) In general.

(1) Civil actions. In any case in which the attorney general of a State has reason to believe that an interest of the residents of that State has been or is threatened or adversely affected by the engagement of any person in a practice that violates any regulation of the Commission prescribed under section 1303(b) *[15 USCS § 6502*(b)], the State, as parens patriae, may bring a civil action on behalf of the residents of the State in a district court of the United States of appropriate jurisdiction to–

(A) enjoin that practice;

(B) enforce compliance with the regulation;

(C) obtain damage, restitution, or other compensation on behalf of residents of the State; or

(D) obtain such other relief as the court may consider to be appropriate.

(2) Notice.

(A) In general. Before filing an action under paragraph (1), the attorney general of the State involved shall provide to the Commission–

(i) written notice of that action; and

(ii) a copy of the complaint for that action.

(B) Exemption.

(i) In general. Subparagraph (A) shall not apply with respect to the filing of an action by an attorney general of a State under this subsection, if the attorney general determines that it is not feasible to provide the notice described in that subparagraph before the filing of the action.

(ii) Notification. In an action described in clause (i), the attorney general of a State shall provide notice and a copy of the complaint to the Commission at the same time as the attorney general files the action.

(b) Intervention.

(1) In general. On receiving notice under subsection (a)(2), the Commission shall have the right to intervene in the action that is the subject of the notice.

(2) Effect of intervention. If the Commission intervenes in an action under subsection (a), it shall have the right–

(A) to be heard with respect to any matter that arises in that action; and

(B) to file a petition for appeal.

(3) Amicus curiae. Upon application to the court, a person whose self-regulatory guidelines have been approved by the Commission and are relied upon as a defense by any defendant to a proceeding under this section may file amicus curiae in that proceeding.

(c) Construction. For purposes of bringing any civil action under subsection (a), nothing in this title shall be construed to prevent an attorney general of a State from exercising the powers conferred on the attorney general by the laws of that State to–

(1) conduct investigations;

(2) administer oaths or affirmations; or

(3) compel the attendance of witnesses or the production of documentary and other evidence.

(d) Actions by the Commission. In any case in which an action is instituted by or on behalf of the Commission for violation of any regulation prescribed under section 1303, no State may, during the pendency of that action, institute an action under subsection (a) against any defendant named in the complaint in that action for violation of that regulation.

(e) Venue; service of process.

(1) Venue. Any action brought under subsection (a) may be brought in the district court of the United States that meets applicable requirements relating to venue under section 1391 of title 28, United States Code.

(2) Service of process. In an action brought under subsection (a), process may be served in any district in which the defendant–

(A) is an inhabitant; or

(B) may be found.

§ 6505. Administration and applicability of Act

(a) In general. Except as otherwise provided, this title [15 USCS § § 6501 et seq.] shall be enforced by the Commission under the Federal Trade Commission Act (15 U.S.C. 41 et seq.).

(b) Provisions. Compliance with the requirements imposed under this title [15 USCS § § 6501 et seq.] shall be enforced under–

(1) section 8 of the Federal Deposit Insurance Act (12 U.S.C. 1818), in the case of–

(A) national banks, and Federal branches and Federal agencies of foreign banks, by the Office of the Comptroller of the Currency;

(B) member banks of the Federal Reserve System (other than national banks), branches and agencies of foreign banks (other than Federal branches, Federal agencies, and insured State branches of foreign banks), commercial lending companies owned or controlled by foreign banks, and organizations operating under section 25 or 25(a) of the Federal Reserve Act (12 U.S.C. 601 et seq. and 611 et seq.), by the Board; and

(C) banks insured by the Federal Deposit Insurance Corporation (other than members of the Federal Reserve System) and insured State branches of foreign banks, by the Board of Directors of the Federal Deposit Insurance Corporation;

(2) section 8 of the Federal Deposit Insurance Act (12 U.S.C. 1818), by the Director of the Office of Thrift Supervision, in the case of a savings association the deposits of which are insured by the Federal Deposit Insurance Corporation;

(3) the Federal Credit Union Act (12 U.S.C. 1751 et seq.) by the National Credit Union Administration Board with respect to any Federal credit union;

(4) part A of subtitle VII of title 49, United States Code [49 USCS § § 40101 et seq.], by the Secretary of Transportation with respect to any air carrier or foreign air carrier subject to that part;

(5) the Packers and Stockyards Act, 1921 (7 U.S.C. 181 et seq.) (except as provided in section 406 of that Act (7 U.S.C. 226, 227)), by the Secretary of Agriculture with respect to any activities subject to that Act; and

(6) the Farm Credit Act of 1971 (12 U.S.C. 2001 et seq.) by the Farm Credit Administration with respect to any Federal land bank, Federal land bank association, Federal intermediate credit bank, or production credit association.

(c) Exercise of certain powers. For the purpose of the exercise by any agency referred to in subsection (a) of its powers under any Act referred to in that subsection, a violation of any requirement imposed under this title shall be deemed to be a violation of a requirement imposed under that Act. In addition to its powers under any provision of law specifically referred to in subsection (a), each of the agencies referred to in that subsection may exercise, for the purpose of enforcing compliance with any requirement imposed under this title [*15 USCS § § 6501* et seq.], any other authority conferred on it by law.

(d) Actions by the Commission. The Commission shall prevent any person from violating a rule of the Commission under section 1303 [*15 USCS § 6502*] in the same manner, by the same means, and with the same jurisdiction, powers, and duties as though all applicable terms and provisions of the Federal Trade Commission Act *(15 U.S.C. 41* et seq.) were incorporated into and made a part of this title. Any entity that violates such rule shall be subject to the penalties and entitled to the privileges and immunities provided in the Federal Trade Commission Act in the same manner, by the same means, and with the same jurisdiction, power, and duties as though all applicable terms and provisions of the Federal Trade Commission Act were incorporated into and made a part of this title [*15 USCS § § 6501* et seq.].

(e) Effect on other laws. Nothing contained in the Act shall be construed to limit the authority of the Commission under any other provisions of law.

FINANCIAL MODERNIZATION
SERVICES ACT (1999) [EXCERPTS]

Summary

The Financial Modernization and Privacy Act (also known as the Gramm-Leach-Bliley Act or GLB) is regarded as the most sweeping legislation affecting banks and other financial institutions since the Depression. The passage of GLB permits banks, insurance companies, and brokerage firms to operate as one entity, transforming them into a "financial supermarket" and enabling them to offer a wider range of products and services.

The consolidation of these financial institutions, however, has great implications for consumer privacy rights. It enables financial institutions to share consumer information with their affiliates (other commonly owned companies) for sales and promotional purposes. Hence, to regulate the disclosure of consumer data amongst affiliates, GLB requires financial institutions to give consumers a Privacy Policy notice informing them of the kind of information it collects about the individual and how it uses that information. It also requires financial institutions to give consumers the right to opt-out or prevent the sale of personal data to third parties. Moreover, GLB requires financial institutions to develop policies to prevent fraudulent access to confidential financial information. July 1, 2001 is the deadline for financial institutions to comply with the notice requirements.

Although GLB prohibits financial institutions from disclosing nonpublic information, such as an individual's account number or access code to a third party non-affiliated company (an outside company), it does not prevent these institutions from selling publicly available information, that is information the financial institution reasonably believes is lawfully made available to the general public, to a non-affiliated telemarketer. Thus, if the consumer does not opt-out, the institution is free to sell, lease or otherwise disclose almost anything in its files about the consumer, including medical information, to non-affiliates.

Under GLB the consumer has no private right of action if a financial institution violates GLB privacy requirements. However, the consumer can complain to one of the seven federal agencies that have jurisdiction and enforcement authority over financial institutions under GLB. Once a complaint is made the enforcing agency will investigate the complaint and may bring a court action or an administrative case against the company. However, the agency cannot represent or give legal advice to the complaining party.

Seven federal agencies enforce the privacy provisions of the GLB. They include the Federal Deposit Insurance Corporation (FDIC), the Federal Reserve, the Office of Thrift Supervision), the Office of Comptroller of the Currency (OCC), the National Credit Union Administration (NCUA), the Securities and Exchange Commission (SEC) and the Federal Trade Commission (FTC).

United States
Financial Modernization Services Act

References

Public Law, 106-102, Gramm-Leach-Bliley Act of 1999
[http://thomas.loc.gov/cgi-bin/query/z?c106:S.900.ENR:]

Senate Report, 106-44, Financial Services Modernization Act of 1999
[http://thomas.loc.gov/cgi-bin/cpquery/R?cp106:FLD010:@1(sr044)]

House Report, 106-434, Gramm-Leach-Bliley Act of 1999
[http://thomas.loc.gov/cgi-bin/cpquery/R?cp106:FLD010:@1(hr434)]

Federal Deposit Insurance Corporation (FDIC)
[http://www.fdic.gov/consumers/questions/customer]

Federal Reserve
[http://www.federalreserve.gov/pubs/complaints]

Office of Thrift Supervision
[http://www.ots.treas.gov/contacts.html]

Office of Comptroller of the Currency (OCC)
[http://www.occ.treas.gov/customer.htm]

National Credit Union Administration (NCUA)
[http://www.ncua.gov/talk2ncua/talk2ncua.html]

The Securities and Exchange Commission (SEC)
[http://www.sec.gov/consumer/compform.htm]

The Federal Trade Commission (FTC)
[http://www.ftc.gov/privacy/]

L. Richard Fischer, *The Law of Financial Privacy* (A.S. Pratt & Sons 2000)

§ 501. Protection of non-public personal information.

(a) Privacy obligation policy. It is the policy of the Congress that each financial institution has an affirmative and continuing obligation to respect the privacy of its customers and to protect the security and confidentiality of those customers' nonpublic personal information.

(b) Financial institutions safeguards. In furtherance of the policy in subsection (a), each agency or authority described in section 505(a) shall establish appropriate standards for the financial institutions subject to their jurisdiction relating to administrative, technical, and physical safeguards--

    (1) to insure the security and confidentiality of customer records and information

    (2) to protect against any anticipated threats or hazards to the security or integrity of such records; and

    (3) to protect against unauthorized access to or use of such records or information which could result in substantial harm or inconvenience to any customer.

§ 502. Obligations with respect to disclosures of personal information.

(a) Notice requirements.

Except as otherwise provided in this subtitle, a financial institution may not, directly or through any affiliate, disclose to a nonaffiliated third party any nonpublic personal information, unless such financial institution provides or has provided to the consumer a notice that complies with section 503.

(b) Opt-out.

    (1) In general. A financial institution may not disclose nonpublic personal information to a nonaffiliated third party unless--

        (A) such financial institution clearly and conspicuously discloses to the consumer, in writing or in electronic form or other form permitted by the regulations prescribed under section 504, that such information may be disclosed to such third party;

        (B) the consumer is given the opportunity, before the time that such information is initially disclosed, to direct that such information not be disclosed to such third party; and

        (C) the consumer is given an explanation of how the consumer can exercise that nondisclosure option.

    (2) Exception. This subsection shall not prevent a financial institution from providing nonpublic personal information to a nonaffiliated third party to perform services for or functions on behalf of the financial institution, including marketing of the financial institution's own products or services, or financial products or services offered pursuant to joint agreements between two or more financial institutions that comply with the requirements imposed by the regulations prescribed under section 504, if the financial institution fully discloses the providing of such information and enters into a contractual agreement with the third party that requires the third party to maintain the confidentiality of such information.

(c) Limits on reuse of information. Except as otherwise provided in this subtitle, a nonaffiliated third party that receives from a financial institution nonpublic personal information under this section shall not, directly or through an affiliate of such receiving third party, disclose such information to any other person that is a nonaffiliated third party of both the financial institution and such receiving third party, unless such disclosure would be lawful if made directly to such other person by the financial institution.

(d) Limitations on the sharing of account number information for marketing purposes. A financial institution shall not disclose, other than to a consumer reporting agency, an account number or similar form of access number or access code for a credit card account, deposit account, or transaction account of a consumer to any nonaffiliated third party for use in telemarketing, direct mail marketing, or other marketing through electronic mail to the consumer.

(e) General exceptions. Subsections (a) and (b) shall not prohibit the disclosure of nonpublic personal information--

> (1) as necessary to effect, administer, or enforce a transaction requested or authorized by the consumer, or in connection with--
>> (A) servicing or processing a financial product or service requested or authorized by the consumer;
>> (B) maintaining or servicing the consumer's account with the financial institution, or with another entity as part of a private label credit card program or other extension of credit on behalf of such entity; or
>> (C) a proposed or actual securitization, secondary market sale (including sales of servicing rights), or similar transaction related to a transaction of the consumer;
> (2) with the consent or at the direction of the consumer;
>> (A) to protect the confidentiality or security of the financial institution's records pertaining to the consumer, the service or product, or the transaction therein;
>> (B) to protect against or prevent actual or potential fraud, unauthorized transactions, claims, or other liability;
>> (C) for required institutional risk control, or for resolving customer disputes or inquiries;
>> (D) to persons holding a legal or beneficial interest relating to the consumer; or
>> (E) to persons acting in a fiduciary or representative capacity on behalf of the consumer;
> (4) to provide information to insurance rate advisory organizations, guaranty funds or agencies, applicable rating agencies of the financial institution, persons assessing the institution's compliance with industry standards, and the institution's attorneys, accountants, and auditors;
> (5) to the extent specifically permitted or required under other provisions of law and in accordance with the Right to Financial Privacy Act of 1978, to law enforcement agencies (including a Federal functional regulator, the Secretary of the Treasury with respect to subchapter II of chapter 53 of title 31, United States Code, and chapter 2 of title I of Public Law 91-508 (12 U.S.C. 1951-1959), a State insurance

authority, or the Federal Trade Commission), self-regulatory organizations, or for an investigation on a matter related to public safety;

(6)(A) to a consumer reporting agency in accordance with the Fair Credit Reporting Act, or (B) from a consumer report reported by a consumer reporting agency;

(7) in connection with a proposed or actual sale, merger, transfer, or exchange of all or a portion of a business or operating unit if the disclosure of nonpublic personal information concerns solely consumers of such business or unit; or

(8) to comply with Federal, State, or local laws, rules, and other applicable legal requirements; to comply with a properly authorized civil, criminal, or regulatory investigation or subpoena or summons by Federal, State, or local authorities; or to respond to judicial process or government regulatory authorities having jurisdiction over the financial institution for examination, compliance, or other purposes as authorized by law.

§ 503. Disclosure of institution privacy

(a) Disclosure required - At the time of establishing a customer relationship with a consumer and not less than annually during the continuation of such relationship, a financial institution shall provide a clear and conspicuous disclosure to such consumer, in writing or in electronic form or other form permitted by the regulations prescribed under section 504, of such financial institution's policies and practices with respect to--

(1) disclosing nonpublic personal information to affiliates and nonaffiliated third parties, consistent with section 502, including the categories of information that may be disclosed;

(2) disclosing nonpublic personal information of persons who have ceased to be customers of the financial institution; and

(3) protecting the nonpublic personal information of consumers.

Such disclosures shall be made in accordance with the regulations prescribed under section 504.

(b) Information to be included - The disclosure required by subsection (a) shall include--

(1) the policies and practices of the institution with respect to disclosing nonpublic personal information to nonaffiliated third parties, other than agents of the institution, consistent with section 502 of this subtitle, and including--

(A) the categories of persons to whom the information is or may be disclosed, other than the persons to whom the information may be provided pursuant to section 502(e); and

(B) the policies and practices of the institution with respect to disclosing of nonpublic personal information of persons who have ceased to be customers of the financial institution;

(2) the categories of nonpublic personal information that are collected by the financial institution;

(3) the policies that the institution maintains to protect the confidentiality and security of nonpublic personal information in accordance with section 501; and

(4) the disclosures required, if any, under section 603(d)(2)(A)(iii) of the Fair Credit Reporting Act.

§ 504. Rulemaking.

(a) Regulatory Authority

(1) Rulemaking- The Federal banking agencies, the National Credit Union Administration, the Secretary of the Treasury, the Securities and Exchange Commission, and the Federal Trade Commission shall each prescribe, after consultation as appropriate with representatives of State insurance authorities designated by the National Association of Insurance Commissioners, such regulations as may be necessary to carry out the purposes of this subtitle with respect to the financial institutions subject to their jurisdiction under section 505.

(2) Coordination, consistency, and comparability - Each of the agencies and authorities required under paragraph (1) to prescribe regulations shall consult and coordinate with the other such agencies and authorities for the purposes of assuring, to the extent possible, that the regulations prescribed by each such agency and authority are consistent and comparable with the regulations prescribed by the other such agencies and authorities.

(3) Procedures and deadline - Such regulations shall be prescribed in accordance with applicable requirements of title 5, United States Code, and shall be issued in final form not later than 6 months after the date of the enactment of this Act.

(b) Authority to grant exceptions - The regulations prescribed under subsection (a) may include such additional exceptions to subsections (a) through (d) of section 502 as are deemed consistent with the purposes of this subtitle.

§ 505. Enforcement.

(a) In general - This subtitle and the regulations prescribed thereunder shall be enforced by the Federal functional regulators, the State insurance authorities, and the Federal Trade Commission with respect to financial institutions and other persons subject to their jurisdiction under applicable law, as follows:

(1) Under section 8 of the Federal Deposit Insurance Act, in the case of--

(A) national banks, Federal branches and Federal agencies of foreign banks, and any subsidiaries of such entities (except brokers, dealers, persons providing insurance, investment companies, and investment advisers), by the Office of the Comptroller of the Currency;

(B) member banks of the Federal Reserve System (other than national banks), branches and agencies of foreign banks (other than Federal branches, Federal agencies, and insured State branches of foreign banks), commercial lending companies owned or controlled by foreign banks, organizations operating under section 25 or 25A of the Federal Reserve Act, and bank holding companies and their nonbank or affiliates (except brokers, dealers, persons providing insurance, investment companies, and investment advisers), by the Board of Governors of the Federal Reserve System;

(C) banks insured by the Federal Deposit Insurance Corporation (other than members of the Federal Reserve System), insured State branches of foreign banks, and any subsidiaries of such entities (except brokers, dealers, persons providing insurance, investment companies, and investment advisers), by the Board of Directors of the Federal Deposit Insurance Corporation; and

(D) savings associations the deposits of which are insured by the Federal Deposit Insurance Corporation, and any subsidiaries of such savings associations (except brokers, dealers, persons providing insurance, investment companies, and investment advisers), by the Director of the Office of Thrift Supervision.

(2) Under the Federal Credit Union Act, by the Board of the National Credit Union Administration with respect to any federally insured credit union, and any subsidiaries of such an entity.

(3) Under the Securities Exchange Act of 1934, by the Securities and Exchange Commission with respect to any broker or dealer.

(4) Under the Investment Company Act of 1940, by the Securities and Exchange Commission with respect to investment companies.

(5) Under the Investment Advisers Act of 1940, by the Securities and Exchange Commission with respect to investment advisers registered with the Commission under such Act.

(6) Under State insurance law, in the case of any person engaged in providing insurance, by the applicable State insurance authority of the State in which the person is domiciled, subject to section 104 of this Act.

(7) Under the Federal Trade Commission Act, by the Federal Trade Commission for any other financial institution or other person that is not subject to the jurisdiction of any agency or authority under paragraphs (1) through (6) of this subsection.

(b) Enforcement of Section 501.

(1) In general - Except as provided in paragraph (2), the agencies and authorities described insubsection (a) shall implement the standards prescribed under section 501(b) in the same manner, to the extent practicable, as standards prescribed pursuant to section 39(a) of the Federal Deposit Insurance Act are implemented pursuant to such section.

(2) Exception - The agencies and authorities described in paragraphs (3), (4), (5), (6), and (7) of subsection (a) shall implement the standards prescribed under section 501(b) by rule with respect to the financial institutions and other persons subject to their respective jurisdictions under subsection (a).

United States
Financial Modernization Services Act

(c) Absence of state action - If a State insurance authority fails to adopt regulations to carry out this subtitle, such State shall not be eligible to override, pursuant to section 47(g)(2)(B)(iii) of the Federal Deposit Insurance Act, the insurance customer protection regulations prescribed by a Federal banking agency under section 47(a) of such Act. Definitions - The terms used in subsection (a)(1) that are not defined in this subtitle or otherwise defined in section 3(s) of the Federal Deposit Insurance Act shall have the same meaning as given in section 1(b) of the International Banking Act of 1978.

§ 506. Protection of fair credit reporting act

(a) Amendment - Section 621 of the Fair Credit Reporting Act (15 U.S.C. 1681s) is amended

(1) in subsection (d), by striking everything following the end of the second sentence; and

(2) by striking subsection (e) and inserting the following:

"(e) Regulatory authority - (1) The Federal banking agencies referred to in paragraphs (1)

and (2) of subsection (b) shall jointly prescribe such regulations as necessary to carry out the purposes of this Act with respect to any persons identified under paragraphs (1) and (2) of subsection (b), and the Board of Governors of the Federal Reserve System shall have authority to prescribe regulations consistent with such joint regulations with respect to bank holding companies and affiliates (other than depository institutions and consumer reporting agencies) of such holding companies. 2) The Board of the National Credit Union Administration shall prescribe such regulations as necessary to carry out the purposes of this Act with respect to any persons identified under paragraph (3) of subsection (b)."

(b) Conforming Amendment - Section 621(a) of the Fair Credit Reporting Act (15 U.S.C. 1681s(a)) is amended by striking paragraph (4).

(c) Relation to other provisions - Except for the amendments made by subsections (a) and (b), nothing in this title shall be construed to modify, limit, or supersede the operation of the Fair Credit Reporting Act, and no inference shall be drawn on the basis of the provisions of this title regarding whether information is transaction or experience information under section 603 of such Act.

§ 507. Relation to state law

(a) In general - This subtitle and the amendments made by this subtitle shall not be construed as superseding, altering, or affecting any statute, regulation, order, or interpretation in effect in any State, except to the extent that such statute, regulation, order, or interpretation is inconsistent with the provisions of this subtitle, and then only to the extent of the inconsistency.

(b) Greater protection under state law - For purposes of this section, a State statute, regulation, order, or interpretation is not inconsistent with the provisions of this subtitle if the protection such statute, regulation, order, or interpretation affords any person is greater than the protection provided under this subtitle and the amendments made by this subtitle, as determined by the Federal Trade Commission, after consultation with the agency or authority with jurisdiction under section 505(a) of either the person that initiated the complaint or that is the subject of the complaint, on its own motion or upon the petition of any interested party.

§ 508. Study of information sharing among financial affiliates.

(a) In general - The Secretary of the Treasury, in conjunction with the Federal functional regulators and the Federal Trade Commission, shall conduct a study of information sharing practices among financial institutions and their affiliates. Such study shall include--

(1) the purposes for the sharing of confidential customer information with affiliates or with nonaffiliated third parties;

(2) the extent and adequacy of security protections for such information;

(3) the potential risks for customer privacy of such sharing of information;

(4) the potential benefits for financial institutions and affiliates of such sharing of information;

(5) the potential benefits for customers of such sharing of information;

(6) the adequacy of existing laws to protect customer privacy;

(7) the adequacy of financial institution privacy policy and privacy rights disclosure under existing law;

(8) the feasibility of different approaches, including opt-out and opt-in, to permit customers to direct that confidential information not be shared with affiliates and nonaffiliated third parties; and

(9) the feasibility of restricting sharing of information for specific uses or of permitting customers to direct the uses for which information may be shared.

(b) Consultation.--The Secretary shall consult with representatives of State insurance authorities designated by the National Association of Insurance Commissioners, and also with financial services industry, consumer organizations and privacy groups, and other representatives of the general public, in formulating and conducting the study required by subsection (a).

(c) Report. On or before January 1, 2002, the Secretary shall submit a report to the Congress containing the findings and conclusions of the study required under subsection (a), together with such recommendations for legislative or administrative action as may be appropriate.

§ 509. Definitions

As used in this subtitle:

United States
Financial Modernization Services Act

(1) Federal banking agency - The term `Federal banking agency' has the same meaning as given in section 3 of the Federal Deposit Insurance Act.

(2) Federal functional regulator - The term `Federal functional regulator' means--

    (A) the Board of Governors of the Federal Reserve System;

    (B) the Office of the Comptroller of the Currency;

    (C) the Board of Directors of the Federal Deposit Insurance Corporation;

    (D) the Director of the Office of Thrift Supervision;

    (E) the National Credit Union Administration Board; and

    (F) the Securities and Exchange Commission.

(3) Financial institution -

    (A) In general - The term `financial institution' means any institution the business of which is engaging in financial activities as described in section 4(k) of the Bank Holding Company Act of 1956.

    (B) Persons subject to CFTC regulation - Notwithstanding subparagraph (A), the term 'financial institution' does not include any person or entity with respect to any financial activity that is subject to the jurisdiction of the Commodity Futures Trading Commission under the Commodity Act.

    (C) Farm credit institutions - Notwithstanding subparagraph (A), the term 'financial institution' does not include the Federal Agricultural Mortgage Corporation or any entity chartered and operating under the Farm Credit Act of 1971.

    (D) Other secondary market institutions - Notwithstanding subparagraph (A), the term `financial institution' does not include institutions chartered by Congress specifically to engage in transactions described in section 502(e)(1)(C), as long as such institutions do not sell or transfer nonpublic personal information to a nonaffiliated third party.

(4) Nonpublic personal information.

    (A) The term "nonpublic personal information" means personally identifiable financial information--

        (i) provided by a consumer to a financial institution;

        (ii) resulting from any transaction with the consumer or any service performed for the consumer; or

        (iii) otherwise obtained by the financial institution.

    (B) Such term does not include publicly available information, as such term is defined by the regulations prescribed under section 504.

    (C) Notwithstanding subparagraph (B), such term--

        (i) shall include any list, description, or other grouping of consumers (and publicly available information pertaining to them) that is derived using any nonpublic personal information other than publicly available information; but

(ii) shall not include any list, description, or other grouping of consumers (and publicly available information pertaining to them) that is derived without using any nonpublic personal information.

(5) Non-affiliated third party - The term "nonaffiliated third party" means any entity that is not an affiliate of, or related by common ownership or affiliated by corporate control with, the financial institution, but does not include a joint employee of such institution.

(6) Affiliate- The term "affiliate" means any company that controls, is controlled by, or is under common control with another company

(7) Necessary to effect, administer, or enforce - The term "as necessary toeffect, administer, or enforce the transaction" means--

(A) the disclosure is required, or is a usual, appropriate, or acceptable method, to carry out the transaction or the product or service business of which the transaction is a part, and record or service or maintain the consumer's account in the ordinary course of providing the financial service or financial product, or to administer or service benefits or claims relating to the transaction or the product or service business of which it is a part, and includes--

(i) providing the consumer or the consumer's agent or broker with a confirmation, statement, or other record of the transaction, or information on the status or value of the financial service of financial product; and

(ii) the accrual or recognition of incentives or bonuses associated with the transaction that are provided by the financial institution or any other party;

(B) the disclosure is required, or is one of the lawful or appropriate methods, to enforce the rights of the financial institution or of other persons engaged in carrying out the financial transaction, or providing the product or service.

(C) the disclosure is required, or is a usual, appropriate, or acceptable method, for insurance underwriting at the consumer's request or for reinsurance purposes, or for any of the following purposes as they relate to a consumer's insurance: Account administration, reporting, investigating, or preventing fraud or material misrepresentation, processing premium payments, processing insurance claims, administering insurance benefits (including utilization review activities), participating in research , or as otherwise required or specifically permitted by Federal or State law; or

(D) the disclosure is required, or is a usual, appropriate or acceptable method, in connection with--

(i) the authorization, settlement, billing, processing, clearing, transferring, reconciling, or collection of amounts charged, debited, or otherwise paid using a debit, credit or other payment card, check, or account number, or by other payment means;

(ii) the transfer of receivables, accounts or interests therein; or

(iii) the audit of debit, credit or other payment information.

(8) State insurance authority - The term "State insurance authority" means, in the case of any person engaged in providing insurance, the State insurance authority of the State in which the person is domiciled.

(9) Consumer - The term "consumer" means an individual who obtains, from a financial institution, financial products or services which are to be used primarily for personal, family, or household purposes, and also means the legal representative of such an individual.

(10) Joint agreement - The term "joint agreement" means a formal written contract pursuant to which two or more financial institutions jointly offer, endorse, or sponsor a financial product or service, and as may be further defined in the regulations prescribed under section 504.

(11) Customer relationship - The term "time of establishing a customer relationship" shall be defined by the regulations prescribed under section 504, and shall, in the case of a financial institution engaged in extending credit directly to consumers to finance purchases of goods or services, mean the time of establishing the credit relationship with the consumer.

§ 510. Effective date

This subtitle shall take effect 6 months after the date on which rules are required to be prescribed under section 504(a)(3), except--

(1) to the extent that a later date is specified in the rules prescribed under section 504; and

(2) that sections 504 and 506 shall be effective upon enactment.

Subtitle B--Fraudulent Access to Financial Information

§ 521. Privacy protection for customer information of financial institutions

(a) Prohibition on obtaining customer information by false pretenses - It shall be a violation of this subtitle for any person to obtain or attempt to obtain, or cause to be disclosed or attempt to cause to be disclosed to any person, customer information of a financial institution relating to another person--

(1) by making a false, fictitious, or fraudulent statement or representation to an officer, employee, or agent of a financial institution;

(2) by making a false, fictitious, or fraudulent statement or representation to a customer of a financial institution; or

(3) by providing any document to an officer, employee, or agent of a financial institution, knowing that the document is forged, counterfeit, lost, or stolen, was fraudulently obtained, or contains a false, fictitious, or fraudulent statement or representation.

(b) Prohibition on solicitation of a person to obtain customer information from financial institution under false pretenses - It shall be a violation of this subtitle to request a person to obtain customer information of a financial institution, knowing that the person will obtain, or attempt to obtain, the information from the institution in any manner described in subsection (a).

(c) Nonapplicability to law enforcement - No provision of this section shall be construed so as to prevent any action by a law enforcement agency, or any officer, employee, or agent of such agency, to obtain customer information of a financial institution in connection with the performance of the official duties of the agency.

(d) Nonapplicability to financial institutions in certain cases - No provision of this section shall be construed so as to prevent any financial institution, or any officer, employee, or agent of a financial institution, from obtaining customer information of such financial institution in the course of--

(1) testing the security procedures or systems of such institution for maintaining the confidentiality of customer information;

(2) investigating allegations of misconduct or negligence on the part of any officer, employee, or agent of the financial institution; or

(3) recovering customer information of the financial institution which was obtained or received by another person in any manner described in subsection (a) or (b).

(e) Nonappliability to insurance institutions for investigation of insurance fraud - No provision of this section shall be construed so as to prevent any insurance institution, or any officer, employee, or agency of an insurance institution, from obtaining information as part of an insurance investigation into criminal activity, fraud, material misrepresentation, or material nondisclosure that is authorized for such institution under State law, regulation, interpretation, or order.

(f) Nonapplicability to certain types of customer information of financial institutions - No provision of this section shall be construed so as to prevent any person from obtaining customer information of a financial institution that otherwise is available as a public record filed pursuant to the securities laws (as defined in section 3(a)(47) of the Securities Exchange Act of 1934).

(g) Nonapplicability to collection of child support judgments No provision of this section shall be construed to prevent any State-licensed private investigator, or any officer, employee, or agent of such private investigator, from obtaining customer information of a financial institution, to the extent reasonably necessary to collect child support from a person adjudged to have been delinquent in his or her obligations by a Federal or State court, and to the extent that such action by a State-licensed private investigator is not unlawful under any other Federal or State law or regulation, and has been authorized by an order or judgment of a court of competent jurisdiction.

§ 522. Administrative enforcement

(a) Enforcement by federal trade commission - Except as provided in subsection (b), compliance with this subtitle shall be enforced by the Federal Trade Commission in the same manner and with the same power and authority as the Commission has under the Fair Debt Collection Practices Act to enforce compliance with such Act.

(b) Enforcement by other agencies in certain cases.

(1) In general - Compliance with this subtitle shall be enforced under--

(A) Section 8 of the Federal Deposit Insurance Act, in the case of--

(i) national banks, and Federal branches and Federal agencies of foreign banks, by the Office of the Comptroller of the Currency;

(ii) member banks of the Federal Reserve System (other than national banks), branches and agencies of foreign banks (other than Federal branches, Federal agencies, and insured State branches of foreign banks), commercial lending companies owned or controlled by foreign banks, and organizations operating under section 25 or 25A of the Federal Reserve Act, by the Board;

(iii) banks insured by the Federal Deposit Insurance Corporation (other than members of the Federal Reserve System and national nonmember banks) and insured State branches of foreign banks, by the Board of Directors of the Federal Deposit Insurance Corporation; and

(iv) savings associations the deposits of which are insured by the Federal Deposit Insurance Corporation, by the Director of the Office of Thrift Supervision; and the Federal Credit Union Act, by the Administrator of the National Credit Union Administration with respect to any Federal credit union.

(2) Violations of this subtitle treated as violations of other laws - For the purpose of the exercise by any agency referred to in paragraph (1) of its powers under any Act referred to in that paragraph, a violation of this subtitle shall be deemed to be a violation of a requirement imposed under that Act. In addition to its powers under any provision of law specifically referred to in paragraph (1), each of the agencies referred to in that paragraph may exercise, for the purpose of enforcing compliance with this subtitle, any other authority conferred on such agency by law.

§ 523. Criminal penalty

(a) In general - Whoever knowingly and intentionally violates, or knowingly and intentionally attempts to violate, section 521 shall be fined in accordance with title 18, United States Code, or imprisoned for not more than 5 years, or both.

(b) Enhanced penalty for aggravated cases - Whoever violates, or attempts to violate, section 521 while violating another law of the United States or as part of a pattern of any illegal activity involving more than $100,000 in a 12-month period shall be fined twice the amount provided in subsection (b)(3) or (c)(3) (as the case may be) of section 3571 of title 18, United States Code, imprisoned for not more than 10 years, or both.

§ 524. Relation to state laws

(a) In general - This subtitle shall not be construed as superseding, altering, or affecting the statutes, regulations, orders, or interpretations in effect in any State, except to the extent that such statutes, regulations, orders, or interpretations are inconsistent with the provisions of this subtitle, and then only to the extent of the inconsistency.

(b) Greater protection under state law - For purposes of this section, a State statute, regulation, order, or interpretation is not inconsistent with the provisions of this subtitle if the protection such statute, regulation, order, or interpretation affords any person is greater than the protection provided under this subtitle as determined by the Federal Trade Commission, after consultation with the agency or authority with jurisdiction under section 522 of either the person that initiated the complaint or that is the subject of the complaint, on its own motion or upon the petition of any interested party.

§ 525. Agency guidance

In furtherance of the objectives of this subtitle, each Federal banking agency (as defined in section 3(z) of the Federal Deposit Insurance Act), the National Credit Union Administration, and the Securities and Exchange Commission or self-regulatory organizations, as appropriate, shall review regulations and guidelines applicable to financial institutions under their respective jurisdictions and shall prescribe such revisions to such regulations and guidelines as may be necessary to ensure that such financial institutions have policies, procedures, and controls in place to prevent the unauthorized disclosure of customer financial information and to deter and detect activities proscribed under section 521.

§ 526. Reports

(a) Report to the Congress - Before the end of the 18-month period beginning on the date of the enactment of this Act, the Comptroller General, in consultation with the Federal Trade Commission, Federal banking agencies, the National Credit Union Administration, the Securities and Exchange Commission, appropriate Federal law enforcement agencies, and appropriate State insurance regulators, shall submit to the Congress a report on the following:

(1) The efficacy and adequacy of the remedies provided in this subtitle in addressing attempts to obtain financial information by fraudulent means or by false pretenses.

(2) Any recommendations for additional legislative or regulatory action to address threats to the privacy of financial information created by attempts to obtain information by fraudulent means or false pretenses.

(b) Annual report by administering agencies - The Federal Trade Commission and the Attorney General shall submit to Congress an annual report on number and disposition of all enforcement actions taken pursuant to this subtitle.

United States
Financial Modernization Services Act

§ 527. Definitions

For purposes of this subtitle, the following definitions shall apply:

(1) Customer - The term "customer" means, with respect to a financial institution, any person (or authorized representative of a person) to whom the financial institution provides a product or service, including that of acting as a fiduciary.

(2) Customer information of a financial institution - The term "customer information of a financial institution" means any information maintained by or for a financial institution which is derived from the relationship between the financial institution and a customer of the financial institution and is identified with the customer.

(3) Document - The term "document" means any information in any form.

(A) In general - The term `financial institution' means any institution engaged in the business of providing financial services to customers who maintain a credit, deposit, trust, or other financial account or relationship with the institution.

(B) Certain financial institutions specifically included - The term "financial institution" includes any depository institution (as defined in section 19(b)(1)(A) of the Federal Reserve), any broker or dealer, any investment adviser or investment company, any insurance company, any loan or finance company, any credit card issuer or operator of a credit card system, and any consumer reporting agency that compiles and maintains files on consumers on a nationwide basis (as defined in section 603(p) of the Consumer Credit Protection Act).

(4) Financial institution.--

(A) In general.--The term ``financial institution'' means any institution engaged in the business of providing financial services to customers who maintain a credit, deposit, trust, or other financial account or with the institution.

(B) Certain financial institutions specifically included.--The term ``financial institution'' includes any depository institution (as defined in section 19(b)(1)(A) of the Federal Reserve Act), any broker or dealer, any investment adviser or investment company, any insurance company, any loan or finance company, any credit card issuer or operator of a credit card system, and any consumer reporting agency that compiles and maintains files on consumers on a nationwide basis (as defined in section 603(p) of the Consumer Credit Protection Act).

(C) Securities institutions.--For purposes of subparagraph (B)--

(i) the terms ``broker'' and ``dealer'' have the same meanings as given in section 3 of the Exchange Act of 1934 (15 U.S.C. 78c);

(ii) the term ``investment adviser'' has the same meaning as given in section 202(a)(11) of the Investment Advisers Act of 1940 (15 U.S.C. 80b-2(a)); and

(iii) the term ``investment company'' has the same meaning as given in section 3 of the Investment Company Act of 1940 (15 U.S.C. 80a-3).

(D) Certain persons and entities specifically excluded.--The term ``financial institution'' does not include any person or entity with respect to any financial activity that is subject to the jurisdiction of the Commodity Futures Trading Commission under the Commodity Exchange Act and does not include the Federal Agricultural Mortgage Corporation or any entity chartered and operating under the Farm Credit Act of 1971.

(E) Further definition by regulation.--The Federal Trade Commission, after consultation with Federal agencies and the Securities and Exchange Commission, may prescribe regulations clarifying or describing the types of institutions which shall be as financial institutions for purposes of this subtitle.

United States
Federal Trade Commission Act

FEDERAL TRADE COMMISSION ACT
(US)

Summary

In 1914 Congress passed the Federal Trade Commission Act (FTCA) to protect consumers from deceptive practices and unfair methods of competition. An unfair method of competition is defined under section 45(n) as "one that causes or is likely to cause substantial injury to consumers which is not reasonably avoidable by consumers themselves and not outweighed by countervailing benefits to consumers or to competition."

The Act created the Federal Trade Commission to regulate and enforce its provisions. It gave the FTC authority to investigate unfair practices, to pursue complaints, to issue reports, and to enforce orders. Thus, if the FTC finds that a practice violates the Act it may issue an order requiring the individual or entity to cease from using such method or practice. The individual or entity subject to the order may request to a court to review the order. If the court finds the practice to be unfair or deceptive it may impose preliminary/permanent injunctions or a penalty of no more than $10,000 for each violation of the FTC order.

References

Federal Trade Commission, Privacy Initiatives
[http://www.ftc.gov/privacy/index.html]

§ 45. Unfair methods of competition unlawful; prevention by Commission

(a) Declaration of unlawfulness; power to prohibit unfair practices; inapplicability to foreign trade

(1) Unfair methods of competition in or affecting commerce, and unfair or deceptive acts or practices in or affecting commerce, are hereby declared unlawful.

(2) The Commission is hereby empowered and directed to prevent persons, partnerships, or corporations, except banks, savings and loan institutions described in section 57a(f)(3) of this title, Federal credit unions described in section 57a(f)(4) of this title, common carriers subject to the Acts to regulate commerce, air carriers and foreign air carriers subject to part A of subtitle VII of title 49, and persons, partnerships, or corporations insofar as they are subject to the Packers and Stockyards Act, 1921, as amended (7 U.S.C. 181 et seq.), except as provided in section 406(b) of said Act (7 U.S.C. 227(b)), from using unfair methods of competition in or affecting commerce and unfair or deceptive acts or practices in or affecting commerce.

(3) This subsection shall not apply to unfair methods of competition involving commerce with foreign nations (other than import commerce) unless -

(A) such methods of competition have a direct, substantial, and reasonably foreseeable effect -

(i) on commerce which is not commerce with foreign nations, or on import commerce with foreign nations; or

(ii) on export commerce with foreign nations, of a person engaged in such commerce in the United States; and

(B) such effect gives rise to a claim under the provisions of this subsection, other than this paragraph. If this subsection applies to such methods of competition only because of the operation of subparagraph (A)(ii), this subsection shall apply to such conduct only for injury to export business in the United States.

(b) Proceeding by Commission; modifying and setting aside orders

Whenever the Commission shall have reason to believe that any such person, partnership, or corporation has been or is using any unfair method of competition or unfair or deceptive act or practice in or affecting commerce, and if it shall appear to the Commission that a proceeding by it in respect thereof would be to the interest of the public, it shall issue and serve upon such person, partnership, or corporation a complaint stating its charges in that respect and containing a notice of a hearing upon a day and at a place therein fixed at least thirty days after the service of said complaint. The person, partnership, or corporation so complained of shall have the right to appear at the place and time so fixed and show cause why an order should not be entered by the Commission requiring such person, partnership, or corporation to cease and desist from the violation of the law so charged in said complaint. Any person, partnership, or corporation may make application, and upon good cause shown may be allowed by the Commission to intervene and appear in said proceeding by counsel or in person. The testimony in any such proceeding shall be reduced to writing and filed in the office of the Commission. If upon such hearing the Commission shall be of the opinion that the method of competition or the act or practice in question is prohibited by this subchapter, it shall make a report in writing in which it shall state its findings as to the facts and shall issue and cause to be served on such person, partnership, or corporation an order requiring such person, partnership, or corporation to cease and desist from using such method of competition or such act or practice. Until the expiration of the time allowed for filing a petition for review, if no such petition has been duly filed within such time, or, if a petition for review has been filed within such time then until the record in the proceeding has been filed in a court of appeals of the United States, as hereinafter provided, the Commission may at any time, upon such notice and in such manner as it shall deem proper, modify or set aside, in whole or in part, any report or any order made or issued by it under this section. After the expiration of the time allowed for filing a petition for review, if no such petition has been duly filed within such time, the Commission may at any time, after notice and opportunity for hearing, reopen and alter, modify, or set aside, in whole or in part any report or order made or issued by it under this section, whenever in the opinion of the Commission conditions of fact or of law have so changed as to require such action or if the public interest shall so require, except that (1) the said person, partnership, or corporation may, within sixty days after service upon him or it of said report or order entered after such a reopening, obtain a review thereof in the appropriate court of appeals of the United States, in the manner provided in subsection (c) of this section; and (2) in the case of an order, the Commission shall reopen any such order to consider whether such order (including any affirmative relief provision contained in such order) should be altered, modified, or set aside, in whole or in part, if the person, partnership, or corporation involved files a request with the Commission which makes a satisfactory showing that changed conditions of law or fact require such order to be altered, modified, or set aside, in whole or in part. The Commission shall determine whether to alter, modify, or set aside any order of the Commission in response to a request made by a person, partnership, or corporation under paragraph (2) not later than 120 days after the date of the filing of such request.

(c) Review of order; rehearing

Any person, partnership, or corporation required by an order of the Commission to cease and desist from using any method of competition or act or practice may obtain a review of such order in the court of appeals of the United States, within any circuit where the method of competition or the act or practice in question was used or where such person, partnership, or corporation resides or carries on business, by filing in the court, within sixty days from the date of the service of such order, a written petition praying that the order of the Commission be set aside. A copy of such petition shall be forthwith transmitted by the clerk of the court to the Commission, and thereupon the Commission shall file in the court the record in the proceeding, as provided in section 2112 of title 28. Upon such filing of the petition the court shall have jurisdiction of the proceeding and of the question determined therein concurrently with the Commission until the filing of the record and shall have power to make and enter a decree affirming, modifying, or setting aside the order of the Commission, and enforcing the same to the extent that such order is affirmed and to issue such writs as are ancillary to its jurisdiction or are necessary in its judgement to prevent injury to the public or to competitors pendente lite. The findings of the Commission as to the facts, if supported by evidence, shall be conclusive. To the extent that the order of the Commission is affirmed, the court shall thereupon issue its own order commanding obedience to the terms of such order of the Commission. If either party shall apply to the court for leave to adduce additional evidence, and shall show to the satisfaction of the court that such additional evidence is material and that there were reasonable grounds for the failure to adduce such evidence in the proceeding before the Commission, the court may order such additional evidence to be taken before the Commission and to be adduced upon the hearing in such manner and upon such terms and conditions as to the court may seem proper. The Commission may modify its findings as to the facts, or make new findings, by reason of the additional evidence so taken, and it shall file such modified or new findings, which, if supported by evidence, shall be conclusive, and its recommendation, if any, for the modification or setting aside of its original order, with the return of such additional evidence. The judgment and decree of the court shall be final, except that the same shall be subject to review by the Supreme Court upon certiorari, as provided in section 1254 of title 28.

(d) Jurisdiction of court

Upon the filing of the record with it the jurisdiction of the court of appeals of the United States to affirm, enforce, modify, or set aside orders of the Commission shall be exclusive.

(e) Exemption from liability

No order of the Commission or judgement of court to enforce the same shall in anywise relieve or absolve any person, partnership, or corporation from any liability under the Antitrust Acts.

(f) Service of complaints, orders and other processes; return

Complaints, orders, and other processes of the Commission under this section may be served by anyone duly authorized by the Commission, either (a) by delivering a copy thereof to the person to be served, or to a member of the partnership to be served, or the president, secretary, or other executive officer or a director of the corporation to be served; or (b) by leaving a copy thereof at the residence or the principal office or place of business of such person, partnership, or corporation; or (c) by mailing a copy thereof by registered mail or by certified mail addressed to such person, partnership, or corporation at his or its residence or principal office or place of business. The verified return by the person so serving said complaint, order, or other process setting forth the manner of said service shall be proof of the same, and the return post office receipt for said complaint, order, or other process mailed by registered mail or by certified mail as aforesaid shall be proof of the service of the same.

(g) Finality of order

An order of the Commission to cease and desist shall become final -

(1) Upon the expiration of the time allowed for filing a petition for review, if no such petition has been duly filed within such time; but the Commission may

thereafter modify or set aside its order to the extent provided in the last sentence of subsection (b).

(2) Except as to any order provision subject to paragraph (4), upon the sixtieth day after such order is served, if a petition for review has been duly filed; except that any such order may be stayed, in whole or in part and subject to such conditions as may be appropriate, by -

(A) the Commission;

(B) an appropriate court of appeals of the United States, if

(i) a petition for review of such order is pending in such court, and (ii) an application for such a stay was previously submitted to the Commission and the Commission, within the 30-day period beginning on the date the application was received by the Commission, either denied the application or did not grant or deny the application; or

(C) the Supreme Court, if an applicable petition for certiorari is pending.

(3) For purposes of subsection (m)(1)(B) of this section and of section 57b(a)(2) of this title, if a petition for review of the order of the Commission has been filed -

(A) upon the expiration of the time allowed for filing a petition for certiorari, if the order of the Commission has been affirmed or the petition for review has been dismissed by the court of appeals and no petition for certiorari has been duly filed;

(B) upon the denial of a petition for certiorari, if the order of the Commission has been affirmed or the petition for review has been dismissed by the court of appeals; or

(C) upon the expiration of 30 days from the date of issuance of a mandate of the Supreme Court directing that the order of the Commission be affirmed or the petition for review be dismissed.

(4) In the case of an order provision requiring a person, partnership, or corporation to divest itself of stock, other share capital, or assets, if a petition for review of such order of the Commission has been filed -

(A) upon the expiration of the time allowed for filing a petition for certiorari, if the order of the Commission has been affirmed or the petition for review has been dismissed by the court of appeals and no petition for certiorari has been duly filed;

(B) upon the denial of a petition for certiorari, if the order of the Commission has been affirmed or the petition for review has been dismissed by the court of appeals; or

(C) upon the expiration of 30 days from the date of issuance of a mandate of the Supreme Court directing that the order of the Commission be affirmed or the petition for review be dismissed.

(h) Modification or setting aside of order by Supreme Court

> If the Supreme Court directs that the order of the Commission be modified or set aside, the order of the Commission rendered in accordance with the mandate of the Supreme Court shall become final upon the expiration of thirty days from the time it was rendered, unless within such thirty days either party has instituted proceedings to have such order corrected to accord with the mandate, in which event the order of the Commission shall become final when so corrected.

(i) Modification or setting aside of order by Court of Appeals

> If the order of the Commission is modified or set aside by the court of appeals, and if (1) the time allowed for filing a petition for certiorari has expired and no such petition has been duly filed, or (2) the petition for certiorari has been denied, or (3) the decision of the court has been affirmed by the Supreme Court, then the order of the Commission rendered in accordance with the mandate of the court of appeals shall become final on the expiration of thirty days from the time such order of the Commission was rendered, unless within such thirty days either party has instituted proceedings to have such order corrected so that it will accord with the mandate, in which event the order of the Commission shall become final when so corrected.

(j) Rehearing upon order or remand

> If the Supreme Court orders a rehearing; or if the case is remanded by the court of appeals to the Commission for a rehearing, and if (1) the time allowed for filing a petition for certiorari has expired, and no such petition has been duly filed, or (2) the petition for certiorari has been denied, or (3) the decision of the court has been affirmed by the Supreme Court, then the order of the Commission rendered upon such rehearing shall become final in the same manner as though no prior order of the Commission had been rendered.

(k) "Mandate" defined

> As used in this section the term "mandate", in case a mandate has been recalled prior to the expiration of thirty days from the date of issuance thereof, means the final mandate.

(l) Penalty for violation of order; injunctions and other appropriate equitable relief

> Any person, partnership, or corporation who violates an order of the Commission after it has become final, and while such order is in effect, shall forfeit and pay to the United States a civil penalty of not more than $10,000 for each violation, which shall accrue to the United States and may be recovered in a civil action brought by the Attorney General of the United States. Each separate violation of such an order shall be a separate offense, except that in a case of a violation through continuing failure to obey or

neglect to obey a final order of the Commission, each day of continuance of such failure or neglect shall be deemed a separate offense. In such actions, the United States district courts are empowered to grant mandatory injunctions and such other and further equitable relief as they deem appropriate in the enforcement of such final orders of the Commission.

(m) *Civil actions for recovery of penalties for knowing violations of rules and cease and desist orders respecting unfair or deceptive acts or practices; jurisdiction; maximum amount of penalties; continuing violations; de novo determinations; compromise or settlement procedure*

(1)(A) The Commission may commence a civil action to recover a civil penalty in a district court of the United States against any person, partnership, or corporation which violates any rule under this chapter respecting unfair or deceptive acts or practices (other than an interpretive rule or a rule violation of which the Commission has provided is not an unfair or deceptive act or practice in violation of subsection (a)(1) of this section) with actual knowledge or knowledge fairly implied on the basis of objective circumstances that such act is unfair or deceptive and is prohibited by such rule. In such action, such person, partnership, or corporation shall be liable for a civil penalty of not more than $10,000 for each violation.

(B) If the Commission determines in a proceeding under subsection (b) of this section that any act or practice is unfair or deceptive, and issues a final cease and desist order, other than a consent order, with respect to such act or practice, then the Commission may commence a civil action to obtain a civil penalty in a district court of the United States against any person, partnership, or corporation which engages in such act or practice -

(1) after such cease and desist order becomes final (whether or not such person, partnership, or corporation was subject to such cease and desist order), and

(2) with actual knowledge that such act or practice is unfair or deceptive and is unlawful under subsection (a)(1)

of this section. In such action, such person, partnership, or corporation shall be liable for a civil penalty of not more than $10,000 for each violation.

(C) In the case of a violation through continuing failure to comply with a rule or with subsection (a)(1) of this section, each day of continuance of such failure shall be treated as a separate violation, for purposes of subparagraphs (A) and (B). In determining the amount of such a civil penalty, the court shall take into account the degree of culpability, any history of prior such conduct, ability to pay, effect on ability to continue to do business, and such other matters as justice may require.

(2) If the cease and desist order establishing that the act or practice is unfair or deceptive was not issued against the defendant in a civil penalty action under paragraph (1)(B) the issues of fact in such action against such defendant shall be tried de novo. Upon request of any party to such an action against such defendant, the court shall also review the determination of law made by the Commission in the proceeding under subsection (b) of this section that the act or practice which was the subject of such proceeding constituted an unfair or deceptive act or practice in violation of subsection (a) of this section.

(3) The Commission may compromise or settle any action for a civil penalty if such compromise or settlement is accompanied by a public statement of its reasons and is approved by the court.

(n) *Standard of proof; public policy consideration*

The Commission shall have no authority under this section or section 57a of this title to declare unlawful an act or practice on the grounds that such act or practice is unfair unless the act or practice causes or is likely to cause substantial injury to consumers which is not reasonably avoidable by consumers themselves and not outweighed by countervailing benefits to consumers or to competition. In determining whether an act or practice is unfair, the Commission may consider established public policies as evidence to be considered with all other evidence. Such public policy considerations may not serve as a primary basis for such determination.

§ 46. Additional powers of Commission

The Commission shall also have power -

(a) *Investigation of persons, partnerships, or corporations*

To gather and compile information concerning, and to investigate from time to time the organization, business, conduct, practices, and management of any person, partnership, or corporation engaged in or whose business affects commerce, excepting banks, savings and loan institutions described in section 57a(f)(3) of this title, Federal credit unions described in section 57a(f)(4) of this title, and common carriers subject to the Act to regulate commerce, and its relation to other persons, partnerships, and corporations.

(b) *Reports of persons, partnerships, and corporations*

To require, by general or special orders, persons, partnerships, and corporations, engaged in or whose business affects commerce, excepting banks, savings and loan institutions described in section 57a(f)(3) of this title, Federal credit unions described in section 57a(f)(4) of this title, and common carriers subject to the Act to regulate commerce, or any class of them, or any of them, respectively, to file with the Commission in such form as the Commission may prescribe annual or special, or both annual and special, reports or answers in writing to specific questions, furnishing to the Commission such information as it may require as to the organization, business, conduct, practices, management, and relation to other corporations, partnerships, and individuals of the respective persons, partnerships, and corporations filing such reports or answers in writing. Such reports and answers shall be made under oath, or otherwise, as the Commission may prescribe, and shall be filed with the Commission within such reasonable period as the Commission may prescribe, unless additional time be granted in any case by the Commission.

(c) *Investigation of compliance with antitrust decrees.*

Whenever a final decree has been entered against any defendant corporation in any suit brought by the United States to prevent and restrain any violation of the antitrust Acts, to make investigation, upon its own initiative, of the manner in which the decree has been or is being carried out, and upon the application of the Attorney General it shall be its duty to make such investigation. It shall transmit to the Attorney General a report embodying its findings and recommendations as a result of any such investigation, and the report shall be made public in the discretion of the Commission.

(d) *Investigations of violations of antitrust statutes*

Upon the direction of the President or either House of Congress to investigate and report the facts relating to any alleged violations of the antitrust Acts by any corporation.

(e) *Readjustment of business of corporations violating antitrust statutes.*

Upon the application of the Attorney General to investigate and make recommendations for the readjustment of the business of any corporation alleged to be violating the antitrust Acts in order that the corporation may thereafter maintain its organization, management, and conduct of business in accordance with law.

(f) *Publication of information; reports*

To make public from time to time such portions of the information obtained by it hereunder as are in the public interest; and to make annual and special reports to the Congress and to submit therewith recommendations for additional legislation; and to provide for the publication of its reports and decisions in such form and manner as may be best adapted for public information and use: Provided, That the Commission shall not have any authority to make public any trade secret or any commercial or financial information which is obtained from any person and which is privileged or confidential, except that the Commission may disclose such information to officers and employees of appropriate Federal law enforcement agencies or to any officer or employee of any State law enforcement agency upon the prior certification of an officer of any such Federal or State law enforcement agency that such information will be maintained in confidence and will be used only for official law enforcement purposes.

(g) Classification of corporations; regulations

From time to time classify corporations and (except as provided in section 57a(a)(2) of this title) to make rules and regulations for the purpose of carrying out the provisions of this subchapter.

(h) Investigations of foreign trade conditions; reports

To investigate, from time to time, trade conditions in and with foreign countries where associations, combinations, or practices of manufacturers, merchants, or traders, or other conditions, may affect the foreign trade of the United States, and to report to Congress thereon, with such recommendations as it deems advisable.

(i) Investigations of foreign antitrust law violations

With respect to the International Antitrust Enforcement Assistance Act of 1994 (15 U.S.C. 6201 et seq.), to conduct investigations of possible violations of foreign antitrust laws (as defined in section 12 of such Act (15 U.S.C. 6211)). Provided, That the exception of "banks, savings and loan institutions described in section 57a(f)(3) of this title, Federal credit unions described in section 57a(f)(4) of this title, and common carriers subject to the Act to regulate commerce" from the Commission's powers defined in clauses (a) and (b) of this section, shall not be construed to limit the Commission's authority to gather and compile information, to investigate, or to require reports or answers from, any person, partnership, or corporation to the extent that such action is necessary to the investigation of any person, partnership, or corporation, group of persons, partnerships, or corporations, or industry which is not engaged or is engaged only incidentally in banking, in business as a savings and loan institution, in business as a Federal credit union, or in business as a common carrier subject to the Act to regulate commerce.

The Commission shall establish a plan designed to substantially reduce burdens imposed upon small businesses as a result of requirements established by the Commission under clause (b) relating to the filing of quarterly financial reports. Such plan shall (1) be established after consultation with small businesses and persons who use the information contained in such quarterly financial reports; (2) provide for a reduction of the number of small businesses required to file such quarterly financial reports; and (3) make revisions in the forms used for such quarterly financial reports for the purpose of reducing the complexity of such forms. The Commission, not later than

United States
Federal Trade Commission Act

December 31, 1980, shall submit such plan to the Committee on Commerce, Science, and Transportation of the Senate and to the Committee on Energy and Commerce of the House of Representatives. Such plan shall take effect not later than October 31, 1981. No officer or employee of the Commission or any Commissioner may publish or disclose information to the public, or to any Federal agency, whereby any line-of-business data furnished by a particular establishment or individual can be identified. No one other than designated sworn officers and employees of the Commission may examine the line-of-business reports from individual firms, and information provided in the line-of-business program administered by the Commission shall be used only for statistical purposes.

Information for carrying out specific law enforcement responsibilities of the Commission shall be obtained under practices and procedures in effect on May 28, 1980, or as changed by law.

Nothing in this section (other than the provisions of clause (c) and clause (d)) shall apply to the business of insurance, except that the Commission shall have authority to conduct studies and prepare reports relating to the business of insurance. The Commission may exercise such authority only upon receiving a request which is agreed to by a majority of the members of the Committee on Commerce, Science, and Transportation of the Senate or the Committee on Energy and Commerce of the House of Representatives. The authority to conduct any such study shall expire at the end of the Congress during which the request for such study was made.

§ 57a. Unfair or deceptive acts or practices rulemaking proceedings.

(a) Authority of Commission to prescribe rules and general statements of policy

    (1) Except as provided in subsection (h) of this section, the Commission may prescribe -

        (A) interpretive rules and general statements of policy with respect to unfair or deceptive acts or practices in or affecting commerce (within the meaning of section 45(a)(1) of this title), and

        (B) rules which define with specificity acts or practices which are unfair or deceptive acts or practices in or affecting commerce (within the meaning of section 45(a)(1) of this title), except that the Commission shall not develop or promulgate any trade rule or regulation with regard to the regulation of the development and utilization of the standards and certification activities pursuant to this section. Rules under this subparagraph may include requirements prescribed for the purpose of preventing such acts or practices.

    (2) The Commission shall have no authority under this subchapter, other than its authority under this section, to prescribe any rule with respect to unfair or deceptive acts or practices in or affecting commerce (within the meaning of section 45(a)(1) of this title). The preceding sentence shall not affect any authority of the

Commission to prescribe rules (including interpretive rules), and general statements of policy, with respect to unfair methods of competition in or affecting commerce.

(b) Procedures applicable

(1) When prescribing a rule under subsection (a)(1)(B) of this section, the Commission shall proceed in accordance with section 553 of title 5 (without regard to any reference in such section to sections 556 and 557 of such title), and shall also

(A) publish a notice of proposed rulemaking stating withparticularity the text of the rule, including any alternatives, which the Commission proposes to promulgate, and the reason for the proposed rule;

(B) allow interested persons to submit written data, views, and arguments, and make all such submissions publicly available;

(C) provide an opportunity for an informal hearing in accordance with subsection (c) of this section; and

(D) promulgate, if appropriate, a final rule based on the matter in the rulemaking record (as defined in subsection (e)(1)(B) of section), together with a statement of basis and purpose.

(2)(A) Prior to the publication of any notice of proposed rulemaking pursuant to paragraph (1)(A), Commission shall publish an advance notice of proposed rulemaking in the Federal Register. Such advance notice shall -

(i) contain a brief description of the area of inquiry under consideration, the objectives which the Commission seeks to achieve, and possible regulatory alternatives under consideration by the Commission; and

(ii) invite the response of interested parties with respect to such proposed rulemaking, including any suggestions or alternative methods for achieving such objectives.

(B) The Commission shall submit such advance notice of proposed rulemaking to the Committee on Commerce, Science, and Transportation of the Senate and to the Committee on Energy and Commerce of the House of Representatives. The Commission may use additional mechanisms as the Commission considers useful to obtain suggestions regarding the content of the area of inquiry before the publication of a general notice of proposed rulemaking under paragraph (1)(A).

(C) The Commission shall, 30 days before the publication of a notice of proposed rulemaking pursuant to paragraph (1)(A), submit such notice to the Committee on Commerce, Science, Transportation of the Senate and to the Committee on Energy and Commerce of the House of Representatives.

(3) The Commission shall issue a notice of proposed rulemaking pursuant to paragraph (1)(A) only where it has reason to believe that the unfair or deceptive acts or practices which are the subject of the proposed rulemaking are prevalent.

United States
Federal Trade Commission Act

The Commission shall make a determination that unfair or deceptive acts or practices are prevalent under this paragraph only if -

(A) it has issued cease and desist orders regarding such acts or practices, or

(B) any other information available to the Commission indicates a widespread pattern of unfair or deceptive acts or practices.

(c) Informal hearing procedure

The Commission shall conduct any informal hearings required by subsection (b)(1)(C) of this section in accordance with the following procedure:

(1) (A) The Commission shall provide for the conduct of proceedings under this subsection by hearing officers who shall perform their functions in accordance with the requirements of this subsection

(B) The officer who presides over the rulemaking proceedings shall be responsible to a chief presiding officer who shall not be responsible to any other officer or employee of the Commission. The officer who presides over the rulemaking proceeding shall make a recommended decision based upon the findings and conclusions of such officer as to all relevant and material evidence, except that such recommended decision may be made by another officer if the officer who presided over the proceeding is no longer available to the Commission.

(C) Except as required for the disposition of ex parte matters as authorized by law, no presiding officer shall consult any person or party with respect to any fact in issue unless such officer gives notice and opportunity for all parties to participate.

(2) Subject to paragraph (3) of this subsection, an interested person is entitled -

(A) to present his position orally or by documentary submission (or both), and

(B) if the Commission determines that there are disputed issues of material fact it is necessary to resolve, to present such rebuttal submissions and to conduct (or have conducted under paragraph (3)(B)) such cross-examination of persons as the Commission determines

(i) to be appropriate, and

(ii) to be required for a full and true disclosure with respect to such issues.

(3) The Commission may prescribe such rules and make such rulings concerning proceedings in such hearings as may tend to avoid unnecessary costs or delay. Such rules or rulings may include

(A) imposition of reasonable time limits on each interested person's oral presentations, and (B) requirements that any cross-examination to which a person may be entitled under paragraph (2) be conducted by the Commission on behalf of that person in such manner as the Commission determines

(i) to be appropriate, and

(ii) to be required for a full and true disclosure with respect to disputed issues of material fact.

(4) (A) Except as provided in subparagraph (B), if a group of persons each of whom under paragraphs (2) and (3) would be entitled to conduct (or have conducted) cross-examination and who are determined by the Commission to have the same or similar interests in the proceeding cannot agree upon a single representative of such interests for purposes of cross-examination, the Commission may make rules and rulings

(i) limiting the representation of such interest, for such purposes, and (ii) governing the manner in which such cross-examination shall be limited.

(B) When any person who is a member of a group with respect to which the Commission has made a determination under subparagraph (A) is unable to agree upon group representation with the other members of the group, then such person shall not be denied under the authority of subparagraph (A) the opportunity to conduct (or have conducted) cross-examination as to issues affecting his particular interests if

(i) he satisfies the Commission that he has made a reasonable and good faith effort to reach agreement upon group representation with the other members of the group and

(ii) the Commission determines that there are substantial and relevant issues which are not adequately presented by the group representative.

(5) A verbatim transcript shall be taken of any oral presentation, and cross-examination, in an informal hearing to which this subsection applies. Such transcript shall be available to the public.

(d) Statement of basis and purpose accompanying rule; "Commission" defined; judicial review of amendment or repeal of rule; violation of rule

(1) The Commission's statement of basis and purpose to accompany a rule promulgated under subsection (a)(1)(B) of this section shall include

(A) a statement as to the prevalence of the acts or practices treated by the rule;

(B) a statement as to the manner and context in which such acts or practices are unfair or deceptive; and

(C) a statement as to the economic effect of the rule, taking into account the effect on small business and consumers.

(2) (A) The term "Commission" as used in this subsection and subsections (b) and (c) of this section includes any person authorized to act in behalf of the Commission in any part of the rulemaking proceeding.

(B) A substantive amendment to, or repeal of, a rule promulgated under subsection (a)(1)(B) of this section shall be prescribed, and subject to judicial review, in the same manner as a rule prescribed under such subsection. An exemption under subsection (g) of this section shall not be treated as an amendment or repeal of a rule.

(3) When any rule under subsection (a)(1)(B) of this section takes effect a subsequent violation thereof shall constitute an unfair or deceptive act or practice in

violation of section 45(a)(1) of this title, unless the Commission otherwise expressly provides in such rule.

(e) Judicial review; petition; jurisdiction and venue; rulemaking record; additional submissions and presentations; scope of review and relief; review by Supreme Court; additional remedies

(1) (A) Not later than 60 days after a rule is promulgated under subsection (a)(1)(B) of this section by the Commission, any interested person (including a consumer or consumer organization) may file a petition, in the United States Court of Appeals for the District of Columbia circuit or for the circuit in which such person resides or has his principal place of business, for judicial review of such rule. Copies of the petition shall be forthwith transmitted by the clerk of the court to the Commission or other officer designated by it for that purpose. The provisions of section 2112 of title 28 shall apply to the filing of the rulemaking record of proceedings on which the Commission based its rule and to the transfer of proceedings in the courts of appeals.

(B) For purposes of this section, the term "rulemaking record" means the rule, its statement of basis and purpose, the transcript required by subsection (c)(5) of this section, any written submissions, and any other information which the Commission considers relevant to such rule.

(2) If the petitioner or the Commission applies to the court for leave to make additional oral submissions or written presentations and shows to the satisfaction of the court that such submissions and presentations would be material and that there were reasonable grounds for the submissions and failure to make such submissions and presentations in the proceeding before the Commission, the court may order the Commission to provide additional opportunity to make such submissions and presentations. The Commission may modify or set aside its rule or make a new rule by reason of the additional submissions and presentations and shall file such modified or new rule, and the rule's statement of basis of purpose, with the return of such submissions and presentations. The court shall thereafter review such new or modified rule.

(3) Upon the filing of the petition under paragraph (1) of this subsection, the court shall have to review the rule in accordance with chapter 7 of title 5 and to grant appropriate relief, including interim relief, as provided in such chapter. The court shall hold unlawful and set aside the rule on any ground specified in subparagraphs (A), (B), (C), or (D) of section 706(2) of title 5 (taking due account of the rule of prejudicial error), or if -

(A) the court finds that the Commission's action is not supported by substantial evidence in the rulemaking record (as defined in paragraph (1)(B) of this subsection) taken as a whole, or

(B) the court finds that -

(i) a Commission determination under subsection (c) of this section that the petitioner is not entitled to conduct cross-examination or make rebuttal submissions, or

(ii) a Commission rule or ruling under subsection (c) of this section limiting the petitioner's cross-examination or rebuttal submissions, has precluded disclosure of disputed material facts which was necessary for fair determination by the Commission of the rulemaking proceeding taken as a whole. The term "evidence", as used in this paragraph, means any matter in the rulemaking record.

(4) The judgment of the court affirming or setting aside, in whole or in part, any such rule shall be final, subject to review by the Supreme Court of the United States upon certiorari or certification, as provided in section 1254 of title 28.

(5) (A) Remedies under the preceding paragraphs of this subsection are in addition to and not in lieu of any other remedies provided by law.

(B) The United States Courts of Appeal shall have exclusive jurisdiction of any action to obtain judicial review (other than in an enforcement proceeding) of a rule prescribed under subsection (a)(1)(B) of this section, if any district court of the United States would have had jurisdiction of such action but for this subparagraph. Any such action shall be brought in the United States Court of Appeals for the District of Columbia circuit, or for any circuit which includes a judicial district in which the action could have been brought but for this subparagraph.

(C) A determination, rule, or ruling of the Commission described in paragraph (3)(B)(i) or (ii) may be reviewed only in a proceeding under this subsection and only in accordance with paragraph (3)(B). Section 706(2)(E) of title 5 shall not apply to any rule promulgated under subsection (a)(1)(B) of this section. The contents and adequacy of any statement required by subsection (b)(1)(D) of this section shall not be subject to judicial review in any respect.

(f) Unfair or deceptive acts or practices by banks, savings and loan institutions, or Federal credit unions; promulgation of regulations by Board of Governors of Federal Reserve System, Federal Home Loan Bank Board, and National Credit Union Administration Board; agency enforcement and compliance proceedings; violations; power of other Federal agencies unaffected; reporting requirements

(1) In order to prevent unfair or deceptive acts or practices in or affecting commerce (including acts or practices which are unfair or deceptive to consumers) by banks or savings and loan institutions described in paragraph (3), each agency specified in paragraph (2) or (3) of this subsection shall establish a separate division of consumer affairs which shall receive and take appropriate action upon complaints with respect to such acts or practices by banks or savings and loan institutions described in paragraph (3) subject to its jurisdiction. The Board of Governors of the Federal Reserve System (with respect to banks) and the Federal Home Loan Bank

Board (with respect to savings and loan institutions described in paragraph (3)) and the National Credit Union Administration Board (with respect to Federal credit unions described in paragraph (4)) shall prescribe regulations to carry out the purposes of this section, including regulations defining with specificity such unfair or deceptive acts or practices, and containing requirements prescribed for the purpose of preventing such acts or practices. Whenever the Commission prescribes a rule under subsection (a)(1)(B) of this section, then within 60 days after such rule takes effect each such Board shall promulgate substantially similar regulations prohibiting acts or practices of banks or savings and loan institutions described in paragraph (3), or Federal credit unions described in paragraph (4), as the case may be, which are substantially similar to those prohibited by rules of the Commission and which impose substantially similar requirements, unless (A) any such Board finds that such acts or practices of banks or savings and loan institutions described in paragraph (3), or Federal credit unions described in paragraph (4), as the case may be, are not unfair or deceptive, or (B) the Board of Governors of the Federal Reserve System finds that implementation of similar regulations with respect to banks, savings and loan institutions or Federal credit unions would seriously conflict with essential monetary and payments systems policies of such Board, and publishes any such finding, and the reasons therefor, in the Federal Register.

(2) Enforcement. - Compliance with regulations prescribed under this subsection shall be enforced under section 1818 of title 12, in the case of - (A) national banks, banks operating under the code of law for the District of Columbia, and Federal branches and Federal agencies of foreign banks, by the division of consumer affairs established by the Office of the Comptroller of the Currency; (B) member banks of the Federal Reserve System (other than national banks and banks operating under the code of law for the District of Columbia), branches and agencies of foreign banks (other than Federal branches, Federal agencies, and insured State branches of foreign banks), commercial lending companies owned or controlled by foreign banks, and organizations operating under section 25 or 25(a) (FOOTNOTE 1) of the Federal Reserve Act (12 U.S.C. 601 et seq., 611 et seq.), by the division of consumer affairs established by the Board of Governors of the Federal Reserve System; and (FOOTNOTE 1) See References in Text note below. (C) banks insured by the Federal Deposit Insurance Corporation (other (FOOTNOTE 2) banks referred to in subparagraph (A) or (B)) and insured State branches of foreign banks, by the division of consumer affairs established by the Board of Directors of the Federal Deposit Insurance Corporation. (FOOTNOTE 2) So in original. Probably should be "(other than".

(3) Compliance with regulations prescribed under this subsection shall be enforced under section 1818 of title 12 with respect to savings associations as defined in section 1813 of title 12.

(4) Compliance with regulations prescribed under this subsection shall be enforced with respect to Federal credit unions under sections 1766 and 1786 of title 12.

(5) For the purpose of the exercise by any agency referred to in paragraph (2) of its powers under any Act referred to in that paragraph, a violation of any regulation prescribed under this subsection shall be deemed to be a violation of a requirement imposed under that Act. In addition to its powers under any provision of law specifically referred to in paragraph (2), each of the agencies referred to in that paragraph may exercise, for the purpose of enforcing compliance with any regulation prescribed under this subsection, any other authority conferred on it by law.

(6) The authority of the Board of Governors of the Federal Reserve System to issue regulations under this subsection does not impair the authority of any other agency designated in this subsection to make rules respecting its own procedures in enforcing compliance with regulations prescribed under this subsection.

(7) Each agency exercising authority under this subsection shall transmit to the Congress each year a detailed report on its activities under this paragraph during the preceding calendar year. The terms used in this paragraph that are not defined in this subchapter or otherwise defined in section 1813(s) of title 12 shall have the meaning given to them in section 3101 of title 12.

(g) Exemptions and stays from application of rules; procedures

(1) Any person to whom a rule under subsection (a)(1)(B) of this section applies may petition the Commission for an exemption from such rule.

(2) If, on its own motion or on the basis of a petition under paragraph (1), the Commission finds that the application of a rule prescribed under subsection (a)(1)(B) of this section to any person or class or (FOOTNOTE 3) persons is not necessary to prevent the unfair or deceptive act or practice to which the rule relates, the Commission may exempt such person or class >from all or part of such rule. Section 553 of title 5 shall apply to action under this paragraph. (FOOTNOTE 3) So in original. Probably should be "of".

(3) Neither the pendency of a proceeding under this subsection respecting an exemption from a rule, nor the pendency of judicial proceedings to review the Commission's action or failure to act under this subsection, shall stay the applicability of such rule under subsection (a)(1)(B) of this section.

(h) Restriction on rulemaking authority of Commission respecting children's advertising proceedings pending on May 28, 1980 The Commission shall not have any authority to promulgate any rule in the children's advertising proceeding pending on May 28, 1980, or in any substantially similar proceeding on the basis of a determination by the Commission that such advertising constitutes an unfair act or practice in or affecting commerce.

(i) Meetings with outside parties

(1) For purposes of this subsection, the term "outside party" means any person other than

(A) a Commissioner;

(B) an officer or employee of the Commission; or

(C) any person who has entered into a contract or any other agreement or arrangement with the Commission to provide any goods or services (including consulting services) to the Commission.

(2) Not later than 60 days after May 28, 1980, the Commission shall publish a proposed rule, and not later than 180 days after May 28, 1980, the Commission shall promulgate a final rule, which shall authorize the Commission or any Commissioner to meet with any outside party concerning any rulemaking proceeding of the Commission. Such rule shall provide that -

(A) notice of any such meeting shall be included in any weekly calendar prepared by the Commission; and

(B) a verbatim record or a summary of any such meeting, or of any communication relating to any such meeting, shall be kept, made available to the public, and included in the rulemaking record.

(j) Communications by investigative personnel with staff of Commission concerning matters outside rulemaking record prohibited Not later than 60 days after May 28, 1980, the Commission shall publish a proposed rule, and not later than 180 days after May 28, 1980, the Commission shall promulgate a final rule, which shall prohibit any officer, employee, or agent of the Commission with any investigative responsibility or other responsibility relating to any rulemaking proceeding within any operating bureau of the Commission, from communicating or causing to be communicated to any Commissioner or to the personal staff of any Commissioner any fact relevant to the merits of such proceeding and which is not on the rulemaking record of such proceeding, unless such communication is made available to the public and is included in the rulemaking record. The provisions of this subsection shall not apply to any communication to the extent such communication is required for the disposition of ex parte matters as authorized by law.

§ 57b. Civil actions for violations of rules and cease and desist orders respecting unfair or deceptive acts or practices.

(a) Suits by Commission against persons, partnerships, or corporations; jurisdiction; relief for dishonest or fraudulent acts

(1) If any person, partnership, or corporation violates any rule under this subchapter respecting unfair or deceptive acts or practices (other than an interpretive rule, or a rule violation of which the Commission has provided is not an unfair or deceptive act or practice in violation of section 45(a) of this title), then the Commission may commence a civil action against such person, partnership, or

corporation for relief under subsection (b) of this section in a United States district court or in any court of competent jurisdiction of a State.

(2) If any person, partnership, or corporation engages in any unfair or deceptive act or practice (within the meaning of section 45(a)(1) of this title) with respect to which the Commission has issued a final cease and desist order which is applicable to such person, partnership, or corporation, then the Commission may commence a civil action against such person, partnership, or corporation in a United States district court or in any court of competent jurisdiction of a State. If the Commission satisfies the court that the act or practice to which the cease and desist order relates is one which a reasonable man would have known under the circumstances was dishonest or fraudulent, the court may grant relief under subsection (b) of this section.

(b) Nature of relief available The court in an action under subsection (a) of this section shall have jurisdiction to grant such relief as the court finds necessary to redress injury to consumers or other persons, partnerships, and corporations resulting from the rule violation or the unfair or deceptive act or practice, as the case may be. Such relief may include, but shall not be limited to, rescission or reformation of contracts, the refund of money or return of property, the payment of damages, and public notification respecting the rule violation or the unfair or deceptive act or practice, as the case may be; except that nothing in this subsection is intended to authorize the imposition of any exemplary or punitive damages.

(c) Conclusiveness of findings of Commission in cease and desist proceedings; notice of judicial proceedings to injured persons, etc.

(1) If

(A) a cease and desist order issued under section 45(b) of this title has become final under section 45(g) of this title with respect to any person's, partnership's, or corporation's rule violation or unfair or deceptive act or practice, and

(B) an action under this section is brought with respect to such person's, partnership's, or corporation's rule violation or act or practice, then the findings of the Commission as to the material facts in the proceeding under section 45(b) of this title with respect to such person's, partnership's, or corporation's rule violation or act or practice, shall be conclusive unless

(i) the terms of such cease and desist order expressly provide that the Commission's findings shall not be conclusive, or

(ii) the order became final by reason of section 45(g)(1) of this title, in which case such finding shall be conclusive if supported by evidence.

(2) The court shall cause notice of an action under this section to be given in a manner which is reasonably calculated, under all of the circumstances, to apprise the persons, partnerships, and corporations allegedly injured by the defendant's rule violation or act or practice of the pendency of such action. Such notice may, in the discretion of the court, be given by publication.

(d) Time for bringing of actions No action may be brought by the Commission under this section more than 3 years after the rule violation to which an action under subsection (a)(1) of this section relates, or the unfair or deceptive act or practice to which an action under subsection (a)(2) of this section relates; except that if a cease and desist order with respect to any person's, partnership's, or corporation's rule violation or unfair or deceptive act or practice has become final and such order was issued in a proceeding under section 45(b) of this title which was commenced not later than 3 years after the rule violation or act or practice occurred, a civil action may be commenced under this section against such person, partnership, or corporation at any time before the expiration of one year after such order becomes final.

(e) Availability of additional Federal or State remedies; other authority of Commission unaffected Remedies provided in this section are in addition to, and not in lieu of, any other remedy or right of action provided by State or Federal law. Nothing in this section shall be construed to affect any authority of the Commission under any other provision of law.

§ 57b-1. Civil investigative demands.

(a) Definitions For purposes of this section:

(1) The terms "civil investigative demand" and "demand" mean any demand issued by the commission under subsection (c)(1) of this section.

(2) The term "Commission investigation" means any inquiry conducted by a Commission investigator for the purpose of ascertaining whether any person is or has been engaged in any unfair or deceptive acts or practices in or affecting commerce (within the meaning of section 45(a)(1) of this title) or in any antitrust violations.

(3) The term "Commission investigator" means any attorney or investigator employed by the Commission who is charged with the duty of enforcing or carrying into effect any provisions relating to unfair or deceptive acts or practices in or affecting commerce (within the meaning of section 45(a)(1) of this title) or any provisions relating to antitrust violations.

(4) The term "custodian" means the custodian or any deputy custodian designated under section 57b-2(b)(2)(A) of this title.

(5) The term "documentary material" includes the original or any copy of any book, record, report, memorandum, paper, communication, tabulation, chart, or other document.

(6) The term "person" means any natural person, partnership, corporation, association, or other legal entity, including any person acting under color or authority of State law.

(7) The term "violation" means any act or omission constituting an unfair or deceptive act or practice in or affecting commerce (within the meaning of section 45(a)(1) of this title) or any antitrust violation.

(8) The term "antitrust violation" means -

(A) any unfair method of competition (within the meaning of section 45(a)(1) of this title);

(B) any violation of the Clayton Act (15 U.S.C. 12 et seq.) or of any other Federal statute that prohibits, or makes available to the Commission a civil remedy with respect to, any restraint upon or monopolization of interstate or foreign trade or commerce;

(C) with respect to the International Antitrust Enforcement Assistance Act of 1994 (15 U.S.C. 6201 et seq.), any violation of any of the foreign antitrust laws (as defined in section 12 of such Act (15 U.S.C. 6211)) with respect to which a request is made under section 3 of such Act (15 U.S.C. 6202); or

(D) any activity in preparation for a merger, acquisition, joint venture, or similar transaction, which if consummated, may result in any such unfair method of competition or in any such violation.

(b) Actions conducted by Commission respecting unfair or deceptive acts or practices in or affecting commerce For the purpose of investigations performed pursuant to this section with respect to unfair or deceptive acts or practices in or affecting commerce (within the meaning of section 45(a)(1) of this title); all actions of the Commission taken under section 46 and section 49 of this title shall be conducted pursuant to subsection (c) of this section.

(c) Issuance of demand; contents; service; verified return; sworn certificate; answers; taking of oral testimony

(1) Whenever the Commission has reason to believe that any person may be in possession, custody, or control of any documentary material or tangible things, or may have any information, relevant to unfair or deceptive acts or practices in or affecting commerce (within the meaning of section 45(a)(1) of this title), or to antitrust violations, the Commission may, before the institution of any proceedings under this subchapter, issue in writing, and cause to be served upon such person, a civil investigative demand requiring such person to produce such documentary material for inspection and copying or reproduction, to submit such tangible things, to file written reports or answers to questions, to give oral testimony concerning documentary material or other information, or to furnish any combination of such material, answers, or testimony.

(2) Each civil investigative demand shall state the nature of the conduct constituting the alleged violation which is under investigation and the provision of law applicable to such violation.

(3) Each civil investigative demand for the production of documentary material shall -

(A) describe each class of documentary material to be produced under the demand with such definiteness and certainty as to permit such material to be fairly identified;

(B) prescribe a return date or dates which will provide a reasonable period of time within which the material so demanded may be assembled and made available for inspection and copying or reproduction; and

(C) identify the custodian to whom such material shall be made available.

(4) Each civil investigative demand for the submission of tangible things shall -

(A) describe each class of tangible things to be submitted under the demand with such definiteness and certainty as to permit such things to be fairly identified;

(B) prescribe a return date or dates which will provide a reasonable period of time within which the things so demanded may be assembled and submitted; and

(C) identify the custodian to whom such things shall be submitted.

(5) Each civil investigative demand for written reports or answers to questions shall -

(A) propound with definiteness and certainty the reports to be produced or the questions to be answered;

(B) prescribe a date or dates at which time written reports or answers to questions shall be submitted; and

(C) identify the custodian to whom such reports or answers shall be submitted.

(6) Each civil investigative demand for the giving of oral testimony shall -

(A) prescribe a date, time, and place at which oral testimony shall be commenced; and

(B) identify a Commission investigator who shall conduct the investigation and the custodian to whom the transcript of such investigation shall be submitted.

(7) (A) Any civil investigative demand may be served by any Commission investigator at any place within the territorial jurisdiction of any court of the United States.

(B) Any such demand or any enforcement petition filed under this section may be served upon any person who is not found within the territorial jurisdiction of any court of the United States, in such manner as the Federal Rules of Civil Procedure prescribe for service in a foreign nation.

(C) To the extent that the courts of the United States have authority to assert jurisdiction over such person consistent with due process, the United States District Court for the District of Columbia shall have the same jurisdiction to take any action respecting compliance with this section by such person that such district court would have if such person were personally within the jurisdiction of such district court.

(8) Service of any civil investigative demand or any enforcement petition filed under this section may be made upon a partnership, corporation, association, or other legal entity by -

(A) delivering a duly executed copy of such demand or petition to any partner, executive officer, managing agent, or general agent of such partnership, corporation, association, or other legal entity, or to any agent of such partnership, corporation, association, or other legal entity authorized by appointment or by law to receive service of process on behalf of such partnership, corporation, association, or other legal entity;

(B) delivering a duly executed copy of such demand or petition to the principal office or place of business of the partnership, corporation, association, or other legal entity to be served; or

(C) depositing a duly executed copy in the United States mails, by registered or certified mail, return receipt requested, duly addressed to such partnership, corporation, association, or other legal entity at its principal office or place of business.

(9) Service of any civil investigative demand or of any enforcement petition filed under this section may be made upon any natural person by -

(A) delivering a duly executed copy of such demand or petition to the person to be served; or

(B) depositing a duly executed copy in the United States mails by registered or certified mail, return receipt requested, duly addressed to such person at his residence or principal office or place of business.

(10) A verified return by the individual serving any civil investigative demand or any enforcement petition filed under this section setting forth the manner of such service shall be proof of such service. In the case of service by registered or certified mail, such return shall be accompanied by the return post office receipt of delivery of such demand or enforcement petition.

(11) The production of documentary material in response to a civil investigative demand shall be made under a sworn certificate, in such form as the demand designates, by the person, if a natural person, to whom the demand is directed or, if not a natural person, by any person having knowledge of the facts and circumstances relating to such production, to the effect that all of the documentary material required by the demand and in the possession, custody, or control of the person to whom the demand is as been produced and made available to the custodian.

(12) The submission of tangible things in response to a civil investigative demand shall be made under a sworn certificate, in such form as the demand designates, by the person to whom the demand is directed or, if not a natural person, by any person having knowledge of the facts and circumstances relating to such production, to the effect that all of the tangible things required by the demand and in the possession, custody, or control of the person to whom the demand is directed have been submitted to the custodian.

(13) Each reporting requirement or question in a civil investigative demand shall be answered separately and fully in writing under oath, unless it is objected to, in which event the reasons for the objection shall be stated in lieu of an answer, and it

shall be submitted under a sworn certificate, in such form as the demand designates, by the person, if a natural person, to whom the demand is directed or, if not a natural person, by any person responsible for answering each reporting requirement or question, to the effect that all information required by the demand and in the possession, custody, control, or knowledge of the person to whom the demand is directed has been submitted.

(14) (A) Any Commission investigator before whom oral testimony is to be taken shall put the witness on oath or affirmation and shall personally, or by any individual acting under his direction and in his presence, record the testimony of the witness. The testimony shall be taken stenographically and transcribed. After the testimony is fully transcribed, the Commission investigator before whom the testimony is taken shall promptly transmit a copy of the transcript of the testimony to the custodian.

(B) Any Commission investigator before whom oral testimony is to be taken shall exclude from the place where the testimony is to be taken all other persons except the person giving the testimony, his attorney, the officer before whom the testimony is to be taken, and any stenographer taking such testimony.

(C) The oral testimony of any person taken pursuant to a civil investigative demand shall be taken in the judicial district of the United States in which such person resides, is found, or transacts business, or in such other place as may be agreed upon by the Commission investigator before whom the oral testimony of such person is to be taken and such person.

(D) (i) Any person compelled to appear under a civil investigative demand for oral testimony pursuant to this section may be accompanied, represented, and advised by an attorney. The attorney may advise such person, in confidence, either upon the request of such person or upon the initiative of the attorney, with respect to any question asked of such person.

(ii) Such person or attorney may object on the record to any question, in whole or in part, and shall briefly state for the record the reason for the objection. An objection may properly be made, received, and entered upon the record when it is claimed that such person is entitled to refuse to answer the question on grounds of any constitutional or other legal right or privilege, including the privilege against self-incrimination. Such person shall not otherwise object to or refuse to answer any question, and shall not himself or through his attorney otherwise interrupt the oral examination. If such person refuses to answer any question, the Commission may petition the district court of the United States pursuant to this section for an order compelling such person to answer such question.

(iii) If such person refuses to answer any question on grounds of the privilege against self-incrimination, the testimony of such person may be compelled in accordance with the provisions of section 6004 of title 18.

(E) (i) After the testimony of any witness is fully transcribed, the Commission investigator shall afford the witness (who may be accompanied by an attorney) a reasonable opportunity to examine the transcript. The transcript shall be read to or by the witness, unless such examination and reading are waived by the witness. Any changes in form or substance which the witness desires to make shall be entered and identified upon the transcript by the Commission investigator with a statement of the reasons given by the witness for making such changes. The transcript shall then be signed by the witness, unless the witness in writing waives the signing, is ill, cannot be found, or refuses to sign.

(ii) If the transcript is not signed by the witness during the 30-day period following the date upon which the witness is first afforded a reasonable opportunity to examine it, the Commission investigator shall sign the transcript and state on the record the fact of the waiver, illness, absence of the witness, or the refusal to sign, together with any reasons given for the failure to sign.

(F) The Commission investigator shall certify on the transcript that the witness was duly sworn by him and that the transcript is a true record of the testimony given by the witness, and the Commission investigator shall promptly deliver the transcript or send it by registered or certified mail to the custodian.

(G) The Commission investigator shall furnish a copy of the transcript (upon payment of reasonable charges for the transcription) to the witness only, except that the Commission may for good cause limit such witness to inspection of the official transcript of his testimony.

(H) Any witness appearing for the taking of oral testimony pursuant to a civil investigative demand shall be entitled to the same fees and mileage which are paid to witnesses in the district courts of the United States.

(d) Procedures for demand material Materials received as a result of a civil investigative demand shall be subject to the procedures established in section 57b-2 of this title.

(e) Petition for enforcement Whenever any person fails to comply with any civil investigative demand duly served upon him under this section, or whenever satisfactory copying or reproduction of material requested pursuant to the demand cannot be accomplished and such person refuses to surrender such material, the Commission, through such officers or attorneys as it may designate, may file, in the district court of the United States for any judicial district in such person resides, is found, or transacts business, and serve upon such person, a petition for an order of such court for the enforcement of this section. All process of any court to which application may be made as provided in this subsection may be served in any judicial district.

(f) Petition for order modifying or setting aside demand

(1) Not later than 20 days after the service of any civil investigative demand upon any person under subsection (c) of this section, or at any time before the return date specified in the demand, whichever period is shorter, or within such period exceeding 20 days after service or in excess of such return date as may be prescribed in writing, subsequent to service, by any Commission investigator named in the demand, such person may file with the Commission a petition for an order by the Commission modifying or setting aside the demand.

(2) The time permitted for compliance with the demand in whole or in part, as deemed proper and ordered by the Commission, shall not run during the pendency of such petition at the Commission, except that such person shall comply with any portions of the demand not sought to be modified or set aside. Such petition shall specify each ground upon which the petitioner relies in seeking such relief, and may be based upon any failure of the demand to comply with the provisions of this section, or upon any constitutional or other legal right or privilege of such person.

(g) Custodial control of documentary material, tangible things, reports, etc. At any time during which any custodian is in custody or control of any documentary material, tangible things, reports, answers to questions, or transcripts of oral testimony given by any person in compliance with any civil investigative demand, such person may file, in the district court of the United States for the judicial district within which the office of such custodian is situated, and serve upon such custodian, a petition for an order of such court requiring the performance by such custodian of any duty imposed upon him by this section or section 57b-2 of this title.

(h) Jurisdiction of court Whenever any petition is filed in any district court of the United States under this section, such court shall have jurisdiction to hear and determine the matter so presented, and to enter such order or orders as may be required to carry into effect the provisions of this section. Any final order so entered shall be subject to appeal pursuant to section 1291 of title 28. Any disobedience of any final order entered under this section by any court shall be punished as a contempt of such court.

(i) Commission authority to issue subpoenas or make demand for information Notwithstanding any other provision of law, the Commission shall have no authority to issue a subpoena or make a demand for information, under authority of this subchapter or any other provision of law, unless such subpoena or demand for information is signed by a Commissioner acting pursuant to a Commission resolution. The Commission shall not delegate the power conferred by this section to sign subpoenas or demands for information to any other person.

(j) Applicability of this section The provisions of this section shall not -

(1) apply to any proceeding under section 45(b) of this title, any proceeding under section 11(b) of the Clayton Act (15 U.S.C. 21(b)), or any adjudicative proceeding under any other provision of law; or

(2) apply to or affect the jurisdiction, duties, or powers of any agency of the Federal Government, other than the Commission, regardless of whether such jurisdiction, duties, or powers are derived in whole or in part, by reference to this subchapter.

§ 57b-2. Confidentiality

(a) Definitions For purposes of this section:

(1) The term "material" means documentary material, tangible things, written reports or answers to questions, and transcripts of oral testimony.

(2) The term "Federal agency" has the meaning given it in section 552(e) (FOOTNOTE 1) of title 5. (FOOTNOTE 1) See References in Text note below.

(b) Procedures respecting documents, tangible things, or transcripts of oral testimony received pursuant to compulsory process or investigation

(1) With respect to any document, tangible thing, or transcript of oral testimony received by the Commission pursuant to compulsory process in an investigation, a purpose of which is to determine whether any person may have violated any provision of the laws administered by the Commission, the procedures established in paragraph (2) through paragraph (7) shall apply.

(2) (A) The Commission shall designate a duly authorized agent to serve as custodian of documentary material, tangible things, or written reports or answers to questions, and transcripts of oral testimony, and such additional duly authorized agents as the Commission shall determine from time to time to be necessary to serve as deputies to the custodian.

(B) Any person upon whom any demand for the production of documentary material has been duly served shall make such material available for inspection and copying or reproduction to the custodian designated in such demand at the principal place of business of such person (or at such other place as such custodian and such person thereafter may agree or prescribe in writing or as the court may direct pursuant to section 57b-1(h) of this title) on the return date specified in such demand (or on such later date as such custodian may prescribe in writing). Such person may upon written agreement between such person and the custodian substitute copies for originals of all or any part of such material.

(3) (A) The custodian to whom any documentary material, tangible things, written reports or answers to questions, and transcripts of oral testimony are delivered shall take physical possession of such material, reports or answers, and transcripts, and shall be responsible for the use made of such material, reports or answers, and transcripts, and for the return of material, pursuant to the requirements of this section.

(B) The custodian may prepare such copies of the documentary material, written reports or answers to questions, and transcripts of oral testimony, and may make tangible things available, as may be required for official use by any duly authorized officer or employee of the Commission under regulations which shall be promulgated by the Commission. Notwithstanding subparagraph (C), such material, things, and transcripts may be used by any such officer or employee in connection with the taking of oral testimony under this section.

(C) Except as otherwise provided in this section, while in the possession of the custodian, no documentary material, tangible things, reports or answers to questions, and transcripts of oral testimony shall be available for examination by any individual other than a duly authorized officer or employee of the Commission without the consent of the person who produced the material, things, or transcripts. Nothing in this section is intended to prevent disclosure to either House of the Congress or to any committee or subcommittee of the Congress, except that the Commission immediately shall notify the owner or provider of any such information of a request for information designated as confidential by the owner or provider.

(D) While in the possession of the custodian and under such reasonable terms and conditions as the Commission shall prescribe -

(i) documentary material, tangible things, or written reports shall be available for examination by the person who produced the material, or by any duly authorized representative of such person; and

(ii) answers to questions in writing and transcripts of oral testimony shall be available for examination by the person who produced the testimony or by his attorney.

(4) Whenever the Commission has instituted a proceeding against a person, partnership, or corporation, the custodian may deliver to any officer or employee of the Commission documentary material, tangible things, written reports or answers to questions, and transcripts of oral testimony for official use in connection with such proceeding. Upon the completion of the proceeding, the officer or employee shall return to the custodian any such material so delivered which has not been received into the record of the proceeding.

(5) If any documentary material, tangible things, written reports or answers to questions, and transcripts of oral testimony have been produced in the course of any investigation by any person pursuant to compulsory process and -

(A) any proceeding arising out of the investigation has been completed; or

(B) no proceeding in which the material may be used has been commenced within a reasonable time after completion of the examination and analysis of all such material and other information assembled in the course of the investigation; then the custodian shall, upon written request of the person who produced the material, return to the person any such material which has not been received into the record of any such proceeding (other than copies of such material made by the custodian pursuant to paragraph (3)(B)).

(6) The custodian of any documentary material, written reports or answers to questions, and transcripts of oral testimony may deliver to any officers or employees of appropriate Federal law enforcement agencies, in response to a written request, copies of such material for use in connection with an investigation or proceeding under the jurisdiction of any such agency. The custodian of any tangible things may make such things available for inspection to such persons on the same basis. Such materials shall not be made available to any such agency until the custodian received certification of any officer of such agency that such information will be maintained in confidence and will be used only for official law enforcement purposes. Such documentary material, results of inspections of tangible things, written reports or answers to questions, and transcripts of oral testimony may be used by any officer or employee of such agency only in such manner and subject to such conditions as apply to the Commission under this section. The custodian may make such materials available to any State law enforcement agency upon the prior certification of any officer of such agency that such information will be maintained in confidence and will be used only for official law enforcement purposes.

(7) In the event of the death, disability, or separation from service in the Commission of the custodian of any documentary material, tangible things, written reports or answers to questions, and transcripts of oral testimony produced under any demand issued under this subchapter, or the official relief of the custodian from responsibility for the custody and control of such material, the Commission promptly shall -

(A) designate under paragraph (2)(A) another duly authorized agent to serve as custodian of such material; and

(B) transmit in writing to the person who produced the material or testimony notice as to the identity and address of the successor so designated. Any successor designated under paragraph (2)(A) as a result of the requirements of this paragraph shall have (with regard to the material involved) all duties and responsibilities imposed by this section upon his predecessor in office with regard to such material, except that he shall not be held responsible for any default or dereliction which occurred before his designation.

(c) Information considered confidential

(1) All information reported to or otherwise obtained by the Commission which is not subject to the requirements of subsection (b) of this section shall be considered confidential when so marked by the person supplying the information and shall not be disclosed, except in accordance with the procedures established in paragraph (2) and paragraph (3).

(2) If the Commission determines that a document marked confidential by the person supplying it may be disclosed because it is not a trade secret or commercial or financial information which is obtained from any person and which is privileged

or confidential, within the meaning of section 46(f) of this title, then the Commission shall notify such person in writing that the Commission intends to disclose the document at a date not less than 10 days after the date of receipt of notification.

(3) Any person receiving such notification may, if he believes disclosure of the document would cause disclosure of a trade secret, or commercial or financial information which is obtained from any person and which is privileged or confidential, within the meaning of section 46(f) of this title, before the date set for release of the document, bring an action in the district court of the United States for the district within which the documents are located or in the United States District Court for the District of Columbia to restrain disclosure of the document. Any person receiving such notification may file with the appropriate district court or court of appeals of the United States, as appropriate, an application for a stay of disclosure. The documents shall not be disclosed until the court has ruled on the application for a stay.

(d) Particular disclosures allowed

(1) The provisions of subsection (c) of this section shall not be construed to prohibit -

(A) the disclosure of information to either House of the Congress or to any committee or subcommittee of the Congress, except that the Commission immediately shall notify the owner or provider of any such information of a request for information designated as confidential by the owner or provider;

(B) the disclosure of the results of any investigation or study carried out or prepared by the Commission, except that no information shall be identified nor shall information be disclosed in such a manner as to disclose a trade secret of any person supplying the trade secret, or to disclose any commercial or financial information which is obtained from any person and which is privileged or confidential;

(C) the disclosure of relevant and material information in Commission adjudicative proceedings or in judicial proceedings to which the Commission is a party; or

(D) the disclosure to a Federal agency of disaggregated information obtained in accordance with section 3512 (FOOTNOTE 1) of title 44, except that the recipient agency shall use such disaggregated information for economic, statistical, or policymaking purposes only, and shall not disclose such information in an individually identifiable form.

(2) Any disclosure of relevant and material information in Commission adjudicative proceedings or in judicial proceedings to which the Commission is a party shall be governed by the rules of the Commission for adjudicative proceedings or by court rules or orders, except that the rules of the Commission shall not be amended in a manner inconsistent with the purposes of this section.

(e) Effect on other statutory provisions limiting disclosureNothing in this section shall supersede any statutory provision which expressly prohibits or limits particular disclosures by the Commission, or which authorizes disclosures to any other Federal agency.

(f) Exemption from disclosure Any material which is received by the Commission in any investigation, a purpose of which is to determine whether any person may have violated any provision of the laws administered by the Commission, and which is provided pursuant to any compulsory process under this subchapter or which is provided voluntarily in place of such compulsory process shall be exempt from disclosure under section 552 of title 5.

§ 57b-3. Rulemaking process

(a) Definitions For purposes of this section:

(1) The term "rule" means any rule promulgated by the Commission under section 46 or section 57a of this title, except that such term does not include interpretive rules, rules involving Commission management or personnel, general statements of policy, or rules relating to Commission organization, procedure, or practice. Such term does not include any amendment to a rule unless the Commission -

(A) estimates that such amendment will have an annual effect on the national economy of $100,000,000 or more;

(B) estimates that such amendment will cause a substantial change in the cost or price of goods or services which are used extensively by particular industries, which are supplied extensively in particular geographic regions, or which are acquired in significant quantities by the Federal Government, or by State or local governments; or

(C) otherwise determines that such amendment will have a significant impact upon persons subject to regulation under such amendment and upon consumers.

(2) The term "rulemaking" means any Commission process for formulating or amending a rule.

(b) Notice of proposed rulemaking; regulatory analysis; contents; issuance

(1) In any case in which the Commission publishes notice of a proposed rulemaking, the Commission shall issue a preliminary regulatory analysis relating to the proposed rule involved. Each preliminary regulatory analysis shall contain -

(A) a concise statement of the need for, and the objectives of, the proposed rule;

(B) a description of any reasonable alternatives to the proposed rule which may accomplish the stated objective of the rule in a manner consistent with applicable law; and

(C) for the proposed rule, and for each of the alternatives described in the analysis, a preliminary analysis of the projected benefits and any adverse economic effects and any other effects, and of the effectiveness of the proposed rule and each alternative in meeting the stated objectives of the proposed rule.

(2) In any case in which the Commission promulgates a final rule, the Commission shall issue a final regulatory analysis relating to the final rule. Each final regulatory analysis shall contain -

(A) a concise statement of the need for, and the objectives of, the final rule;

(B) a description of any alternatives to the final rule which were considered by the Commission;

(C) an analysis of the projected benefits and any adverse economic effects and any other effects of the final rule;

(D) an explanation of the reasons for the determination of the Commission that the final rule will attain its objectives in a manner consistent with applicable law and the reasons the particular alternative was chosen; and

(E) a summary of any significant issues raised by the comments submitted during the public comment period in response to the preliminary regulatory analysis, and a summary of the assessment by the Commission of such issues.

(3) (A) In order to avoid duplication or waste, the Commission is authorized to - (i) consider a series of closely related rules as one rule for purposes of this subsection; and

(ii) whenever appropriate, incorporate any data or analysis contained in a regulatory analysis issued under this subsection in the statement of basis and purpose to accompany any rule promulgated under section 57a(a)(1)(B) of this title, and incorporate by reference in any preliminary or final regulatory analysis information contained in a notice of proposed rulemaking or a statement of basis and purpose.

(B) The Commission shall include, in each notice of proposed rulemaking and in each publication of a final rule, a statement of the manner in which the public may obtain copies ofthe preliminary and final regulatory analyses. The Commission may charge a reasonable fee for the copying and mailing of regulatory analyses. The regulatory analyses shall be furnished without charge or at a reduced charge if the Commission determines that waiver or reduction of the fee is in the public interest because furnishing the information primarily benefits the general public.

(4) The Commission is authorized to delay the completion of any of the requirements established in this subsection by publishing in the Federal Register, not later than the date of publication of the final rule involved, a finding that the final rule is being promulgated in response to an emergency which makes timely compliance with the provisions of this subsection impracticable. Such publication shall include a statement of the reasons for such finding.

(5) The requirements of this subsection shall not be construed to alter in any manner the substantive standards applicable to any action by the Commission, or the procedural standards otherwise applicable to such action.

(c) Judicial review

(1) The contents and adequacy of any regulatory analysis prepared or issued by the Commission under this section, including the adequacy of any procedure involved in such preparation or issuance, shall not be subject to any judicial review in any court, except that a court, upon review of a rule pursuant to section 57a(e) of this title, may set aside such rule if the Commission has failed entirely to prepare a regulatory analysis.

(2) Except as specified in paragraph (1), no Commission action may be invalidated, remanded, or otherwise affected by any court on account of any failure to comply with the requirements of this section.

(3) The provisions of this subsection do not alter the substantive or procedural standards otherwise applicable to judicial review of any action by the Commission.

(d) Regulatory agenda; contents; publication dates in Federal Register

(1) The Commission shall publish at least semiannually a regulatory agenda. Each regulatory agenda shall contain a list of rules which the Commission intends to propose or promulgate during the 12-month period following the publication of the agenda. On the first Monday in October of each year, the Commission shall publish in the Federal Register a schedule showing the dates during the current fiscal year on which the semiannual regulatory agenda of the Commission will be published. (2) For each rule listed in a regulatory agenda, the Commission shall -

(A) describe the rule;

(B) state the objectives of and the legal basis for the rule; and

(C) specify any dates established or anticipated by the Commission for taking action, including dates for advance notice of proposed rulemaking, notices of proposed rulemaking, and final action by the Commission.

(3) Each regulatory agenda shall state the name, office address, and office telephone number of the Commission officer or employee responsible for responding to any inquiry relating to each rule listed.

(4) The Commission shall not propose or promulgate a rule which was not listed on a regulatory agenda unless the Commission publishes with the rule an explanation of the reasons the rule was omitted from such agenda.

International Privacy Law

UNIVERSAL DECLARATION OF
HUMAN RIGHTS (1948)

Summary

On December 10, 1948 the General Assembly of the United Nations adopted and proclaimed the Universal Declaration of Human Rights. The Declaration sets forth a comprehensive list of the rights to which all people are entitled. Because nations initially resisted the creation of a legally binding instrument defining these human rights and fundamental freedoms, the Universal Declaration of Human Rights at its inception was viewed by the nations as a non-binding agreement, without the force of law. However, with passage of time, the UDHR has acquired the force of law through its incorporation into national laws, and because its language and ideas have been included in subsequent, binding treaties on human rights.

Article 12 of the Universal Declaration recognizes the right to privacy. It states: "No one shall be subjected to arbitrary interference with his privacy, family, home or correspondence, nor to attacks upon his honour and reputation. Everyone has the right to the protection of the law against such interference or attacks. Article 12 was the first statement of privacy as a basic human right that ought to be recognized by all nations."

The privacy right envisioned by the Declaration is a universal right that seeks to safeguard the individual across a wide range of activities, including family life, physical residence, and correspondence. The privacy right is coupled with a right to freedom from attacks upon honor and reputation, thereby linking the idea of privacy with human dignity. It is also worth noting that the second sentence of Article 12 imposes a duty upon states to establish rights in law to protect citizens against arbitrary interference with privacy.

Many subsequent international agreements have recognized the right to privacy outlined in Article 12. Article 17 of the International Covenant on Civil and Political Rights adopts the language verbatim. The European Convention on Human Rights, the U.N. Convention on the Rights of the Child, and the American Convention on Human Rights also incorporate a right to privacy based on Article 12.

References

United Nations, Universal Declaration of Human Rights
[http://www.un.org/Overview/rights.html]

UN, Office of the High Commission for Human Rights
[http://www.unhchr.ch/udhr/lang/eng.htm]

International
Universal Declaration of Human Rights

ADOPTED BY THE UNITED NATIONS GENERAL ASSEMBLY 10 DECEMBER 1948

WHEREAS recognition of the inherent dignity and of the equal and inalienable rights of all members of the human family is the foundation of freedom, justice and peace in the world,

WHEREAS disregard and contempt for human rights have resulted in barbarous acts which have outraged the conscience of mankind, and the advent of a world in which human beings shall enjoy freedom of speech and belief and freedom from fear and want has been proclaimed as the highest aspiration of the common people,

WHEREAS it is essential, if man is not to be compelled to have recourse, as a last resort, to rebellion against tyranny and oppression, that human rights should be protected by the rule of law,

WHEREAS it is essential to promote the development of friendly relations between nations,

WHEREAS the peoples of the United Nations have in the Charter reaffirmed their faith in fundamental human rights, in the dignity and worth of the human person and in the equal rights of men and women and have determined to promote social progress and better standards of life in larger freedom,

WHEREAS Member States have pledged themselves to achieve, in co-operation with the United Nations, the promotion of universal respect for and observance of human rights and fundamental freedoms,

WHEREAS a common understanding of these rights and freedoms is of the greatest importance for the full realisation of this pledge,

Now, therefore, THE GENERAL ASSEMBLY proclaims this Universal Declaration of Human Rights as a common standard of achievement for all peoples and all nations, to the end that every individual and every organ of society, keeping this Declaration constantly in mind, shall strive by teaching and education to promote respect for these rights and freedoms and by progressive measures, national and international, to secure their universal and effective recognition and observance, both among the peoples of the Member States themselves and among the peoples of territories under their jurisdiction.

ARTICLE 1. All human beings are born free and equal in dignity and rights. They are endowed with reason and conscience and should act towards one another in a spirit of brotherhood.

International
Universal Declaration of Human Rights

ARTICLE 2. Everyone is entitled to all the rights and freedoms set forth in this Declaration, without distinction of any kind, such as race, colour, sex, language, religion, political or other opinion, national or social origin, property, birth or other status.

Furthermore, no distinction shall be made on the basis of the political, jurisdictional or international status of the country or territory to which a person belongs, whether it be independent, trust, non-self-governing or under any other limitation of sovereignty.

ARTICLE 3. Everyone has the right to life, liberty and security of person.

ARTICLE 4. No one shall be held in slavery or servitude; slavery and the slave trade shall be prohibited in all their forms.

ARTICLE 5. No one shall be subjected to torture or to cruel, inhuman or degrading treatment or punishment.

ARTICLE 6. Everyone has the right to recognition everywhere as a person before the law.

ARTICLE 7. All are equal before the law and are entitled without any discrimination to equal protection of the law. All are entitled to equal protection against any discrimination in violation of this Declaration and against any incitement to such discrimination.

ARTICLE 8. Everyone has the right to an effective remedy by the competent national tribunals for acts violating the fundamental rights granted him by the constitution or by law.

ARTICLE 9. No one shall be subjected to arbitrary arrest, detention or exile.

ARTICLE 10. Everyone is entitled in full equality to a fair and public hearing by an independent and impartial tribunal, in the determination of his rights and obligations and of any criminal charge against him.

ARTICLE 11. (1) Everyone charged with a penal offence has the right to be presumed innocent until proved guilty according to law in a public trial at which he has had all the guarantees necessary for his defence. (2) No one shall be held guilty of any penal offence on account of any act or omission which did not constitute a penal offence, under national or international law, at the time when it was committed. Nor shall a heavier penalty be imposed than the one that was applicable at the time the penal offence was committed.

ARTICLE 12. No one shall be subjected to arbitrary interference with his privacy, family, home or correspondence, nor to attacks upon his honour and reputation. Everyone has the right to the protection of the law against such interference or attacks.

ARTICLE 13. (1) Everyone has the right to freedom of movement and residence within the borders of each State. (2) Everyone has the right to leave any country, including his own, and to return to his country.

ARTICLE 14. (1) Everyone has the right to seek and to enjoy in other countries asylum from persecution. (2) This right may not be invoked in the case of prosecutions genuinely arising form non-political crimes or from acts contrary to the purposes and principles of the United Nations.

ARTICLE 15. (1) Everyone has the right to a nationality. (2) No one shall be arbitrarily deprived of his nationality nor denied the right to change his nationality.

ARTICLE 16. (1) Men and women of full age, without any limitation due to race, nationality or religion, have the right to marry and to found a family. They are entitled to equal rights as to marriage, during marriage and at its dissolution. (2) Marriage shall be entered into only with the free and full consent of the intending spouses. (3) The family is the natural and fundamental group unit of society and is entitled to protection by society and the State.

ARTICLE 17. (1) Everyone has the right to own property alone as well as in association with others. (2) No one shall be arbitrarily deprived of his property.

ARTICLE 18. Everyone has the right to freedom of thought, conscience and religion; this right includes freedom to change his religion or belief, and freedom, either alone or in community with others and in public or private, to manifest his religion or belief in teaching, practice, worship and observance.

ARTICLE 19. Everyone has the right to freedom of opinion and expression; this right includes freedom to hold opinions without interference and to seek, receive and impart information and ideas through any media and regardless of frontiers.

ARTICLE 20. (1) Everyone has the right to freedom of peaceful assembly and association. (2) No one may be compelled to belong to an association.

ARTICLE 21. (1) Everyone has the right to take part in the government of his country, directly or through chosen representatives. (2) Everyone has the right of equal access to public service in his country. (3) The will of the people shall be the basis of the authority of government; this will shall be expressed in periodic and genuine elections which shall be held by universal and equal suffrage and shall be held by secret vote or by equivalent free voting procedures.

ARTICLE 22. Everyone, as a member of society, has the right to social security and is entitled to realisation, through national effort and international co-operation and in accordance with the organisation and resources of each State, of the economic, social and cultural rights indispensable for his dignity and the free development of his personality.

ARTICLE 23. (1) Everyone has the right to work, to free choice of employment, to just and favourable conditions of work and to protection against unemployment. (2) Everyone, without any discrimination, has the right to equal pay for equal work. (3) Everyone has the right to just and favourable remuneration ensuring for himself and his family an existence worthy of human dignity, and supplemented, if necessary, by other means of social protection. (4) Everyone has the right to form and to join trade unions for the protection of his interests.

ARTICLE 24. Everyone has the right to rest and leisure, including reasonable limitation of working hours and periodic holidays with pay.

ARTICLE 25. (1) Everyone has the right to a standard of living adequate for the health and well-being of himself and of his family, including food, clothing, housing and medical care and necessary social services, and the right to security in the event of unemployment, sickness, disability, widowhood, old age and other lack of livelihood in circumstances beyond his control. (2) Motherhood and childhood are entitled to special care and assistance. All children, whether born in or out of wedlock, shall enjoy the same social protection.

ARTICLE 26. (1) Everyone has the right to education. Education shall be free, at least in the elementary and fundamental stages. Elementary education shall be compulsory. Technical and professional education shall be made generally available and higher education shall be equally accessible to all on the basis of merit. (2) Education shall be directed to the full development of the human personality and to the strengthening of respect for human rights and fundamental freedoms. It shall promote understanding, tolerance and friendship among all nations, racial or religious groups, and shall further the activities of the United Nations for the maintenance of peace. (3) Parents have a prior right to choose the kind of education that shall be given their children.

ARTICLE 27. (1) Everyone has the right to freely participate in the cultural life of the community, to enjoy the arts and to share in scientific advancement and its benefits. (2) Everyone has the right to the protection of the moral and material interests resulting from any scientific, literary or artistic production of which he is the author.

ARTICLE 28. Everyone is entitled to a social and international order in which the rights and freedoms set forth in this Declaration can be fully realised.

ARTICLE 29. (1) Everyone has duties to the community in which alone the free and full development of is personality is possible. (2) In the exercise of his rights and freedoms, everyone shall be subject only to such limitations as are determined by law solely for the purpose of securing due recognition and respect for the rights and freedoms of others and of meeting the just requirements of morality, public order and the general welfare in a democratic society. (3) These rights and freedoms may in no case be exercised contrary to the purposes and principles of the United Nations.

ARTICLE 30. Nothing in this Declaration may be interpreted as implying for any State, group or person any right to engage in any activity or to perform any act aimed at the destruction of any of the rights and freedoms set forth herein.

International
Council of Europe Convention on Human Rights

COUNCIIL OF EUROPE CONVENTION FOR THE PROTECTION OF HUMAN RIGHTS AND FUNDAMENTAL FREEDOMS (1950)[i]

Summary

The Council of Europe Convention for the Protection of Human Rights was adopted shortly after the Universal Declaration of Human Rights of the United Nations. Article 8 in the Council of Europe Convention addresses the right to respect for private and family life.

References

> Council of Europe, Legal Affairs, Treaty Office
> http://conventions.coe.int/Treaty/EN/CadreListeTraites.htm
> http://conventions.coe.int/treaty/en/Treaties/Word/005.doc

The text of the Convention had been amended according to the provisions of Protocol No. 3 (ETS No. 45), which entered into force on 21 September 1970, of Protocol No. 5 (ETS No. 55), which entered into force on 20 December 1971 and of Protocol No. 8 (ETS No. 118), which entered into force on 1 January 1990, and comprised also the text of Protocol No. 2 (ETS No. 44) which, in accordance with Article 5, paragraph 3 thereof, had been an integral part of the Convention since its entry into force on 21 September 1970. All provisions which had been amended or added by these Protocols are replaced by Protocol No. 11 (ETS No. 155), as from the date of its entry into force on 1 November 1998. As from that date, Protocol No. 9 (ETS No. 140), which entered into force on 1 October 1994, is repealed and Protocol No. 10 (ETS no. 146) has lost its purpose.

The governments signatory hereto, being members of the Council of Europe,
Considering the Universal Declaration of Human Rights proclaimed by the General Assembly of the United Nations on 10th December 1948;
Considering that this Declaration aims at securing the universal and effective recognition and observance of the Rights therein declared;
Considering that the aim of the Council of Europe is the achievement of greater unity between its members and that one of the methods by which that aim is to be pursued is the maintenance and further realisation of human rights and fundamental freedoms;
Reaffirming their profound belief in those fundamental freedoms which are the foundation of justice and peace in the world and are best maintained on the one hand by an effective political democracy and on the other by a common understanding and observance of the human rights upon which they depend;

Being resolved, as the governments of European countries which are like-minded and have a common heritage of political traditions, ideals, freedom and the rule of law, to take the first steps for the collective enforcement of certain of the rights stated in the Universal Declaration, Have agreed as follows:

Article 1 – Obligation to respect human rights

The High Contracting Parties shall secure to everyone within their jurisdiction the rights and freedoms defined in Section I of this Convention.

Section I– Rights and freedoms

Article 2 – Right to life

1. Everyone's right to life shall be protected by law. No one shall be deprived of his life intentionally save in the execution of a sentence of a court following his conviction of a crime for which this penalty is provided by law.

2. Deprivation of life shall not be regarded as inflicted in contravention of this article when it results from the use of force which is no more than absolutely necessary:

   a) in defence of any person from unlawful violence;

   b) in order to effect a lawful arrest or to prevent the escape of a person lawfully detained;

   c) in action lawfully taken for the purpose of quelling a riot or insurrection.

Article 3 – Prohibition of torture

No one shall be subjected to torture or to inhuman or degrading treatment or punishment.

Article 4 – Prohibition of slavery and forced labour

1. No one shall be held in slavery or servitude.

2. No one shall be required to perform forced or compulsory labour.

3. For the purpose of this article the term "forced or compulsory labour" shall not include:

   a) any work required to be done in the ordinary course of detention imposed according to the provisions of Article 5 of this Convention or during conditional release from such detention;

   b) any service of a military character or, in case of conscientious objectors in countries where they are recognised, service exacted instead of compulsory military service;

   c) any service exacted in case of an emergency or calamity threatening the life or well-being of the community;

   d) any work or service which forms part of normal civic obligations.

Article 5 – Right to liberty and security

1. Everyone has the right to liberty and security of person. No one shall be deprived of his liberty save in the following cases and in accordance with a procedure prescribed by law:

a) the lawful detention of a person after conviction by a competent court;

b) the lawful arrest or detention of a person for non- compliance with the lawful order of a court or in order to secure the fulfilment of any obligation prescribed by law;

c) the lawful arrest or detention of a person effected for the purpose of bringing him before the competent legal authority on reasonable suspicion of having committed an offence or when it is reasonably considered necessary to prevent his committing an offence or fleeing after having done so;

d) the detention of a minor by lawful order for the purpose of educational supervision or his lawful detention for the purpose of bringing him before the competent legal authority;

e) the lawful detention of persons for the prevention of the spreading of infectious diseases, of persons of unsound mind, alcoholics or drug addicts or vagrants;

f) the lawful arrest or detention of a person to prevent his effecting an unauthorised entry into the country or of a person against whom action is being taken with a view to deportation or extradition.

2. Everyone who is arrested shall be informed promptly, in a language which he understands, of the reasons for his arrest and of any charge against him.

3. Everyone arrested or detained in accordance with the provisions of paragraph 1.c of this article shall be brought promptly before a judge or other officer authorised by law to exercise judicial power and shall be entitled to trial within a reasonable time or to release pending trial. Release may be conditioned by guarantees to appear for trial.

4. Everyone who is deprived of his liberty by arrest or detention shall be entitled to take proceedings by which the lawfulness of his detention shall be decided speedily by a court and his release ordered if the detention is not lawful.

5. Everyone who has been the victim of arrest or detention in contravention of the provisions of this article shall have an enforceable right to compensation.

Article 6 – Right to a fair trial

1. In the determination of his civil rights and obligations or of any criminal charge against him, everyone is entitled to a fair and public hearing within a reasonable time by an independent and impartial tribunal established by law. Judgment shall be pronounced publicly but the press and public may be excluded from all or part of the trial in the interests of morals, public order or national security in a democratic society, where the interests of juveniles or the protection of the private life of the parties so require, or to the extent strictly necessary in the opinion of the court in special circumstances where publicity would prejudice the interests of justice.

2. Everyone charged with a criminal offence shall be presumed innocent until proved guilty according to law.

3. Everyone charged with a criminal offence has the following minimum rights:

a) to be informed promptly, in a language which he understands and in detail, of the nature and cause of the accusation against him;

b) to have adequate time and facilities for the preparation of his defence;

c) to defend himself in person or through legal assistance of his own choosing or, if he has not sufficient means to pay for legal assistance, to be given it free when the interests of justice so require;

d) to examine or have examined witnesses against him and to obtain the attendance and examination of witnesses on his behalf under the same conditions as witnesses against him;

e) to have the free assistance of an interpreter if he cannot understand or speak the language used in court.

Article 7 – No punishment without law

1. No one shall be held guilty of any criminal offence on account of any act or omission which did not constitute a criminal offence under national or international law at the time when it was committed. Nor shall a heavier penalty be imposed than the one that was applicable at the time the criminal offence was committed.

2. This article shall not prejudice the trial and punishment of any person for any act or omission which, at the time when it was committed, was criminal according to the general principles of law recognised by civilised nations.

Article 8 – Right to respect for private and family life

1. Everyone has the right to respect for his private and family life, his home and his correspondence.

2. There shall be no interference by a public authority with the exercise of this right except such as is in accordance with the law and is necessary in a democratic society in the interests of national security, public safety or the economic well-being of the country, for the prevention of disorder or crime, for the protection of health or morals, or for the protection of the rights and freedoms of others.

Article 9 – Freedom of thought, conscience and religion

1. Everyone has the right to freedom of thought, conscience and religion; this right includes freedom to change his religion or belief and freedom, either alone or in community with others and in public or private, to manifest his religion or belief, in worship, teaching, practice and observance.

2. Freedom to manifest one's religion or beliefs shall be subject only to such limitations as are prescribed by law and are necessary in a democratic society in the interests of public safety, for the protection of public order, health or morals, or for the protection of the rights and freedoms of others.

Article 10 – Freedom of expression

1. Everyone has the right to freedom of expression. This right shall include freedom to hold opinions and to receive and impart information and ideas without interference by public

authority and regardless of frontiers. This article shall not prevent States from requiring the licensing of broadcasting, television or cinema enterprises.

The exercise of these freedoms, since it carries with it duties and responsibilities, may be subject to such formalities, conditions, restrictions or penalties as are prescribed by law and are necessary in a democratic society, in the interests of national security, territorial integrity or public safety, for the prevention of disorder or crime, for the protection of health or morals, for the protection of the reputation or rights of others, for preventing the disclosure of information received in confidence, or for maintaining the authority and impartiality of the judiciary.

Article 11 – Freedom of assembly and association

1. Everyone has the right to freedom of peaceful assembly and to freedom of association with others, including the right to form and to join trade unions for the protection of his interests.
2. No restrictions shall be placed on the exercise of these rights other than such as are prescribed by law and are necessary in a democratic society in the interests of national security or public safety, for the prevention of disorder or crime, for the protection of health or morals or for the protection of the rights and freedoms of others. This article shall not prevent the imposition of lawful restrictions on the exercise of these rights by members of the armed forces, of the police or of the administration of the State.

Article 12 – Right to marry

Men and women of marriageable age have the right to marry and to found a family, according to the national laws governing the exercise of this right.

Article 13 – Right to an effective remedy

Everyone whose rights and freedoms as set forth in this Convention are violated shall have an effective remedy before a national authority notwithstanding that the violation has been committed by persons acting in an official capacity.

Article 14 – Prohibition of discrimination

The enjoyment of the rights and freedoms set forth in this Convention shall be secured without discrimination on any ground such as sex, race, colour, language, religion, political or other opinion, national or social origin, association with a national minority, property, birth or other status.

Article 15 – Derogation in time of emergency

1. In time of war or other public emergency threatening the life of the nation any High Contracting Party may take measures derogating from its obligations under this Convention to the extent strictly required by the exigencies of the situation, provided that such measures are not inconsistent with its other obligations under international law.

2. No derogation from Article 2, except in respect of deaths resulting from lawful acts of war, or from Articles 3, 4 (paragraph 1) and 7 shall be made under this provision.

3. Any High Contracting Party availing itself of this right of derogation shall keep the Secretary General of the Council of Europe fully informed of the measures which it has taken and the reasons therefor. It shall also inform the Secretary General of the Council of Europe when such measures have ceased to operate and the provisions of the Convention are again being fully executed.

Article 16 – Restrictions on political activity of aliens

Nothing in Articles 10, 11 and 14 shall be regarded as preventing the High Contracting Parties from imposing restrictions on the political activity of aliens.

Article 17 – Prohibition of abuse of rights

Nothing in this Convention may be interpreted as implying for any State, group or person any right to engage in any activity or perform any act aimed at the destruction of any of the rights and freedoms set forth herein or at their limitation to a greater extent than is provided for in the Convention.

Article 18 – Limitation on use of restrictions on rights

The restrictions permitted under this Convention to the said rights and freedoms shall not be applied for any purpose other than those for which they have been prescribed.

OECD PRIVACY GUIDELINES (1980)

Summary

On September 23, 1980, the Organization for Economic Cooperation and Development, a group of leading industrial countries concerned with global economic and democratic development, issued guidelines for privacy protection in the transfer of personal information across national borders. These are the Guidelines on the Protection of Privacy and Transborder Flows of Personal Data. The OECD Privacy Guidelines outline an eight-fold path to privacy.

First is the principle of collection limitation. This principle states that there should be limits to the collection of personal data; any such data collected should be obtained by lawful means and with the consent of the data subject, where appropriate. Second is the principle of data quality. This principle embodies the notion that collected data should be relevant to a specific purpose, and be accurate, complete, and up-to-date. Third is the principle of purpose specification; that is, the purpose for collecting data should be settled at the outset. The fourth principle, use limitation, works in tandem with the third. It states that the use of personal data ought be limited to specified purposes, and that data acquired for one purpose ought not be used for others. The fifth principle is security: data must be collected and stored in a way reasonably calculated to prevent its loss, theft, or modification. The sixth principle is openness. There should be a general position of transparency with respect to the practices of handling data. The seventh principle is individual participation: individual should have the right to access, confirm, and demand correction of their personal data. The eighth and last principle is accountability. Those in charge of handling data should be responsible for complying with the principles of the privacy guidelines.

In developing the guidelines, the OECD worked closely with the Council of Europe , which was at that time drafting its own Convention on Privacy. Examination of both the Guidelines and the Convention will show that they have much in common, as well as pointing to the general concern for individual privacy protection that arose in the late 1970s. Since the Guidelines' release, many OECD countries have enacted laws to implement them. In 1985, OECD extended the guidelines to cover transborder data flow. Although the OECD Guidelines are nonbinding on signatories, the eight privacy principles have had a significant impact on the development of privacy law around the globe.

References

OECD, Guidelines on the Protection of Privacy and Transborder Flows of Personal Data (1980)

http://www.oecd.org/dsti/sti/it/secur/prod/PRIV-EN.HTM

OECD, Declaration on Transborder Data Flows (1985)

http://www.oecd.org/dsti/sti/it/secur/prod/e_dflow.htm

OECD, Ministerial Declaration on the Protection of Privacy on Global Networks (1998)

http://appli1.oecd.org/olis/1998doc.nsf/linkto/dsti-iccp-reg(98)10-final

OECD RECOMMENDATION CONCERNING AND GUIDELINES GOVERNING THE PROTECTION OF PRIVACY AND TRANSBORDER FLOWS OF PERSONAL DATA

RECOMMENDATION OF THE COUNCIL CONCERNING GUIDELINES GOVERNING THE PROTECTION OF PRIVACY AND TRANSBORDER FLOWS OF PERSONAL DATA

The Council, Having regard to articles 1(c), 3(a) and 5(b) of the Convention on the Organisation for Economic Co-operation and Development of 14th December, 1960;

Recognising:

> that, although national laws and policies may differ, Member countries have a common interest in protecting privacy and individual liberties, and in reconciling fundamental but competing values such as privacy and the free flow of information;

> that automatic processing and transborder flows of personal data create new forms of relationships among countries and require the development of compatible rules and practices;

> that transborder flows of personal data contribute to economic and social development;

> that domestic legislation concerning privacy protection and transborder flows of personal data may hinder such transborder flows;

Determined to advance the free flow of information between Member countries and to avoid the creation of unjustified obstacles to the development of economic and social relations among Member countries;

RECOMMENDS

1. That Member countries take into account in their domestic legislation the principles concerning the protection of privacy and individual liberties set forth in the Guidelines contained in the Annex to this Recommendation which is an integral part thereof;

2. That Member countries endeavour to remove or avoid creating, in the name of privacy protection, unjustified obstacles to transborder flows of personal data;

3. That Member countries co-operate in the implementation of the Guidelines set forth in the Annex;

International
OECD Privacy Guidelines

4. That Member countries agree as soon as possible on specific procedures of consultation and co-operation for the application of these Guidelines.

ANNEX

GUIDELINES GOVERNING THE PROTECTION OF PRIVACY AND TRANSBORDER FLOWS OF PERSONAL DATA

GENERAL

Definitions

1. For the purposes of these Guidelines:

(a) "data controller" means a party who, according to domestic law, is competent to decide about the contents and use of personal data regardless of whether or not such data are collected, stored, processed or disseminated by that party or by an agent on its behalf;

(b) "personal data" means any information relating to an identified or identifiable individual (data subject);

(c) "transborder flows of personal data" means movements of personal data across national borders.

Scope of Guidelines

2. These Guidelines apply to personal data, whether in the public or private sectors, which, because of the manner in which they are processed, or because of their nature or the context in which they are used, pose a danger to privacy and individual liberties.

3. These Guidelines should not be interpreted as preventing:

(a) the application, to different categories of personal data, of different protective measures depending upon their nature and the context in which they are collected, stored, processed or disseminated;

(b) the exclusion from the application of the Guidelines of personal data which obviously do not contain any risk to privacy and individual liberties; or

(c) the application of the Guidelines only to automatic processing of personal data.

4. Exceptions to the Principles contained in Parts Two and Three of these Guidelines, including those relating to national sovereignty, national security and public policy ("ordre public"), should be:

(a) as few as possible, and

(b) made known to the public.

5. In the particular case of Federal countries the observance of these Guidelines may be affected by the division of powers in the Federation.

6. These Guidelines should be regarded as minimum standards which are capable of being supplemented by additional measures for the protection of privacy and individual liberties.

BASIC PRINCIPLES OF NATIONAL APPLICATION

Collection Limitation Principle

7. There should be limits to the collection of personal data and any such data should be obtained by lawful and fair means and, where appropriate, with the knowledge or consent of the data subject:

Data Quality Principle

8. Personal data should be relevant to the purposes for which they are to be used, and, to the extent necessary for those purposes, should be accurate, complete and kept up-to-date.

Purpose Specification Principle

9. The purposes for which personal data are collected should be specified not later than at the time of data collection and the subsequent use limited to the fulfilment of those purposes or such others as are not incompatible with those purposes and as are specified on each occasion of change of purpose.

Use Limitation Principle

10. Personal data should not be disclosed, made available or otherwise used for purposes other than those specified in accordance with Paragraph 9 except: (a) with the consent of the data subject; or (b) by the authority of law.

Security Safeguards Principle

11. Personal data should be protected by reasonable security safeguards against such risks as loss or unauthorised access, destruction, use, modification or disclosure of data.

Openness Principle

12. There should be a general policy of openness about developments, practices and policies with respect to personal data. Means should be readily available of establishing the existence

and nature of personal data, and the main purposes of their use, as well as the identity and usual residence of the data controller.

Individual Participation Principle

13. An individual should have the right:

> (a) to obtain from a data controller, or otherwise, confirmation of whether or not the data controller has data relating to him;

> (b) to have communicated to him, data relating to him (i) within a reasonable time; (ii) at a charge, if any, that is not excessive; (iii) in a reasonable manner; and (iv) in a form that is readily intelligible to him;

> (c) to be given reasons if a request made under subparagraphs (a) and (b) is denied, and to be able to challenge such denial; and

> (d) to challenge data relating to him and, if the challenge is successful, to have the data erased, rectified, completed or amended.

Accountability Principle

14. A data controller should be accountable for complying with measures which give effect to the principles stated above.

BASIC PRINCIPLES OF INTERNATIONAL APPLICATION: FREE FLOW AND LEGITIMATE RESTRICTIONS

15. Member countries should take into consideration the implications for other Member countries of domestic processing and re-export of personal data.

16. Member countries should take all reasonable and appropriate steps to ensure that transborder flows of personal data, including transit through a Member country, are uninterrupted and secure.

17. A Member country should refrain from restricting transborder flows of personal data between itself and another Member country except where the latter does not yet substantially observe these Guidelines or where the re-export of such data would circumvent its domestic privacy legislation. A Member country may also impose restrictions in respect of certain categories of personal data for which its domestic privacy legislation includes specific

regulations in view of the nature of those data and for which the other Member country provides no equivalent protection.

18. Member countries should avoid developing laws, policies and practices in the name of the protection of privacy and individual liberties, which would create obstacles to transborder flows of personal data that would exceed requirements for such protection.

NATIONAL IMPLEMENTATION

19. In implementing domestically the principles set forth in Parts Two and Three, Member countries should establish legal, administrative or other procedures or institutions for the protection of privacy and individual liberties in respect of personal data. Member countries should in particular endeavour to:

> (a) adopt appropriate domestic legislation;
>
> (b) encourage and support self-regulation, whether in the form of codes of conduct or otherwise;
>
> (c) provide for reasonable means for individuals to exercise their rights;
>
> (d) provide for adequate sanctions and remedies in case of failures to comply with measures which implement the principles set forth in Parts Two and Three; and
>
> (e) ensure that there is no unfair discrimination against data subjects.

INTERNATIONAL CO-OPERATION

20. Member countries should, where requested, make known to other Member countries details of the observance of the principles set forth in these Guidelines. Member countries should also ensure that procedures for transborder flows of personal data and for the protection of privacy and individual liberties are simple and compatible with those of other Member countries which comply with these Guidelines.

21. Member countries should establish procedures to facilitate: (i) information exchange related to these Guidelines, and (ii) mutual assistance in the procedural and investigative matters involved.

22. Member countries should work towards the development of principles, domestic and international, to govern the applicable law in the case of transborder flows of personal data.

APPENDIX

EXPLANATORY MEMORANDUM

Introduction

International
OECD Privacy Guidelines

A feature of OECD Member countries over the past decade has been the development of laws for the protection of privacy. These laws have tended to assume different forms in different countries, and in many countries are still in the process of being developed. The disparities in legislation may create obstacles to the free flow of information between countries. Such flows have greatly increased in recent years and are bound to continue to grow as a result of the introduction of new computer and communication technology.

The OECD, which had been active in this field for some years past, decided to address the problems of diverging national legislation and in 1978 instructed a Group of Experts to develop Guidelines on basic rules governing the transborder flow and the protection of personal data and privacy, in order to facilitate the harmonization of national legislation. The Group has now completed its work.

The Guidelines are broad in nature and reflect the debate and legislative work which has been going on for several years in Member countries. The Expert Group which prepared the Guidelines has considered it essential to issue an accompanying Explanatory Memorandum. Its purpose is to explain and elaborate the Guidelines and the basic problems of protection of privacy and individual liberties. It draws attention to key issues that have emerged in the discussion of the Guidelines and spells out the reasons for the choice of particular solutions.

The first part of the Memorandum provides general background information on the area of concern as perceived in Member countries. It explains the need for international action and summarises the work carried out so far by the OECD and certain other international organisations. It concludes with a list of the main problems encountered by the Expert Group in its work.

Part Two has two subsections. The first contains comments on certain general features of the Guidelines, the second detailed comments on individual paragraphs.

This Memorandum is an information document, prepared to explain and describe generally the work of the Expert Group. It is subordinate to the Guidelines themselves. It cannot vary the meaning of the Guidelines but is supplied to help in their interpretation and application.

I GENERAL BACKGROUND

The Problems

1. The 1970s may be described as a period of intensified investigative and legislative activities concerning the protection of privacy with respect to the collection and use of personal data. Numerous official reports show that the problems are taken seriously at the political level and at the same time that the task of balancing opposing interests is delicate and unlikely to be

accomplished once and for all. Public interest has tended to focus on the risks and implications associated with the computerised processing of personal data and some countries have chosen to enact statutes which deal exclusively with computers and computer-supported activities. Other countries have preferred a more general approach to privacy protection issues irrespective of the particular data processing technology involved.

2. The remedies under discussion are principally safeguards for the individual which will prevent an invasion of privacy in the classical sense, i.e. abuse or disclosure of intimate personal data; but other, more or less closely related needs for protection have become apparent. Obligations of record-keepers to inform the general public about activities concerned with the processing of data, and rights of data subjects to have data relating to them supplemented or amended, are two random examples. Generally speaking, there has been a tendency to broaden the traditional concept of privacy ("the right to be left alone") and to identify a more complex synthesis of interests which can perhaps more correctly be termed privacy and individual liberties.

3. As far as the legal problems of automatic data processing (ADP) are concerned, the protection of privacy and individual liberties constitutes perhaps the most widely debated aspect. Among the reasons for such widespread concern are the ubiquitous use of computers for the processing of personal data, vastly expanded possibilities of storing, comparing, linking, selecting and accessing personal data, and the combination of computers and telecommunications technology which may place personal data simultaneously at the disposal of thousands of users at geographically dispersed locations and enables the pooling of data and the creation of complex national and international data networks. Certain problems require particularly urgent attention, e.g. those relating to emerging international data networks, and to the need of balancing competing interests of privacy on the one hand and freedom of information on the other, in order to allow a full exploitation of the potentialities of modern data processing technologies in so far as this is desirable.

Activities at national level

4. Of the OECD Member countries more than one-third have so far enacted one or several laws which, among other things, are intended to protect individuals against abuse of data relating to them and to give them the right of access to data with a view to checking their accuracy and appropriateness. In federal states, laws of this kind may be found both at the national and at the state or provincial level. Such laws are referred to differently in different countries. Thus, it is common practice in continental Europe to talk about "data laws" or "data protection laws" (lois sur la protection des donnees), whereas in English speaking countries they are usually known as "privacy protection laws". Most of the statutes were enacted after 1973 and the present period may be described as one of continued or even widened legislative activity. Countries which already have statutes in force are turning to new areas of protection or are

engaged in revising or complementing existing statutes. Several other countries are entering the area and have bills pending or are studying the problems with a view to preparing legislation. These national efforts, and not least the extensive reports and research papers prepared by public committees or similar bodies, help to clarify the problems and the advantages and implications of various solutions. At the present stage, they provide a solid basis for international action.

5. The approaches to protection of privacy and individual liberti s adopted by the various countries have many common features. Thus, it is possible to identify certain basic interests or values which are commonly considered to be elementary components of the area of protection. Some core principles of this type are: setting limits to the collection of personal data in accordance with the objectives of the data collector and similar criteria; restricting the usage of data to conform with openly specified purposes; creating facilities for individuals to learn of the existence and contents of data and have data corrected; and the identification of parties who are responsible for compliance with the relevant privacy protection rules and decisions. Generally speaking, statutes to protect privacy and individual liberties in relation to personal data attempt to cover the successive stages of the cycle, beginning with the initial collection of data and ending with erasure or similar measures, and to ensure to the greatest possible extent individual awareness, participation and control.

6. Differences between national approaches as apparent at present in laws, bills or proposals for legislation, refer to aspects such as the scope of legislation, the emphasis placed on different elements of protection, the detailed implementation of the broad principles indicated above, and the machinery of enforcement. Thus, opinions vary with respect to licensing requirements and control mechanisms in the form of special supervisory bodies ("data inspection authorities"). Categories of sensitive data are defined differently, the means of ensuring openness and individual participation vary, to give just a few instances. Of course, existing traditional differences between legal systems are a cause of disparity, both with respect to legislative approaches and the detailed formulation of the regulatory framework for personal data protection.

International aspects of privacy and data banks

7. For a number of reasons the problems of developing safeguards for the individual in respect of the handling of personal data cannot be solved exclusively at the national level. The tremendous increase in data flows across national borders and the creation of international data banks (collections of data intended for retrieval and other purposes) have highlighted the need for concerted national action and at the same time support arguments in favour of free flows of information which must often be balanced against requirements for data protection and for restrictions on their collection, processing and dissemination.

8. One basic concern at the international level is for consensus on the fundamental principles on which protection of the individual must be based. Such a consensus would obviate or diminish reasons for regulating the export of data and facilitate resolving problems of conflict of laws. Moreover, it could constitute a first step towards the development of more detailed, binding international agreements.

9. There are other reasons why the regulation of the processing of personal data should be considered in an international context: the principles involved concern values which many nations are anxious to uphold and see generally accepted; they may help to save costs in international data traffic; countries have a common interest in preventing the creation of locations where national regulations on data processing can easily be circumvented; indeed, in view of the international mobility of people, goods and commercial and scientific activities, commonly accepted practices with regard to the processing of data may be advantageous even where no transborder data traffic is directly involved.

Relevant international activities

10. There are several international agreements on various aspects of telecommunications which, while facilitating relations and co-operation between countries, recognise the sovereign right of each country to regulate its own telecommunications (The International Telecommunications Convention of 1973). The protection of computer data and programmes has been investigated by, among others, the World Intellectual Property Organisation which has developed draft model provisions for national laws on the protection of computer software. Specialised agreements aiming at informational co-operation may be found in a number of areas, such as law enforcement, health services, statistics and judicial services (e.g. with regard to the taking of evidence).

11. A number of international agreements deal in a more general way with the issues which are at present under discussion, viz. the protection of privacy and the free dissemination of information. They include the European Convention on Human Rights of 4th November, 1950 and the International Covenant on Civil and Political Rights (United Nations, 19th December, 1966).

12. However, in view of the inadequacy of existing international instruments relating to the processing of data and individual rights, a number of international organisations have carried out detailed studies of the problems involved in order to find more satisfactory solutions.

13. In 1973 and 1974 the Committee of Ministers of the Council of Europe adopted two resolutions concerning the protection of the privacy of individuals vis-a-vis electronic data banks in the private and public sectors respectively. Both resolutions recommend that the governments of the Member states of the Council of Europe take steps to give effect to a

number of basic principles of protection relating to the obtaining of data, the quality of data, and the rights of individuals to be informed about data and data processing activities.

14. Subsequently the Council of Europe, on the instructions of its Committee of Ministers, began to prepare an international Convention on privacy protection in relation to data processing abroad and transfrontier data processing. It also initiated work on model regulations for medical data banks and rules of conduct for data processing professionals. According to present plans, work on the Convention is to be completed before 30th June, 1980. The draft Convention seeks to establish basic principles of data protection to be enforced by Member countries, to reduce restrictions on transborder data flows between the Contracting Parties on the basis of reciprocity, to bring about co- operation between national data protection authorities, and to set up a Consultative Committee for the application and continuing development of the convention.

15. The European Community has carried out studies concerning the problems of harmonization of national legislations within the Community in relation to transborder data flows and possible distortions of competition, the problems of data security and confidentiality, and the nature of transborder data flows. A sub-committee of the European Parliament held a public hearing on data processing and the rights of the individual in early 1978. Its work has resulted in a report to the European Parliament in spring 1979. The report, which was adopted by the European Parliament in May 1979, contains a resolution on the protection of the rights of the individual in the face of technical developments in data processing.

Activities of the OECD

16. The OECD programme on transborder data flows derives from computer utilisation studies in the public sector which were initiated in 1969. A Group of Experts, the Data Bank Panel, analysed and studied different aspects of the privacy issue, e.g. in relation to digital information, public administration, transborder data flows, and policy implications in general. In order to obtain evidence on the nature of the problems, the Data Bank Panel organised a Symposium in Vienna in 1977 which provided opinions and experience from a diversity of interests, including government, industry, users of international data communication networks, processing services, and interested intergovernmental organisations.

17. A number of guiding principles were elaborated in a general framework for possible international action. These principles recognised (a) the need for generally continuous and uninterrupted flows of information between countries, (b) the legitimate interests of countries in preventing transfers of data which are dangerous to their security or contrary to their laws on public order and decency or which violate the rights of their citizens, (c) the economic value of information and the importance of protecting "data trade" by accepted rules of fair

competition, (d) the needs for security safeguards to minimise violations of proprietary data and misuse of personal information, and (e) the significance of a commitment of countries to a set of core principles for the protection of personal information.

18. Early in 1978 a new ad hoc Group of Experts on Transborder Data Barriers and Privacy Protection was set up within the OECD which was instructed to develop guidelines on basic rules governing the transborder flow and the protection of personal data and privacy, in order to facilitate a harmonization of national legislations, without this precluding at a later date the establishment of an international Convention. This work was to be carried out in close co-operation with the Council of Europe and the European Community and to be completed by 1st July, 1979.

19. The Expert Group, under the chairmanship of the Honourable Mr. Justice Kirby, Australia, and with the assistance of Dr. Peter Seipel (Consultant), produced several drafts and discussed various reports containing, for instance, comparative analyses of different approaches to legislation in this field. It was particularly concerned with a number of key issues set out below.

(a) The specific, sensitive facts issue The question arises as to whether the Guidelines should be of a general nature or whether they should be structured to deal with different types of data or activities (e.g. credit reporting). Indeed, it is probably not possible to identify a set of data which are universally regarded as being sensitive.

(b) The ADP issue The argument that ADP is the main cause for concern is doubtful and, indeed, contested. (c) The legal persons issue Some, but by no means all, national laws protect data relating to legal persons in a similar manner to data related to physical persons.

(d) The remedies and sanctions issue The approaches to control mechanisms vary considerably: for instance, schemes involving supervision and licensing by specially constituted authorities might be compared to schemes involving voluntary compliance by record-keepers and reliance on traditional judicial remedies in the Courts.

(e) The basic machinery or implementation issue The choice of core principles and their appropriate level of detail presents difficulties. For instance, the extent to which data security questions (protection of data against unauthorised interference, fire, and similar occurrences) should be regarded as part of the privacy protection complex is debatable; opinions may differ with regard to time limits for the retention, or requirements for the erasure, of data, and the same applies to requirements that data be relevant to specific purposes. In particular, it is difficult to draw a clear dividing line between the level of basic principles or objectives and lower level "machinery" questions which should be left to domestic implementation.

(f) The choice of law issue The problems of choice of jurisdiction, choice of applicable law and recognition of foreign judgements have proved to be complex in the context of transborder data flows. The question arises, however, whether and to what extent it should be attempted at this stage to put forward solutions in Guidelines of a non-binding nature.

(g) The exceptions issue Similarly, opinions may vary on the question of exceptions. Are they required at all? If so, should particular categories of exceptions be provided for or should general limits to exceptions be formulated?

(h) The bias issue Finally, there is an inherent conflict between the protection and the free transborder flow of personal data. Emphasis may be placed on one or the other, and interests in privacy protection may be difficult to distinguish from other interests relating to trade, culture, national sovereignty, and so forth.

20. During its work the Expert Group has maintained close contacts with corresponding organs of the Council of Europe. Every effort has been made to avoid unnecessary differences between the texts produced by the two organisations; thus, the set of basic principles of protection are in many respects similar. On the other hand, a number of differences do occur. To begin with, the OECD Guidelines are not legally binding, whereas the Council of Europe has produced a convention which, if adopted, would be legally binding among those countries which ratify it. This in turn means that the question of exceptions has been dealt with in greater detail by the Council of Europe. As for the area of application, the Council of Europe Convention deals primarily with the automatic processing of personal data whereas the OECD Guidelines apply to personal data which involve dangers to privacy and individual liberties, irrespective of the methods and machinery used in their handling. At the level of details, the basic principles of protection proposed by the two organisations are not identical and the terminology employed differs in some respects. The institutional framework for continued co-operation is treated in greater detail in the Council of Europe Convention than in the OECD Guidelines.

21. The Expert Group also maintained co-operation with the Commission of the European Communities as required by its mandate.

II. THE GUIDELINES

A. Purpose and Scope

General

22. The Preamble of the Recommendation expresses the basic concerns calling for action. The Recommendation affirms the commitment of Member countries to protect privacy and individual liberties and to respect the transborder flows of personal data.

23. The Guidelines set out in the Annex to the Recommendation consist of five parts. Part One contains a number of definitions and specifies the scope of the Guidelines, indicating that they represent minimum standards. Part Two contains eight basic principles (Paragraphs 7-14) relating to the protection of privacy and individual liberties at the national level. Part Three deals with principles of international application, i.e. principles which are chiefly concerned with relationships between Member countries.

24. Part Four deals, in general terms, with means of implementing the basic principles set out in the preceding parts and specifies that these principles should be applied in a non-discriminatory manner. Part Five concerns matters of mutual assistance between Member countries, chiefly through the exchange of information and by avoiding incompatible national procedures for the protection of personal data. It concludes with a reference to issues of applicable law which may arise when flows of personal data involve several Member countries.

Objectives

25. The core of the Guidelines consists of the principles set out in Part Two of the Annex. It is recommended to Member countries that they adhere to these principles with a view to
    (a) achieving acceptance by Member countries of certain minimum standards of protection of privacy and individual liberties with regard to personal data;
    (b) reducing differences between relevant domestic rules and practices of Member countries to a minimum;
    (c) ensuring that in protecting personal data they take into consideration the interests of other Member countries and the need to avoid undue interference with flows of personal data between Member countries; and
    (d) eliminating, as far as possible, reasons which might induce Member countries to restrict transborder flows of personal data because of the possible risks associated with such flows. As stated in the Preamble, two essential basic values are involved: the protection of privacy and individual liberties and the advancement of free flows of personal data. The Guidelines attempt to balance the two values against one another; while accepting certain restrictions to free transborder flows of personal data, they seek to reduce the need for such restrictions and thereby strengthen the notion of free information flows between countries.

26. Finally, Parts Four and Five of the Guidelines contain principles seeking to ensure:
    (a) effective national measures for the protection of privacy and individual liberties;
    (b) avoidance of practices involving unfair discrimination between individuals; and
    (c) bases for continued international co-operation and compatible procedures in any regulation of transborder flows of personal data.

Level of detail

27. The level of detail of the Guidelines varies depending upon two main factors, viz. (a) the extent of consensus reached concerning the solutions put forward, and (b) available knowledge and experience pointing to solutions to be adopted at this stage. For instance, the Individual Participation Principle (Paragraph 13) deals specifically with various aspects of protecting an individual's interest, whereas the provision on problems of choice of law and related matters (Paragraph 22) merely states a starting-point for a gradual development of detailed common approaches and international agreements. On the whole, the Guidelines constitute a general framework for concerted actions by Member countries: objectives put forward by the Guidelines may be pursued in different ways, depending on the legal instruments and strategies preferred by Member countries for their implementation. To conclude, there is a need for a continuing review of the Guidelines, both by Member countries and the OECD. As and when experience is gained, it may prove desirable to develop and adjust the Guidelines accordingly.

Non-Member countries

28. The Recommendation is addressed to Member countries and this is reflected in several provisions which are expressly restricted to relationships between Member countries (see Paragraphs 15, 17 and 20 of the Guidelines). Widespread recognition of the Guidelines is, however, desirable and nothing in them should be interpreted as preventing the application of relevant provisions by Member countries to non-Member countries. In view of the increase in transborder data flows and the need to ensure concerted solutions, efforts will be made to bring the Guidelines to the attention of non-Member countries and appropriate international organisations.

The broader regulatory perspective

29. It has been pointed out earlier that the protection of privacy and individual liberties constitutes one of many overlapping legal aspects involved in the processing of data. The Guidelines constitute a new instrument, in addition to other, related international instruments governing such issues as human rights, telecommunications, international trade, copyright, and various information services. If the need arises, the principles set out in the Guidelines could be further developed within the framework of activities undertaken by the OECD in the area of information, computer and communications policies.

30. Some Member countries have emphasized the advantages of a binding international Convention with a broad coverage. The Mandate of the Expert Group required it to develop guidelines on basic rules governing the transborder flow and the protection of personal data and privacy, without this precluding at a later stage the establishment of an international Convention of a binding nature. The Guidelines could serve as a starting-point for the development of an international Convention when the need arises.

Legal persons, groups and similar entities

31. Some countries consider that the protection required for data relating to individuals may be similar in nature to the protection required for data relating to business enterprises, associations and groups which may or may not possess legal personality. The experience of a number of countries also shows that it is difficult to define clearly the dividing line between personal and non-personal data. For example, data relating to a small company may also concern its owner or owners and provide personal information of a more or less sensitive nature. In such instances it may be advisable to extend to corporate entities the protection offered by rules relating primarily to personal data.

32. Similarly, it is debatable to what extent people belonging to a particular group (e.g. mentally disabled persons, immigrants, ethnic minorities) need additional protection against the dissemination of information relating to that group.

33. On the other hand, the Guidelines reflect the view that the notions of individual integrity and privacy are in many respects particular and should not be treated in the same way as the integrity of a group of persons, or corporate security and confidentiality. The needs for protection are different and so are the policy frameworks within which solutions have to be formulated and interests balanced against one another. Some members of the Expert Group suggested that the possibility of extending the Guidelines to legal persons (corporations, associations) should be provided for. This suggestion has not secured a sufficient consensus. The scope of the Guidelines is therefore confined to data relating to individuals and it is left to Member countries to draw dividing lines and decide policies with regard to corporations, groups and similar bodies (cf. paragraph 49 below).

Automated and non-automated data

34. In the past, OECD activities in privacy protection and related fields have focused on automatic data processing and computer networks. The Expert Group has devoted special attention to the issue of whether or not these Guidelines should be restricted to the automatic and computer-assisted processing of personal data. Such an approach may be defended on a number of grounds, such as the particular dangers to individual privacy raised by automation and computerised data banks, and increasing dominance of automatic data processing methods, especially in transborder data flows, and the particular framework of information, computer and communications policies within which the Expert Group has set out to fulfil its Mandate.

35. On the other hand, it is the conclusion of the Expert Group that limiting the Guidelines to the automatic processing of personal data would have considerable drawbacks. To begin with, it is difficult, at the level of definitions, to make a clear distinction between the automatic and non- automatic handling of data. There are, for instance, "mixed" data processing systems, and there are stages in the processing of data which may or may not lead to automatic treatment. These difficulties tend to be further complicated by ongoing technological developments, such

as the introduction of advanced semi-automated methods based on the use of microfilm, or microcomputers which may increasingly be used for private purposes that are both harmless and impossible to control. Moreover, by concentrating exclusively on computers the Guidelines might lead to inconsistency and lacunae, and opportunities for record-keepers to circumvent rules which implement the Guidelines by using non- automatic means for purposes which may be offensive.

36. Because of the difficulties mentioned, the Guidelines do not put forward a definition of "automatic data processing" although the concept is referred to in the preamble and in paragraph 3 of the Annex. It may be assumed that guidance for the interpretation of the concept can be obtained from sources such as standard technical vocabularies.

37. Above all, the principles for the protection of privacy and individual liberties expressed in the Guidelines are valid for the processing of data in general, irrespective of the particular technology employed. The Guidelines therefore apply to personal data in general or, more precisely, to personal data which, because of the manner in which they are processed, or because of their nature or context, pose a danger to privacy and individual liberties.

38. It should be noted, however, that the Guidelines do not constitute a set of general privacy protection principles; invasions of privacy by, for instance, candid photography, physical maltreatment, or defamation are outside their scope unless such acts are in one way or another associated with the handling of personal data. Thus, the Guidelines deal with the building-up and use of aggregates of data which are organised for retrieval, decision-making, research, surveys and similar purposes. It should be emphasized that the Guidelines are neutral with regard to the particular technology used; automatic methods are only one of the problems raised in the Guidelines although, particularly in the context of transborder data flows, this is clearly an important one.

B. Detailed Comments

General

39. The comments which follow relate to the actual Guidelines set out in the Annex to the Recommendation. They seek to clarify the debate in the Expert Group.

Paragraph 1: Definitions

40. The list of definitions has been kept short. The term "data controller" is of vital importance. It attempts to define a subject who, under domestic law, should carry ultimate responsibility for activities concerned with the processing of personal data. As defined, the data controller is a party who is legally competent to decide about the contents and use of data, regardless of whether or not such data are collected, stored, processed or disseminated by that party or by an agent on its behalf. The data controller may be a legal or natural person, public

authority, agency or any other body. The definition excludes at least four categories which may be involved in the processing of data, viz. (a) licensing authorities and similar bodies which exist in some Member countries and which authorise the processing of data but are not entitled to decide (in the proper sense of the word) what activities should be carried out and for what purposes; (b) data processing service bureaux which carry out data processing on behalf of others; (c) telecommunications authorities and similar bodies which act as mere conduits; and (d) "dependent users" who may have access to data but who are not authorised to decide what data should be stored, who should be able to use them, etc. In implementing the Guidelines, countries may develop more complex schemes of levels and types of responsibilities. Paragraphs 14 and 19 of the Guidelines provide a basis for efforts in this direction.

41. The terms "personal data" and "data subject" serve to underscore that the Guidelines are concerned with physical persons. The precise dividing line between personal data in the sense of information relating to identified or identifiable individuals and anonymous data may be difficult to draw and must be left to the regulation of each Member country. In principle, personal data convey information which by direct (e.g. a civil registration number) or indirect linkages (e.g. an address) may be connected to a particular physical person.

42. The term "transborder flows of personal data" restricts the application of certain provisions of the Guidelines to international data flows and consequently omits the data flow problems particular to federal states. The movements of data will often take place through electronic transmission but other means of data communication may also be involved. Transborder flows as understood in the Guidelines includes the transmission of data by satellite.

Paragraph 2: Area of application

43. The Section of the Memorandum dealing with the scope and purpose of the Guidelines introduces the issue of their application to the automatic as against non-automatic processing of personal data. Paragraph 2 of the Guidelines, which deals with this problem, is based on two limiting criteria. The first is associated with the concept of personal data: the Guidelines apply to data which can be related to identified or identifiable individuals. Collections of data which do not offer such possibilities (collections of statistical data in anonymous form) are not included. The second criterion is more complex and relates to a specific risk element of a factual nature, viz. that data pose a danger to privacy and individual liberties. Such dangers can arise because of the use of automated data processing methods (the manner in which data are processed), but a broad variety of other possible risk sources is implied. Thus, data which are in themselves simple and factual may be used in a context where they become offensive to a data subject. On the other hand, the risks as expressed in Paragraph 2 of the Guidelines are intended to exclude data collections of an obviously innocent nature (e.g. personal notebooks). The dangers referred to in Paragraph 2 of the Guidelines should relate to privacy and individual

liberties. However, the protected interests are broad (cf. paragraph 2 above) and may be viewed differently by different Member countries and at different times. A delimitation as far as the Guidelines are concerned and a common basic approach are provided by the principles set out in Paragraphs 7 to 13.

44. As explained in Paragraph 2 of the Guidelines, they are intended to cover both the private and the public sector. These notions may be defined differently by different Member countries.

Paragraph 3: Different degrees of sensitivity

45. The Guidelines should not be applied in a mechanistic way irrespective of the kind of data and processing activities involved. The framework provided by the basic principles in Part Two of the Guidelines permits Member countries to exercise their discretion with respect to the degree of stringency with which the Guidelines are to be implemented, and with respect to the scope of the measures to be taken. In particular, Paragraph 3(b) provides for many "trivial" cases of collection and use of personal data (cf. above) to be completely excluded from the application of the Guidelines. Obviously this does not mean that Paragraph 3 should be regarded as a vehicle for demolishing the standards set up by the Guidelines. But, generally speaking, the Guidelines do not presuppose their uniform implementation by Member countries with respect to details. For instance, different traditions and different attitudes by the general public have to be taken into account. Thus, in one country universal personal identifiers may be considered both harmless and useful whereas in another country they may be regarded as highly sensitive and their use restricted or even forbidden. In one country, protection may be afforded to data relating to groups and similar entities whereas such protection is completely non-existent in another country, and so forth. To conclude, some Member countries may find it appropriate to restrict the application of the Guidelines to the automatic processing of personal data. Paragraph 3(c) provides for such a limitation.

Paragraph 4: Exceptions to the Guidelines

46. To provide formally for exceptions in Guidelines which are part of a non- binding Recommendation may seem superfluous. However, the Expert Group has found it appropriate to include a provision dealing with this subject and stating that two general criteria ought to guide national policies in limiting the application of the Guidelines: exceptions should be as few as possible, and they should be made known to the public (e.g. through publication in an official government gazette). General knowledge of the existence of certain data or files would be sufficient to meet the second criterion, although details concerning particular data etc. may have to be kept secret. The formula provided in Paragraph 4 is intended to cover many different kinds of concerns and limiting factors, as it was obviously not possible to provide an exhaustive list of exceptions - hence the wording that they include national sovereignty, national security and public policy ("ordre public"). Another overriding national concern would

be, for instance, the financial interests of the State ("credit public"). Moreover, Paragraph 4 allows for different ways of implementing the Guidelines: it should be borne in mind that Member countries are at present at different stages of development with respect to privacy protection rules and institutions and will probably proceed at different paces, applying different strategies, e.g. the regulation of certain types of data or activities as compared to regulation of a general nature ("omnibus approach").

47. The Expert Group recognised that Member countries might apply the Guidelines differentially to different kinds of personal data. There may be differences in the permissible frequency of inspection, in ways of balancing competing interests such as the confidentiality of medical records versus the individual's right to inspect data relating to him, and so forth. Some examples of areas which may be treated differently are credit reporting, criminal investigation and banking. Member countries may also choose different solutions with respect to exceptions associated with, for example, research and statistics. An exhaustive enumeration of all such situations and concerns is neither required nor possible. Some of the subsequent paragraphs of the Guidelines and the comments referring to them provide further clarification of the area of application of the Guidelines and of the closely related issues of balancing opposing interests (compare with Paragraphs 7, 8, 17 and 18 of the Guidelines). To summarise, the Expert Group has assumed that exceptions will be limited to those which are necessary in a democratic society.

Paragraph 5: Federal countries

48. In Federal countries, the application of the Guidelines is subject to various constitutional limitations. Paragraph 5, accordingly, serves to underscore that no commitments exist to apply the Guidelines beyond the limits of constitutional competence.

Paragraph 6: Minimum standards

49. First, Paragraph 6 describes the Guidelines as minimum standards for adoption in domestic legislation. Secondly, and in consequence, it has been agreed that the Guidelines are capable of being supplemented by additional measures for the protection of privacy and individual liberties at the national as well as the international level.

Paragraph 7: Collection Limitation Principle

50. As an introductory comment on the principles set out in Paragraphs 7 to 14 of the Guidelines it should be pointed out that these principles are interrelated and partly overlapping. Thus, the distinctions between different activities and stages involved in the processing of data which are assumed in the principles, are somewhat artificial and it is essential that the principles are treated together and studied as a whole. Paragraph 7 deals with two issues, viz. (a) limits to the collection of data which, because of the manner in which they are to be

processed, their nature, the context in which they are to be used or other circumstances, are regarded as specially sensitive; and (b) requirements concerning data collection methods. Different views are frequently put forward with respect to the first issue. It could be argued that it is both possible and desirable to enumerate types or categories of data which are per se sensitive and the collection of which should be restricted or even prohibited. There are precedents in European legislation to this effect (race, religious beliefs, criminal records, for instance). On the other hand, it may be held that no data are intrinsically "private" or "sensitive" but may become so in view of their context and use. This view is reflected, for example, in the privacy legislation of the United States.

51. The Expert Group has discussed a number of sensitivity criteria, such as the risk of discrimination, but has not found it possible to define any set of data which are universally regarded as sensitive. Consequently, Paragraph 7 merely contains a general statement that there should be limits to the collection of personal data. For one thing, this represents an affirmative recommendation to lawmakers to decide on limits which would put an end to the indiscriminate collection of personal data. The nature of the limits is not spelt out but it is understood that the limits may relate to:
  - data quality aspects (i.e. that it should be possible to derive information of sufficiently high quality from the data collected, that data should be collected in a proper information framework, etc.);
  - limits associated with the purpose of the processing of data (i.e. that only certain categories of data ought to be collected and, possibly, that data collection should be restricted to the minimum necessary to fulfil the specified purpose);
  - "earmarking" of specially sensitive data according to traditions and attitudes in each Member country;
  - limits to data collection activities of certain data controllers;
  - civil rights concerns.

52. The second part of Paragraph 7 (data collection methods) is directed against practices which involve, for instance, the use of hidden data registration devices such as tape recorders, or deceiving data subjects to make them supply information. The knowledge or consent of the data subject is as a rule essential, knowledge being the minimum requirement. On the other hand, consent cannot always be imposed, for practical reasons. In addition, Paragraph 7 contains a reminder ("where appropriate") that there are situations where for practical or policy reasons the data subject's knowledge or consent cannot be considered necessary. Criminal investigation activities and the routine up-dating of mailing lists may be mentioned as examples. Finally, Paragraph 7 does not exclude the possibility of a data subject being represented by another party, for instance in the case of minors, mentally disabled persons, etc.

Paragraph 8: Data Quality Principle

53. Requirements that data be relevant can be viewed in different ways. In fact, some members of the Expert Group hesitated as to whether such requirements actually fitted into the framework of privacy protection. The conclusion of the Group was to the effect, however, that data should be related to the purpose for which they are to be used. For instance, data concerning opinions may easily be misleading if they are used for purposes to which they bear no relation, and the same is true of evaluative data. Paragraph 8 also deals with accuracy, completeness and up-to-dateness which are all important elements of the data quality concept. The requirements in this respect are linked to the purposes of data, i.e. they are not intended to be more far- reaching than is necessary for the purposes for which the data are used. Thus, historical data may often have to be collected or retained; cases in point are social research, involving so-called longitudinal studies of developments in society, historical research, and the activities of archives. The "purpose test" will often involve the problem of whether or not harm can be caused to data subjects because of lack of accuracy, completeness and up-dating.

Paragraph 9: Purpose Specification Principle

54. The Purpose Specification Principle is closely associated with the two surrounding principles, i.e. the Data Quality Principle and the Use Limitation Principle. Basically, Paragraph 9 implies that before, and in any case not later than at the time of data collection it should be possible to identify the purposes for which these data are to be used, and that later changes of purposes should likewise be specified. Such specification of purposes can be made in a number of alternative or complementary ways, e.g. by public declarations, information to data subjects, legislation, administrative decrees, and licences provided by supervisory bodies. According to Paragraphs 9 and 10, new purposes should not be introduced arbitrarily; freedom to make changes should imply compatibility with the original purposes. Finally, when data no longer serve a purpose, and if it is practicable, it may be necessary to have them destroyed (erased) or given an anonymous form. The reason is that control over data may be lost when data are no longer of interest; this may lead to risks of theft, unauthorised copying or the like.

Paragraph 10: Use Limitation Principle

55. This paragraph deals with uses of different kinds, including disclosure, which involve deviations from specified purposes. For instances, data may be transmitted from one computer to another where they can be used for unauthorised purposes without being inspected and thus disclosed in the proper sense of the word. As a rule the initially or subsequently specified purposes should be decisive for the uses to which data can be put. Paragraph 10 foresees two general exceptions to this principle: the consent of the data subject (or his representative - see Paragraph 52 above) and the authority of law (including, for example, licences granted by supervisory bodies). For instance, it may be provided that data which have been collected for purposes of administrative decision-making may be made available for research, statistics and social planning.

Paragraph 11: Security Safeguards Principle

56. Security and privacy issues are not identical. However, limitations on data use and disclosure should be reinforced by security safeguards. Such safeguards include physical measures (locked doors and identification cards, for instance), organisational measures (such as authority levels with regard to access to data) and, particularly in computer systems, informational measures (such as enciphering and threat monitoring of unusual activities and responses to them). It should be emphasized that the category of organisational measures includes obligations for data processing personnel to maintain confidentiality. Paragraph 11 has a broad coverage. The cases mentioned in the provision are to some extent overlapping (e.g. access/disclosure). "Loss" of data encompasses such cases as accidental erasure of data, destruction of data storage media (and thus destruction of data) and theft of data storage media. "Modified" should be construed to cover unauthorised input of data, and "use" to cover unauthorised copying.

Paragraph 12: Openness Principle

57. The Openness Principle may be viewed as a prerequisite for the Individual Participation Principle (Paragraph 13); for the latter principle to be effective, it must be possible in practice to acquire information about the collection, storage or use of personal data. Regular information from data controllers on a voluntary basis, publication in official registers of descriptions of activities concerned with the processing of personal data, and registration with public bodies are some, though not all, of the ways by which this may be brought about. The reference to means which are "readily available" implies that individuals should be able to obtain information without unreasonable effort as to time, advance knowledge, travelling, and so forth, and without unreasonable cost.

Paragraph 13: Individual Participation Principle

58. The right of individuals to access and challenge personal data is generally regarded as perhaps the most important privacy protection safeguard. This view is shared by the Expert Group which, although aware that the right to access and challenge cannot be absolute, has chosen to express it in clear and fairly specific language. With respect to the individual sub-paragraphs, the following explanations are called for:

59. The right to access should as a rule be simple to exercise. This may mean, among other things, that it should be part of the day-to-day activities of the data controller or his representative and should not involve any legal process or similar measures. In some cases it may be appropriate to provide for intermediate access to data; for example, in the medical area a medical practitioner can serve as a go-between. In some countries supervisory organs, such as data inspection authorities, may provide similar services. The requirement that data be

communicated within reasonable time may be satisfied in different ways. For instance, a data controller who provides information to data subjects at regular intervals may be exempted from obligations to respond at once to individual requests. Normally, the time is to be counted from the receipt of a request. Its length may vary to some extent from one situation to another depending on circumstances such as the nature of the data processing activity. Communication of such data "in a reasonable manner" means, among other things, that problems of geographical distance should be given due attention. Moreover, if intervals are prescribed between the times when requests for access must be met, such intervals should be reasonable. The extent to which data subjects should be able to obtain copies of data relating to them is a matter of implementation which must be left to the decision of each Member country.

60. The right to reasons in Paragraph 13(c) is narrow in the sense that it is limited to situations where requests for information have been refused. A broadening of this right to include reasons for adverse decisions in general, based on the use of personal data, met with sympathy in the Expert Group. However, on final consideration a right of this kind was thought to be too broad for insertion in the privacy framework constituted by the Guidelines. This is not to say that a right to reasons for adverse decisions may not be appropriate, e.g. in order to inform and alert a subject to his rights so that he can exercise them effectively.

61. The right to challenge in 13(c) and (d) is broad in scope and includes first instance challenges to data controllers as well as subsequent challenges in courts, administrative bodies, professional organs or other institutions according to domestic rules of procedure (compare with Paragraph 19 of the Guidelines). The right to challenge does not imply that the data subject can decide what remedy or relief is available (rectification, annotation that data are in dispute, etc.): such matters will be decided by domestic law and legal procedures. Generally speaking, the criteria which decide the outcome of a challenge are those which are stated elsewhere in the Guidelines.

Paragraph 14: Accountability Principle

62. The data controller decides about data and data processing activities. It is for his benefit that the processing of data is carried out. Accordingly, it is essential that under domestic law accountability for complying with privacy protection rules and decisions should be placed on the data controller who should not be relieved of this obligation merely because the processing of data is carried out on his behalf by another party, such as a service bureau. On the other hand, nothing in the Guidelines prevents service bureaux personnel, "dependent users" (see paragraph 40) and others from also being held accountable. For instance, sanctions against breaches of confidentiality obligations may be directed against all parties entrusted with the handling of personal information (cf. Paragraph 19 of the Guidelines). Accountability under Paragraph 14 refers to accountability supported by legal sanctions, as well as to accountability established by codes of conduct, for instance.

International
OECD Privacy Guidelines

Paragraphs 15-18: Basic Principles of International Application

63. The principles of international application are closely interrelated. Generally speaking, Paragraph 15 concerns respect by Member countries for each other's interest in protecting personal data, and the privacy and individual liberties of their nationals and residents. Paragraph 16 deals with security issues in a broad sense and may be said to correspond, at the international level, to Paragraph 11 of the Guidelines. Paragraphs 17 and 18 deal with restrictions on free flows of personal data between Member countries; basically, as far as protection of privacy and individual liberties is concerned, such flows should be admitted as soon as requirements of the Guidelines for the protection of these interests have been substantially, i.e. effectively, fulfilled. The question of other possible bases of restricting transborder flows of personal data is not dealt with in the Guidelines.

64. For domestic processing Paragraph 15 has two implications. First, it is directed against liberal policies which are contrary to the spirit of the Guidelines and which facilitate attempts to circumvent or violate protective legislation of other Member countries. However, such circumvention or violation, although condemned by all Member countries, is not specifically mentioned in this Paragraph as a number of countries felt it to be unacceptable that one Member country should be required to directly or indirectly enforce, extraterritorially, the laws of other Member countries. - It should be noted that the provision explicitly mentions the re-export of personal data. In this respect, Member countries should bear in mind the need to support each other's efforts to ensure that personal data are not deprived of protection as a result of their transfer to territories and facilities for the processing of data where control is slack or non-existent.

65. Secondly, Member countries are implicitly encouraged to consider the need to adapt rules and practices for the processing of data to the particular circumstances which may arise when foreign data and data on non-nationals are involved. By way of illustration, a situation may arise where data on foreign nationals are made available for purposes which serve the particular interests of their country of nationality (e.g. access to the addresses of nationals living abroad).

66. As far as the Guidelines are concerned, the encouragement of international flows of personal data is not an undisputed goal in itself. To the extent that such flows take place they should, however, according to Paragraph 16, be uninterrupted and secure, i.e. protected against unauthorised access, loss of data and similar events. Such protection should also be given to data in transit, i.e. data which pass through a Member country without being used or stored with a view to usage in that country. The general commitment under Paragraph 16 should, as far as computer networks are concerned, be viewed against the background of the International Telecommunications Convention of Malaga-Torremolinos (25th October, 1973). According to that convention, the members of the International Telecommunications Union, including the OECD Member countries, have agreed, inter alia, to ensure the establishment, under the best

technical conditions, of the channels and installations necessary to carry on the rapid and uninterrupted exchange of international telecommunications. Moreover, the members of ITU have agreed to take all possible measures compatible with the telecommunications system used to ensure the secrecy of international correspondence. As regards exceptions, the right to suspend international telecommunications services has been reserved and so has the right to communicate international correspondence to the competent authorities in order to ensure the application of internal laws or the execution of international conventions to which members of the ITU are parties. These provisions apply as long as data move through telecommunications lines. In their context, the Guidelines constitute a complementary safeguard that international flows of personal data should be uninterrupted and secure.

67. Paragraph 17 reinforces Paragraph 16 as far as relationships between Member countries are concerned. It deals with interests which are opposed to free transborder flows of personal data but which may nevertheless constitute legitimate grounds for restricting such flows between Member countries. A typical example would be attempts to circumvent national legislation by processing data in a Member country which does not yet substantially observe the Guidelines. Paragraph 17 establishes a standard of equivalent protection, by which is meant protection which is substantially similar in effect to that of the exporting country, but which need not be identical in form or in all respects. As in Paragraph 15, the re-export of personal data is specifically mentioned - in this case with a view to preventing attempts to circumvent the domestic privacy legislation of Member countries. - The third category of grounds for legitimate restrictions mentioned in Paragraph 17, concerning personal data of a special nature, covers situations where important interests of Member countries could be affected. Generally speaking, however, Paragraph 17 is subject to Paragraph 4 of the Guidelines which implies that restrictions on flows of personal data should be kept to a minimum.

68. Paragraph 18 attempts to ensure that privacy protection interests are balanced against interests of free transborder flows of personal data. It is directed in the first place against the creation of barriers to flows of personal data which are artificial from the point of view of protection of privacy and individual liberties and fulfil restrictive purposes of other kinds which are thus not openly announced. However, Paragraph 18 is not intended to limit the rights of Member countries to regulate transborder flows of personal data in areas relating to free trade, tariffs, employment, and related economic conditions for international data traffic. These are matters which were not addressed by the Expert Group, being outside its Mandate.

Paragraph 19: National Implementation

69. The detailed implementation of Parts Two and Three of the Guidelines is left in the first place to Member countries. It is bound to vary according to different legal systems and traditions, and Paragraph 19 therefore attempts merely to establish a general framework indicating in broad terms what kind of national machinery is envisaged for putting the

Guidelines into effect. The opening sentence shows the different approaches which might be taken by countries, both generally and with respect to control mechanisms (e.g. specially set-up supervisory bodies, existing control facilities such as courts, public authorities, etc.).

70. In Paragraph 19(a) countries are invited to adopt appropriate domestic legislation, the word "appropriate" foreshadowing the judgement by individual countries of the appropriateness or otherwise of legislative solutions. Paragraph 19(b) concerning self-regulation is addressed primarily to common law countries where non-legislative implementation of the Guidelines would complement legislative action. Paragraph 19(c) should be given a broad interpretation; it includes such means as advice from data controllers and the provision of assistance, including legal aid. Paragraph 19(d) permits different approaches to the issue of control mechanisms: briefly, either the setting-up of special supervisory bodies, or reliance on already existing control facilities, whether in the form of courts, existing public authorities or otherwise. Paragraph 19(e) dealing with discrimination is directed against unfair practices but leaves open the possibility of "benign discrimination" to support disadvantaged groups, for instance. The provision is directed against unfair discrimination on such bases as nationality and domicile, sex, race, creed, or trade union affiliation.

Paragraph 20: Information Exchange and Compatible Procedures

71. Two major problems are dealt with here, viz. (a) the need to ensure that information can be obtained about rules, regulations, decisions, etc. which implement the Guidelines, and (b) the need to avoid transborder flows of personal data being hampered by an unnecessarily complex and disparate framework of procedures and compliance requirements. The first problem arises because of the complexity of privacy protection regulation and data policies in general. There are often several levels of regulation (in a broad sense) and many important rules cannot be laid down permanently in detailed statutory provisions; they have to be kept fairly open and left to the discretion of lower-level decision-making bodies.

72. The importance of the second problem is, generally speaking proportional to the number of domestic laws which affect transborder flows of personal data. Even at the present stage, there are obvious needs for co-ordinating special provisions on transborder data flows in domestic laws, including special arrangements relating to compliance control and, where required, licences to operate data processing systems.

Paragraph 21: Machinery for Co-operation

73. The provision on national procedures assumes that the Guidelines will form a basis for continued co-operation. Data protection authorities and specialised bodies dealing with policy issues in information and data communications are obvious partners in such a co-operation. In particular, the second purpose of such measures, contained in Paragraph 21(ii), i.e. mutual aid

in procedural matters and requests for information, is future-oriented: its practical significance is likely to grow as international data networks and the complications associated with them become more numerous.

Paragraph 22: Conflicts of Laws

74. The Expert Group has devoted considerable attention to issues of conflicts of laws, and in the first place to the questions as to which courts should have jurisdiction over specific issues (choice of jurisdiction) and which system of law should govern specific issues (choice of law). The discussion of different strategies and proposed principles has confirmed the view that at the present stage, with the advent of such rapid changes in technology, and given the non-binding nature of the Guidelines, no attempt should be made to put forward specific, detailed solutions. difficulties are bound to arise with respect to both the choice of a theoretically sound regulatory model and the need for additional experience about the implications of solutions which in themselves are possible.

75. As regards the question of choice of law, one way of approaching these problems is to identify one or more connecting factors which, at best, indicate one applicable law. This is particularly difficult in the case of international computer networks where, because of dispersed location and rapid movement of data, and geographically dispersed data processing activities, several connecting factors could occur in a complex manner involving elements of legal novelty. Moreover, it is not evident what value should presently be attributed to rules which by mechanistic application establish the specific national law to be applied. For one thing, the appropriateness of such a solution seems to depend upon the existence of both similar legal concepts and rule structures, and binding commitments of nations to observe certain standards of personal data protection. In the absence of these conditions, an attempt could be made to formulate more flexible principles which involve a search for a "proper law" and are linked to the purpose of ensuring effective protection of privacy and individual liberties. Thus, in a situation where several laws may be applicable, it has been suggested that one solution could be to give preference to the domestic law offering the best protection of personal data. On the other hand, it may be argued that solutions of this kind leave too much uncertainty, not least from the point of view of the data controllers who may wish to know, where necessary in advance, by which national systems of rules an international data processing system will be governed.

76. In view of these difficulties, and considering that problems of conflicts of laws might best be handled within the total framework of personal and non- personal data, the Expert Group has decided to content itself with a statement which merely signals the issues and recommends that Member countries should work towards their solution.

Follow-up

77. The Expert Group called attention to the terms of Recommendation 4 on the Guidelines which suggests that Member countries agree as soon as possible on specific procedures of consultation and co-operation for the application of the Guidelines.

COUNCIL OF EUROPE CONVENTION
ON PRIVACY (1981)

Summary

The Council of Europe concluded the Convention for the Protection of Individuals with Regard to Automatic Processing of Personal Data in 1981, and it entered into force in 1985. The Council negotiated the Convention in response to the rapid rise of automated data processing, and advances in computer technology that were allowing more and more records to be stored and transferred digitally. The Council also noted that there was a lack of rules generally applicable across Europe for dealing with the legal issues that might arise from computerized data transfer.

The convention's point of departure is that certain rights of the individual may have to be protected vis-à-vis the free flow of information regardless of frontiers, the latter principle being enshrined in international and European instruments on human rights. To this end, the convention consists of three main parts: substantive law provisions in the form of basic principles; special rules on transborder data flows; and mechanisms for mutual assistance and consultation between the Parties.

The Council of Europe worked closely with the OECD in drafting the Convention. The result is that both privacy frameworks are similar.

References

Council of Europe, Legal Affairs, Treaty Office, Convention No. 108 (1981)
http://conventions.coe.int/Treaty/EN/CadreListeTraites.htm

CONVENTION FOR THE PROTECTION OF INDIVIDUALS WITH REGARD TO AUTOMATIC PROCESSING OF PERSONAL DATA

ENTERED INTO FORCE OCTOBER 1, 1985

The Member States of the Council of Europe, signatory hereto,

Considering that the aim of the Council of Europe is to achieve greater unity between its members, based in particular on respect for the rule of law, as well as human rights and fundamental freedoms;

Considering that it is desirable to extend the safeguards for everyone's rights and fundamental freedoms, and in particular the right to the respect for privacy, taking account of the increasing flow across frontiers of personal data undergoing automatic processing;

Reaffirming at the same time their commitment to freedom of information regardless of frontiers;

International
Council of Europe Convention on Privacy

Recognising that it is necessary to reconcile the fundamental values of the respect for privacy and the free flow of information between peoples,

Have agreed as follows:

CHAPTER I – GENERAL PROVISIONS

Article 1: Object and purpose

The purpose of this convention is to secure in the territory of each Party for every individual, whatever his nationality or residence, respect for his rights and fundamental freedoms, and in particular his right to privacy, with regard to automatic processing of personal data relating to him ("data protection").

Article 2: Definitions

For the purposes of this convention:

a. "personal data" means any information relating to an identified or identifiable individual ("data subject");

b. "automated data file" means any set of data undergoing automatic processing;

c. "automatic processing" includes the following operations if carried out in whole or in part by automated means: storage of data, carrying out of logical and/or arithmetical operations on those data, their alteration, erasure, retrieval or dissemination;

d. "controller of the file" means the natural or legal person, public authority, agency or any other body who is competent according to the national law to decide what should be the purpose of the automated data file, which categories of personal data should be stored and which operations should be applied to them.

Article 3: Scope

1. The Parties undertake to apply this convention to automated personal data files and automatic processing of personal data in the public and private sectors.

2. Any State may, at the time of signature or when depositing its instrument of ratification, acceptance, approval or accession, or at any later time, give notice by a declaration addressed to the Secretary General of the Council of Europe:

a. that it will not apply this convention to certain categories of automated personal data files, a list of which will be deposited. In this list it shall not include, however, categories of automated data files subject under its domestic law to data protection provisions. Consequently, it shall amend this list by a new declaration whenever additional categories of automated personal data files are subjected to data protection provisions under its domestic law;

b. that it will also apply this convention to information relating to groups of persons, associations, foundations, companies, corporations and any other bodies consisting directly or indirectly of individuals, whether or not such bodies possess legal personality;

c. that it will also apply this convention to personal data files which are not processed automatically.

3. Any State which has extended the scope of this convention by any of the declarations provided for in sub-paragraph 2.b or c above may give notice in the said declaration that such extensions shall apply only to certain categories of personal data files, a list of which will be deposited.

4. Any Party which has excluded certain categories of automated personal data files by a declaration provided for in sub-paragraph 2.a above may not claim the application of this convention to such categories by a Party which has not excluded them.

5. Likewise, a Party which has not made one or other of the extensions provided for in sub-paragraph 2.b and c above may not claim the application of this convention on these points with respect to a Party which has made such extensions.

6. The declarations provided for in paragraph 2 above shall take effect from the moment of the entry into force of the convention with regard to the State which has made them if they have been made at the time of signature or deposit of its instrument of ratification, acceptance, approval or accession, or three months after their receipt by the Secretary General of the Council of Europe if they have been made at any later time. These declarations may be withdrawn, in whole or in part, by a notification addressed to the Secretary General of the Council of Europe. Such withdrawals shall take effect three months after the date of receipt of such notification.

CHAPTER II - BASIC PRINCIPLES FOR DATA PROTECTION

Article 4: Duties of the Parties

1. Each Party shall take the necessary measures in its domestic law to give effect to the basic principles for data protection set out in this chapter.

2. These measures shall be taken at the latest at the time of entry into force of this convention in respect of that Party.

Article 5: Quality of data

Personal data undergoing automatic processing shall be:

a. obtained and processed fairly and lawfully;

b. stored for specified and legitimate purposes and not used in a way incompatible with those purposes;

c. adequate, relevant and not excessive in relation to the purposes for which they are stored;

d. accurate and, where necessary, kept up to date

e. preserved in a form which permits identification of the data subjects for no longer than is required for the purpose for which those data are stored.

International
Council of Europe Convention on Privacy

Article 6: Special categories of data

Personal data revealing racial origin, political opinions or religious or other beliefs, as well as personal data concerning health or sexual life, may not be processed automatically unless domestic law provides appropriate safeguards. The same shall apply to personal data relating to criminal convictions.

Article 7: Data security

Appropriate security measures shall be taken for the protection of personal data stored in automated data files against accidental or unauthorised destruction or accidental loss as well as against unauthorised access, alteration or dissemination.

Article 8: Additional safeguards for the data subject

Any person shall be enabled:

a. to establish the existence of an automated personal data file, its main purposes, as well as the identity and habitual residence or principal place of business of the controller of the file;

b. to obtain at reasonable intervals and without excessive delay or expense confirmation of whether personal data relating to him are stored in the automated data file as well as communication to him of such data in an intelligible form;

c. to obtain, as the case may be, rectification or erasure of such data if these have been processed contrary to the provisions of domestic law giving effect to the basic principles set out in Articles 5 and 6 of this convention;

d. to have a remedy if a request for confirmation or, as the case may be, communication, rectification or erasure as referred to in paragraphs b and c of this article is not complied with.

Article 9: Exceptions and restrictions

1. No exception to the provisions of Articles 5, 6 and 8 of this convention shall be allowed except within the limits defined in this article.

2. Derogation from the provisions of Articles 5, 6 and 8 of this convention shall be allowed when such derogation is provided for by the law of the Party and constitutes a necessary measure in a democratic society in the interests of:

a. protecting State security, public safety, the monetary interests of the State or the suppression of criminal offences;

b. protecting the data subject or the rights and freedoms of others. 3. Restrictions on the exercise of the rights specified in Article 8, paragraphs b, c and d, may be provided by law with respect to automated personal data files used for statistics or for scientific research purposes when there is obviously no risk of an infringement of the privacy of the data subjects.

Article 10: Sanctions and remedies

Each Party undertakes to establish appropriate sanctions and remedies for violations of provisions of domestic law giving effect to the basic principles for data protection set out in this chapter.

Article 11: Extended protection

None of the provisions of this chapter shall be interpreted as limiting or otherwise affecting the possibility for a Party to grant data subjects of wider measure of protection than that stipulated in this convention.

CHAPTER III – TRANSBORDER DATA FLOWS

Article 12: Transborder flows of personal data and domestic law

1. The following provisions shall apply to the transfer across national borders, by whatever medium, of personal data undergoing automatic processing or collected with a view to their being automatically processed.

2. A Party shall not, for the sole purpose of the protection of privacy, prohibit or subject to special authorisation transborder flows of personal data going to the territory of another Party.

3. Nevertheless, each Party shall be entitled to derogate from the provisions of paragraph 2:

a. insofar as its legislation includes specific regulations for certain categories of personal data or of automated personal data files, because of the nature of those data or those files, except where the regulations of the other Party provide an equivalent protection;

b. when the transfer is made from its territory to the territory of a non-Contracting State through the intermediary of the territory of another Party, in order to avoid such transfers resulting in circumvention of the legislation of the Party referred to at the beginning of this paragraph.

CHAPTER IV – MUTUAL ASSISTANCE

Article 13: Co-operation between Parties

1. The Parties agree to render each other mutual assistance in order to implement this convention.

2. For that purpose:

a. each Party shall designate one or more authorities, the name and address of each of which it shall communicate to the Secretary General of the Council of Europe;

b. each Party which has designated more than one authority shall
specify in its communication referred to in the previous sub-paragraph the competence of each authority.

3. An authority designated by a Party shall at the request of an authority designated by another Party:

International
Council of Europe Convention on Privacy

a. furnish information on its law and administrative practice in the field of data protection;

b. take, in conformity with its domestic law and for the sole purpose of protection of privacy, all appropriate measures for furnishing factual information relating to specific automatic processing carried out in its territory, with the exception however of the personal data being processed.

Article 14: Assistance to data subjects resident abroad

1. Each Party shall assist any person resident abroad to exercise the rights conferred by its domestic law giving effect to the principles set out in Article 8 of this convention. 2. When such a person resides in the territory of another Party he shall be given the option of submitting his request through the intermediary of the authority designated by that Party. 3. The request for assistance shall contain all the necessary particulars, relating inter alia to:

a. the name, address and any other relevant particulars identifying the person making the request;

b. the automated personal data file to which the request pertains, or its controller;

c. the purpose of the request.

Article 15: Safeguards concerning assistance rendered by designated authorities

1. An authority designated by a Party which has received information from an authority designated by another Party either accompanying a request for assistance or in reply to its own request for assistance shall not use that information for purposes other than those specified in the request for assistance.

2. Each Party shall see to it that the persons belonging to or acting on behalf of the designated authority shall be bound by appropriate obligations of secrecy or confidentiality with regard to that information.

3. In no case may a designated authority be allowed to make under Article 14, paragraph 2, a request for assistance on behalf of a data subject resident abroad, of its own accord and without the express consent of the person concerned.

Article 16: Refusal of requests for assistance

A designated authority to which a request for assistance is addressed under Articles 13 or 14 of this convention may not refuse to comply with it unless:

a. the request is not compatible with the powers in the field of data protection of the authorities responsible for replying;

b. the request does not comply with the provisions of this convention

c. compliance with the request would be incompatible with the sovereignty, security or public policy (ordre public) of the Party by which it was designated, or with the rights and fundamental freedoms of persons under the jurisdiction of that Party.

Article 17: Costs and procedures of assistance

1. Mutual assistance which the Parties render each other under Article 13 and assistance they render to data subjects abroad under Article 14 shall not give rise to the payment of any costs or fees other than those incurred for experts and interpreters. The latter costs or fees shall be borne by the Party which has designated the authority making the request for assistance.

2. The data subject may not be charged costs or fees in connection with the steps taken on his behalf in the territory of another Party other than those lawfully payable by residents of that Party.

3. Other details concerning the assistance relating in particular to the forms and procedures and the languages to be used, shall be established directly between the Parties concerned.

CHAPTER V – CONSULTATIVE COMMITTEE

Article 18: Composition of the committee

1. A Consultative Committee shall be set up after the entry into force of this convention.

2. Each Party shall appoint a representative to the committee and a deputy representative. Any member State of the Council of Europe which is not a Party to the convention shall have the right to be represented on the committee by an observer.

3. The Consultative Committee may, by unanimous decision, invite any non-member State of the Council of Europe which is not a Party to the convention to be represented by an observer at a given meeting.

Article 19: Functions of the committee

The Consultative Committee:

a. may make proposals with a view to facilitating or improving the application of the convention;

b. may make proposals for amendment of this convention in accordance with Article 21;

c. shall formulate its opinion on any proposal for amendment of this convention which is referred to it in accordance with Article 21, paragraph 3;

d. may, at the request of a Party, express an opinion on any question concerning the application of this convention.

Article 20: Procedure

1. The Consultative Committee shall be convened by the Secretary General of the Council of Europe. Its first meeting shall be held within twelve months of the entry into force of this convention. It shall subsequently meet at least once every two years and in any case when one-third of the representatives of the Parties request its convocation.

2. A majority of representatives of the Parties shall constitute a quorum for a meeting of the Consultative Committee.

3. After each of its meetings, the Consultative Committee shall submit to the Committee of Ministers of the Council of Europe a report on its work and on the functioning of the convention.

4. Subject to the provisions of this convention, the Consultative Committee shall draw up its own Rules of Procedure.

CHAPTER VI – AMENDMENTS

Article 21: Amendments

1. Amendments to this convention may be proposed by a Party, the Committee of Ministers of the Council of Europe or the Consultative Committee.

2. Any proposal for amendment shall be communicated by the Secretary General of the Council of Europe to the member States of the Council of Europe and to every non-member State which has acceded to or has been invited to accede to this convention in accordance with the provisions of Article 23.

3. Moreover, any amendment proposed by a Party or the Committee of Ministers shall be communicated to the Consultative Committee, which shall submit to the Committee of Ministers its opinion on that proposed amendment.

4. The Committee of Ministers shall consider the proposed amendment and any opinion submitted by the Consultative Committee and may approve the amendment.

5. The text of any amendment approved by the Committee of Ministers in accordance with paragraph 4 of this article shall be forwarded to the Parties for acceptance.

6. Any amendment approved in accordance with paragraph 4 of this article shall come into force on the thirtieth day after all Parties have informed the Secretary General of their acceptance thereof.

CHAPTER VII – FINAL CLAUSES

Article 22: Entry into force

1. This convention shall be open for signature by the member States of the Council of Europe. It is subject to ratification, acceptance or approval. Instruments of ratification, acceptance or approval shall be deposited with the Secretary General of the Council of Europe.

2. This convention shall enter into force on the first day of the month following the expiration of a period of three months after the date on which five member States of the Council of Europe have expressed their consent to be bound by the convention in accordance with the provisions of the preceding paragraph.

3. In respect of any member State which subsequently expresses its consent to be bound by it, the convention shall enter into force on the first day of the month following the expiration of a period of three months after the date of the deposit of the instrument of ratification, acceptance or approval.

Article 23: Accession by non-member States

1. After the entry into force of this convention, the Committee of Ministers of the Council of Europe may invite any State not a member of the Council of Europe to accede to this convention by a decision taken by the majority provided for in Article 20.d of the Statute of the Council of Europe and by the unanimous vote of the representatives of the Contracting States entitled to sit on the committee.

2. In respect of any acceding State, the convention shall enter into force on the first day of the month following the expiration of a period of three months after the date of deposit of the instrument of accession with the Secretary General of the Council of Europe.

Article 24: Territorial clause

1. Any State may at the time of signature or when depositing its instrument of ratification, acceptance, approval or accession, specify the territory or territories to which this convention shall apply.

2. Any State may at any later date, by a declaration addressed to the Secretary General of the Council of Europe, extend the application of this convention to any other territory specified in the declaration. In respect of such territory the convention shall enter into force on the first day of the month following the expiration of a period of three months after the date of receipt of such declaration by the Secretary General. 3. Any declaration made under the two preceding paragraphs may, in respect of any territory specified in such declaration, be withdrawn by a notification addressed to the Secretary General. The withdrawal shall become effective on the first day of the month following the expiration of a period of six months after the date of receipt of such notification by the Secretary General.

Article 25: Reservations

No reservation may be made in respect of the provisions of this convention.

Article 26: Denunciation

1. Any Party may at any time denounce this convention by means of a notification addressed to the Secretary General of the Council of Europe.

2. Such denunciation shall become effective on the first day of the month following the expiration of a period of six months after the date of receipt of the notification by the Secretary General.

Article 27: Notifications

The Secretary General of the Council of Europe shall notify the member States of the Council and any State which has acceded to this convention of

a. any signature;

b. the deposit of any instrument of ratification, acceptance, approval or accession

c. any date of entry into force of this convention in accordance with Articles 22, 23 and 24;

d. any other act, notification or communication relating to this convention.

In witness whereof the undersigned, being duly authorised thereto, have signed this Convention.

Done at Strasbourg, the 28th day of January 1981, in English and in French, both texts being equally authoritative, in a single copy which shall remain deposited in the archives of the Council of Europe. The Secretary General of the Council of Europe shall transmit certified copies to each member State of the Council of Europe and to any State invited to accede to this Convention.–

UN GUIDELINES FOR THE
REGULATION OF COMPUTERIZED
PERSONAL FILES (1990)

Summary

Adopted December 14, 1990 as General Assembly Resolution 45/95, the Guidelines for the Regulation of Computerized Personal Files provide ten principles concerning the minimum privacy guarantees that ought to be reflected in national privacy laws. These mirror the OECD's eight guidelines, but parse them out in slightly different ways. For example, both instruments contain provisions on lawful collection, accuracy, purpose specification, access and enforcement.

Unlike the OECD guidelines, however, the UN guidelines specify that no data ought to be collected which is likely to give rise to unlawful or arbitrary discrimination, such as information on religion, sex life, and race. The UN guidelines also contain a humanitarian clause stating that a nation may depart from the principles espoused by the guidelines when to do so would promote human rights.

References

United Nations, General Assembly Resolution 45/95, Guidelines for the regulation of computerized personal data files (14 December 1999)
http://www.un.org/documents/ga/res/45/a45r095.htm

UN, Report of the Secretary-General on the Follow-up to the Guidelines for the Regulation of Computerized Personal Data Files:
http://www.hri.ca/fortherecord1997/documentation/commission/e-cn4-1997-67.htm

The procedures for implementing regulations concerning computerized personal data files are left to the initiative of each State subject to the following orientations:

A. PRINCIPLES CONCERNING THE MINIMUM GUARANTEES THAT SHOULD BE PROVIDED IN NATIONAL LEGISLATIONS

1. Principle of lawfulness and fairness

Information about persons should not be collected or processed in unfair or unlawful ways, nor should it be used for ends contrary to the purposes and principles of the Charter of the United Nations.

International
UN Guidelines for Personal Data Files

2. *Principle of accuracy*

Persons responsible for the compilation of files or those responsible for keeping them have an obligation to conduct regular checks on the accuracy and relevance of the data recorded and to ensure that they are kept as complete as possible in order to avoid errors of omission and that they are kept up to date regularly or when the information contained in a file is used, as long as they are being processed.

3. *Principle of the purpose-specification*

The purpose which a file is to serve and its utilization in terms of that purpose should be specified, legitimate and, when it is established, receive a certain amount of publicity or be brought to the attention of the person concerned, in order to make it possible subsequently to ensure that:

    (a) All the personal data collected and recorded remain relevant and adequate to the purposes so specified;

    (b) None of the said personal data is used or disclosed, except with the consent of the person concerned, for purposes incompatible with those specified;

    (c) The period for which the personal data are kept does not exceed that which would enable the achievement of the purposes so specified.

4. *Principle of interested-person access*

Everyone who offers proof of identity has the right to know whether information concerning him is being processed and to obtain it in an intelligible form, without undue delay or expense, and to have appropriate rectifications or erasures made in the case of unlawful, unnecessary or inaccurate entries and, when it is being communicated, to be informed of the addressees. Provision should be made for a remedy, if need be with the supervisory authority specified in principle 8 below. The cost of any rectification shall be borne by the person responsible for the file. It is desirable that the provisions of this principle should apply to everyone, irrespective of nationality or place of residence.

5. *Principle of non-discrimination*

Subject to cases of exceptions restrictively envisaged under principle 6, data likely to give rise to unlawful or arbitrary discrimination, including information on racial or ethnic origin, colour, sex life, political opinions, religious, philosophical and other beliefs as well as membership of an association or trade union, should not be compiled.

6. *Power to make exceptions*

Departures from principles 1 to 4 may be authorized only if they are necessary to protect national security, public order, public health or morality, as well as, inter alia, the rights and freedoms of others, especially persons being persecuted (humanitarian clause) provided that such departures are expressly specified in a law or equivalent regulation promulgated in accordance with the internal legal system which expressly states their limits and sets forth appropriate safeguards.

Exceptions to principle 5 relating to the prohibition of discrimination, in addition to being subject to the same safeguards as those prescribed for exceptions to principles I and 4, may be authorized only within the limits prescribed by the International Bill of Human Rights and the other relevant instruments in the field of protection of human rights and the prevention of discrimination.

7. Principle of security

Appropriate measures should be taken to protect the files against both natural dangers, such as accidental loss or destruction and human dangers, such as unauthorized access, fraudulent misuse of data or contamination by computer viruses.

8. Supervision and sanctions

The law of every country shall designate the authority which, in accordance with its domestic legal system, is to be responsible for supervising observance of the principles set forth above. This authority shall offer guarantees of impartiality, independence vis-a-vis persons or agencies responsible for processing and establishing data, and technical competence. In the event of violation of the provisions of the national law implementing the aforementioned principles, criminal or other penalties should be envisaged together with the appropriate individual remedies.

9. Transborder data flows

When the legislation of two or more countries concerned by a transborder data flow offers comparable safeguards for the protection of privacy, information should be able to circulate as freely as inside each of the territories concerned. If there are no reciprocal safeguards, limitations on such circulation may not be imposed unduly and only in so far as the protection of privacy demands.

10. Field of application

The present principles should be made applicable, in the first instance, to all public and private computerized files as well as, by means of optional extension and subject to appropriate adjustments, to manual files. Special provision, also optional, might be made to extend all or part of the principles to files on legal persons particularly when they contain some information on individuals.

B. APPLICATION OF THE GUIDELINES TO PERSONAL DATA FILES KEPT BY GOVERNMENTAL INTERNATIONAL ORGANIZATIONS

International
UN Guidelines for Personal Data Files

The present guidelines should apply to personal data files kept by governmental international organizations, subject to any adjustments required to take account of any differences that might exist between files for internal purposes such as those that concern personnel management and files for external purposes concerning third parties having relations with the organization.

Each organization should designate the authority statutorily competent to supervise the observance of these guidelines.

Humanitarian clause: a derogation from these principles may be specifically provided for when the purpose of the file is the protection of human rights and fundamental freedoms of the individual concerned or humanitarian assistance.

A similar derogation should be provided in national legislation for governmental international organizations whose headquarters agreement does not preclude the implementation of the said national legislation as well as for non-governmental international organizations to which this law is applicable.

EUROPEAN UNION DATA PROTECTION DIRECTIVE (1995)

Summary

The European Union Data Protection Directive of 1995 establishes common rules for data protection among Member States of the European Union in order to facilitate the free flow of personal data within the EU. The Directive imposes obligations on the processors of personal data. It requires technical security and the notification of individuals whose data are being collected, and outlines circumstances under which data transfer may occur. The directive also gives individual substantial rights to control the use of data about themselves. These rights include the right to be informed that their personal data is being transferred, the need to obtain "unambiguous" consent from the individual for the transfer of certain data, the opportunity to make corrections in the data, and the right to object to the transfer. Data regulatory authority, enforcement provisions, and sanctions are also key elements of the directive. Following passage of the directive, the various national governments of the EU amended their own national data protection legislation to bring it into line with the Directive.

The Directive extends privacy safeguards to personal data that is transferred outside of the European Union. Article 25 of the Directive states that data can only be transferred to third countries that provide an "adequate level of data protection." As a result implementation focuses on both the adoption of adequate methods for privacy protection in third party countries.

References

EUR-Lex- Community Legislation in Force – Document 395L0046
http://europa.eu.int/eur-lex/en/lif/dat/1995/en_395L0046.html

Data Protection: Implementation of Directive95/46
http://www.europa.eu.int/comm/internal_market/en/dataprot/law/impl.htm

DIRECTIVE OF THE EUROPEAN PARLIAMENT AND THE COUNCIL OF EUROPE

ON THE PROTECTION OF INDIVIDUALS WITH REGARD TO THE PROCESSING OF PERSONAL DATA AND ON THE FREE MOVEMENT OF SUCH DATA

[As amended and approved by The Council of the European Union, Brussels, 20 July 1995]

THE EUROPEAN PARLIAMENT AND THE COUNCIL OF THE EUROPEAN UNION,

International
European Union Data Protection Directive

Having regard to the Treaty establishing the European Community, and in particular Article 100a thereof,

Having regard to the proposal from the Commission (1),

Having regard to the Opinion of the Economic and Social Committee (2),

Acting in accordance with the procedure referred to in Article 189b of the Treaty (3)

(1) Whereas the objectives of the Community, as laid down in the Treaty, as amended by the Treaty on European Union, include establishing an ever closer union among the people of Europe, fostering closer relations between the States belonging to the Community, ensuring economic and social progress by common action to eliminate the barriers which divide Europe, encouraging the constant improvement of the living conditions of its people, preserving and strengthening peace and liberty and promoting democracy on the basis of the fundamental rights recognized in the constitutions and laws of the Member States and in the European Convention for the Protection of Human Rights and Fundamental Freedoms;

(2) Whereas data-processing systems are designed to serve man; whereas they must, whatever the nationality or residence of natural persons, respect the fundamental freedoms and rights of individuals, notably the right to privacy, and contribute to economic and social progress, trade expansion and the well-being of individuals;

(3) Whereas the establishment and functioning of an internal market in which, in accordance with Article 7a of the Treaty, the free movement of goods, persons, services and capital is ensured require not only that personal data should be able to flow freely from one Member State to another, but also that the fundamental rights of individuals should be safeguarded.

(4) Whereas increasingly frequent recourse is being had in the Community to the processing of personal data in the various spheres of economic and social activity; whereas the progress made in information technology is making the processing and exchange of such data considerably easier;

(5) Whereas the economic and social integration resulting from the establishment and functioning of the internal market within the meaning of Article 7a of the Treaty will necessarily lead to a substantial increase in cross-border flows of personal data between all those involved in a private or public capacity in economic and social activity in the Member States; whereas the exchange of personal data between undertakings in different Member States is set to increase; whereas the national authorities in the various Member States are being called upon by virtue of Community law to collaborate and exchange personal data so as to be able to perform their duties or carry out tasks on behalf of an authority in another Member State within the context of the area without internal frontiers as constituted by the Internal Market;

(6) Whereas, furthermore, the increase in scientific and technical cooperation and the coordinated introduction of new telecommunications networks in the Community necessitate and facilitate cross-border flows of personal data;

(7) Whereas the difference in levels of protection of the rights and freedoms of individuals, notably the right to privacy, with regard to the processing of personal data afforded in the Member States may prevent the transmission of such data from the territory of one Member

State to that of another Member State; whereas this difference may therefore constitute an obstacle to the pursuit of a number of economic activities at Community level, distort competition and impede authorities in the discharge of their responsibilities under Community law; whereas this difference in levels of protection is due to the existence of a wide variety of national laws, regulations and administrative provisions;

(8) Whereas, in order to remove the obstacles to flows of personal data, the level of protection of the rights and freedoms of individuals with regard to the processing of such data must be equivalent in all the Member States; whereas this objective is vital to the internal market but cannot be achieved by Member States alone, especially in view of the scale of the divergences which currently exist between the relevant laws in the Member States and the need to coordinate the laws of the Member States so as to ensure that the cross-border flow of personal data is regulated in a consistent manner that is in keeping with the objective of the internal market as provided for in Article 7a of the Treaty; whereas Community action to approximate those laws is therefore needed;

(9) Whereas, given the equivalent protection resulting from the approximation of national laws, the Member States will no longer be able to inhibit the free movement between them of personal data on grounds relating to protection of the rights and freedoms of individuals, and in particular the right to privacy; whereas Member States will be left a margin for manoeuvre, which may, in the context of implementation of the Directive, also be exercised by the business and social partners; whereas Member States will therefore be able to specify in their national law the general conditions governing the lawfulness of data processing; whereas in doing so the Member States shall strive to improve the protection currently provided by their legislation; whereas, within the limits of this margin for manoeuvre and in accordance with Community law, disparities could arise in the implementation of the Directive, and this could have an effect on the movement of data within a Member State as well as within the Community;

(10) Whereas the object of the national laws on the processing of personal data is to protect fundamental rights and freedoms, notably the right to privacy, which is recognized both in Article 8 of the European Convention for the Protection of Human Rights and Fundamental Freedoms and in the general principles of Community law; whereas, for that reason, the approximation of those laws must not result in any lessening of the protection they afford but must, on the contrary, seek to ensure a high level of protection in the Community;

(11) Whereas the principles of the protection of the rights and freedoms of individuals, notably the right to privacy, which are contained in this Directive, give substance to and amplify those contained in the Council of Europe Convention of 28 January 1981 for the Protection of Individuals with regard to Automatic Processing of Personal Data;

(12) Whereas the protection principles must apply to all processing of personal data by any person whose activities are governed by Community law; whereas there should be excluded the processing of data carried out by a natural person in the exercise of activities which are exclusively personal or domestic, such as correspondence and the holding of records of addresses;

International
European Union Data Protection Directive

(13) Whereas the activities referred to in Titles V and VI of the Treaty on European Union regarding public safety, defence, State security or the activities of the State in the area of criminal law fall outside the scope of Community law, without prejudice to the obligations incumbent upon Member States under Article 56(2), Article 57 or Article 100a of the Treaty establishing the European Community; whereas the processing of personal data that is necessary to safeguard the economic well-being of the State does not fall within the scope of this Directive where such processing relates to State security matters;

(14) Whereas, given the importance of the developments under way, in the framework of the information society, of the techniques used to capture, transmit, manipulate, record, store or communicate sound and image data relating to natural persons, this Directive should be applicable to processing involving such data;

(15) Whereas the processing of such data is covered by this Directive only if it is automated or if the data processed are contained or are intended to be contained in a filing system structured according to specific criteria relating to individuals, so as to permit easy access to the personal data in question;

(16) Whereas the processing of sound and image data, such as in cases of video surveillance, does not come within the scope of this Directive if it is carried out for the purposes of public security, defence, national security or in the course of State activities relating to the area of criminal law or of other activities which do not come within the scope of Community law;

(17) Whereas as far as the processing of sound and image data carried out for purposes of journalism or the purposes of literary or artistic expression is concerned, in particular in the audiovisual field, the principles of the Directive are to apply in a restricted manner according to the provisions laid down in Article 9,

(18) Whereas, in order to ensure that individuals are not deprived of the protection to which they are entitled under this Directive, any processing of personal data in the Community must be carried out in accordance with the law of one of the Member States; whereas, in this connection, processing carried out under the responsibility of a controller who is established in a Member State should be governed by the law of that State;

(19) Whereas establishment on the territory of a Member State implies the effective and real exercise of activity through the means of a stable set-up; whereas the legal form of such an establishment, whether a simple branch or a subsidiary with a legal personality, is not the determinate factor in this respect; whereas, when a single controller is established on the territory of several Member States, particularly be means of a subsidiary, he must ensure, in order to avoid any circumvention of national rules, that each of the establishments fulfils the obligations imposed by the national law applicable to its activities;

(20) Whereas the fact that processing is carried out by a person established in a third country must not stand in the way of the protection of individuals provided for in this Directive; whereas, in these cases, the processing should be governed by the law of the Member State in which the means used are located, and there should be guarantees to ensure that the rights and obligations provided for in this Directive are respected in practice;

(21) Whereas this Directive is without prejudice to the rules of territoriality applicable in criminal matters;

(22) Whereas Member States shall more precisely define in the laws they enact or when bringing into force the measures taken under this Directive, the general circumstances in which processing is lawful; whereas in particular Article 5, in conjunction with Articles 7 and 8, allows Member States, independently of general rules, to provide for special processing conditions for specific sectors and for the various categories of data covered by Article 8;

(23) Whereas Member States are empowered to ensure the implementation of the protection of individuals both by means of a general law on the protection of individuals against the processing of personal data and by sectorial laws such as those relating, for example, to Institutes for Statistics;

(24) Whereas the legislation concerning the protection of legal persons with regard to the processing of data which concern them is not affected by this Directive;

(25) Whereas the principles of protection must be reflected, on the one hand, in the obligations imposed on persons, public authorities, enterprises, agencies or other bodies responsible for processing, in particular regarding data quality, technical security, notification to the supervisory authority, and the circumstances under which processing can be carried out, and, on the other hand, in the rights conferred on individuals, the data on whom are the subject of processing, to be informed that processing is taking place, to consult the data, to request corrections and even to object to processing in certain circumstances;

(26) Whereas the principles of protection must apply to any information concerning an identified or identifiable person; whereas, to determine whether a person is identifiable, account should be taken of all the means likely reasonably to be used either by the controller or by any other person to identify the said person; whereas the principles of protection shall not apply to data rendered anonymous in such a way that the data subject is no longer identifiable; whereas codes of conduct within the meaning of Article 27 may be a useful instrument in providing guidance as to the way in which data may be rendered anonymous and retained in a form in which identification of the data subject is no longer possible;

(27) Whereas the protection of individuals must apply as much to automatic processing of data as to manual processing; whereas the scope of this protection must not in effect depend on the techniques used, otherwise this would create a serious risk of circumvention; whereas, nonetheless, as regards manual processing, this Directive covers only filing systems, not according to specific criteria relating to individuals allowing easy access to the personal data; whereas, in line with the definition in Article 2(c) the different criteria for determining the constituents of a structured set of personal data, and the different criteria governing access to such a set, can be laid down by each Member State; whereas files or sets of files as well as their cover pages, which are not structured according to specific criteria, shall under no circumstances fall within the scope of this Directive;

(28) Whereas any processing of personal data must be lawful and fair to the individual concerned; whereas, in particular, the data must be adequate, relevant and not excessive in relation to the purposes for which they are processed; whereas such purposes must be explicit

and legitimate and must be determined at the time of collection of the data; whereas the purposes of processing further to collection shall not be incompatible with the purposes as they were originally specified;

(29) Whereas the further processing of personal data for historical, statistical, or scientific purposes is not generally to be considered incompatible with the purposes for which the data have previously been collected provided that Member States furnish suitable guarantees; whereas these guarantees must in particular rule out the use of data for taking measures or decisions regarding any particular individual;

(30) Whereas, in order to be lawful, the processing of personal data must in addition be carried out with the consent of the data subject or be necessary with a view to the conclusion or performance of a contract binding on the data subject, or be required by law, by the performance of a task in the public interest or in the exercise of official authority, or by the interest of a natural or legal person provided that the interests or the rights and freedoms of the data subject are not overriding; whereas, in particular, in order to maintain a balance between the interests involved while guaranteeing effective competition, Member States remain free to determine the circumstances in which personal data may be used or disclosed to a third party in the context of the legitimate ordinary business activities of companies and other bodies; whereas Member States may similarly specify the conditions under which personal data may be disclosed to a third party for the purposes of marketing whether carried out commercially or b a charitable organization or by any other association or foundation, of a political nature for example, subject to the provisions allowing a data subject to object to the processing of data regarding him, at no cost and without having to state his reasons;

(31) Whereas the processing of personal data must equally be regarded as lawful where it is carried out in order to protect an interest which is essential for the data subject's life;

(32) Whereas it is for national legislation to determine whether the controller performing a task carried out in the public interest or in the exercise of official authority should be a public administration or another national or legal person governed by public law or by private law or such as a professional association;

(33) Whereas data which are capable by their nature of infringing fundamental freedoms or privacy should not be processed unless the data subject gives his explicit consent; whereas, however, derogation from this prohibition must be explicitly provided for in respect of specific needs, in particular where the processing of these data is carried out for certain health-related purposes by individuals subject to a legal obligation of professional secrecy or in the course of legitimate activities by certain associations or foundations the purpose of which is to permit the exercise of fundamental freedoms;

(34) Whereas Member States must Also be authorized, when justified by grounds of important public interest, to derogate from the prohibition on processing sensitive categories of data where important reasons of public interest so justify in areas such as public health and social protection, especially as regards the assurance of quality and cost-effectiveness, and as regards the procedures used for settling claims for benefits and services in the health insurance system, scientific research and government statistics; whereas it is incumbent on them, however, to

provide specific and suitable safeguards so as to protect the fundamental rights and the privacy of individuals;

(35) Whereas, moreover, the processing of personal data by official authorities for achieving aims, laid down in constitutional law or international public law, of officially recognized religious associations is carried out on important grounds of public interest;

(36)Whereas where, in the course of electoral activities, the operation of the democratic system requires in certain Member States that political parties compile data on people's political opinions, the processing of such data can be permitted for reasons of important public interest, provided that appropriate safeguards are established;

(37) Whereas the processing of personal data for purposes of journalism or for purposes of literary or artistic expression, in particular in the audiovisual field, should qualify for exemption from the requirements of certain provisions of this Directive insofar as this is necessary to reconcile the fundamental rights of individuals with freedom of information and notably the right to receive and impart information, as guaranteed in particular in Article 10 of the European Convention for the Protection of Human Rights and Fundamental Freedoms; whereas Member States should therefore lay down exemptions and derogations necessary for the purposes of balance between fundamental rights as regards general measures on the legitimacy of data processing, measures on the transfer of data to third countries and the powers of supervisory authority; whereas this should not, however, lead Member States to lay down exemptions from the measures to ensure security of processing; whereas the supervisory authority responsible for this sector should also be provided at least with certain ex-post powers, e.g. to publish a regular report or to refer matters to the judicial authorities;

(38) Whereas, if the processing of data is to be fair, the data subject must be in a position to learn of the existence of a processing operation and, where data are collected from him, must be given accurate and full information, bearing in mind the circumstances of the collection;

(39) Whereas certain processing operations involve data which the controller has not collected directly from the data subject; whereas, furthermore, data can be legitimately disclosed to a third party, even if the disclosure was not anticipated at the time the data were collected from the data subject; whereas, in all these cases, the data subject should be informed when the data are recorded or at the latest when the data are first disclosed to a third party;

(40) Whereas, however, it is not necessary to impose this obligation if the data subject already knows the information; whereas, moreover, this obligation is not provided for if the recording or disclosure are expressly provided for by law or if the provision of information proves impossible or involved disproportionate efforts, which could be the case where processing is for historical, statistical or scientific purposes; whereas, in this regard, the number of data subjects, the age of the data, and any compensatory measures adopted may be taken into consideration;

(41) Whereas any person must be able to exercise the right of access to data relating to him which are being processed, in order to verify in particular the accuracy of the data and the lawfulness of the processing; whereas, for the same reasons, every data subject must also have the right to know the logic involved in the automatic processing of data concerning him, at

least in the case of the automated decisions referred to in Article 15(1); whereas this right must not be adversely affect business confidentiality or intellectual property and in particular the copyright protecting the software; whereas these considerations must not, however, result in the data subject being refused all information;

(42) Whereas Member States may, in the interest of the data subject or so as to protect the rights and freedoms of others, restrict rights of access and information; whereas they may, for example, specify that access to medical data may be obtained only through a health professional;

(43) Whereas restrictions on the rights of access and information and on certain obligations of the controller may similarly be imposed by Member States insofar as they are necessary to safeguard, for example, national security, defence, public safety, or important economic or financial interests of a Member State or the Union, as well as criminal investigations and prosecutions and action in respect of breaches of ethics in the regulated professions; whereas the list of exceptions and limitations should include the tasks of monitoring, inspection or regulation necessary in three last-mentioned areas concerning public security, economic or financial interests and crime prevention; whereas the listing of tasks in these three areas does not affect the legitimacy of exceptions or restrictions for reasons of State security or defence;

(44) Whereas Member States may also be led, by virtue of the provisions of Community law, to derogate from the provisions of this Directive concerning the right of access, the obligation to inform individuals and the quality of data, in order to safeguard certain purposes among those referred to above;

(45) Whereas, in cases of processing lawfully data pursued on grounds of public interest, official authority or the legitimate interests of a natural or legal person, any data subject should nevertheless be entitled, on legitimate and compelling grounds relating to his particular situation, to object to the processing of any data relating to himself; whereas Member States nevertheless have the possibility of laying down national provisions to the contrary;

(46) Whereas the protection of the rights and freedoms of data subjects with regard to the processing of personal data requires that appropriate technical and organizational measures be taken, both at the time of the design of the processing system and at the time of the processing itself, particularly in order to maintain security and thereby to prevent any unauthorized processing; whereas it is incumbent on the Member States to ensure that controllers comply with these measures; whereas these measures must ensure an appropriate level of security, taking into account the state of the technology and the cost of its use in view of the risks inherent in the processing and the nature of the data to be protected;

(47) Whereas where a message containing personal data is transmitted by means of a telecommunications or electronic mail service, the sole purpose of which is the transmission of such messages, the controller in respect of the personal data contained in the message will normally be considered to be the person from whom the message originates, rather than the person offering the transmission services; whereas, nevertheless, those offering such services will normally be considered controllers in respect of the processing of the additional personal data necessary for the operation of the service;

(48) Whereas the notification procedures are designed to ensure disclosure of the purposes and main features of any processing operation for the purpose of verification that the operation is in accordance with the national measures taken under this Directive;

(49) Whereas, in order to avoid unsuitable administrative formalities, exemptions from the obligation to notify and simplification of the notification required may be provided for by Member States in cases where processing is unlikely to adversely affect the rights and freedoms of data subjects, provided that it is in accordance with a measure taken by a Member State specifying its limits; whereas in an equivalent way exemption or simplification can similarly be provided for by Member States where a person appointed by the controller ensures that the processing carried out is not likely adversely to affect the rights and freedoms of data subjects; whereas such an official, whether or not an employee of the controller, must be in a position to exercise his functions in complete independence;

(50) Whereas exemption or simplification could be provided for in cases of processing operations whose sole purpose is the keeping of a register intended, according to national law, to provide information to the public and open to consultation by the public or by any person demonstrating a legitimate interest;

(51) Whereas, nevertheless, simplification or exemption from the obligation to notify shall not release the controller from any of the other obligations resulting from this Directive;

(52) Whereas, in this context, ex post facto verification by the competent authorities must be in general be considered a sufficient measure;

(53) Whereas, however, certain processing operations are likely to pose specific risks to the rights and freedoms of data subjects by virtue of their nature, their scope or their purposes, such as the purpose of excluding individuals from a right, benefit or contract, or by virtue of the specific use of new technologies; whereas it is for Member States, if they so wish, to specify such risks in their legislation;

(54) Whereas with regard to all the processing undertaken in society, the amount posing such specific risks should be very limited; whereas Member States must provide that the supervisory authority, or the data protection official in cooperation with the authority, check such processing prior to it being carried out; whereas following this prior check, the supervisory authority may, according to its national law, give an opinion or an authorization regarding the processing; whereas such checking may equally take place in the course of the preparation of a legislative measure adopted by the national parliament or on the basis of such a measure, defining the nature of the processing and specifying suitable safeguards;

(55) Whereas, if the controller fails to respect the rights of data subjects, national legislation must provide for a judicial remedy; whereas any damage which a person may suffer as a result of unlawful processing must be compensated for by the controller, who may be exempted from liability if he proves that he is not responsible for the damage, in particular in cases where he reports an error on the part of the data subject or in a case of force majeure; whereas sanctions must be imposed on any person, whether governed by private or public law, who fails to comply with the national measures taken under this Directive;

(56) Whereas cross-border flows of personal data are necessary to the expansion of international trade; whereas the protection of individuals guaranteed in the Community by this Directive does not stand in the way of transfers of personal data to third countries which ensure an adequate level of protection; whereas the adequacy of the level of protection afforded by a third country must be assessed in the light of all the circumstances surrounding the transfer operation or set of transfer operations;

(57) Whereas, on the other hand, the transfer of personal data to a third country which does not ensure an adequate level of protection must be prohibited;

(58) Whereas provision should be made for exemptions from this prohibition in certain circumstances where the data subject has given his consent, where the transfer is necessary in relation to a contract or a legal claim, where protection of an important public interest so requires, for example in cases of international transfers of data between tax or customs administrations or between services competent for social security matters, or where the transfer is made from a register established by law and intended for consultation by the public or persons having a legitimate interest; whereas in this case such a transfer should not involve the entirety of the data or entire categories of the data contained in the register and, when the register is intended for consultation by persons having a legitimate interest, the transfer should be made only at the request of the same persons or if the latter are the recipients;

(59) Whereas particular measures may be taken to compensate for the lack of protection in a third country in cases where the person responsible for the processing offers appropriate assurances; whereas, moreover, provision must be made for procedures for negotiations between the Community and such third countries;

(60) Whereas, in any event, transfers to third countries may only be effected in full compliance with the provisions adopted by the Member States pursuant to this Directive, and in particular Article 8 thereof;

(61) Whereas Member States and the Commission, in their respective spheres of competence, must encourage the trade associations and other representative organizations concerned to draw up codes of conduct so far as to facilitate the application of this Directive, taking account of the specific characteristics of the processing carried out in certain sectors, and respecting the national provisions adopted for its implementation;

(62) Whereas the establishment in Member States of supervisory authorities, exercising their functions with complete independence, is an essential component of the protection of individuals with regard to the processing of personal data;

(63) Whereas such authorities must have the necessary means to perform their duties, including powers of investigation and intervention, particularly in cases of complaints from individuals, and powers to engage in legal proceedings; whereas such authorities must help to ensure transparency of processing in the Member States within those jurisdiction they fall;

(64) Whereas the authorities in the different Member States will need to assist one another in performing their duties so as to ensure that the rules of protection are properly respected throughout the European Union;

(65) Whereas, at Community level, a Working Party on the Protection of Individuals with regard to the Processing of Personal Data must be set up and be completely independent in the performance of its functions; whereas, having regard to its specific nature, it must advise the Commission and, in particular, contribute to the uniform application of the national rules adopted pursuant to this Directive;

(66) Whereas, with regard to the transfer of data to third countries, the application of this Directive calls for the conferment of powers of implementation on the Commission and the establishment of a procedure in accordance with the procedures laid down in Council Decision 87/373/EEC(1);

(67) Whereas an agreement on a "modus vivendi" between the European Parliament, the Council and the Commission concerning the implimenting measures for acts adopted in accordance with the procedure laid down in Article 189b of the EC Treaty was reached on 20 December 1994;

(68) Whereas the principles set out in this Directive regarding the protection of the rights and freedoms of individuals, notably their right to privacy, with regard to the processing of personal data may be supplemented or clarified, in particular as far as certain sectors are concerned, by specific rules based on those principles;

(69) Whereas Member States should be allowed a period of not more than three years from the entry into force of the national measures transposing this Directive in which to apply such new national rules gradually to all processing operations already under way; whereas, in order to facilitate cost-efficient implementation, a further period expiring twelve years after the date on which this Directive is adopted will be allowed to Member States to ensure the conformity of existing manual filing systems with certain of the Directive's provisions; whereas data contained in such filing systems actively processed during this extended transition period should nevertheless be brought into conformity with these provisions at the time of such further active processing;

(70) Whereas it is not necessary for the data subject to give his consent again so as to allow the controller to continue to process, after the national provisions taken pursuant to this Directive enter into force, any sensitive data necessary for the performance of a contract concluded on the basis of free and informed consent before the entry into force of these provisions;

(71) Whereas this Directive does not stand in the way of a Member State's regulating marketing activities aimed at consumers residing in its territory insofar as much as such regulation does not concern the protection of individuals with regard to the processing of personal data;

(72) Whereas the Directive allows the principle of public access to official documents to be taken into account when implementing the principles set out in this Directive,

HAVE ADOPTED THIS DIRECTIVE:

International
European Union Data Protection Directive

CHAPTER I: GENERAL PROVISIONS

Article 1 Object of the Directive

1. In accordance with this Directive, Member States shall protect the fundamental rights and freedoms of natural persons, and in particular their right to privacy, with respect to the processing of personal data.

2. Member States shall neither restrict nor prohibit the free flow of personal data between Member States for reasons connected with the protection afforded under paragraph 1.

Article 2 Definitions

For the purposes of this Directive

(a) "personal data" shall mean any information relating to an identified or identifiable natural person ("data subject"); an identifiable person is one who can be identified, directly or indirectly, in particular by reference to an identification number or to one or more factors specific to his physical, physiological, mental, economic, cultural or social identity;

(b) "processing of personal data" ("processing") shall mean any operation or set of operations which is performed upon personal data, whether or not by automatic means, such as collection, recording, organization, storage, adaptation or alteration, retrieval, consultation, use, disclosure by transmission, dissemination or otherwise making available, alignment or combination, blocking, erasure or destruction;

(c) "personal data filing system" ("filing system") shall mean any structured set of personal data which are accessible according to specific criteria, whether centralized, decentralized or dispersed on a functional or geographical basis;

(d) "controller" shall mean the natural or legal person, public authority, agency or any other body which alone or jointly with others determines the purposes and means of the processing of personal data. Where the purposes and means of processing are determined by national or Community laws or regulations, the controller or the specific criteria for his nomination may be designated by a national or Community law.

(e) "processor" shall mean the natural or legal person, public authority, agency or any other body which processes personal data on behalf of the controller;

(f) "third party" shall mean the natural or legal person, public authority, agency or any other body other than the data subject, the controller, the processor and the persons who, under the direct authority of the controller or the processor, are authorized to process the data;

(g) "recipient" shall mean the natural or legal person, public authority, agency or any other body to whom data are disclosed, whether a third party or not; however, authorities which may receive data in the framework of a particular inquiry shall not be regarded as recipients;

(h) "the data subject's consent" shall mean any freely given specific and informed indication of his wishes by which the data subject signifies his agreement to personal data relating to him being processed.

Article 3 Scope

1. This Directive shall apply to the processing of personal data wholly or partly by automatic means, and to the processing otherwise than by automatic means of personal data which form part of a filing system or are intended to form part of a filing system.

2. This Directive shall not apply to the processing of personal data:

- in the course of an activity which falls outside the scope of community law, such as those provided for by Titles V and VI of the Treaty on European Union and in any case to processing operations concerning public security, defence, State security (including the economic well-being of the State when the processing operation related to State security matters) and the activities of the State in areas of criminal law;

- by a natural person in the course of a purely personal or household activity.

Article 4 National law applicable

1. Each Member State shall apply the national provisions it adopts pursuant to this Directive to the processing of personal data where:

(a) the processing is carried out in the context of the activities of an establishment of the controller on the territory of the Member State; when the same controller is established on the territory of several Member States, he must take the necessary measures to ensure that each of these establishments complies with the obligations laid down by the national law applicable;

(b) the controller is not established on the Member State's territory, but in a place where its national law applies by virtue of international public law;

(c) the controller is not established on Community territory and, for purposes of processing personal data makes use of equipment, automated or otherwise, situated on the territory of said Member State, unless such equipment is used only for purposes of transit through the territory of the Community.

2. In the circumstances referred to in paragraph 1(c), the controller must designate a representative established in the territory of that Member State, without prejudice to legal actions which could be initiated against the controller himself.

CHAPTER II: GENERAL RULES ON THE LAWFULNESS OF THE PROCESSING OF PERSONAL DATA

Article 5

Member States shall, within the limits of the provisions of this Chapter, determine more precisely the conditions under which the processing of personal data is lawful.

International
European Union Data Protection Directive

SECTION 1: PRINCIPLES RELATING TO DATA QUALITY

Article 6

1. Member States shall provide that personal data must be:

(a) processed fairly and lawfully;

(b) collected for specified, explicit and legitimate purposes and not further processed in a way incompatible with those purposes. Further processing of data for historical, statistical or scientific purposes shall not be considered as incompatible provided that Member States provide appropriate safeguards;

(c) adequate, relevant and not excessive in relation to the purposes for which they are collected and/or for which they are further processed;

(d) accurate and, where necessary, kept up to date; every reasonable step must be taken to ensure that data which are inaccurate or incomplete, having regard to the purposes for which they were collected or for which they are further processed, are erased or rectified;

(e) kept in a form which permits identification of data subjects for no longer that is necessary for the purposes for which the data were collected or for which they are further processed. Member Sates shall lay down appropriate safeguards for personal data stored for longer periods for historical, statistical or scientific use.

2. It shall be for the controller to ensure that paragraph 1 is complied with.

SECTION II PRINCIPLES RELATING TO THE REASONS FOR MAKING DATA PROCESSING LEGITIMATE

Article 7

Member States shall provide that personal data may be processed only if:

(a) the data subject has given his consent unambiguously; or

(b) processing is necessary for the performance of a contact to which the data subject is party or in order to take steps at the request of the data subject entering into a contract.; or

(c) processing is necessary for compliance with a legal obligation to which the controller is subject; or

(d) processing is necessary in order to protect the vital interests of the data subject; or

(e) processing is necessary for the performance of a task carried out in the public interest or in the exercise of official authority vested in the controller or in a third party to whom the data are disclosed; or

(f) processing is necessary for the purposes of the legitimate interests pursued by the controller or by the third party or parties to whom the data are disclosed, except where such interests are overridden by the interests or fundamental rights and freedoms of the data subject which require protection under Article 1(1).

SECTION III SPECIAL CATEGORIES OF PROCESSING

Article 8 The processing of special categories of data

1. Member States shall prohibit the processing of personal data revealing racial or ethnic origin, political opinions, religious or philosophical beliefs, trade-union membership, and the processing of data concerning health or sex life.

2. Paragraph 1 shall not apply where:

   (a) the data subject has given his explicit consent to the processing of those data, except where the laws of the Member State provide that the prohibition referred to in paragraph 1 may not be waived by the data subject giving his consent.; or

   (b) processing is necessary for the purposes of carrying out the obligations and specific rights of the controller in the field of employment law insofar as it is authorized by national law providing for adequate safeguards; or

   (c) processing is necessary to protect the vital interests of the data subject or of another person where the data subject is physically or legally incapable of giving his consent; or

   (d) processing is carried out in the course of its legitimate activities with appropriate guarantees by a foundation, association or any other non-profit-seeking body with a political, philosophical, religious or trade-union aim and on condition that the processing relates solely to the members of the body or to persons who have regular contact with it in connection with its purposes and that the data are not disclosed to a third party without the consent of the data subjects; or

   (e) the processing relates to data which are manifestly made public by the data subject or is necessary for the establishment, exercise or defense of legal claims.

3. Paragraph 1 shall not apply where processing of the data is required for the purposes of preventive medicine, medical diagnosis, the provision of care or treatment or the management of health-care services, and where those data are processed by a health professional subject under national law or rules established by national competent bodies to the obligation of professional secrecy or by another person also subject to an equivalent obligation of secrecy.

4. Subject to the provision of suitable safeguards, Member States may lay down for reasons of important public interest, exemptions in addition to those laid down in paragraph 2 either by national law or by decision of the supervisory authority.

5. Processing of data relating to offences, criminal convictions or security measures may be carried out only under the control of official authority, or if suitable specific safeguards are provided under national law, subject to derogations which may be granted by the Member State under national provisions providing suitable specific safeguards. However, a complete register of criminal convictions may be kept only under the control of official authority. Member States may provide that data relating to administrative sanctions or civil trials shall also be processed under the control of official authority.

6. Derogations from paragraph 1 provided for in paragraphs 4 and 5 shall be notified to the Commission.

7. Member States shall determine the conditions under which a national identification number or any other identifier of general application may be processed. Article 9 Processing of personal data and freedom of expression Member States shall provide for exemptions or derogations from the provisions of this Chapter, Chapter IV and Chapter VI for the processing of personal data carried out solely for journalistic purposes or the purpose of artistic or literary expression only if they are necessary to reconcile the right to privacy with the rules governing freedom of expression.

Article 9 Processing of personal data and freedom of expression

Member States shall provide for exemptions or derogations from the provisions of this Chapter, Chapter IV and Chapter VI for the processing of personal data carried out solely for journalistic purposes or the purpose of artistic or literary expression only if they are necessary to reconcile the right to privacy with the rules governing freedom of expression.

SECTION IV INFORMATION TO BE GIVEN TO THE DATA SUBJECT

Article 10 Information in cases of collection of data from the data subject

Member States shall provide that the controller or his representative must provide a data subject from whom data relating to himself are collected with at least the following information, except where he already knows:

(a) the identity of the controller and of his representative, if any,

(b) the purposes of the processing for which the data are intended,

(c) any further information such as - the recipients or categories of recipients of the data; - whether replies to the questions are obligatory or voluntary, as well as the possible consequences of the failure to reply; - the existence of the right of access to and the right to rectify the data concerning him insofar as they are necessary, having regard to the specific circumstances in which the data are collected, to guarantee fair processing in respect of the data subject.

Article 11 Information where the data have not been obtained from the data subject

1. Where the data have not been obtained from the data subject, Member States shall provide that the controller or his representative must at the time of undertaking the recording of personal data or if a disclosure to a third party is envisaged, no later than the time when the data are first disclosed provide the data subject with at least the following information, except where he already knows:

(a) the identity of the controller and of his representative, if any,

(b) the purposes of the processing,

(c) any further information such as

- the categories of data concerned
- the recipients or categories of recipients;
- the existence of the right of access to and the right to rectify the data concerning him insofar as they are necessary, having regard to the specific circumstances in which the data are processed, to guarantee fair processing in respect of the data subject.

2. Paragraph 1 shall not apply where, in particular for processing for statistical purposes or for the purposes of historical or scientific research, the provision of information proves impossible or involves a disproportionate effort or if recording or disclosure is expressly laid down by law. In these cases Member States shall provide appropriate safeguards.

SECTION V THE DATA SUBJECT'S RIGHT OF ACCESS TO DATA

Article 12 Right of access

Member States shall guarantee for every data subject the right to obtain from the controller:

1. without constraint at reasonable intervals and without excessive delay or expense:
   - confirmation as to whether or not data relating to him are processed and information at least as to the purposes of the processing, the categories of data concerned, and the recipients or categories of recipients to whom the data are disclosed;
   - communication to him in an intelligible form of the data undergoing processing and of any available information as to their source;
   - knowledge of the logic involved in any automatic processing of data concerning him at least in the case of the automated decisions referred to in Article 15(1);

2. as appropriate the rectification, erasure or blocking of data, the processing of which does not comply with the provisions of this Directive, in particular because of the incomplete or inaccurate nature of the data;

3. notification to third parties to whom the data have been disclosed of any rectification, erasure or blocking carried out in compliance with paragraph 2, unless this proves impossible or involves a disproportionate effort.

SECTION VI: EXEMPTIONS AND RESTRICTIONS

Article 13: Exemptions and restrictions

1. Member States may adopt legislative measures to restrict the scope of the obligations and rights provided for in Articles 6(1), 10, 11(1), 12 and 21 when such a restriction constitutes a necessary measure to safeguard:

   (a) national security;
   (b) defence;

(c) public security;

(d) the prevention, investigation, detection and prosecution of criminal offences, or of breaches of ethics for regulated professions;

(e) an important economic or financial interest of a Member State or of the European Union, including monetary, budgetary and taxation matters;

(f) a monitoring, inspection or regulatory function connected, even occasionally, with the exercise of official authority in cases referred to in (c), (d) and (e);

(g) the protection of the data subject or of the rights and freedoms of others.

2. Subject to adequate legal guarantees, in particular that the data are not used for taking measures or decisions regarding any particular individual data subject, Member States may restrict, by a legislative measure, the rights provided for in Article 12 when data are processed solely for purposes of scientific research or are kept in personal form for a period which does not exceed the period necessary for the sole purpose of creating statistics.

SECTION VII: THE DATA SUBJECT'S RIGHT TO OBJECT

Article 14 The data subject's right to object

Member States shall grant the data subject the right:

(a) at least in the cases referred to in Article 7(e) and (f), to object at any time on compelling legitimate grounds relating to his particular situation to the processing of data relating to him, save where otherwise

provided by national legislation. Where there is a justified objection, the processing instigated by the controller may no longer involve those data;

(b) to object, on request and free of charge, to the processing of personal data relating to him which the controller anticipates being processed for the purposes of direct marketing; or to be informed before personal data are disclosed for the first time to third parties or used on their behalf for the purposes of direct marketing, and to be expressly offered the right to object free of charge to such disclosures or uses.

Member States shall take the necessary measures to ensure that data subjects are aware of the existence of the right referred to in the first subparagraph of (b).

Article 15: Automated individual decisions

1. Member States shall grant the right to every person not to be subject to a decision which produces legal effects concerning him or significantly affects him and which is based solely on automated processing of data intended to evaluate certain personal aspects relating to him, such as his performance at work, creditworthiness, reliability, conduct, etc.

2. Subject to the other Articles of this Directive, Member States shall provide that a person may be subjected to a decision of the kind referred to in paragraph 1 if that decision:

> (a) is taken in the course of entering into or performance of a contract, provided the request by the data subject has been satisfied, or that there are suitable measures to safeguard his legitimate interests, such as arrangements allowing him to defend his point of view; or

> (b) is authorized by a law which also lays down measures to safeguard the data subject's legitimate interests.

SECTION VIII: CONFIDENTIALITY AND SECURITY OF PROCESSING

Article 16 Confidentiality of processing

Any person acting under the authority of the controller or of the processor, including the processor himself, who has access to personal data must not process them except on instructions from the controller, unless he is required to do so by law.

Article 17 Security of processing

1. Member States shall provide that the controller must implement appropriate technical and organizational measures to protect personal data against accidental or unlawful destruction or accidental loss and against unauthorized alteration, disclosure or access, in particular where the processing involves the transmission of data over a network, and against all other unlawful forms of processing. Having regard to the state of the art and the costs of their implementation, such measures shall ensure a level of security appropriate to the risks represented by the processing and the nature of the data to be protected.

2. The Member States shall provide that the controller must, where processing is carried out on his behalf, choose a processor who provides sufficient guarantees in respect of the technical security measures and organizational measures governing the processing to be carried out and must ensure compliance with those measures.

3. The carrying out of processing by way of a processor must be governed by a contract or legal act binding the processor to the controller and stipulating in particular that:

> - the processor shall act only on instructions from the controller;
> - the obligations set out in paragraph 1, as defined by the law of the Member State in which the processor is established, shall also be incumbent on the processor.

4. For the purposes of keeping proof, the parts of the contract or legal act relating to data protection and the requirements relating to the measures referred to in paragraph 1 shall be in writing or in another equivalent form.

International
European Union Data Protection Directive

SECTION IX: NOTIFICATION

Article 18 Obligation to notify the supervisory authority

1. Member States shall provide that the controller or his representative, if any, must notify the supervisory authority referred to in Article 28 before carrying out any wholly or partly automatic processing operation or set of such operations intended to serve a single purpose or several related purposes.

2. Member States may provide for the simplification of or exemption from notification only in the following cases and under the following conditions:

- where, for categories of processing operations which are unlikely, taking account of the data to be processed, to affect adversely the rights and freedoms of data subjects, they specify the purposes of the processing, the data or categories of data undergoing processing, the category or categories of data subject, the recipients or categories of recipient to whom the data are to be disclosed and the length of time the data are to be stored and/or

- where the controller appoints, in compliance with the national law which governs him, a data protection official, responsible in particular

= for ensuring in an independent manner the internal application of the national provisions taken pursuant to this Directive

= for keeping the register of processing operations carried out by the controller, containing the items of information referred to in Article 21(2), thereby ensuring that the rights and freedoms of the data subjects are unlikely to be adversely affected by the processing operations.

3. Member States may provide that paragraph 1 does not apply to processing whose sole purpose is the keeping of a register, which according to laws or regulations is intended to provide information to the public and which is open to consultation either by the public in general or by any person demonstrating a legitimate interest.

4. Member States may provide for an exemption from the obligation to notify or a simplification of the notification in the case or processing operations referred to in Article 8(2)(d).

5. Member States may stipulate that certain or all non-automatic processing operations involving personal data shall be notified, or provide for these processing operations to be subject to a simplified notification.

Article 19 Contents of notification

1. Member States shall specify the information to be given in the notification. It shall include at least:

(a) the name and address of the controller and of his representative, if any;

(b) the purpose or purposes of the processing;

(c) a description of the category or categories of data subject and of the data or categories of data relating to them;

(d) the recipients or categories of recipient to whom the data might be disclosed;

(e) proposed transfers of data to third countries;

(f) a general description allowing a preliminary assessment to be made of the appropriateness of the measures taken pursuant to Article 17 to ensure security of processing.

2. Member States shall specify the procedures under which any change affecting the information referred to in paragraph 1 must be notified to the supervisory authority.

Article 20 Prior checking

1. Member States shall determine the processing operations likely to present specific risks for the rights and freedoms of data subjects and shall check that these processing operations are examined prior to the start thereof.

2. Such prior checks shall be carried out by the supervisory authority following receipt of a notification from the controller or by the data protection official, who in cases of doubt must consult the supervisory authority.

3. Member States may also carry out such checks in the context of preparation of a measure decided on by the national parliament or based on such a decision, defining the nature of the processing operation and laying down appropriate safeguards.

Article 21 Publicizing of processing operations

1. Member States shall take measures to ensure that processing operations are publicized.

2. Member States shall provide that a register of processing operations notified in accordance with Article 18 shall be kept by the supervisory authority. The register shall contain at least the information listed in Article 19(1)(a) to (e). The register may be inspected by any person.

3. Member States shall provide, in relation to processing operations not subject to notification, that controllers or another body appointed by the Member States make available at least the information referred to in Article 19(1)(a) to (e) in an appropriate fashion to any person on request. Member States may provide that this provision does not apply to processing whose sole purpose is the keeping of a register, which according to laws or regulations is intended to provide information to the public and which is open to consultation either by the public in general or by any person who can provide proof of a legitimate interest.

CHAPTER III JUDICIAL REMEDIES, LIABILITY AND PENALTIES

Article 22 Remedies

Without prejudice to any administrative remedy for which provision may be made, inter alia before the supervisory authority referred to in Article 28, prior to referral to the judicial authority, Member States shall provide for the right of every person to a judicial remedy for any breach of the rights guaranteed him by the national law applicable to the processing in question.

Article 23 Liability

1. Member States shall provide that any person who has suffered damage as a result of an unlawful processing operation or of any act incompatible with the national provisions adopted pursuant to this Directive is entitled to receive compensation from the controller for the damage suffered.

2. The controller may be exempted from this liability, in whole or in part, if he proves that he is not responsible for the event giving rise to the damage.

Article 24 Sanctions

The Member States shall adopt suitable measures to ensure the full implementation of the provisions of this Directive and shall in particular lay down the sanctions to be imposed in case of infringement of the provisions adopted pursuant to this Directive.

CHAPTER IV TRANSFER OF PERSONAL DATA TO THIRD COUNTRIES

Article 25 Principles

1. Member States shall provide that the transfer to a third country of personal data which are undergoing processing or are intended for processing after transfer may take place only if, without prejudice to compliance with the national provisions adopted pursuant to the other provisions of this Directive, the third country in question ensures an adequate level of protection.

2. The adequacy of the level of protection afforded by a third country shall be assessed in the light of all the circumstances surrounding a data transfer operation or set of data transfer operations; particular consideration shall be given to the nature of the data, the purpose and duration of the proposed processing operation or operations, the country of origin and country of final destination, the rules of law, both general and sectoral, in force in the third country in question and the professional rules and security measures which are complied with in those countries.

3. Member States and the Commission shall inform each other of cases where the consider that a third country does not ensure an adequate level of protection within the meaning of paragraph 2.

4. Where the Commission finds, under the procedure provided for in Article 31(2), that a third country does not ensure an adequate level of protection within the meaning of paragraph 2 of this Article Member States shall take the measures necessary to prevent the transfer of data of the same type to the third country in question.

5. At the appropriate time, the Commission shall enter into negotiations with a view to remedying the situation resulting from the funding made pursuant to paragraph 4.

6. The Commission may find, in accordance with the procedure referred to in Article 31(2), that a third country ensures an adequate level of protection within the meaning of paragraph 2 of this Article, by reason of its domestic law or of the international commitments it has entered into, particularly upon conclusion of the negotiations referred to in paragraph 5, for the protection of the private lives and basic freedoms and rights of individuals. Member States shall take the measures necessary to comply with the Commission's decision.

Article 26 Derogations

1. By way of derogation from Article 25 and save where otherwise provided by domestic law governing particular cases, Member States shall provide that a transfer or a set of transfers of personal data to a third country which does not ensure an adequate level of protection within the meaning of Article 25(2) may take place on condition that:

   1) the data subject has given his consent unambiguously to the proposed transfer, or

   2) the transfer is necessary for the performance of a contract between the data subject and the controller or the implementation of precontractual measures taken in response to the data subject's request, or

   3) the transfer is necessary for the conclusion or for the performance of a contract concluded in the interest of the data subject between the controller and a third party, or

   4) the transfer is necessary or legally required on important public interest grounds, or for the establishment, exercise or defence of legal claims, or

   5) the transfer is necessary in order to protect the vital interests of the data subject, or

   6) the transfer is made from a register which according to laws or regulations is intended to provide information to the public and which is open to consultation either by the public in general or by any person who can demonstrate legitimate interest, to the extent that the conditions laid down in law for consultation are fulfilled in the particular case.

2. Without prejudice to paragraph 1, a Member State may authorize a transfer or a set of transfers of personal data to a third country which does not ensure an adequate level of protection within the meaning of Article 25(2), where the controller adduces sufficient guarantees with respect to the protection of the privacy and fundamental rights and freedoms of individuals and as regards the exercise of the corresponding rights; such guarantees may in particular result from appropriate contractual clauses.

3. The Member State shall inform the Commission and the other Member States of the authorizations granted pursuant to paragraph 2. If a Member State or the Commission objects on justified grounds involving the protection of the privacy and fundamental rights and freedoms of individuals, the Commission shall take appropriate measures in

accordance with the procedure laid down in Article 31(2). Member States shall take the necessary measures to comply with the Commission's decision.

4. Where the Commission decides, in accordance with the procedure referred to in Article 31(2), that certain standard contractual clauses offer sufficient guarantees required by paragraph 2, Member States shall take the necessary measures to comply with the Commission's decision.

CHAPTER V CODES OF CONDUCT

Article 27

1. The Member States and the Commission shall encourage the drawing up of codes of conduct intended to contribute to the proper implementation of the national provisions adopted by the Member States pursuant to this Directive, taking account of the specific features of the various sectors.

2. Member States shall make provision for trade associations and other bodies representing other categories of controllers which have drawn up draft national codes or which have the intention of amending or extending existing national codes to be able to submit them to the opinion of the national authority. Member States shall make provision for this authority to ascertain, among other things, whether the drafts submitted to it are in accordance with the national provisions adopted pursuant to this Directive. If it sees fit, the authority shall seek the views of data subjects or their representatives.

3. Draft Community codes, and amendments or extensions to existing Community codes, may be submitted to the Working Party referred to in Article 29. This Working Party shall determine, among other things, whether the drafts submitted to it are in accordance with the national provisions adopted pursuant to this Directive. If it sees fit, the authority shall seek the views of data subjects or their representatives. The Commission may ensure appropriate publicity for the codes which have been approved by the Working Party.

CHAPTER VI SUPERVISORY AUTHORITY AND WORKING PARTY ON THE PROTECTION OF INDIVIDUALS WITH REGARD TO THE PROCESSING OF PERSONAL DATA

Article 28 Supervisory authority

1. Each Member State shall provide that one or more public authorities are responsible for monitoring the application within its territory of the provisions adopted by the Member States pursuant to this Directive. These authorities shall act with complete independence in exercising the functions entrusted to them.

2. Each Member State shall provide that the supervisory authorities are consulted when drawing up administrative measures or regulations relating to the protection of individuals' rights and freedoms with regard to the processing of personal data.

3. Each authority shall in particular be endowed with:

- investigative powers, such as powers of access to data forming the subject-matter of processing operations and powers to collect all the information necessary for the performance of its supervisory duties;

- effective powers of intervention, such as, for example, that of delivering opinions in accordance with Article 20, before processing operations are carried out and ensuring appropriate publication of such opinions, or that of ordering the blocking, erasure or destruction of data, or of imposing a temporary or definitive ban on processing, or that of warning or admonishing the controller or that of referring the matter to national parliaments or other political institutions;

- the power to engage in legal proceedings where the national provisions adopted pursuant to this Directive have been violated or to bring these violations to the attention of the judicial authorities. Decisions by the supervisory authority which give rise to complaints may be appealed against through the courts.

4. Each supervisory authority shall hear claims lodged by any person, or by an association representing that person, concerning the protection of his rights and freedoms in regard to the processing of personal data. The person concerned shall be informed of the outcome of the claim. Each supervisory authority shall, in particular, hear claims for checks on the lawfulness of data processing lodged by any person when the national provisions adopted pursuant to Article 13 of this Directive apply. The person shall at any rate be informed that a check has taken place.

5. Each supervisory authority shall draw up a report on its activities at regular intervals. The report shall be made public.

6. Each supervisory authority is competent, whatever the national law applicable to the processing in question, for exercising, on the territory of its own Member State, the powers attributed to it in accordance with paragraph 3. Each authority may be requested to exercise its powers by an authority of another Member State. The supervisory authorities shall cooperate with one another to the extent necessary for the performance of their duties, in particular by exchanging all useful information.

7. Member States shall provide that the members and staff of the supervisory authority, even after their employment has ended, are to be subject to a duty of professional secrecy with regard to confidential information to which they have access.

Article 29 Working Party on the Protection of Individuals with regard to the Processing of Personal Data

1. A Working Party on the Protection of Individuals with regard to the Processing of Personal Data, hereinafter referred to as "the Working Party", is hereby set up. It shall have advisory status and act independently.

2. The Working Party shall be composed of a representative of the supervisory authority or authorities designated by each Member State and of a representative of the authority or authorities established for Community institutions and bodies, and of a representative of the Commission. Each member of the Working Party shall be designated by the institution, authority or authorities which he represents. Where a Member State designates more than one supervisory authority, they shall nominate a joint representative. The same shall apply for the authorities established for Community institutions and bodies.

3. The Working Party shall take decisions by a simple majority of the representatives of the supervisory authorities.

4. The Working Party shall elect its chairman. The chairman's term of office shall be two years. His appointment shall be renewable.

5. The Working Party's secretariat shall be provided by the Commission.

6. The Working Party shall adopt its own rules of procedure.

7. The Working Party shall consider items placed on its agenda by its chairman, either on his own initiative or at the request of a representative of the supervisory authorities or at the Commission's request.

Article 30

1. The Working Party shall:

(a) examine any question covering the application of the national measures adopted under this Directive in order to contribute to the uniform application of such measures;

(b) give the Commission an opinion on the level of protection in the Community and in third countries;

(c) advise the Commission on any proposed amendment of this Directive, on any additional or specific measures to safeguard the rights and freedoms of natural persons with regard to the processing of personal data and on any other proposed Community measures affecting such rights and freedoms;

(d) give an opinion on codes of conduct drawn up at Community level.

2. If the Working Party finds that divergences likely to affect the equivalence of protection for persons with regard to the processing of personal data in the Community are arising between the laws or practices of Member States, it shall inform the Commission accordingly.

3. The Working Party may, on its own initiative, make recommendations on all matters relating to the protection of persons with regard to the processing of personal data in the Community.

4. The Working Party's opinions and recommendations shall be forwarded to the Commission and to the committee referred to in Article 31.

5. The Commission shall inform the Working Party of the action it has taken in response to its opinions and recommendations. It shall do so in a report which shall

also be forwarded to the European Parliament and the Council. The report shall be made public.

6. The Working Party shall draw up an annual report on the situation regarding the protection of natural persons with regard to the processing of personal data in the Community and in third countries, which it shall transmit to the Commission, the European Parliament and the Council. The report shall be made public.

CHAPTER VII COMMUNITY IMPLEMENTING MEASURES

Article 31 The Committee

1. The Commission shall be assisted by a committee composed of the representatives of the Member States and chaired by the representative of the Commission.

2. The representative of the Commission shall submit to the committee a draft of the measures to be taken. The committee shall deliver its opinion on the draft within a time limit which the chairman may lay down according to the urgency of the matter. The opinion shall be delivered by the majority laid down in Article 148(2) of the Treaty. The votes of the representatives of the Member States within the committee shall be weighted in the manner set out in that Article. The chairman shall not vote. The Commission shall adopt measures which shall apply immediately. However, if these measures are not in accordance with the opinion of the committee, they shall be communicated by the Commission to the Council forthwith. In that event: The Commission shall defer application of the measures which it has decided for a period to be laid down in each act adopted by the Council, but which may in on case exceed three months from the date of communication. The Council, acting by a qualified majority, may take a different decision within the time limit referred to in the previous paragraph.

FINAL PROVISIONS

Article 32

1. Member States shall bring into force the laws, regulations and administrative provisions necessary to comply with this Directive at the latest at the end of a period of three years from the adoption of the Directive. When Member States adopt these measures, they shall contain a reference to this Directive or be accompanied by such reference on the occasion of their official publication. The methods of making such reference shall be laid down by the Member States.

2. Member States shall ensure that processing already underway on the date the national provisions adopted pursuant to this Directive enter into force, is brought into conformity with these provisions within 3 years of this date. By way of derogation from the preceding subparagraph, Member States may provide that the processing of data already held in manual filing systems on the date of entry into force of the national provisions adopted in implementation of this Directive shall be brought into

conformity with Articles 6,7 and 8 within 12 years of the date on which this Directive is adopted. Member States shall, however, grant the data subject the right to obtain, at his request and in particular at the time of exercising his right of access, the rectification, erasure or blocking of data which are incomplete, inaccurate or stored in a way incompatible with the legitimate purposes pursued by the controller.

3. By way of derogation from paragraph 2, Member States may provide, subject to suitable safeguards, that data kept for the sole purpose of historical research are not brought into conformity with Articles 6,7 and 8 of this Directive.

4. Member States shall communicate to the Commission the provisions of national law which they adopt in the field covered by this Directive.

Article 33

The Commission shall report to the Council and the European Parliament at regular intervals, starting not later than three years after the date referred to in Article 32(1), on the implementation of this Directive, attaching to its report, if necessary, suitable proposals for amendments. The report shall be made public.

The Commission shall examine, in particular, the application of this Directive to the data processing of sound and image data relating to natural persons and shall submit any appropriate proposals which prove to be necessary, taking account of developments in information technology and in the light of the state of progress in the information society.

Article 34

This Directive is addressed to the Member States

EUROPEAN UNION DIRECTIVE FOR THE PROTECTION OF PRIVACY IN THE TELECOMMUNICATIONS SECTOR (1997)

Summary

In December 1997, the EU adopted the Directive of the European Parliament and of the Council concerning the processing of personal data and protection of privacy in the telecommunications sector (Directive 97/66/EC)." The Directive obliges the Member States to lay down implementing regulations by October of 1998. The Telecommunications Directive establishes specific protections covering telephone, digital television, mobile networks and other telecommunications systems.

The Directive restricts the use to which personal information gathered on subscribers to telecommications systems can be put. The Directive also mandates that such information can only be stored to the extent necessary for billing. The Telecommunications Directive (97/66/EC) imposes wide-ranging obligations on carries and service providers to ensure the privacy of users' communications, including Internet-related activities. Access to billing data is severely restricted, as is telemarketing activity.

Several principles of data protection are strengthened under the Directive: the right to know where the data originated, the right to have inaccurate data rectified, a right of recourse in the event of unlawful processing and the right to withhold permission to use data in some circumstances. The provider of a generally available telecommunication service must take technical and organizational measures to safeguard security of its services. Security measures should be appropriate to the risk presented, keeping in mind the state of the art and economic feasibility. If there is any particular risk of a breach of security, service providers must inform their subscribers of the risk and what remedies may be taken, including the cost involved.

The directive mandates that Member States pass national regulations to ensure the confidentiality of communication over public telecommunication networks and publicly available telecommunication services. They are also directed to prohibit bugging, tapping, storage or other kinds of interception or surveillance of communications, by anyone other than a user, and without the consent of a user, except when legally authorized.

References

EUR-LEX: Community legislation in force *Document 395L0046*

http://europa.eu.int/eur-lex/en/lif/dat/1995/en_395L0046.html

DIRECTIVE 97/66/EC OF THE EUROPEAN PARLIAMENT AND OF THE COUNCIL of 15 December 1997

International
European Union Telecommunications Privacy Directive

THE EUROPEAN PARLIAMENT AND THE COUNCIL OF THE EUROPEAN UNION,

Having regard to the Treaty establishing the European Community, and in particular Article 100a thereof,

Having regard to the proposal from the Commission (1),

Having regard to the opinion of the Economic and Social Committee (2),

Acting in accordance with the procedure laid down in Article 189b of the Treaty (3), in the light of the joint text approved by the Conciliation Committee on 6 November 1997,

(1) Whereas Directive 95/46/EC of the European Parliament and of the Council of 24 October 1995 on the protection of individuals with regard to the processing of personal data and on the free movement of such data (4) requires Member States to ensure the rights and freedoms of natural persons with regard to the processing of personal data, and in particular their right to privacy, in order to ensure the free flow of personal data in the Community;

(2) Whereas confidentiality of communications is guaranteed in accordance with the international instruments relating to human rights (in particular the European Convention for the Protection of Human Rights and Fundamental Freedoms) and the constitutions of the Member States;

(3) Whereas currently in the Community new advanced digital technologies are introduced in public telecommunications networks, which give rise to specific requirements concerning the protection of personal data and privacy of the user; whereas the development of the information society is characterised by the introduction of new telecommunications services; whereas the successful cross-border development of these services, such as video-on-demand, interactive television, is partly dependent on the confidence of the users that their privacy will not be at risk;

(4) Whereas this is the case, in particular, with the introduction of the Integrated Services Digital Network (ISDN) and digital mobile networks;

(5) Whereas the Council, in its Resolution of 30 June 1988 on the development of the common market for telecommunications services and equipment up to 1992 (5), called for steps to be taken to protect personal data, in order to create an appropriate environment for the future development of telecommunications in the Community; whereas the Council re-emphasised the importance of the protection of personal data and privacy in its Resolution of 18 July 1989 on the strengthening of the coordination for the introduction of the Integrated Services Digital Network (ISDN) in the European Community up to 1992 (6);

(6) Whereas the European Parliament has underlined the importance of the protection of personal data and privacy in the telecommunications networks, in particular with regard to the introduction of the Integrated Services Digital Network (ISDN);

(7) Whereas, in the case of public telecommunications networks, specific legal, regulatory, and technical provisions must be made in order to protect fundamental rights and freedoms of natural persons and legitimate interests of legal persons, in particular with regard to the increasing risk connected with automated storage and processing of data relating to subscribers and users;

(8) Whereas legal, regulatory, and technical provisions adopted by the Member States concerning the protection of personal data, privacy and the legitimate interest of legal persons, in the telecommunications sector, must be harmonised in order to avoid obstacles to the internal market for telecommunications in conformity with the objective set out in Article 7a of the Treaty; whereas the harmonisation is limited to requirements that are necessary to guarantee that the promotion and development of new telecommunications services and networks between Member States will not be hindered;

(9) Whereas the Member States, providers and users concerned, together with the competent Community bodies, should cooperate in introducing and developing the relevant technologies where this is necessary to apply the guarantees provided for by the provisions of this Directive.

(10) Whereas these new services include interactive television and video on demand;

(11) Whereas, in the telecommunications sector, in particular for all matters concerning protection of fundamental rights and freedoms, which are not specifically covered by the provisions of this Directive, including the obligations on the controller and the rights of individuals, Directive 95/46/EC applies; whereas Directive 95/46/EC applies to non-publicly available telecommunications services;

(12) Whereas this Directive, similarly to what is provided for by Article 3 of Directive 95/46/EC, does not address issues of protection of fundamental rights and freedoms related to activities which are not governed by Community law; whereas it is for Member States to take such measures as they consider necessary for the protection of public security, defence, State security (including the economic well-being of the State when the activities relate to State security matters) and the enforcement of criminal law; whereas this Directive shall not affect the ability of Member States to carry out lawful interception of telecommunications, for any of these purposes;

(13) Whereas subscribers of a publicly available telecommunications service may be natural or legal persons; whereas the provisions of this Directive are aimed to protect, by supplementing Directive 95/46/EC, the fundamental rights of natural persons and particularly their right to privacy, as well as the legitimate interests of legal persons; whereas these provisions may in no case entail an obligation for Member States to extend the application of Directive 95/46/EC to the protection of the legitimate interests of legal persons; whereas this protection is ensured within the framework of the applicable Community and national legislation;

(14) Whereas the application of certain requirements relating to presentation and restriction of calling and connected line identification and to automatic call forwarding to subscriber lines connected to analogue exchanges must not be made mandatory in specific cases where such application would prove to be technically impossible or would require a disproportionate economic effort; whereas it is important for interested parties to be informed of such cases and the Member States should therefore notify them to the Commission;

(15) Whereas service providers must take appropriate measures to safeguard the security of their services, if necessary in conjunction with the provider of the network, and inform

subscribers of any special risks of a breach of the security of the network; whereas security is appraised in the light of the provision of Article 17 of Directive 95/46/EC;

(16) Whereas measures must be taken to prevent the unauthorised access to communications in order to protect the confidentiality of communications by means of public telecommunications networks and publicly available telecommunications services; whereas national legislation in some Member States only prohibits intentional unauthorized access to communications;

(17) Whereas the data relating to subscribers processed to establish calls contain information on the private life of natural persons and concern the right to respect for their correspondence or concern the legitimate interests of legal persons; whereas such data may only be stored to the extent that is necessary for the provision of the service for the purpose of billing and for interconnection payments, and for a limited time; whereas any further processing which the provider of the publicly available telecommunications services may want to perform for the marketing of its own telecommunications services may only be allowed if the subscriber has agreed to this on the basis of accurate and full information given by the provider of the publicly available telecommunications services about the types of further processing he intends to perform;

(18) Whereas the introduction of itemized bills has improved the possibilities for the subscriber to verify the correctness of the fees charged by the service provider; whereas, at the same time, it may jeopardise the privacy of the users of publicly available telecommunications services; whereas therefore, in order to preserve the privacy of the user, Member States must encourage the development of telecommunications service options such as alternative payment facilities which allow anonymous or strictly private access to publicly available telecommunications services, for example calling cards and facilities for payment by credit card; whereas, alternatively, Member States may, for the same purpose, require the deletion of a certain number of digits from the called numbers mentioned in itemized bills;

(19) Whereas it is necessary, as regards calling line identification, to protect the right of the calling party to withhold the presentation of the identification of the line from which the call is being made and the right of the called party to reject calls from unidentified lines; whereas it is justified to override the elimination of calling line identification presentation in specific cases; whereas certain subscribers, in particular helplines and similar organizations, have an interest in guaranteeing the anonymity of their callers; whereas it is necessary, as regards connected line identification, to protect the right and the legitimate interest of the called party to withhold the presentation of the identification of the line to which the calling party is actually connected, in particular in the case of forwarded calls; whereas the providers of publicly available telecommunications services must inform their subscribers of the existence of calling and connected line identification in the network and of all services which are offered on the basis of calling and connected line identification and about the privacy options which are available; whereas this will allow the subscribers to make an informed choice about the privacy facilities they may want to use; whereas the privacy options which are offered on a per-line basis do not necessarily have to be available as an automatic network service but may

be obtainable through a simple request to the provider of the publicly available telecommunications service;

(20) Whereas safeguards must be provided for subscribers against the nuisance which may be caused by automatic call forwarding by others; whereas, in such cases, it must be possible for subscribers to stop the forwarded calls being passed on to their terminals by simple request to the provider of the publicly available telecommunications service;

(21) Whereas directories are widely distributed and publicly available; whereas the right to privacy of natural persons and the legitimate interest of legal persons require that subscribers are able to determine the extent to which their personal data are published in a directory; whereas Member States may limit this possibility to subscribers who are natural persons;

(22) Whereas safeguards must be provided for subscribers against intrusion into their privacy by means of unsolicited calls and telefaxes; whereas Member States may limit such safeguards to subscribers who are natural persons;

(23) Whereas it is necessary to ensure that the introduction of technical features of telecommunications equipment for data protection purposes is harmonised in order to be compatible with the implementation of the internal market;

(24) Whereas in particular, similarly to what is provided for by Article 13 of Directive 95/46/EC, Member States can restrict the scope of subscribers' obligations and rights in certain circumstances, for example by ensuring that the provider of a publicly available telecommunications service may override the elimination of the presentation of calling line identification in conformity with national legislation for the purpose of prevention or detection of criminal offences or State security;

(25) Whereas where the rights of the users and subscribers are not respected, national legislation must provide for judicial remedy; whereas sanctions must be imposed on any person, whether governed by private or public law, who fails to comply with the national measures taken under this Directive;

(26) Whereas it is useful in the field of application of this Directive to draw on the experience of the Working Party on the protection of individuals with regard to the processing of personal data composed of representatives of the supervisory authorities of the Member States, set up by Article 29 of Directive 95/46/EC;

(27) Whereas, given the technological developments and the attendant evolution of the services on offer, it will be necessary technically to specify the categories of data listed in the Annex to this Directive for the application of Article 6 of this Directive with the assistance of the Committee composed of representatives of the Member States set up in Article 31 of Directive 95/46/EC in order to ensure a coherent application of the requirements set out in this Directive regardless of changes in technology; whereas this procedure applies solely to specifications necessary to adapt the Annex to new technological developments, taking into consideration changes in market and consumer demand; whereas the Commission must duly inform the European Parliament of its intention to apply this procedure and whereas, otherwise, the procedure laid down in Article 100a of the Treaty shall apply;

International
European Union Telecommunications Privacy Directive

(28) Whereas, to facilitate compliance with the provisions of this Directive, certain specific arrangements are needed for processing of data already under way on the date that national implementing legislation pursuant to this Directive enters into force,

HAVE ADOPTED THIS DIRECTIVE:

Article 1 - Object and scope

1. This Directive provides for the harmonisation of the provisions of the Member States required to ensure an equivalent level of protection of fundamental rights and freedoms, and in particular the right to privacy, with respect to the processing of personal data in the telecommunications sector and to ensure the free movement of such data and of telecommunications equipment and services in the Community.

2. The provisions of this Directive particularise and complement Directive 95/46/EC for the purposes mentioned in paragraph 1. Moreover, they provide for protection of legitimate interests of subscribers who are legal persons.

3. This Directive shall not apply to the activities which fall outside the scope of Community law, such as those provided for by Titles V and VI of the Treaty on European Union, and in any case to activities concerning public security, defence, State security (including the economic well-being of the State when the activities relate to State security matters) and the activities of the State in areas of criminal law.

Article 2 - Definitions

In addition to the definitions given in Directive 95/46/EC, for the purposes of this Directive:

(a) 'subscriber` shall mean any natural or legal person who or which is party to a contract with the provider of publicly available telecommunications services for the supply of such services;

(b) 'user` shall mean any natural person using a publicly available telecommunications service, for private or business purposes, without necessarily having subscribed to this service;

(c) 'public telecommunications network` shall mean transmission systems and, where applicable, switching equipment and other resources which permit the conveyance of signals between defined termination points by wire, by radio, by optical or by other electromagnetic means, which are used, in whole or in part, for the provision of publicly available telecommunications services;

(d) 'telecommunications service` shall mean services whose provision consists wholly or partly in the transmission and routing of signals on telecommunications networks, with the exception of radio- and television broadcasting.

Article 3 - Services concerned

1. This Directive shall apply to the processing of personal data in connection with the provison of publicly available telecommunications services in public

telecommunications networks in the Community, in particular via the Integrated Services Digital Network (ISDN) and public digital mobile networks.

2. Articles 8, 9 and 10 shall apply to subscriber lines connected to digital exchanges and, where technically possible and if it does not require a disproportionate economic effort, to subscriber lines connected to analogue exchanges.

3. Cases where it would be technically impossible or require a disproportionate investment to fulfil the requirements of Articles 8, 9 and 10 shall be notified to the Commission by the Member States.

Article 4 - Security

1. The provider of a publicly available telecommunications service must take appropriate technical and organisational measures to safeguard security of its services, if necessary in conjunction with the provider of the public telecommunications network with respect to network security. Having regard to the state of the art and the cost of their implementation, these measures shall ensure a level of security appropriate to the risk presented.

2. In case of a particular risk of a breach of the security of the network, the provider of a publicly available telecommunications service must inform the subscribers concerning such risk and any possible remedies, including the costs involved.

Article 5 - Confidentiality of the communications

1. Member States shall ensure via national regulations the confidentiality of communications by means of a public telecommunications network and publicly available telecommunications services. In particular, they shall prohibit listening, tapping, storage or other kinds of interception or surveillance of communications, by others than users, without the consent of the users concerned, except when legally authorised, in accordance with Article 14 (1).

2. Paragraph 1 shall not affect any legally authorised recording of communications in the course of lawful business practice for the purpose of providing evidence of a commercial transaction or of any other business communication.

Article 6 - Traffic and billing data

1. Traffic data relating to subscribers and users processed to establish calls and stored by the provider of a public telecommunications network and/or publicly available telecommunications service must be erased or made anonymous upon termination of the call without prejudice to the provisions of paragraphs 2, 3 and 4.

2. For the purpose of subscriber billing and interconnection payments, data indicated in the Annex may be processed. Such processing is permissible only up to the end of the period during which the bill may lawfully be challenged or payment may be pursued.

International
European Union Telecommunications Privacy Directive

3. For the purpose of marketing its own telecommunications services, the provider of a publicly available telecommunications service may process the data referred to in paragraph 2, if the subscriber has given his consent.

4. Processing of traffic and billing data must be restricted to persons acting under the authority of providers of the public telecommunications networks and/or publicly available telecommunications services handling billing or traffic management, customer enquiries, fraud detection and marketing the provider's own telecommunications services and it must be restricted to what is necessary for the purposes of such activities.

5. Paragraphs 1, 2, 3 and 4 shall apply without prejudice to the possibility for competent authorities to be informed of billing or traffic data in conformity with applicable legislation in view of settling disputes, in particular interconnection or billing disputes.

Article 7 - Itemized billing

1. Subscribers shall have the right to receive non-itemized bills.

2. Member States shall apply national provisions in order to reconcile the rights of subscribers receiving itemised bills with the right to privacy of calling users and called subscribers, for example by ensuring that sufficient alternative modalities for communications or payments are available to such users and subscribers.

Article 8 - Presentation and restriction of calling and connected line identification

1. Where presentation of calling-line identification is offered, the calling user must have the possibility via a simple means, free of charge, to eliminate the presentation of the calling-line identification on a per-call basis. The calling subscriber must have this possibility on a per-line basis.

2. Where presentation of calling-line identification is offered, the called subscriber must have the possibility via a simple means, free of charge for reasonable use of this function, to prevent the presentation of the calling line identification of incoming calls.

3. Where presentation of calling line identification is offered and where the calling line identification is presented prior to the call being established, the called subscriber must have the possibility via a simple means to reject incoming calls where the presentation of the calling line identification has been eliminated by the calling user or subscriber.

4. Where presentation of connected line identification is offered, the called subscriber must have the possibility via a simple means, free of charge, to eliminate the presentation of the connected line identification to the calling user.

5. The provisions set out in paragraph 1 shall also apply with regard to calls to third countries originating in the Community; the provisions set out in paragraphs 2, 3 and 4 shall also apply to incoming calls originating in third countries.

6. Member States shall ensure that where presentation of calling and/or connected line identification is offered, the providers of publicly available telecommunications services inform the public thereof and of the possibilities set out in paragraphs 1, 2, 3 and 4.

Article 9 - Exceptions

Member States shall ensure that there are transparent procedures governing the way in which a provider of a public telecommunications network and/or a publicly available telecommunications service may override the elimination of the presentation of calling line identification:

> (a) on a temporary basis, upon application of a subscriber requesting the tracing of malicious or nuisance calls; in this case, in accordance with national law, the data containing the identification of the calling subscriber will be stored and be made available by the provider of a public telecommunications network and/or publicly available telecommunications service;

> (b) on a per-line basis for organisations dealing with emergency calls and recognized as such by a Member State, including law enforcement agencies, ambulance services and fire brigades, for the purpose of answering such calls.

Article 10 - Automatic call forwarding

Member States shall ensure that any subscriber is provided, free of charge and via a simple means, with the possibility to stop automatic call forwarding by a third party to the subscriber's terminal.

Article 11 - Directories of subscribers

> 1. Personal data contained in printed or electronic directories of subscribers available to the public or obtainable through directory enquiry services should be limited to what is necessary to identify a particular subscriber, unless the subscriber has given his unambiguous consent to the publication of additional personal data. The subscriber shall be entitled, free of charge, to be omitted from a printed or electronic directory at his or her request, to indicate that his or her personal data may not be used for the purpose of direct marketing, to have his or her address omitted in part and not to have a reference revealing his or her sex, where this is applicable linguistically.

> 2. Notwithstanding paragraph 1, Member States may allow operators to require a payment from subscribers wishing to ensure that their particulars are not entered in a directory, provided that the sum involved does not act as a disincentive to the exercise of this right, and that, taking account of the quality requirements of the public directory in the light of the universal service, it is limited to the actual costs incurred by the operator for the adaptation and updating of the list of subscribers not to be included in the public directory.

> 3. The rights conferred by paragraph 1 shall apply to subscribers who are natural persons. Member States shall also guarantee, in the framework of Community law and

applicable national legislation, that the legitimate interests of subscribers other than natural persons with regard to their entry in public directories are sufficiently protected.

Article 12 - Unsolicited calls

1. The use of automated calling systems without human intervention (automatic calling machine) or facsimile machines (fax) for the purposes of direct marketing may only be allowed in respect of subscribers who have given their prior consent.

2. Member States shall take appropriate measures to ensure that, free of charge, unsolicited calls for purposes of direct marketing, by means other than those referred to in paragraph 1, are not allowed either without the consent of the subscribers concerned or in respect of subscribers who do not wish to receive these calls, the choice between these options to be determined by national legislation.

3. The rights conferred by paragraphs 1 and 2 shall apply to subscribers who are natural persons. Member States shall also guarantee, in the framework of Community law and applicable national legislation, that the legitimate interests of subscribers other than natural persons with regard to unsolicited calls are sufficiently protected.

Article 13 - Technical features and standardisation

1. In implementing the provisions of this Directive, Member States shall ensure, subject to paragraphs 2 and 3, that no mandatory requirements for specific technical features are imposed on terminal or other telecommunications equipment which could impede the placing of equipment on the market and the free circulation of such equipment in and between Member States.

2. Where provisions of this Directive can be implemented only by requiring specific technical features, Member States shall inform the Commission according to the procedures provided for by Directive 83/189/EEC (7) which lays down a procedure for the provision of information in the field of technical standards and regulations.

3. Where required, the Commission will ensure the drawing up of common European standards for the implementation of specific technical features, in accordance with Community legislation on the approximation of the laws of the Member States concerning telecommunications terminal equipment, including the mutual recognition of their conformity, and Council Decision 87/95/EEC of 22 December 1986 on standardisation in the field of information technology and telecommunications (8).

Article 14 - Extension of the scope of application of certain provisions of Directive 95/46/EC

1. Member States may adopt legislative measures to restrict the scope of the obligations and rights provided for in Articles 5, 6 and Article 8(1), (2), (3) and (4), when such restriction constitutes a necessary measure to safeguard national security, defence, public security, the prevention, investigation, detection and prosecution of

criminal offences or of unauthorised use of the telecommunications system, as referred to in Article 13(1) of Directive 95/46/EC.

2. The provisions of Chapter III on judicial remedies, liability and sanctions of Directive 95/46/EC shall apply with regard to national provisions adopted pursuant to this Directive and with regard to the individual rights derived from this Directive.

3. The Working Party on the Protection of Individuals with regard to the Processing of Personal Data established according to Article 29 of Directive 95/46/EC shall carry out the tasks laid down in Article 30 of the abovementioned Directive also with regard to the protection of fundamental rights and freedoms and of legitimate interests in the telecommunications sector, which is the subject of this Directive.

4. The Commission, assisted by the Committee established by Article 31 of Directive 95/46/EC, shall technically specify the Annex according to the procedure mentioned in this Article. The aforesaid Committee shall be convened specifically for the subjects covered by this Directive.

Article 15 - Implementation of the Directive

1. Member States shall bring into force the laws, regulations and administrative provisions necessary for them to comply with this Directive not later than 24 October 1998. By way of derogation from the first subparagraph, Member States shall bring into force the laws, regulations and administrative provisions necessary for them to comply with Article 5 of this Directive not later than 24 October 2000. When Member States adopt these measures, they shall contain a reference to this Directive or shall be accompanied by such a reference at the time of their official publication. The procedure for such reference shall be adopted by Member States.

2. By way of derogation from Article 6(3), consent is not required with respect to processing already under way on the date the national provisions adopted pursuant to this Directive enter into force. In those cases the subscribers shall be informed of this processing and if they do not express their dissent within a period to be determined by the Member State, they shall be deemed to have given their consent.

3. Article 11 shall not apply to editions of directories which have been published before the national provisions adopted pursuant to this Directive enter into force.

4. Member States shall communicate to the Commission the text of the provisions of national law which they adopt in the field governed by this Directive.

Article 16 - Addressees

This Directive is addressed to the Member States.

Done at Brussels, 15 December 1997.
For the European Parliament
The President

International
European Union Telecommunications Privacy Directive

J. M. GIL-ROBLES
For the Council
The President
J.-C. JUNCKER

(1) OJ C 200, 22.7.1994, p. 4.
(2) OJ C 159, 17.6.1991, p. 38.
(3) Opinion of the European Parliament of 11 March 1992 (OJ C 94, 13.4.1992, p. 198). Council Common Position of 12 September 1996 (OJ C 315,
24.10.1996, p. 30) and Decision of the European Parliament of 16 January 1997 (OJ C 33, 3.2.1997, p. 78). Decision of the European Parliament of
20 November 1997 (OJ C 371, 8.12.1997). Council Decision of 1 December 1997.
(4) OJ L 281, 23.11.1995, p. 31.
(5) OJ C 257, 4.10.1988, p. 1.
(6) OJ C 196, 1.8.1989, p. 4.
(7) OJ L 109, 26.4.1983, p. 8. Directive as last amended by Directive 94/10/EC (OJ L 100, 19.4.1994, p. 30).
(8) OJ L 36, 7.2.1987, p. 31. Decision as last amended by the 1994 Act of Accession.

ANNEX - List of data

For the purpose referred to in Article 6(2) the following data may be processed:
Data containing the:

> number or identification of the subscriber station,
> address of the subscriber and the type of station,
> total number of units to be charged for the accounting period,
> called subscriber number,
> type, starting time and duration of the calls made and/or the data volume transmitted,
> date of the call/service,
> other information concerning payments such as advance payment, payments by instalments, disconnection and reminders.

OECD CRYPTOGRAPHY GUIDELINES
(1997)

Summary

The unprecedented growth of communication networks and associated technologies for privacy and security created a need for an international policy framework to harmonize national policies and promote techniques to safeguard communication networks . In 1997 the OECD, an international body of 29 countries, adopted the Guidelines for Cryptography Policy. The Guidelines are a non-binding agreement identifying the policy goals that countries should implement when drawing up cryptography policies at the national and international levels.

The Guidelines set out eight principles for cryptography policy: (i) Cryptographic methods should be trustworthy in order to generate confidence in the use of information and communications systems; (ii) Users should have a right to choose any cryptographic method, subject to applicable law; (iii) Cryptographic methods should be developed in response to the needs, demands and responsibilities of individuals, businesses and governments; (iv) Technical standards, criteria and protocols for cryptographic methods should be developed and promulgated at the national and international level; (v) The fundamental rights of individuals to privacy, including secrecy of communications and protection of personal data, should be respected in national cryptography policies and in the implementation and use of cryptographic methods; (vi) National cryptography policies may allow lawful access to plain-text, or cryptographic keys, of encrypted data. These policies must respect the other principles contained in the guidelines to the greatest extent possible; (vii) Whether established by contract or legislation, the liability of individuals and entities that offer cryptographic services or hold or access cryptographic keys should be clearly stated; (viii) Governments should co-operate to co-ordinate cryptography policies. As part of this effort, governments should remove, or avoid creating in the name of cryptography policy, unjustified obstacles to trade.

During deliberations a proposal for the adoption of key escrow techniques that would enable routine law enforcement access to computer communications was put forward. The OECD member countries firmly rejected the recommendation. Reasons given disfavoring the proposal were that key escrow would undermine trust and could not be included in a nation-wide card system. In the end, member states adopted the OECD Guidelines as a coordinated effort to facilitate the smooth development of an efficient secure information infrastructure and to address issues of privacy, law enforcement, national security, technology development and commerce.

International
OECD Cryptography Guidelines

References

OECD, *Cryptography Policy: The Guidelines and the Issues* (1999)
[http://www.oecd.org/dsti/sti/it/secur/prod/e-crypto.htm]
OECD, *Report on Background and Issues of Cryptography Policy* (1997)
[http://www.oecd.org/dsti/sti/it/secur/prod/crypto3.htm]
EPIC, *Cryptography & Liberty 2000: An International Survey of Encryption Policy,* (EPIC 2000)
[http://www2.epic.org/reports/crypto2000/]

RECOMMENDATION OF THE COUNCIL CONCERNING GUIDELINES FOR CRYPTOGRAPHY POLICY

27 March 1997

THE COUNCIL, HAVING REGARD TO:

* the Convention on the Organisation for Economic Co-operation and Development of 14 December 1960, in particular, articles 1 b), 1 c), 3 a) and 5 b) thereof;

* the Recommendation of the Council concerning Guidelines Governing the Protection of Privacy and Transborder Flows of Personal Data of 23 September 1980 [C(80)58(Final)];

* the Declaration on Transborder Data Flows adopted by the Governments of OECD Member countries on 11 April 1985 [Annex to C(85)139];

* the Recommendation of the Council concerning Guidelines for the Security of Information Systems of 26-27 November 1992 [C(92)188/FINAL];

* the Directive [95/46/EC] of the European Parliament and of the Council of the European Union of 24 October 1995 on the protection of individuals with regard to the processing of personal data and on the free movement of such data;

* the Wassenaar Arrangement on Export Controls for Conventional Arms and Dual-use Goods and Technologies agreed on 13 July 1996;

* the Regulation [(EC) 3381/94] and the Decision [94/942/PESC] of the Council of the European Union of 19 December 1994 concerning the control of the export of dual-use goods;

* and the Recommendation [R(95)13] of the Council of Europe of 11 September 1995 concerning problems of criminal procedural law connected with information technology;

CONSIDERING:

* that national and global information infrastructures are developing rapidly to provide a seamless network for world-wide communications and access to data;

* that this emerging information and communications network is likely to have an important impact on economic development and world trade;

* that the users of information technology must have trust in the security of information and communications infrastructures, networks and systems; in the confidentiality, integrity, and availability of data on them; and in the ability to prove the origin and receipt of data;

* that data is increasingly vulnerable to sophisticated threats to its security, and ensuring the security of data through legal, procedural and technical means is fundamentally important in order for national and international information infrastructures to reach their full potential;

RECOGNISING:

* that, as cryptography can be an effective tool for the secure use of information technology by ensuring confidentiality, integrity and availability of data and by providing authentication and

non-repudiation mechanisms for that data, it is an important component of secure information and communications networks and systems;

* that cryptography has a variety of applications related to the protection of privacy, intellectual property, business and financial information, public safety and national security, and the operation of electronic commerce, including secure anonymous payments and transactions;

* that the failure to utilise cryptographic methods can adversely affect the protection of privacy, intellectual property, business and financial information, public safety and national security and the

operation of electronic commerce because data and communications may be inadequately protected from unauthorised access, alteration, and improper use, and, therefore, users may not trust information and communications systems, networks and infrastructures;

* that the use of cryptography to ensure integrity of data, including authentication and non-repudiation mechanisms, is distinct from its use to ensure confidentiality of data, and that each of these uses presents different issues;

- that the quality of information protection afforded by cryptography depends not only on the selected technical means, but also on good managerial, organisational and operational procedures;

-

AND FURTHER RECOGNISING:

* that governments have wide-ranging responsibilities, several of which are specifically implicated in the use of cryptography, including protection of privacy and facilitating information and communications systems security; encouraging economic well-being by, in part, promoting commerce; maintaining public safety; and enabling the enforcement of laws and the protection of national security;

* that although there are legitimate governmental, commercial and individual needs and uses for cryptography, it may also be used by individuals or entities for illegal activities, which can affect public safety, national security, the enforcement of laws, business interests, consumer interests or privacy; therefore governments, together with industry and the general public, are challenged to develop balanced policies;

* that due to the inherently global nature of information and communications networks, implementation of incompatible national policies will not meet the needs of individuals, business and governments and may create obstacles to economic co-operation and development; and, therefore, national policies may require international co-ordination;

* that this Recommendation of the Council does not affect the sovereign rights of national governments and that the Guidelines contained in the Annex to this Recommendation are always subject to the requirements of national law;

On the proposal of the Committee for Information, Computer and Communications Policy;

RECOMMENDS THAT MEMBER COUNTRIES:

1. establish new, or amend existing, policies, methods, measures, practices and procedures to reflect and take into account the Principles concerning cryptography policy set forth in the Guidelines contained in the Annex to this Recommendation (hereinafter "the Guidelines"), which is an integral part hereof; in so doing, also take into account the Recommendation of the Council concerning Guidelines Governing the Protection of Privacy and Transborder Flows of Personal Data of 23 September 1980 [C(80)58(Final)] and the Recommendation of the Council concerning Guidelines for the Security of Information Systems of 26-27 November 1992 [C(92)188/FINAL];

2. consult, co-ordinate and co-operate at the national and international level in the implementation of the Guidelines;

3. act on the need for practical and operational solutions in the area of international cryptography policy by using the Guidelines as a basis for agreements on specific issues related to international cryptography policy;

4. disseminate the Guidelines throughout the public and private sectors to promote awareness of the issues and policies related to cryptography;

5. remove, or avoid creating in the name of cryptography policy, unjustified obstacles to international trade and the development of information and communications networks;

6. state clearly and make publicly available, any national controls imposed by governments relating to the use of cryptography;

7. review the Guidelines at least every five years, with a view to improving international co-operation on issues relating to cryptography policy.

ANNEX

GUIDELINES FOR CRYPTOGRAPHY POLICY

I. AIMS

The Guidelines are intended:
* to promote the use of cryptography:
    o to foster confidence in information and communication infrastructures, networks and systems and the manner in which they are used;
    o to help ensure the security of data, and to protect privacy, in national and global information and communications infrastructures, networks and systems;
* to promote this use of cryptography without unduly jeopardising public safety, law enforcement, and national security;
* to raise awareness of the need for compatible cryptography policies and laws, as well as the need for interoperable, portable and mobile cryptographic methods in national and global information and communications networks;
* to assist decision-makers in the public and private sectors in developing and implementing coherent national and international policies, methods, measures, practices and procedures for the effective use of cryptography;
* to promote co-operation between the public and private sectors in the development and implementation of national and international cryptography policies, methods, measures, practices and procedures;
* to facilitate international trade by promoting cost-effective, interoperable, portable and mobile cryptographic systems;
* to promote international co-operation among governments, business and research communities, and standards-making bodies in achieving co-ordinated use of cryptographic methods.

II. SCOPE

The Guidelines are primarily aimed at governments, in terms of the policy recommendations herein, but with anticipation that they will be widely read and followed by both the private and public sectors.

It is recognised that governments have separable and distinct responsibilities for the protection of information which requires security in the national interest; the Guidelines are not intended for application in these matters.

III. DEFINITIONS

For the purposes of the Guidelines:

International
OECD Cryptography Guidelines

* "Authentication" means a function for establishing the validity of a claimed identity of a user, device or another entity in an information or communications system.

* "Availability" means the property that data, information, and information and communications systems are accessible and usable on a timely basis in the required manner.

* "Confidentiality" means the property that data or information is not made available or disclosed to unauthorised individuals, entities, or processes.

* "Cryptography" means the discipline which embodies principles, means, and methods for the transformation of data in order to hide its information content, establish its authenticity, prevent its undetected modification, prevent its repudiation, and/or prevent its unauthorised use.

* "Cryptographic key" means a parameter used with a cryptographic algorithm to transform, validate, authenticate, encrypt or decrypt data.

* "Cryptographic methods" means cryptographic techniques, services, systems, products and key management systems.

* "Data" means the representation of information in a manner suitable for communication, interpretation, storage, or processing.

* "Decryption" means the inverse function of encryption.

* "Encryption" means the transformation of data by the use of cryptography to produce unintelligible data (encrypted data) to ensure its confidentiality.

* "Integrity" means the property that data or information has not been modified or altered in an unauthorised manner.

* "Interoperability" of cryptographic methods means the technical ability of multiple cryptographic methods to function together.

* "Key management system" means a system for generation, storage, distribution, revocation, deletion, archiving, certification or application of cryptographic keys.

* "Keyholder" means an individual or entity in possession or control of cryptographic keys. A keyholder is not necessarily a user of the key.

* "Law enforcement" or "enforcement of laws" refers to the enforcement of all laws, without regard to subject matter.

* "Lawful access" means access by third party individuals or entities, including governments, to plaintext, or cryptographic keys, of encrypted data, in accordance with law.

* "Mobility" of cryptographic methods only means the technical ability to function in multiple countries or information and communications infrastructures.

* "Non-repudiation" means a property achieved through cryptographic methods, which prevents an individual or entity from denying having performed a particular action related to data (such as mechanisms for non-rejection of authority (origin); for proof of obligation, intent, or commitment; or for proof of ownership).

* "Personal data" means any information relating to an identified or identifiable individual.

* "Plaintext" means intelligible data.

* "Portability" of cryptographic methods means the technical ability to be adapted and function in multiple systems.

IV. INTEGRATION

The principles in Section V of this Annex, each of which addresses an important policy concern, are interdependent and should be implemented as a whole so as to balance the various interests at stake. No principle should be implemented in isolation from the rest.

V. PRINCIPLES

1. TRUST IN CRYPTOGRAPHIC METHODS

CRYPTOGRAPHIC METHODS SHOULD BE TRUSTWORTHY IN ORDER TO GENERATE CONFIDENCE IN THE USE OF INFORMATION AND COMMUNICATIONS SYSTEMS.

Market forces should serve to build trust in reliable systems, and government regulation, licensing, and use of cryptographic methods may also encourage user trust. Evaluation of cryptographic methods, especially against market-accepted criteria, could also generate user trust.

In the interests of user trust, a contract dealing with the use of a key management system should indicate the jurisdiction whose laws apply to that system.

2. CHOICE OF CRYPTOGRAPHIC METHODS

USERS SHOULD HAVE A RIGHT TO CHOOSE ANY CRYPTOGRAPHIC METHOD, SUBJECT TO APPLICABLE LAW.

Users should have access to cryptography that meets their needs, so that they can trust in the security of information and communications systems, and the confidentiality and integrity of data on those systems. Individuals or entities who own, control, access, use or store data may have a responsibility to protect the confidentiality and integrity of such data, and may therefore be responsible for using appropriate cryptographic methods. It is expected that a variety of cryptographic methods may be needed to fulfil different data security requirements. Users of cryptography should be free, subject to applicable law, to determine the type and level of data security needed, and to select and implement appropriate cryptographic methods, including a key management system that suits their needs.

International
OECD Cryptography Guidelines

In order to protect an identified public interest, such as the protection of personal data or electronic commerce, governments may implement policies requiring cryptographic methods to achieve a sufficient level of protection.

Government controls on cryptographic methods should be no more than are essential to the discharge of government responsibilities and should respect user choice to the greatest extent possible. This principle should not be interpreted as implying that governments should initiate legislation which limits user choice.

3. MARKET DRIVEN DEVELOPMENT OF CRYPTOGRAPHIC METHODS

CRYPTOGRAPHIC METHODS SHOULD BE DEVELOPED IN RESPONSE TO THE NEEDS, DEMANDS AND RESPONSIBILITIES OF INDIVIDUALS, BUSINESSES AND GOVERNMENTS.

The development and provision of cryptographic methods should be determined by the market in an open and competitive environment. Such an approach would best ensure that solutions keep pace with changing technology, the demands of users and evolving threats to information and communications systems security. The development of international technical standards, criteria and protocols related to cryptographic methods should also be market driven. Governments should encourage and co-operate with business and the research community in the development of cryptographic methods.

4. STANDARDS FOR CRYPTOGRAPHIC METHODS

TECHNICAL STANDARDS, CRITERIA AND PROTOCOLS FOR CRYPTOGRAPHIC METHODS SHOULD BE DEVELOPED AND PROMULGATED AT THE NATIONAL AND INTERNATIONAL LEVEL.

In response to the needs of the market, internationally-recognised standards-making bodies, governments, business and other relevant experts should share information and collaborate to develop and promulgate interoperable technical standards, criteria and protocols for cryptographic methods. National standards for cryptographic methods, if any, should be consistent with international standards to facilitate global interoperability, portability and mobility. Mechanisms to evaluate conformity to such technical standards, criteria and protocols for interoperability, portability and mobility of cryptographic methods should be developed. To the extent that testing of conformity to, or evaluation of, standards may occur, the broad acceptance of such results should be encouraged.

5. *PROTECTION OF PRIVACY AND PERSONAL DATA*

THE FUNDAMENTAL RIGHTS OF INDIVIDUALS TO PRIVACY, INCLUDING SECRECY OF COMMUNICATIONS AND PROTECTION OF PERSONAL DATA, SHOULD BE RESPECTED IN NATIONAL CRYPTOGRAPHY POLICIES AND IN THE IMPLEMENTATION AND USE OF CRYPTOGRAPHIC METHODS.

Cryptographic methods can be a valuable tool for the protection of privacy, including both the confidentiality of data and communications and the protection of the identity of individuals. Cryptographic methods also offer new opportunities to minimise the collection of personal data, by enabling secure but anonymous payments, transactions and interactions. At the same time, cryptographic methods to ensure the integrity of data in electronic transactions raise privacy implications. These implications, which include the collection of personal data and the creation of systems for personal identification, should be considered and explained, and, where appropriate, privacy safeguards should be established.

The OECD Guidelines for the Protection of Privacy and Transborder Flows of Personal Data provide general guidance concerning the collection and management of personal information, and should be applied in concert with relevant national law when implementing cryptographic methods.

6. *LAWFUL ACCESS*

NATIONAL CRYPTOGRAPHY POLICIES MAY ALLOW LAWFUL ACCESS TO PLAINTEXT, OR CRYPTOGRAPHIC KEYS, OF ENCRYPTED DATA. THESE POLICIES MUST RESPECT THE OTHER PRINCIPLES CONTAINED IN THE GUIDELINES TO THE GREATEST EXTENT POSSIBLE.

If considering policies on cryptographic methods that provide for lawful access, governments should carefully weigh the benefits, including the benefits for public safety, law enforcement and national security, as well as the risks of misuse, the additional expense of any supporting infrastructure, the prospects of technical failure, and other costs. This principle should not be interpreted as implying that governments should, or should not, initiate legislation that would allow lawful access.

Where access to the plaintext, or cryptographic keys, of encrypted data is requested under lawful process, the individual or entity requesting access must have a legal right to possession of the plaintext, and once obtained the data must only be used for lawful purposes. The process through which lawful access is obtained should be recorded, so that the disclosure of the cryptographic keys or the data can be audited or reviewed in accordance with national law. Where lawful access is requested and obtained, such access should be granted within designated time limits appropriate to the circumstances. The conditions of lawful access should be stated clearly and published in a way that they are easily available to users, keyholders and providers of cryptographic methods.

Key management systems could provide a basis for a possible solution which could balance the interest of users and law enforcement authorities; these techniques could also be used to recover data, when keys are lost. Processes for lawful access to cryptographic keys must recognise the distinction between keys which are used to protect confidentiality and keys which are used for other purposes only. A cryptographic key that provides for identity or integrity only (as distinct from a cryptographic key that verifies identity or integrity only) should not be made available without the consent of the individual or entity in lawful possession of that key.

7. LIABILITY

WHETHER ESTABLISHED BY CONTRACT OR LEGISLATION, THE LIABILITY OF INDIVIDUALS AND ENTITIES THAT OFFER CRYPTOGRAPHIC SERVICES OR HOLD OR ACCESS CRYPTOGRAPHIC KEYS SHOULD BE CLEARLY STATED.

The liability of any individual or entity, including a government entity, that offers cryptographic services or holds or has access to cryptographic keys, should be made clear by contract or where appropriate by national legislation or international agreement. The liability of users for misuse of their own keys should also be made clear. A keyholder should not be held liable for providing cryptographic keys or plaintext of encrypted data in accordance with lawful access. The party that obtains lawful access should be liable for misuse of cryptographic keys or plaintext that it has obtained.

8. INTERNATIONAL CO-OPERATION

GOVERNMENTS SHOULD CO-OPERATE TO CO-ORDINATE CRYPTOGRAPHY POLICIES. AS PART OF THIS EFFORT, GOVERNMENTS SHOULD REMOVE, OR AVOID CREATING IN THE NAME OF CRYPTOGRAPHY POLICY, UNJUSTIFIED OBSTACLES TO TRADE.

In order to promote the broad international acceptance of cryptography and enable the full potential of the national and global information and communications networks, cryptography policies adopted by a country should be co-ordinated as much as possible with similar policies of other countries. To that end, the Guidelines should be used for national policy formulation.

If developed, national key management systems must, where appropriate, allow for international use of cryptography.

Lawful access across national borders may be achieved through bilateral and multilateral co-operation and agreement.

No government should impede the free flow of encrypted data passing through its jurisdiction merely on the basis of cryptography policy. In order to promote international trade, governments should avoid developing cryptography policies and practices which create unjustified obstacles to global electronic commerce. Governments should avoid creating unjustified obstacles to international availability of cryptographic methods.

International
GATT

GENERAL AGREEMENT ON TRADE IN SERVICES (1994) [EXCERPT]

Reference

WTO I Legal Texts – The WTO Agreements
http://www.wto.org/english/docs_e/legal_e/final_e.htm

Article XIV General Exceptions

Subject to the requirement that such measures are not applied in a manner which would constitute a means of arbitrary or unjustifiable discrimination between countries where like conditions prevail, or a disguised restriction on trade in services, nothing in this Agreement shall be construed to prevent the adoption or enforcement by any Member of measures:

(a) necessary to protect public morals or to maintain public order;[1]

(b) necessary to protect human, animal or plant life or health;

(c) necessary to secure compliance with laws or regulations which are not inconsistent with the provisions of this Agreement including those relating to:

(i) the prevention of deceptive and fraudulent practices or to deal with the effects of a default on services contracts;

(ii) the protection of the privacy of individuals in relation to the processing and dissemination of personal data and the protection of confidentiality of individual records and accounts;

(iii) safety;

(d) inconsistent with Article XVII, provided that the difference in treatment is aimed at ensuring the equitable or effective [2]imposition or collection of direct taxes in respect of services or service suppliers of other Members;

---

[1] The public order exception may be invoked only where a genuine and sufficiently serious threat is posed to one of the fundamental interests of society.

[2] Measures that are aimed at ensuring the equitable or effective imposition or collection of direct taxes include measures taken by a Member under its taxation system which:

(i) apply to non-resident service suppliers in recognition of the fact that the tax obligation of non-residents is determined with respect to taxable items sourced or located in the Member's territory; or

(ii) apply to non-residents in order to ensure the imposition or collection of taxes in the Member's territory; or

(iii) apply to non-residents or residents in order to prevent the avoidance or evasion of taxes, including compliance measures; or

(iv) apply to consumers of services supplied in or from the territory of another Member in order to ensure the imposition or collection of taxes on such consumers derived from sources in the Member's territory; or

(e) inconsistent with Article II, provided that the difference in treatment is the result of an agreement on the avoidance of double taxation or provisions on the avoidance of double taxation in any other international agreement or arrangement by which the Member is bound.

(v) distinguish service suppliers subject to tax on worldwide taxable items from other service suppliers, in recognition of the difference in the nature of the tax base between them; or

(vi) determine, allocate or apportion income, profit, gain, loss, deduction or credit of resident persons or branches, or between related persons or branches of the same person, in order to safeguard the Member's tax base.

Tax terms or concepts in paragraph (d) of Article XIV and in this footnote are determined according to tax definitions and concepts, or equivalent or similar definitions and concepts, under the domestic law of the Member taking the measure.

International
ILO Code of Practice

PROTECTION OF WORKERS'
PERSONAL DATA (1996)

International Labour Office Geneva

CODE OF PRACTICE ON THE PROTECTION OF WORKERS' PERSONAL DATA

1. Preamble

Employers collect personal data on job applicants and workers for a number of purposes: to comply with law; to assist in selection for employment, training and promotion; to ensure personal safety, personal security, quality control, customer service and the protection of property. Various national laws and international standards have established binding procedures for the processing of personal data. Computerized retrieval techniques, automated personnel information systems, electronic monitoring, genetic screening and drug testing illustrate the need to develop data protection provisions which specifically address the use of workers' personal data in order to safeguard the dignity of workers, protect their privacy and guarantee their fundamental right to determine who may use which data for what purposes and under what conditions.

2. Purpose

The purpose of this code of practice is to provide guidance on the protection of worker's personal data. This code does not having binding force. It does not replace national laws, regulations, international labour standards or other accepted standards. It can be used in the development of legislation, regulations, collective agreements, work rules, policies and practical measures.

3. Definitions

In this code:

3.1. The term "personal data" means any related to an identified or identifiable worker information.

3.2. The term "processing" includes the collection, storage, combination, communication or any other use of personal data.

3.3. The term "monitoring" includes, but is not limited to, the use of devices such as computers, cameras, video equipment, sound devices, telephones and other communication equipment, various methods of establishing identity and location, or any other method of surveillance.

3.4. The term "worker" includes any current or former worker or applicant for employment.

4. Scope of application

4.1. This code applies to:

(a) the public and private sectors;

(b) the manual and automatic processing of all workers' personal data.

5. General principles

5.1. Personal data should be processed lawfully and fairly, and only for reasons directly relevant to the employment of the worker.

5.2. Personal data should, in principle, be used only for the purposes for which they were originally collected.

5.3. If personal data are to be processed for purposes other than those for which they were collected, the employer should ensure that they are not used in a manner incompatible with the original purpose, and should take the necessary measures to avoid any misinterpretations caused by a change of context.

5.4. Personal data collected in connection with technical or organizational measures to ensure the security and proper operation of automated information systems should not be used to control the behaviour of workers.

5.5. Decisions concerning a worker should not be based solely on the automated processing of that worker's personal data.

5.6. Personal data collected by electronic monitoring should not be the only factors in evaluating worker performance.

5.7. Employers should regularly assess their data processing practices:

(a) to reduce as far as possible the kind and amount of personal data collected; and

(b) to improve ways of protecting the privacy of workers.

5.8. Workers and their representatives should be kept informed of any data collection process, the rules that govern that process, and their rights.

5.9. Persons who process personal data should be regularly trained to ensure an understanding of the data collection process and their role in the application of the principles in this code.

5. 10. The processing of personal data should not have the effect of unlawfully discriminating in employment or occupation.

5.11. Employers, workers and their representatives should cooperate in protecting personal data and in developing policies on workers' privacy consistent with the principles in this code.

5.12. All persons, including employers, workers' representatives, employment agencies and workers, who have access to personal data, should be bound to a rule of confidentiality consistent with the performance of their duties and the principles in this code.

5.13. Workers may not waive their privacy rights.

6. Collection of personal data

6.1. All personal data should, in principle, be obtained from the individual worker.

6.2. If it is necessary to collect personal data from third parties, the worker should be informed in advance, and give explicit consent. The employer should indicate the purposes of the processing, the sources and means the employer intends to use, as well as the type of data to be gathered, and the consequences, if any, of refusing consent.

6.3. If the worker is asked to sign a statement authorizing the employer or any other person or organization to collect or disclose information about the worker, the statement should be in plain language and specific as to the persons, institutions or organizations to be addressed, the personal data to be disclosed, the purposes for which the personal data will be collected, and the period of time within which the statement will be used.

6.4. When an employer has obtained a worker's consent for the collection of personal data, the employer should :ensure that any persons or organizations required by the employer to collect the data or conduct an investigation are at all times clear about the purpose of the inquiry and that they ,avoid all false or misleading representation.

6.5 (1) An employer should not collect personal data concerning a worker's:

(a) sex life;

(b) political, religious or other beliefs; (c) criminal convictions.

(2) In exceptional circumstances, an employer may collect personal data concerning those in (1) above, if the data are directly relevant to an employment decision and in conformity with national legislation.

6.6. Employers should not collect personal data concerning the worker's membership in a workers' organization or the worker's trade union activities, unless obliged or allowed to do so by law or a collective agreement.

6.7. Medical personal data should not be collected except in conformity with national legislation, medical confidentiality and the general principles of occupational health and safety, and only as needed:

(a) to determine whether the worker is fit for a particular employment;

(b) to fulfil the requirements of occupational health and safety; and

(c) to determine entitlement to, and to grant, social benefits.

6.8. If a worker is asked questions that are inconsistent with principles 5.1, 5.10, 6.5, 6.6 and 6.7 of this code and the worker gives an inaccurate or incomplete answer, the worker should not be subject to termination of the employment relationship or any other disciplinary measure.

6.9. Personal data provided by the worker which go beyond or are irrelevant to the request for personal data because the worker has misunderstood the request should not be processed.

6.10. Polygraphs, truth verification equipment or any other similar testing procedure should not be used.

6. 11. Personality tests or similar testing procedures should be consistent with the provisions of this code, provided that the worker may object to the testing.

6.12. Genetic screening should be prohibited or limited to cases explicitly authorized by national legislation.

6.13. Drug testing should be undertaken only in conformity with national law and practice or international standards. Examples of ILO guidance include the code of practice on

Management of alcohol and drug-related issues in the workplace and the "Guiding principles on drug and alcohol testing in the workplace".[1]

6.14 (1) If workers are monitored they should be informed in advance of the reasons for monitoring, the time schedule, the methods and techniques used and the data to be collected, and the employer must minimize the intrusion on the privacy of workers.

(2) Secret monitoring should be permitted only: if it is in conformity with national legislation; or if there is suspicion on reasonable grounds of criminal activity or other serious wrongdoing.

(3) Continuous monitoring should be permitted only if required for health and safety or the protection of property.

7. Security of personal data

7.1. Employers should ensure that personal data are protected by such security safeguards as are reasonable in the circumstances to guard against loss and unauthorized access, use, modification or disclosure.

8. Storage of personal data

8.1. The storage of personal data should be limited to data gathered consistent with the principles on the collection of personal data in this Code.

8.2. Personal data covered by medical confidentiality should be stored only by personnel bound by rules on medical secrecy and should be maintained apart from all other personal data.

8.3. Employers should provide general information, regularly reviewed, listing types of personal data held on individual workers and on the processing of that data.

8.4. Employers should verify periodically that the personal data stored is accurate, up to date and complete.

8.5. Personal data should be stored only for so long as it is justified by the specific purposes for which they have been collected unless:

(a) a worker wishes to be on a list of potential job candidates for a specific period;

(b) the personal data are required to be kept by national legislation; or

(c) the personal data are required by an employer or a worker for any legal proceedings to prove any matter to do with an existing or former employment relationship.

8.6. Personal data should be stored and coded in a manner:

(a) that the worker can understand; and

(b) that does not ascribe any characteristics to the worker that have the effect of discrimination against the worker.

---

[1] ILO: Management of alcohol and drug-related issues in the workplace: An ILO code of practice (Geneva, 1996); "Guiding principles on drug and alcohol testing in the workplace", in Drug and alcohol testing in the workplace (Geneva, 1993), as adopted by the ILO Interregional Tripartite Experts Meeting on Drug and Alcohol Testing in the Workplace, 10-14 May 1993, Oslo (Honefoss), Norway (also reproduced as Appendix V of the above-mentioned code of practice).

International
ILO Code of Practice

9. Use of personal data

9.1. Personal data should be used consistent with the principles in this code that apply to its collection, communication and storage.

10. Communication of personal data

10.1. Personal data should not be communicated to third parties without the worker's explicit consent unless the communication is:

(a) necessary to prevent serious and imminent threat to life or health;

(b) required or authorized by law; necessary for the conduct of the employment relationship;

(d) required for the enforcement of criminal law.

10.2. A worker's personal data should not be communicated for commercial or marketing purposes without the worker's informed and explicit consent.

10.3. The rules applicable to communications to third parties should apply to the communication of personal data between employers in the same group and between different agencies of government.

10.4. Employers should instruct those who receive a worker's personal data that the personal data can be used only for the purposes for which the data are communicated, and should request confirmation that the instructions have been followed. This does not apply to regular communications pursuant to any statutory obligation.

10.5. Internal communications of personal data should be limited to those explicitly drawn to the attention of the worker.

10.6. Personal data should be internally available only to specifically authorized users, who should have access only to such personal data as are needed for the fulfilment of their particular tasks.

10.7. An interconnection of files containing workers' personal data should be prohibited unless strict compliance with the provisions of this code on internal communications has been secured.

10.8. In the case of a medical examination, the employer should be informed only of the conclusions relevant to the particular employment decision.

10.9. The conclusions should contain no information of a medical nature. They might, as appropriate, indicate fitness for the proposed assignment or specify the kinds of jobs and the conditions of work which are medically contra-indicated, either temporarily or permanently.

10.10. The communication of personal data to workers' representatives should take place only in conformity with national legislation or a collective agreement in accordance with national practice, and should be limited to the personal data necessary to fulfil the representatives' specific functions.

10.11. Employers should adopt procedures for monitoring the internal flow of personal data and for ensuring that the processing complies with this code.

11. Individual rights

11.1. Workers should have the right to be regularly notified of the personal data held about them and the processing of that personal data.

11.2. Workers should have access to all their personal data, 'irrespective of whether the personal data are processed by automated systems or are kept in a particular manual file regarding the individual worker or in any other file which includes workers' personal data

11.3. The workers' right to know about the processing of their personal data should include the right to examine and obtain a copy of any records to the extent that the data contained in the record includes that worker's personal data

11.4. Workers should have the right of access to their personal data during normal working hours. If access cannot be arranged during normal working hours, other arrangements should be made that take into account the interests of the worker ,and the employer.

11.5. Workers should be entitled to designate a workers' representative or a co-worker of their choice to assist them in the exercise of their right of access.

11.6. Workers should have the right to have access to medical data concerning them through a medical professional of their choice.

11.7. Employers should not charge workers for granting access to or copying their own records.

11.8. Employers should, in the event of a security investigation, have the right to deny the worker access to that worker's personal data until the close of the investigation and to the extent that the purposes of the investigation would be threatened. No decision concerning the employment relationship should be taken, however, before the worker has had access to all the worker's personal data.

11.9. Workers should have the right to demand that incorrect or incomplete personal data, and personal data processed inconsistently with the provisions of this code, be deleted or rectified.

11.10. In case of a deletion or rectification of personal data, employers should inform all parties who have been previously provided with the inaccurate or incomplete personal data of the corrections made, unless the worker agrees that this is not necessary.

11.11. If the employer refuses to correct the personal data, the worker should be entitled to place a statement on or with the record setting out the reasons for that worker's disagreement. Any subsequent use of the personal data should include the information that the personal data are disputed, and the worker's statement.

11.12. In the case of judgmental personal data, if deletion or rectification is not possible, workers should have the right to supplement the stored personal data by a statement expressing their own view. The statement should be included in all communications of the personal data, unless the worker agrees that this is not necessary.

11.13. In any legislation, regulation, collective agreement, work rules or policy developed consistent with the provisions of this code, there should be specified an avenue of redress for workers to challenge the employer's compliance with the instrument. Procedures should be established to receive and respond to any complaint lodged by workers. The complaint process should be easily accessible to workers and be simple to use.

12. Collective rights

12.1. All negotiations concerning the processing of workers' personal data should be guided and bound by the principles in this code that protect the individual worker's right to know and decide which personal data concerning that worker should be used, under which conditions, and for which purposes.

12.2. The workers' representatives, where they exist, and in conformity with national law and practice, should be informed and consulted:

(a) concerning the introduction or modification of automated systems that process worker's personal data;

(b) before the introduction of any electronic monitoring of workers' behaviour in the workplace;

(c) about the purpose, contents and the manner of administering and interpreting any questionnaires and tests concerning the personal data of the workers.

13. Employment agencies

13.1. If the employer uses employment agencies to recruit workers, the employer should request the employment agency to process personal data consistently with the provisions of this code.

PERSONAL DATA PROTECTION LAW

The *Saeima*[1] has adopted and
the President has proclaimed the following law:

CHAPTER I-GENERAL PROVISIONS

Section 1

The purpose of this Law is to protect the fundamental human rights and freedoms of natural persons, in particular the inviolability of private life, with respect to the processing of data regarding natural persons (hereinafter – personal data).

Section 2

The following terms are used in this Law:

1) data subject – a natural person who may be directly or indirectly identified using data available within a data processing system;

2) consent of a data subject – a freely, unmistakably expressed affirmation of the wishes of a data subject, by which the data subject allows his or her personal data to be processed;

3) personal data – any information related to an identified or identifiable natural person;

4) personal data processing – any operations carried out regarding personal data, including data collection, registration, recording, storing, arrangement, transformation, utilisation, transfer, transmission and dissemination, blockage or erasure;

5) personal data processing system – a structured body of personal data recorded in any form that is accessible on the basis of relevant criteria;

6) processor of personal data – a person authorised by a system controller, who carries out personal data processing upon the instructions of the system controller;

7) recipient of personal data – a natural or a legal person to whom personal data are disclosed;

8) sensitive personal data - personal data which indicate the race, ethnic origin, religious, philosophical or political convictions, or trade union membership of a person, or provide information as to the health or sexual life of a person;

9) system controller – a natural or a legal person who manages a personal data processing system and determines its purposes and the means of processing; and

10) third person – any natural or legal person except for a data subject, a system controller, a system processor and persons who have been directly authorised by a system controller or a processor of personal data.

International
Personal Data Protection Law (Latvia)

Section 3

(1) This Law applies to the processing of all types of personal data, and to any natural and legal person involved in personal data processing, except in the cases set out in Paragraphs two and three of this Section.

(2) This Law does not apply to the information systems made by natural persons in which personal data are processed for personal or household and family purposes and in which the personal data collected are not disclosed to other persons.

(3) This Law does not apply to the processing of personal data carried out by public institutions in the fields of national security and criminal law.

Section 4

The protection of personal data which have been declared to be official secret matters shall be regulated by the Law on Official Secrets.

Section 5

(1) Sections 7, 8, 9 and 11 of this Law shall not apply if personal data are processed for journalistic, artistic or literary purposes, and it is not prescribed otherwise by law.

(2) In applying the provisions of Paragraph one of this Section, regard shall be had to the rights of persons to inviolability of private life and freedom of expression.

CHAPTER II - GENERAL PRINCIPLES FOR PERSONAL DATA PROCESSING

Section 6

Every natural person has the right to protection of his or her personal data.

Section 7

Personal data processing is permitted only if not prescribed otherwise by law, and at least one of the following conditions exist:

1) the data subject has given his or her consent;

2) the personal data processing results from contractual obligations of the data subject;

3) the data processing is necessary to a system controller for the performance of his or her lawful obligations;

4) the data processing is necessary to protect vitally important interests of the data subject, including life and health;

5) the data processing is necessary in order to ensure that the public interest is complied with, or to fulfil functions of public authority for whose performance the personal data have been transferred to a system controller or transmitted to a third person; and

6) the data processing is necessary in order to, complying with the fundamental human rights and freedoms of the data subject, exercise lawful interests of the system controller or of such third person as the personal data have been disclosed to.

Section 8

(1) When collecting personal data from a data subject, a system controller has an obligation to provide a data subject with the following information unless it is already available to the data subject:

1) the designation, or name and surname, and address of the system controller;

2) the intended purpose and basis for the personal data processing;

3) the possible recipients of the personal data;

4) the rights of the data subject to gain access to his or her personal data and the possibility of rectifying such data; and

5) whether providing an answer is mandatory or voluntary, as well as possible consequences of failing to provide an answer.

(2) Paragraph one of this Section is not applicable, if the conducting of personal data processing without disclosing its purpose is authorised by law.

Section 9

(1) If personal data have not been obtained from the data subject, a system controller, prior to disclosing the data to third persons, is obliged to provide the data subject with the following information:

1) the designation, or name and surname, and address of the system controller;

2) the intended purpose for the personal data processing;

3) the possible recipients of the personal data;

4) the source of the personal data; and

5) the rights of data subjects to gain access to his or her personal data and the possibility of rectifying such data.

(2) Paragraph one of this Section is not applicable, if:

1) the law provides for the processing of personal data without informing the data subject thereof; and

2) when processing personal data for scientific, historical or statistical research, the informing of the data subject requires inordinate effort or is impossible.

Section 10

(1) In order to protect the interests of a data subject, a system controller shall ensure that:

1) the personal data processing takes place lawfully;

2) the personal data are collected in accordance with the intended purpose and to the extent required therefor;

3) the personal data are stored so that the data subject is identifiable during a relevant period of time, which does not exceed the time period prescribed for the intended purpose of the data processing; and

4) the personal data are accurate and that they are updated, rectified or erased in a timely manner if such personal data are incomplete or inaccurate.

(2) Personal data processing for purposes other than those originally intended is permissible if it does not violate the rights of the data subject and is carried out for the needs of scientific or statistical research only in accordance with the conditions mentioned in Section 9 and Section 10, Paragraph one of this Law.

Section 11

The processing of sensitive personal data is prohibited, except in cases where:

1) the data subject has given his or her written consent for the processing of his or her sensitive personal data;

2) special processing of personal data, without requesting the consent of the data subject, is provided for by regulatory enactments which regulate legal relations regarding employment, and such regulatory enactments guarantee the protection of personal data;

3) personal data processing is necessary to protect the life and health of the data subject or another person, and the data subject is not legally or physically able to express his or her consent;

4) personal data processing is necessary to achieve the lawful, non-commercial objectives of public organisations and their associations, if such data processing is only related to the members of these organisations or their associations and the personal data are not transferred to third parties;

5) personal data processing is necessary for the purposes of medical treatment, is carried out by a medical practitioner or a medical treatment institution and an adequate level of protection of personal data is ensured; or

6) the processing concerns such personal data as necessary for the protection of lawful rights and interests of natural or legal persons in court proceedings.

Section 12

If personal data relate to disciplinary and administrative violations or judgments in civil matters, only officials authorised by State or local government institutions are entitled to process such data.

Section 13

(1) A system controller is obliged to disclose personal data in cases provided for by law to officials of State and local government institutions. The system controller shall

disclose the personal data only to such officials of the State and local government institutions as he or she has identified prior to the disclosure of such data.

(2) Personal data may be disclosed on the basis of a written application or agreement, stating the purpose for using the data, if not prescribed otherwise by law. The application for personal data shall set out information as will allow identification of the applicant for the data and the data subject, as well as the scope of the personal data requested.

(3) The personal data received may be used only for the purposes for which they are intended.

Section 14

(1) A system controller may entrust personal data processing to a personal data processor provided a written contract is entered into between them.

(2) A personal data processor may process personal data entrusted to him or her only within the scope determined in the contract and in accordance with the purposes provided for therein.

(3) Prior to commencing personal data processing, a personal data processor shall perform safety measures determined by the system controller for the protection of the system in accordance with the requirements of this Law.

CHAPTER III - RIGHTS OF A DATA SUBJECT

Section 15

(1) In addition to the rights mentioned in Sections 8 and 9 of this Law, a data subject has the right to obtain all information that has been collected concerning himself or herself in any system for personal data processing, unless the disclosure of such information is prohibited by law.

(2) A data subject has the right to obtain information concerning those natural or legal persons who within a prescribed time period have received information from a system controller concerning this data subject. In the information to be provided to the data subject, it is prohibited to include State institutions, which administer criminal procedures, investigatory operations authorities or other institutions concerning which the disclosure of such information is prohibited by law.

(3) A data subject also has the right to request the following information:

    1) the designation, or name and surname, and address of the system controller;

    2) the purpose, scope and method of the personal data processing;

    3) the date when the personal data concerning the data subject were last rectified;

    4) the source from which the personal data were obtained unless the disclosure of such information is prohibited by law; and

    5) the processing methods utilised for the automated processing systems, concerning the application of which individual automated decisions are taken.

(4) A data subject has the right, within a period of one month from the date of submission of the relevant request (not more frequently than two times a year), to receive the information specified in this Section in writing free of charge.

Section 16

(1) A data subject has the right to request that his or her personal data be supplemented or rectified, as well as that their processing be suspended or that the data be destroyed if the personal data are incomplete, outdated, false, unlawfully obtained or are no longer necessary for the purposes for which they were collected. If the data subject is able to substantiate that the personal data included in the personal data processing system are incomplete, outdated, false, unlawfully obtained or no longer necessary for the purposes for which they were collected, the system controller has an obligation to rectify this inaccuracy or violation without delay and notify third parties who have previously received the processed data of such.

(2) If information has been retracted, a system controller shall ensure the accessibility of both the new and the retracted information, and that the information mentioned is received simultaneously by recipients thereof.

Section 17

Sections 15 and 16 of this Law are not applicable if the processed data are used only for the needs of scientific and statistical research and, on the basis of such, no activities are carried out and no decisions are taken regarding the data subject.

Section 18

A person is not required to comply with an individual decision which has been taken only upon the basis of data processed automatically. The person may be made subject to such aforementioned decision if it has been taken in accordance with law or a contract entered into with the data subject.

Section 19

A data subject has the right to object to the processing of his or her personal data if such will be used for commercial purposes.

Section 20

A data subject has the right to appeal to the State Data Inspection the refusal of a system controller to provide the information mentioned in Section 15 of this Law or perform the activities mentioned in Section 16 of this Law.

CHAPTER IV - REGISTRATION AND PROTECTION OF A PERSONAL DATA PROCESSING SYSTEM

Section 21

(1) All State and local government institutions, and other natural persons and legal persons which carry out or wish to commence carrying out personal data processing, and establish systems for personal data processing, shall register such in accordance with the procedures prescribed in this Law unless otherwise prescribed by law.

(2) The registration procedure prescribed by this Law is not applicable to the personal data processing carried out in the areas of public safety, combating of crime or national security and defence, by institutions specially authorised by law.

Section 22

(1) The institutions and persons mentioned in Section 21 of this Law which wish to commence personal data processing and establish a system for personal data processing shall submit an application for registration to the State Data Inspection which includes the following information:

1) the designation (name and surname), registration code, address and telephone number of the institution or person (system controller);

2) the name, surname, personal identity number, address and telephone number of a person authorised by the system controller;

3) the legal basis for the operation of the personal data processing system;

4) the type of personal data to be included in the system, the purposes for which it is intended and the scope of personal data to be processed;

5) the categories of data subjects;

6) the categories of recipients of personal data;

7) the intended method of personal data processing;

8) the planned method of obtaining personal data and a mechanism for the control of their quality;

9) other data processing systems which will be connected with the system to be registered;

10) what personal data connected systems will be able to obtain from the system to be registered, and what data the system to be registered will be able to obtain from connected systems;

11) the method for transferring data from the system to be registered to another system;

12) the identification codes of natural persons as will be used by the system to be registered;

13) the method for exchanging information with the data subject;

14) the procedures whereby a personal data subject is entitled to obtain information concerning himself or herself and other information mentioned in Sections 8 and 9 of this Law;

15) the procedures for supplementing and updating of personal data;

16) technical and organisational measures ensuring the protection of personal data; and

17) what personal data will be transferred to other states.

(2) Prior to registration of a personal data processing system, the State Data Inspection shall perform an inspection of the personal data processing system.

(3) When registering a personal data processing system, the State Data Inspection shall issue a certificate of registration of the personal data processing system to a system controller or to a person authorised by him or her.

(4) Prior to changes being made to the information mentioned in Paragraph one of this Section, they shall be registered in the State Data Inspection.

Section 23

The State Data Inspection may refuse to register a personal data processing system, if:

1) all of the information mentioned in Section 22 of this Law is not submitted; or

2) on inspection of the personal data processing system, violations are determined.

Section 24

(1) The State Data Inspection shall include the information mentioned in Section 22 of this Law in the register for personal data processing systems. The register shall be accessible to the general public.

(2) Information concerning the registered personal data processing systems shall be published in accordance with the procedures prescribed in regulatory enactments.

Section 25

(1) A system controller has an obligation to apply the necessary technical and organisational measures to protect personal data and prevent their illegal processing.

(2) A system controller shall control the form of personal data entered in the personal data processing system and the time of recording and is responsible for the actions of persons who carry out personal data processing.

Section 26

The mandatory technical and organisational requirements for the protection of personal data processing systems shall be determined by the Cabinet.

Section 27

(1) Natural persons involved in personal data processing shall make a commitment in writing to preserve and not, in an unlawful manner, disclose personal data. Such persons have a duty not to disclose the personal data even after termination of legal employment or other contractually specified relations.

(2) A system controller is obliged to record the persons mentioned in Paragraph one of this Section.

(3) When processing personal data, a processor of the personal data shall comply with the instructions of the system controller.

Section 28

(1) Personal data may be transferred to another state if that state ensures such level of data protection as corresponds to the relevant level of the data protection in effect in Latvia and written consent has been obtained from the State Data Inspection.

(2) Exemption from compliance with the requirements of Paragraph one of this Section is permissible if at least one of the following conditions is complied with:

1) the data subject has given consent to the transfer of the data to another state;

2) the transfer of the data is required to fulfil an agreement between the data subject and the system controller, or the personal data are required to be transferred in accordance with contractual obligations binding upon the data subject;

3) the transfer of the data is required and requested, pursuant to prescribed procedures, in accordance with significant state or public interests, or is required for judicial proceedings;

4) the transfer of the data is necessary to protect the life and health of the data subject; or

5) the transfer of the data concerns such personal data as are public or have been accumulated in a publicly accessible register.

Section 29

(1) The protection of personal data shall be carried out by the State Data Inspection which shall be subject to the supervision of the Ministry of Justice. The State Data Inspection shall be managed by a director who shall be appointed and released from his or her position by the Cabinet pursuant to the recommendation of the Minister for Justice.

(2) The State Data Inspection shall act in accordance with by-laws approved by the Cabinet. Every year the State Data Inspection shall submit a report on its activities to the Cabinet and shall publish it in the newspaper *Latvijas Vetsnesis* [Official gazette of the Government of Latvia].

(3) The duties of the State Data Inspection in the field of personal data protection are as follows:

1) to ensure compliance of personal data processing in the State with the requirements of this Law;

2) to take decisions and review complaints regarding the protection of personal data;

3) to register personal data processing systems;

4) to propose and carry out activities aimed at raising the effectiveness of personal data protection; and

5) together with the Office of the Director General of the State Archives of Latvia, to decide on the transfer of personal data processing systems to the State archives for preservation thereof.

(4) In the field of personal data protection, the rights of the State Data Inspection are as follows:

1) in accordance with the procedures prescribed by regulatory enactments, to receive, free of charge, information from natural persons and legal persons as is necessary for the performance of functions pertaining to inspection;

2) to perform inspection of a personal data processing system prior to its registration;

3) to require that data be blocked, that incorrect or unlawfully obtained data be erased or destroyed, or to order a permanent or temporary prohibition of data processing; and

4) to bring an action in court for violations of this Law.

Section 30

(1) In order to perform the duties mentioned in Section 29, Paragraph three of this Law, the director of the State Data Inspection and the inspectors authorised by the director, upon presenting their official identification cards, have the right:

1) to freely enter any non-residential premises where personal data processing systems are located, and in the presence of a representative of the system controller carry out necessary inspections or other measures in order to determine the compliance of the personal data processing procedure with law;

2) to require written or verbal explanations from any natural or legal person involved in personal data processing;

3) to require that documents are produced and other information is provided which relate to the personal data processing system being inspected;

4) to require inspection of a personal data processing system, or of any facility or information carrier of such, and to determine that an expert examination be conducted regarding questions subject to investigation;

5) to request assistance of officials of law enforcement institutions, if required, in order to ensure performance of its duties; and

6) to prepare and submit materials to law enforcement institutions in order for offenders to be held to liability, if required.

(2) The officials of the State Data Inspection involved in registration and inspections shall ensure that the information obtained in the process of registration and inspections is not disclosed, except information accessible to the general public. Such prohibition shall also remain in effect after the officials have ceased to fulfil their official functions.

Section 31

Decisions by the State Data Inspection may be appealed to a court.

Section 32

If, in violating this Law, harm or losses have been caused to a person, he or she has the right to receive commensurate compensation.

Transitional provisions

11 Chapter IV of this Law, "Registration and Protection of a Personal Data Processing System", shall come into force on 1 January 2001.

2. The institutions and persons mentioned in Section 21 of this Law, which have commenced operations before the coming into force of this Law, shall register with the State Data Inspection by 1 January 2002. After expiry of this term, unregistered systems shall cease operations.

This Law has been adopted by the *Saeima* on 23 March 2000.

President
V. V__e-Freiberga
Riga, 6 April 2000

PROTECTION OF THE PERSONAL DATA
(2000)

The Parliament has enacted the following Act of the Czech Republic:

PART ONE

PERSONAL DATA PROTECTION

CHAPTER I
INTRODUCTORY PROVISIONS

Article 1 - Purpose of the Act

The Act regulates the protection of personal data of natural persons, the rights and obligations arising within the data processing and specifies the conditions under which the personal data may be transferred to other countries.

Article 2

A Personal Data Protection Office with its seat in Prague (hereinafter referred to as the "Office") is being established.

Article 3 - Scope of the Act

(1) This Act shall apply to the personal data which are processed by state authorities, regional and other self-administration authorities, other public administration bodies, as well as natural and legal persons, unless this Act or a specific Act stipulates otherwise.

(2) This Act shall apply to all personal data processing, whether being executed in an automatic or other manner.

(3) This Act shall not apply to the personal data processing which is executed by a natural person exclusively for this natural person's needs.

(4) This Act shall not apply to the random personal data collection, provided that such data is not further processed.

(5) Processing of the personal data for statistical and archival purposes shall be regulated by specific Acts[1],[2].

(6) The provisions of articles 5, 9, 11, 16, and 27 of this Act shall not apply to processing of the personal data carried out by:

      -the intelligence services[3];

---

[1] Act No. 89/1995 Coll., on the State Statistical Service.
Act No. 158/1999 Coll., on Census of Citizens, Houses and Flats in 2001.

[2] Act No. 97/1974 Coll., on Archives, as Amended by Act No. 343/1992 Coll.

[3] Act No. 153/1994 Coll., on Intelligence Service of the Czech Republic, as Amended by Act No. 118/1995 Coll.

-the Police of the Czech Republic, including the National Centre of Interpol the Police of the Czech Republic, whilst detecting criminal acts[4],

-the Ministry of Finance within the framework of the financial and analytical activity according to a specific Act[5],

-the National Security Office (NBU) when executing a security screening according to a specific Act [6].

-the Ministry of Interior upon issuing certifications under a specific Act[7], upon issuing covert documents[8] and in the activity of the Inspection Division of the Ministry of Interior [9].

Article 4 - Definition of Terms

For the purposes of this Act:

"personal data" shall mean any data relating to an identified or identifiable data subject. A data subject shall be considered to be identified or identifiable if his identity may be directly or indirectly ascertained on the basis of one or more items of the personal data. Data shall not be considered the personal data if a disproportionate quantity of time, effort or material resources are required to determine the identity of the data subject;

"sensitive data" shall mean the personal data revealing nationality, racial and/or ethnic origin, political attitudes, membership in political parties and/or movements, or trade union or employee organisations, religious and philosophical beliefs, criminal activity, health, and sexual life of the data subject;

"anonymous data" shall mean the data which can be related to an identified or identifiable data subject neither in its original form nor following its processing;

"data subject" shall mean a natural person to whom the personal data is relating to;

"personal data processing" shall mean any operation or a set of operations which is being systematically executed by an controller or processor with the personal data in an automatic or other manner. The personal data processing shall mean, in particular, the collection of the data, its storage on information carriers, retrieval, modification or

---

4 Act No. 283/1991 Coll., on the Police of the Czech Republic, as Subsequently Amended.

5 Act No. 61/1996 Coll., on Certain Measures against Legalisation of Proceeds from Criminal Activity and on Amendments and Changes of Some Related Acts, as Amended by Act No. 15/1998 Coll.

6 Act No. 148/1998 Coll., on Protection of Classified Information and on Amendments of Some Related Acts, as Subsequently Amended.

7 Act No. 451/1991 Coll. Specifying Some Additional Prerequisites for the Performance of Certain Positions in State Authorities and Organisations of the Czech and Slovak Federal Republic, the Czech Republic and the Slovak Republic, as Subsequently Amended.
Act No. 279/1992 Coll. on Some Additional Prerequisites for the Performance of Certain Positions Staffed on the Basis of Assignment or Appointment of Officers of the Police of the Czech Republic and of the Correctional Service Corps of the Czech Republic, as Subsequently Amended.

8 Article 34a of Act No. 283/1991 Coll.

9 Article 2(4) of Act No. 283/1991 Coll.

alteration, searching, using, transferring, distributing, publishing, preserving, exchanging, sorting or combining, blocking and liquidating;

"**personal data collection**" shall mean a systematic procedure or a set of procedures, whose aim shall be to obtain the personal data for the purpose of its further storage on a data carrier for its immediate or subsequent processing;

"**personal data preserving**" shall mean keeping the data in the manner that permits its further processing;

"**personal data blocking**" shall mean establishing that condition in which the personal data shall be inaccessible for a certain period of time and may not be otherwise processed;

"**personal data liquidating**" shall mean a physical destruction of the data carrier, the data physical deletion or the data permanent exclusion from further processing;

"**controller**" shall mean any subject which specifies the purpose and the means of the personal data processing, executes such processing and is responsible for it. The controller may authorise or assign a processor to process the personal data, unless a specific Act stipulates otherwise;

"**processor**" shall mean any subject processing the personal data pursuant to this Act on the basis of a specific Act or authorisation by the controller;

"**published personal data**" shall mean the personal data which is made accessible, in particular, by the mass media, other form of public communication, or as a part of a public list.

CHAPTER II
RIGHTS AND OBLIGATIONS WHILST PROCESSING THE PERSONAL DATA

Article 5

(1) The controller shall be obligated to:

-specify the purpose for which the personal data are to be processed;

-specify the means and manners of the personal data processing;

-process only authentic and accurate personal data, which he obtained in conformity with this Act. The controller shall be obligated to verify whether the personal data is authentic and accurate. If the controller finds that the data being processed by him is not authentic or accurate with respect to the specified purpose, in particular, in relation to an objection raised by the data subject, the controller must block the personal data and repair or supplement it without undue delay. If the data cannot be corrected or supplemented, the controller must liquidate it without undue delay. Inauthentic, inaccurate, or unverified personal data may be processed only in the case that a specific Act stipulates so[10]. This data must be duly designated and kept separately from the remaining personal data;

---

[10] E.g., Act No. 89/1995 Coll., Act No. 153/1994 Coll., as Amended by Act No. 118/1995 Coll., and Act No. 283/1991 Coll., as Subsequently Amended.

-collect the personal data corresponding exclusively to the specified purpose and in the extent which is necessary for the fulfilment of the specified purpose;

-keep the personal data only for the time period which is necessary for the purpose of its processing. After expiry of this period the personal data may be kept solely for statistical, scientific and archival purposes. When used for the purposes specified above, it is necessary to respect the right to protect the private and personal life of the data subject from unauthorised infringement;

-process the personal data only in conformity with the purpose for which the data was collected, unless a specific Act stipulates otherwise. The personal data may be processed for a different purpose only if the data subject has given his consent thereto;

-collect the personal data only in an open manner; collecting data on the pretence of another purpose or another activity is prohibited, unless a specific Act stipulates otherwise;

-ensure that the personal data which was obtained for different purposes shall not be combined, unless a specific Act stipulates otherwise.

(2) The controller may process the personal data only with the consent of the data subject. Without this consent the controller may process the data,

-if he is executing the data processing specified by a specific Act or required to comply with the duties specified by a specific Act[11];

-if it is essential that the data subject could enter into negotiations on a contractual relationship or that the data subject could comply with the arrangements arising from the agreements concluded with the controller;

-if it is essential, inter alia, for the protection of important interests of the data subject. Should this be the case, the data subject's consent must be obtained without undue delay. Should not the consent be granted, the controller must terminate the processing and liquidate the data;

-if this is the case when the personal data has been justifiably published pursuant to a specific Act[12]. Nevertheless, this shall not affect the data subject's right to protect his private and personal life;

-if it is essential for the protection of the rights of the controller; however, such personal data processing may not be in contradiction with the data subject's right to protect his private and personal life

---

[11] E.g. Act No. 111/1998 Coll., on Universities and on Changes and Amendments of other Acts (the Universities Act); Act No. 564/1990 Coll., on the State Administration and Self-administration in Education, as Subsequently Amended; Act No. 153/1994 Coll., as Amended by Act No. 118/1995 Coll. and Act No. 61/1996 Coll., as Amended by Act No. 15/1998 Coll.

[12] Act No. 81/1966 Coll., on the Periodical Press and Other Media of Mass Information, as Subsequently Amended.

(3) If a controller processes the personal data on the basis of a specific Act[11], the controller shall be obligated to respect the data subject's right to protect the data subject's private and personal life.

(4) Without the data subject's consent, the personal data may be processed for statistical or scientific purposes. When being processed for the above specified purposes, the personal data must be made anonymous as soon as possible. Nevertheless, when the personal data is being processed for these purposes, the level of its protection required under article 13 must be ensured.

(5) However, the consent under paragraph (2) shall not affect the duties referred to in paragraph (1) (c) and (g). The consent must be granted in writing and it must clearly specify the scope of the consent, to whom and for what purpose, for what period of time and by whom the consent is being granted. The consent may be revoked at any time. The controller shall keep the consent for the period of the personal data processing, for the processing thereof the consent was granted.

(6) If the controller or the processor executes the personal data processing for the purpose of offering the data subject's business opportunities or services, the data subject's name, surname and address may be used for this purpose on condition that the data was acquired from a public list or in relation with the activity of an controller or a processor. The controller or processor, however, may not further process the data stated above if the data subject has expressed his dissent therefrom. The dissent from the processing must be executed in writing. No additional personal data may be attached to the stated data without the data subject's consent.

Article 6

If the authorisation does not ensue from a legal regulation, the controller may conclude with the processor a contract on the personal data processing. The contract must be in writing, otherwise it shall be considered null and void. The contract shall explicitly state the scope, purpose and period of time for which the contract is being concluded. Should the processor fail to grant in the contract sufficient guarantees on technical and organisational provisions ensuring the personal data protection, the contract shall be considered null and void.

Article 7

The obligations specified in article 5 shall apply mutatis mutandis to a processor.

Article 8

Should a processor find out that an controller breaches the obligations stipulated by this Act, the processor shall be obligated to notify the controller of this fact without delay and to terminate the personal data processing. Should the processor fail to do so, the processor and the data controller shall be liable jointly and severally for any damage incurred to the data subject. The processor's liability ensuing from this Act shall not be affected herewith.

Article 9 - Sensitive Data

The sensitive data may be processed if:

-the data subject has granted the explicit consent to such processing. The consent must be granted in writing, it must be signed by the data subject and it must clearly specify the data with respect of which the consent is being granted; as well as to which controller, for what purpose and what period of time the consent is being granted and by whom it is being granted.

The data subject may revoke his consent at any time. The controller shall be obligated to instruct the data subject in advance of the data subject's rights. The controller shall be obligated to keep the consent for the time period of the personal data processing for the processing of which the consent had been granted;

-it is unavoidable in order to preserve the life or health of the data subject or of another person or to ward off an immediate danger threatening to their property, if this person's consent may not be obtained, in particular, due to this person's physical, mental or legal lack of capacity, or in the case that the data subject is missing or in other similar cases.

The controller shall be obligated to terminate the data processing as soon as the mentioned above reasons cease to exist and the controller shall liquidate the data, unless the data subject grants his consent for further processing;

-this is the case of providing the health care[13], as well as another examination of the health conditions pursuant to a specific Act, especially for the social security purposes[14];

-a specific Act[15] stipulates so.

Article 10

Upon the personal data processing, the controller and processor shall ensure that the data subject's rights has not been breached, in particular, the data subject's right to preserve human dignity; and the controller and processor shall ensure that the data subject's private and personal life shall be protected from unjustifiable intervention herein.

Article 11

(1) The controller shall be obligated to notify the data subject in a timely and duly manner of the fact that the controller is collecting the data about the data subject, the

---

[13] Act No. 20/1966 Coll., on the Care of the People's Health, as Subsequently Amended.

[14] E.g. Act No. 582/1991 Coll., on Organisation and Implementation of the Social Security, as Subsequently Amended.

[15] E.g. Act No. 48/1997 Coll., on Public Health Insurance and on Changes and Amendments of Some Related Acts, as Subsequently Amended; Act No. 280/1992 Coll., on Ministry, Branch, Undertaking and Other Health Insurance Companies, as Subsequently Amended; Act No. 551/1992 Coll., on the General Health Insurance Company of the Czech Republic, as Subsequently Amended; and Act No. 158/1999 Coll.

scope of the data and the purpose, who will do the data further processing and for what purpose, to whom the data may be disclosed, or for whom the data are designated. This information must also include the controller's registered office, or the processor's registered office, if appropriate.

(2) The controller must further instruct the data subject on whether the data subject is obligated under the law to provide the personal data for processing, what consequences will follow if the data subject rejects to do so, and when the data subject is entitled to reject to provide the personal data or whether the provision of the personal data is voluntary.

(3) The controller must notify the data subject on the data subject's right to access to the personal data, as well on other rights stipulated in article 21 of this Act.

(4) If the controller did not obtain the personal data from the data subject, the controller shall notify the data subject, in addition to the information under paragraphs (1) and (2), prior to the personal data further processing, on who provided the data to the controller, as well as the information on the type of the personal data and the content of the data.

(5) The controller shall not be obligated to provide the information under paragraph (1) if:

the controller is processing the personal data exclusively for statistical, scientific or archival purposes;

the law stipulates the obligation of the controller to process the personal data;

a specific Act[16] stipulates that the controller is not obligated to provide the personal data.

(6) Neither adjudication of a body of a public authority nor any other act may be issued or executed without verification on the basis of an exclusively automated personal data processing. This shall not apply to the case when such adjudication or act was executed in favour of the data subject.

(7) The provisions stated above shall not affect the right of the data subject to demand the information pursuant to specific Acts[17].

(8) When processing the personal data under article 5 paragraph (2)(e), the controller shall be obligated to inform the data subject on this procedure without undue delay.

Article 12

(1) The information under article 11 paragraphs (1) to (4) shall be provided to the data subject in writing, in an intelligible form and without undue delay. Nevertheless, the information shall not be provided if it is a part of the instruction pursuant to a legal regulation.

---

[16] E.g. Act No. 153/1994 Coll., as Amended by Act No.118/1995 Coll.; Act No. 61/1966 Coll., as Amended by Act No. 15/1998 Coll., and Act No. 283/1991 Coll., as Subsequently Amended.

[17] E.g. Act No. 123/1998 Coll., on the Right to Information on the Environment; Act No. 367/1990 Coll., on Municipalities (the Municipality System), as Subsequently Amended; Act No. 106/1999 Coll., on Free Access to Information.

(2) Unless stipulated otherwise by or a specific Act[16], based on the data subject's request in writing, the controller shall be obligated to provide the data subject with the information on the personal data being processed about the data subject; the information provision being free of charge if provided once a calendar year, otherwise any time for a reasonable compensation not exceeding the costs incurred for the provision of the information.

Article 13 - Obligations of Persons when Securing the Personal Data

The controller and the processor are obligated to adopt the measures which shall prevent any unauthorised or accidental access to the personal data; alteration, destruction or loss, unauthorised transmissions, other unauthorised processing, or other abuse of the personal data. This obligation shall be in force even after terminating the personal data processing.

Article 14

Employees of the controller or processor or third persons who are involved in the personal data processing on the basis of a contract concluded with the controller or processor, may process the personal data only under the conditions and scope specified by the controller or the processor.

Article 15

(1) The employees of the controller or processor, other natural persons who are involved in the personal data processing on the basis of a contract concluded with the controller or processor and other persons who, within the scope of fulfilling their legally mandated competencies and responsibilities, come into contact with the personal data at the premises of the controller or the processor, shall be obligated to maintain confidentiality on the personal data and security arrangements whose public disclosure would endanger the security of the personal data. The obligation to maintain confidentiality shall persist even after terminating the employment relationship or the applicable work.

(2) The provisions of the preceding paragraph shall not affect any obligation to maintain confidentiality pursuant to specific Acts[18].

(3) The obligation to maintain confidentiality shall not apply to the notification obligation pursuant to specific Acts[19].

Article 16 - Notification Obligation

---

[18] E.g. Act No. 148/1998 Coll., as Subsequently Amended; Act No. 89/1995 Coll.; Act No. 20/1966, as Subsequently Amended; Act No. 15/1998 Coll., on the Securities Commission and on Changes and Amendments to Some Related Acts.

[19] E.g. articles 167 and 168 of Act No. 140/1961 Coll., the Criminal Code, as Subsequently Amended; Act No. 21/1992 Coll., on Banks, as Subsequently Amended; Act No. 20/1966 Coll., as Subsequently Amended.

(1) Whoever intends to process the personal data shall be obligated to notify the Office of this fact prior to commencing the personal data processing. The controller shall also be obligated to notify the Office if he intends to alter the personal data processing. The notification must be executed in writing.

(2) The notification must include the following information:

the name of the controller, the address of his registered office and the identification number if it has been assigned;

-the purpose or purposes of the processing;

-the categories of the data subjects and the personal data which relate to these subjects;

-the sources of the personal data;

-the description of the method the personal data are processing;

-the location or locations where the personal data shall be processed if the location/locations differ from the address of the controller's registered office;

-the recipient or a category of recipients to whom the personal data may be accessible or disclosed;

-the assumed personal data transfers to other countries;

-the description of measures adopted for securing the required personal data protection pursuant to article 13;

-the links to other controllers or processors.

(3) Within 30 days as of the delivery of the notification, the Office shall be obligated to communicate to the notifier that the Office has registered his notification, or to issue an adjudication under article 17.

(4) If the Office has registered the notification, the notifier may commence the personal data processing as of the date of the registration.

(5) Should the Office fail to inform the notifier within the period of time specified in paragraph (3) that it has registered the notification or to issue an adjudication, it is presumed that the Office has registered the notification.

Article 17

(1) Should the Office ascertain that the notifier does not meet the conditions specified by this Act, the Office shall not permit the personal data processing.

(2) Should the notification not contain all the required information, the Office shall invite the notifier to complete it within a specified time limit.

(3) Should a reasonable doubt arise with respect to the notification that this Act might be breached when processing the personal data, the Office shall invite the notifier to supplement the notification within a specified time limit, or the Office shall perform its own on site investigation, if appropriate.

(4) After the expiry of the time limit specified under paragraphs (2) and (3), the Office shall either register the notification or issue an adjudication prohibiting the personal data processing.

Article 18

The notification obligation pursuant to article 16 shall not apply to the personal data processing:

(a) which is a part of open to the public records;

(b) whose processing is mandated to the controller by Act[20].

Article 19

Should the controller intend to terminate his activity the controller must notify the Office without delay how the controller has disposed of the personal data, if its processing is subject to the notification obligation.

Article 20 - Liquidation of the Personal Data

(1) The controller or the processor, acting on the basis of the controller's instructions, shall be obligated to carry out the liquidation of the personal data as soon as the purpose for which the personal data was processed ceases to exist or on the basis of a request by the data subject pursuant to article 21.

(2) A specific Act shall specify the exceptions relating to the storage of the personal data for archival purposes and to the exercise of rights in civil judicial proceedings, criminal proceedings and administrative proceedings.

Article 21 - Protection of the Data Subjects' Rights

(1) If the data subject ascertains that the controller or processor breached his obligations, the data subject shall be entitled to address the Office and demand that remedial measures be adopted.

(2) If the controller or the processor breached his obligations, the data subject has the right to require:

-that the controller or the processor desist from such activity, rectify the condition thus incurred or provide at the controller or the processor's own expense an apology or other satisfaction;

-that the controller or processor execute a correction or completion of the personal data in that manner that the personal data be authentic and accurate;

-that the personal data be blocked or liquidated;

-the payment of financial compensation, if the data subject's right to human dignity, personal honour, good reputation or the right to protect his name was violated.

(3) Whoever proves that he could not prevent the breach of the obligation despite using best efforts that might have been required of him, shall be relieved of the liability under paragraph (2). Nevertheless, the data subject may demand that the controller or the

---

20 E.g., Act No. 153/1994 Coll.; Act No. 61/1996 Coll., as amended by Act No. 15/1998 Coll.; Act No. 283/1991 Coll., as Subsequently Amended; and Act No. 158/1999 Coll.

processor desist from his wrongful acts, remove a defective condition, execute a remedy, supplementation, blockage or liquidation of the personal data.

(4) Should the controller or processor cause damage to the data subject, the controller and the processor shall be liable jointly and severally pursuant to specific Acts[21].

(5) Should a breach of obligations stipulated by this Act occurred both on the part of the controller and on the part of the processor, the controller and the processor shall be liable jointly and severally. The data subject may sue his claims from either of them.

Article 22

The data subject may not demand the right to block or liquidate the personal data if the controller is obligated to process the personal data pursuant to a specific Act or if this could result in a detriment of the rights of third parties.

Article 23 - Remedy of Non-material Detriment

(1) If a person executing an activity on behalf of the controller or processor on the basis of a contract breaches the bestowed obligations, the data subject has the right to demand that:

- this person desist from this activity, rectify the condition thus arisen or provide an apology or other satisfaction at his own expense;
- this person liquidate the personal data that he is processing without authorisation;
- this person pay a financial compensation for the detriment that resulted from the breach of the data subject's right to human dignity, personal honour, good reputation or the right to protect the name.

(2) Should this person fail to provide an apology or other satisfaction at his own expense or to pay the financial compensation, the controller or the processor shall be obligated to meet this obligation instead of the stated above person.

(3) Should a person who is in a working relationship to the controller or the processor breach the bestowed obligations, this person's liability shall be governed by the Labour Code.

Article 24

The persons referred to in article 23 shall be relieved of the liability if they prove that they did not cause the breach of the regulations. Nevertheless, the data subject may demand that they desist from the activity breaching the bestowed obligations, rectify the condition arisen from such activity and liquidate the personal data that they are processing without authorisation .

Article 25 - Indemnity

---

[21] E.g. Act No. 40/1964 Coll., the Civil Code, as Subsequently Amended; Act No. 82/1998 Coll., on Liability for Damage Caused by Resolution or Incorrect Official Procedure while Executing Public Authority; Act No. 358/1992 Coll., on Notaries and Their Activity (the Notaries Procedure Act), as Subsequently Amended.

General legal regulations with respect to indemnity [22],[23] shall apply to the matters not specified by this Act.

Article 26

The obligations under articles 21 to 25 shall apply mutatis mutandis to the persons who have collected the personal data without authorisation.

CHAPTER III
TRANSFER OF THE PERSONAL DATA TO OTHER COUNTRIES

Article 27

(1) The personal data may be transferred to other countries on condition that the national legislation of the country where the personal data is to be processed correspond to the requirements stipulated by this Acts.

(2) If the condition under paragraph (1) is not met, the transfer of the personal data may be executed if:

-the transfer of the personal data is carried out with the consent of, or on the basis of an instruction of, the data subject who is entitled to grant it;

it is essential for the protection of the data subject's rights or setting up the data subject's claims;

-the personal data concerned is a part of public registers or registers accessible to everyone who proves a legal interest; nevertheless, this shall apply only to the individually determined data or pieces of the data;

the transfer ensues from an international treaty which is binding for the Czech Republic;

-the transfer is necessary for the conclusion or performance of a contract between the data subject and the controller or of a contract which is being concluded in the interest of the data subject;

-it is essential for protecting the life of or providing the health care to the data subject.

(3) The transfer of the personal data may be carried out in other cases, if it is done for the benefit of the data subject and if it ensues from a bilateral contract between the controller and the recipient that the recipient shall secure the required personal data protection.

(4) The controller shall be obligated to apply to the Office for a single or multiple permit to transfer the personal data to other countries. The Office shall rule on the application without delay, however, within 7 calendar days as the latest. Should the Office fail to make a ruling within this period of time it shall be presumed that the Office gives consent to the transfer of the personal data; the consent being granted for

---

22 Act No. 40/1964 Coll., as Subsequently Amended.

23 Act No. 513/1991 Coll., the Commercial Code, as Subsequently Amended.

the period stated in the application. If there is danger in delay the Office shall issue its ruling without delay. An appeal against the ruling does not have a suspensory effect.

(5) If the Office issues a ruling on transfer of the personal data, the Office shall also specify the time limit within which the controller may perform the transfer. If the controller breaches the obligations stipulated by this Act, the Office shall revoke this permit. An appeal against the ruling does not have a suspensory effect.

(6) The controller does not have the obligations under paragraphs (4) and (5) in the event that a specific Act stipulates so[24].

CHAPTER IV
POSITION AND COMPETENCE OF THE OFFICE

Article 28

(1) The Office is an independent authority. In its activity, it shall act independently and shall be governed solely by Acts and other legislation.

(2) The Office's activity may be intervened exclusively on the basis of the law.

(3) The activity of the Office is covered from a special chapter of the state budget of the Czech Republic.

Article 29

(1) The Office:

-performs supervision over the fulfilling the obligations stipulated by this Act in the course of the personal data processing;

-keeps records of notifications executed under article 16 and the register of permitted personal data processing (hereinafter referred to as "the register");

-accepts the citizens' incentives and complaints with regards to breach of this Act;

-prepares an annual report of its activity and makes it available to the public;

-exercises other authorities mandated to it by law;

-investigates misdemeanours and other administrative offences and imposes penalties pursuant to this Act;

-secures fulfilment of requirements ensuing from international treaties which are binding for the Czech Republic;

-provides consultations in the area of the personal data protection;

-co-operates with its similar supervisory authorities in other countries.

(2) The procedure followed in performing supervision activity in the form of an inspection is stipulated by a specific Act[25].

---

[24] E.g. Act No. 153/1994 Coll., as Amended by Act No. 118/1995 Coll.; Act 61/1996 Coll., as Amended by Act No. 15/1998 Coll.; and Act 283/1991 Coll., as Subsequently Amended.

[25] Act No. 552/1991 Coll., on State Inspection, as Subsequently Amended.

(3) A supervision over the personal data processing which is performed by intelligence services is stipulated by a specific Act [26].

CHAPTER V
ORGANISATION OF THE OFFICE

Article 30

(1) The Office consists of:

    (a) a chairman;

    (b) inspectors; and

    (c) employees.

(2) The supervisory activity of the Office shall be carried out by inspectors and authorised employees (hereinafter referred to as "the supervisors").

(3) The provisions of the Labour Code shall apply to the chairman, inspectors and employees of the Office, unless this Act stipulates otherwise.

(4) The salaries of the Office's employees shall be governed by legal regulations specifying salaries of civil employees [27].

(5) The Office's employees shall be entitled to compensation of travel expenses pursuant to a specific Act [28].

Article 31

The supervisory activity of the Office shall be executed on the basis of an internal supervisory plan or on the basis of the citizens' incentives and complaints.

Article 32 - Chairman of the Office

(1) The Office is managed by a chairman who is appointed and recalled by the President of the Czech Republic based on a proposal of the Senate of the Parliament of the Czech Republic.

(2) The Chairman of the Office is appointed for a period of 5 years. The Chairman may be appointed for the maximum of two successive periods.

(3) Only the citizen of the Czech Republic may be appointed the Office's chairman who:

-enjoys legal capacity;

---

[26] Article 12 of Act No. 153/1994 Coll.

[27] Act No. 143/1992 Coll., on Salaries and Remuneration for Emergency Readiness in Budgetary and Some Other Organisations and Authorities, as Subsequently Amended.
Government Decree No. 253/1992 Coll., on Salaries of Employees of Authorities of State Administration, Some Other Authorities and Municipalities, as Subsequently Amended.

[28] Act No. 119/1992 Coll., on Travel Expenses Compensation, as Subsequently Amended.

-has no criminal records, meets the conditions prescribed by a specific Act [29] and whose knowledge, experience and moral qualities establish a prerequisite that he will properly serve in his position; and

-is a university graduate.

(4) For the purpose of this Act, a natural person shall be considered having no criminal records who has not been lawfully sentenced for a wilful criminal act or for a crime committed by negligence in relation to the personal data processing.

(5) The position of the Office chairman shall not be compatible with the positions of a deputy or senator, judge, state attorney, any position in the state administration, a position of a member of the local self-administration authorities and a membership in political parties and movements.

(6) The Office chairman may not hold any other paid position, be in other employment, or execute any gainful activity, with the exception of the administration of his own property and scientific, pedagogical, literal, journalistic and artistic activities, if such activity does not impair the dignity of the Office or threaten confidence in the independence and impartiality of the Office.

(7) The Office chairman shall be recalled from his position if he ceases to meet any of the conditions of his appointment.

(8) The Office chairman may also be recalled from his position if he fails to perform his position for a period of 6 months.

Article 33 - The Office's Inspectors

(1) The inspector is appointed and recalled by the President of the Czech Republic based on a proposal of the Senate of the Parliament of the Czech Republic.

(2) The inspector is appointed for the period of 10 years period. He/she may be appointed repeatedly.

(3) The inspector carries out inspections, manages inspections, prepares the inspection report and performs other tasks related to the Office's tasks.

(4) The activities of the Office under paragraph (3) are carried out by 7 inspectors.

Article 34

(1) Only the citizen of the Czech Republic may be appointed the inspector who enjoys legal capacity, has no criminal records, meets the conditions prescribed by a specific Act[29] and is a university graduate.

(2) The position of the inspector shall not be compatible with the positions of a deputy or senator, judge, state attorney, any position in the state administration, a position of a member of the local self-administration authorities and a membership in political parties and movements. The inspector may not hold any other paid position, be in other

---

[29] Act No. 451/1991 Coll.
[29] Act No. 451/1991 Coll.

employment, or execute any gainful activity, with the exception of the administration of his own property and scientific, pedagogical, literal, journalistic and artistic activities, if such activity does not impair the dignity of the Office or threaten confidence in the independence and impartiality of the Office.

(3) The inspector shall be recalled from his position if he ceases to meet any of the conditions of his appointment.

CHAPTER VI
ACTIVITY OF THE OFFICE

Article 35

Registration

(1) The data ensuing from notifications under article 16 paragraph (2) are recorded in the Register of the permitted personal data processing.

(2) A registration or a revocation thereof shall be published by the Office in the Office Bulletin not later than within 2 months, unless a specific Act stipulates that the registration or the revocation thereof shall not to be officially published. A notification on registration or the revocation thereof may also be published by the Office in other suitable manner.

(3) The register is publicly accessible, with the exception of the data specified under article 16 paragraph (2)(e) and (i).

Article 36 - Annual Report

(1) The Office's annual report includes, in particular, the information on performed inspection activity and its evaluation, the information and evaluation on the course of the personal data processing and protection in the Czech Republic and the evaluation of the Office's other activities.

(2) The annual report is being submitted by the Office Chairman for the informational purposes to the Chamber of the Deputies and the Senate of the Parliament of the Czech Republic and to the Government of the Czech Republic; the annual report being submitted within two months after the end of the business year and published in the Office Bulletin.

Article 37 - Authorities of the Supervisors

(1) When executing inspections, the supervisors shall be entitled to:

-enter the premises, facilities and plant establishments, lands and other areas of the controllers and processors, who are being inspected, and/or everyone who processes the personal data (hereinafter referred to as "the supervisee") if entering the areas specified above is related to the subject of the inspection; the supervisors may enter residential premises only in the event that the residential premises are also used for carrying on the business activity;

-require that the supervisee and other persons submit, within the specified time limits, the original documents and other written materials, data records on computer-readable media, transcripts and software source codes, if they have them in their possession, transcripts and copies of the data (hereinafter referred to as "the documents"), if these documents are related to the subject of the inspection; the supervisors shall also be entitled to execute their own documentation;

get acquainted with the classified information under the conditions determined by a specific Act[30], as well as with other facts which are protected by the obligation to maintain confidentiality;

-demand from natural and/or legal persons the provision of authentic and complete information of the facts which are being ascertained and which related to the matter;

-seize documents in justified cases; the act of taking over the documents must be confirmed in writing and handed to the supervisee; at the supervisee's request, the copies of the seized documents must be left with the supervisee;

-make copies of the contents of computer-readable media found at the location of the supervisee which include the personal data;

-demand that the supervisees submit a written report on elimination of any ascertained deficiencies within a specified time limit;

-use the telecommunications facilities of the supervisees in the cases where the use thereof is essential for ensuring the inspection.

Article 38 - Obligations of the Supervisors

(1) Those supervisors may not perform inspections who arise reasonable doubts as to their prejudice with respect to their relationship with supervisees or the matter of supervision.

(2) Immediately upon learning the facts indicating his prejudice, a supervisor shall be obligated to notify the Office chairman thereof.

(3) An objection to prejudice at the part of supervisor shall be ruled upon by the Office chairman without undue delay. Prior to the decision of the objection to prejudice, the supervisor shall undertake only those acts that can brook no delay.

(4) No appeal lies against the decision on objection to prejudice.

(5) The supervisors shall be obligated to:

-identify themselves to the supervisee by the supervisor's licence;

-notify the supervisee that an inspection has commence;

-respect the rights and legally protected interests of the supervisees;

-return the seized documents and copies of the computer-readable media to the - supervisee as soon as the reasons for their seizure have passed;

-protect properly the seized documents against loss, destruction, damage or misuse;

-execute an inspection protocol on results of the inspection;

---

[30] Act No. 148/1998 Coll., as Subsequently Amended.

-keep in secrecy the facts ascertained within discharge of the inspection and not to misuse knowledge of these facts. The obligation to maintain confidentiality shall not affect the notification obligation under specific Acts. The obligation to maintain confidentiality shall remain effective even after terminating the employment relationship to the Office. The Office chairman may release the supervisor from confidentiality. The obligation to maintain confidentiality shall not apply to anonymous and generalised information.

(6) The inspection protocol shall include, in particular, a description of the ascertained facts, together with the deficiencies and indication of provisions of the regulations which were breached and the measures that were imposed for a remedy and indication of the time limits by which the remedies shall be performed. The inspection protocol shall contain the indication of the Office and the names of the supervisors participating in the inspection, the indication of the supervisee, the place and time of executing the inspection, the subject of the inspection, the conditions found, the indication of documents and other documentation and the findings that form the substance of the protocol. The inspection protocol shall be signed by the supervisors who participated in the inspection.

(7) The supervisors shall be obligated to apprise the supervisees of the contents of the inspection protocol and to submit them the duplicate thereof. The supervisees shall confirm their having been apprised of the inspection protocol and taking over the duplicate thereof by signing the inspection protocol. Should a supervisee refuse to be apprised of the contents of the inspection protocol or to confirm the fact of having been apprised, these facts shall be noted in the inspection protocol.

Article 39

In relation to the discharge of the inspection, everybody shall be obligated to render necessary assistance to the supervisors in their activity.

Article 40 - Remedial Measures

(1) If a supervisor determines that the obligations stipulated by this Act were breached, the inspector shall determine which measures shall be adopted in order to eliminate the ascertained deficiencies and shall specify a time limit for their elimination.

(2) If a liquidation of the personal data was imposed, the personal data shall be blocked until their liquidation. The controller may file an objection to the Office chairman against imposing the liquidation. The personal data shall be blocked until a decision is adopted with regard to the objection. An action may be filed against the chairman's decision in accordance with the administrative law regulations. The data shall be blocked until a decision is adopted by the court.

(3) The supervisee shall be obligated to submit a report on adopted measures within the specified time limit.

International
Protection of Personal Data Act (Czech Republic)

Article 41

Unless stipulated otherwise by this Act, the procedures on matters specified under this Act shall be governed by the Administrative Code[31].

Article 42

The operation of information systems which treats the personal data pursuant to the existing legislative provisions shall mean the personal data processing.

Article 43 - Authorities and Responsibilities in the Course of Inspection

The authorities and responsibilities of the supervisors and supervisees shall be governed by a specific Act[25], unless stipulated otherwise by this Act.

CHAPTER VII
PENALTIES

Article 44 - Offences

(1) A person who is in an employment or a similar relationship to the controller or the processor or who carries out activities on behalf of the controller or the processor on the basis of an agreement, or a person who, as a part of fulfilling legally mandated competencies and obligations, comes into contact with the controller's or processor's personal data shall be considered to have committed an offence and shall be punished by a penalty of up to CZK 50,000 if he breaches the obligation of maintain confidentiality stipulated by this Act.

(2) The person referred to in paragraph (1) shall be considered to have committed an offence and shall be punished by a penalty of up to CZK 25,000 if he breaches another obligation stipulated by this Act.

(3) Offences and their hearing shall be governed by a specific Act[32].

(4) The Office shall be the authority competent to hear the offences.

Article 45 - Disciplinary Penalty

A disciplinary penalty of up to CZK 25,000 may be imposed, even repeatedly, on a person which shall not render the Office necessary assistance within the performance of the Office's supervisory activity.

Article 46 - Penalties to Controllers and Processors

(1) An controller and/or a processor who breaches the obligation stipulated by this Act shall be punished by a penalty of up to CZK 10.000.000.

---

[31] Act No.71/1967 Coll., on Administrative Processes (the Administrative Code), as Amended by Act No. 29/2000 Coll.

[32] Act No. 200/1990 Coll., on Offences, as Subsequently Amended.

(2) If an controller and/or a processor repeatedly breaches the obligation stipulated by this Act within one year as of the day when the decision of imposition the penalty came into force, he may be liable to a penalty of up to CZK 20.000.000.

(3) An controller and/or a processor who obstructs the supervision executed by the Office may be punished by a disciplinary penalty of up to CZK 1.000.000, even repeatedly.

(4) Any breaches of obligations shall be heard by the Office.

(5) When imposing penalty pursuant to this Act, the Office shall ensue, in particular, from the character, seriousness, manner of activity, degree of blame, duration and consequences of the unlawful activity.

(6) The penalty may be imposed within one year as of the day when the respective authority ascertained the breach of the obligation, nevertheless, within 3 years as of the day when the breach occurred as the latest.

(7) The penalty shall be collected by the Office. The penalty shall be levied by the local competent financial office in accordance with a specific Act[33].

(8) The revenues from the penalties shall constitute the income to the State budget of the Czech Republic.

CHAPTER VIII
COMMON, TRANSITIONAL AND CONCLUSING PROVISIONS

Article 47 - Measures for a Transitional Period

(1) Everyone who shall process the personal data as of the day when this Act comes into force and who shall be subject to the notification obligation under article 16 shall be obligated to fulfil the notification obligation within 6 months as of the day of the effectiveness of this Act as the latest.

(2) The personal data processing carried out prior to the effectiveness of this Act shall be brought into harmony with this Act within 1 year as of the effective date that this Act.

Article 48 - Repealing Provision

Act No. 256/1992 Coll., on Protection of the Personal Data in Information Systems is hereby repealed.

PART TWO

Article 49 - Amendment to the Criminal Code

Act No.140/1961 Coll., the Criminal Code, as amended, shall be changed as follows:

(1) Article 178 paragraph (1) reads as follows:

---

33 Act No.337/1992 Coll., on Administration of Taxes and Charges, as Subsequently Amended.

" (1) Whoever, be it through negligence, shall unjustifiably disclose, make accessible, otherwise process or appropriate personal data on another person which were collected in connection with the execution of public administration, shall be punished by imprisonment of up to three years or by a prohibition of activity or by a financial penalty.".

(2) In article 178 paragraph (2), the word "personal " shall be inserted after the word "who".

PART THREE

Article 50 - Amendment of the Act on Free Access to Information

Act No. 106/1999 Coll., on Free Access to Information, shall be amended as follows:

(1) Article 2 paragraph (3), including the footnote No.1 shall read as follows:

"(3) The Act shall not apply to providing the personal data and information in accordance with a specific Act.[34]

(2) In article 5 paragraph (3), the second sentence is being replaced by a sentence which shall read as follows, including the footnote No. 3a: "For this purpose, the obligation to avoid combining information in accordance with a specific Act shall not apply to these subjects.[35][3a]

(3) In article 8, paragraphs (1) and (2), including the heading and footnote No. 5, are hereby repealed.

PART FOUR

Article 51 - Effectiveness

This Act shall become effective on the 1st June 2000, with the exception of provisions of articles 16, 17 and 35, which shall become effective on the 1st December 2000.

Klaus autograph

Havel autograph

Zeman autograph

---

[34] 1E.g., Act No. 101/2000 Coll., on Protection of the Personal Data and Amendments to Some Related Acts and Act No. 123/1998 Coll., on the Right to Information about the Environment.".

[35] [3a]Article 5 (1) (h) of Act No. 101/2000 Coll., on Protection of the Personal Data and Amendments to Some Related Acts.".

Recent Developments

OPINION 4/2001 ON THE COUNCIL OF EUROPE'S DRAFT CONVENTION ON CYBER-CRIME

Adopted on 22 March 2001

THE WORKING PARTY ON THE PROTECTION OF INDIVIDUALS WITH REGARD TO THE PROCESSING OF PERSONAL DATA

set up by Directive 95/46/EC of the European Parliament and of the Council of 24 October 1995[1],
having regard to Articles 29 and 30 paragraphs 1 (a) and 3 of that Directive,
having regard to its Rules of Procedure and in particular to articles 12 and 14 thereof,
has adopted the present **Opinion:**

Introduction

Cyber-crime is part of the seamy side of the Information Society. The use of new technologies bring not only enormous benefits for societies. They also provide the opportunity to commit new kinds of crimes or traditional crimes using new means. States and various instances are conscious of this issue which is therefore dealt with for example in the European Union,[2] the G8,[3] the OECD, the United Nations and the Council of Europe. The objective of these initiatives is to create an information society where citizens can enjoy freedom and security.

The Council of Europe has a longstanding experience and tradition both in international co-operation in criminal matters as well as in Human Rights. It is working since 1997 on a draft convention on cyber-crime. The committee of experts on crime in cyberspace (PC-CY) has finished its work in December 2000 and the Parliamentary Assembly of the Council of Europe will have to give its opinion (expected for Spring 2001) before the text is to be submitted to the Committee of Ministers of the Council of Europe for adoption. Depending on the opinion of the Assembly, a drafting group will be mandated to modify the text accordingly.

---

[1] Official Journal no. L 281 of 23/11/1995, p. 31, available at: http://europa.eu.int/comm/internal_market/en/media/dataprot/index.htm

[2] See Communication from the European Commission to the Council and the European Parliament "Creating a Safer Information Society by Improving the Security of Information Infrastructures and Combating Computer-related Crime" (adopted on 26th January 2001, available at http://europa.eu.int/ISPO/eif/InternetPoliciesSite/Crime/crime1.html).

[3] See Recommendation 3/99 on the preservation of traffic data by Internet Service Providers for law enforcement purposes. Adopted on 7 September 1999. WP 25, available at http://europa.eu/comm/internal_market/en/media/dataprot/wpdocs/index.htm

Recent Developments
Opinion on Draft Cyber-Crime Convention (EC)

This draft Convention can be signed by countries which are not members of the Council of Europe. The United States, Canada, Japan and South Africa are already actively participating in the drafting process.

Since April 2000, different versions of the draft Convention have been made available to the public on the web site of the Council of Europe. The draft Explanatory memorandum was published for the first time only recently in February 2001. The drafting process on both documents is continuing. This Opinion only comments on the text of the draft convention as published on 22nd December 2000 (version 25 public)[4], not on the explanatory memorandum.

The Working Party notes the efforts being made in many areas to combat cyber crime and supports the general objectives of these efforts in the way they can contribute to improve the security level for all citizens and in particular for the processing of personal data. It would nevertheless like to give a strong message that a fair balance must be struck between anti cyber crime efforts and the fundamental rights to privacy and personal data protection of individuals as regards the extent to which measures are proposed in the whole of the draft convention. These rights are notably enshrined in the Council of Europe's European Convention on Human Rights, the 1981 Council of Europe Convention for the Protection of Individuals with regard to Automatic Processing of Personal Data, Recommendation N° R (87) 15 regulating the use of personal data in the police sector, Recommendation N° R (95) 4 on the protection of personal data in the field of telecommunications services, in particular as regards telephone services, the EU Charter on Fundamental Rights, the EU Data Protection Directives and the 1966 United Nations International Covenant on Civil and Political Rights.

For these reasons the Working Party offers the following observations on the current draft of the Council of Europe's cyber crime convention.

The Draft Convention

The content of this draft Convention as regards harmonisation of procedural measures (Chapter II) and international mutual assistance (Chapter III) results in the exchange of personal data (traffic data, content of communications and all other kinds) in the course of international co-operation in criminal matters which are not exclusively linked to cyber-crime.

Chapter III concerns international co-operation "for the purposes of investigations or proceedings concerning criminal offences related to computer systems and data or for the collection of evidence in electronic form of a criminal offence". Most obligations for mutual assistance laid down there may concern any crime for which they are sought, be it computer-related or not. The obligations include mutual assistance regarding extradition, spontaneous

---

[4] See http://coe.fr

information, preservation of computer data and traffic data, disclosure of and access to computer and traffic data, transborder access to stored data as well as real-time collection of traffic data and interception of communications. This chapter also provides for possibilities to make requests for mutual assistance by expedited means of communications including fax and e-mail. Formal confirmation has only to follow if requested by the requested Party.

The draft Convention (Chapter II section 2) also requests the Parties to harmonise their procedural law with a view to ensuring that the following measures are available: expedited preservation of stored computer data, expedited preservation and disclosure of traffic data, order a person to submit computer data under his control and a service provider to submit subscriber information under his control, search and seizure of stored computer data, real-time collection of traffic data and interception of content data.

Concerning the substantive penal law, the draft Convention (Chapter II section 1) requests parties to consider specific acts as crimes with all consequences, in particular the exercise of specific investigative powers that usually exist for criminal investigations. This is for example the case for illegal access to computer data, illegal interception, misuse of devices such as computer programs or passwords, computer related forgery and fraud, offences related to child pornography or infringements of copyright and related rights. The Working Party regrets that no provision is made on the incrimination of violation of data protection rules.

Human Rights, Privacy and Data Protection

The preamble of the draft Convention refers to the 1950 Council of Europe Convention for the Protection of Human Rights and Fundamental Freedoms (ECHR), to the 1966 United Nations International Covenant on Civil and Political Rights, (in brackets) to the 1981 Council of Europe Convention for the Protection of Individuals with regard to Automatic Processing of Personal Data, and (in brackets) to Recommendation N° R (87) 15 regulating the use of personal data in the police sector.

However, the draft Convention does not harmonise the safeguards and conditions that shall apply to the measures envisaged on the basis of the texts referred to. Though the draft convention (article 15) mentions in the context of procedural law that the "establishment, implementation and application of the powers and procedures provided in this section (Chapter II section 2), shall be subject to the conditions and safeguards provided for under the domestic law of each Party concerned", it does not require such safeguards and conditions effectively being in place.

Council of Europe countries are obliged to implement the ECHR (granting the right to privacy and data protection, secrecy of correspondence, fair trial, no punishment without law, freedom of expression and imposing precise conditions in clear legal texts to lawfully limit those rights) and other relevant instruments. They must therefore have safeguards and conditions in place, though the concrete nature and scope of those may not be identical in all member countries. However, since the draft Convention is intended to be signed also by non-Council of Europe countries, those countries are not subject to the same obligations as the Council of Europe members and this draft convention does not oblige them to introduce safeguards and conditions in accordance with International Human Rights texts.

Furthermore, the formulation in article 15 of the draft Convention could create the impression that the protection of human rights shall only be considered when it is "due" and shall only be "adequate". Furthermore, considerations on the proportionality of the powers or procedure to the nature and circumstances of the offence are not referred to as a matter of principle but only "where applicable". If this could be interpreted as limiting the safeguards and procedures, it would considerably lower, if not fully undermine, the protection of fundamental rights.

In Chapter III on International Co-operation, there is a similar lack of harmonisation of the conditions and safeguards. Some of the obligations to help the requesting party are subject to the conditions and safeguards provided for under national law (real-time collection of traffic data and interceptions of content data).[5] The other obligations are not subject to any further conditions. This means that a Council of Europe member could not refuse co-operation. It could only do so in the two cases where violation of its "ordre public" is recognised as a ground for refusal.[6] And the requirement of dual criminality (another very important safeguard) can only be invoked in limited cases.[7] As a result, in general and irrespective of national or wider concepts on safeguards and conditions, the requested party shall deliver the information, material etc. as requested by the other party. This is a desirable objective in terms of effective law enforcement and fight against crime. However, it may not pass the test of necessity, appropriateness and proportionality as required by Human Rights instruments implemented into constitutional and specific national law.

In this context, the Working Party also notes that throughout the draft Convention,[8] reference is made to "law and other measures" that the signatories are obliged to take in order to implement the Convention. The Working Party would like to draw the attention of the Council of Europe, in particular its instances currently dealing with the draft, and all potential signatories to the fact that these terms have to be interpreted in the light of the jurisprudence

---

[5] See articles 33 and 34 of draft convention.

[6] See article 27 (4b) in case no mutual legal assistance treaty applies but this chapter of the draft convention. See article 29 (5b) for expedited preservation of stored computer data and article 30 (2b) for expedited disclosure of preserved traffic data.

[7] See article 29 (3) and (4) regarding expedited preservation of stored computer data and article 30 on expedited disclosure of preserved traffic data.

[8] See articles 14, 16, 17, 18, 19, 20 on real time collection of traffic data (i.e. without a warrant or similar basis), 21 on interception of content data, 23 and 26 of the draft Convention.

of the European Court of Human Rights if the measures based on them are to be lawful limitations of the fundamental rights and freedoms.

Several EU Member States implement Directive 95/46/EC also in the "third pillar", i.e. for processing of personal data in criminal matters. Their national laws thus require that personal data can in principle only be sent to non-EU countries if this country does provide an adequate level of protection of individuals with regard to the processing of their personal data. These countries therefore need to be able to check the adequacy of the level of protection in the third country. In case no adequate protection is found, a transfer of personal data may nevertheless be necessary to fight against crime. National law may have provided for this by allowing exceptions to the principle of adequacy. The same need to set conditions may arise in other countries on the basis of their constitutional and procedural laws. Therefore, the draft Convention should, as a bare minimum, provide for the possibility to reconcile both objectives by allowing the requested party to impose specific safeguards and conditions in order make the transfer happen. Otherwise, conflicts could arise between the obligation to assist and the obligation to respect fundamental rights as granted by the European instruments and relevant jurisprudence.

Apparently Article 27bis together with Article 27(6) are intended to address this issue, but it is not fully clear how. Article 27bis as such does not explicitly mention personal data protection but "confidentiality and limitation on use" concerning "information or material". It provides only for the possibility ("may", no obligation) that the requested party subjects the furnishing of information or material to confidentiality or use limitations. At the same time, these possibilities seem to be substantially restricted: as footnote 48 indicates, confidentiality may not be granted if procedural law requires publication. Footnote 49 explains that Article 27bis is without prejudice to Article 27 on mutual assistance in the absence of international agreements. Article 27 (4) allows to refuse mutual assistance for the reasons enumerated there such as if the execution of the request is likely to prejudice its "ordre public", sovereignty, security or other essential interests. Before refusing or postponing assistance, the requested party shall consider whether the request may be granted partially or subject to (Article 27 (6)). However, it is unclear whether data protection conditions could be based on this provision since it is related to the grounds for refusal enumerated in Article 27 (4) which do not necessarily include data protection.

The Working Party is of the opinion that these provisions and their limitations are not sufficient to fully safeguard the fundamental rights to privacy and personal data protection. Citizens may not be able to foresee when and how their fundamental rights are to be restricted. The draft Convention should therefore contain at least data protection provisions outlining the protection that must be afforded to individuals who are subject of all the measures envisaged in the draft Convention. In addition, signatories should be requested to sign up to the Council of Europe's Convention 108[9] which is open for non-Council of Europe countries.

In particular Article 27bis and its relation to Article 27 (4) and (6) should be clarified in light of the preceding comments. In view of the fact that Directive 95/46/EC is typically implemented in a seamless way, i.e. including the processing of personal data in the "third pillar", there are strong arguments to conclude that the notion of "ordre public" may also cover situations where an inadequate level of protection of individuals with regard to the processing of their personal data in a requesting country would jeopardize the rights and freedoms of the persons concerned. In this context, explicit reference is made to the fact that the right to the protection of one's personal data has recently been laid down in Article 8 of the EU Charter of Fundamental Rights. The existence or non-existence of an adequate level of protection in a third country is also mentioned in the Europol Convention as an important criterium to decide on whether, and if so to what extent, personal data may be communicated by Europol to that third country for law enforcement purposes.

Whilst Article 27bis, if clarified and amended as suggested, may go some way towards addressing confidentiality and purpose limitation issues in the specific context of transfer of personal data to non Council of Europe or non EU countries, it is the Working Party's view that a signatory commitment to satisfying the requirements of Article 27bis will not necessarily constitute an adequate commitment to privacy (see above). The inclusion of data protection provisions will help to codify and clarify the test to be made regarding necessity, appropriateness and proportionality required by the instruments cited above.

It is also the Working Party's view that signatories to the convention must satisfy the requirements of data protection provisions prior to being considered to provide an adequate level of protection for the rights and freedoms of data subjects. Such an approach will assist in ensuring harmonisation of the safeguards and conditions that shall apply to the measures envisaged in the draft convention. If a party in a third country is to enjoy the benefits of a transfer of personal data to it, it must accept proper responsibility for ensuring that the fundamental rights of the individuals concerned are adequately protected once the data have been received.

Traffic data

The Working Party welcomes that, contrary to previous drafts, the current version of the Convention (version n° 25) does not include anymore a general surveillance obligation consisting in the routine retention of all traffic data. This is in line with the Working Party's

---

[9] This proposal follows the Schengen model where mutual assistance among police services for specific purposes and the exchange of personal data are based on the adherence to Convention 108 and data protection provision in the Schengen agreement itself.

Recommendation 3/99 on the preservation of traffic data by Internet Service Providers for law enforcement purposes, adopted on 7 September 1999[10], which explains the legal arguments[11] opposing such general obligation.

Also the EU Data Protection Commissioners at their Spring 2000 Conference in Stockholm took a strong position against such measure. They adopted a resolution expressing that they "note with concern proposals that ISPs should routinely retain traffic data beyond the requirements of billing purposes in order to permit access by law enforcement bodies. The Conference emphasises that such retention would be an improper invasion of the fundamental rights guaranteed to individuals by Article 8 of the European Convention on Human Rights. Where traffic data are to be retained in specific cases, there must be a demonstrable need, the period of retention must be as short as possible and the practice must be clearly regulated by law."

The views on this issue are converging. Other institutions and groups such as the International Working Group on Data Protection in Telecommunications in its Common Position on data protection aspects in the draft convention.[12] Have also expressed substantial reservations.

Nevertheless, the provisions in the draft Convention concerning traffic data raise serious concerns: Articles 29 and 30 on expedited preservation and disclosure of traffic and other data do not provide for the possibility for the requested party to refuse such assistance for data protection reasons, but only for the similar general grounds as discussed above ("ordre public" etc.). At the same time, the obligations that stored computer data and traffic data are to be preserved upon request for at least 60 days in order to allow a decision being taken on why they are needed and how they should be used, present a considerable burden on business (telecommunications operators, internet service providers and all others) and private persons. Similar concerns apply to Article 20 which obliges service providers to collect or record within their technical capability traffic data in real-time.

Generally speaking, business may need more legal security as to their obligations and their concrete implementation. They may fear that consumers cannot have sufficient trust and confidence in their products and services in case it is not clear who and when does access confidential information and communications.

---

[10] Available at: http://europa.eu.int/comm/internal-_market/en/media/dataprot/wpdocs/index.htm

[11] Referring in particular to Directive 97/66/EC.

[12] International Working Group on Data Protection in Telecommunications, Common Position on Data Protection aspects in the Draft Convention on Cyber-crime of the Council of Europe, adopted at its 28th meeting on 13/14 September 2000 in Berlin,. Available at:, http://www.datenschutz-berlin.de/doc/int/iwgdpt/cy_en.htm.

Recent Developments
Opinion on Draft Cyber-Crime Convention (EC)

Conclusions

The Working Party emphasises the Council of Europe's important role as efficient guardian of fundamental rights and freedoms for decades. The Working Party takes the view that the Council of Europe, in promoting international co-operation in matters of cyber-crime outside its own membership, needs to pay particular attention to the protection of fundamental rights and freedoms, especially the right to privacy and personal data protection.

The Working Party therefore sees a need for clarification of the text of the articles of the draft convention because their wording is often too vague and confusing and may not qualify as a sufficient basis for relevant laws and mandatory measures that are intended to lawfully limit fundamental rights and freedoms. Explanations in the explanatory memorandum cannot replace legal clarity of the text itself.

Most of the provisions of the draft Convention have a strong impact on the fundamental rights to privacy and personal data protection. As described above, the choices expressed in the current text of the draft Convention do, to a certain extent, anticipate the result of the examination necessary if the fundamental right to privacy (Article 8 of ECHR) and others are to be restricted.[13] One of the basic questions in this respect is whether a measure is necessary in a specific case, if so, whether it is appropriate, proportionate and not excessive. Some of the elements of the draft Convention are completely new and their impact on the fundamental rights, in particular the right to privacy and data protection, may not have been sufficiently evaluated by the committee of experts on crime in cyber-space (PC-CY). The Working Party sees a need to improve the justification of the measures envisaged in terms of necessity, appropriateness and proportionality as required by the Human Rights and Data Protection instruments referred to above.

The Working Party strongly recommends that the draft Convention should contain data protection provisions outlining the protections that must be afforded to individuals who are subject of the information to be processed in connection with all the measures envisaged in the draft Convention. Article 27bis should also be included (thus delete the brackets) and improved as indicated. The inclusion of data protection provisions will help to codify and clarify the requirements of necessity, appropriateness and proportionality required by the "acquis" of the Council of Europe and EU Member States.

The Working Party is furthermore of the opinion that the reference to Convention 108 should be included into the preamble (thus the brackets to be deleted), though this has no binding effect, and signatories to the Cyber crime Convention should be invited to sign up to

---

[13] For example interception of communications and traffic data fully break the secrecy of correspondence (see Malone judgement of the European Court of Human Rights).

Convention 108 on the Protection of Individuals with regard to Automated Processing of Personal Data.

Furthermore, the Working Party regrets that no provision is made in the draft Convention on the incrimination of violations of data protection rules.

The Working Party sees a discrepancy in treatment of Council of Europe countries and others because Council of Europe members have to respect their obligations following from the European Convention Human Rights, Convention 108, relevant Council of Europe Recommendations, the EU Charter on Fundamental Rights, the EU Data Protection Directives and relevant national legislation whereas non Council of Europe countries have, on the basis of the current draft convention, not the same or similar obligations.

The Working Party furthermore takes the view that signatories to the Convention must accept proper responsibility for ensuring that the fundamental rights of individuals are adequately protected once the data concerning them have been received from the European Union and Council of Europe member countries.

The position proposed in the current draft convention (public version 25) not to oblige signatories to compel service providers to retain traffic data of all communications should in no way be revised.

The Working Party regrets the very late release of relevant documents. The Working Party considers it highly desirable that the public debate be prolonged involving all parties concerned (human rights organisations, industry etc.) before the Parliamentary Assembly of the Council of Europe debates and decides.

The Working Party is of the view that a large number of the deficiencies highlighted before in this opinion, apparently result from the fact that the Council of Europe has not made the best possible use of the available expertise in data protection matters. The Working Party therefore invites the Council of Europe, and especially the EU Member States, to consult their data protection experts before finalising their position on the draft Convention, and to make the best possible use of their contributions.

The Working Party invites the Council of Europe, the European Commission, the European Parliament and Member States to take into account this opinion.

The Working Party reserves the possibility to issue further comments.

Done at Brussels, 22 March 2001

Recent Developments
Opinion on Draft Cyber-Crime Convention (EC)

For the Working Party
The Chairman
Stefano RODOTA

OPINION 3/2001 ON THE LEVEL OF PROTECTION OF THE AUSTRALIAN PRIVACY AMENDMENT (PRIVATE SECTOR) ACT 2000

Adopted on 26th January 2001

THE WORKING PARTY ON THE PROTECTION OF INDIVIDUALS WITH REGARD TO THE PROCESSING OF PERSONAL DATA

set up by Directive 95/46/EC of the European Parliament and of the Council of 24 October 1995[1]

having regard to Articles 29 and 30 paragraphs 1 (a) and 3 of that Directive,

having regard to its Rules of Procedure and in particular to articles 12 and 14 thereof

has adopted the following **OPINION**:

Introduction

Australia has had legislation covering the Commonwealth (federal) public sector since 1988 where the Privacy Act sets down detailed Information Privacy Principles (IPPs) based on the 1980 OECD Guidelines. The Privacy Act also applies to the private sector to the extent that it includes provisions and guidelines governing the consumer credit industry and restricting the use of tax file number information.[2] The Privacy Act created the Office of the Privacy Commissioner as a member of the Human Rights and Equal Opportunity Commission but since 1st July 2000, the Privacy Commissioner is established as a separate statutory agency.

The Privacy Amendment (Private Sector) Bill 2000 was passed by the Australian Parliament on 6 December 2000 and received Royal Assent on 21 December 2000. The new legislation contains amendments to the Commonwealth Privacy Act 1988 that will regulate the handling of personal information by private sector organisations. It will come into effect on 21 December 2001.

The Act implements the National Privacy Principles based on the National Principles for Fair Handling of Personal Information (NPPs) developed by the Federal Privacy Commissioner and released first in 1998 after extensive consultation with businesses and consumers. In the Act, the national principles provide a default framework setting out minimum standards in relation to how organisations should collect, use and disclose personal information. Private sector

---

[1] Official Journal no. L 281 of 23/11/1995, p. 31, available at: http://europa.eu.int/comm/internal_market/en/media/dataprot/index.htm

[2] Other Commonwealth laws contain specific privacy provisions relating to information about health insurance claims, data matching, information about old criminal convictions and personal information disclosed by telecommunications companies (Telecommunications Act 1997)

organisations are bound by the national principles unless they have their own privacy code that has been approved by the Privacy Commissioner. For ease of reference the National Principles are attached in annex 1.

Privacy Amendment (Private Sector) Act 2000

The working party welcomes the adoption of the Act and the work carried out in the past two years by the Privacy Commissioner, the Government and all interested parties which first led to the drafting of the National Principles for the Handling of Personal Information. It supports the Australian government goal to enhance the protection of personal data processed by the private sector and considers this work of great importance towards the fulfilment of Australia's commitment to abide by the 1980 OECD guidelines. It recognises the innovative value s of the co-regulatory scheme which aims at bridging the gap between legislation and self-regulation by giving the latter the force of law.

From an European perspective, national data protection commissioners welcome developments that strengthen privacy protection in third countries as a means of meeting the requirements laid down in Articles 25 and 26 of the EU directive for data to flow to third countries. The working party also notes with interest it is possible for organisations to apply to the Privacy Commissioner to have a Privacy code approved which would operate in place of the standards in the legislation and that the Privacy Commissioner may only approve a code if it provides at least the same standard of privacy protection as the NPPs.

Sectors and activities excluded

The working party notes with concern that some sectors and activities are excluded from the protections of the Act. In particular:

Small business: only small businesses deemed to pose a high risk to privacy are required to comply with the legislation.[3]

Moreover small business operators may choose to fall within the scope of the Act and to that effect notify their adherence to its provisions to the privacy Commissioner who keeps a register to that effect. Even though this possibility allows to identity the small business that

---

[3] These small businesses are identified in Section 6D of the Act as those that have an annual turnover of $3.000.000 or less and :

    -provide a health service to another individual and hold health information except in an employee record, or ·

    -collect from third parties or/and disclose personal information about another individual to third parties for a benefit, service or advantage unless the collection/disclosure is carried out with the individual's consent or as required or authorized by legislation or
    -are contracted to provide a service to the Commonwealth

voluntarily fall under the Act, the complexity of this exemption is such that it makes it very difficult to determine: a) what Australian business is a small business and b) whether or not it is exempt from the provisions of the Act.

The working party notes that this uncertainty renders it necessary to assume that all data transfers to Australian businesses are potentially to a small business operator which is not subject to the law, unless the name of the small business is inserted in the Privacy Commissioner's Register.

Employee data:

An Act or practice engaged in by an organisation that is or was an employer of an individual is exempt from the Act if the act or practice is directly related to:

>   a) a current or former employment relationship between the employer and the individual, and
>
>   b) an employee record held by the organisation and relating to that individual

Employee records are defined in subsection 6 (1) in the broadest sense including information about the engagement, terms and conditions of contract, evaluative material over the performance of the contract, employee's emergency contacts, trade union membership, recreation long leave, taxation, banking affairs, etc.

The working party notes that employee related data often contains sensitive data and sees no reason to exclude it at least from the protection given by NPP 10 for sensitive information. Moreover the exemptions allows information about previous employers to be collected and disclosed to a third party (eg a future employer) without the employee being informed.

It is the working party's opinion that the risk of privacy violations makes it all the more important to impose additional safeguards when exporting this type of data to Australia[4] and recommends that operators put into place appropriate means to do so (for example through contractual clauses).

Exceptions:

Exceptions to substantive data protection principles on the grounds that it is authorised by law:

National Privacy Principle NPP 2.1 (g) allows information to be used or disclosed for a secondary purpose where the use or disclosure is required or authorised by or under law.[5]

---

[4] There is no exemption for employee records in the 1988 Privacy Act for the public sector.

[5] According to the Explanatory Memorandum page 119, the reference to "authorised encompasses circumstances where the law permits, but does not require, use or disclosure". The reference to law (instead of legislation) is broad and may include any binding act

Recent Developments
Opinion on the Australian Privacy Act (EC)

In the working party's view it is acceptable to provide for an exception when organisations are faced with conflicting legal obligations, but to widen the exception to cover all options offered by sector specific laws, past present and future, risks undermining legal certainty and devoid the content of the basic protection. The wording "authorized" as opposed to "specifically authorized" which existed in the January 1999 edition of the National Principles can also be read to mean that all secondary purposes that are not forbidden are allowed. In the working party's view such a wide exemption would virtually devoid the purpose limitation principle of any value.

Publicly available data:

The collection of data for the purpose of including it in a generally available publication fall within the scope of NPPs1 (collection) but once the information is compiled in a format such that it comes within the definition of a generally available publication, the remaining Privacy Principles are not applied. This excludes all individual rights such as access and correction.

The working party notes that excluding publicly available personal data and in particular the secondary uses thereof from any protection is contrary to line taken by the directive. Moreover the 1980 OECD guidelines contain no such general exemption.

Transparency to data subjects:

NPP 1.3 (collection) allows for organisations to inform individuals before or at the time of collection but also adds that, if this is not practicable, it may inform individuals as soon as practicable thereafter.

The working party notes that allowing organisations to inform individuals after collection has been carried out is contrary to Principle 9 of the OECD Guidelines.[6] This issue is of importance particularly with regard to sensitive data - where consent is one of the triggers for collection to be lawful in NPP 10.1.

Collection and use of data in particular with regard to direct marketing

NPPs 1 (collection) and 2 (use and disclosure) cover the purpose limitation principle by requiring collection of personal information to be necessary and by fair and lawful means,[7] and by placing limits and conditions on use and disclosure.[8]

---

[6] The purposes for which personal data are collected should be specified not later than at the time of data collection and the subsequent use limited to the fulfilment of those purposes or such others as are not incompatible with those purposes and as are specified on each occasion of change of purpose

[7] Privacy Amendment (Private Sector) Act 2000, Schedule 3, NPP1.1 & 1.2

[8] Privacy Amendment (Private Sector) Act 2000, Schedule 3, NPP2

But the limitations with regard to use and disclosure concern only the secondary purpose. Processing for the 'primary' purpose of collection and 'related purposes within the reasonable expectation of the individual' are allowed provided that the individual has been given notice - consent is not required.

A practical result of this set up is that to use personal data for direct marketing it is not necessary to obtain the individual's consent (or respect any of the other limitations in NPP 2) if direct marketing is the primary purpose of collection. If instead it is the secondary purpose, opt-out must be provided every time the organisation sends the individual direct marketing material.

The working party recalls its opinion on "Transfers of personal data to third countries - WP 12" where it determined that allowing personal data to be used for direct marketing without an opt-out being offered cannot in any circumstance be considered adequate.

Sensitive data

National Privacy Principle 10 (sensitive information) places limitations only to the collection of sensitive data. There are no special restrictions or conditions on the use or disclosure of such data - other than health data, for which there are some provisions in NPP 2. The Act therefore allows most sensitive information which has been collected for a legitimate purpose to be used for other purposes subject only to the normal restrictions that apply to all types of data.

The working party notes that in the EU it is forbidden to process (i.e. collect, use and disclose) sensitive data unless one of a number of specific exemptions apply.

Lack of correction rights for EU citizens

Section 41 (4) allows the Privacy Commissioner to investigate an act or practice under NPP 6 or 7 only if it is an interference with the privacy of Australian citizens and the permanent residents. As a result, EU citizens that are no permanent residents in Australia but whose data was transferred from the EU to Australia may not exercise access and correction rights in relation to their data.

Onward transfers from Australia to other third countries

NPP 9 prohibits exports of personal information by an organisation to someone in a foreign country (other than an affiliate of the organisation itself) unless one of six conditions applies.

With reference to NPP 9 (a) : (applicable when recipient of the information is subject to a law, binding scheme or contract which effectively upholds principles for fair handling of the information that are substantially similar to the National Privacy Principles) the working party is of the opinion that the assistance of the Privacy Commissioner in indicating what third country regime can be considered as substantially similar to the Australian domestic situation is advisable.

With reference to NPP 9(f): (which applies when all the other five conditions are not applicable, hence when the recipient is not subject to a law, binding scheme or contract) the working party notes that this provision does not take into account the individuals' right to see his rights enforced.Moreover, the working party notes that Section 5 on the extra territorial operation of the Act, applies only to Australians and does not extend the protection of NPP9 to non-Australians. This means that an Australian company can import data from European citizens and subsequently export it to a country with no privacy laws without the Australian Act applying. Such a measure would make it possible to circumvent the EU Directive, if Australia was recognised as providing adequate protection.

Conclusions

On the basis of the above, the working party considers that data transfers to Australia could be regarded as adequate only if appropriate safeguards were introduced to meet the above mentioned concerns. This could be done for example through voluntary codes of conduct foreseen in Part IIIAA of the Act taking into account that the enforcement of voluntary codes is done either by the Privacy Commissioner himself or by an independent adjudicator.

But with a view to obtain a more comprehensive adequacy assessment, the working party encourages the Commission to continue to follow the issue to seek improvements of general application and to keep the Working Party informed of developments.

Done at Brussels, 26th January 2001
For the Working Party
The Chairman
Stefano RODOTA

OPINION 2/2001 ON THE ADEQUACY OF THE CANADIAN PERSONAL INFORMATION AND ELECTRONIC DOCUMENTS ACT

Adopted on 26th January 2001

THE WORKING PARTY ON THE PROTECTION OF INDIVIDUALS WITH REGARD TO THE PROCESSING OF PERSONAL DATA

set up by Directive 95/46/EC of the European Parliament and of the Council of 24 October 1995,[1]

having regard to Articles 29 and 30 paragraphs 1 (a) and 3 of that Directive,

having regard to its Rules of Procedure and in particular to articles 12 and 14 thereof

has adopted the following **OPINION**:

Introduction

Canada has had federal legislation to protect personal information in the public sector since the 1983 Privacy Act. The Act establishes rules applying to information collected and used by government and introduces a fair information code to regulate government handling of personal records. It also gives the Federal Privacy Commissioner broad powers to investigate individuals' complaints, to launch complaints and to audit federal agencies' compliance. Most provinces (with the exception of Prince Edward island) have similar provisions. The Privacy Act is currently being reviewed.

As for the private sector, the Personal Information and Electronic Documents Act received Royal Assent on 13 April 2000. The Act will apply to private sector organisations that collect, use or disclose personal information in the course of commercial activities. It enter into force in three stages:

Stage 1 : On 1st January 2001, the Act will apply to every organisation which operates as a federal work, undertaking or business. It will apply to personal information of clients and employees in the federally regulated private sector, such as airlines, banking, broadcasting, inter-provincial transportation and telecommunications. The law will also apply to all

---

[1]   Official Journal no. L 281 of 23/11/1995, p. 31, available at: http://europa.eu.int/comm/internal_market/en/media/dataprot/index.htm

organisations that disclose personal information for consideration outside a province or outside Canada.

Stage 2 : On 1st January 2002, the law will apply to personal health information for the organisations and activities already covered in the first stage (i.e. federally regulated private sector or out of province/country exchanges).

Stage 3: As from 1st January 2004, the law will extend to every organisation that collects, uses or discloses personal information in the course of a commercial activity within a province, whether or not the organisation is a federally-regulated business or not. Where and whenever a province adopts legislation that is substantially similar, the organisations, classes of organisations or activities covered will be exempted from the application of the federal law for intra-provincial transactions.

The Personal Information and Electronic Documents Act The privacy provisions in Schedule 1 of the Act are those of the CSA Model Code for the Protection of Personal Information, recognised as the Canadian national standard in 1996.

These provisions have been compared with the main provisions of the directive taking into account the Working Party's opinion on "Transfers of personal data to third countries : Applying Articles 25 and 26 of the EU data protection directive.[2]

Below are some specific issues to which the Working Party draws the Commission's attention:

Scope of the Act

Organisations covered: The Act applies to every organisation and in its first stage to organisations that operate as a federal work, undertaking or business. An organisation includes an association, a partnership, a person and a trade union. The Act contains a non-exhaustive list of federal works subject to the Act. Although most federally regulated organisations are captured under this definition, not all types of organisations are federal works. For instance, insurance companies and credit unions are not federal works for the purposes of the Act.[3]

---

[2] WP12 - adopted by the Working Party on 24 July 1998, available at: http://www.europa.eu.int/comm/internal_market/en/media/dataprot/wpdocs/index.htm

[3] See « Your privacy responsabilities - A guide for businesses and organisations » issued by the Federal privacy Commissionner, page 3 available at http://www.privcom.gc.ca

Recent Developments
Opinion on the Canadian Personal Information Act (EC)

Commercial activity: The Act applies to information that is collected, used or disclosed in the course of commercial activities. These include any transaction or any regular course of conduct that is of a commercial character including the selling, battering or leasing of donor, membership of other fund-raising lists.

Non-profit organisations and charities are therefore not subject to the Act unless they engage in a commercial activity.

Furthermore, the Act does not apply when an organisation uses personal information solely for journalistic, artistic or literary purposes, nor does it apply to personal information used solely for personal or domestic purposes. Organisations to which the federal Privacy Act applies are also not covered.

Sensitive Data:

The Working Party notes that sensitive data is not identified as such. Data is regarded as sensitive depending on the context in which it is used. There is no prohibition on the collection of sensitive data. However, clause 4.3.4 of Schedule 1 requires organizations to take into account the sensitivity of the information in determining the form of the consent sought for its collection. Clause 4.3.6 recommends that an organisation "should" generally seek express consent when the information is likely to be considered sensitive. Furthermore, clause 4.7.2 of Schedule 1 states that more sensitive information should be safeguarded by a higher level of protection.

The Working Party would welcome the systematic use of highest level of protection when sensitive data is processed and encourages the Canadian authorities and in particular the Privacy Commissioner to work towards this goal.

The Act also lists several specific situations (sections 7(1), (2) and (3)) where personal information (including data that can be considered sensitive in Europe) may be collected, used or disclosed without the knowledge or consent of the individual. Having examined them, the Working Party considers that the specific circumstances warrant these exceptions.

In particular, the Working Party draws attention to the Section 7(1)(d), (2)(c.1) or (3)(h.1) which allows the use and disclosure of personal information, without the knowledge or consent of the individual, if the information is publicly available and is specified by the

Regulations. The Regulations issued by Industry Canada limit the secondary uses of the data and provide sufficient and adequate safeguards for this type of data.[4]

Health data : The legislation exempts "personal health information" from its ambit for one year after the legislation comes into force(2.1), that is in January 1, 2002. Personal health information, with respect to an individual, whether living or deceased, is defined as follows:

> information concerning the physical or mental health of the individual; information concerning any health service provided to the individual; information concerning the donation by the individual of any body part or any bodily substance of the individual or information derived from the testing or examination of a body part or bodily substance of the individual; information that is collected in the course of providing health services to the individual; or information that is collected incidentally to the provision of health services to the individual.

The Working Party draws the attention to the fact that the Privacy Act applies to all public sector health institutions. Moreover, most of the health information in private organisations will not be covered by the Personal Information and Electronic Documents Act until 2004, when the Act applies to provincial organizations in the commercial sector where most such information is found.

Health Canada is coordinating the efforts of a federal/provincial/territorial working group, the Protection of Personal Health Information Working Group, which is currently developing a Harmonization Resolution for the treatment of personal health information in Canada. This resolution is not legally binding but outlines a set of voluntary principles for the protection of personal health information across Canada. It applies to the health system whether in the public or private sector. As part of this process, provinces and territories are being asked to conduct a review of personal health information protection in their respective jurisdiction, and where necessary, to work towards developing legislation and/or other measures consistent with the Resolution.

Attached for information purposes is a paper released by Industry Canada on the status of the provisions currently in force or being debated throughout Canada (annex 1).
The Working Party encourages all efforts aiming for a comprehensive and coherent rules for health throughout Canada.

Employment data

---

[4] 4 See « The regulations specifying publicly available information and investigative bodies », published in Part 1 of the Canada Gazette and available at http://www.canada.gc.ca/gazette/part1/

Initially the Act applies will only apply to personal information about an employee of organisations which collects, uses or discloses personal information in connection with the operation of a federal work undertaking or businesses. As from 1st January 2004, the application of the Act will extent to all organisations whether or not they are federally regulated.

Personal information is defined as information about an identifiable individual but it does not include the name, title, business address or telephone number of an employee of an organisation.[5] This type of information is therefore excluded from the application of the Act. But should this information be combined with personal information, the Act will apply.

Also as from 1 January 2001, the Act will apply to disclosures of personal data across outside a province for consideration (where the personal information itself is the subject of the trade).

Considering the specific case of employee data exported from the EU to Canada, the Working Party notes that this will fall under the Act as from 1st January 2001, if the data is about an employee of a Canadian federally related work or if the exchange of information is carried out for a commercial purpose. In all other cases, the Act will apply as of 1st January 2004.

Interaction with Provincial legislation and Onward transfers

Given the progressive entry into force of the Act and its interaction with other provisions, the Working Party draws the attention of the Commission to flows of personal data within Canada (eg from an organisation subject to the Act company to one beyond its scope) or outside Canada.

Clause 4.1.3 of Schedule 1 states that an organisation is responsible for information that has been transferred to a third party for processing. An organization needs consent to collect personal information from another organization if the personal information is collected during the course of commercial activity. The organization also needs consent to use this personal information and to disclose it to another organization. In the example above, an insurance company would need consent before they were allowed to disclose personal information to another organization, regardless of whether the receiving organization was outside or inside the scope of the Act. Clause 4.1.3 also indicates that an organisation shall use contractual or other means to provide a comparable level of protection while the information is being processed by a third party.

---

[5] See Chapter 5, Part I, 2 (1)

Recent Developments
Opinion on the Canadian Personal Information Act (EC)

The Working Party is of the opinion that the transfer of data outside Canada would require the use of contractual or other binding provisions able to provide a comparable level of protection and encourages the Canadian authorities to issue guidance to this effect.

Substantially similar process: If a province passes a law that is deemed substantially similar to the federal Act, the organisations or activities covered by the provincial law will no longer be subject to the federal law for intra provincial transactions. The federal Act will continue to apply to all interprovincial and international collections, uses and disclosures of personal information.

Before establishing the formal procedure for substantially similar determination, Industry Canada has indicated that it will consult with stakeholders and provincial governments on the procedures that would be most appropriate in implementing the substantially similar provision of the Act. Key issues include the matter of who could initiate such a process, the criteria for meeting the substantially similar test, and the nature of public involvement in the process. In January, 2001 Industry Canada will likely release a position paper outlining options on these key questions.

Conclusions

In light of the issues raised, the Working Party

draws the attention of the Commission and the Art. 31 Committee to the fact that the Act only applies to private sector organisations that collect, use or discloses personal information in the course of commercial activities. Moreover the Act will enter into force in three stages, full implementation being scheduled only for 2004.

It recommends therefore that any adequacy finding for the Personal Information and Electronic Documents Act should reflect the limitations in scope and the implementation timetable.

Moreover, the Working Party invites the Commission and the Art. 31 Committee to look into the process leading to the definition of "substantially similar" and to ascertain whether it is appropriate to individually recognise provincial laws as providing an adequate level of protection or if the same objective can be attained at the Federal level through an Order in Council. This issue is of particular importance in the case of Quebec where the "Loi sur la protection des renseignements personnels dans le secteur Privé" is currently in force.

The Working Party also invites the Commission to follow the process with regard to health data and encourages any initiatives that will foster coherence of rules throughout Canada.

Finally the Working Party welcomes any initiative on the part of the Canadian authorities with a view to provide the highest possible protection for sensitive data and ensure that a comparable level of protection is provided for when data is transferred from Canada to the another country.

Done at Brussels, 26th January 2001

For the Working Party
The Chairman
Stefano RODOTA

Annex 1 Provincial and Territorial Information Protection Legislation

BRITISH COLUMBIA

Public Sector Legislation

The Freedom of Information and Protection of Privacy Act applies to most provincial government, local government, and self-governing professional bodies in British Columbia. These public bodies are ministries, agencies, boards, and crown corporations; hospitals, municipalities, regional districts, municipal police, school districts, universities, and colleges; and numerous professional bodies, such as the British Columbia College of Teachers, the College of Physicians and Surgeons, and the Law Society of British Columbia.

The Act provides individuals with specific information and privacy rights with regards to information that is collected or controlled by public bodies in British Columbia. Individuals have two major rights under the Act: the right of access to records in the custody or under the control of a public body, including one's own personal information, and the right of protection of the privacy of one's personal information in the custody or under the control of a public body. The Act contains rules that a public body must follow when it wants to collect, use, or disclose an individual's personal information. Individuals also have the right to request correction of their personal information if they think it is inaccurate, and the right to ask the Information and Privacy Commissioner to investigate if they think their rights are not being upheld.
URL: http://www.oipcbc.org/BCLAW.html

Other Privacy Legislation

In late 1999, the province released a discussion paper titled Protecting Personal Privacy in the Private Sector. A Special Committee on Information Privacy in the Private Sector input has conducted consultations and hearings on this paper. A report from the Committee has yet to be released.

The province's public sector privacy legislation is the Freedom of Information and Protection of Privacy Act. Its coverage includes health information by all publicly funded health organizations and health care providers, including clinics, universities, hospitals. Only practitioners in private practice and private clinics fall outside the scope of this Act. It is expected that private sector legislation, which would also be broad and non-specific would apply to the private health care sector.

ALBERTA

Public Sector Legislation

Alberta's Freedom of Information and Protection of Privacy Act applies to departments, branches or offices of the Government of Alberta, including agencies, boards, commissions, and corporations. It applies to local public bodies (educational, health care or municipal government) as well as health care bodies (hospitals, nursing homes, health boards, community health councils, etc) and educational bodies (universities, colleges, technical institutes, charter schools, etc).

With respect to privacy, the Act controls the manner in which a public body may collect personal information from individuals, to control the use that a public body may make of that information and to control the disclosure by a public body of that information. It allows individuals, subject to limited and specific exception, the right to access their personal information when it is held by a public body, and it allows individuals a right to request corrections to this information. It provides for independent reviews of decisions made by public bodies under the Act and the resolution of complaints.

URL: http://www.gov.ab.ca/foip/legislation/foip_act/index.cfm

Other Privacy Legislation

The province's Bill 40, Health Information Act was assented to in December 1999, but has not yet come into force. The Act applies primarily to the publicly funded health sector, but it also covers pharmacists and physicians, regardless of how they're paid. Currently, physicians and pharmacists are not subject to any law.

The province's Freedom of Information and Protection of Privacy Act currently covers the province's Department of Health and the health authorities, which are subject to the Act as public bodies. When the new Health Information Act comes into force the health authorities and the Department of Health will be subject to its provisions, just like physicians and pharmacists.

SASKATCHEWAN

Public Sector Legislation

The Freedom of Information and Protection of Privacy Act covers all government institutions, including the office of Executive Council and any department, secretariat or other similar agency of the executive government of Saskatchewan. It also covers boards, commissions, Crown corporations and bodies of government. The Act The Freedom of Information and Protection of Privacy Act allows people to apply for access to information possessed or controlled by government, subject to certain exemptions. The Act also establishes privacy rules for how the government may collect and use personal information.
URL: http://www.qp.gov.sk.ca/orphan/legislation/F22-01.htm

The Local Authority Freedom of Information and Protection of Privacy Act allows people, subject to certain exemptions, to apply for access to information possessed or controlled by a local authority, such as a municipality, board of education, hospital or special-care home. The Act also establishes privacy rules for how a local authority may collect and use personal information. Local authorities are defined as rural, urban or northern municipalities, their boards, commissions.
URL: http://www.qp.gov.sk.ca/orphan/Legislation/L27-1.htm

Other Privacy Legislation

Saskatchewan's The Health Information Protection Act was assented to in May 1999, but has not yet come into force. It applies to the entire health care sector, both public and private.

MANITOBA

Public Sector Legislation

The Freedom of Information and Protection of Privacy Act (FIPPA) provides Manitobans and others with a right of access to records of public bodies, subject to certain specified exceptions, and with protection for personal information held by public bodies. FIPPA sets out requirements that public bodies must follow to protect the personal information that they hold. These requirements embody the principles of 'fair information practices'. These rules cover the collection, use, disclosure and management of personal information. Individuals are provided access to their information and have the opportunity to correct this information. Principles of openness and accountability also apply. The Act states that there should be an avenue of independent review for individuals concerned about the personal information policies, practices or holdings of an organization. The Act also provides for independent review by the Manitoba Ombudsman of the decisions and actions of public bodies relating to access to records and personal information protection.

Recent Developments
Opinion on the Canadian Personal Information Act (EC)

FIPPA applies to Manitoba government departments and agencies and covers all local governments, school divisions, community colleges, universities, regional health authorities and hospitals.

Records specifically dealt with under the Personal Health Information Act are not covered by FIPPA.

URL: http://www.gov.mb.ca/chc/fippa/actandregs/index.html

Other Privacy Legislation

The province's The Personal Health Information Act came into force in 1997. It applies to the entire health care sector in Manitoba, public and private.

ONTARIO

Public Sector Legislation

The Freedom of Information and Protection of Privacy Act applies to Ontario's provincial ministries and agencies, boards and most commissions, as well as community colleges and district health councils.

The Act requires that the government protect the privacy of an individual's personal information existing in government records. It establishes rules regarding the collection, retention, use, disclosure and disposal of personal information in its custody or control. If an individual feels his or her privacy has been compromised by a government organization governed by the Act, he or she may complain to the Information and Privacy Commissioner who may investigate the complaint. The Act also gives individuals the right to request access to government information, including most general records and records containing their own personal information.

URL: http://www.ipc.on.ca/english/acts/prov-act.htm

The Municipal Freedom of Information and Protection of Privacy Act applies to municipalities, local boards, agencies and commissions. This may include information held by a city clerk, a school board, board of health, public utility or police commission. The Act requires that local government organizations protect the privacy of an individual's personal information existing in government records. It establishes rules regarding the collection, retention, use, disclosure and disposal of personal information in its custody or control. If an individual feels his or her privacy has been compromised by a government organization governed by the Act, he or she may complain to the Information and Privacy Commissioner who may investigate the complaint. It also gives individuals the right to request access to municipal government information, including most general records and records containing their own personal information.

URL: http://www.ipc.on.ca/english/acts/mun-act.htm

Other Privacy Legislation

Ontario is currently undertaking consultation on two proposed privacy laws. The first is a proposed Ontario Privacy Act and the second is a proposed Personal Health Information Privacy Legislation for the Health Sector.

The province is at this time receiving input from various stakeholders on these proposed legislation.

QUEBEC

Public Sector Legislation

Loi sur l'accès aux documents des organismes publics et sur la protection des renseignements personnels - details to come.
URL: http://www.cai.gouv.qc.ca/loi.htm

Other Privacy Legislation

Quebec's Act respecting the Protection of Personal Information in the Private Sector is not sector specific. As such, it covers personal health information in the private sector. The Act respecting Access to documents held by public bodies and the protection of personal information applies to the remainder of the health care sector.

NEW BRUNSWICK

Details on possible public sector still to come.

A Protection of Personal Information Act was assented to in 1998. It will come into force on January 1, 2001. The Act is specific to the public sector, and will cover private information including personal health information. It applies to organizations like the Ministry of Health, hospitals, universities, and labs (which are all publicly funded in New-Brunswick). However, health care providers, even those offering publicly funded health care, are not covered.

NOVA SCOTIA

Public Sector Legislation

The Freedom of Information and Protection of Privacy Act provides access to most records under the control of the provincial government while protecting the privacy of individuals who do not want their personal information made public. Privacy protection rules cover the collection, use and release of personal information. The Act also gives individuals the right to correct personal information about themselves. They also have the right to appeal decisions if the requested changes were not made. The Act does not apply to records of the Legislature, municipalities and educational institutions.

URL: http://www.gov.ns.ca/govt/foi/act.htm

Other Privacy Legislation

Province has no legislation specific to health information in the private sector. Its Freedom of Information and Protection of Privacy Act covers personal information in the hands of public sector bodies, including hospitals. However, the handling of patient records is covered by the provinces Hospitals Act, section 71.

PRINCE EDWARD ISLAND

The province has no privacy legislation, covering neither the public or private sector. A Freedom of Information and Protection of Privacy Act, which would have covered the public sector, died on the Order Paper and is not in force

NEWFOUNDLAND AND LABRADOR

The province has no privacy legislation, neither for the public or private sector.

NORTHWEST TERRITORIES (NWT)

Northwest Territories has an Access to Information and Protection of Privacy Act which covers personal information held in the public sector, including personal health information. The Act applies to government bodies and Health Boards, which are public sector bodies responsible for administering the delivery health care in NWT through nursing stations and public health care clinics. The hospital in Yellowknife is also run by a Health Board. All organizations under the responsibility of the health boards fall under the Act including their employees. Private health clinics currently fall beyond the scope of the Act, even though practitioners bill the government for services rendered. These clinics are likely to be purchased by the government in the near future. However, it is yet uncertain how the Act will apply to them.

The government is presently at the initial stages of preparing for the development of a Health Information Act.

YUKON

Yukon's Access to Information and Protection of Personal Information Act covers all public sector organizations and their employees. Its coverage includes personal health information. The government of Yukon's Ministry of Health and Social Services serves a dual function. It not only funds health care in the Yukon, it also acts as a Regional Health Authority which delivers health services directly to residents of the Territory. As such, health care providers which deliver services for the Ministry are covered by the Act.

NUNAVUT

Nunavut has an Access to Information and Protection of Privacy Act which covers personal information (including personal health information) in the public sector. Nunavut's Medical Care Act covers personal health information held by health care providers and all employees engaged in the administration of the Act.

The Act applies to government bodies and Regional Offices, which are public sector bodies responsible for administering the delivery health care in Nunavut through nursing stations and public health care clinics. All organizations under the responsibility of the Regional Offices (including hospitals) fall under the Act, including their employees. Private health clinics currently fall beyond the scope of the Act.

OPINION 7/2000 ON THE EUROPEAN COMMISSION PROPOSAL FOR A DIRECTIVE OF THE EUROPEAN PARLIAMENT AND OF THE COUNCIL CONCERNING THE PROCESSING OF PERSONAL DATA AND THE PROTECTION OF PRIVACY IN THE ELECTRONIC COMMUNICATIONS SECTOR OF 12 JULY 2000 COM (2000) 385

Reference

http://www.europa.eu.int/comm/internal_market/en/dataprot/wpdocs/wp36en.htm

Adopted on 2nd November 2000

THE WORKING PARTY ON THE PROTECTION OF INDIVIDUALS WITH REGARD TO THE PROCESSING OF PERSONAL DATA

set up by Directive 95/46/EC of the European Parliament and of the Council of 24 October 1995,[1]

having regard to Articles 29 and 30 paragraphs 1 (a) and 3 of that Directive,

having regard to its Rules of Procedure and in particular to articles 12, 13 and 14 thereof,

has adopted the present **Opinion 7/2000**:

1. Introduction

In the context of the 1999 review of the Community's telecommunications regulatory framework,[2] the Commission has adopted on 12 July 2000 proposals for new Directives in the area of electronic communications, intended to replace the existing regulatory framework. One of the five envisaged proposals concerns a revision of Directive 97/66/EC of the European Parliament and the Council of 15 December 1997 on the processing of personal data and the protection of privacy in the telecommunications sector.

---

[1] Official Journal no. L 281 of 23/11/1995, p. 31, available at: http://europa.eu.int/comm/dg15/en/media/dataprot/index.htm

[2] The 1999 Review was launched by a Commission Communication in November 1999 followed by a broad public consultation. The results of this consultation were summarised in a second Communication adopted by the Commission on 26 April. All documents concerning the review and the draft directives are available at: http://www.ispo.cec.be/infosoc/telecompolicy/review99/Welcome.html

Following its Opinion 2/2000 concerning the general review of the telecommunications legal framework,[3] the Working Party now wishes to contribute to the discussions on the draft directive in the European Parliament and in the Council.

2. Analysis of the draft directive

The Working Party's main concerns relate to personal data processing over and via the Internet that needs to be addressed in a more specific way as well as to new issues arising from the liberalised telecommunications market.

Article 1 - Objective and Scope and Article 3 - Services concerned

The Working Party understands that no change is proposed as to the scope and services concerned. The specific provisions of the new directive would thus apply to the provision of publicly available electronic communications services in public communication networks in the Community. Personal data processing for the use of closed/private networks would fall solely under the general Directive 95/46/EC. This is regrettable because private networks are gaining an increasing importance in every day life and communications of citizens, for example in the context of their work, and the risks to privacy that such networks are raising are accordingly increasing and becoming more specific (e.g. monitoring of employee behaviour by means of traffic data, lack of confidentiality of communications).

Processing of personal data in connection with the delivery of services using public communication services and networks[4] such as the content of broadcasting transmission and Information Society services is not covered either by the proposed new directive. This means that data processing in the latter case is subject only to Directive 95/46/EC as are all matters not covered by the specific privacy directive (see recital 9 which is identical to the relevant recital of the present Directive 97/66/EC).

However, interactive television services would be covered.[5]

These points could usefully be clarified either in the text of the relevant articles of the various directives or in the recitals.

---

[3] All documents adopted by the Working Party are available at: http://europa.eu.int/comm/internal_market/en/media/dataprot/wpdocs/index.htm

[4] This follows from Article 3 of this draft directive and Article 2 of the draft directive on the general framework. The Working Party notes that "public communications service" is not defined in either document and that the definition of "electronic communications service" in the draft directive on privacy is not complete compared to the one in the framework text.

[5] It would also be useful to know whether text messaging in mobile phones is covered.

Recent Developments
Opinion on the Proposed Communications Privacy Directive (EC)

Article 2 - Definitions

The Working Party welcomes the effort to clarify terminology. It notes that the proposed directive accommodates the view the Working Party had taken in its Working Document: Processing of Personal Data on the Internet that both Data Protection Directives fully apply to data processing on the Internet.[6]

Traffic data are defined as "any data processed in the course of or for the purpose of the transmission of a communication over an electronic communications network". This definition does not contain a "necessity" clause. The Working Party welcomes this approach which leads to the result that all traffic data generated during a communication, whether they are necessary to establish the communication or not, have to be erased as soon as the communication is transmitted (see Article 6 paragraph 1). The definition includes location data generated during the transmission of a communication. It also includes "navigation data " (such as URLs/Unique Resource Locator) which might reveal an individual's personal interests (e.g. web sites visited that give indications about an individual's religious beliefs, political opinions, health or sex life). Because they show precisely which pages on a web site have been visited they effectively reveal the actual content that the individual has accessed.

Since traffic data might include this kind of personal information on the individual, they should in addition enjoy the confidentiality provided for communications (see Article 5 and below).[7]

The Working Party understands that the proposed definition of "call" does not cover voice telephony over the Internet but only traditional circuit switched voice telephony.

Although the Working Party welcomes the way in which the proposed directive defines "call", it emphasises that it will continue to take the view that in the existing Directive 97/66/EC "call" includes use of the Internet. This view seems to be shared by the European Commission as follows from the explanatory memorandum to the draft directive.

The Working Party notes that the term "subscriber" is not defined anymore though it is used throughout the draft directive. Instead the term "user" is defined, but excludes legal persons. The Working Party would like to know the reasons for these changes.

---

[6] See Article 2-definitions, draft recital (5), Article-3 services concerned, as well as definition of "electronic communications networks "in the document on a framework where "IP networks" could be added to the examples given.

[7] An additional aspect that would need further discussion is that some of these data could also be considered as sensitive data in the sense of Article 8 of the general Data Protection Directive 95/46/EC, the processing of which is in principle prohibited.

The draft directive no longer refers to "telecommunications services", but to "electronic communications services". The explanatory memorandum to the proposal mentions that this change was necessary to align the terminology with the proposed directive establishing a common framework for electronic communications services and networks.[8]

The term "electronic communications services" is not defined in the proposed privacy directive but in Article 2 b) of the proposed directive establishing a common framework for electronic communications services and networks.

The new definition reads as follows: Electronic communications services means services provided for remuneration which consist wholly or mainly in the transmission and routing of signals on electronic communications networks, including telecommunications services and transmission services in networks used for broadcasting, but excluding services providing, or exercising editorial control over, content transmitted using electronic communications networks and services.

The new definition is actually based on the same core idea as the previous one (the transmission and routing of signals on electronic communications services) but the inclusion of a list of examples of services included and excluded from the definition is very helpful as it sheds light on the discussions outlined in the previous sections.

It can be concluded from the list included in the new definition that those who provide content transmitted using electronic communications networks and services will not fall within the scope of application of the privacy draft directive. This is confirmed by the preamble to the proposed directive establishing a common framework for electronic communications services and networks (recital 7) in which it is stated that it is necessary to separate the regulation of transmission from the regulation of content. It is, however, stated that this separation should not overlook the links existing between them.

The main consequence of this separation is that additional services such as those which provide content to a portal or a web site (but not host them) are covered not by this directive, but only by the general data protection directive. It also means that Internet Service Providers are covered by the specific directive insofar as they act as Access Providers and provide connection to the Internet, and are only covered by the general directive when acting as content providers.

The advantage of the clear separation between regulation of content and transmission is the clarity that it brings with it. In practice, however, it will be less easy to work with such a separation (for example in case an Internet Service Provider that also provides content, by

---

8 COM (2000) 393.

hosting its own portal site. This ISP will then have to apply the general directive to all its activities and the specific directive (which entails specific obligations) to the activities in which it plays the role of access provider.

Another interesting aspect of the new definition of "electronic communications services" is the reference to the fact that the service should be provided for remuneration. Neither the preamble nor the explanatory memorandum refer to the inclusion of this term or give any guidance as to how to interpret it. This could be interpreted as meaning that Free Access Providers would fall outside the scope of application of the revised privacy and telecommunications directive, as they do not receive remuneration (or at least not financial) from Internet users.

This interpretation is however not correct since it has been made clear in the jurisprudence of the European Court of Justice, when dealing with services in the sense of article 50 (ex article 60) of the EC Treaty,[9] that the remuneration does not necessarily has to be paid by the recipient of the service. It can for instance also be paid by advertisers.

In the case of the Free Access Providers, those who place advertisements or banners in the Internet pages are the ones who in fact offer a remuneration to the providers. It is therefore clear that these services fall under the definition of electronic communications service and therefore under the scope of the directive.

It would however be desirable to clarify this issue in the text of the directive since no every reader of the text is aware of the interpretation of this term given by the European Court of Justice.[10]

Article 4 - Security

The Working Party welcomes the explanation in recital (13) as regards security measures such as encryption. It proposes to consider the need for more specific obligations on network operators and service providers on the basis of an analysis of national laws implementing security requirements with a view to facilitating free flow of data and equipment (software and hardware). It would also be useful to indicate more specifically the risks at stake, and this not only concerning the Internet, but also other communication environments since the security obligations are imposed on all network and service providers.

---

[9] Case C-109/92 Wirth [1993] ECR I-6447 , 15.

[10] This could be done for instance by adding the word "normally against remuneration" in the text of the definition and to explain in the respective recital the meaning of these terms in the sense of the jurisprudence cited above.

Article 5 - Confidentiality of Communications

The Working Party recalls the commonly shared view that confidentiality of communications is part of the most important elements of the protection of the fundamental right to privacy and data protection as well as of secrecy of communications. Any exception to this right and obligation should be limited to what is strictly necessary in a democratic society and clearly defined by law in accordance with the conditions set out in Article 15 and Article 13 of Directive 95/46/EC.

Since the wording of the proposed Article 5 par. 2 is too vague and thus allows exemptions to confidentiality without respecting the basic conditions, this paragraph should be deleted.

In this context, the Working Party recalls its Recommendation 2/99 emphasising that "telecommunications operators and telecommunications service providers must take the measures needed to make the interception of telecommunications by unauthorised parties impossible, or as technically difficult as the current state of the technology allows. The Working Party stresses in this respect that the implementation of effective means of intercepting communications, using precisely the most advanced techniques, must not result in a lowering of the level of confidentiality of communication and protection of the privacy of individuals.

These obligations take on a special meaning when telecommunications between individuals located on the territory of the Member States pass or may pass outside European territory, in particular when satellites or the Internet are used."

Confidentiality of communications (including behaviour on the Internet) must be the rule, not the exception.

Article 6 - Traffic data and billing data

The Working Party is of the opinion that the opportunity should be used to review the provision on traffic data more thoroughly. Given the wide definition of traffic data it should be made clear that it is not necessarily acceptable to treat all items of traffic data in the same way. It should be clear for what purposes and to what extent particular types of traffic data (in the sense of the new wider definition) may be generated, collected, stored at all, and for what purposes they might be further used. The Working Party would like to stress that, in case processing be allowed for a specific purpose on the basis of the subscriber's consent, the subscriber does not give up his/her rights to privacy and data protection once and for all. The Working Party also recalls that the level of protection granted by the present Directive 97/66/EC should in any case be maintained, if not strengthened.

Recent Developments
Opinion on the Proposed Communications Privacy Directive (EC)

Concerning Article 6 (2): On the basis of the current text proposal allowing processing of traffic data which are necessary for billing purposes, the Working Party notes that the draft directive does not propose any harmonisation of the period during which the bill may lawfully be challenged. The Working Party wishes to know how the Commission intends to follow up the Working Party's Recommendation 3/99 which recommended to the European Commission to harmonise this period in order to set a limit to the storage of traffic data for this specified billing purpose with a view to strengthening the fundamental right to privacy of citizens. The Working Party invites the European Parliament and the Council to set a clear time limit which should be the shortest possible. Any processing of traffic data for additional purposes creates new risks to the fundamental right to privacy. It can only be considered provided appropriate safeguards are in place. The Working Party therefore recommends to include a " necessity" test in Article 6 par.3 for the possibility to process traffic data for the provider's own marketing.

As regards the proposal to allow processing of traffic data for the provision of "added value services", the Working Party considers that this term is not clear enough with a view to guaranteeing the limitation of the purpose. Neither definition nor indications in the recital are given as to the full range of such services. Since the context compared to marketing of the provider's own services is different, different safeguards may be needed.

The Working Party supports the new provision in Article 6 par. 4 concerning the information to be given to the individual. It proposes to add in the relevant recital that the individual also be informed about his right to object to the processing (Article 14 of Directive 95/46/EC).

Article 7 - Itemised billing

The Working Party welcomes the explicit reference to alternative privacy enhancing modalities for itemised billing in the relevant Article. At the same time, it regrets that one of these modalities (deletion of the digits, recital 18 of Directive 97/66/EC) is not mentioned any longer in the draft recital. The Working Party wishes confirmation in the sense that this continues to be a lawful means and recommends its integration into the recital.

Article 9 - Location data

Since more clarity about added value services is needed (see above), the use of location data (traffic data) for such purposes should be examined in the light of the in-depth review of the rules on traffic data as proposed above. In principle location data should not be processed for the provision of added value services. They may be processed exceptionally for clearly specified purposes which technically require that location data are used and provided that safeguards appropriate to the privacy risks are provided.

Without anticipating the Working Party's final view on the substance concerning processing of location data for added value services,[11] it considers that the proposed technical possibility to deny the processing of location data as proposed in Article 9 (2) is not a satisfactory solution. Given the sensitivity of location data with respect to freedom of movement and the fact that the location data covered here are not necessary to establish the communication, the user/subscriber must have full control over their processing. The rule should thus be the inverse: the subscriber must have the possibility, via simple means, to freely allow the processing of location data for each delivery of an added value service (including if necessary connection to the network or transmission or a communication). The technical implementation of this right must be embedded within the equipment of the user/subscriber, not in the network (contrary to calling line identification).

Article 10 - Exceptions

The Working Party considers that this Article may need additional safeguards in order to avoid circumvention of the stricter rules in Article 15 together with Article 13 of Directive 95/46/EC. Since the "old" terminology of "call" is maintained here, the Working Party understands that this Article only covers voice telephony over fixed and mobile networks, but excludes voice telephony over the Internet, IP addresses and e-mails.

    (a) As regards the proposed possibility to override the choice of the subscriber not to be identified[12] at subscriber requests in order to trace malicious or nuisance calls, a procedural safeguard should be provided for that guarantees to check whether a call was indeed malicious or nuisance.

    (b) The overriding of elimination of CLI and the use of location data against the wish of the subscriber/user or without him/her knowing is not specific enough: firstly it should be clarified which kind of location data (traffic data) are meant here. Secondly, in order to avoid a circumvention of Article 15, the law enforcement agencies that are authorised to respond emergency calls should be specified and the obligation to delete the data after the objective of help is achieved should be laid down.

In this context, the Working Party notes that Article 22 (3) of the draft directive on universal service and users' rights[13] obliges "Member States to ensure that network operators make caller location available to emergency services authorities, where technically feasible for all '112' calls." Though there is no doubt that the services ready to rescue persons in emergency situations shall have all the information they need to identify the caller, the Working Party

---

[11] Or more generally concerning the disclosure of location data to users of the networks.

[12] Elimination of calling line identification (CLI) means that the subscriber can choose to remain anonymous vis à vis the person receiving the call. Overriding this right means that the caller's line can be identified even against his/her wish. As regards emergency calls, it is proposed that this also applies to location data even in case the subscriber has not given consent to any processing of such data.

[13] Available on the web site indicated in footnote 2

draws the attention of the Commission to the need to ensure coherence with data protection principles. The understanding and definition of "emergency services authorities" should be the same in both texts. And the obligation to provide location data to these authorities should be limited to what is necessary to identify the person in trouble. But given the sensitivity of location data (see comments on Articles 2 and 9 above), it may be worth considering to some extent that the "112" emergency feature should be classified as a service with the consequence that the necessary location data only of those callers who have consented to this service are provided to the "112" emergency number.

Article 12-Directories of Subscribers

The Working Party supports the proposed choice of subscribers to decide whether or not they want to be included in directories in electronic or paper form. In addition, given the dimension of electronic directories in particular in today's information society, subscribers should be informed about possible uses of directories and the data they can include should be limited to what is necessary in order to identify them, but not to reveal more private information.

This requirement is linked to an issue, which is not yet addressed in the draft directive : several Data Protection Authorities are currently handling cases of reverse searches in directories. These are new services in the liberalised telecommunications market and they consist in offering easily and at a low cost extended capabilities for the processing of all information contained in telephone directories. It is for example possible to find out by means of the telephone number the name and address of a given person or the names and telephone numbers of all people living in the same street by means of the name of the street. It is possible to learn much more about an individual than he/she would imagine when accepting to have his/her telephone number in the telephone directory. As much information as usually appears on a business card (full name, address, profession, job) can be found. Moreover, the simple knowledge of a citizen's itemised billing, where only called telephone numbers appear, would allow to get a list of the names and addresses of all persons called by him/her during a specific period of time. Other search products contain geographical information ("location data", see comments above on Articles 2 and 9) such as city maps and databases with photographs of all the dwellings of a city. This information could easily be associated to the address appearing in the telephone directory that allows for multi-criteria search.

This is a new purpose of the directories which is not compatible with the initial purpose. It is furthermore not legal unless the data subject has given his/her consent to process his/her personal data for such new purposes. The Working Party has adopted a common position on this subject and considers it important that the draft directive explicitly addresses this issue in the sense that the informed consent of the data subject for inclusion of his/her data in public directories for reversed searches is required.

Another important aspect is that directories can be edited by everybody. It is therefore necessary to ensure that transmissions of data from a provider/operator for the purposes of directories or other uses of the data contained therein respect the choices expressed (free of charge) by users/subscribers to the initial provider/operator. The initial provider/operator has to inform the user/subscriber about these uses (commercial use, reverse directories etc.) before the subscription.

Furthermore, the cession of data in form of CD Roms raise an additional problem in some cases as regards the duration of the licence: the duration of the licence should be determined in a way that does not allow the use of data which are outdated as regards the choices made by the persons concerned.

Article 13 - Unsolicited Communications

Spamming is the practice of sending unsolicited e-mails, usually of a commercial nature, in large numbers and repeatedly to individuals with whom the sender has no previous contact. Spam constitutes a specific form of privacy violation: the user has no human interface, supports the costs of the communication and normally receives spam within the protected area of his private home.

Not surprisingly consumers prefer solicited and targeted commercial communications instead of spam which is annoying, time consuming to read and to delete, and costs money. Nuisance caused by junk e-mailers undermines customer's confidence in e-commerce.

But industry also requests legal certainty: unsolicited e-mail puts ISPs in the unacceptable position of being forced to provide the bandwidth and equipment to deliver junk e-mail that the huge majority of its customers do not want. Removing spam from the servers and dealing with angry customers also involves considerable costs. Systems sometimes collapse under the sheer bulk of unsolicited commercial e-mail that is sent, thereby blocking and delaying legitimate traffic. Most ISPs try to filter out spam and have clauses in their contracts with subscribers that the latter shall not send or relay spam. Registers exist of suspect servers, which are known as source of junk e-mail. But the filters, which they use, are not 100% accurate and they also cause legitimate traffic to be blocked if it is sent from a server which happens to be on the black list. However, since there is no legal ban on spam, this practice puts ISPs in a difficult legal position. A legal ban would facilitate more targeted action against junk e-mailers.

Recent market trends suggest that leading on-line direct marketers in the US operate on the basis of "permission based marketing" (opt-in) because the data provided on that basis are of better quality and the level of positive responses is significantly higher. Some practice even "double opt-in": though the individual had agreed to receive commercial communications (for example by indicating this wish on a web site), in the following first (solicited) e-mail contact he is again asked to confirm his wish to the marketer.

The Internet offers ample opportunities to collect e-mail addresses of users who are interested in receiving commercial communications by e-mail on specific topics and willing to give their consent for that purpose. Any mailings, which are based on consent, are likely to reach far more potential customers than Spam.

In five Member States (Germany, Austria, Italy, Finland and Danemark) it is unlawful to send unsolicited commercial communications . In the other Member States, either an opt-out system exists or the situation is not fully clear. Companies in opt-out countries may target e-mail addresses not only within their own country but as well to consumers in Member States with an opt-in system. Moreover, since e-mail addresses very often give no indication of the country of residence of the recipients, a system of divergent regimes within the internal market does not provide a common solution for the protection of consumer's privacy.

Opt-in is a well-balanced and efficient solution in order to remove obstacles to the provision of commercial communications whilst protecting the fundamental right of privacy of consumers. The Working Party thus welcomes and supports the proposal to address unsolicited electronic mail in the same way as automatic calling machines and facsimile machines. In all these situations, the subscriber has no human interface and supports parts or the whole of the costs of the communication. The degree of invasion into privacy and the economic burden are comparable (see Opinion 1/2000).

Article 14 - Technical features and standardisation (and recital 22)

The Working Party welcomes and supports the proposal to develop specific measures at Community level if necessary in order to ensure a harmonised implementation of the data protection rules.

Since technology develops in a "bottom up" way, it could be useful to recall industry their interest in integrating privacy-compliant and even privacy-enhancing features right from start into the design of software and hardware. The Working Party takes the view that technology must comply with the legal requirements and facilitate their implementation, in particular the data minimisation principle following from Articles 6 and 7 of Directive 95/46/EC, and the exercise of the data subject's rights. Taking into account experience in various Member States as well as the Working Party's Recommendation 3/97 on Anonymity on the Internet and its Recommendation 1/99 on Invisible and Automatic Processing of Personal Data on the Internet Performed by Software and Hardware, it is proposed to add a paragraph along the following lines:

The design and selection of data processing technologies, including hardware and software, shall conform to the objective of processing no or as less personal data as possible and shall facilitate the exercise of the data subject's rights. Where possible and not disproportionate with a view to the protection intended, anonymous and pseudonymous data should be used.

Transparency

The Working Party is of the opinion that, though it is clear that the obligations of the general data protection directive to inform the individual apply,[14] it would provide added value to explicitly oblige providers to inform the subscriber/user before the subscription/use and also afterwards about their rights and thus give them the opportunity to exercise at any time all options/rights they have in accordance with the data protection directives. This information concerns the purposes of the intended processing, the controller, the recipients in case a third party is involved, the rights of the individual etc. It is proposed that the providers/operators publish this information in order to enable the subscriber/user to choose at any time all available options to exercise his/her rights. This could be done for example in form of posting a privacy policy on a web site.

3. Conclusions

The Working Party welcomes the revision aiming at ensuring that the same service is regulated in an equivalent manner irrespective of the means by which it is delivered. This also implies that consumers and users should enjoy the same level of protection concerning their personal data and privacy regardless of the technology by which a particular service is delivered. The Working Party shares and fully supports the Commission's view that maintaining a high level of data protection and privacy for citizens is one of the declared aims. The Working Party furthermore recognises that considerable amount of adaptations are proposed to increase the level of data protection in all electronic communications.

The Working Party recommends the Commission, the European Parliament and the Council to take into account its comments. It invites the Commission to clarify outstanding issues so to allow the Working Party to contribute to the ongoing process.

The Working Party suggests that this draft directive be discussed in the Council's working group "economic questions - data protection". This would allow to speed up the process to adopt all directives proposed for the telecom review and it would bring this text to the competent experts.

The Working Party reserves the possibility to comment on the draft directive as it evolves.

---

14 see Articles 10, 11, 12, 14 etc. of Directive 95/46/EC referred to in recital 9 of the draft directive, as well as Articles 4 (2), 6(4), 7, 8, 9, 11, 12, 13 of the draft directive

Recent Developments
Opinion on the Proposed Communications Privacy Directive (EC)

Done at Brussels, 2nd November 2000
For the Working Party
The Chairman
Stefano RODOTA

COMMISSION DECISION ON STANDARD CONTRACTUAL CLAUSES FOR THE TRANSFER OF PERSONAL DATA TO THIRD COUNTRIES UNDER DIRECTIVE 95/46/EC

Reference

Commission Decision on Standard Contractual Clauses
http://europa.eu.int/comm/internal_market/en/dataprot/news/sccproc.pdf

Standard contractual clauses for the transfer of personal data to third countries - frequently asked questions
http://europa.eu.int/comm/internal_market/en/dataprot/news/clauses2faq.htm

Data protection: Commission approves standard contractual clauses for data transfers to non-EU countries
http://europa.eu.int/comm/internal_market/en/dataprot/news/clauses2.htm

Having regard to the Treaty establishing the European Community,

Having regard to Directive 95/46/EC of the European Parliament and of the Council of 24 October 1995 on the protection of individuals with regard to the processing of personal data and on the free movement of such data,[1] and in particular Article 26(4) thereof,

Whereas:

(1) Pursuant to Directive 95/46/EC, Member States are required to provide that a transfer of personal data to a third country may only take place if the third country in question ensures an adequate level of data protection and the Member States' laws, which comply with the other provisions of the Directive, are respected prior to the transfer.

(2) However, Article 26(2) of Directive 95/46/EC provides that Member States may authorise, subject to certain safeguards, a transfer or a set of transfers of personal data to third countries which do not ensure an adequate level of protection. Such safeguards may in particular result from appropriate contractual clauses.

(3) Pursuant to Directive 95/46/EC, the level of data protection should be assessed in the light of all the circumstances surrounding the data transfer operation or set of data transfer operations. The Working Party on Protection of Individuals with regard to the

---

[1] OJ L 281, 23.11.1995, p. 31.

Recent Developments
Standard Contractual Clauses for Transfer of Personal Data (EC)

Processing of Personal Data established under that Directive[2] has issued guidelines to aid with the assessment.[3]

(4) Article 26(2) of Directive 95/46/EC, which provides flexibility for an organisation wishing to transfer data to third countries, and Article 26(4), which provides for standard contractual clauses, are essential for maintaining the necessary flow of personal data between the Community and third countries without unnecessary burdens for economic operators. Those articles are particularly important in view of the fact that the Commission is unlikely to adopt adequacy findings under Article 25(6) for more than a limited number of countries in the short or even medium term.

(5) The standard contractual clauses are only one of several possibilities under Directive 95/46/EC, together with Article 25 and Article 26(1) and (2), for lawfully transferring personal data to a third country. It will be easier for organisations to transfer personal data to third countries by incorporating the standard contractual clauses in a contract. The standard contractual clauses relate only to data protection. The Data Exporter and the Data Importer are free to include any other clauses on business related issues, such as clauses on mutual assistance in cases of disputes with a Data Subject or a Supervisory Authority, which they consider as being pertinent for the contract as long as they do not contradict the standard contractual clauses.

(6) This Decision should be without prejudice to national authorisations Member States may grant in accordance with national provisions implementing Article 26(2) of Directive 95/46/EC. The circumstances of specific transfers may require that data controllers provide different safeguards within the meaning of Article 26(2). In any case, this Decision only has the effect of requiring the Member States not to refuse to recognise as providing adequate safeguards the contractual clauses described in it and does not therefore have any effect on other contractual clauses.

(7) The scope of this Decision is limited to establishing that the clauses in the Annex may be used by a controller established in the Community in order to adduce sufficient safeguards within the meaning of Article 26(2) of Directive 95/46/EC. The transfer of personal data to third countries is a processing operation in a Member State, the lawfulness of which is subject to national law. The Data Protection Supervisory

---

[2] The web address of the Working Party is: http://www.europa.eu.int/comm/internal_market/en/media/dataprot/wpdocs/index.htm.

[3] WP 4 (5020/97) "First orientations on Transfers of Personal Data to Third Countries – Possible Ways Forward in Assessing Adequacy", a discussion document adopted by the Working Party on 26 June 1997; WP 7 (5057/97) Working document: "Judging industry self-regulation: when does it make a meaningful contribution to the level of data protection in a third country?", adopted by the Working Party on 14 January 1998; WP 9 (5005/98) Working Document: "Preliminary views on the use of contractual provisions in the context of transfers of personal data to third countries", adopted by the Working Party on 22 April 1998; WP 12: Transfers of personal data to third countries: Applying Articles 25 and 26 of the EU data protection directive, adopted by the Working Party on 24 July 1998, available in the web site "europa.eu.int/comm/internal_markt/en/media.dataprot/wpdocs/wp12/en" hosted by the European Commission.

Authorities of the Member States, in the exercise of their functions and powers under Article 28 of Directive 95/46/EC, should remain competent to assess whether the Data Exporter has complied with national legislation implementing the provisions of Directive 95/46/EC and, in particular, any specific rules as regards the obligation of providing information under that Directive.

(8) This Decision does not cover the transfer of personal data by controllers established in the Community to recipients established outside the territory of the Community who act only as processors. Those transfers do not require the same safeguards because the processor acts exclusively on behalf of the controller. The Commission intends to address that type of transfer in a subsequent decision.

(9) It is appropriate to lay down the minimum information that the parties must specify in the contract dealing with the transfer. Member States should retain the power to particularise the information the parties are required to provide. The operation of this Decision should be reviewed in the light of experience.

(10) The Commission will also consider in the future whether standard contractual clauses submitted by business organisations or other interested parties offer adequate safeguards in accordance with Directive 95/46/EC.

(11) While the parties should be free to agree on the substantive data protection rules to be complied with by the Data Importer, there are certain data protection principles which should apply in any event.

(12) Data should be processed and subsequently used or further communicated only for specified purposes and should not be kept longer than necessary.

(13) In accordance with Article 12 of Directive 95/46/EC, the Data Subject should have the right of access to all data relating to him and as appropriate to rectification, erasure or blocking of certain data.

(14) Further transfers of personal data to another controller established in a third country should be permitted only subject to certain conditions, in particular to ensure that data subjects are given proper information and have the opportunity to object, or in certain cases to withold their consent.

(15) In addition to assessing whether transfers to third countries are in accordance with national law, Supervisory Authorities should play a key role in this contractual mechanism in ensuring that personal data are adequately protected after the transfer. In specific circumstances, the Supervisory Authorities of the Member States should retain the power to prohibit or suspend a data transfer or a set of transfers based on the standard contractual clauses in those exceptional cases where it is established that a transfer on contractual basis is likely to have a substantial adverse effect on the guarantees providing adequate protection to the data subject.

(16) The standard contractual clauses should be enforceable not only by the organisations which are parties to the contract, but also by the Data Subjects, in particular, where the Data Subjects suffer damage as a consequence of a breach of the contract.

(17) The governing law of the contract should be the law of the Member State in which the Data Exporter is established, enabling a third-party beneficiary to enforce a contract. Data Subjects should be allowed to be represented by associations or other bodies if they so wish and if authorised by national law.

(18) To reduce practical difficulties which Data Subjects could experience when trying to enforce their rights under the standard contractual clauses, the Data Exporter and the Data Importer should be jointly and severally liable for damages resulting from any violation of those provisions which are covered by the third-party beneficiary clause.

(19) The Data Subject is entitled to take action and receive compensation from the Data Exporter, the Data Importer or from both for any damage resulting from any act incompatible with the obligations contained in the standard contractual clauses. Both parties may be exempted from that liability if they prove that neither of them was responsible.

(20) Joint and several liability does not extend to those provisions not covered by the third-party beneficiary clause and does not need to leave one party paying for the damage resulting from the unlawful processing of the other party. Although mutual indemnification between the parties is not a requirement for the adequacy of the protection for the Data Subjects and may therefore be deleted, it is included in the standard contractual clauses for the sake of clarification and to avoid the need for the parties to negotiate indemnification clauses individually.

(21) In the event of a dispute between the Parties and the Data Subject which is not amicably resolved and where the Data Subject invokes the third-party beneficiary clause, the parties agree to provide the Data Subject with the choice between mediation, arbitration or litigation. The extent to which the Data Subject will have an effective choice will depend on the availability of reliable and recognised systems of mediation and arbitration. Mediation by the Supervisory Authorities of a Member State should be an option where they provide such a service.

(22) The Working Party on the Protection of Individuals with regard to the processing of Personal Data established under Article 29 of Directive 95/46/EC has delivered an Opinion on the level of protection provided under the standard contractual clauses annexed to this Decision, which has been taken into account in the preparation of this Decision.[4]

(23) The measures provided for in this Decision are in accordance with the opinion of the Committee established under Article 31 of Directive 95/46/EC,

HAS ADOPTED THIS DECISION:

Article 1

---

4 Opinion No 1/2001 adopted by the Working Party on 26 January 2001 (DG MARKT 5102/00 WP 38), available in the web site "Europa" hosted by the European Commission.

Standard Contractual Clauses for Transfer of Personal Data (EC)

The standard contractual clauses set out in the Annex are considered as offering adequate safeguards with respect to the protection of the privacy and fundamental rights and freedoms of individuals and as regards the exercise of the corresponding rights as required by Article 26(2) of Directive 95/46/EC.

Article 2

This Decision concerns only the adequacy of protection provided by the standard contractual clauses for the transfer of personal data set out in the Annex. It does not affect the application of other national provisions implementing Directive 95/46/EC that pertain to the processing of personal data within the Member States.

This Decision shall not apply to the transfer of personal data by controllers established in the Community to recipients established outside the territory of the Community who act only as processors.

Article 3

For the purposes of this Decision:

(a) the definitions in Directive 95/46/EC shall apply;

(b) "special categories of data" means the data referred to in Article 8 of that Directive;

(c) "Supervisory Authority" means the Authority referred to in Article 28 of that Directive;

(d) "Data Exporter" means the controller who transfers the Personal Data;

(e) "Data Importer" means the controller who agrees to receive from the Data Exporter personal data for further processing in accordance with the terms of this Decision.

Article 4

1. Without prejudice to their powers to take action to ensure compliance with national provisions adopted pursuant to Chapters II, III, V and VI of Directive 95/46/EC, the competent authorities in the Member States may exercise their existing powers to prohibit or suspend data flows to third countries in order to protect individuals with regard to the processing of their personal data in cases where:

(a) it is established that the law to which the Data Importer is subject imposes upon him requirements to derogate from the relevant data protection rules which go beyond the restrictions necessary in a democratic society as provided for in Article 13 of Directive 95/46/EC where those requirements are likely to have a substantial adverse effect on the guarantees provided by the standard contractual clauses, or

(b) a competent authority has established that the Data Importer has not respected the contractual clauses, or

(c) there is a substantial likelihood that the standard contractual clauses in the Annex are not being or will not be complied with and the continuation of transfer would create an imminent risk of grave harm to the Data Subjects.

2. The prohibition or suspension pursuant to paragraph 1 shall be lifted as soon as the reasons for the prohibition or suspension no longer exist.

3. When Member States adopt measures pursuant to paragraphs 1 and 2, they shall without delay inform the Commission which will forward the information to the other Member States.

Article 5

The Commission shall evaluate the operation of this Decision on the basis of available information three years after its notification to the Member States. It shall submit a report on the findings to the Committee established under Article 31 of Directive 95/46/EC. It shall include any evidence that could affect the evaluation concerning the adequacy of the standard contractual clauses in the Annex and any evidence that this Decision is being applied in a discriminatory way.

Article 6

This Decision shall apply from 3 rd September 2001.

Article 7

This Decision is addressed to the Member States.
Done at Brussels,
For the Commission
Member of the Commission

ANNEX

Standard contractual clauses

for the purposes of Article 26(2) of Directive 95/46/EC for the transfer of personal data to third countries which do not ensure an adequate level of protection

Name of the data exporting organisation:

_____

Address:

_____
_____
_____

Tel: _____   fax: _____ e-mail: _____

Other information needed to identify the organisation ("the Data Exporter")

_____
_____
_____

and

Name of the data importing organization

_____

Address:

_____
_____
_____

Tel: _____   fax: _____ e-mail: _____

Other information needed to identify the organisation ("the Data Importer"):

_____
_____
_____

HAVE AGREED on the following contractual clauses ('the Clauses') in order to adduce adequate safeguards with respect to the protection of privacy and fundamental rights and freedoms of individuals for the transfer by the Data Exporter to the Data Importer of the personal data specified in Appendix 1.

Clause 1 - Definitions

For the purposes of the Clauses:

(a) "personal data", "special categories of data", "process/processing", "controller", "processor", "Data Subject" and "Supervisory Authority" shall have the same meaning as in Directive 95/46/EC of 24 October 1995 on the protection of individuals with regard to the processing of personal data and on the free movement of such data ("the Directive"); (b) "the Data Exporter" shall mean the Controller who transfers the Personal Data;

(c) "the Data Importer" shall mean the Controller who agrees to receive from the Data Exporter personal data for further processing in accordance with the terms of these Clauses and who is not subject to a third country's system ensuring adequate protection.

Clause 2 - Details of the Transfer

Recent Developments
Standard Contractual Clauses for Transfer of Personal Data (EC)

The details of the transfer, and in particular the categories of personal data and the purposes for which they are transferred, are specified in Appendix 1 which forms an integral part of the Clauses.

Clause 3 - Third-party beneficiary clause

The Data Subjects can enforce this Clause, Clause 4 (b), (c) and (d), Clause 5 (a), (b), (c) and (e), Clause 6 (1) and (2), and Clauses 7, 9 and 11 as third-party beneficiaries. The parties do not object to the Data Subjects being represented by an association or other bodies if they so wish and if permitted by national law.

Clause 4 - Obligations of the Data Exporter

The Data Exporter agrees and warrants:

(a) that the processing, including the transfer itself, of the personal data by him has been and, up to the moment of the transfer, will continue to be carried out in accordance with all the relevant provisions of the Member State in which the Data Exporter is established (and where applicable has been notified to the relevant Authorities of that State) and does not violate the relevant provisions of that State;

(b) that if the transfer involves special categories of Data the Data Subject has been informed or will be informed before the transfer that his data could be transmitted to a third country not providing adequate protection;

(c) to make available to the Data Subjects upon request a copy of the Clauses; and

(d) to respond in a reasonable time and to the extent reasonably possible to enquiries from the Supervisory Authority on the processing of the relevant Personal Data by the Data Importer and to any enquiries from the Data Subject concerning the processing of his Personal Data by the Data Importer.

Clause 5 - Obligations of the Data Importer

The Data Importer agrees and warrants:

(a) that he has no reason to believe that the legislation applicable to him prevents him from fulfilling his obligations under the contract and that in the event of a change in that legislation which is likely to have a substantial adverse effect on the guarantees provided by the Clauses, he will notify the change to the Data Exporter and to the Supervisory Authority where the Data Exporter is established, in which case the Data Exporter is entitled to suspend the transfer of data and/or terminate the contract;

(b) to process the Personal Data in accordance with the Mandatory Data Protection Principles set out in Appendix 2;

or, if explicitly agreed by the parties by ticking below and subject to compliance with the Mandatory Data Protection Principles set out in Appendix 3, to process in all other respects the data in accordance with:

the relevant provisions of national law (attached to these Clauses) protecting the fundamental rights and freedoms of natural persons, and in particular their right to privacy with respect to the processing of personal data applicable to a Data Controller in the country in which the Data Exporter is established, or,

the relevant provisions of any Commission decision under Article 25(6) of Directive 95/46/EC finding that a third country provides adequate protection in certain sectors of activity only, if the Data Importer is based in that third country and is not covered by those provisions, in so far those provisions are of a nature which makes them applicable in the sector of the transfer;

(c) to deal promptly and properly with all reasonable inquiries from the Data Exporter or the Data Subject relating to his processing of the Personal Data subject to the transfer and to cooperate with the competent Supervisory Authority in the course of all its inquiries and abide by the advice of the Supervisory Authority with regard to the processing of the data transferred;

(d) at the request of the Data Exporter to submit its data processing facilities for audit which shall be carried out by the Data Exporter or an inspection body composed of independent members and in possession of the required professional qualifications, selected by the Data Exporter, where applicable, in agreement with the Supervisory Authority;

(e) to make available to the Data Subject upon request a copy of the Clauses and indicate the office which handles complaints.

Clause 6 - Liability

• The Parties agree that a Data Subject who has suffered damage as a result of any violation of the provisions referred to in Clause 3 is entitled to receive compensation from the parties for the damage suffered. The Parties agree that they may be exempted from this liability only if they prove that neither of them is responsible for the violation of those provisions.

• The Data Exporter and the Data Importer agree that the y will be jointly and severally liable for damage to the Data Subject resulting from any violation referred to in paragraph 1. In the event of such a violation, the Data Subject may bring an action before a court against either the Data Exporter or the Data Importer or both.

• The parties agree that if one party is held liable for a violation referred to in paragraph 1 by the other party, the latter will, to the extent to which it is liable, indemnify the first party for any cost, charge, damages, expenses or loss it has incurred*.

[* paragraph 3 is optional]

Clause 7 - Mediation and Jurisdiction

i) The parties agree that if there is a dispute between a Data Subject and either party which is not amicably resolved and the Data Subject invokes the third-party beneficiary provision in Clause 3, they accept the decision of the Data Subject:

(a) to refer the dispute to mediation by an independent person or, where applicable, by the Supervisory Authority;

(b) to refer the dispute to the courts in the Member State in which the Data Exporter is established.

ii)   The Parties agree that by agreement between a Data Subject and the relevant party a dispute can be referred to an arbitration body, if that party is established in a country which has ratified the New York Convention on enforcement of arbitration awards.

iii)   The parties agree that paragraphs 1 and 2 apply without prejudice to the Data Subject's substantive or procedural rights to seek remedies in accordance with other provisions of national or international law.

Clause 8 - Cooperation with Supervisory Authorities

The parties agree to deposit a copy of this contract with the Supervisory Authority if it so requests or if such deposit is required under national law.

Clause 9 - Termination of the Clauses

The parties agree that the termination of the Clauses at any time, in any circumstances and for whatever reason does not exempt them from the obligations and/or conditions under the Clauses as regards the processing of the data transferred.

Clause 10 - Governing Law

The Clauses shall be governed by the law of the Member State in which the Data Exporter is established, namely

Clause 11 - Variation of the contract

The parties undertake not to vary or modify the terms of the Clauses.

On behalf of the Data Exporter:

Name (written out in full):

_____

Position:

_____

Address:

_____
_____
_____

Other information necessary in order for the contract to be binding (if any):

_____

_____

_____

Signature:

_____

(stamp of organisation)

On behalf of the Data Importer:

Name (written out in full):

_____

Position:

_____

Address:

_____

_____

_____

Other information necessary in order for the contract to be binding (if any):

_____

_____

_____

Signature:

_____

(stamp of organisation)

APPENDIX 1 to the Standard Contractual Clauses

This Appendix forms part of the Clauses and must be completed and signed by the parties (*The Member States may complete or specify, according to their national procedures, any additional necessary information to be contained in this Appendix)

Data Exporter
The Data Exporter is (please specify briefly your activities relevant to the transfer):

_____

_____

_____

Recent Developments
Standard Contractual Clauses for Transfer of Personal Data (EC)

Data Importer

The Data Importer is (please specify briefly your activities relevant to the transfer):

_____

_____

_____

Data Subjects

The personal data transferred concern the following categories of Data Subjects (please specify):

_____

_____

_____

Purposes of the transfer

The transfer is necessary for the following purposes (please specify):

_____

_____

_____

Categories of data

The personal data transferred fall within the following categories of data (please specify):

_____

_____

_____

Sensitive Data (if appropriate)

The personal data transferred fall within the following categories of sensitive data (please specify):

_____

_____

_____

Recipients

The personal data transferred may be disclosed only to the following recipients or categories of recipients (please specify):

_____

_____

_____

Storage limit

The personal data transferred may be stored for no more than (please indicate):

_____

(months/years)

| DATA EXPORTER | DATA IMPORTER |

Name: _____   _____

Authorised Signature _____   _____

APPENDIX 2 to the Standard Contractual Clauses

Mandatory Data Protection Principles referred to in the first paragraph of Clause 5(b).

These data protection principles should be read and interpreted in the light of the provisions (principles and relevant exceptions) of Directive 95/46/EC [5]

They shall apply subject to the mandatory requirements of the national legislation applicable to the Data Importer which do not go beyond what is necessary in a democratic society on the basis of one of the interests listed in Article 13(1) of Directive 95/46/EC, that is, if they constitute a necessary measure to safeguard national security, defence, public security, the prevention, investigation, detection and prosecution of criminal offences or of breaches of ethics for the regulated professions, an important economic or financial interest of the State or the protection of the Data Subject or the rights and freedoms of others.

(1) Purpose limitation
Data must be processed and subsequently used or further communicated only for the specific purposes in Appendix 1 to the Clauses. Data must not be kept longer than necessary for the purposes for which they are transferred.

(2) Data quality and proportionality
Data must be accurate and, where necessary, kept up to date. The data must be adequate, relevant and not excessive in relation to the purposes for which they are transferred and further processed.

(3) Transparency

---

[5] 1 Directive 95/46/EC of the European Parliament and of the Council of 24 of October 1995 on the protection of individuals with regard to the processing of personal data and on the free movement of such data, Official Journal of the European Communities, L 281, 23.11.1995, p. 31.

Recent Developments
Standard Contractual Clauses for Transfer of Personal Data (EC)

Data Subjects must be provided with information as to the purposes of the processing and the identity of the data controller in the third country, and other information insofar as this is necessary to ensure fair processing, unless such information has already been given by the Data Exporter.

(4) Security and confidentiality

Technical and organisational security measures must be taken by the data controller that are appropriate to the risks, such as unauthorised access, presented by the processing. Any person acting under the authority of the data controller, including a processor, must not process the data except on instructions from the controller.

(5) Rights of access, rectification, erasure and blocking of data

As provided for in Article 12 of Directive 95/46/EC, the Data Subject must have a right of access to all data relating to him that are processed and, as appropriate, the right to the rectification, erasure or blocking of data the processing of which does not comply with the principles set out in this Appendix, in particular because the data are incomplete or inaccurate. He should also be able to object to the processing of the data relating to him on compelling legitimate grounds relating to his particular situation.

(6) Restrictions on onward transfers

Further transfers of personal data from the Data Importer to another controller established in a third country not providing adequate protection or not covered by a Decision adopted by the Commission pursuant to Article 25(6) of Directive 95/46/EC (onward transfer) may take place only if either:

> (a) Data Subjects have, in the case of special categories of data, given their unambiguous consent to the onward transfer or, in other cases, have been given the opportunity to object. The minimum information to be provided to Data Subjects must contain in a language understandable to them:
>> -the purposes of the onward transfer,
>> -the identification of the Data Exporter established in the Community,
>> -the categories of further recipients of the data and the countries of destination, and
>> -an explanation that, after the onward transfer, the data may be processed by a controller established in a country where there is not an adequate level of protection of the privacy of individuals;

or

> (b) the Data Exporter and the Data Importer agree to the adherence to the Clauses of another controller which thereby becomes a party to the Clauses and assumes the same obligations as the Data Importer.

(7) Special categories of data

Where data revealing racial or ethnic origin, political opinions, religious or philosophical beliefs or trade union memberships and data concerning health or sex life and data relating to offences, criminal convictions or security measures are processed, additional safeguards should be in place within the meaning of Directive 95/46/EC, in particular, appropriate security measures such as strong encryption for transmission or such as keeping a record of access to sensitive data.

(8) Direct marketing

Where data are processed for the purposes of direct marketing, effective procedures should exist allowing the Data Subject at any time to 'opt-out' from having his data used for such purposes.

(9) Automated individual decisions

Data Subjects are entitled not to be subject to a decision which is based solely on automated processing of data, unless other measures are taken to safeguard the individual's legitimate interests as provided for in Article 15(2) of Directive 95/46/EC. Where the purpose of the transfer is the taking of an automated decision as referred to in Article 15 of Directive 95/46/EC, which produces legal effects concerning the individual or significantly affects him and which is based solely on automated processing of data intended to evaluate certain personal aspects relating to him, such as his performance at work, creditworthiness, reliability, conduct, etc., the individual should have the right to know the reasoning for this Decision.

APPENDIX 3 to the Standard Contractual Clauses

Mandatory Data Protection Principles referred to in the second paragraph of Clause 5(b).

Purpose limitation

Data must be processed and subsequently used or further communicated only for the specific purposes in Appendix 1 to the Clauses. Data must not be kept longer than necessary for the purposes for which they are transferred.

(2) Rights of access, rectification, erasure and blocking of data

As provided for in Article 12 of Directive 95/46/EC, the Data Subject must have a right of access to all data relating to him that are processed and, as appropriate, the right to the rectification, erasure or blocking of data the processing of which does not comply with the principles set out in this Appendix, in particular because the data is incomplete or inaccurate. He should also be able to object to the processing of the data relating to him on compelling legitimate grounds relating to his particular situation.

(3) Restrictions on onward transfers

Recent Developments
Standard Contractual Clauses for Transfer of Personal Data (EC)

Further transfers of personal data from the Data Importer to another controller established in a third country not providing adequate protection or not covered by a Decision adopted by the Commission pursuant to Article 25(6) of Directive 95/46/EC (onward transfer) may take place only if either:

(a) Data Subjects have, in the case of if special categories of data, given their unambiguous consent to the onward transfer, or, in other cases, have been given the opportunity to object. The minimum information to be provided to Data Subjects must contain in a language understandable to them:

-the purposes of the onward transfer,

-the identification of the Data Exporter established in the Community,

-the categories of further recipients of the data and the countries of destination, and,

-an explanation that, after the onward transfer, the data may be processed by a controller established in a country where there is not an adequate level of protection of the privacy of individuals;

or

(b) the Data Exporter and the Data Importer agree to the adherence to the Clauses of another controller which thereby becomes a party to the Clauses and assumes the same obligations as the Data Importer.

MATERIALS ON SAFE HARBOR
ARRANGEMENT (2000)

Reference

US Department of Commerce, Safe Harbor
[http://www.export.gov/safeharbor/]

SAFE HARBOR PRIVACY PRINCIPLES ISSUED BY THE U.S. DEPARTMENT OF COMMERCE ON JULY 21, 2000

The European Union's comprehensive privacy legislation, the Directive on Data Protection (the Directive), became effective on October 25, 1998. It requires that transfers of personal data take place only to non-EU countries that provide an "adequate" level of privacy protection. While the United States and the European Union share the goal of enhancing privacy protection for their citizens, the United States takes a different approach to privacy from that taken by the European Union. The United States uses a sectoral approach that relies on a mix of legislation, regulation, and self regulation. Given those differences, many U.S. organizations have expressed uncertainty about the impact of the EU-required "adequacy standard" on personal data transfers from the European Union to the United States.

To diminish this uncertainty and provide a more predictable framework for such data transfers, the Department of Commerce is issuing this document and Frequently Asked Questions ("the Principles") under its statutory authority to foster, promote, and develop international commerce. The Principles were developed in consultation with industry and the general public to facilitate trade and commerce between the United States and European Union. They are intended for use solely by U.S. organizations receiving personal data from the European Union for the purpose of qualifying for the safe harbor and the presumption of "adequacy" it creates. Because the Principles were solely designed to serve this specific purpose, their adoption for other purposes may be inappropriate. The Principles cannot be used as a substitute for national provisions implementing the Directive that apply to the processing of personal data in the Member States.

Decisions by organizations to qualify for the safe harbor are entirely voluntary, and organizations may qualify for the safe harbor in different ways. Organizations that decide to adhere to the Principles must comply with the Principles in order to obtain and retain the benefits of the safe harbor and publicly declare that they do so. For example, if an organization joins a self- regulatory privacy program that adheres to the Principles, it qualifies for the safe harbor. Organizations may also qualify by developing their own self- regulatory privacy policies provided that they conform with the Principles. Where in complying with the

Recent Developments
Safe Harbor Arrangement (EU-US)

Principles, an organization relies in whole or in part on self- regulation, its failure to comply with such self- regulation must also be actionable under Section 5 of the Federal Trade Commission Act prohibiting unfair and deceptive acts or another law or regulation prohibiting such acts. *(See the annex for the list of U.S. statutory bodies recognized by the EU.)* In addition, organizations subject to a statutory, regulatory, administrative or other body of law (or of rules) that effectively protects personal privacy may also qualify for safe harbor benefits. In all instances, safe harbor benefits are assured from the date on which each organization wishing to qualify for the safe harbor self-certifies to the Department of Commerce (or its designee) its adherence to the Principles in accordance with the guidance set forth in the Frequently Asked Question on Self-Certification.

Adherence to these Principles may be limited: (a) to the extent necessary to meet national security, public interest, or law enforcement requirements; (b) by statute, government regulation, or case law that create conflicting obligations or explicit authorizations, provided that, in exercising any such authorization, an organization can demonstrate that its non-compliance with the Principles is limited to the extent necessary to meet the overriding legitimate interests furthered by such authorization; or (c) if the effect of the Directive or Member State law is to allow exceptions or derogations, provided such exceptions or derogations are applied in comparable contexts. Consistent with the goal of enhancing privacy protection, organizations should strive to implement these Principles fully and transparently, including indicating in their privacy policies where exceptions to the Principles permitted by (b) above will apply on a regular basis. For the same reason, where the option is allowable under the Principles and/or U.S. law, organizations are expected to opt for the higher protection where possible.

Organizations may wish for practical or other reasons to apply the Principles to all their data processing operations, but they are only obligated to apply them to data transferred after they enter the safe harbor. To qualify for the safe harbor, organizations are not obligated to apply these Principles to personal information in manually processed filing systems. Organizations wishing to benefit from the safe harbor for receiving information in manually processed filing systems from the EU must apply the Principles to any such information transferred after they enter the safe harbor. An organization that wishes to extend safe harbor benefits to human resources personal information transferred from the EU for use in the context of an employment relationship must indicate this when it self-certifies to the Department of Commerce (or its designee) and conform to the requirements set forth in the Frequently Asked Question on Self-Certification. Organizations will also be able to provide the safeguards necessary under Article 26 of the Directive if they include the Principles in written agreements with parties transferring data from the EU for the substantive privacy provisions, once the other provisions for such model contracts are authorized by the Commission and the Member States.

U.S. law will apply to questions of interpretation and compliance with the Safe Harbor Principles (including the Frequently Asked Questions) and relevant privacy policies by safe harbor organizations, except where organizations have committed to cooperate with European Data Protection Authorities. Unless otherwise stated, all provisions of the Safe Harbor Principles and Frequently Asked Questions apply where they are relevant.

"Personal data" and "personal information" are data about an identified or identifiable individual that are within the scope of the Directive, received by a U.S. organization from the European Union, and recorded in any form.

NOTICE: An organization must inform individuals about the purposes for which it collects and uses information about them, how to contact the organization with any inquiries or complaints, the types of third parties to which it discloses the information, and the choices and means the organization offers individuals for limiting its use and disclosure. This notice must be provided in clear and conspicuous language when individuals are first asked to provide personal information to the organization or as soon thereafter as is practicable, but in any event before the organization uses such information for a purpose other than that for which it was originally collected or processed by the transferring organization or discloses it for the first time to a third party.[1]

CHOICE: An organization must offer individuals the opportunity to choose (opt out) whether their personal information is (a) to be disclosed to a third party(1) or (b) to be used for a purpose that is incompatible with the purpose(s) for which it was originally collected or subsequently authorized by the individual. Individuals must be provided with clear and conspicuous, readily available, and affordable mechanisms to exercise choice.

For sensitive information (i.e. personal information specifying medical or health conditions, racial or ethnic origin, political opinions, religious or philosophical beliefs, trade union membership or information specifying the sex life of the individual), they must be given affirmative or explicit (opt in) choice if the information is to be disclosed to a third party or used for a purpose other than those for which it was originally collected or subsequently authorized by the individual through the exercise of opt in choice. In any case, an organization should treat as sensitive any information received from a third party where the third party treats and identifies it as sensitive.

ONWARD TRANSFER: To disclose information to a third party organizations must apply the Notice and Choice Principles. Where an organization wishes to transfer information

---

[1] It is not necessary to provide notice or choice when disclosure is made to a third party that is acting as an agent to perform task(s) on behalf of and under the instructions of the organization. The Onward Transfer Principle, on the other hand, does apply to such disclosures.

Recent Developments
Safe Harbor Arrangement (EU-US)

to a third party that is acting as an agent, as described in the endnote, it may do so if it first either ascertains that the third party subscribes to the Principles or is subject to the Directive or another adequacy finding or enters into a written agreement with such third party requiring that the third party provide at least the same level of privacy protection as is required by the relevant Principles. If the organization complies with these requirements, it shall not be held responsible (unless the organization agrees otherwise) when a third party to which it transfers such information processes it in a way contrary to any restrictions or representations, unless the organization knew or should have known the third party would process it in such a contrary way and the organization has not taken reasonable steps to prevent or stop such processing.

SECURITY: Organizations creating, maintaining, using or disseminating personal information must take reasonable precautions to protect it from loss, misuse and unauthorized access, disclosure, alteration and destruction.

DATA INTEGRITY: Consistent with the Principles, personal information must be relevant for the purposes for which it is to be used. An organization may not process personal information in a way that is incompatible with the purposes for which it has been collected or subsequently authorized by the individual. To the extent necessary for those purposes, an organization should take reasonable steps to ensure that data is reliable for its intended use, accurate, complete, and current.

ACCESS: Individuals must have access to personal information about them that an organization holds and be able to correct, amend, or delete that information where it is inaccurate, except where the burden or expense of providing access would be disproportionate to the risks to the individual's privacy in the case in question, or where the rights of persons other than the individual would be violated.

ENFORCEMENT: Effective privacy protection must include mechanisms for assuring compliance with the Principles, recourse for individuals to whom the data relate affected by non-compliance with the Principles, and consequences for the organization when the Principles are not followed. At a minimum, such mechanisms must include (a) readily available and affordable independent recourse mechanisms by which each individual's complaints and disputes are investigated and resolved by reference to the Principles and damages awarded where the applicable law or private sector initiatives so provide; (b) follow up procedures for verifying that the attestations and assertions businesses make about their privacy practices are true and that privacy practices have been implemented as presented; and (c) obligations to remedy problems arising out of failure to comply with the Principles by organizations announcing their adherence to them and consequences for such organizations. Sanctions must be sufficiently rigorous to ensure compliance by organizations.

Frequently Asked Questions

FAQ 1 - Sensitive Data

Q: Must an organization always provide explicit (opt in) choice with respect to sensitive data?

A: No, such choice is not required where the processing is: (1) in the vital interests of the data subject or another person; (2) necessary for the establishment of legal claims or defenses; (3) required to provide medical care or diagnosis; (4) carried out in the course of legitimate activities by a foundation, association or any other non-profit body with a political, philosophical, religious or trade-union aim and on condition that the processing relates solely to the members of the body or to the persons who have regular contact with it in connection with its purposes and that the data are not disclosed to a third party without the consent of the data subjects; (5) necessary to carry out the organization's obligations in the field of employment law; or (6) related to data that are manifestly made public by the individual.

FAQ 2 - Journalistic Exceptions

Q: Given U.S. constitutional protections for freedom of the press and the Directive's exemption for journalistic material, do the Safe Harbor Principles apply to personal information gathered, maintained, or disseminated for journalistic purposes?

A: Where the rights of a free press embodied in the First Amendment of the U. S. Constitution intersect with privacy protection interests, the First Amendment must govern the balancing of these interests with regard to the activities of U.S. persons or organizations. Personal information that is gathered for publication, broadcast, or other forms of public communication of journalistic material, whether used or not, as well as information found in previously published material disseminated from media archives, is not subject to the requirements of the Safe Harbor Principles.

FAQ 3 - Secondary Liability

Q: Are Internet service providers (ISPs), telecommunications carriers, or other organizations liable under the Safe Harbor Principles when on behalf of another organization they merely transmit, route, switch or cache information that may violate their terms?

A: No. As is the case with the Directive itself, the safe harbor does not create secondary liability. To the extent that an organization is acting as a mere conduit for data transmitted by third parties and does not determine the purposes and means of processing those personal data, it would not be liable.

FAQ 4 - Investment banking and audits

Q: The activities of auditors and investment bankers may involve processing personal data without the consent or knowledge of the individual. Under what circumstances is this permitted by the Notice, Choice, and Access Principles?

Recent Developments
Safe Harbor Arrangement (EU-US)

A: Investment bankers or auditors may process information without knowledge of the individual only to the extent and for the period necessary to meet statutory or public interest requirements and in other circumstances in which the application of these Principles would prejudice the legitimate interests of the organization. These legitimate interests include the monitoring of companies' compliance with their legal obligations and legitimate accounting activities, and the need for confidentiality connected with possible acquisitions, mergers, joint ventures, or other similar transactions carried out by investment bankers or auditors.

FAQ 5 - The Role of the Data Protection Authorities

Q: How will companies that commit to cooperate with European Union Data Protection Authorities (DPAs) make those commitments and how will they be implemented?

A: Under the safe harbor, U.S. organizations receiving personal data from the EU must commit to employ effective mechanisms for assuring compliance with the Safe Harbor Principles. More specifically as set out in the Enforcement Principle, they must provide (a) recourse for individuals to whom the data relate, (b) follow up procedures for verifying that the attestations and assertions they have made about their privacy practices are true, and (c) obligations to remedy problems arising out of failure to comply with the Principles and consequences for such organizations. An organization may satisfy points (a) and (c) of the Enforcement Principle if it adheres to the requirements of this FAQ for cooperating with the DPAs.

An organization may commit to cooperate with the DPAs by declaring in its safe harbor certification to the Department of Commerce (see FAQ 6 on self-certification) that the organization:

- elects to satisfy the requirement in points (a) and (c) of the Safe Harbor Enforcement Principle by committing to cooperate with the DPAs;
- will cooperate with the DPAs in the investigation and resolution of complaints brought under the safe harbor; and
- will comply with any advice given by the DPAs where the DPAs take the view that the organization needs to take specific action to comply with the Safe Harbor Principles, including remedial or compensatory measures for the benefit of individuals affected by any non-compliance with the Principles, and will provide the DPAs with written confirmation that such action has been taken. The cooperation of the DPAs will be provided in the form of information and advice in the following way:

iv)   The advice of the DPAs will be delivered through an informal panel of DPAs established at the European Union level, which will *inter alia* help ensure a harmonised and coherent approach.

v)   The panel will provide advice to the U.S. organizations concerned on unresolved complaints from individuals about the handling of personal information that has been transferred from the EU under the safe harbor. This advice will be designed to ensure that the Safe Harbor Principles are being correctly applied and will include any remedies for the individual(s) concerned that the DPAs consider appropriate.

vi) The panel will provide such advice in response to referrals from the organizations concerned and/or to complaints received directly from individuals against organizations which have committed to cooperate with DPAs for safe harbor purposes, while encouraging and if necessary helping such individuals in the first instance to use the in-house complaint handling arrangements that the organization may offer.

vii) Advice will be issued only after both sides in a dispute have had a reasonable opportunity to comment and to provide any evidence they wish. The panel will seek to deliver advice as quickly as this requirement for due process allows. As a general rule, the panel will aim to provide advice within 60 days after receiving a complaint or referral and more quickly where possible.

viii) The panel will make public the results of its consideration of complaints submitted to it, if it sees fit.

ix) The delivery of advice through the panel will not give rise to any liability for the panel or for individual DPAs.

As noted above, organizations choosing this option for dispute resolution must undertake to comply with the advice of the DPAs. If an organization fails to comply within 25 days of the delivery of the advice and has offered no satisfactory explanation for the delay, the panel will give notice of its intention either to submit the matter to the Federal Trade Commission or other U.S. federal or state body with statutory powers to take enforcement action in cases of deception or misrepresentation, or to conclude that the agreement to cooperate has been seriously breached and must therefore be considered null and void. In the latter case, the panel will inform the Department of Commerce (or its designee) so that the list of safe harbor participants can be duly amended. Any failure to fulfill the undertaking to cooperate with the DPAs, as well as failures to comply with the Safe Harbor Principles, will be actionable as a deceptive practice under Section 5 of the FTC Act or other similar statute.

Organizations choosing this option will be required to pay an annual fee which will be designed to cover the operating costs of the panel, and they may additionally be asked to meet any necessary translation expenses arising out of the panel's consideration of referrals or complaints against them. The annual fee will not exceed $500 and will be less for smaller companies.

The option of co-operating with the DPAs will be available to organizations joining the safe harbor during a three-year period. The DPAs will reconsider this arrangement before the end of that period if the number of U.S. organizations choosing this option proves to be excessive.

Recent Developments
Safe Harbor Arrangement (EU-US)

FAQ 6 - *Self-Certification*

MADE PUBLIC

Q: How does an organization self-certify that it adheres to the Safe Harbor Principles?

A: Safe harbor benefits are assured from the date on which an organization self-certifies to the Department of Commerce (or its designee) its adherence to the Principles in accordance with the guidance set forth below.

To self-certify for the safe harbor, organizations can provide to the Department of Commerce (or its designee) a letter, signed by a corporate officer on behalf of the organization that is joining the safe harbor, that contains at least the following information:

- name of organization, mailing address, email address, telephone and fax numbers;
- description of the activities of the organization with respect to personal information received from the EU; and
- description of the organization's privacy policy for such personal information, including:
- where the privacy policy is available for viewing by the public,
- its effective date of implementation,
- a contact office for the handling of complaints, access requests, and any other issues arising under the safe harbor,
- the specific statutory body that has jurisdiction to hear any claims against the organization regarding possible unfair or deceptive practices and violations of laws or regulations governing privacy (and that is listed in the annex to the Principles),
- name of any privacy programs in which the organization is a member,
- method of verification (e.g. in-house, third party)*, and
- the independent recourse mechanism that is available to investigate unresolved complaints.

Where the organization wishes its safe harbor benefits to cover human resources information transferred from the EU for use in the context of the employment relationship, it may do so where there is a statutory body with jurisdiction to hear claims against the organization arising out of human resources information that is listed in the annex to the Principles. In addition the organization must indicate this in its letter and declare its commitment to cooperate with the EU authority or authorities concerned in conformity with FAQ 9 and FAQ 5 as applicable and that it will comply with the advice given by such authorities.

The Department (or its designee) will maintain a list of all organizations that file such letters, thereby assuring the availability of safe harbor benefits, and will update such list on the basis of annual letters and notifications received pursuant to FAQ 11. Such self-certification letters should be provided not less than annually. Otherwise the organization will be removed from the list and safe harbor benefits will no longer be assured. Both the list and the self-certification letters submitted by the organizations will be made publicly available. All organizations that self- certify for the safe harbor must also state in their relevant published privacy policy statements that they adhere to the Safe Harbor Principles.

The undertaking to adhere to the Safe Harbor Principles is not time-limited in respect of data received during the period in which the organization enjoys the benefits of the safe harbor. Its undertaking means that it will continue to apply the Principles to such data for as long as the organization stores, uses or discloses them, even if it subsequently leaves the safe harbor for any reason.

An organization that will cease to exist as a separate legal entity as a result of a merger or a takeover must notify the Department of Commerce (or its designee) of this in advance. The notification should also indicate whether the acquiring entity or the entity resulting from the merger will (1) continue to be bound by the Safe Harbor Principles by the operation of law governing the takeover or merger or (2) elect to self-certify its adherence to the Safe Harbor Principles or put in place other safeguards, such as a written agreement that will ensure adherence to the Safe Harbor Principles. Where neither (1) nor (2) applies, any data that has been acquired under the safe harbor must be promptly deleted.

An organization does not need to subject all personal information to the Safe Harbor Principles, but it must subject to the Safe Harbor Principles all personal data received from the EU after it joins the safe harbor.

Any misrepresentation to the general public concerning an organization's adherence to the Safe Harbor Principles may be actionable by the Federal Trade Commission or other relevant government body. Misrepresentations to the Department of Commerce (or its designee) may be actionable under the False Statements Act (18 U.S.C. § 1001).

*See FAQ 7 on verification

↪ certified until not certified

FAQ 7 - Verification

Q: How do organizations provide follow up procedures for verifying that the attestations and assertions they make about their safe harbor privacy practices are true and those privacy practices have been implemented as represented and in accordance with the Safe Harbor Principles?

A: To meet the verification requirements of the Enforcement Principle, an organization may verify such attestations and assertions either through self-assessment or outside compliance reviews.

Under the self- assessment approach, such verification would have to indicate that an organization's published privacy policy regarding personal information received from the EU is accurate, comprehensive, prominently displayed, completely implemented and accessible. It would also need to indicate that its privacy policy conforms to the Safe Harbor Principles; that individuals are informed of any in-house arrangements for handling complaints and of the independent mechanisms through which they may pursue complaints; that it has in place procedures for training employees in its implementation, and disciplining them for failure to follow it; and that it has in place internal procedures for periodically conducting objective reviews of compliance with the above. A statement verifying the self-assessment should be signed by a corporate officer or other authorized representative of the organization at least once a year and made available upon request by individuals or in the context of an investigation or a complaint about non-compliance.

Organizations should retain their records on the implementation of their safe harbor privacy practices and make them available upon request in the context of an investigation or a complaint about non-compliance to the independent body responsible for investigating complaints or to the agency with unfair and deceptive practices jurisdiction.

Where the organization has chosen outside compliance review, such a review needs to demonstrate that its privacy policy regarding personal information received from the EU conforms to the Safe Harbor Principles, that it is being complied with and that individuals are informed of the mechanisms through which they may pursue complaints. The methods of review may include without limitation auditing, random reviews, use of "decoys," or use of technology tools as appropriate. A statement verifying that an outside compliance review has been successfully completed should be signed either by the reviewer or by the corporate officer or other authorized representative of the organization at least once a year and made available upon request by individuals or in the context of an investigation or a complaint about compliance.

FAQ 8 - Access

ACCESS PRINCIPLE:

Individuals must have access to personal information about them that an organization holds and be able to correct, amend or delete that information where it is inaccurate, except where the burden or expense of providing access would be disproportionate to the risks to the individual's privacy in the case in question, or where the legitimate rights of persons other than the individual would be violated.

1. Q: Is the right of access absolute?

1. A: No. Under the Safe Harbor Principles, the right of access is fundamental to privacy protection. In particular, it allows individuals to verify the accuracy of information held about them. Nonetheless, the obligation of an organization to provide access to the personal information it holds about an individual is subject to the principle of proportionality or reasonableness and has to be tempered in certain instances. Indeed, the Explanatory Memorandum to the 1980 OECD Privacy Guidelines makes clear that an organization's access

obligation is not absolute. It does not require the exceedingly thorough search mandated, for example, by a subpoena, nor does it require access to all the different forms in which the information may be maintained by the organization.

Rather, experience has shown that in responding to individuals' access requests, organizations should first be guided by the concern(s) that led to the requests in the first place. For example, if an access request is vague or broad in scope, an organization may engage the individual in a dialogue so as to better understand the motivation for the request and to locate responsive information. The organization might inquire about which part(s) of the organization the individual interacted with and/or about the nature of the information (or its use) that is the subject of the access request. Individuals do not, however, have to justify requests for access to their own data.

Expense and burden are important factors and should be taken into account but they are not controlling in determining whether providing access is reasonable. For example, if the information is used for decisions that will significantly affect the individual (e.g., the denial or grant of important benefits, such as insurance, a mortgage, or a job), then consistent with the other provisions of these FAQs, the organization would have to disclose that information even if it is relatively difficult or expensive to provide.

If the information requested is not sensitive or not used for decisions that will significantly affect the individual (e.g., non-sensitive marketing data that is used to determine whether or not to send the individual a catalog), but is readily available and inexpensive to provide, an organization would have to provide access to factual information that the organization stores about the individual. The information concerned could include facts obtained from the individual, facts gathered in the course of a transaction, or facts obtained from others that pertain to the individual.

Consistent with the fundamental nature of access, organizations should always make good faith efforts to provide access. For example, where certain information needs to be protected and can be readily separated from other information subject to an access request, the organization should redact the protected information and make available the other information. If an organization determines that access should be denied in any particular instance, it should provide the individual requesting access with an explanation of why it has made that determination and a contact point for any further inquiries.

2. Q: What is confidential commercial information and may organizations deny access in order to safeguard it?

2. A: Confidential commercial information (as that term is used in the Federal Rules of Civil Procedure on discovery) is information which an organization has taken steps to protect from disclosure, where disclosure would help a competitor in the market. The particular computer

program an organization uses, such as a modeling program, or the details of that program may be confidential commercial information. Where confidential commercial information can be readily separated from other information subject to an access request, the organization should redact the confidential commercial information and make available the non-confidential information. Organizations may deny or limit access to the extent that granting it would reveal its own confidential commercial information as defined above, such as marketing inferences or classifications generated by the organization, or the confidential commercial information of another where such information is subject to a contractual obligation of confidentiality in circumstances where such an obligation of confidentiality would normally be undertaken or imposed.

3. Q: In providing access, may an organization disclose to individuals personal information about them derived from its data bases or is access to the data base itself required?

3. A: Access can be provided in the form of disclosure by an organization to the individual and does not require access by the individual to an organization's data base.

4. Q: Does an organization have to restructure its data bases to be able to provide access?

4. A: Access needs to be provided only to the extent that an organization stores the information. The access principle does not itself create any obligation to retain, maintain, reorganize, or restructure personal information files.

5. Q: These replies make clear that access may be denied in certain circumstances. In what other circumstances may an organization deny individuals access to their personal information?

5. A: Such circumstances are limited, and any reasons for denying access must be specific. An organization can refuse to provide access to information to the extent that disclosure is likely to interfere with the safeguarding of important countervailing public interests, such as national security; defense; or public security. In addition, where personal information is processed *solely* for research or statistical purposes, access may be denied. Other reasons for denying or limiting access are:

- interference with execution or enforcement of the law, including the prevention, investigation or detection of offenses or the right to a fair trial;
- interference with private causes of action, including the prevention, investigation or detection of legal claims or the right to a fair trial;
- disclosure of personal information pertaining to other individual(s) where such references cannot be redacted;
- breaching a legal or other professional privilege or obligation;
- breaching the necessary confidentiality of future or ongoing negotiations, such as those involving the acquisition of publicly quoted companies;
- prejudicing employee security investigations or grievance proceedings;

- prejudicing the confidentiality that may be necessary for limited periods in connection with employee succession planning and corporate re-organizations; or

- prejudicing the confidentiality that may be necessary in connection with monitoring, inspection or regulatory functions connected with sound economic or financial management; or

- other circumstances in which the burden or cost of providing access would be disproportionate or the legitimate rights or interests of others would be violated.

- An organization which claims an exception has the burden of demonstrating its applicability (as is normally the case). As noted above, the reasons for denying or limiting access and a contact point for further inquires should be given to individuals.

6. Q: Can an organization charge a fee to cover the cost of providing access?

6. A: Yes. The OECD Guidelines recognize that organizations may charge a fee, provided that it is not excessive. Thus organizations may charge a reasonable fee for access. Charging a fee may be useful in discouraging repetitive and vexatious requests.

Organizations that are in the business of selling publicly available information may thus charge the organization's customary fee in responding to requests for access. Individuals may alternatively seek access to their information from the organization that originally compiled the data.

Access may not be refused on cost grounds if the individual offers to pay the costs.

7. Q: Is an organization required to provide access to personal information derived from public records?

7. A: To clarify first, public records are those records kept by government agencies or entities at any level that are open to consultation by the public in general. It is not necessary to apply the Access Principle to such information as long as it is not combined with other personal information, apart from when small amounts of non-public record information are used for indexing or organizing public record information. However, any conditions for consultation established by the relevant jurisdiction are to be respected. Where public record information is combined with other non-public record information (other than as specifically noted above), however, an organization must provide access to all such information, assuming it is not subject to other permitted exceptions.

8. Q: Does the Access Principle have to be applied to publicly available personal information?

8. A: As with public record information (see Q7), it is not necessary to provide access to information that is already publicly available to the public at large, as long as it is not combined with non-publicly available information.

9. Q: How can an organization protect itself against repetitious or vexatious requests for access?

9. A: An organization does not have to respond to such requests for access. For these reasons, organizations may charge a reasonable fee and may set reasonable limits on the number of times within a given period that access requests from a particular individual will be met. In setting such limitations, an organization should consider such factors as the frequency with which information is updated, the purpose for which the data are used, and the nature of the information.

10. Q: How can an organization protect itself against fraudulent requests for access?
10. A: An organization is not required to provide access unless it is supplied with sufficient information to allow it to confirm the identity of the person making the request.

11. Q: Is there a time within which responses must be provided to access requests?
11. A: Yes, organizations should respond without excessive delay and within a reasonable time period. This requirement may be satisfied in different ways as the explanatory memorandum to the 1980 OECD Privacy Guidelines states. For example, a data controller who provides information to data subjects at regular intervals may be exempted from obligations to respond at once to individual requests.

FAQ 9 - Human Resources

1.Q. Is the transfer from the EU to the United States of personal information collected in the context of the employment relationship covered by the safe harbor?
1. A: Yes, where a company in the EU transfers personal information about its employees (past or present) collected in the context of the employment relationship, to a parent, affiliate, or unaffiliated service provider in the United States participating in the safe harbor, the transfer enjoys the benefits of the safe harbor. In such cases, the collection of the information and its processing prior to transfer will have been subject to the national laws of the EU country where it was collected, and any conditions for or restrictions on its transfer according to those laws will have to be respected.

The Safe Harbor Principles are relevant only when individually identified records are transferred or accessed. Statistical reporting relying on aggregate employment data and/or the use of anonymized or pseudonymized data does not raise privacy concerns.

2. Q: How do the Notice and Choice Principles apply to such information?
2. A: A U.S. organization that has received employee information from the EU under the safe harbor may disclose it to third parties and/or use it for different purposes only in accordance with the Notice and Choice Principles. For example, where an organization intends to use personal information collected through the employment relationship for non-employment-related purposes, such as marketing communications, the U.S. organization must provide the affected individuals with choice before doing so, unless they have already authorized the use of

the information for such purposes. Moreover, such choices must not be used to restrict employment opportunities or take any punitive action against such employees.

It should be noted that certain generally applicable conditions for transfer from some Member States may preclude other uses of such information even after transfer outside the EU and such conditions will have to be respected.

In addition, employers should make reasonable efforts to accommodate employee privacy preferences. This could include, for example, restricting access to the data, anonymizing certain data, or assigning codes or pseudonyms when the actual names are not required for the management purpose at hand.

To the extent and for the period necessary to avoid prejudicing the legitimate interests of the organization in making promotions, appointments, or other similar employment decisions, an organization does not need to offer notice and choice.

3. Q: How does the Access Principle apply?

3. A: The FAQs on access provide guidance on reasons which may justify denying or limiting access on request in the human resources context. Of course, employers in the European Union must comply with local regulations and ensure that European Union employees have access to such information as is required by law in their home countries, regardless of the location of data processing and storage. The safe harbor requires that an organization processing such data in the United States will cooperate in providing such access either directly or through the EU employer.

4. Q: How will enforcement be handled for employee data under the Safe Harbor Principles?

4. A: In so far as information is used only in the context of the employment relationship, primary responsibility for the data vis-à-vis the employee remains with the company in the EU. It follows that, where European employees make complaints about violations of their data protection rights and are not satisfied with the results of internal review, complaint, and appeal procedures (or any applicable grievance procedures under a contract with a trade union), they should be directed to the state or national data protection or labor authority in the jurisdiction where the employee works. This also includes cases where the alleged mishandling of their personal information has taken place in the United States, is the responsibility of the U.S. organization that has received the information from the employer and not of the employer and thus involves an alleged breach of the Safe Harbor Principles, rather than of national laws implementing the Directive. This will be the most efficient way to address the often overlapping rights and obligations imposed by local labor law and labor agreements as well as data protection law.

Recent Developments
Safe Harbor Arrangement (EU-US)

A U.S. organization participating in the safe harbor that uses EU human resources data transferred from the Europe Union in the context of the employment relationship and that wishes such transfers to be covered by the safe harbor must therefore commit to cooperate in investigations by and to comply with the advice of competent EU authorities in such cases. The DPAs that have agreed to cooperate in this way will notify the European Commission and the Department of Commerce. If a U.S. organization participating in the safe harbor wishes to transfer human resources data from a Member State where the DPA has not so agreed, the provisions of FAQ 5 will apply.

FAQ 10 - Article 17 contracts

Q: When data is transferred from the EU to the United States only for processing purposes, will a contract be required, regardless of participation by the processor in the safe harbor ?

A: Yes. Data controllers in the European Union are always required to enter into a contract when a transfer for mere processing is made, whether the processing operation is carried out inside or outside the EU. The purpose of the contract is to protect the interests of the data controller, i.e. the person or body who determines the purposes and means of processing, who retains full responsibility for the data *vis-à-vis* the individual(s) concerned. The contract thus specifies the processing to be carried out and any measures necessary to ensure that the data are kept secure.

A U.S. organization participating in the safe harbor and receiving personal information from the EU merely for processing thus does not have to apply the Principles to this information, because the controller in the EU remains responsible for it *vis-à-vis* the individual in accordance with the relevant EU provisions (which may be more stringent than the equivalent Safe Harbor Principles).

Because adequate protection is provided by safe harbor participants, contracts with safe harbor participants for mere processing do not require prior authorization (or such authorization will be granted automatically by the Member States) as would be required for contracts with recipients not participating in the safe harbor or otherwise not providing adequate protection.

FAQ 11 - Dispute Resolution and Enforcement

Q: How should the dispute resolution requirements of the Enforcement Principle be implemented, and how will an organization's persistent failure to comply with the Principles be handled?

A: The Enforcement Principle sets out the requirements for safe harbor enforcement. How to meet the requirements of point (b) of the Principle is set out in the FAQ on verification (FAQ 7). This FAQ 11 addresses points (a) and (c), both of which require independent recourse mechanisms. These mechanisms may take different forms, but they must meet the Enforcement Principle's requirements. Organizations may satisfy the requirements through the following: (1) compliance with private sector developed privacy programs that incorporate the Safe Harbor Principles into their rules and that include effective enforcement mechanisms of the type described in the Enforcement Principle; (2) compliance with legal or regulatory supervisory authorities that provide for handling of individual complaints and dispute resolution; or (3) commitment to cooperate with data protection authorities located in the European Union or their authorized representatives. This list is intended to be illustrative and not limiting. The private sector may design other mechanisms to provide enforcement, so long as they meet the requirements of the Enforcement Principle and the FAQs. Please note that the Enforcement Principle's requirements are additional to the requirement set forth in paragraph 3 of the introduction to the Principles that self- regulatory efforts must be enforceable under Article 5 of the Federal Trade Commission Act or similar statute.

Recourse Mechanisms. Consumers should be encouraged to raise any complaints they may have with the relevant organization before proceeding to independent recourse mechanisms. Whether a recourse mechanism is independent is a factual question that can be demonstrated in a number of ways, for example, by transparent composition and financing or a proven track record. As required by the enforcement principle, the recourse available to individuals must be readily available and affordable. Dispute resolution bodies should look into each complaint received from individuals unless they are obviously unfounded or frivolous. This does not preclude the establishment of eligibility requirements by the organization operating the recourse mechanism, but such requirements should be transparent and justified (for example to exclude complaints that fall outside the scope of the program or are for consideration in another forum), and should not have the effect of undermining the commitment to look into legitimate complaints. In addition, recourse mechanisms should provide individuals with full and readily available information about how the dispute resolution procedure works when they file a complaint. Such information should include notice about the mechanism's privacy practices, in conformity with the Safe Harbor Principles.(1) They should also co-operate in the development of tools such as standard complaint forms to facilitate the complaint resolution process.

Remedies and Sanctions. The result of any remedies provided by the dispute resolution body should be that the effects of noncompliance are reversed or corrected by the organization, in so far as feasible, and that future processing by the organization will be in conformity with the Principles and, where appropriate, that processing of the personal data of the individual who has brought the complaint will cease. Sanctions need to be rigorous enough to ensure compliance by the organization with the Principles. A range of sanctions of varying degrees of severity will allow dispute resolution bodies to respond appropriately to varying degrees of non-compliance. Sanctions should include both publicity for findings of non-compliance and the requirement to delete data in certain circumstances.(2) Other sanctions could include suspension and removal of a seal, compensation for individuals for losses incurred as a result of non-compliance and injunctive orders. Private sector dispute resolution bodies and self-regulatory bodies must notify failures of safe harbor organizations to comply with their rulings to the governmental body with applicable jurisdiction or to the courts, as appropriate, and to notify the Department of Commerce (or its designee).

FTC Action. The FTC has committed to reviewing on a priority basis referrals received from privacy self-regulatory organizations, such as BBBOnline and TRUSTe, and EU Member States alleging non-compliance with the Safe Harbor Principles to determine whether Section 5 of the FTC Act prohibiting unfair or deceptive acts or practices in commerce has been violated. If the FTC concludes that it has reason[s] to believe Section 5 has been violated, it may resolve the matter by seeking an administrative cease and desist order prohibiting the challenged practices or by filing a complaint in a federal district court, which if successful could result in a federal court order to same effect. The FTC may obtain civil penalties for violations of an administrative cease and desist order and may pursue civil or criminal contempt for violation of a federal court order. The FTC will notify the Department of Commerce of any such actions it takes. The Department of Commerce encourages other government bodies to notify it of the final disposition of any such referrals or other rulings determining adherence to the Safe Harbor Principles.

Persistent Failure to Comply. If an organization persistently fails to comply with the Principles, it is no longer entitled to benefit from the safe harbor. Persistent failure to comply arises where an organization that has self-certified to the Department of Commerce (or its designee) refuses to comply with a final determination by any self- regulatory or government body or where such a body determines that an organization frequently fails to comply with the Principles to the point where its claim to comply is no longer credible. In these cases, the organization must promptly notify the Department of Commerce (or its designee) of such facts. Failure to do so may be actionable under the False Statements Act(18 U.S.C. § 1001).

The Department (or its designee) will indicate on the public list it maintains of organizations self-certifying adherence to the Safe Harbor Principles any notification it receives of persistent failure to comply, whether it is received from the organization itself, from a self- regulatory body, or from a government body, but only after first providing thirty (30) days' notice and an opportunity to respond to the organization that has failed to comply. Accordingly, the public list maintained by the Department of Commerce (or its designee) will make clear which organizations are assured and which organizations are no longer assured of safe harbor benefits.

An organization applying to participate in a self-regulatory body for the purposes of re-qualifying for the safe harbor must provide that body with full information about its prior participation in the safe harbor.

1 Dispute resolution bodies are not required to conform with the enforcement principle. They may also derogate from the Principles where they encounter conflicting obligations or explicit authorizations in the performance of their specific tasks.

2 Dispute resolutions bodies have discretion about the circumstances in which they use these sanctions. The sensitivity of the data concerned is one factor to be taken into consideration in deciding whether deletion of data should be required, as is whether an organization has collected, used or disclosed information in blatant contravention of the Principles.

FAQ 12 - Choice - Timing of Opt Out

Q: Does the Choice Principle permit an individual to exercise choice only at the beginning of a relationship or at any time?

A: Generally, the purpose of the Choice Principle is to ensure that personal information is used and disclosed in ways that are consistent with the individual's expectations and choices. Accordingly, an individual should be able to exercise "opt out" (or choice) of having personal information used for direct marketing at any time subject to reasonable limits established by the organization, such as giving the organization time to make the opt out effective. An organization may also require sufficient information to confirm the identity of the individual requesting the "opt out." In the United States, individuals may be able to exercise this option through the use of a central "opt out" program such as the Direct Marketing Association's Mail Preference Service. Organizations that participate in the Direct Marketing Association's Mail Preference Service should promote its availability to consumers who do not wish to receive commercial information. In any event, an individual should be given a readily available and affordable mechanism to exercise this option.

Similarly, an organization may use information for certain direct marketing purposes when it is impracticable to provide the individual with an opportunity to opt out before using the information, if the organization promptly gives the individual such opportunity at the same time (and upon request at any time) to decline (at no cost to the individual) to receive any further direct marketing communications and the organization complies with the individual's wishes.

FAQ 13 - Travel Information

Q: When can airline passenger reservation and other travel information, such as frequent flyer or hotel reservation information and special handling needs, such as meals to meet religious requirements or physical assistance, be transferred to organizations located outside the EU?

A: Such information may be transferred in several different circumstances. Under Article 26 of the Directive, personal data may be transferred "to a third country which does not ensure an adequate level of protection within the meaning of Article 25(2)" on the condition that it (1) is necessary to provide the services requested by the consumer or to fulfill the terms of an agreement, such as a "frequent flyer" agreement; or (2) has been unambiguously consented to by the consumer. U.S. organizations subscribing to the safe harbor provide adequate protection for personal data and may therefore receive data transfers from the EU without meeting those conditions or other conditions set out in Article 26 of the Directive. Since the safe harbor includes specific rules for sensitive information, such information (which may need to be collected, for example, in connection with customers' needs for physical assistance) may be included in transfers to safe harbor participants. In all cases, however, the organization transferring the information has to respect the law in the EU Member State in which it is operating, which may *inter alia* impose special conditions for the handling of sensitive data.

FAQ 14 - Pharmaceutical and Medical Products

1. Q: If personal data are collected in the EU and transferred to the United States for pharmaceutical research and/or other purposes, do Member State laws or the Safe Harbor Principles apply?

1. A: Member State law applies to the collection of the personal data and to any processing that takes place prior to the transfer to the United States. The Safe Harbor Principles apply to the data once they have been transferred to the United States. Data used for pharmaceutical research and other purposes should be anonymized when appropriate.

2. Q: Personal data developed in specific medical or pharmaceutical research studies often play a valuable role in future scientific research. Where personal data collected for one research study are transferred to a U.S. organization in the safe harbor, may the organization use the data for a new scientific research activity?

2. A: Yes, if appropriate notice and choice have been provided in the first instance. Such a notice should provide information about any future specific uses of the data, such as periodic follow-up, related studies, or marketing. It is understood that not all future uses of the data can be specified, since a new research use could arise from new insights on the original data, new medical discoveries and advances, and public health and regulatory developments. Where appropriate, the notice should therefore include an explanation that personal data may be used in future medical and pharmaceutical research activities that are unanticipated. If the use is not consistent with the general research purpose(s) for which the data were originally collected, or to which the individual has consented subsequently, new consent must be obtained.

3. Q: What happens to an individual's data if a participant decides voluntarily or at the request of the sponsor to withdraw from the clinical trial?

3. A: Participants may decide or be asked to withdraw from a clinical trial at any time. Any data collected previous to withdrawal may still be processed along with other data collected as part of the clinical trial, however, if this was made clear to the participant in the notice at the time he or she agreed to participate.

4. Q: Pharmaceutical and medical device companies are allowed to provide personal data from clinical trials conducted in the EU to regulators in the United States for regulatory and supervision purposes. Are similar transfers allowed to parties other than regulators, such as company locations and other researchers?

4. A: Yes, consistent with the Principles of Notice and Choice.

5. Q: To ensure objectivity in many clinical trials, participants, and often investigators, as well, cannot be given access to information about which treatment each participant may be receiving. Doing so would jeopardize the validity of the research study and results. Will participants in such clinical trials (referred to as "blinded" studies) have access to the data on their treatment during the trial?

5. A: No, such access does not have to be provided to a participant if this restriction has been explained when the participant entered the trial and the disclosure of such information would jeopardize the integrity of the research effort. Agreement to participate in the trial under these conditions is a reasonable forgoing of the right of access. Following the conclusion of the trial and analysis of the results, participants should have access to their data if they request it. They should seek it primarily from the physician or other health care provider from whom they received treatment within the clinical trial, or secondarily from the sponsoring company.

6. Q: Does a pharmaceutical or medical device firm have to apply the Safe Harbor Principles with respect to notice, choice, onward transfer, and access in its product safety and efficacy monitoring activities, including the reporting of adverse events and the tracking of patients/subjects using certain medicines or medical devices (e.g. a pacemaker)?

6. A: No, to the extent that adherence to the Principles interferes with compliance with regulatory requirements. This is true both with respect to reports by, for example, health care providers, to pharmaceutical and medical device companies, and with respect to reports by pharmaceutical and medical device companies to government agencies like the Food and Drug Administration.

7. Q: Invariably, research data are uniquely key-coded at their origin by the principal investigator so as not to reveal the identity of individual data subjects. Pharmaceutical companies sponsoring such research do not receive the key. The unique key code is held only by the researcher, so that he/she can identify the research subject under special circumstances (e.g. if follow-up medical attention is required). Does a transfer from the EU to the United States of data coded in this way constitute a transfer of personal data that is subject to the Safe Harbor Principles?

7. A: No. This would not constitute a transfer of personal data that would be subject to the Principles.

FAQ 15- Public Record and Publicly Available Information

Q: Is it necessary to apply the Notice, Choice and Onward Transfer Principles to public record information or publicly available information?

A: It is not necessary to apply the Notice, Choice or Onward Transfer Principles to public record information, as long as it is not combined with non-public record information and as long as any conditions for consultation established by the relevant jurisdiction are respected.

Recent Developments
Safe Harbor Arrangement (EU-US)

Also, it is generally not necessary to apply the Notice, Choice or Onward Transfer Principles to publicly available information unless the European transferor indicates that such information is subject to restrictions that require application of those Principles by the organization for the uses it intends. Organizations will have no liability for how such information is used by those obtaining such information from published materials.

Where an organization is found to have intentionally made personal information public in contravention of the Principles so that it or others may benefit from these exceptions, it will cease to qualify for the benefits of the safe harbor.

Letter from U.S. Department of Commerce to Commission Services transmitting the Safe Harbor Privacy Principles and FAQs, etc.

July 17, 2000

Mr. John Mogg
Director DG Internal Market
European Commission
Office C 107-6/72
Rue de la Loi, 200
1049 Brussels
BELGIUM

Dear Mr. Mogg:

I am pleased to provide you with several documents: 1) the "Safe Harbor Privacy Principles," issued by the U.S. Department of Commerce on July 21, 2000; 2) Frequently Asked Questions (FAQs) that supplement the Safe Harbor Principles; 3) an overview on how organizations' safe harbor commitments will be enforced in the United States; 4) a memorandum on damages available to individuals; 5) the July 14, 2000 letter from the Federal Trade Commission; and 6) the July 14, 2000 letter from the U.S. Department of Transportation.

The Department is providing these documents under its authority to foster, promote, and develop international commerce. Both the Safe Harbor Principles and the FAQs ("the Principles") are intended to serve as authoritative guidance to U.S. companies and other organizations receiving personal data from the European Union and wishing to establish a predictable basis for the continuation of such transfers. The enforcement overview and other supporting documents are intended to explain how U.S. enforcement mechanisms, based either on law and regulation or self-regulation, will satisfy the requirements of the Enforcement Principle and ensure that an organization's commitment to adhere to the Principles will be effectively enforced. The safe harbor documents of course need to be read against the U.S. legal system and its well known features, such as class actions and contingency fees, which allow consumers even with novel claims relatively ready and inexpensive access to the courts and damages where justified.

Organizations can be assured of the benefits of the safe harbor by self-certifying that they adhere to the Principles. The Department of Commerce will arrange for a list to be maintained of all organizations that self-certify their adherence to the Principles. Both the list and the notifications submitted by organizations containing information with regard to their implementation of the Principles will be made publicly available as will any proper and final adverse determination made by a U.S. enforcement body and notified to the Department of Commerce (or its designee) that a safe harbor organization has persistently failed to comply with the Principles. Where in complying with the Principles, an organization relies in whole or in part on self-regulation, its failure to comply with such self-regulation must also be actionable under Section 5 of the Federal Trade Commission Act prohibiting unfair and deceptive acts or another law or regulation prohibiting such acts.

On the basis of these documents, our expectation is that the European Commission will determine that this safe harbor framework provides adequate protection for the purposes of Article 25.1 of the Data Protection Directive and data transfers from the European Union would continue to organizations that participate in the safe harbor. As a result, adherence to the Principles on these terms will reduce the uncertainty about the impact of the "adequacy" standard on personal data transfers to such organizations from EU Member States.

On the basis of our dialogue, we understand that the Commission and Member States will use the flexibility of Article 26 and any discretion regarding enforcement to avoid disrupting data flows to U.S. organizations during the implementation phase of the safe harbor and that the situation will be reviewed in mid 2001. This will give U.S. organizations an opportunity to decide whether to enter the safe harbor and (if necessary) to update their information practices. We will encourage U.S. organizations to enter the safe harbor as soon as possible to enhance privacy protection and because participation in the safe harbor provides greater certainty that data flows will continue without interruption.

During the dialogue, you sought assurances that where the United States enacted privacy legislation providing greater privacy protection than the safe harbor, such protection should be applied to safe harbor data too, in cases where the law applied with respect to U.S. citizens only, but was silent on its applicability with respect to non-U.S. citizens. You noted that the EU Directive on Data Protection applies to all personal information processed in Europe, regardless of the individuals' citizenship or residency. I would like to confirm that we agree that privacy legislation should not apply differently on the basis of nationality, as provided for in paragraph 19(e) of the OECD guidelines and paragraph 70 of the explanatory memorandum and to assure you that if such legislation were proposed in Congress, we would work within the legislative process to avoid any such effects. We will also continue our efforts, in line with our general commitment to regulatory co-operation in the context of the Transatlantic Economic Partnership, to keep you informed of legislative and other developments in the United States in the field of privacy protection of which we are aware, with particular attention to any such developments that may create allowable exceptions to the Principles. Of course, you can raise any concerns about these issues under the review arrangements provided for.

Similarly, on a number of occasions I raised with you the concerns of U.S. industry about the possible effects of the safe harbor as regards jurisdiction and applicable law. I would like to confirm that it is the U.S. intention that participation in the safe harbor does not change the *status quo ante* for any organization with respect to jurisdiction, applicable law and liability in the European Union. Moreover, our discussions with respect to the safe harbor have not resolved nor prejudged the questions of jurisdiction or applicable law with respect to websites. All existing rules, principles, conventions and treaties relating to international conflicts of law continue to apply and are not prejudiced in any way by the safe harbor arrangement.

Finally, the Department of Commerce will notify the Commission in advance of any proposed FAQs or revisions to existing ones.

Sincerely,

Robert S. LaRussa, Acting

Safe Harbor Enforcement Overview

July 14, 2000

Safe Harbor Enforcement Overview
Federal and State "Unfair and Deceptive Practices" Authority and Privacy

This memorandum outlines the authority of the Federal Trade Commission (FTC) under Section 5 of the Federal Trade Commission Act (15 U.S.C. §§ 41-58, as amended) to take action against those who fail to protect the privacy of personal information in accordance with their representations and/or commitments to do so. It also addresses the exceptions to that authority and the ability of other federal and state agencies to take action where the FTC does not have authority.(1)

FTC Authority over Unfair or Deceptive Practices

Section 5 of the Federal Trade Commission Act declares "unfair or deceptive acts or practices in or affecting commerce" to be illegal. 15 U.S.C. § 45(a)(1). Section 5 confers on the FTC the plenary power to prevent such acts and practices. 15 U.S.C. § 45(a)(2). Accordingly, the FTC may, upon conducting a formal hearing, issue a "cease and desist" order to stop the offending conduct. 15 U.S.C. § 45(b). If it would be in the public interest to do so, the FTC can also seek a temporary restraining order or temporary or permanent injunction in U.S. district court. 15 U.S.C. § 53(b). In cases where there is a widespread pattern of unfair or deceptive acts or practices, or where it has already issued cease and desist orders on the matter, the FTC may promulgate an administrative rule prescribing the acts or practices involved. 15 U.S.C. § 57a.

Anyone who does not comply with an FTC order is subject to a civil penalty of up to $11,000, with each day of a continuing violation constituting a separate violation.(2) 15 U.S.C. § 45(l). Likewise, anyone who knowingly violates an FTC rule is liable for $11,000 for each violation. 15 U.S.C. § 45(m). Enforcement actions can be brought by either the Department of Justice, or if it declines by the FTC. 15 U.S.C. § 56.

FTC Authority and Privacy

In exercising its Section 5 authority, the FTC takes the position that misrepresenting why information is being collected from consumers or how the information will be used constitutes a deceptive practice.(3) For example, in 1998, the FTC filed a complaint against GeoCities for disclosing information it had collected on its Web site to third parties for purposes of solicitation, and without prior permission, despite its representations to the contrary.(4) The FTC staff has also asserted that the collection of personal information from children, and sale and disclosure of that information, without the parents' consent is likely to be an unfair practice.(5)

In a letter to Director General John Mogg of the European Commission, FTC Chairman Pitofsky noted the limitations on the FTC's authority to protect privacy where there has not been a misrepresentation (or no representation at all) as to how the information collected will be used. FTC Chairman Pitofsky letter to John Mogg (September 23, 1998). However, companies that want to avail themselves of the proposed "safe harbor" will have to certify that they will protect the information they collect in accordance with prescribed guidelines. Consequently, where a company certifies that it will safeguard the privacy of information and then fails to do so, such action would be a misrepresentation and a "deceptive practice" within the meaning of Section 5.

Recent Developments
Safe Harbor Arrangement (EU-US)

As the FTC's jurisdiction extends to unfair or deceptive acts or practices "in or affecting commerce," the FTC will not have jurisdiction over the collection and use of personal information for noncommercial purposes, charitable fund-raising for example. *See* Pitofsky letter, p. 3. However, the use of personal information in any commercial transaction will satisfy this jurisdictional predicate. Thus, for example, the sale by an employer of personal information on its employees to a direct marketer would bring the transaction within the purview of Section 5.

Section 5 Exceptions

Section 5 establishes exceptions to the FTC's authority over unfair or deceptive acts or practices with respect to:

- financial institutions, including banks, savings and loans, and credit unions;
- telecommunications and interstate transportation common carriers;
- air carriers; and
- packers and stockyard operators.

See 15 U.S.C. § 45(a)(2). We discuss each exception, and the regulatory authority that takes its place, below.

Financial Institutions(6)

The first exception applies to "banks, savings and loan institutions described in section 18(f)(3) [15 U.S.C. § 57a(f)(3)]" and "Federal credit unions described in section 18(f)(4) [15 U.S.C. § 57a(f)(4)]."(7) These financial institutions are instead subject to regulations issued by the Federal Reserve Board, the Office of Thrift Supervision(8), and the National Credit Union Administration Board, respectively. *See* 15 U.S.C. § 57a(f). These regulatory agencies are directed to prescribe the regulations necessary to prevent unfair and deceptive practices by these financial institutions(9) and to establish a separate division to handle consumer complaints. 15 U.S.C. § 57a(f)(1). Finally, authority for enforcement derives from section 8 of the Federal Deposit Insurance Act (12 U.S.C. § 1818), for banks and savings and loans, and sections 120 and 206 of the Federal Credit Union Act, for Federal credit unions. 15 U.S.C. §§ 57a(f)(2)-(4).

Although the insurance industry is not specifically included in the list of exceptions in Section 5, the McCarran-Ferguson Act (15 U.S.C. § 1011 *et seq.*) generally leaves the regulation of the business of insurance to the individual states.(10) Furthermore, pursuant to section 2(b) of the McCarran-Ferguson Act, no federal law will invalidate, impair, or supersede state regulation "unless such Act specifically relates to the business of insurance." 15 U.S.C. § 1012(b). However, the provisions of the FTC Act apply to the insurance industry "to the extent that such business is not regulated by State law." *Id*. It should also be noted that McCarran-Ferguson defers to the states only with respect to "the business of insurance." Therefore, the FTC retains residual authority over unfair or deceptive practices by insurance companies when they are not engaged in the business of insurance. This could include, for example, when insurers sell personal information about their policy holders to direct marketers of non-insurance products.(11)

Common Carriers

The second Section 5 exception extends to those common carriers that are "subject to the Acts to regulate commerce." 15 U.S.C. § 45(a)(2). In this case, the "Acts to regulate commerce" refer to subtitle IV of Title 49 of the United States Code and to the Communications Act of 1934 (47 U.S.C. § 151 *et seq.*) (the Communications Act). *See* 15 U.S.C. § 44.

49 U.S.C. subtitle IV (Interstate Transportation) covers rail carriers, motor carriers, water carriers, brokers, freight forwarders, and pipeline carriers. 49 U.S.C. § 10101 *et seq.* These various common carriers are subject to regulation by the Surface Transportation Board, an independent agency within the Department of Transportation. 49 U.S.C. §§ 10501, 13501, and 15301. In each instance, the carrier is prohibited from disclosing information about the nature, destination, and other aspects of its cargo that might be used to the shipper's detriment. *See* 49 U.S.C. §§ 11904, 14908, and 16103. We note that these provisions refer to information regarding the shipper's cargo and thus do not appear to extend to personal information about the shipper that is unrelated to the shipment in question.

As for the Communications Act, it provides for the regulation of "interstate and foreign commerce in communication by wire and radio" by the Federal Communications Commission (FCC). *See* 47 U.S.C. §§ 151 and 152. In addition to common carrier telecommunications companies, the Communications Act also applies to companies such as television and radio broadcasters and cable service providers which are not common carriers. As such, these latter companies do not qualify for the exception under Section 5 of the FTC Act. Thus, the FTC has jurisdiction to investigate these companies for unfair and deceptive practices, while the FCC has concurrent jurisdiction to enforce its independent authority in this area as described below.

Under the Communications Act, "every telecommunications carrier," including local exchange carriers, has a duty to protect the privacy of customer proprietary information.(12) 47 U.S.C. § 222(a). In addition to this general privacy-protection authority, the Communications Act was amended by the Cable Communications Policy Act of 1984 (the Cable Act), 47 U.S.C. § 521 *et seq.*, to mandate specifically that cable operators protect the privacy of "personally identifiable information" on cable subscribers. 47 U.S.C. § 551.(13) The Cable Act restricts the collection of personal information by cable operators and requires the cable operator to notify the subscriber of the nature of the information collected and how that information will be used. The Cable Act gives subscribers the right of access to the information about them and requires cable operators to destroy that information when it's no longer needed.

The Communications Act empowers the FCC to enforce these two privacy provisions, either at its own initiation or in response to an outside complaint.(14) 47 U.S.C. §§ 205, 403; *id.* § 208. If the FCC determines that a telecommunications carrier (including a cable operator) has violated the privacy provisions of section 222 or section 551, there are three basic actions it may take. First, after a hearing and determination of violation, the Commission may order the carrier to pay *monetary damages*.(15) 47 U.S.C. § 209. Alternatively, the FCC may order the carrier to *cease and desist* from the offending practice or omission. 47 U.S.C. § 205(a). Finally, the Commission may also order an offending carrier to *"conform to and observe [any] regulation or practice"* that the FCC may prescribe. *Id.*

Private persons who believe a telecommunications carrier or cable operator has violated the relevant provisions of the Communications Act or the Cable Act may either file a complaint with the FCC or take their claims to a federal district court. 47 U.S.C. § 207. A complainant who prevails in a federal court action against a telecommunications carrier for failure to protect customer proprietary information under the broader section 222 of the Communications Act may be awarded actual damages and attorneys' fees. 47 U.S.C. § 206. A complainant who files suit claiming a privacy violation under the cable-specific section 551 of the Cable Act may, in addition to actual damages and attorneys' fees, also be awarded punitive damages and reasonable litigation costs. 47 U.S.C. § 551(f).

The FCC has adopted detailed rules to implement section 222. *See* 47 CFR 64.2001-2009. The rules set out specific safeguards to protect against unauthorized access to customer proprietary network information. The regulations require telecommunications carriers to:

- develop and implement software systems that "flag" a customer's notice/approval status when the customer's service record first comes on-screen;
- maintain an electronic "audit trail" to track access to a customer's account, including when a customer's record is opened, by whom, and for what purpose;
- train their personnel on the authorized use of customer proprietary network information, with appropriate disciplinary processes in place;
- establish a supervisory review process to ensure compliance when conducting outbound marketing; and
- certify to the FCC, on an annual basis, how they are complying with these regulations.

Air Carriers

U.S. and foreign air carriers that are subject to Federal Aviation Act of 1958 are also exempt from Section 5 of the FTC Act. *See* 15 U.S.C. § 45(a)(2). This includes anyone who provides interstate or foreign transportation of goods or passengers, or who transports mail, by aircraft. *See* 49 U.S.C. § 40102. Air carriers are subject to the authority of the Department of Transportation. In this regard, the Secretary of Transportation is authorized to take action "preventing unfair, deceptive, predatory, or anticompetitive practices in air transportation." 49 U.S.C. § 40101(a)(9). The Secretary of Transportation can investigate whether a U.S. or foreign air carrier, or a ticket agent, has engaged in an unfair or deceptive practice if it is in the public interest. 49 U.S.C. § 41712. After a hearing, the Secretary of Transportation can issue an order to stop the illegal practice. *Id.* To our knowledge, the Secretary of Transportation has not exercised this authority to address the issue of protecting the privacy of personal information about airline customers.(16)

There are two provisions protecting the privacy of personal information that apply to air carriers in specific contexts. First, the Federal Aviation Act protects the privacy of pilot applicants. *See* 49 U.S.C. § 44936(f). While allowing air carriers to obtain an applicant's employment records, the Act gives the applicant the right to notice that the records have been requested, to give consent to the request, to correct inaccuracies, and to have the records divulged only to those involved in the hiring decision. Second, DOT regulations require passenger manifest information collected for government use in the event of an aviation disaster to "be kept confidential and released only to the U.S. Department of State, the National Transportation Board (upon the NTSB's request), and the U.S. Department of Transportation." 14 CFR part 243, § 243.9(c) (as added by 63 FR 8258).

Packers and Stockyards

With regard to the Packers and Stockyards Act of 1921 (7 U.S.C. § 181 *et seq.*), the Act makes it unlawful for "any packer with respect to livestock, meats, meat food products, or livestock products in unmanufactured form, or for any live poultry dealer with respect to live poultry, to engage in or use any unfair, unjustly discriminatory, or deceptive practice or device." 7 U.S.C. § 192(a); *see also* 7 U.S.C. § 213(a) (prohibiting "any unfair, unjustly discriminatory, or deceptive practice or device" in connection with livestock). The Secretary of Agriculture has the primary responsibility to enforce these provisions, while the FTC retains jurisdiction over retail transactions and those involving the poultry industry. 7 U.S.C. § 227(b)(2).

It is not clear whether the Secretary of Agriculture will interpret the failure by a packer or stockyard operator to protect personal privacy in accordance with stated policy to be a "deceptive" practice under the Packers and Stockyards Act. However, the Section 5 exception applies to persons, partnerships, or corporations only "insofar as they are subject to the Packers and Stockyards Act," Therefore, if personal privacy is not an issue within the purview of the Packers and Stockyards Act, then the exception in Section 5 may very well not apply and packers and stockyard operators would be subject to the authority of the FTC in that regard.

State "Unfair and Deceptive Practices" Authority

According to an analysis prepared by FTC staff, "All fifty states plus the District of Columbia, Guam, Puerto Rico, and the U.S. Virgin Islands have enacted laws more or less like the Federal Trade Commission Act ("FTCA") to prevent unfair or deceptive trade practices." FTC fact sheet, reprinted in Comment, Consumer Protection: The Practical Effectiveness of State Deceptive Trade Practices Legislation, *59 Tul. L. Rev. 427 (1984)*. In all cases, an enforcement agency has the authority "to conduct investigations through the use of subpoenas or civil investigative demands, obtain assurances of voluntary compliance, to issue cease and desist orders or obtain court injunctions preventing the use of unfair, unconscionable or deceptive trade practices." *Id.* In 46 jurisdictions, the law allows private actions for actual, double, treble, or punitive damages and, in some cases, recovery of costs and attorney's fees. *Id.*

Florida's Deceptive and Unfair Trade Practices Act, for example, authorizes the attorney general to investigate and file civil actions against "unfair methods of competition, unfair, unconscionable or deceptive trade practices," including false or misleading advertising, misleading franchise or business opportunities, fraudulent telemarketing, and pyramid schemes. *See also* N.Y. General Business Law § 349 (prohibiting unfair acts and deceptive practices carried out in the course of business).

A survey conducted this year by the National Association of Attorneys General (NAAG) confirms these findings. Of forty-three states that responded, all have "mini-FTC" statutes or other statutes that provide comparable protection. Also according to the NAAG survey, 39 states indicated they would have the authority to hear complaints by non-residents. With respect to consumer privacy, in particular, 37 out of forty-one states that responded indicated that they would respond to complaints alleging that a company within their jurisdiction was not adhering to its self-declared privacy policy.

ENDNOTES
1. We do not discuss here all the various Federal statutes that address privacy in specific contexts or state statutes and common law that might apply. Statutes at the federal level that regulate the commercial collection and use of personal information include the Cable Communications Policy Act (47 U.S.C. § 551), the Driver's Privacy Protection Act (18 U.S.C. § 2721), the Electronic Communications Privacy Act (18 U.S.C. § 2701 *et seq.*), the Electronic Funds Transfer Act (15 U.S.C. §§ 1693, 1693m), the Fair Credit Reporting Act (15 U.S.C. § 1681 *et seq.*), the Right to Financial Privacy Act (12 U.S.C. § 3401 *et seq.*),

the Telephone Consumer Protection Act (47 U.S.C. § 227), and the Video Privacy Protection Act (18 U.S.C. § 2710), among others. Many states have analogous legislation in these areas. *See, e.g.,* Mass. Gen. Laws ch. 167B, § 16 (prohibiting financial institutions from disclosing customer's financial records to a third party without either the customer's consent or legal process), N.Y. Pub. Health Law § 17 (limiting use and disclosure of medical or mental health records and giving patients the right of access thereto).

2. In such an action, the United States district court can also order injunctive and equitable relief appropriate to enforcing the FTC order. 15 U.S.C. § 45(l)

3. "Deceptive practice" is defined as a representation, omission or practice that is likely to mislead reasonable consumers in a material fashion.

4. *See* www.ftc.gov/opa/1998/9808/geocitie.htm.

5. *See* staff letter to Center for Media Education, www.ftc.gov/os/1997/9707/cenmed.htm. In addition, the Children's Online Privacy Protection Act of 1998 confers on the FTC specific legal authority to regulate the collection of personal information from children by website and online service operators. *See* 15 U.S.C. §§ 6501-6506. In particular, the act requires online operators to give notice and to obtain verifiable parental consent before collecting, using, or disclosing personal information from children. *Id.*, § 6502(b). The act also gives parents a right of access and to refuse permission for the continued use of the information. *Id.*

6. On November 12, 1999, President Clinton signed the Gramm-Leach-Bliley Act (Pub. L. 106-102, codified at 15 U.S.C. § 6801 *et seq.*) into law. The Act limits the disclosure by financial institutions of personal information about their customers. The Act requires financial institutions to, *inter alia*, notify all customers of their privacy policies and practices with respect to the sharing of personal information with affiliates and non-affiliates. The Act authorizes the FTC, the Federal banking authorities and other authorities to promulgate regulations to implement the privacy protections required by the statute. The agencies have issued proposed regulations for this purpose.

7. By its terms, this exception does not apply to the securities sector. Therefore, brokers, dealers and others in the securities industry are subject to the concurrent jurisdiction of the Securities and Exchange Commission and the FTC with respect to unfair or deceptive acts and practices.

8. The exception in Section 5 originally referred to the Federal Home Loan Bank Board which was abolished in August 1989 by the Financial Institutions Reform, Recovery and Enforcement Act of 1989. Its functions were transferred to the Office of Thrift Supervision and to the Resolution Trust Corporation, the Federal Deposit Insurance Corporation, and the Housing Finance Board.

9. While removing financial institutions from the FTC's jurisdiction, Section 5 also stipulates that whenever the FTC issues a rule on unfair or deceptive acts and practices, the financial regulatory Boards should adopt parallel regulations within 60 days. *See* 15 U.S.C. § 57a(f)(1).

10. "The business of insurance, and every person engaged therein, shall be subject to the laws of the several States which relate to the regulation or taxation of such business." 15 U.S.C. § 1012(a).

11. The FTC has exercised jurisdiction over insurance companies in different contexts. In one case, the FTC took action against a firm for deceptive advertising in a state in which it was not licensed to do business. The FTC's jurisdiction was upheld on the basis that there was no effective state regulation because the firm was effectively beyond the reach of the state. *See* FTC v. Travelers Health Association, 362 U.S. 293 (1960).

As for the states, seventeen have adopted the model "Insurance Information and Privacy Protection Act" prepared by the National Association of Insurance Commissioners (NAIC). The Act includes provisions for notice, use and disclosure, and access. Also, almost all states have adopted the NAIC's model "Unfair Insurance Practices Act," which specifically targets unfair trade practices in the insurance industry.

12. The term "customer proprietary network information" means information that relates to "the quantity, technical configuration, type, destination, and amount of use of a telecommunications service" by a customer and telephone billing information. 47 U.S.C. § 222(f)(1). However, the term does not include subscriber list information. *Id.*

13. The legislation does not expressly define "personally identifiable information."

14. This authority encompasses the right to redress for privacy violations under both section 222 of the Communications Act or, with respect to cable subscribers, under section 551 of the Cable Act amendment to the Act. *See also* 47 U.S.C. § 551(f)(3) (civil action in federal district court is a nonexclusive remedy, offered "in addition to any other lawful remedy available to a cable subscriber.")

15. However, the absence of direct damage to a complainant is not grounds to dismiss a complaint. 47 U.S.C. § 208(a).

16. We understand there are efforts underway within the industry to address the privacy issue. Industry representatives have discussed the proposed safe harbor principles and their possible application to air carriers. The discussion has included a proposal to adopt an industry privacy policy with participating firms expressly subjecting themselves to DOT authority.

Department of Commerce Memorandum on Damages for Breaches of Privacy, Legal Authorizations and Mergers and Takeovers in U.S. Law
July 14, 2000

Damages for Breaches of Privacy, Legal Authorizations
and Mergers and Takeovers in U.S. Law

This responds to the request by the European Commission for clarification of U.S. law with respect to (a) claims for damages for breaches of privacy, (b) "explicit authorizations" in U.S. law for the use of personal information in a manner inconsistent with the safe harbor principles, and (c) the effect of mergers and takeovers on obligations undertaken pursuant to the safe harbor principles.

A. Damages for Breaches of Privacy

Failure to comply with the safe harbor principles could give rise to a number of private claims depending on the relevant circumstances. In particular, safe harbor organizations could be held liable for misrepresentation for failing to adhere to their stated privacy policies. Private causes of action for damages for breaches of privacy are also available under common law. Many federal and state statutes on privacy also provide for the recovery of damages by private individuals for violations.

The right to recover damages for invasion of personal privacy is well established under U.S. common law.

Use of personal information in a manner inconsistent with the safe harbor principles can give rise to legal liability under a number of different legal theories. For example, both the transferring data controller and the individuals affected could sue the safe harbor organization which fails to honor its safe harbor commitments for misrepresentation. According to the Restatement of the Law, Second, Torts(1):

One who fraudulently makes a misrepresentation of fact, opinion, intention or law for the purpose of inducing another to act or to refrain from action in reliance upon it, is subject to liability to the other in deceit for pecuniary loss caused to him by his justifiable reliance upon the misrepresentation.

Restatement, § 525. A misrepresentation is "fraudulent" if it is made with the knowledge or in the belief that it is false. *Id.*, § 526. As a general rule, the maker of a fraudulent misrepresentation is potentially liable to everyone who he intends or expects to rely on that misrepresentation for any pecuniary loss they might suffer as a result. *Id.* 531. Furthermore, a party who makes a fraudulent misrepresentation to another could be liable to a third-party if the tortfeasor intends or expects that his misrepresentation would be repeated to and acted upon by the third-party. *Id.*, § 533.

In the context of the safe harbor, the relevant representation is the organization's public declaration that it will adhere to the safe harbor principles. Having made such a commitment, a conscious failure to abide by the principles could be grounds for a cause of action for misrepresentation by those who relied on the misrepresentation. Because the commitment to adhere to the principles is made to the public at large, the individuals who are the subjects of that information as well as the data controller in Europe that transfers personal information to the U.S. organization could all have causes of action against the U.S. organization for misrepresentation.(2) Moreover, the U.S. organization remains liable to them for the "continuing misrepresentation" for as long as they rely on the misrepresentation to their detriment. Restatement, § 535.

Those who rely on a fraudulent misrepresentation have a right to recover damages. According to the Restatement:

The recipient of a fraudulent misrepresentation is entitled to recover as damages in an action of deceit against the maker the pecuniary loss to him of which the misrepresentation is a legal cause.

Restatement, § 549. Allowable damages include actual out-of-pocket loss as well as the lost "benefit of the bargain" in a commercial transaction. *Id.; see, e.g.,* Boling v. Tennessee State Bank, 890 S.W.2d 32 (1994) (bank liable to borrowers for $14,825 in compensatory damages for disclosing borrowers' personal information and business plans to bank president who had a conflicting interest).

Whereas fraudulent misrepresentation requires either actual knowledge or at least the belief that the representation is false, liability can also attach for negligent misrepresentation. According to the Restatement, whoever makes a false statement in the course of his business, profession, or employment, or in any pecuniary transaction can be held liable "if he fails to exercise reasonable care or competence in obtaining or communicating the information." Restatement, § 552(1). In contrast with fraudulent misrepresentations, damages for negligent misrepresentation are limited to out-of-pocket loss. *Id.*, § 552B(1).

In a recent case, for example, the Superior Court of Connecticut held that a failure by an electric utility to disclose its reporting of customer payment information to national credit agencies sustained a cause of action for misrepresentation. *See* Brouillard v. United Illuminating Co., 1999 Conn. Super. LEXIS 1754. In that case, the plaintiff was denied credit because the defendant reported payments not received within thirty days of the billing date as "late". The plaintiff alleged that he had not been informed of this policy when he opened a residential electric service account with the defendant. The court specifically held that "a claim for negligent misrepresentation may be based on the defendant's failure to speak when he has a duty to do so." This case also shows that "scienter" or fraudulent intent is not a necessary element in a cause of action for negligent misrepresentation. Thus, a U.S. organization which negligently fails to fully disclose how it will use personal information received under the safe harbor could be held liable for misrepresentation.

Insofar as a violation of the safe harbor principles entailed a misuse of personal information, it could also support a claim by the data subject for the common law tort of invasion of privacy. American law has long recognized causes of action relating to invasions of privacy. In a 1905 case,(3) the Georgia Supreme Court found a right to privacy rooted in natural law and common law precepts in holding for a private citizen whose photograph had been used by a life insurance company, without his consent or knowledge, to illustrate a commercial advertisement. Articulating now-familiar themes in American privacy jurisprudence, the court found that the usage of the photograph was "malicious," "false," and tended to "bring plaintiff into ridicule before the world."(4) The foundations of the *Pavesich* decision have prevailed with minor variations to become the bedrock of American law on this topic. State courts have consistently upheld causes of action in the realm of invasion of privacy, and at least 48 states now judicially recognize some such cause of action.(5) Moreover, at least twelve states have constitutional provisions safeguarding their citizens' right to be free from intrusive actions,(6) which in some cases could extend to protect against intrusion by non-governmental entities. *See, e.g.,* Hill v. NCAA, 865 P.2d 633 (Ca. 1994); *see also* S. Ginder, Lost and Found in Cyberspace: Informational Privacy in the Age of the Internet, 34 S.D. L. Rev. 1153 (1997) ("Some state constitutions include privacy protections which surpass privacy protections in the U.S. Constitution. Alaska, Arizona, California, Florida, Hawaii, Illinois, Louisiana, Montana, South Carolina, and Washington have broader privacy protection.")

The Second Restatement of Torts provides an authoritative overview of the law in this area. Reflecting common judicial practice, the Restatement explains that the "right to privacy" encompasses four distinct causes of action in tort under that umbrella. *See* Restatement, § 652A. First, a cause of action for "intrusion upon seclusion" may lie against a defendant who intentionally intrudes, physically or otherwise, upon the solitude or seclusion of another or his private affairs or concerns.(7) Second, an "appropriation" case may exist when one takes the name or likeness of another for his own use or benefit.(8) Third, the "publication of private facts" is actionable when the matter publicized is of a kind that would be highly offensive to a reasonable person and is not of legitimate concern to the public.(9) Lastly, an action for "false light publicity" is appropriate when the defendant knowingly or recklessly places another before the public in a false light that would be highly offensive to a reasonable person.(10)

In the context of the safe harbor framework, "intrusion upon seclusion" could encompass the unauthorized collection of personal information whereas the unauthorized use of personal information for commercial purposes could give rise to a claim of appropriation. Similarly, the disclosure of personal information that is inaccurate would give rise to a tort of "false light publicity" if the information meets the standard of being highly offensive to a reasonable person. Finally, the invasion of privacy that results from the publication or disclosure of sensitive personal information could give rise to a cause of action for "publication of private facts." (*See* examples of illustrative cases below.)

On the issue of damages, invasions of privacy give the injured party the right to recover damages for:

(a) the harm to his interest in privacy resulting from the invasion;

(b) his mental distress proved to have been suffered if it is of a kind that normally results from such an invasion; and

(c) special damage of which the invasion is a legal cause.

Restatement, § 652H. Given the general applicability of tort law and the multiplicity of causes of action covering different aspects of privacy interests, monetary damages are likely to be available to those who suffer invasion of their privacy interests as a result of a failure to adhere to the safe harbor principles.

Indeed, state courts are replete with cases alleging invasion of privacy in analogous situations. Ex Parte AmSouth Bancorporation et al., 717 So. 2d 357, for example, involved a class action that alleged the defendant "exploited the trust depositors placed in the Bank, by sharing confidential information regarding Bank depositors and their accounts" to enable a bank affiliate to sell mutual funds and other investments. Damages are often awarded in such cases. In Vassiliades v. Garfinckel's, Brooks Bros., 492 A.2d 580 (D.C.App. 1985), an appellate court reversed a lower court judgement to hold that the use of photographs of the plaintiff "before" and "after" plastic surgery in a presentation in a department store constituted an invasion of privacy through the publication of private facts. In Candebat v. Flanagan, 487 So.2d 207 (Miss. 1986), the defendant insurance company used an accident in which plaintiff's wife was seriously injured in an advertising campaign. Plaintiff sued for invasion of privacy. The court held that plaintiff could recover damages for emotional distress and appropriation of identity. Actions for misappropriation can be maintained even if the plaintiff is not personally famous. See, e.g.,Staruski v. Continental Telephone Co., 154 Vt. 568 (1990) (defendant derived commercial benefit in using employee's name and photograph in newspaper advertisement). In Pulla v. Amoco Oil Co., 882 F.Supp. 836 (S.D Iowa 1995), an employer intruded on plaintiff employee's seclusion by having another employee investigate his credit card records in order to verify his sick day absences. The court upheld a jury award of $2 in actual damages and $500,000 in punitive damages. Another employer was held liable for publishing a story in the company newspaper about an employee who was terminated for allegedly falsifying his employment records. See Zinda v. Louisiana-Pacific Corp., 140 Wis.2d 277 (Wis.App. 1987). The story invaded the plaintiff's privacy by publication of a private matter because the newspaper circulated in the community. Finally, a college which tested students for HIV after telling them the blood test was for rubella only was held liable for intrusion upon seclusion. See Doe v. High-Tech Institute, Inc., 972 P.2d 1060 (Colo.App. 1998). (For other reported cases, see Restatement, § 652H, Appendix.)

The United States is often criticized for being overly litigious, but this also means that individuals actually can, and do, pursue legal recourse when they believe they have been wronged. Many aspects of the U.S. judicial system make it easy for plaintiffs to bring suit, either individually or as a class. The legal bar, comparatively larger than in most other countries, makes professional representation readily available. Plaintiffs' counsel representing individuals in private claims will typically work on a contingency fee basis, allowing even poor or indigent plaintiffs to seek redress. This brings up an important factor - in the United States, each side typically bears its own lawyers' fees and other costs. This contrasts with the prevailing rule in Europe wherein the losing party has to reimburse the other side for costs. Without debating the relative merits of the two systems, the U.S. rule is less likely to deter legitimate claims by individuals who would not be able to pay the costs on both sides if they should lose.

Individuals can sue for redress even if their claims are relatively small. Most, if not all U.S. jurisdictions, have small claims courts which provide simplified and less costly procedures for disputes below the statutory limits.(11) The potential for punitive damages also offers a financial reward for individuals who might have suffered little direct injury to bring suit against reprehensible misconduct. Finally, individuals who have been injured in the same way can marshal their resources as well as their claims to bring a class-action lawsuit.

A good example of the ability of individuals to bring suit to obtain redress is the pending litigation against Amazon.com for invasion of privacy. Amazon.com, the large online retailer, is the target of a class action, in which the plaintiffs allege that they were not told about, and did not consent to, the collection of personal information about them when they used a software program owned by Amazon called "Alexa." In that case, plaintiffs have alleged violations of the Computer Fraud and Abuse Act in unlawful access to their stored communications and of the Electronic Communications Privacy Act for unlawful interception of their electronic and wire communications. They also claim an invasion of privacy under common law. This stems from a complaint filed by an Internet security expert in December. The suit seeks damages of $1,000 per class member, plus attorneys' fees and profits earned as a result of violations of laws. Given that the number of class members could be in the millions, damages could total billions of dollars. The FTC is also investigating the charges.

Federal and state privacy legislation often provides private causes of action for money damages.

In addition to giving rise to civil liability under tort law, noncompliance with the safe harbor principles could also violate one or another of the hundreds of federal and state privacy laws. Many of these laws, which address both government and private-sector handling of personal information, allow individuals to sue for damages when violations occur. For example:

Electronic Communications Privacy Act of 1986. The ECPA prohibits the unauthorized interception of cellular telephone calls and computer-to-computer transmissions. Violations can result in civil liability of not less than $100 for each day of violation. The protection of the ECPA also extends to unauthorized access or disclosure of stored electronic communications. Violators are liable for damages suffered or forfeiture of profits generated by a violation.

Telecommunications Act of 1996. Under section 702, customer proprietary network information (CPNI) may not be used for any purpose other than to provide telecommunications services. Service subscribers can either submit a complaint to the Federal Communications Commission or file suit in federal district court to recover damages and attorneys' fees.

Consumer Credit Reporting Reform Act of 1996. The 1996 Act amended the Fair Credit Reporting Act of 1970 (FCRA) to require improved notice and right of access for credit reporting subjects. The Reform Act also imposed new restrictions on resellers of consumer credit reports. Consumers can recover damages and attorneys' fees for violations.

State laws also protect personal privacy in a broad range of situations. Areas where the states have taken action include bank records, cable television subscriptions, credit reports, employment records, government records, genetic information and medical records, insurance records, school records, electronic communications, and video rentals.(12)

B. Explicit Legal Authorizations

The safe harbor principles contain an exception where statute, regulation or case law create "conflicting obligations or explicit authorizations, provided that, in exercising any such authorization, an organization can demonstrate that its non-compliance with the principles is limited to the extent necessary to meet the overriding legitimate interests further by such authorization." Clearly, where U.S. law imposes a conflicting obligation, U.S. organizations whether in the safe harbor or not must comply with the law. As for explicit authorizations, while the safe harbor principles are intended to bridge the differences between the U.S. and European regimes for privacy protection, we owe deference to the legislative prerogatives of our elected lawmakers. The limited exception from strict adherence to the safe harbor principles seeks to strike a balance to accommodate the legitimate interests on each side.

The exception is limited to cases where there is an explicit authorization. Therefore, as a threshold matter, the relevant statute, regulation or court decision must affirmatively authorize the particular conduct by safe harbor organizations.(13) In other words, the exception would not apply where the law is silent. In addition, the exception would apply only if the explicit authorization conflicts with adherence to the safe harbor principles. Even then, the exception "is limited to the extent necessary to meet the overriding legitimate interests furthered by such authorization." By way of illustration, where the law simply authorizes a company to provide personal information to government authorities, the exception would not apply. Conversely, where the law specifically authorizes the company to provide personal information to government agencies without the individual's consent, this would constitute an "explicit authorization" to act in a manner that conflicts with the safe harbor principles. Alternatively, specific exceptions from affirmative requirements to provide notice and consent would fall within the exception (since it would be the equivalent of a specific authorization to disclose the information without notice and consent). For example, a statute which authorizes doctors to provide their patients' medical records to health officials without the patients' prior consent might permit an exception from the notice and choice principles. This authorization would not permit a doctor to provide the same medical records to health maintenance organizations or commercial pharmaceutical research laboratories, which would be beyond the scope of the purposes authorized by the law and therefore beyond the scope of the exception.(14) The legal authority in question can be a "stand alone" authorization to do specific things with personal information, but, as the examples below illustrate, it is likely to be an exception to a broader law which proscribes the collection, use, or disclosure of personal information.

Telecommunications Act of 1996

In most cases, the authorized uses are either consistent with the requirements of the Directive and the principles, or would be permitted by one of the other allowed exceptions. For example, section 702 of the Telecommunications Act (codified at 47 U.S.C. § 222) imposes a duty on telecommunications carriers to maintain the confidentiality of personal information that they obtain in the course of providing their services to their customers. This provision specifically allows telecommunications carriers to:

- use customer information to provide telecommunications service, including the publication of subscriber directories;
- provide customer information to others at the written request of the customer; and
- provide customer information in aggregate form.

See 47 U.S.C. § 222(c)(1)-(3). The Act also allows telecommunications carriers an exception to use customer information:

- to initiate, render, bill, and collect for their services;
- to protect against fraudulent, abusive or illegal conduct; and
- to provide telemarketing, referral or administrative services during a call initiated by the customer.(15)

Id., § 222(d)(1)-(3). Finally, telecommunications carriers are required to provide subscriber list information, which can only include the names, addresses, telephone numbers and line of business for commercial customers to publishers of telephone directories. *Id.*, § 222(e).

Recent Developments
Safe Harbor Arrangement (EU-US)

The exception for "explicit authorizations" might come into play when telecommunications carriers use CPNI to prevent fraud or other unlawful conduct. Even here, such actions could qualify as being in the "public interest" and allowed by the principles for that reason.

Department of Health and Human Services Proposed Rules

The Department of Health and Human Services (HHS) has proposed rules regarding standards for the privacy of individually identifiable health information. *See* 64 Fed. Reg. 59,918 (Nov. 3, 1999) (to be codified at 45 C.F.R. pts. 160-164). The rules would implement the privacy requirements of the Health Insurance Portability and Accountability Act of 1996, Pub. L. 104-191. The proposed rules generally would prohibit covered entities (i.e. health plans, health care clearinghouses, and health providers that transmit health information in electronic format) from using or disclosing protected health information without individual authorization. *See* proposed 45 C.F.R. § 164.506. The proposed rules would require disclosure of protected health information for only two purposes: 1) to permit individuals to inspect and copy health information about themselves, *see id*. at § 164.514; and 2) to enforce the rules, *see id*. at § 164.522.

The proposed rules would permit use or disclosure of protected health information, without specific authorization by the individual, in limited circumstances. These include for example oversight of the health care system, law enforcement, and emergencies. *See id*. at § 164.510. The proposed rules set out in detail the limits on these uses and disclosures. Moreover, permitted uses and disclosures of protected health information would be limited to the minimum amount of information necessary. *See id*. at § 164.506.

The permissive uses explicitly authorized by the proposed regulations are generally consistent with the safe harbor principles or are otherwise allowed by another exception. For example, law enforcement and judicial administration are permitted, as is medical research. Other uses, such as oversight of the health care system, public health function, and government health data systems, serve the public interest. Disclosures to process health care payments and premiums are necessary to the provision of health care. Uses in emergencies, to consult with next-of-kin regarding treatment where the patient's consent "cannot practicably or reasonably be obtained," or to determine the identity or cause of death of the deceased protect the vital interests of the data subject and others. Uses for the management of active duty military and other special classes of individuals aid the proper execution of the military mission or similar exigent situations; and in any event, such uses will have little if any application to consumers in general.

This leaves only the use of personal information by health care facilities to produce patient directories. While such use might not rise to the level of a "vital" interest, the directories do benefit patients and their friends and relations. Also, the scope of this authorized use is inherently limited. Therefore, reliance on the exception in the principles for uses "explicitly authorized" by law for this purpose presents minimal risk to the privacy of patients.

Fair Credit Reporting Act

The European Commission has expressed the concern that the "explicit authorizations" exception would "effectively create an adequacy finding" for the Fair Credit Reporting Act (FCRA). This would not be the case. In the absence of a specific adequacy finding for the FCRA, those U.S. organizations that would otherwise rely on such a finding, would have to promise to adhere to the safe harbor principles in all respects. This means that where FCRA requirements exceed the level of protection embodied in the principles, the U.S. organizations need only to obey the FCRA. Conversely, where the FCRA might fall short, then those organizations would need to bring their information practices into conformity with the principles. The exception would not alter this basic assessment. By its terms, the exception applies only where the relevant law explicitly authorizes conduct that would be inconsistent with the safe harbor principles. The exception would not extend to where FCRA requirements merely do not meet the safe harbor principles.(16)

In other words, we do not intend the exception to mean that whatever is not required is therefore "explicitly authorized." Furthermore, the exception applies only when what is explicitly authorized by U.S. law <u>conflicts</u> with the requirements of the safe harbor principles. The relevant law must meet both of these elements before non-adherence with the principles would be permitted.

Section 604 of the FCRA, for example, explicitly authorizes consumer reporting agencies to issue consumer reports in various enumerated situations. *See* FCRA, § 604. If in so doing, section 604 authorizes credit reporting agencies to act in conflict with the safe harbor principles, then the credit reporting agencies would need to rely on the exception (unless, of course, some other exception applied). Credit reporting agencies must obey court orders and grand jury subpoenas, and use of credit reports by government licensing, social and child support enforcement agencies serves a public purpose. *Id.*, § 604(a)(1), (3)(D), and (4). Consequently, the credit reporting agency would not need to rely on the "explicit authorization" exception for these purposes. Where it acts in accordance with written instructions by the consumer, the consumer reporting agency would be fully in compliance with the safe harbor principles. *Id.*, § 604(a)(2). Likewise, consumer reports can be procured for employment purposes only with the consumer's written authorization (*id.*, §§ 604(a)(3)(B) and (b)(2)(A)(ii)) and for credit or insurance transactions that are not initiated by the consumer only if the consumer had not opted out from such solicitations (*id.*, § 604(c)(1)(B)). Also, FCRA prohibits credit reporting agencies from providing medical information for employment purposes without the consent of the consumer. *Id.*, § 604(g). Such uses comport with the notice and choice principles. Other purposes authorized by section 604 entail transactions involving the consumer and would be permitted by the principles for that reason. *See id.*, § 604(a)(3)(A) and (F).

The remaining use "authorized" by section 604 relates to secondary credit markets. *Id.*, § 604(a)(3)(E). There is no conflict between use of consumer reports for this purpose and the safe harbor principles *per se*. It is true that the FCRA does not require credit reporting agencies, for example, to give notice and consent to consumers when they issue reports for this purpose. However, we reiterate the point that the absence of a requirement does not connote an "explicit authorization" to act in a manner other than as required. Similarly, section 608 allows credit reporting agencies to provide some personal information to government agencies. This "authorization" would not justify a credit reporting agency ignoring its commitments to adhere to the safe harbor principles. This contrasts with our other examples where exceptions from affirmative notice and choice requirements operate to explicitly authorize uses of personal information without notice and choice.

Conclusion

A distinct pattern emerges even from our limited review of these statutes:

- The "explicit authorization" in the law generally permits the use or disclosure of personal information without the individual's prior consent; thus, the exception would be limited to the notice and choice principles.
- In most cases, the exceptions authorized by the law are narrowly drawn to apply in specific situations for specific purposes. In all cases, the law otherwise prohibits the unauthorized use or disclosure of personal information that does not fall within these limits.
- In most cases, reflecting their legislative character, the authorized use or disclosure serves a public interest.
- In almost all cases, the authorized uses are either fully consistent with the safe harbor principles or fall into one of the other allowed exceptions.

In conclusion, the exception for "explicit authorizations" in the law will, by its nature, likely be rather limited in scope.

C. Mergers and Takeovers

The Article 29 Working Party expressed concern over situations where an organization within the safe harbor is taken over by, or merged with, a firm which has not made a commitment to follow the safe harbor principles. The Working Party, however, appears to have assumed that the surviving firm would not be bound to apply the safe harbor principles to personal information held by the firm that is taken over, but that is not necessarily the case under U.S. law. The general rule in the United States as to mergers and takeovers is that a company which acquires the outstanding stock of another corporation generally assumes the obligations and liabilities of the acquired firm. *See* 15 *Fletcher Cyclopedia of the Law of Private Corporations* § 7117 (1990); *see also Model Bus. Corp. Act* § 11.06(3) (1979) ("the surviving corporation has all liabilities of each corporation party to the merger"). In other words, the surviving firm in a merger or takeover of a safe harbor organization by this method would be bound by the latter's safe harbor commitments.

Moreover, even if the merger or takeover were effectuated through the acquisition of assets, the liabilities of the acquired enterprise could nevertheless bind the acquiring firm in certain circumstances. 15 *Fletcher,* § 7122. Even where liabilities did not survive the merger, however, it is worth noting that they also would not survive a merger where the data were transferred from Europe pursuant to a contract -- the only viable alternative to the safe harbor for data transfers to the United States. In addition, the safe harbor documents as revised now require any safe harbor organization to notify the Department of Commerce of any takeover and permit data to continue to be transferred to the successor organization only if the successor organization joins the safe harbor. *See FAQ 6.* Indeed, the United States has now revised the safe harbor framework to require U.S. organizations in this situation to delete information they have received under the safe harbor framework if their safe harbor commitments will not continue or other suitable safeguards are not put in place.

Endnotes

1. Second Restatement of the Law - Torts; American Law Institute (1997).
2. This might be the case, for example, where the individuals relied on the U.S. organization's safe harbor commitments in giving their consent to the data controller to transfer their personal information to the United States.
3. *Pavesich v. New England Life Ins. Co.,* 50 S.E. 68 (Ga. 1905)
4. *Id.,* at 69.
5. An electronic search of the Westlaw database found 2703 reported cases of civil actions in state courts that pertained to "privacy" since 1995. We have previously provided the results of this search to the Commission.
6. *See, e.g.,* Alaska Constitution, Art. 1 Sec. 22; Arizona, Art. 2, Sec. 8; California, Art. 1, Sec. 1; Florida, Art. 1, Sec. 23; Hawaii, Art. 1, Sec. 5; Illinois, Art. 1, Sec. 6; Louisiana, Art. 1, Sec. 5; Montana, Art. 2, Sec. 10; New York, Art. 1, Sec. 12; Pennsylvania, Art. 1, Sec. 1; South Carolina, Art. 1, Sec. 10; and Washington, Art. 1, Sec 7.
7. *Id.,* at Chapter 28, Section 652B.
8. *Id.,* at Chapter 28, Section 652C.
9. *Id.,* at Chapter 28, Section 652D.
10. *Id.,* at Chapter 28, Section 652E.

Recent Developments
Safe Harbor Arrangement (EU–US)

11. We had previously provided the Commission with information on small-claims actions.

12. A recent electronic search of the Westlaw database yielded 994 reported states cases that related to damages and invasion of privacy.

13. As a point of clarification, the relevant legal authority will <u>not</u> have to specifically reference the safe harbor principles.

14. Similarly, the doctor in this example could not rely on the statutory authority to override the individual's exercise of the opt-out from direct marketing provided by FAQ 12. The scope of any exception for "explicit authorizations" is necessarily limited to the scope of the authorization under relevant law.

15. The scope of this exception is very limited. By its terms, the telecommunications carrier can use CPNI only <u>during</u> a call initiated by the customer. Furthermore, we have been advised by the FCC that the telecommunications carrier may not use CPNI to market services beyond the scope of the customer's inquiry. Finally, since the customer must approve the use of CPNI for this purpose, this provision is not really an "exception" at all.

16. Our discussion here should not be taken as an admission that the FCRA does not provide "adequate" protection. Any assessment of the FCRA must consider the protection provided by the statute in its entirety and not focus only on the exceptions as we do here.

Letter from the Federal Trade Commission concerning its jurisdiction over consumer privacy issues

July 14, 2000

John Mogg
Director, DG XV
European Commission
Office C 107-6/72
Rue de la Loi, 200
1049 Brussels
BELGIUM

Dear Mr. Mogg:

I understand a number of questions have arisen with regard to my letter to you of March 29, 2000. To clarify our authority on those areas where questions have arisen, I am sending this letter, which, for future ease of reference, adds to and recapitulates some of the text of previous correspondence.

In your visits to our offices and in your correspondence, you have raised several questions about the United States Federal Trade Commission's authority in the online privacy area. I thought it would be useful to summarize my prior responses and to provide additional information about the agency's jurisdiction over consumer privacy issues raised in your most recent letter. Specifically, you ask whether: (1) the FTC has jurisdiction over transfers of employment-related data if done in violation of the U.S. safe harbor principles; (2) the FTC has jurisdiction over non-profit privacy "seal" programs; (3) the FTC Act applies equally to the offline as well as online world; and (4) what happens when the FTC's jurisdiction overlaps with other law enforcement agencies.

FTC Act Application to Privacy

The Federal Trade Commission's legal authority in this area is found in Section 5 of the Federal Trade Commission Act ("FTC Act"), which prohibits "unfair or deceptive acts or practices" in or affecting commerce.(1) A deceptive practice is defined as a representation, omission or practice that is likely to mislead reasonable consumers in a material fashion. A practice is unfair if it causes, or is likely to cause, substantial injury to consumers which is not reasonably avoidable and is not outweighed by countervailing benefits to consumers or competition.(2)

Certain information collection practices are likely to violate the FTC Act. For example, if a web site falsely claims to comply with a stated privacy policy or a set of self-regulatory guidelines, Section 5 of the FTC Act provides a legal basis for challenging such a misrepresentation as deceptive. Indeed, we have successfully enforced the law to establish this principle.(3) In addition, the Commission has taken the position it may challenge particularly egregious privacy practices as unfair under Section 5 if such practices involve children, or the use of highly sensitive information, such as financial records(4) and medical records. The Federal Trade Commission has and will continue to pursue such law enforcement actions through our active monitoring and investigative efforts, and through referrals we receive from self-regulatory organizations and others, including European Union member states.

Backstop Self-Regulation

The FTC will give priority to referrals of non-compliance with self-regulatory guidelines received from organizations such as BBBOnline and TRUSTe.(5) This approach would be consistent with our longstanding relationship with the National Advertising Review Board (NARB) of the Better Business Bureau, which refers advertising complaints to the FTC. The National Advertising Division (NAD) of NARB resolves complaints, through an adjudicative process, concerning national advertising. When a party refuses to comply with an NAD decision, a referral is made to the FTC. FTC staff reviews the challenged advertising on a priority basis to determine if it violates the FTC Act, and often is successful in stopping the challenged conduct or convincing the party to return to the NARB process.

Similarly, the FTC will give priority to referrals of non-compliance with safe harbor principles from EU member states. As with referrals from U.S. self-regulatory organizations, our staff will consider any information bearing upon whether the conduct complained of violates Section 5 of the FTC Act. This commitment can also be found in the safe harbor principles under the Frequently Asked Question (FAQ 11) on enforcement.

GeoCities: The FTC's First Online Privacy Case

The Federal Trade Commission's first Internet privacy case, GeoCities, was based on the Commission's authority under Section 5.(6) In that case, the FTC alleged that GeoCities misrepresented, both to adults and children, how their personal information would be used. The Federal Trade Commission's complaint alleged that GeoCities represented that certain personal identifying information it collected on its Web site was to be used only for internal purposes or to provide consumers with the specific advertising offers and products or services they requested, and that certain additional "optional" information would not be released to anyone without the consumer's permission. In fact, this information was disclosed to third parties who used it to target members for solicitations beyond those agreed to by the member. The complaint also charged that GeoCities engaged in deceptive practices relating to its collection of information from children. According to the FTC's complaint, GeoCities represented that it operated a children's area on its Web site and that the information collected there was maintained by GeoCities. In fact, those areas on the Web site were run by third-parties who collected and maintained the information.

The settlement prohibits GeoCities from misrepresenting the purpose for which it collects or uses personal identifying information from or about consumers, including children. The order requires the company to post on its Web site a clear and prominent Privacy Notice, telling consumers what information is being collected and for what purpose, to whom it will be disclosed, and how consumers can access and remove the information. To ensure parental control, the settlement also requires GeoCities to obtain parental consent before collecting personal identifying information from children 12 and under. Under the order, GeoCities is required to notify its members and provide them with an opportunity to have their information deleted from GeoCities' and any third parties' databases. The settlement specifically requires GeoCities to notify the parents of children 12 and under and to delete their information, unless a parent affirmatively consents to its retention and use. Finally, GeoCities also is required to contact third parties to whom it previously disclosed the information and request that those parties delete that information as well.(7)

ReverseAuction.com

In January 2000, the Commission approved a complaint against, and consent agreement with, ReverseAuction.com, an online auction site that allegedly obtained consumers' personally identifying information from a competitor site (eBay.com) and then sent deceptive, unsolicited e-mail messages to those consumers seeking their business.(8) Our complaint alleged that ReverseAuction violated Section 5 of the FTC Act in obtaining the personally identifiable information, which included eBay users' e-mail addresses and personalized user identification names ("user IDs"), and in sending out the deceptive e-mail messages.

As described in the complaint, before obtaining the information, ReverseAuction registered as an eBay user and agreed to comply with eBay's User Agreement and Privacy Policy. The agreement and policy protect consumers' privacy by prohibiting eBay users from gathering and using personal identifying information for unauthorized purposes, such as sending unsolicited commercial e-mail messages. Thus, our complaint first alleged that ReverseAuction misrepresented that it would comply with eBay's User Agreement and Privacy Policy, a deceptive practice under Section 5. In the alternative, the complaint alleged that ReverseAuction's use of the information to send the unsolicited commercial e-mail, in violation of the User Agreement and Privacy Policy, was an unfair trade practice under Section 5.

Second, the complaint alleged that the e-mail messages to consumers contained a deceptive subject line informing each of them that his or her eBay user ID "will expire soon." Finally, the complaint alleged that the e-mail messages falsely represented that eBay directly or indirectly provided ReverseAuction with eBay users' personally identifiable information, or otherwise participated in dissemination of the unsolicited e-mail.

The settlement obtained by the FTC bars ReverseAuction from committing these violations in the future. It also requires ReverseAuction to provide notice to consumers who, as a result of receiving ReverseAuction's e-mail, registered or will register with ReverseAuction. The notice informs these consumers that their eBay users IDs were not about to expire on eBay, and that eBay did not know of, or authorize, ReverseAuction's dissemination of the unsolicited e-mail. The notice also provides these consumers with the opportunity to cancel registration with ReverseAuction and have their personal identifying information deleted from ReverseAuction's database. In addition, the order requires ReverseAuction to delete, and refrain from using or disclosing, the personal identifying information of eBay members who received ReverseAuction's e-mail but who have not registered with ReverseAuction. Finally, consistent with prior privacy orders obtained by this agency, the settlement requires ReverseAuction to disclose its own privacy policy on its Internet site, and contains comprehensive record keeping provisions to allow the FTC to monitor compliance.

The ReverseAuction case demonstrates that the FTC is committed to using enforcement to buttress industry self-regulatory efforts in the area of online consumer privacy. Indeed, this case directly challenged conduct that undermined a Privacy Policy and User Agreement protecting consumers' privacy, and that could erode consumer confidence in privacy measures undertaken by online companies. Because this case involved the misappropriation by one company of consumer information protected by another company's privacy policy, it also may have particular relevance to the privacy concerns raised by the transfer of data between companies in different countries.

Notwithstanding the Federal Trade Commission's law enforcement actions in GeoCities, Liberty Financial Cos., and ReverseAuction, the agency's authority in some areas of online privacy is more limited. As noted above, to be reachable under the FTC Act, the collection and use of personal information without consent must constitute either a deceptive or unfair trade practice. Thus, the FTC Act likely would not address the practices of a Web site that collected personally identifiable information from consumers, but neither misrepresented the purpose for which the information was collected, nor used or released the information in a way that was likely to cause substantial injury to consumers. Also, it currently may not be within the FTC's power to broadly require that entities collecting information on the Internet adhere to a privacy policy or to any particular privacy policy.(9) As stated above, however, a company's failure to abide by a stated privacy policy is likely to be a deceptive practice.

Furthermore, the FTC's jurisdiction in this area covers unfair or deceptive acts or practices only if they are "in or affecting commerce." Information collection by commercial entities that are promoting products or services, including collecting and using information for commercial purposes, would presumably meet the "commerce" requirement. On the other hand, many individuals or entities may be collecting information online without any commercial purpose, and thereby may fall outside the Federal Trade Commission's jurisdiction. An example of this limitation involves "chat rooms" if operated by noncommercial entities, e.g., a charitable organization.

Finally, there are a number of full or partial statutory exclusions from the FTC's basic jurisdiction over commercial practices that limit the FTC's ability to provide a comprehensive response to Internet privacy concerns. These include exemptions for many information intensive consumer businesses such as banks, insurance companies and airlines. As you are aware, other federal or state agencies would have jurisdiction over those entities, such as the federal banking agencies or the Department of Transportation.

In cases where it does have jurisdiction, the FTC accepts and, resources permitting, acts on consumer complaints received by mail and telephone in its Consumer Response Center ("CRC") and, more recently, on its Web site.(10) The CRC accepts complaints from all consumers, including those residing in European Union member states. The FTC Act provides the Federal Trade Commission equitable power to obtain injunctive relief against future violations of the FTC Act, as well as redress for injured consumers. We would, however, look to see whether the company has engaged in a pattern of improper conduct, as we do not resolve individual consumer disputes. In the past, the Federal Trade Commission has provided redress for citizens of both the United States and other countries.(11) The FTC will continue to assert its authority, in appropriate cases, to provide redress to citizens of other countries who have been injured by deceptive practices under its jurisdiction.

Employment Data

Your most recent letter sought additional clarification concerning the FTC's jurisdiction in the area of employment data. First, you pose the question whether the FTC could take action under Section 5 against a company that represents it complies with U.S. safe harbor principles but transfers or uses employment-related data in a manner that violates these principles. We want to assure you that we have carefully reviewed the FTC authorizing legislation, related documents, and relevant case law and have concluded that the FTC has the same jurisdiction in the employment-related data situation as it would generally under Section 5 of the FTC Act.(12) That is to say, assuming a case met our existing criteria (unfairness or deception) for a privacy-related enforcement action, we could take action in the employment-related data situation.

We also would like to dispel any view that the FTC's ability to take privacy-related enforcement action is limited to situations where a company has deceived individual consumers. In fact, as the Commission's recent action in the ReverseAuction(13) matter makes clear, the FTC will bring privacy-related enforcement actions in situations involving data transfers between companies, where one company allegedly has acted unlawfully vis a vis another company, leading to possible injury to both consumers and companies. We expect this situation is the one in which the employment issue is most likely to arise, as employment data about Europeans is transferred from European companies to American companies that have pledged to abide by the safe harbor principles.

We do wish to note one circumstance in which FTC action would be circumscribed, however. This would occur in situations in which the matter is already being addressed in a traditional labor law dispute resolution context, most likely a grievance/arbitration claim or an unfair labor practice complaint at the National Labor Relations Board. This would occur, for example, if an employer had made a commitment in a collective bargaining agreement regarding the use of personal data and an employee or union claimed that the employer had breached that agreement. The Commission would likely defer to that proceeding.(14)

Jurisdiction Over "Seal" Programs

Second, you ask whether the FTC would have jurisdiction over "seal" programs administering dispute resolution mechanisms in the United States that misrepresented their role in enforcing the "safe harbor" principles and handling individual complaints, even if such entities were technically "not for profit." In determining whether we have jurisdiction over an entity that holds itself out as a non-profit, the Commission closely analyzes whether the entity, while not seeking a profit for itself, furthers the profit of its members. The Commission has successfully asserted jurisdiction over such entities and as recently as May 24, 1999, the United States Supreme Court, in <u>California Dental Association v. Federal Trade Commission</u>, unanimously affirmed the Commission's jurisdiction over a voluntary nonprofit association of local dental societies in an antitrust matter. The Court held:

The FTC Act is at pains to include not only an entity "organized to carry on business for its own profit," 15 U. S. C. §44, but also one that carries on business for the profit "of its members." . . . . It could, indeed, hardly be supposed that Congress intended such a restricted notion of covered supporting organizations, with the opportunity this would bring with it for avoiding jurisdiction where the purposes of the FTC Act would obviously call for asserting it.

In sum, determining whether to assert jurisdiction over a particular "non-profit" entity administering a seal program would require a factual review of the extent to which the entity provided economic benefit to its for-profit members. If such an entity operated its seal program in a manner that provided an economic benefit to its members, the FTC likely would assert its jurisdiction. As a separate point, the FTC likely would have jurisdiction over a fraudulent seal program that misrepresents its status as a non-profit entity.

<u>Privacy in the Offline World</u>

Third, you note that our prior correspondence has focused on privacy in the online world. While online privacy has been a major concern of the FTC as a critical component to the development of electronic commerce, the FTC Act dates back to 1914 and applies equally in the offline world. Thus, we can pursue offline firms that engage in unfair or deceptive trade practices with regard to consumers' privacy.(15) In fact, in a case brought by the Commission last year, <u>FTC v. TouchTone Information, Inc.</u>,(16) an "information broker" was charged with illegally obtaining and selling consumers' private financial information. The Commission alleged that Touch Tone obtained consumers' information by "pretexting," a term of art coined by the private investigation industry to describe the practice of getting personal information about others under false pretenses, typically on the telephone. The case, filed April 21, 1999, in federal court in Colorado, seeks an injunction and all illegally gained profits.

This law enforcement experience, as well as recent concerns about the merging of offline and online databases, the blurring of distinctions between online and offline merchants, and the fact that a vast amount of personal identifying information is collected and used offline, make clear that significant attention to offline privacy issues is warranted.

<u>Overlapping Jurisdiction</u>

Finally, you pose the question of the interplay of the FTC's jurisdiction with that of other law enforcement agencies, particularly in cases where there is potentially overlapping jurisdiction. We have developed strong working relationships with numerous other law enforcement agencies, including the federal banking agencies and the state attorneys general. We very often coordinate investigations to maximize our resources in instances of overlapping jurisdiction. We also often refer matters to the appropriate federal or state agency for investigation.

I hope this review is helpful. Please let me know if you need any further information.

Sincerely,

Robert Pitofsky

Endnotes

1. 15 U.S.C. § 45. The Fair Credit Reporting Act would also apply to Internet data collection and sales that meet the statutory definitions of "consumer report" and "consumer reporting agency."

2. 15 U.S.C. § 45(n).

3. *See* GeoCities, Docket No. C-3849 (Final Order Feb. 12, 1999) (available at www.ftc.gov/os/1999/9902/9823015d%26o.htm); Liberty Financial Cos., Docket No. C-3891 (Final Order Aug. 12, 1999) (available at www.ftc.gov/opa/1999/9905/younginvestor.htm). *See also* Children's Online Privacy Protection Act Rule (COPPA), 16 C.F.R. Part 312 (available at www.ftc.gov/opa/1999/9910/childfinal.htm). The COPPA Rule, which became effective last month, requires operators of Web sites directed to children under 13, or who knowingly collect personal information from children under 13, to implement the fair information practice standards enunciated in the Rule.

4. *See* FTC v. Touch Tone, Inc., Civil Action No. 99-WM-783 (D.Co.) (filed April 21, 1999) at <www.ftc.gov/opa/1999/9904/touchtone.htm>. Staff Opinion Letter, July 17, 1997, issued in response to a petition filed by the Center for Media Education, at <www.ftc.gov/os/1997/9707/cenmed.htm>.

5. Indeed, the FTC recently filed a complaint in federal district court against a TRUSTe sealholder, Toysmart.com, seeking injunctive and declaratory relief to prevent the sale of confidential, personal customer information collected on the company Web site in violation of its own privacy policy. The FTC learned of this possible law violation directly from TRUSTe. FTC v. Toysmart.com, LLC, Civil Action No. 00-11341-RGS (D.Ma.) (filed July 11, 2000) (available at www.ftc.gov/opa/2000/07/toysmart.htm).

6. GeoCities, Docket No. C-3849 (Final Order Feb. 12, 1999) (available at www.ftc.gov/os/1999/9902/9823015d%26o.htm).

7. The Commission subsequently settled another matter involving the collection of personal information from children online. Liberty Financial Companies, Inc., operated the Young Investor website which was directed to children and teens, and focused on issues relating to money and investing. The Commission alleged that the site falsely represented that personal information collected from children in a survey would be maintained anonymously, and that participants would be sent an e-mail newsletter as well as prizes. In fact, the personal information about the child and the family's finances was maintained in an identifiable manner, and no newsletter or prizes were sent. The consent agreement prohibits such misrepresentations in the future and requires Liberty Financial to post a privacy notice on its children's sites and obtain verifiable parental consent before collecting personal identifying information from children. Liberty Financial Cos., Docket No. C-3891 (Final Order Aug. 12, 1999) (available at www.ftc.gov/opa/1999/9905/younginvestor.htm).

8. See ReverseAuction.com, Inc., Civil Action No. 000032 (D.D.C.) (filed January 6, 2000) (press release and pleadings at www.ftc.gov/opa/2000/01/reverse4.htm).

9. For this reason, the Federal Trade Commission stated in Congressional testimony that additional legislation probably would be required to mandate that all U.S. commercial Web sites directed toward consumers abide by specified fair information practices. "Consumer Privacy on the World Wide Web," Before the Subcommittee on Telecommunications, Trade and Consumer Protection of the House Committee on Commerce United States House of Representatives, July 21, 1998 (the testimony can be found at www.ftc.gov/os/9807/privac98.htm). The FTC deferred calling for such legislation in order to give self-regulatory efforts the opportunity to demonstrate widespread adoption of fair information practices on Web sites. In the Federal Trade Commission's report to Congress on online privacy, "Privacy Online: A Report to Congress," June 1998 (the report can be found at www.ftc.gov/reports/privacy3/toc.htm), the FTC recommended legislation to require that commercial Web sites obtain parental consent before collecting personally identifiable information from children under 13 years old. See footnote 3 supra. Last year, the FTC's report, "Self-Regulation and Privacy Online: A Federal Trade Commission Report to Congress," July 1999 (the report can be found at www.ftc.gov/os/1999/9907/index.htm#13,) found sufficient progress in self-regulation and, accordingly, chose not to recommend legislation at that time.

In May 2000, the Commission issued a third report to Congress, "Privacy Online: Fair Information Practices in the Electronic Marketplace," (the report can be found at www.ftc.gov/os/2000/05/index.htm#22) which discusses the FTC's recent survey of commercial Web sites and their compliance with fair information practices. The report also recommended (by a majority of the Commission) that Congress enact legislation that would set forth a basic level of privacy protection for consumer-oriented commercial Web sites.

10. *See* https://www.ftc.gov/ftc/complaint.htm for the Federal Trade Commission's online complaint form.

11. For example, in a recent case involving an Internet pyramid scheme, the Commission obtained refunds for 15,622 consumers totaling approximately $5.5 million. The consumers resided in the United States and 70 foreign countries. *See* www.ftc.gov/opa/9807/fortunar.htm; www.ftc.gov/opa/9807/ftcrefund01.htm.

12. Except as specifically excluded by the FTC's authorizing statute, the FTC's jurisdiction under the FTC Act over practices "in or affecting commerce" is coextensive with the constitutional power of Congress under the Commerce Clause, United States v. American Building Maintenance Industries, 422 U.S. 271, 277 n. 6 (1975). The FTC's jurisdiction would thus encompass employment-related practices in firms and industries in international commerce.

13. *See* "Online Auction Site Settles FTC Privacy Charges," FTC News Release (Jan. 6, 2000), *available at* http://www.ftc.gov/opa/2000/01/reverse4.htm.

14. The determination whether conduct is an "unfair labor practice" or a violation of a collective bargaining agreement is a technical one that is ordinarily reserved to the expert labor tribunals who will hear the complaints, such as arbitrators and the NRLB.

15. As you know from earlier discussions, the Fair Credit Reporting Act also gives the FTC the authority to protect consumers' financial privacy within the purview of the Act and the Commission recently issued a decision pertaining to this issue. *See* In the Matter of Trans Union, Docket No. 9255 (March 1, 2000) (press release and opinion available at www.ftc.gov/os/2000/03/index.htm#1).

16. Civil Action 99-WM-783 (D.Colo.)(available at http://www.ftc.gov/opa/1999/9904/touchtone.htm) (tentative consent decree pending).

Letter from the Department of Transportation concerning its authority in protecting the privacy of consumers with respect to information

July 14, 2000

John Mogg
Director, DG XV
European Commission
Office C 107-6/72
Rue de la Loi, 200
1049 Brussels
BELGIUM

Dear Director General Mogg:

Recent Developments
Safe Harbor Arrangement (EU-US)

I am providing you this letter at the request of the U.S. Department of Commerce to explain the role of the Department of Transportation in protecting the privacy of consumers with respect to information provided by them to airlines.

The Department of Transportation encourages self-regulation as the least intrusive and most efficient means of ensuring the privacy of information provided by consumers to airlines and accordingly supports the establishment of a "safe harbor" regime that would enable airlines to comply with the requirements of the European Union's privacy directive as regards transfers outside the EU. The Department recognizes, however, that for self-regulatory efforts to work, it is essential that the airlines that commit to the privacy principles set forth in the "safe harbor" regime in fact abide by them. In this regard, self-regulation should be backed by law enforcement. Therefore, using its existing consumer protection statutory authority, the Department will ensure airline compliance with privacy commitments made to the public, and pursue referrals of alleged non-compliance that we receive from self-regulatory organizations and others, including European Union member states.

The Department's authority to take enforcement action in this area is found in 49 U.S.C. 41712 which prohibits a carrier from engaging in "an unfair or deceptive practice or an unfair method of competition" in the sale of air transportation that results or is likely to result in consumer harm. Section 41712 is patterned after Section 5 of the Federal Trade Commission Act (15 U.S.C. 45). However, air carriers are exempt from Section 5 regulation by the Federal Trade Commission under 15 U.S.C. 45(a)(2).

My office investigates and prosecutes cases under 49 U.S.C. 41712. (See, *e.g.*, DOT Orders 99-11-5, November 9, 1999; 99-8-23, August 26, 1999; 99-6-1, June 1, 1999; 98-6-24, June 22, 1998; 98-6-21, June 19, 1998; 98-5-31, May 22, 1998; and 97-12-23, December 18, 1997.) We institute such cases based on our own investigations, as well as on formal and informal complaints we receive from individuals, travel agents, airlines, and U.S. and foreign government agencies.

I would point out that the failure by a carrier to maintain the privacy of information obtained from passengers would not be a *per se* violation of section 41712. However, once a carrier formally and publicly commits to the "safe harbor" principles of providing privacy to the consumer information it obtains, then the Department would be empowered to use the statutory powers of section 41712 to ensure compliance with those principles. Therefore, once a passenger provides information to a carrier that has committed to honoring the "safe harbor" principles, any failure to do so would likely cause consumer harm and be a violation of section 41712. My office would give the investigation of any such alleged activity and the prosecution of any case evidencing such activity a high priority. We will also advise the Department of Commerce of the outcome of any such case.

Violations of section 41712 can result in the issuance of cease and desist orders and the imposition of civil penalties for violations of those orders. Although we do not have the authority to award damages or provide pecuniary relief to individual complainants, we do have the authority to approve settlements resulting from investigations and cases brought by the Department that provide items of value to consumers either in mitigation or as an offset to monetary penalties otherwise payable. We have done so in the past, and we can and will do so in the context of the safe harbor principles when circumstances warrant. Repeated violations of section 41712 by any U.S. airline would also raise questions regarding the airline's compliance disposition which could, in egregious situations, result in an airline being found to be no longer fit to operate and, therefore, losing its economic operating authority. (See, DOT Orders 93-6-34, June 23, 1993, and 93-6-11, June 9, 1993. Although this proceeding did not involve section 41712, it did result in the revocation of the operating authority of a carrier for a complete disregard for the provisions of the Federal Aviation Act, a bilateral agreement, and the Department's rules and regulations.)

I hope that this information proves helpful. If you have any questions or need further information, please feel free to contact me.

Sincerely,

Samuel Podberesky
Assistant General Counsel for
Aviation Enforcement and Proceeding

EU

Letter from Commission Services transmitting the European Commission's Adequacy Finding

EUROPEAN COMMISSION
Internal Market DG
Director-General
Brussels, 28.01.00 4074
DG Markt/E-1 D(2000)168

Mr. Robert LaRussa
Under Secretary for International Trade of
the United States Department of Commerce
Washington D.C. 20230
United States of America

Recent Developments
Safe Harbor Arrangement (EU-US)

Dear Mr. LaRussa,

Thank you for your letter of 17 July with which you enclosed the "Safe Harbor Privacy Principles" and the frequently asked questions and answers (the principles) issued by the Department of Commerce on 21 July and related material concerning enforcement by public bodies in the United States. I am pleased to inform you that the Commission, exercising the powers conferred on it by Article 25.6 of the Data Protection Directive (95/46/EC), has found that these arrangements would provide adequate protection for the purposes of Article 25.1 of the Directive regarding the transfer of personal data to countries outside the European Union. I enclose a copy of the Commission decision C(2000) 2441 for your information. The Member States are required to comply with decisions of the Commission taken on the basis of Article 25.6.

The Commission decision

The decision provides that data controllers in the EU can transfer personal data processed in accordance with MS law, without providing additional safeguards to ensure their protection, to US-based organisations declaring their adherence to the "safe harbor" principles, provided that they are subject to the statutory powers of a public body empowered to investigate complaints and to obtain relief against unfair or deceptive practices or otherwise effectively ensure compliance with the principles. The effect of this decision is also that any requirements for the prior authorisation of transborder data transfers as provided for under Member State law will be waived, or that approval will be automatically and promptly granted, as regards such transfers to organisations qualifying for the safe harbor. The Directive and Member States' laws implementing it still of course govern the lawfulness of processing in the EU, and Article 25.6 decisions do not affect that in any way. This means that violations of Member State laws by data exporters can result in the blocking of data transfers, notwithstanding the existence of relevant Article 25.6 decisions.

List of Participating US-based Organisations

The Commission welcomes the fact that the Department of Commerce will provide for the maintenance of a list, to be made publicly available and kept up to date on a regular basis, of the US-based organisations which have declared their adherence to the "safe harbor" principles and which notify this to the Department of Commerce or the organisation the Department designates for this purpose. We note also that the Department of Commerce or its designee will make public any proper and final adverse determinations notified to it pertaining to non-compliance with the principles by a "safe harbor" organisation or to other events that might bring to an end an organisation's participation in the "safe harbor", such as a takeover or a merger. This will ensure transparency and clarity about which US-based organisations enjoy "safe harbor" benefits.

Date of entry into effect

Member States are required to ensure that the decision is effective 90 days after its notification to them. After this, US organisations self-certifying their adherence to the "safe harbor" will be assured of "safe harbor" benefits from the date that they notify the Department of Commerce (or its designee) and publicly announce that they have taken the measures necessary to comply with the principles. The Commission and the Member States recognise that US organisations will need some time to consider whether to participate in the "safe harbor" and, if so, to implement privacy policies to put the principles into effect. During the course of our discussions, Member States have demonstrated their willingness to use the flexibility offered by Article 26 of the Directive to avoid interruptions in data flows, so as not to call into question the good faith efforts being made to secure adequate protection for data transferred from the EU. The Commission and the Member States have confirmed their willingness to continue to use this flexibility during the implementation phase of the "safe harbor", so that US organisations have time to decide whether to participate in the "safe harbor" and (if necessary) to update their information processing policies and practices accordingly. If Member States become aware that action needs to be taken which will interrupt data flows to the United States, they will inform the Commission immediately, if possible before such action is taken, and the Department of Commerce will be informed. In this connection, I would draw your attention to the enclosed extract from the minutes of the Article 31 Committee. The situation will be reviewed in the middle of 2001.

In deciding whether to participate in the "safe harbor", organisations should consider that the "safe harbor" represents clear advantages over the existing situation, in terms of speedier transfers, lighter administrative burdens and greater legal certainty. These advantages will benefit the EU transferers of data as well as the US recipients. US organisations may of course join the "safe harbor" at any time, but we consider that the resulting benefits represent strong arguments for their entering the "safe harbor" as quickly as possible.

The proposed review of the implementation phase will take into account the particular needs of the financial services sector. The EU side shares the US goal of identifying a predictable framework for data transfers in and bringing the benefits of the "safe harbor" to the financial services sector, given its economic importance and the high volume of personal data flows in this sector. More time is however needed for further examination of recent developments in US laws governing privacy in the financial sector and of their interaction with the "safe harbor," and specifically for completion in the United States of the Financial Modernization Act regulations. On our side, we shall seek to maintain the momentum developed in the "safe harbor" discussions and, as indicated above, thanks to the flexibility allowed by the Directive itself we do not anticipate problems with interruptions in data flows while good faith efforts continue to address these issues.

Recent Developments
Safe Harbor Arrangement (EU-US)

Complaint Procedures

It can be expected that claims will arise from time to time that an organisation which has entered the "safe harbor" is not in fact complying with the "safe harbor" principles. As for all cases where complaints concern recipients falling within the scope of a decision taken on the basis of Article 25.6 of the Directive, it will be for the appropriate US bodies to determine whether such claims are founded and if so, to ensure that the organisation takes the measures necessary to come into compliance with the principles as quickly as possible, or is removed from the "safe harbor". Reliance on US enforcement arrangements to ensure a good general level of compliance with the principles is a fundamental aspect of the "adequacy" finding. As indicated by Article 2 of the decision, evidence that any enforcement body in the United States responsible for compliance with the principles is failing to secure compliance may trigger action by the Commission, in consultation with the Member States through the Article 31 Committee, and after informing the Department of Commerce, to reverse, suspend or limit the scope of the decision with respect to such enforcement body. Measures to suspend specific data transfers for reasons connected with compliance problems in the United States can be taken at the national level only in the circumstances and in the manner set out in Article 2, paragraph 1. Moreover, such measures can have only a temporary effect, pending a resolution of the problem by the appropriate enforcement bodies in the United States. These arrangements as a whole reflect our shared twin objectives of avoiding the interruption of transborder data flows and maintaining high data protection standards.

Jurisdiction

During our dialogue, you raised with me the concerns of US industry about the possible effects of the "safe harbor" as regards jurisdiction and applicable law in the European Union. I would like to confirm that it is the Commission's intention that participation in the "safe harbor" does not change the *status quo ante* for any organisation with respect to jurisdiction, applicable law or liability in the European Union. Moreover, our discussions with respect to the "safe harbor" have not resolved nor prejudged the questions of jurisdiction or applicable law with respect to websites. All existing rules, principles, conventions and treaties relating to international conflicts of law continue to apply and are not prejudiced in any way by the "safe harbor" arrangement.

Use of Contracts - Commission decisions based on Article 26 of the data protection Directive

I should also add that the establishment of the "safe harbor" does not affect the ability of Member States to authorise transfers on the basis of safeguards adduced by the data exporter in accordance with Article 26.2. This means organisations not wishing to qualify for the "safe harbor" could put in place the safeguards necessary for transfers of personal data from the EU to the United States by means of binding written agreements between the transferers and the recipients of data. The Commission may approve model clauses for such agreements under Article 26.4 of the Directive which are binding on the Member States. The Commission and the Member States are of the view that the "safe harbor" principles may be used in such agreements for the substantive provisions on data protection. Such agreements may need to include other provisions on issues such as liability and enforcement, on which decisions have not yet been taken. The Commission has initiated discussions with the Member States in the Article 31 Committee regarding these other provisions, with the aim of adopting a decision under Article 26.4 authorising model agreements which rely on the "safe harbor" principles for the provisions on data processing and other contractual provisions as necessary. Such a decision would mean that transfers covered by contracts in the approved form would be automatically authorised. The Commission is working with the Article 31 Committee to finalise such a decision as soon as possible.

Our dialogue has proved extremely useful in clarifying rules and practices on both sides, identifying much common ground and exchanging information on procedures. The continuation of this dialogue would seem desirable, on a periodic basis and/or when a particular problem makes it necessary. This will allow us to continue to exchange information on relevant developments concerning the implementation of Articles 25 and 26 and developments in the United States, in line with our general commitment to regulatory co-operation in the context of the TransAtlantic Economic Partnership. Thank you for the confirmation in your letter that you believe that privacy legislation should not discriminate on the basis of nationality and your assurance that you will work within the legislative process to avoid any such discrimination resulting from legislation proposed in Congress. We also welcome your offer to continue your efforts to keep us informed about legislative and other developments in the United States in the privacy field of which you may be aware. We shall of course do the same as regards EU legislation and developments in the privacy field. We have accepted the language in the introduction to the principles on explicit authorisations in US law permitting exceptions to be made to the principles in the expectation that these will in practice most frequently reflect a public interest concern and not fall outside the scope of exceptions allowed by the Directive. We would wish the matter to be taken up through the review arrangement in the event that this expectation proved to be incorrect or in the event that discriminatory privacy legislation were adopted in the United States.

As you know, the Commission and the Member States are committed to implementing and enforcing these provisions and any decisions based on them in an even-handed and non-discriminatory manner as between US organisations and those located in other third countries and in the EU and agree that we should monitor whether they have been implemented and enforced in this manner in our continuing dialogue (I enclose an extract from the minutes of the Article 31 Committee on this point, together with a text adopted by the working party established under Article 29 of the Directive.) It is also important to recall that the "safe harbor" reflects a number of features which may be unique to the US constitutional model and legal system and which were taken into account in the US context, but which are not necessarily present outside this context. We continue to prefer legally binding data protection rules, for which the Directive and the OECD guidelines must remain our principal benchmarks and any proposal to regard the "safe harbor" as providing adequate protection outside the US context would have to be examined by the Commission in the light of all the relevant circumstances.

The European Commission and the Member States have committed themselves to conducting an evaluation of the implementation of the decision in 2003 as indicated in Article 3 of the decision, and we hope that the US Government will participate in this review. In any event, the European Commission will inform the US Government before taking any action to modify the decision.

This letter is for your information only and of itself creates no legally binding effects.

(signed)
John F. Mogg

Extract from the minutes of the Article 31 Committee, 22 June 2000

All members of the Committee emphasised that there was no legal basis in the Directive (apart from Article 32 paragraph 2) for a delayed application of the rules or for differentiated treatment as regards a particular group of third country recipients, except in so far as the latter were covered by a decision under Article 25 paragraph 6. This being said, the Committee recalled the different ways in which data transfers were allowable under Article 26 even where protection in the third country in question was not generally adequate. These provisions had ensured that data flows had continued uninterrupted up to now and the Committee expected no change during the implementation phase of the "safe harbor". US organisations will thus have time to decide whether to participate in the "safe harbor" and (if necessary) to update their information processing policies and practices accordingly.

European Commission's decision C(2000) 2441 finding the safe harbor to provide adequate protection

COMMISSION OF THE EUROPEAN COMMUNITIES

COMMISSION DECISION

of

pursuant to Directive 95/46/EC of the European Parliament and of the Council

on the adequacy of the protection provided by the Safe Harbor Privacy Principles and related
Frequently Asked Questions issued by
the US Department of Commerce
(Text with EEA relevance)

THE COMMISSION OF THE EUROPEAN COMMUNITIES,

Having regard to the Treaty establishing the European Community,

Having regard to Directive 95/46/EC of the European Parliament and of the Council of 24 October 1995 on the protection of individuals with regard to the processing of personal data and on the free movement of such data(1), and in particular Article 25(6) thereof,

Whereas:

(1) Pursuant to Directive 95/46/EC Member States are required to provide that the transfer of personal data to a third country may take place only if the third country in question ensures an adequate level of protection and the Member State laws implementing other provisions of the Directive are respected prior to the transfer.

(2) The Commission may find that a third country ensures an adequate level of protection. In that case personal data may be transferred from the Member States without additional guarantees being necessary.

(3) Pursuant to Directive 95/46/EC the level of data protection should be assessed in the light of all the circumstances surrounding a data transfer operation or a set of data transfer operations and in respect of given conditions. The Working Party on Protection of Individuals with regard to the processing of Personal Data established under that Directive(2) has issued guidance on the making of such assessments(3).

(4) Given the different approaches to data protection in third countries, the adequacy assessment should be carried out and any decision based on Article 25(6) of Directive 95/46/EC should be enforced in a way that does not arbitrarily or unjustifiably discriminate against or between third countries where like conditions prevail nor constitute a disguised barrier to trade taking into account the Community's present international commitments.

(5) The adequate level of protection for the transfer of data from the Community to the United States recognised by this Decision, should be attained if organisations comply with the Safe Harbor Privacy Principles for the protection of personal data transferred from a Member State to the United States (hereinafter "the Principles") and the Frequently Asked Questions (hereinafter "the FAQs") providing guidance for the implementation of the Principles issued by the Government of the United States on 21.07.2000. Furthermore the organisations should publicly disclose their privacy policies and be subject to the jurisdiction of the Federal Trade Commission (FTC) under Section 5 of the Federal Trade Commission Act which prohibits unfair or deceptive acts or practices in or affecting commerce, or that of another statutory body that will effectively ensure compliance with the Principles implemented in accordance with the FAQs.

Recent Developments
Safe Harbor Arrangement (EU-US)

(6) Sectors and/or data processing not subject to the jurisdiction of any of the government bodies in the United States listed in Annex VII to this Decision should fall outside the scope of this Decision.

(7) To ensure the proper application of this Decision, it is necessary that organisations adhering to the Principles and the FAQs can be recognised by interested parties, such as data subjects, data exporters and data protection authorities. To this end the US Department of Commerce or its designee should undertake to maintain and make available to the public a list of organisations self-certifying their adherence to the Principles implemented in accordance with the FAQs and falling within the jurisdiction of at least one of the government bodies listed in Annex VII to this Decision.

(8) In the interests of transparency and in order to safeguard the ability of the competent authorities in the Member States to ensure the protection of individuals as regards the processing of their personal data, it is necessary to specify in this Decision the exceptional circumstances in which the suspension of specific data flows should be justified, notwithstanding the finding of adequate protection.

(9) The "safe harbor" created by the Principles and the FAQs, may need to be reviewed in the light of experience, of developments concerning the protection of privacy in circumstances in which technology is constantly making easier the transfer and processing of personal data and in the light of reports on implementation by enforcement authorities involved.

(10) The Working Party on Protection of Individuals with regard to the processing of Personal Data established under Article 29 of Directive 95/46/EC has delivered Opinions on the level of protection provided by the "safe harbor" Principles in the United States which have been taken into account in the preparation of the present Decision(4).

(11) The measures provided for in this Decision are in accordance with the opinion of the Committee established under Article 31 of Directive 95/46/EC,

HAS ADOPTED THIS DECISION:

Article 1

1. For the purposes of Article 25(2) of Directive 95/46/EC, for all the activities falling within the scope of that Directive, the "Safe Harbor Privacy Principles" (hereinafter "the Principles"), as set out in Annex I to this Decision, implemented in accordance with the guidance provided by the Frequently Asked Questions (hereinafter "the FAQs") issued by the US Department of Commerce on 21.07.2000 as set out in Annex II to this Decision are considered to ensure an adequate level of protection for personal data transferred from the Community to organisations established in the United States, having regard to the following documents issued by the US Department of Commerce:

(a) the safe harbor enforcement overview set out in Annex III,

(b) a memorandum on damages for breaches of privacy and explicit authorisations in US law set out in Annex IV,

(c) a letter from the Federal Trade Commission set out in Annex V,

(d) a letter from the US Department of Transportation set out in Annex VI.

2. In relation to each transfer of data the following conditions shall be met:

(a) the organisation receiving the data has unambiguously and publicly disclosed its commitment to comply with the Principles implemented in accordance with the FAQs, and

(b) the organisation is subject to the statutory powers of a government body in the United States listed in Annex VII to this Decision which is empowered to investigate complaints and to obtain relief against unfair or deceptive practices as well as redress for individuals, irrespective of their country of residence or nationality, in case of non-compliance with the Principles implemented in accordance with the FAQs.

3. The conditions set out in paragraph 2 are considered to be met for each organisation that self-certifies its adherence to the Principles implemented in accordance with the FAQs from the date on which the organisation notifies to the US Department of Commerce (or its designee) the public disclosure of the commitment referred to in paragraph 2(a) and the identity of the government body referred to in paragraph 2(b).

Article 2

This Decision concerns only the adequacy of protection provided in the United States under the Principles implemented in accordance with the FAQs with a view to meeting the requirements of Article 25(1) of Directive 95/46/EC and does not affect the application of other provisions of that Directive that pertain to the processing of personal data within the Member States, in particular Article 4 thereof.

Article 3

1. Without prejudice to their powers to take action to ensure compliance with national provisions adopted pursuant to provisions other than Article 25 of Directive 95/46/EC, the competent authorities in Member States may exercise their existing powers to suspend data flows to an organisation that has self-certified its adherence to the Principles implemented in accordance with the FAQs in order to protect individuals with regard to the processing of their personal data in cases where:

(a) the government body in the United States referred to in Annex VII to this Decision or an independent recourse mechanism within the meaning of letter a) of the Enforcement Principle set out in Annex I to this Decision has determined that the organisation is violating the Principles implemented in accordance with the FAQs; or

(b) there is a substantial likelihood that the Principles are being violated, there is a reasonable basis for believing that the enforcement mechanism concerned is not taking or will not take adequate and timely steps to settle the case at issue, the continuing transfer would create an imminent risk of grave harm to data subjects, and the competent authorities in the Member State have made reasonable efforts under the circumstances to provide the organisation with notice and an opportunity to respond.

The suspension shall cease as soon as compliance with the Principles implemented in accordance with the FAQs is assured and the competent authorities concerned in the Community are notified thereof.

2. Member States shall inform the Commission without delay when measures are adopted on the basis of paragraph 1.

3. The Member States and the Commission shall also inform each other of cases where the action of bodies responsible for ensuring compliance with the Principles implemented in accordance with the FAQs in the United States fails to secure such compliance.

4. If the information collected under paragraphs 1, 2 and 3 provides evidence that any body responsible for ensuring compliance with the Principles implemented in accordance with the FAQs in the United States is not effectively fulfilling its role, the Commission shall inform the US Department of Commerce and, if necessary, present draft measures in accordance with the procedure referred to in Article 31 of Directive 95/46/EC with a view to reversing or suspending the present Decision or limiting its scope.

Article 4

1. This Decision may be adapted at any time in the light of experience with its implementation and/or if the level of protection provided by the Principles and the FAQs is overtaken by the requirements of US legislation.

The Commission shall in any case evaluate the implementation of the present Decision on the basis of available information three years after its notification to the Member States and report any pertinent findings to the Committee established under Article 31 of Directive 95/46/EC, including any evidence that could affect the evaluation that the provisions set out in Article 1 of this Decision provide adequate protection within the meaning of Article 25 of Directive 95/46/EC and any evidence that the present Decision is being implemented in a discriminatory way.

2. The Commission shall, if necessary, present draft measures in accordance with the procedure referred to in Article 31 of Directive 95/46/EC.

Article 5

Member States shall take all the measures necessary to comply with this Decision at the latest at the end of a period of ninety days from the date of its notification to the Member States.

Article 6

This Decision is addressed to the Member States.

Done at Brussels, *For the Commission*

Member of the Commission

Annex VII

With reference to Article 1(2)(b), the government bodies in the United States empowered to investigate complaints and to obtain relief against unfair or deceptive practices as well as redress for individuals, irrespective of their country of residence or nationality, in case of non-compliance with the Principles implemented in accordance with the FAQs are:

1. The Federal Trade Commission, and

2. The US Department of Transportation.

The Federal Trade Commission acts on the basis of its authority under Section 5 of the Federal Trade Commission Act. The jurisdiction of the Federal Trade Commission under Section 5 is excluded with respect to: banks, saving and loans and credit unions; telecommunications and interstate transportation common carriers, air carriers and packers and stockyard operators. Although the insurance industry is not specifically included in the list of exceptions in Section 5, the McCarran-Ferguson Act(5) leaves the regulation of the business of insurance to the individual states. However, the provisions of the FTC Act apply to the insurance industry to the extent that such business is not regulated by State law. The FTC retains residual authority over unfair or deceptive practices by insurance companies when they are not engaged in the business of insurance.

The US Department of Transportation acts on the basis of its authority under Title 49 United States Code Section 41712. The US Department of Transportation institutes cases based on its own investigations as well as formal and informal complaints received from individuals, travel agents, airlines, US and foreign government agencies.

Endnotes

1 OJ L 281, 23.11.1995, p. 31.

2 The web address of the Working Party is: http://www.europa.eu.int/comm/internal_market/en/media/dataprot/wpdocs/index.htm

3 WP12: Transfers of personal data to third countries: Applying Articles 25 and 26 of the EU data protection directive, adopted by the Working Party on 24 July 1998.

4 WP 15: Opinion 1/99 concerning the level of data protection in the United States and the ongoing discussions between the European Commission and the United States.

WP 19: Opinion 2/99 on the Adequacy of the "International Safe Harbor Principles" issued by the US Department of Commerce on 19 April 1999.

WP 21: Opinion 4/99 on the Frequently Asked Questions to be issued by the US Department of Commerce in relation to the proposed "Safe Harbor Principles" on the Adequacy of the "International Safe Harbor Principles".

WP 23: Working document on the current state of play of the ongoing discussions between the European Commission and the United States Government concerning the "International Safe Harbor Principles".

Recent Developments
Safe Harbor Arrangement (EU-US)

WP 27: Opinion 7/99 on the Level of Data Protection provided by the "Safe Harbor" Principles as published together with the Frequently Asked Questions (FAQs) and other related documents on 15 and 16 November 1999 by the US Department of Commerce.
WP 31: Opinion 3/2000 on the EU/US dialogue concerning the "Safe Harbor" arrangement.
WP 32: Opinion 4/2000 on the level of protection provided by the "Safe Harbor Principles".
5 15 USC. § 1011 *et seq.*

Text on Non-Discrimination adopted by the Article 31 Committee on May 31, 2000

Non-discriminatory and even-handed implementation of Articles 25 and 26 of the Directive and decisions taken on the basis of these provisions

The Committee is mindful of the interest which third countries are showing in the implementation of Articles 25 and 26 of the Directive and in particular in the effects of findings of "adequacy" under Article 25(6). It recognises that some third countries have raised concerns that enforcement actions in the EU may be more severe *vis-à-vis* third country entities than they are *vis-à-vis* EU data controllers and that there may also be discrimination between the entities from different third countries.

The Committee is confident that these concerns will prove to be unfounded. It recalls the standard text in the recitals of the Commission's decisions under Article 25(6)(1) and the views of the Article 29 working party on this issue, as expressed at the wp's meeting on 3 February.

For its part, the Committee regards it as necessary to be even-handed in implementing the provisions of the Directive that deal with third countries. The Committee express its commitment to the principle of non-discrimination and recall that the general principle of equality, of which the prohibition of discrimination on grounds of nationality is a specific enunciation, is one of the fundamental principles of Community law. This principle requires that similar situations shall not be treated differently unless differentiation is objectively justified(2). The Committee also recalls obligations emanating from other international instruments, in particular the European Convention of Human Rights. Article 14 of the ECHR requires that the rights and freedoms set forth in the Convention (which include the right to respect for privacy - Article 8) be secured without discrimination on any ground, including *inter alia* national origin.

The Committee also regards it as important to be able to judge different situations on their merits and not to regard the equal treatment principle as imposing a single model on third countries. Such an interpretation of the principle would fly in the face of the deliberately flexible wording of Article 25 (which requires "adequate" protection in third countries and which allows circumstances to be judged on a case by case basis) and of the need to take into account different countries' varied approaches to achieving effective data protection. This approach means that adequacy findings may sometimes be made despite certain weaknesses in a particular system, provided of course that such a system can be assessed as adequate overall, for example because of compensating strengths in other areas. The principle of equal treatment does not mean that allowances made to take account of the particular traditions of one country, as described above, are automatically applicable to or acceptable in the cases of other third countries. It does mean that assessments of adequacy should be made broadly by reference to the same standard.

The Committee will respect the principle of equality of treatment in any opinions it may be called upon to issue involving data transfers to third countries which are the subject of Commission draft measures for adequacy findings under Article 25(6) or which are already the subject of Article 25(6) decisions (notably under Article 2 paragraph 5 of such decisions) and welcomes the Commission's intention to be particularly vigilant in this regard (see Article 3 of the draft Article 25(6) decision). The Committee wishes to be informed of any instances of allegedly arbitrary and/or unjustified discriminatory actions and to have the opportunity to discuss and contribute to resolving them, including consideration of the views of the third country concerned.

As befits an instrument aiming to protect fundamental rights, the Directive's enforcement should, in the Committee's view, be impartial both as between different third countries and as between third countries' and EU entities. The Committee notes in this context that complaints handling is a major part of the enforcement of data protection rules, including the Directive. Member States as well as the third countries which benefit from an Article 25.6 decision are subject to an obligation to respond to complaints in an appropriate manner and in respect of the applicable law or rules. Fulfilling this obligation cannot be held to be incompatible with an undertaking to enforce Articles 25 and 26 in an even-handed manner. It is also useful to recall in this regard that under Community law non-compliance with the law by one entity cannot be accepted as legitimate defence for non-compliance by another entity(3).

Endnotes

1 " Given the different approaches to data protection in third countries, the adequacy assessment has to be carried out, and any decision based on Article 25 paragraph 6 has to be enforced, in a way that does not arbitrarily or unjustifiably discriminate against or between third countries where like conditions prevail nor constitute a disguised barrier to trade taking into account the Community's present international commitments"

2 ECJ judgement of 8 October 1980 in case 810/79, Peter Überschär v Bundesversicherungsanstalt für Angestellte.

3 Cases 52/75, 78/76, 232/78, 325/82 and 38/89.

Recent Developments
Safe Harbor Arrangement (EU-US)

Text on Non-Discrimination adopted by the Article 29 Working Party on February 3, 2000

Non-discriminatory and even-handed implementation of Articles 25 and 26 of the Directive and decisions taken on the basis of these provisions

The working party is mindful of the interest which third countries are showing in the implementation of Articles 25 and 26 of the Directive and in particular in the effects of findings of "adequacy" under Article 25(6). It recognises that concerns exist in some third countries that enforcement actions in the EU may be more severe *vis-à-vis* third country entities than they are *vis-à-vis* EU data controllers and that there may also be discrimination among the entities from different third countries.

The working party is confident that these concerns will prove to be unfounded. The data protection supervisory authorities themselves work in the framework of legal and judicial systems that are impartial and the emphasis that is placed on their independence by the Directive and by national law serves to reinforce this. The general principle of equality, of which the prohibition of discrimination on grounds of nationality is a specific enunciation, is one of the fundamental principles of Community law and requires that similar situations shall not be treated differently unless differentiation is objectively justified(1). The members of the working party also recall that one of the purposes of the working party's deliberations is to help ensure the harmonious and thus even-handed implementation of the directive.

The working party fully recognises the necessity to be even-handed in dealing with third countries. The working party notes the commitment of its members to a non-discriminatory and even-handed approach in any actions they may take involving third country recipients covered by Article 25(6) decisions, both among such recipients and between such recipients and data controllers in the EU. The working party wishes to discuss and to contribute to resolving any issues relating to possible discrimination which are drawn to their attention, consulting as necessary with enforcement bodies in the third country or countries concerned.

In the context of ensuring impartial enforcement, the working party recalls that complaints handling is a major part of the enforcement of data protection rules, including the Directive. Member States authorities, as well as the third countries which benefit from an Article 25.6 decision, are subject to an obligation to respond to complaints in an appropriate manner and in respect of the applicable law or rules. Fulfilling this obligation cannot be held to be incompatible with an undertaking to enforce Articles 25 and 26 in an even-handed manner. It is also useful to recall in this regard that under Community law non-compliance with the law by one entity cannot be accepted as legitimate defence for non-compliance by another entity(2).

Endnotes

1 ECJ ruling ..../. Überschär

2 Cases 52/75, 78/76, 232/78, 325/82 and 38/89

European Parliament resolution on the Draft Commission Decision on the adequacy of the protection provided by the Safe Harbour Privacy Principles and related Frequently Asked Questions issued by the US Department of Commerce

Adopted by the European Parliament on 5 July 2000

The European Parliament,

– having regard to European Parliament and Council Directive 95/46/EC on the protection of individuals with regard to the processing of personal data and on the free movement of such data [1], (hereinafter referred to as "the Directive"), in particular Article 25 thereof,

– having regard to the draft Commission Decision (C5-0280/2000),

– having regard to the opinion (WP 32) on this subject adopted unanimously on 16 May 2000 by the working party provided for in Article 29 of the Directive and to the opinions delivered previously on the same question (WP12 and WP27),

– having regard to the opinion of 31 May 2000 delivered by the Committee provided for in Article 31 of the Directive,

– having regard to Council Decision 1999/468/EC laying down the procedures for the exercise of the implementing powers conferred on the Commission[2], and in particular Article 8 thereof concerning implementing measures,

– having regard to Rule 88 of its Rules of Procedure,

– having regard to the report by the Committee on Citizens' Freedoms and Rights, Justice and Home Affairs (A5-0177/2000),

The meaning of data protection in the framework of the competences of the Union

A. whereas

(a) the development of the information society and electronic commerce have led at global level to an exponential increase in the movement of data and the risks involved in the misuse of such data;

[1] OJ L 281, 23.11.1995, p. 31.

[2] OJ L 184, 17.7.1999, p. 23.

(b) such abuses not only act as a brake on the development of e-commerce in that they undermine the confidence of consumers, but also often constitute an infringement of the rights and freedoms of persons and, in particular, an invasion of privacy;

(c) protecting data means protecting the people to whom the information being processed relates, and such protection is one of the fundamental rights recognised by the Union (Article 8 of the European Convention for the Protection of Human Rights, referred to in Article 6 of the Treaty on European Union and Article 286 of the Treaty establishing the European Community);

(d) the Directive, which is modelled on Council of Europe Convention No. 108 (1981) and the OECD (1980) and UN (1990) guidelines, is based on identifying rights for the data subject and corresponding obligations on those who process data or who exercise control over such processing;

(e) such protection would be useless if it were confined to the territory of the Union and did not also provide adequate protection, as provided for by the Directive, in the third countries to which the data is transferred;

(f) an adequate level of protection for personal data in all the countries to which data can be transferred is also required, in order to avoid a situation where different levels of protection allow distortions in the use of data and relocation of its processing in violation of the GATS agreements;

(g) the Commission must ensure, on behalf of the citizens of the Union and its Member States, that 'adequate' protection exists in the third countries;

The role of the Commission and the measures and criteria that it must adopt in order to evaluate the 'adequacy' of the protection provided by third countries

B. whereas:

(a) in evaluating the 'adequacy' of the protection provided by third countries, the Commission must take account of the varying levels of legal, economic and technological development of the third countries in relation to European standards;

(b) 'adequate' protection does not mean per se that the third country should have the same rules as the Union but that, regardless of the type of legislative protection in force in the third country, the data subject must be effectively protected;

(c) in a third country protection should be considered effective when its effectiveness can be measured with reference to objective data, such as the possibility of identifying the person on whom the obligations are incumbent, the type of data processed, the uses that may be made of it and the mechanisms created to guarantee protection;

(d) in this context, the protection provided by a third country must comply with the following minimum requirements set out by the data control authorities of the EU Member States (opinion WP12 of June 1998):

"(1) the purpose limitation principle - data should be processed for a specific purpose and subsequently used or further communicated only insofar as this is not incompatible with the purpose of the transfer. The only exemptions to this rule would be those necessary in a democratic society on one of the grounds listed in Article 13 of the Directive.

(2) the data quality and proportionality principle - data should be accurate and, where necessary, kept up to date. The data should be adequate, relevant and not excessive in relation to the purposes for which they are transferred or further processed.

(3) the transparency principle - individuals should be provided with information as to the purpose of the processing and the identity of the data controller in the third country, and other information insofar as this is necessary to ensure fairness. The only exemptions permitted should be in line with Articles 11(2)[3] and 13 of the Directive.

(4) the security principle - technical and organisational security measures should be taken by the data controller that are appropriate to the risks presented by the processing. Any person acting under the authority of the data controller, including a processor, must not process data except on instructions from the controller.

(5) the rights of access, rectification and opposition - the data subject should have a right to obtain a copy of all data relating to him/her that are processed, and a right to rectification of those data where they are shown to be inaccurate. In certain situations he/she should also be able to object to the processing of the data relating to him/her. The only exemptions to these rights should be in line with Article 13 of the Directive.

(6) restrictions on onward transfers - further transfers of the personal data by the recipient of the original data transfer should be permitted only where the second recipient (i.e. the recipient of the onward transfer) is also subject to rules affording an adequate level of protection. The only exceptions permitted should be in line with Article 26(1) of the Directive.

C. whereas, with reference to the guarantees concerning effective implementation, it is also necessary to secure the following objectives, particularly if the rules relating to the processing of data subject to assessment are based on a system of self-regulation:

"- The instrument must have mechanisms which effectively ensure a good level of general compliance. A system of dissuasive and punitive sanctions is one way of achieving this. Mandatory external audits are another.

- The instrument must provide support and help to individual data subjects who are faced with a problem involving the processing of their personal data. An easily accessible, impartial and independent body to hear complaints from data subjects and adjudicate on breaches of the code must therefore be in place.

- The instrument must guarantee appropriate redress in cases of non-compliance. A data subject must be able to obtain a remedy for his/her problem and compensation as appropriate";

---

[3] Article 11(2) stipulates that when data are collected from someone other than the data subject, information need not be provided to the data subject if this proves impossible, involves a disproportionate effort, or if the recording or disclosure of the data is expressly required by law.";

Recent Developments
Safe Harbor Arrangement (EU-US)

The data protection system used in the United States

D. whereas in the United States:

(a) there is not at present any generally applicable legal data protection in the private sector and virtually all data are currently processed without specific guarantees of judicial protection;

(b) there are, however, numerous legislative proposals pending before Congress and the President of the United States himself recently referred to the need for further legislative measures, while the Federal Trade Commission expressed the same opinion in its third report to Congress on the functioning of the system of self-regulation in the electronic marketplace;

(c) the guidelines approved by the OECD (signed by the USA in 1980 and ratified at the Ottawa OECD Conference in September 1998) must in any case be applied in the area of personal data protection;

The nature and scope of the enforceability of the safe harbour

E. whereas, rather than encouraging a legislative approach, the US Department of Commerce intends to propose to companies 'safe harbour privacy principles' (and the Frequently Asked Questions (FAQs) arising from such principles), which:

(a) will apply only to personal data of EU origin, with the status of the voluntary 'standard' suggested to the businesses intending to receive data from the EU, but are binding on those businesses that opt to adhere to them and are enforceable by private dispute resolution bodies and government bodies with powers to obtain relief against unfair or deceptive practices;

(b) relate only to firms which fall within the competence of the Federal Trade Commission and the Department of Transportation (so that, for example, firms in the banking and telecommunications sectors are excluded);

(c) are subject to exceptions (FAQ 15) as regards public record and publicly available data (e.g. land register, telephones, tax declarations, electoral rolls), which are protected by Community legislation;

(d) use ambiguous terms such as 'organisation' (which may refer both to businesses and business conglomerates) and 'explicit authorisations' (which allow exemptions to the principles);

(e) do not provide a right of effective, personal appeal to a public body (FAQ 11);

(f) do not allow it to be concluded with certainty that it will be possible to obtain compensation for individual damage suffered as a result of possible violations of the safe harbour principles;

1. As a preliminary matter, and irrespective of the question of the draft decision submitted to Parliament:

(a) Notes with concern that, almost two years after the Directive's entry into force, data relating to EU citizens are circulating in third countries without any effective control by the Commission or the Member States;

(b) Wonders to what extent data relating to EU citizens may have been misused already;

(c) Requests the Member States and the Commission to inform EU citizens of the risks attached to the circulation of data in countries where data protection is not ensured or the Commission has not yet completed the process of assessing the adequacy of any such protection;

(d) Considers that the Commission was responsible for a serious omission in failing to draw up, before the Directive's entry into force, standard contractual clauses that EU citizens could invoke in the courts of third countries;

(e) Establishes 30 September 2000 as the date by which the proposed standard clauses should be submitted to the Committee set up under Article 31 of the Directive;

(f) Reserves the right, in the event of failure to comply, to launch the procedures provided for in the Treaty in respect of failure to act;

The draft decision submitted to the European Parliament

2. Points out that the draft decision does not describe a situation currently in existence in the United States, but is based on a draft of the safe harbour principles (with the relevant explanations) which the US Department of Commerce will issue for the guidance of companies wishing to meet the adequate protection requirement of the Directive;

3. Draws the Commission's attention to the risk that the exchange of letters between the Commission and the US Department of Commerce on the implementation of the 'safe harbour' principles could be interpreted by the European and/or United States judicial authorities as having the substance of an international agreement adopted in breach of Article 300 of the Treaty establishing the European Community and the requirement to seek Parliament's assent (Judgment of the Court of Justice of 9 August 1994: French Republic v. the Commission – Agreement between the Commission and the United States regarding the application of their competition laws (Case C-327/91))[4];

4. Regrets that, in the course of the last two years, there has been no consultation of European undertakings with regard to the risk of discrimination in relation to US undertakings which would be subject to less onerous data protection requirements than those with which European undertakings must comply;

5. Regrets that, in contrast with the US authorities' consultation of NGOs active in the field of consumer protection, the Commission has not embarked on any such consultation of European NGOs;

6. Insists on the importance of providing the best possible level of consumer protection and, in this regard, urges the Commission to ensure and assist continuous monitoring of the safe harbour principles;

7. Calls into question the existence in the US of two different protection systems depending on whether or not the owners of the data are European, and wonders whether such a dual system complies with the clause prohibiting discrimination on the grounds of nationality contained in the relevant international (OECD) agreements;

---

4 [1994] ECR p. I-3641.

Recent Developments
Safe Harbor Arrangement (EU-US)

8. Considers that the situation in the US as regards privacy protection is likely to evolve rapidly over the coming few years, that new legislation is likely to be enacted there which could introduce standards of protection that are higher than those required by the safe harbour principles and that the safe harbour arrangement will therefore need to be adapted in order not to be overtaken by these developments;

9. Takes the view that, if issued and implemented by individual firms, such principles and the relevant explanations could be considered adequate protection under the terms of Article 25 of the Directive provided that the following changes are made to them:

  - recognition of an individual right of appeal to an independent public body instructed to consider any appeal relating to an alleged violation of the principles;
  - an obligation on participating firms to compensate for the damage, whether moral or to property, suffered by those involved, in the event of violations of the principles, and an undertaking by the firms to cancel personal data obtained or processed in an unlawful manner;
  - ease of identification of the steps to be taken to ensure data are cancelled and to obtain compensation for any damage suffered;
  - provision of a preliminary check by the Commission on the proper functioning of the system within six months of its entry into force and presentation of a report on the outcome of the check and any problems encountered to the working party provided for in Article 29 and the Committee provided for in Article 31 of the Directive, as well as to the relevant committee of the European Parliament;

10. Calls on the Commission to ensure that the operation of the safe harbour system is closely monitored, especially but not only as regards the points raised in Paragraphs 8 and 9 above and to make periodic reports to the working party provided for in Article 29 and the Committee provided for in Article 31 of the Directive, as well as to the relevant committee of the European Parliament;

11. Takes the view that the free movement of data cannot be authorised until all the components of the safe harbour system are operational and the United States authorities have informed the Commission that these conditions have been fulfilled;

12. Calls on the Commission and the Member States:

  - to provide appropriate information (in the Official Journal and via the Internet) for European citizens on the 'safe harbour', making clear that differences may continue to exist between the 'safe harbour' and European law as regards the processing of personal data;
  - to set up help-lines (freephone numbers, advice centres) to the relevant national authorities and the Commission to deal with any practical difficulties encountered (e.g. translations of appeals, forms, etc.);
  - to review the decision in good time in the light of experience and of any legislative developments;

13. Insists that the European Commission append this resolution to its transmission letter to the United States authorities, thereby clearly emphasising Parliament's concern about the

absence of an individual right of judicial appeal and the failure of an agreement to oblige companies to pay compensation for unlawfully processed data;

14. Instructs its President to forward this resolution to the Commission and the Parliaments and Governments of the Member States.

ARTICLE 29 WORKING GROUP - FOURTH ANNUAL REPORT

ON THE SITUATION REGARDING THE PROTECTION OF INDIVIDUALS WITH REGARD TO THE PROCESSING OF PERSONAL DATA AND PRIVACY IN THE COMMUNITY AND IN THIRD COUNTRIES

COVERING THE YEAR 1999

Adopted on 17.5.2001

THE WORKING PARTY ON THE PROTECTION OF INDIVIDUALS WITH REGARD TO THE PROCESSING OF PERSONAL DATA

set up by Directive 95/46/EC of the European Parliament and of the Council of 24 October 1995 [1] ,

given Article 29 and Article 30(6) of the aforementioned directive,

given its Rules of procedure and, in particular, Articles 12, 13 and 15,

adopted this report:

1. INTRODUCTION

This is the fourth annual report of the Working Party on the Protection of Individuals with regard to the Processing of Personal Data [2] covering the year 1999. The report is addressed to the Commission, the European Parliament, the Council as well as to the public at large. The Working Party is the independent EU advisory body on data protection and privacy [3] . Its report is intended to give an overview on the situation of the protection of individuals concerning the processing of personal data in the Community and in third countries [4] .

The general Data Protection Directive 95/46/EC of the European Parliament and of the Council on the protection of individuals with regard to the processing of personal data and on the free movement of such data (hereinafter "the Directive") was adopted on 24 October 1995

---

[1] Directive 95/46/EC of the European Parliament and of the Council of 24 October 1995 on the protection of individuals with regard to the processing of personal data and the free movement of such data, Official Journal n° L 281 of 23.11.1995, p. 31, available at: http://europa.eu.int/comm/internal_market/en/dataprot/law/index.htm

[2] Established by Article 29 of Directive 95/46/EC. Its tasks are laid down in Article 30 and in Article 14 (3) of Directive 97/66/EC .

[3] See Article 29 (1) second sentence of Directive 95/46/EC.

[4] See Article 30 paragraph 6 of Directive 95/46/EC.

and required implementation not later than three years after this date (24 October 1998)[5]. The specific Directive 97/66/EC concerning the processing of personal data and the protection of privacy in the telecommunications sector, adopted by the European Parliament and the Council on 15 December 1997, aligned the date for its transposition on the one of the General Directive.

The first report explained the composition and tasks of the Working Party and covered the main facts observed in 1996 in the field of data protection [6] . The second report covered the year 1997 and essentially followed the structure of the first report, in order to facilitate analysis of developments. The third annual report continued this tradition: it first presented an overview of main developments in the European Union, both in the Member States and at Community level and addressed then the work of the Council of Europe. The report further informed about the main developments in third countries and other developments at international level.

This fourth report received a new structure with a view both to improving its reader friendliness and emphasising the Working Party's activities during the year 1999, which are now presented in a separate chapter (2.3). The Article 29 Data Protection Working Party's annual report will complement rather than summarise the national annual reports of data protection supervisory authorities. Moreover, as privacy and data protection have increased in importance over the years and more and more people in the European Union are becoming interested in the developments in these areas in the Community, it was further agreed that more emphasis should be placed on EU related questions.

Main issues addressed during the year 1999 at Community level concern transfers of personal data to third countries, in particular to the United States of America, Switzerland and Hungary, and Internet and telecommunications related issues.

In 1999, the Article 29 Data Protection Working Party met eight times. It thus doubled the number of meetings per year compared to the first three years (in 1996, 1997 and 1998 it met four times per year). The Working Party was dealing with 72 items on its agenda and treated about 280 documents in the various official languages in cause of the preparation of its opinions, recommendations and working papers. In 1999, the Working Party was chaired by Mr Peter J. HUSTINX, Chairman of the Dutch data protection authority (*Registratiekamer*), re-elected at the 9 th meeting on 10 and 11 March 1998 for a period of two years. At the same meeting, Prof. Stefano RODOTA, Chairman of the Italian data protection authority (*Garante*

---

[5] This date is different from the date of entry into force: Since the Directive does not specify the date of its entry into force, it came into force on the 20 th day following the day of its publication (see Article 254 (1) of the Treaty).

[6] WP 3 (5023/97): First annual report, adopted on 25 June 1997, available at:
http://europa.eu.int/comm/internal_market/en/dataprot/wpdocs/index.htm

per la protezione dei dati personali), was elected Vice-chairman of the Working Party after the retirement of Ms Louise CADOUX (*Commission National de l'Informatique et des Libertés, CNIL*).

The Working Party's opinions and recommendations were transmitted to the Commission and to the Article 31 Committee and where appropriate to the presidents of the Council and the European Parliament and others.

The Secretariat of the Working Party is provided by the

European Commission
Directorate General Internal Market
Unit "Data protection".

The documents adopted by the Working Party are available in all official languages at this unit's web page on the Website "Europa" of the European Commission at:
http://www.europa.eu.int/comm/internal_market/en/dataprot/wpdocs/index.htm

2. DEVELOPMENTS IN EU ON PRIVACY AND DATA PROTECTION

2.1 Directive 95/46/EC

2.1.1 Implementation into national law

The national data protection supervisory authorities were invited to inform about the implementation of the data protection directives as well as any other developments in the field of data protection in their countries. The state of implementation is presented below in chapters 2.1 and 2.2. The other developments are explained in chapter 2.4.

Austria

The Data Protection Act 2000, BGBl. I No 165/1999, was adopted in 1999 to implement the Data Protection Directive and entered into force on 1 January 2000. Austria is a federal state and because of the allocation of responsibilities between Bund and Länder, Directive 95/46/EC can only be implemented at federal level in those areas where the Bund has the power to legislate. It is not possible for the federal legislator to transpose the full field of application of Directive 95/46/EC. Where data are processed for purposes which fall within the sphere where the Land has power to legislate, it is the task of the Länder to implement the directives' data protection provisions. The first data protection laws at level of the Länder were adopted in 2000 (at present, there are six data protection laws at level of the Länder.)

Belgium

The law of 11 December 1998 transposing Directive 95/46/EC was published in the Official Journal (Moniteur Belge) on 3 February 1999. The law will enter into force the sixth month after the publication in the Official Journal of its Executive Decree, i.e. the 1 st of September 2001 (the Executive Decree has been published on 13 March 2001).

Denmark

No transposition was made in 1999.

Finland

The Directive 95/46/EC of the European Parliament and of the Council on the protection of individuals with regard to the processing of personal data and on the free movement of such data came into force in Finland on 1 June 1999, when the Personal Data Act (523/1999) became effective.

France

No transposition was made in 1999.

In late June 2000, the French government informed the *Commission Nationale de l'informatique et des Libertés* ("National Commission for Informatics and Freedom", CNIL) of the preliminary draft law transposing Directive 95/46/EC. The CNIL then submitted its opinion to the government in mid-September. The Council of State must now give its opinion before the draft law is adopted by the government and presented to the Parliament. This draft law should simplify the system for notifying the supervisory authority in advance of processing, while at the same time increasing its ex-post powers.

Germany

As to Directive 95/46/EC, the German government has so far missed the implementation deadline. It is now following a two phase approach: In a first step, it is planned to implement Directive 95/46/EC and to take some additional data protection issues on board, such as provisions on video surveillance, chip cards, anonymization, pseudonymization and data protection audit. This work is expected to be completed by mid-2001. In a second step, a general revision of German data protection law is planned. A master plan to achieve this objective is expected for 2002.

Italy

Various regulatory instruments were enacted in 1999 in order to lay down precise rules supplementing those issued in connection with the transposition of Directive WP 3 (5023/97): First annual report, adopted on 25 June 1997, available at: 95/46/EC as made via the Data Protection Act no. 675 of 31.12.96 – as also related to processing operations that had been initially excluded from the scope of application of the relevant provisions in order to extend the time-limit for compliance by certain controllers. New laws were enacted, in particular concerning the processing operations which are referred to in Article 8 of Directive

95/46/EC; this applied especially to public bodies, which had been allowed by the General Data Protection Act (no. 675/1996) to continue their processing operations on a provisional basis, and to the sectors in which the minimum security measures required for preventive purposes were to be set out in pursuance of Article 17 of the Directive.

Legislative decree no. 135 of 11.05.99 laid down the general principles to be followed by public bodies when processing either sensitive data (including data disclosing health) or information related to judicial measures. The cases were specified in which the processing could be considered to serve a substantial public interest and was therefore automatically allowed with a view to achieving that purpose. Additionally, the general principles laid down in the DPA (no. 675/1996) were strengthened by specifying that public bodies are allowed to only process such data as are absolutely necessary in order to discharge those official tasks that cannot be fulfilled by using anonymised data – based on a case by case assessment. Processing of data concerning health and sex life was made the subject of specific obligations including the use of either encryption technology or identification codes allowing data subjects to be only identified in case of necessity, and specific arrangements for keeping this information.

In a decree of 30.07.99, no. 281, specific provisions were made in connection with the processing of personal data for historical, scientific research and statistics purposes. Account was taken in this decree of the principles laid down in the relevant Council of Europe Recommendations (No. R(83) 10 and R(97) 18); special emphasis was put on the role played by codes of conduct and ethics. The group drafting such codes has been working during both 1999 and 2000 under the auspices of the Garante; a draft Code of conduct for the processing of personal data for historical purposes can be found on the Garante's Website, in both Italian and English.

Decree no. 282 was also enacted on the same day (30.07.99) to regulate the processing of medical data by either public health care bodies (in addition to the provisions made in decree no. 135/1999) or health care organisations or professionals discharging their functions on the basis of either an agreement with or the formal recognition of the national health service. The contribution given by the relevant stakeholders via their associations in developing effective sectored self-regulation under the auspices and guidance of the Garante proved to be an useful tool with a view to achieving the protection of personal data by supplementing legislative measures – which is fully consistent with Article 27 of Directive 95/46/EC.

As to security measures, regulations were enacted in decree no. 318 of 28.07.99 to set out the minimum-security measures for the processing of personal data. Different measures were provided for depending on the use of electronic or stringent obligations apply if the data are processed for exclusively personal purposes). Compliance with these measures is mandatory under penalty of criminal punishment pursuant to Article 36 of the DPA (no. 675/1996).

Ireland

No transposition of this Directive into Irish law was made in 1999. The transposition is envisaged to take place in early 2001.

Luxembourg

Luxembourg has not yet transposed this directive in 1999. The draft Luxembourg law will be transmitted to Parliament in October 2000 for vote in 2001.

Portugal

The Directive 95/46/Ec was transposed into national law in 1998 by Act 67/98 of 26 October – Data Protection Act.

Spain

The Organic Law No. 15/1999 of 13 December 1999 on the protection of personal data modified the existing data protection Act (Organic Law 5/1992) with a view to bringing it fully in line with the Directive and then to complete its transposition (organic refers to to the fact that all laws regulating the fundamental rights granted by the Spanish Institution are called "organicas" and must be voted by the Parliament by absolute majority.

Sweden

The EC Directive 95/46 was implemented into Swedish law in 1998 when the Personal Data Act (1998:204) was adopted. In 1999, the Parliament decided to amend section 33 (transfer to third countries), so that it would follow the Directive more closely. The new wording of section 33 means that personal data may be transferred to a third country on condition that this country has an adequate level of protection for personal data. In a second paragraph have been added the circumstances that should be considered when assessing whether the level of protection is adequate. The original wording of section 33 meant an absolute prohibition against third country transfers with exception only for certain specific situations stated in section 34.

The Netherlands

Directive 95/46/EC was not transposed into national law in 1999. The Wet Bescherming Persoonsgegevens (WBP or Personal Data Protection Act) of 6 July 2000, which was under discussions in 1999 in the Parliament, will enter into force in 2001.

The United Kingdom

The United Kingdom spent much of 1999 establishing the regulatory and technical measures required to implement the Data Protection Act 1998.

Recent Developments
Article 29 WG 4th Annual Report (EC)

2.1.2 Infringement proceedings

The European Commission decided in July 1999 to send reasoned opinions to France, Luxembourg, the Netherlands, Germany, the United Kingdom, Ireland, Denmark, Spain and Austria for failure to comply with the obligation flowing from Art. 32 par. 4 to notify all the measures necessary to implement Directive 95/46/EC. The reasoned opinions represent the second stage of formal infringement proceedings under Article 226 of the EC Treaty. Since the Commission did not receive a satisfactory response within two months of receipt by France, Luxembourg, Germany, Ireland and the Netherlands, it decided in December 1999 to take these countries to the European Court of Justice for failure to notify all the measures necessary to implement Directive 95/46/EC. This step represents the third formal stage of formal infringement proceedings under Article 226 of the EC Treaty.

2.2 Directive 97/66/EC

2.2.1 Implementation into national law

The national data protection supervisory authorities were invited to inform about the Implementation of the data protection directives as well as any other developments in the field of data protection in their countries. The state of implementation is presented in this chapter. The other developments are explained in chapter 2.4.

Austria

Austria implemented Directive 97/66/EC by means of the Telecommunications Act, BGBl. I No 100/1997.

Belgium

The provisions of Directive 97/66/EC have been integrated in Belgian law by the way of amendments to already existing legislation.

Articles 78-79 of the Consumer Protection Act of 14/07/91 have been amended in order to provide for the regulation of unsolicited calls for the purposes of direct marketing. The new provisions have entered into force on 01/10/99 ((*Moniteur Belge* (hereinafter M.B.) 23/06/99)). Article 9 of the Royal Decree on telecommunications of 22/06/98 has been amended on 08/07/99, in order to integrate the provisions of the Directive regarding the Calling Line Identification system. The amendments entered into force on 01/09/99 (M.B. 01/09/99). A Royal Decree on directories was adopted on 14/09/99. It entered into force on 18/09/99 (M.B. 18/09/99). It provides for the conditions of publication of personal data in directories.

The Article 105nonies of the law of 21 March 1991 on Public Economic Companies has been completely amended in order to implement the provision of Directive 97/66/EC related to the handling and preservation of traffic data by telecom operators and telecom service providers. It has entered into force on 21 December 1999 (M.B. 21.12.99).

Denmark

No transposition was made in 1999.

Finland

The Directive 97/66/EC concerning the processing of personal data and the protection of privacy in the telecommunications sector became effective when the Act on the Protection of Privacy and Data Security in Telecommunications came into force on 1 July 1999.

France

The French government informed the CNIL of the preliminary draft law-transposing Directive 97/66/EC in December 1999, then - in June 2000 - provided information on its draft regulations. The CNIL submitted its opinions on these two texts to the government in January 2000 and July 2000, respectively.

Germany

Directive 97/66/EC was implemented into national law as explained in the third annual report (p. 10).

Italy

Directive 97/66/EC was transposed into national law by legislative decree no. 171 of 13.05.1998 (as already explained in the 3 rd Annual Report).

Ireland

No transposition was made in 1999. The transposition of the Directive into Irish law is envisaged to take place in early 2001.

Luxembourg

Up to now no text for transposition of the directive has been elaborated. The transposition of this directive will only be possible in early 2002.

Portugal

The Directive 97/66/EC was transposed into national law also in 1998 by Act 69/98 of 28 October.

Spain

It was already transposed in 1998 by the General Telecommunications Law 11/1998 and by the Royal Decree 1736/1998 which adopted the Regulation developing Title III of the aforementioned Law.

Recent Developments
Article 29 WG 4th Annual Report (EC)

Sweden

Directive 97/66/EC was implemented into Swedish law in 1999 through amendments of the Telecommunications Act (1993:597) and the Telecommunications Ordinance (1997:399).

Article 12 on unsolicited commercial communications has been implemented in March 2000 through an amendment in the Marketing Practices Act (1995:450).

The Netherlands

Directive 97/66/EC was transposed into national law by the Telecommunicatiewet ('Wet van 19 oktober 1998, houdende de regels inzake de telecommunicatie').

The United Kingdom

The Telecommunications (Data Protection and Privacy) (Direct Marketing) Regulation 1998 came into force on 1 March 1999, which implemented Article 12 of the EU Telecommunications Directive 97/46/EC on unsolicited commercial communications.

2.2.2 Infringement proceedings

Eight Member States (Germany, Spain, Italy, the Netherlands, Austria, Portugal, Finland and Sweden) have notified implementing measures for the Protection of Personal Data Directive (97/66/EC). The proceedings against the Netherlands, Austria, Portugal, Finland and Sweden were therefore dropped in 1999, whereas reasoned opinions were sent to Belgium, Denmark [7] and Ireland. In December 1999 the Commission also decided to start court action against Greece, France, Luxembourg and the United Kingdom for failure to notify it of full national implementing measures.

2.3 Issues addressed by the Article 29 Data Protection Working Party

The main issues on which the Working Party took a position in 1999 are highlighted and concern the transfer of data to third countries, internet and telecommunications, the P3P seminar, the public sector information, the codes of conduct as well as the EU Charta on Fundamental Rights.

2.3.1 Transfer of data to third countries

The Directive establishes rules designed to ensure that data is only transferred to third countries when the third country ensures an adequate level of protection of individuals with regard to the processing of their personal data or when certain specific exemptions apply (Articles 25 and 26 of Directive 95/46/EC). Without such rules, the high standards of data protection established by the Directive would quickly be undermined, given the ease with which data can be moved around on international networks.

---

[7] Since Denmark had notified, the procedure was closed in 2000.

The Directive provides for the blocking of specific transfers where necessary, but this is a solution of last resort and there are several other ways of ensuring that data continues to be adequately protected while not causing disruption to international data flows and the commercial transactions with which they are associated.

The Commission may find, together with the Committee established by Article 31 of Directive 95/46/EC which is composed of Member States representatives that a third country ensures an adequate level of protection. It has to consult the Article 29 Working Party who has to deliver an opinion on the level of protection in third countries.

On 24 July 1998, the Working Party adopted a working document on transfers of personal data to third countries [8] which explains the requirements of Directive 95/46/EC and lists the concrete factors which should be taken into account when assessing whether or not there is an adequate level of protection.

Where no adequate level of protection exists, contractual clauses may provide sufficient safeguards with respect to the protection of the fundamental rights and freedoms of individuals in order to allow transfers to such countries[9].

During 1999, the Working Party devoted most of its attention to the issue of data transfers to third countries. It dealt in particularly with the the United States of America, Switzerland and Hungary.

2.3.1.1 *United States of America: Safe Harbor Principles*

The underlying rational for the Safe Harbor Principles is that the United States takes a different approach to privacy from that taken by the European Community. The United States uses a sectored approach that relies on a mix of legislation, regulation and self regulation which in the opinion of the Article 29 Working Party cannot be relied upon to provide adequate protection in all cases for personal data transferred from the European Union. On 4 November 1998, the Department of Commerce (DoC) issued a set of privacy principles with the view to establish a permanent framework for the transfer of personal data between the US and the EU.

Following that initiative, the year 1999 was dedicated to a series of extensive discussions on a bilateral basis between the American government and the European Commission. Informal dialogues with Mr Mogg, Director General of the Internal Market Directorate General and Under-secretary for Commerce, Aaron (DoC), took place in March, May, and November 1999.

---

[8] Available on the website under:
http://europa.eu.int/comm/internal_market/en/dataprot/news/clauses2faq.htm.
[9] See Article 26(2) and (4) of the Directive 95/46/EC.

Recent Developments
Article 29 WG 4th Annual Report (EC)

The Commission kept the Working Party thoroughly informed of the discussions and asked for its advice on a number of points in order to improve and clarify the text of the Safe Harbor principles and frequently asked questions originated by the DoC, and to contribute to a text offering 'adequate protection' as required by the Directive 95/46/EC. This work led to four public opinions and one public working document.

January 1999

The Working Party adopted on 26 January 1999 its first opinion (Opinion 1/99 [10]) on the *'level of data protection in the US and the ongoing discussions between the European Commission and the US government'*, urging the parties and the representatives of EU Member States meeting in the Committee established by Article 31 of Directive 95/46/EC to take into account the following shortcomings in the US draft text:

- the "individual's right of access", limited in the US text to that which is "reasonable" whereas the OECD Privacy Guidelines do not limit the right itself but request that it be exercised "in a reasonable manner");
- the absence of "purpose specification principle", present in the OECD Privacy Guidelines;
- "proprietary data "and any "manually processed data" which were entirely outside of the scope of the US principles;
- the vagueness of terms like 'risk management' and 'information security'.

April-May

Following a revised version of the "Safe Harbor" Principles released by the DoC on 19 April, the Working Party issued on 3 May its second opinion, (Opinion 2/99 [11]), on the *'Adequacy of the International Safe Harbor Principles'*.

It acknowledged progress in a number of areas, such as the definition of personal data (referring now to an 'identified or identifiable individual'), and onward transfers (differentiating between transfers amongst organisations adhering to the principles and transfers to third parties outside the "Safe Harbor" scheme). Concerns were raised on the exceptions provided for in Member States law' as this could lead to the interpretation of national implementation measures by organisations adhering to a third country's self-regulatory scheme. With regard to 'manual' data, the Working Party considered that there should be equal treatment for automated and manually processed data held in filing systems. Finally, the following principles where discussed in-depth : Notice, Choice, Onward transfer, Access and Enforcement.

---

[10] WP 15 (5092/98): Opinion 1/99 concerning the level of data protection in the United States and the ongoing discussions between the European Commission and the United States Government. Adopted on 26 January 1999.

[11] WP 19 (5047/99): Opinion 2/99 on the Adequacy of the 'International Safe Harbor Principles'

June

The 'Frequently asked Questions (FAQs)' developed from six to 15 during the months of April, May, and June 1999. Following which, the Working Party adopted on 7 June its third opinion (Opinion 4/99 [12]) specifically on the FAQ's, estimating that:

- the FAQs should have authoritative status provided that they are consistent with and are considered together with the 'Safe Harbor Principles';
- the final list of FAQs should be exhaustive and no change to the FAQ should be introduced unilaterally;
- the FAQs should be looked at in the light of experience in any review of the implementation of the "Safe Harbor" arrangement and may need to be adapted and/or supplemented.

Furthermore, the opinion examined in detail FAQs 1 (Sensitive Data), 2 (Journalistic exceptions), 3 (Secondary liability), 4 (Head-hunters), 5 (Role of Data Protection authorities), 6 (Self-certification), 11 (independent investigation of complaints) and 13 (opt-out choice).

July 1999

On 7 July, a working document[13] on the 'Current state of play of the ongoing discussions between the European Commission and the United States Government concerning the 'International Safe Harbor Principles on 1 June 1999' was adopted by the Working Party. It consists of a messages addressed to the Committee created by Article 31 (representatives of the EU Member States) of the Directive.

It drew the Commission's attention to the need:

- to ensure a solid legal basis of Article 25 of the Directive 95/46/EC
- to clarify the scope of the "Safe Harbor" arrangement in several areas;
- to specify the condition of the implementation and enforcement of the "Safe Harbor" arrangement principles and
- to elaborate the contents of principles 1 (notice), 2 (choice) and 6 (access)

December 1999

---

[12] WP 21 (5066/99): Opinion 4/99 on the Frequently asked Questions to be issued by the US Department of Commerce in relation to the proposed "Safe Harbor Principles". Adopted on 7 June1999 (in EN).

[13] WP 23 (5075/99): Working document on the current state of play of the ongoing discussions between the European Commission and the United Stated States Government concerning the 'International Safe Harbor Principles' issued by the US Department of Commerce on 1 June 1999, adopted on 7 July 1999.

Recent Developments
Article 29 WG 4th Annual Report (EC)

In its fourth opinion, adopted on 3 December 1999 (Opinion 7/99[14]) on the 'Level of Data Protection provide by the "Safe Harbor" Principles as published together with the FAQs and other related documents on 15 and 16 November 1999', the Working Party confirmed its general concerns on the "Safe Harbor" arrangement, and invited the Commission to urge the US to make a number of key improvements, notably:

- to clarify the scope of the "Safe Harbor" and in particular to remove any possible misunderstanding that US organisations can choose to rely on the "Safe Harbor" principles in circumstances when the Directive itself applies;
- to provide more reliable arrangements allowing "Safe Harbor" participants to be identified with certainty and avoiding the risk that "Safe Harbor" benefits will continue to be accorded after "Safe Harbor" status has, for one reason or another, been lost;
- to make it absolutely clear that enforcement by an appropriately empowered public body is in place for all participants in the "Safe Harbor";
- to make it the rule that private sector dispute resolution bodies must refer unresolved complaints to such a public body;
- to make the allowed exceptions and exemptions less sweeping and less open-ended so that exceptions are precisely that – that is, they apply only where and to the extent necessary and are not general invitations to override the principles; a particularly important point as regards the right of access;
- to strengthen the Choice principle, which represented the lynchpin of the US approach.

The Working Party also invited the Commission to revise Article 2 of the draft Commission decision of 24 November and to accelerate the work on standard contractual clauses with a view to a decision under Article 26 (4) of Directive 95/46/EC (safeguards for transfers to areas where adequate protection is not otherwise guaranteed).

2.3.1.2 Switzerland

The Working Party was informed that the European Commission is drafting a proposal for a Decision based on Article 25(6) of Directive 95/46/EC stating that, by reason of its domestic law, Switzerland ensures an adequate level of protection within the meaning of Article 25(2) of the aforementioned Directive. With a view to drawing up an opinion for the European Commission, assisted by the Committee set up under Article 31 of Directive 95/46/EC, the Working Party has carried out an analysis of the data protection rules applied in Switzerland 15 .

---

[14] WP 27 (5146/99): Opinion 7/99 on the level of Data Protection provided by the "Safe Harbor" Principles as published together with the Frequently Asked Questions (FAQ) and other related developments. Adopted on 3 December 1999 .

[15] In order to obtain more specific information on certain points, the Chairman of the Working Party sent a letter to the Federal Data Protection Commissioner on 15 March 1999, who replied on

Given the division of powers between the Confederation and the cantons, the Federal Law (Law on Data Protection of 19 June 1992, as subsequently amended and supplemented by the ruling of the Swiss Federal Council of 14 June 1993) applies to the processing of personal data by the entire Swiss private sector and by the federal public authorities. The cantonal provisions, on the other hand, govern the processing of personal data by public sector bodies at canton or commune level. The cantons are responsible, for instance, for processing in the following sectors: policing, education, health and in particular public hospitals. In the interests of completeness, it should be pointed out that the cantons are also responsible for processing certain types of personal data in accordance with federal law, e.g. for the purposes of federal tax collection.

Both the federal and cantonal legislation, are designed to be compatible with:
1.- the Council of Europe Convention for the Protection of Individuals with Regard to Automatic Processing of Personal Data (Convention No 108), which was ratified by Switzerland on 2 October 1997 and which, while not directly applicable, establishes international commitments for both the Federation and the cantons;

2.- the Federal Constitution (amended by referendum on 18 April last), as interpreted in the case law of the Federal Supreme Court. It should be pointed out that the amended Constitution gives every person the right to privacy and, in particular, the right to be protected against the misuse of data concerning them (Article 13 on the protection of the private sphere).

In conclusion, the Working Party recommended that the Commission and the Committee set up under Article 31 of Directive 95/46/EC should conclude that Switzerland ensures an adequate level of protection within the meaning of Article 25(6) of the Directive.

2.3.1.3 *Hungary*

With a view to delivering an opinion to the European Commission, assisted by the Committee created by Article 31 of Directive 95/46/EC, the Working Party carried out an analysis of data protection provisions applicable in Hungary [16].

The legislative situation as regards protection of personal data is governed by Act LXIII promulgated on 17 November 1992, which entered into force on 1 May 1993 and was

---

24 March 1999. There have also been informal contacts between the Secretariat of the Working Party and the Federal Commissioner.

[16] With a view to obtaining more precise information on certain matters, an exchange of correspondence took place between the Chairman of the Working Party and the Hungarian ombudsman (letters of 22 March and 19 April 1999 and replies of 25 March and 23 April 1999 respectively).

subsequently amended [17] . The scope of this law is broader than the protection of personal data, since the Act also lays down the procedure applicable to public access to administrative documents. The Ombudsman, whose powers are established by the Act and who was appointed by Parliament on 30 June 1995, is responsible for monitoring the application of these two regulations.

As regards the protection of personal data, the following should also be noted:
- Hungary's international commitments resulting from the ratification, on 8 October 1997, of the Council of Europe Convention for the protection of individuals with regard to automatic processing of personal data (Convention N° 108),
- the protection of privacy at constitutional level, in particular with regard to the processing of personal data [18] ,
-the existence of sectored laws containing provisions on the protection of personal data in fields as diverse as the secret services, statistics, commercial canvassing, scientific research and, more recently, the health sector.

In the Working Party's opinion, the Hungarian law on data protection ensures an adequate level of protection recommended the Commission and the Committee established by Article 31 of Directive 95/46/EC to note that Hungary ensures an adequate level of protection within the meaning of Article 25(6) of this Directive.

2.3.1.4 The Working Party entered into preliminary discussions on the level of protection in Hong Kong, Norway and Iceland.

2.3.2 Working documents [19] about the ICC and CBI model contractual clauses

The International Chamber of Commerce drafted clauses with the aim of ensuring transborder data flows whilst efficiently protecting personal data worldwide in the sense of article 26(2) and (4) of Directive 95/46/EC.

The original version of the clauses in question were submitted to the Directorate General XV of the European Commission in September 1998, with a view to being adopted as a

---

[17] See the recent Act LXXII of 22 June 1999 which introduces the concept of "subcontractor" into Hungarian legislation.

[18] The English translation, drawn up by the Hungarian authorities, of Article 59 of the constitution reads as follows: "(1) In the Republic of Hungary everyone is entitled to the protection of his or her reputation and to privacy of the home, of personal effects, particulars, papers, records and data, and to the privacy of personal affairs and secrets. (2) For the acceptance of the law on the protection of the security of personal data and records, the votes of two thirds of the MPs present are necessary. "

[19] These documents were not published but directly sent to respectively ICC and CBI with a view to influencing their internal discussions at a very early stage.

Commission's decision according to the Directive 95/46/EC. A revised version of the clauses was submitted to the Directorate General XV on 18 December 1998.

The Working Party analysed the ICC clauses and made further suggestions and comments. It proposed in particular that the ICC clauses should apply to controller – controller situations. This means that the clauses should provide for safeguards in the case where personal data were to be sold from the EU to new responsible abroad. Here, the individual has no protection. So far, the ICC text addresses only controller – processor situations that are, to a certain extent, covered by Article 17 (3) of Directive 95/46/EC. The Working Party invited the ICC to revise its text in the light of the comments made.

The Confederation of British Industry similarly drafted contractual clauses for the transfer of personal data from the European Union to third countries. The CBI paper (version 15 December 1998), comprising a set of model contractual clauses together with explanatory material, was submitted to the Director-General of the Directorate General XV of the European Commission on 23 December 1998. In its Working document the Working Party encouraged the European Commission to take up the CBI's invitation to discuss these issues further taking into account the shortcomings identified.

2.3.3 Internet and Telecommunications

The Working Party adopted several recommendations dealing with major aspects of the Internet and Telecommunications :

2.3.3.1 Working document on processing of personal data on the Internet

The European Conference of Data Protection Commissioners held in Dublin on 23 and 24 April 1998, expressed the wish that the Working Party may develop the subject in a more systematic approach to clarify the issues at stake and provide for solutions with a view to contributing to a development of the internet and related services that respects the user's right to privacy and thus provides for confidence and trust both for commercial and private applications. The Commissioners recalled that the rules following from the EU Data Protection legislation fully apply, according to appropriate modalities, to personal data processing on the internet, irrespective of the technical tools used.

The Working Party shares [20] the view of the EU Data Protection Commissioners Conference. The Internet is not a legal vacuum. Processing of personal data on the Internet has to respect data protection principles just as in the off-line world [21] . This does not constitute a

---

[20] WP 16 (5013/99): Working document: Processing of Personal Data on the Internet. Adopted on 23.2.1999.

[21] See also Ministerial Declaration of the Bonn Conference on Global Networks, June 1997, available at : http://www2.echo.lu/bonn/conference.html

limitation of the uses of the Internet, but is on the contrary part of the essentials aiming at ensuring trust and confidence of users in the functioning of the Internet and the services provided over it. Data protection on the Internet is thus and indispensable condition for the take-up of electronic commerce.

The general data protection directive 95/46/EC applies to any processing of personal data falling under its scope, irrespective of the technical means used. Personal data processing on the Internet therefore has to be considered in the light of the directive.

The specific directive 97/66/EC on the protection of privacy and personal data in the telecommunications sector complements the general directive 95/46/EC by establishing specific legal and technical provisions.[22] The Internet is a network of computers open to all. It thus forms part of the public telecommunications sector. The provisions of Directive 97/66/EC therefore apply to the processing of personal data in connection with the provision of publicly available telecommunication services in public telecommunications networks in the Community [23] .

2.3.3.2 Recommendation on Invisible and Automated Processing on the Internet

The underlying rational for such a recommendation[24] was that various kinds of processing of personal data is taking place on the Internet performed by means of software or hardware and without the individual concerned knowing about it. They are thus "invisible" to the user. For example the so-called « cookies » technology permits a server to store and retrieve in an invisible way some particular data on the hard disk of the Internet user. Similarly, the common Internet software (this include namely browsing, FTP [25] , email, news and chat programs) collect, link and disseminate various kinds of personal data of the user and thus allow creating user profiles without his knowledge. These techniques allow the creation of clicktrails about the Internet user. Clicktrails consist of information about an individual's behaviour, identity, pathway or choices expressed while visiting a Website. They contain the links that a user has followed and are logged in the web server. The Working Party noted that the various practices on processing personal data on the Internet were not in conformity with the EU Data Protection Directive, in particular with the requirement that the data subject is informed and thus made aware of the processing in question. The Working Party therefore

---

[22] To all matters which are not specifically covered by Directive 97/66/EC, such as the obligations on the controller and the rights of individuals or non-publicly available telecommunications services, Directive 95/46/EC applies (see recital 11 of Directive 97/66/EC).

[23] See article 3 paragraph 1 of Directive 97/66/EC.

[24] WP 17 (5093/98): Recommendation 1/99 on Invisible and Automatic Processing of Personal Data on the Internet Performed by Software and Hardware; Adopted by the Working Party on 23 February 1999

[25] FTP = File Transfer Protocol

recommended to the Internet industry to adapt their programmes and products according to the data protection principles specified in this document, notably by configuring of hard-and software in a way that they do not, by default, allow to collect, store or send a client's persistent information. This would allow to give the user the choice.

2.3.3.3 *Recommendation 2/99 on privacy in interceptions*

In the context of discussions in the Council of the European Union interception and the resolutions of the European Parliament on the Echelon spy-system, the Working Party considered it necessary to contribute with its expertise to the public debate.

The Working Party points out that each telecommunication interception, defined as a third party acquiring knowledge of the content and/or data relating to private telecommunications between two or more correspondents, and in particular of traffic data concerning the use of telecommunication services, constitutes a violation of the individuals' right to privacy and of the confidentiality of correspondence. It follows that interceptions are unacceptable unless they fulfil three fundamental criteria in accordance with Article 8 (2) of the European Convention for the Protection of Human Rights and Fundamental Freedoms of 4 November 1950 [26] , and the European Court of Human Rights' interpretation of this provision: a legal basis, the need for the measure in a democratic society and conformity with one of the legitimate aims listed in the Convention [27] .

The legal basis must precisely define the limits and the means of applying the measure through clear and detailed rules, which are particularly necessary owing to the continuous improvement of the technical means available. The text of the law must be accessible to the public so that citizens may be informed of the consequences of their behavior. In this legal context, exploratory or general surveillance on a large scale must be proscribed.

Within the European Union, Directive 95/46/EC establishes the principle of the protection of the right to privacy enshrined in the legal systems of the Member States. This Directive specifies the principles contained in the European Convention for the Protection of Human Rights of 4 November 1950 and in Council of Europe Convention No. 108 of 28 January 1981 Convention for the Protection of Individuals with regard to Automatic Processing of

---

[26] It should be stressed that the fundamental guarantees recognised by the Council of Europe on the interception of telecommunications create obligations for Member States regardless of the distinctions made at European Union level according to the Community or intergovernmental nature of the fields addressed.

[27] Council of Europe Convention No 108 also stipulates that interference may be tolerated only when it constitutes a necessary measure in a democratic society for the protection of the national interests listed in Article 9 (2) of that Convention (NB the national interests listed in Convention 108 and in the Convention for the Protection of Human Rights are not exactly the same), and when it is strictly defined in terms of this purpose.

Personal Data. Directive 97/66/EC [28] gives concrete expression to the provisions of this Directive by specifying the Member States' obligation to ensure through national regulations the confidentiality of communications carried out by means of a publictelecommunications network or by means of publicly available telecommunication services.

The purpose of this recommendation is to indicate how the principles of the protection of the fundamental rights and freedoms of natural persons, particularly of their private lives and secrecy of communications, is to be applied to the measures concerning the interception of telecommunications adopted at European level. The scope of the recommendation covers interceptions in a large sense comprising interception of the content of telecommunications as well as data related to telecommunications, in particular any preparatory measures (such as monitoring and data mining of traffic data) which may be envisaged in order to decide whether an interception is advisable.

The Working Party stresses in particular that the obligations of security and confidentiality of data to which telecommunication operators, service providers and Member States are subject to on the basis of Articles 17 (1) and (2) of Directive 95/46 and Articles 4, 5 and 6 of Directive 97/66/EC respectively are the rule and not the exception. Telecommunications operators and telecommunications service providers must take the measures needed to make the interception of telecommunications by unauthorized parties impossible, or as technically difficult as the current state of the technology allows.

The Working Party concluded with a checklist on how to respect fundamental rights and freedoms by authorities with regard to interceptions.

2.3.3.4 Recommendation 3/99 on the preservation of traffic data by the Internet Service Providers for law enforcement purposes

Combating computer-related crime, is an issue that has been acquiring increasing international attention. The G8 countries[29] adopted a 10-point action plan, which was being implemented in 1999 with the help of a specialised high-tech crime subgroup consisting of representatives of the G8 law enforcement agencies. One of the outstanding and most controversial issues was the preservation of historic and future traffic data by Internet Service Providers for law enforcement purposes and disclosure of such data to law enforcement authorities. The G8 high-tech crime subgroup intended to propose recommendations to ensure the possibility of preserving and disclosing traffic data. In parallel, the Council of Europe is working on a draft Convention on Cybercrime.

---

[28] Directive of 15 December 1997 concerning the processing of personal data and the protection of privacy in the telecommunications sector, OJ L 24, 30 January 1998, p. 1.

[29] G8 countries are: Canada, France, Germany, Italy, Japan, the United Kingdom, the United States of America and Russia.

Acknowledging the important role that traffic data can play in the context of the investigation of crimes perpetrated over the Internet, the Working Party however wishes to remind the national governments about the principles on the protection of the fundamental rights and freedoms of natural persons, and in particular of their privacy and the secrecy of their correspondence which need to be taken into account in this context.

The Working Party is also conscious of the burdens that may be put on telecommunication operators and service providers.

As the Working Party already stated in its Recommendation 2/99 on the respect of privacy in the context of interception of telecommunications adopted on 3 May 1999 [30] , the fact that a third party acquires knowledge of traffic data concerning the use of telecommunication services has generally been considered as a telecommunication interception and constitutes therefore a violation of the individuals' right to privacy and of the confidentiality of correspondence as guaranteed by Article 5 of Directive 97/66/EC. In addition, such disclosure of traffic data is incompatible with Article 6 of that directive. The Working Party considered that the most effective means to reduce unacceptable risks to privacy while recognising the needs for effective law enforcement is that traffic data should in principle not be kept only for law enforcement purposes.

2.3.4 P3P seminar

The European Commission hosted a seminar with the World Wide Web Consortium (W3C) which is developing the Platform for Privacy Preferences (P3P) and the Article 29 Data Protection Working Party. P3P conceives of privacy and data protection as something to be agreed between the Internet user, whose data are collected, and the Website that collects the data. The philosophy is based on the idea that the user consents to the collection of his personal data by a site, provided that the site's declared privacy practices, such as the purposes for which data are collected and whether or not data are used for secondary purposes or passed on to third parties, satisfy the user's requirements. The World Wide Web Consortium has sought to develop a single vocabulary through which a user's preferences and the site's practices are articulated. The P3P seminar was the follow-up to the Working Party's Opinion 1/98. The goal was to discuss how the Platform for Privacy Preferences (P3P) can take into account the legal requirements of the Data Protection Directive for its implementation within the EU.

---

[30] Available at http://europa.eu.int/comm/internal_market/en/dataprot/wpdocs/index.htm.

2.3.5 Public sector information

The European Commission has submitted a Green Paper entitled "Public sector information: a key resource for Europe" for public consultation [31] . The main objective of the Green Paper is to encourage discussion on how public sector information can be made more accessible to citizens and business, and on whether

or not national rules in this area need to be harmonised. One of the key aspects of the Green Paper is the availability of public sector information. The Green Paper does not ignore the protection of personal data, even though such protection would not appear to be its primary focus.

The Working Party contributed with Opinion 3/99 to the consultation process [32] .

The objective of this Opinion is to provide input for the discussion on the protection of personal data, a dimension which must be taken into consideration when undertaking to grant greater access to public sector data, where such data relates to individuals. However, the Opinion does not claim to provide answers to all of the questions raised by the need for a balance between improved access to public sector data, based on a desire for increased transparency by the State with regard to its citizens, on the one hand, and the protection of personal data as defined by Directive 95/46/EC, on the other hand. Drawing on Directive 95/46/EC and on practical illustrations using the best-known public registers of personal data, the aim of this Opinion is to provide, on the basis of concrete examples, a number of terms of reference which are advisable to take into account when concrete decisions are taken.

The purpose principle (Article 6 of Directive 95/46/EC) requires that personal data are collected for specific, explicit and legitimate purposes and are not subsequently processed in a manner, which is incompatible with these purposes. This principle therefore plays a key role in the accessibility of personal data held by the public sector.

In particular, a case-by-case examination is required of the extent to which a law makes publication or public access to personal data mandatory or permissible. Is the law intended to ensure access to the data in their entirety with no time limitation? Can the data be used for any purpose, regardless of the initial purpose or, conversely, does the law allow only some parties to access the data and/or does it require that the data can be used for a purpose linked to the initial purpose for which they were made public? Consequently, personal data to be made

---

[31] COM (1998)585, available at: http://europa.eu.int/servlet/portail/RenderServlet?model=xml

[32] WP 20 (5026/99/FR + 5055/99 all other languages): Opinion No 3/99 on Public sector information and the protection of personal data; Contribution to the consultation initiated by the European Commission in its Green Paper entitled "Public sector information: a key resource for Europe", COM (1998) 585; Adopted on 3 May 1999.

public do not constitute a homogeneous category, which can be dealt with uniformly from a data protection point of view, nor does the individual concerned loose his rights when his personal data are made public Instead, a step-by-step analysis is needed of the rights of the data subject and the right of the public to access the data respectively. While there may be public access to data, such access may be subject to certain conditions (such as proof of legitimate interest). Alternatively, the purposes for which the data may be used, for example for commercial purposes or by the media, may be restricted. Many examples are given to illustrate these points.

2.3.6 *Codes of conduct*

Article 27 of Directive 95/46/EC provides that the Commission and Member States shall encourage the drawing-up of codes of conduct intended to contribute to the proper implementation of national laws transposing the directive, taking into account the specific features of the various sectors. Concerning Community codes, they may be submitted to the Article 29 Working Party which determines among other things, whether the drafts are in accordance with the national laws or not. The Commission may ensure appropriate publicity for the codes approved by the Working Party. The Working Party has elaborated a working document [33] laying down the procedure and elements of substance for the consideration of Community codes. The Chairman, the Secretariat (provided by the Commission) and the members have their respective roles until the adoption of a final opinion. No code has been approved so far. The Working Party and the submitting organisations are still in discussions about the final shape of the codes.

FEDMA

The Federation of European Direct Marketing (FEDMA) represents the direct marketing sector at the European level and has submitted a draft Community code of practice for the use of personal data in direct marketing [34] . Its national members are the Direct Marketing Associations (DMAs) of 12 countries of the European Union (all except Luxembourg, Denmark and Greece) and Switzerland, Hungary, Poland, Czech and Slovak Republic, which represent users, service providers and media/carriers of direct marketing. FEDMA also has about 500 direct company members and represents directly, or indirectly through the trade associations, a total of around 10,000 European direct marketing practitioners.

The Working Party has established a subgroup on the FEDMA code which had submitted its first report to the Working Party on 3 December 1998. It commented the first version of the

---

[33] WP 13 (5004/98): Future work on codes of conduct: Working Document on the procedure for the consideration by the Working Party of Community codes of conduct. Adopted on 10 September 1998.

[34] This draft code does not address questions of on-line marketing and e-commerce on which FEDMA is working separately. The subgroup on FEDMA is of the view that the e-commerce code should also be submitted to the Working Party.

draft European Code of Practice presented by FEDMA on 18 August 1998. The conclusion of this report was that the draft code is in many points not in line with the directive and that it does not present enough added value. It was also proposed to FEDMA to meet in order to discuss the issues at stake. These comments were sent to FEDMA (and not published). FEDMA elaborated a revised version and submitted it to the subgroup on 12 July 1999. The subgroup has again analysed the text and concluded that though important improvements were made, the draft code still is not fully in line with the directive and could provide more added value (e.g. in particular as regards processing operations typical for the direct marketing sector and the handling of individual complaints cross-borders).

IATA

In 1997, the International Air Transport Association (IATA) submitted to the Working Party "Recommended Practice 1774 - Protection of privacy and transborder data flows of personal data used in international air transport of passengers and cargo" (RP 1174). These guidelines are recommended by IATA to its members for years. In light of directive 95/46/EC, IATA revised RP 1774 with the aim to comply with the directive and possibly contribute to free flow of personal data amongst its international members.

2.3.7 EU Charta on Fundamental Rights

The Working Party strongly recommended the Convention elaborating the European Charter on Fundamental Rights to incorporate the fundamental right to data protection in addition to the right to privacy into the Charter . [35]

2.4 Main developments in Member States

As in previous years, the national data protection supervisory authorities were invited to inform about any data protection developments in their countries in the year 1999. These are summarised below. The addresses of the respective Websites where the full texts of the Data Protection Authorities' own annual report can be obtained, are also published below and listed in Annex 3.

The only difference from last year is that were asked to fill in a questionnaire as opposed to writing a summary of the main developments in their country. The questionnaire allowed focusing contributions on five specific topics, namely :

A: Legislative measures adopted in 1999 in the country under the first pillar of the EU, which had an impact on privacy and data protection (excluding Directive 95/46/EC and 97/66/EC)
B: Changes, which were made in 1999 in their country in the area of data protection and privacy under the second and third pillar of the EU.

---

[35] WP 26 (5143/99): Recommendation 4/99 on the inclusion of the fundamental right to data protection in the European catalogue of fundamental rights. Adopted on 7 September 1999.

C: Case law (national courts) /jurisprudence : Listing the leading judicial cases in their countries in 1999 on privacy and data protection, in particular cases which have a cross border element.

D: Specific issues e.g. Data Protection Authority Actions : Listing any issues in the field of data protection which posed a problem in their country in 1999 or any other issues which they thought were of importance in the field of data protection and privacy in that year and which needed to be addressed (for example measures of the authority) either in their country or at EU level.

E: The respective web addresses of where their annual reports and other information can be obtained.

AUSTRIA

A. Legislative measures adopted in Austria under the first pillar (this is excluding Directive 95/46/EC and 97/66/EC)

Together with the Data Protection Act (DSG) 2000, Parliament adopted the Federal Statistics Act (Bundesstatistikgesetz) 2000, BGBl. I No 163/1999, the Federal Archives Act (Bundesarchivgesetz), BGBl. I No 162/1999 and the amendment to the Insurance Contract Act (Versicherungsvertragsgesetz), BGBl. I No 150/1999. The aim of the Federal Statistics Act is to create a legal basis for obtaining data for statistical surveys from public registers and administrative authorities, firstly in order to relieve the burden on respondents and secondly to permit a more rational compilation of statistics by the Austrian Federal Statistical Institute. In addition, the law lays down quality criteria and principles to be adhered to when compiling statistics and national accounts, with corresponding control mechanisms, in order to guarantee objective official statistics which can meet international standards and stand up to scientific scrutiny.

The Austrian Federal Law on the Protection, Storage and Use of federal archive material (Federal Archive Act) also entered into force on 1 January 2000. The purpose of this law is to establish a legal definition of archive material which also encompasses the current technical possibilities for creating written records and also to lay down clear legal provisions on the protection and storage of historically valuable documents and/or to create legal bases for access to the archive. This falls within the field of federal tasks.

The Data Protection Directive was also, inter alia, the immediate ground for the amendment to the Insurance Contract Act, since it was not clear to what extent private insurers could use health information. For this reason, a legal basis for the use of health information by insurers was introduced in Section 11a of the Insurance Contract Act. The provision stipulates when and for what purposes insurers may use health information and to whom this may be transmitted. In addition, provisions were introduced to protect the rights of the individual concerned.

Recent Developments
Article 29 WG 4th Annual Report (EC)

In BGBl. I No 190/1999, the Federal law on electronic signatures (Signaturgesetz-SIG) was adopted in Austria and, by transposing Directive 1999/93/EC, thereby provides the legal framework for generating and using electronic signatures and for providing signature and certification services.

B. Changes made in Austria under the second and third pillar

The amended Security Police Act (Sicherheitspolizeigesetznovelle) 1999, BGBl. I No 146/1999, regulates, inter alia, the following areas: To compensate for the abolition of border controls on Austria's accession to the Schengen Implementing Agreement, provisions are proposed to check persons and goods in the context of international travel (so-called "Schleierfahndung" - checks not based on suspicion). Provisions were also introduced governing police records involving the use of genetic information obtained through DNA analyses. Since several international regulations (EURATOM Regulation No 3, European Commission Decision of 30 November 1994, Council Decision of 27 April 1998, Europol-Convention) require the conduct of high quality security checks, the number of cases where security checks are permitted was increased and also, in special circumstances, it has become possible to conduct intelligence investigations for the purpose of a security check. In addition, a Human Rights Advisory Council has been established in the Interior Ministry to advise the Minister on issues relating to respect for human rights.

BELGIUM

A. Legislative measures adopted in Belgium under the first pillar (excluding Directive 95/46/EC and 97/66/EC)

None

B. Changes made in Belgium under the second and third pillar

With a view to strengthening the fight against crime, several legislative actions have been initiated in 1999, focused on the one hand on cyber crime, and on the other hand, on crimes related to child pornography and human trade.

Draft legislation has been prepared during the course of 1999, which have been submitted for advice to the Privacy Commission. One of the drafts regarded the collaboration of telecommunication providers in the framework of interception of telecommunications. The Commission has given a negative opinion on that draft, considering in particular that the scope of application of the draft, and the circumstances in which the judicial authorities could request and have access to the data were too wide. Regarding another draft law on cybercrime, the Commission raised concern, in particular with regard to the obligation of preservation of traffic data upon telecommunication operators, and the risks linked to the development of a generalised system of surveillance of telecommunication data[36].

The Commission has also given an opinion on the processing of personal data in the framework of "VICLAS" (Violent Crime Linkage Analysis System). The system relies on the analysis of data related to the victim and the author of serious – and possible serial crimes (e.g. murders, sexual violence) in order to establish possiblelinks between these crimes. The system is used in several countries inside and outside the EU. While its useful character has not been put in question, the Commission has made several comments regarding its compliance with the Belgian privacy legislation. It has in particular emphasised the urgent need for a legal framework allowing the processing of sensitive and medical data included in VICLAS by judicial authorities. It has also pointed some information about the victim, which should not be collected systematically when they are not necessary. As regards DNA information, the Commission is opposed to the proliferation of DNA databanks and considers that VICLAS should not create its own DNA databank, but follow the existing procedure as regards the consultation and utilisation of such data. The Commission has finally recommended a storage of the data for a limited period depending on the quality of the data, and not, as it was foreseen, for a general period of 30 years.

C. Major case law

No major cases in the sphere of privacy and data protection.

D. Specific issues

Official positions have been taken, as stated above, regarding the development of measures in order to fight against crime (interception of telecommunications, collection of criminal information, etc.)

Considering the growing number of requests to the Commission regarding the conditions of use of video surveillance, the Commission has issued at its own initiative an opinion on that subject, which updates a former opinion of 1995 on the same subject. This opinion interprets and clarifies the application of the new privacy legislation to the processing of images, and in particular to the use of cameras.

Regular meetings have taken place with members of the Belgian Commission responsible for a study on the goods of Jewish people, which have been spoliated during the Second World War. The Privacy Commission has defined the conditions according to which banks and insurance companies should co-operate and transfer their data to the Study Commission.

---

[36] The definitive text of these laws has been drafted and adopted (as regards cybercrime) in the course of the year 2000.

Recent Developments
Article 29 WG 4th Annual Report (EC)

The Commission has also examined the question of the <u>application of the privacy legislation to deceased persons</u>, and has concluded that there was at the present time a lack of adequate provisions which would allow the protection of personal data of a deceased person and which would permit e.g. a right of access to some data by heirs of that person (e.g. in case there is a need to check the medical file of that person when there is possibly a medical error at the origin of the death). The Commission has expressed the <u>wish that legislative action is taken</u> in order to remedy that situation.

The Commission has adopted an opinion from its own initiative regarding <u>new utilisation of directories</u>, and in particular the publication of directories on-line, allowing reverse searches e.g. on the basis of a telephone number. The Commission has stressed that such publication could only be made according to specific conditions, among which prior information and consent of the data subject.

E. Website

http://www.privacy.fgov.be

DENMARK

A. Legislative measures adopted in Denmark under the first pillar (excluding Directives 95/46/EC and Directive 97/66/EC)

Each year, several laws and regulations with impact on privacy and data protection are adopted. It is not possible to list all of them here. Especially in the field of telecommunication, several new regulations were adopted in 1999.

B. Changes made in Denmark under the second and third pillar of the EU
None

C. Major case law

All cases concerning the two Registration Acts were in 1999 decided administratively by the Danish Data Protection Agency.

D. Specific issues

In 1999, the Danish Data Protection Agency had two cases concerning the question of monitoring employees' and students' use of Internet by using a log. The Danish Data Protection Agency found in both cases that the logging of students' and employees' use of Internet formed a register which fell within the scope of the Public Authorities Registers Act. The Danish Data Protection Agency found that the registration was legal if it had a reasoned purpose and the employees and students were informed about the registration in advance.

The Danish Data Protection Agency also gave an account about the safety in relation to the fact that many governmental bodies' registers - including registers with sensitive data - are operated by the private enterprise "Computer Science Corporation" (CSC). The Danish Data Protection Agency found that there were no safety problems in relation to CSC as long as CSC complies with the law. It did not have any importance that CSC is a private enterprise.

In 1999, the Danish Data Protection Agency also made a statement to The Ministry of Justice concerning the plans for making a DNA register, a register with persons accused, charged or convicted for certain serious crimes. The Danish Data Protection Agency found that the admission of non-convicted persons into the register was not contradictory to The Public Authorities Registers Act. Nevertheless the Danish Data Protection Agency recommended that the register was authorized by law.

E. Website

www.datatilsynet.dk (only available in Danish)

FINLAND

A. Legislative measures adopted in Finland under the first pillar (excluding

Directives 95/46/EC and 97/66/EC)

In order to transpose the principles of the Directive, inspection continued in different fields of legislation. For example, the provisions of the Population Information Act, which governs the national population information system, were under inspection in 1999. The Act on Electric Identity Card came into force in December 1999. Parliament passed the Act on Electronic Service in Administration at the end of 1999, and which became effective on 1 January 2000. The Act on Openness of Government Activities, which came into force on 1 December 1999, regulates the disclosure of personal data from administrative files, the secrecy rules of documents and personal data, and good practice in information management.

B. Changes made in Finland under the second and third pillar

The EU Data Protection Directive is also taken into account when dealing with issues under the second or third pillar. Among other things, inspection of legislation pertaining to personal data files maintained by the police was initiated in 1999.

C. Major case law

In accordance with Finnish law, public prosecutors are obliged to hear the Data Protection Ombudsman prior to bringing charges on procedures in violation of the Personal Data Act. The courts of justice are obliged to provide an opportunity for the Data Protection Ombudsman to be heard when trying a case related to this. The Data Protection Ombudsman issued a statement on 15 cases. The cases concerned, e.g. illegal file-keeping, use of the personal data file in violation of its purpose, computer break-in, disclosure and secrecy.

D. Specific issues

Recent Developments
Article 29 WG 4th Annual Report (EC)

The Office of the Data Protection Ombudsman was mostly occupied with data protection issues related to health-care and working life. From the viewpoint of the protection of privacy, electronic services and customer contacts, electronic commerce on the Internet, the use of the Internet and, generally, the questions related to electronic data transmission, telecommunications and the use of new technologies saw the most prominent increase. The general problem was the introduction of IT and new technology without the legislative requirements being investigated in advance and the processing of personal data not being planned appropriately.

The main aim of the Office of the Data Protection Ombudsman was to prevent violations of data protection. For this reason, the Office produced guidelines and information material on the new Personal Data Act (15 brochures in total) and took part in approximately 140 educational seminars. The Office expressed its opinion, or was heard in Parliament, in a total of 55 government bills concerning processing of personal data.

The Office strived to promote the drawing-up of codes of conduct taking into account the various sectors as per Article 27 of the EU Data Protection Directive. Work related to codes of conduct was initiated in different sectors. The codes of conduct concerning indemnity and life assurance companies and sports were already completed in 1999. The private health-care organisations, in particular, completed guidelines concerning processing of personal data. Several central administration authorities drew up guidelines, which can be classified as codes of conduct to their administrative fields.

Owing to the EU Data Protection Directive taking effect, the cases of disclosing data to recipients abroad were less than in previous years. The disclosures to non-EU countries were mainly carried out for direct marketing purposes. In one case, the Data Protection Ombudsman notified the European Commission of the approved transfer.

E. Website

www.tietosuoja.fi

FRANCE

A. Legislative measures adopted in France under the first pillar (excluding Directives 95/46/EC and 97/66/EC)

Data protection is an increasingly important issue in the news, from epidemiological research on HIV, to setting up files of sex offenders' genetic fingerprints, to the CNIL's active policy on ensuring Internet sites comply with the law. Two new national laws led to intense public debate in France in 1999 on two social issues with major repercussions for data protection.

The first matter for debate was the setting-up of a national file on genetic fingerprints pursuant to the Law of 17 June 1998 on the prevention and prosecution of sex offences and the protection of minors. This file contains only the fingerprints of persons convicted of sexual offences, not those of suspects. In addition to security issues, the implementation measures taken after the CNIL gave its opinion focus particularly on ensuring that only non-coding DNA segments are used for identification purposes, that is, segments from which it is impossible to determine the organic, physiological or morphological characteristics of the individuals concerned.

The second issue was the setting-up of registers of persons who have concluded a *pacte civil de solidarité* ("Civil Solidarity Pact", PACS) which, pursuant to the Law of 15 November 1999, grants rights to unmarried couples who are co-habiting, whether they are of the same or different sexes (e.g. joint tax declaration, social security entitlements, right to housing, particularly in the case of the death of one of the partners, etc.). The ultimate purpose of these registers is to enable an individual who is applying for a PACS to confirm that his partner has not already signed a pact with someone else. After the CNIL gave its opinion, it was agreed that these registers could legitimately be consulted by the public or private bodies who were responsible for dealing with the rights this innovative legislation granted to individuals (the Treasury, social security, credit institutions). On the other hand, as the data processed in this way generally concern morals, and are therefore quite sensitive, they should not be accessible to others, such as landlords or family members. Moreover, the CNIL expressed a desire, which was adopted, that the information system be designed so that it could not produce a list of partners according to sexual orientation. Lastly, thanks to the CNIL, no "PACS certificate" would be issued to individuals, thus preventing employers or landlords from pressuring individuals to produce it and obtaining private information in that way.

In addition, the Parliament adopted legislative provisions to enable the tax authorities to use social security numbers for establishing the base of, checking and collecting taxes (Article 107 of the Finance Law for 1999). The Constitutional Council was asked to rule on this provision, and has accepted it, as the goal was limited and guaranteed that the "informatics and freedom" law would be fully applied were included. The implementation measures, which are subject to prior checks by the CNIL, lay down that this number cannot be used as an identifier for all the files held by the tax authorities. Moreover, if there are serious infringements on freedom, the files set up using this number may be destroyed.

B. Changes made in France under the second and third pillar

None.

C. Major case law

The CNIL referred to two cases to the courts. The first concerned the provision of a list of the members of a regional religious youth group to a far-right-wing organisation, which sells nazi memorabilia. The other concerned the comment "does not have the right profile, homosexual" in a staff recruitment file of a large company.

The courts have not yet ruled on these cases.

D. Specific issues

Other than the public debates on the two issues mentioned above, in which the CNIL took part, the most significant occurrences of the year were:
- an increase in requests to access security files (by police, for the most part) of more than 67%, that is, 671 requests, resulting in 1100 checks and on-site verifications of the files in question;
- a general increase in the number of complaints (by 31%) and in new processing declarations (250 per day);
- a great deal of activity in retailing and telecommunications, in conjunction with the players in those fields.

The CNIL was the driving force behind the adoption of a fourth professional code of conduct, drawn up by major retailers. Specifically, this provides for two check boxes to appear on on-line purchasing forms. The first allows the person in question to refuse to be sent any advertising material by the retailer in question, while the second enables them to refuse to allow their data to be sold to a third party.

The CNIL has continued its year-old active policy of education and checking Websites. A list of Websites declaring they comply with the law has been published on the CNIL's Website.

The CNIL also carried out a study on spamming which was made available to the public on 14 October 1999 (www.cnil.fr). In the CNIL's opinion, it is completely unlawful to collect email from public areas of the Internet and use it for canvassing of any kind if the individual concerned has not been clearly informed that this may be done and been given the opportunity to refuse such use on-line when the data was collected.

With regard to telecommunications, a recommendation was made concerning the new mobile services which allow reduced-rate calls if the subscriber allows an advertisement to be played during the call. It was made public and sent to all mobile operators. Specifically, the service on offer must allow the subscriber to make calls without having advertisements played. If the advertisement can be heard by the person who has been called, that person must be informed of this ahead of time, and be able to refuse.

A report has also been drawn up on the data on the location of mobiles. The CNIL is of the opinion that location data is highly sensitive in terms of the freedom to come and go as one pleases. Under no circumstances should it be kept for longer than is required for invoicing purposes. In addition, this time should be set at the same length for all operators. With regard to the use of location data for communicating with third parties, whether these are individuals or value-added "local" services, the CNIL concluded that the location data could not be provided by default, except to emergency services. The caller must, on a case-by-case basis, be given a clear and simple opportunity to permit to transmit this information.

E. Website

www.cnil.fr, click on "publications", then on "rapports annuels"

GERMANY

A. Legislative measures adopted in Germany under the first pillar (excluding Directives 95/46/EC and 97/66/EC)

A law on the protection against infection was adopted. It regulates the processing of personal data in the field of disease control.

A law on traffic statistics with the Law on inland water transport was adopted. It regulates data protection in the field of transport statistics and inland water transport.

B. Changes made in Germany under the second and third pillar

Law amending the Law on DNA testing of 2 June 1999 (Federal Law Gazette I, page 1242).

Law on the basis in criminal procedural law of the settlement between offender and victim of 28 December 1999 (Federal Law Gazette I, page 2491).

Prolongation of paragraph 12 of the Law on telecommunications equipment (FAG) until 31 December 2001 (Federal Law Gazette I, page 2492).

C. Major case law

1. Judgement of the Federal Constitutional Court of 14 July 1999 on the 1994 Law on combating crime/G 10 Law/telecommunications surveillance by the Federal Intelligence Service (BVerfGE 100, 313).
2. Decision of the Federal Constitutional Court of 27 October 1999 on the right of administrative courts to consult confidential documents (BVerfGE 101, 106).

D. Specific issues

- Creation of a nation-wide data bank containing pictures of buildings
- Data protection in cases of company mergers and divisions
- Transparency in the scoring procedure relating to the Schufa company
- Data protection when converting from registered shares to bearer shares
- Conflict between data protection and independence in the media

Recent Developments
Article 29 WG 4th Annual Report (EC)

- Linked file on DNA analysis: information stored only on the basis of a court order or with the permission of the person concerned
- Money-laundering file: There is disagreement about the volume of data to be stored on suspect persons
- Video surveillance by police forces

E. Website

www.bfd.bund.de or www.datenschutz.bund.de (including links to Länder websites)

GREECE

During 2000, the Hellenic Data Protection Authority adopted the following most important decisions:

Conditions for the lawful processing of personal data as regards the purposes of direct marketing/advertising and the ascertainment of credibility

As far as trading of personal data for the purpose of direct marketing and/or promotion of sales is concerned, processing of the said data shall be considered lawful under limitations. Collection of personal data shall be effected either following consent of the data subject or arising from catalogues addressed to the public such as telephone directories and trade fair catalogues provided that the subjects have granted their consent for the inclusion of their data in the said catalogues or published their data for similar purposes. Collection of data shall also be considered lawful if the said data is collected from sources available to the public and only if conditions regarding lawful access are kept. Data collected for the aforementioned purposes may include full name, address and profession. The agent of collection has the obligation to consult the special Register of the Data Protection Authority with which those who do not wish to have their data involved in activities concerning direct advertising and promotion of sales are registered following application and are, thus, exempted from any collection of their data whatsoever.

As soon as the first letter is sent to the subject, the sender shall inform the addressee regarding the source of his/her information and ask for the said subject's consent in order to use the data. The decision of the Data Protection Authority also mentions the Act on consumer protection regarding the banning of transmission of advertising messages via telephone, fax, electronic mail or other electronic means without the explicit consent of the consumer.

Concerning the processing of personal data for the purpose of ascertainment of credibility, the Data Protection Authority shall set conditions in order to reduce processing that takes place without the consent of the subject. In particular, the collection of the following data shall be permitted: petitions in bankruptcy; decisions regarding petitions in bankruptcy; bills of exchange; auction programs concerning movable property and real estate; changes in firms, societies anonymous, limited companies and joint ventures; mortgages and securing by mortgage; seizures and checks under Presidential Decree No. 1923; dud checks; protested bills of exchange and protested bills payable to order.

Special time limits concerning keeping the said data and limitations regarding the recording of the ensuing changes in relation to the said data e.g. immediate recording of the settlement of a due check shall be set for the aforementioned categories.

Following collection, companies in charge shall have the obligation to inform the data subjects as regards to the recording of data. In case the data subjects object to it and ask for deletion of information, the said companies shall be obliged to delete the data and inform the data subjects of consequences that may arise and may affect their behavior in terms of exchanges. Only businesspeople using the data according to the provisions for lawful use shall be the recipients of the aforementioned data. It is emphasized that recipient companies shall have the right to collect only the unfavorable data mentioned above. Favorable data relating to the financial position such as real estate shall only be collected following consent of the data subject. Thus, the creation of financial position overall profiles without the knowledge of the data subjects is avoided.

Thanks to the said decision, the Data Protection Authority intends to set the conditions of processing credibility-related information taking always into account the citizen's protection from the processing of personal data as well as the right of the businesspeople of the country to lawful access to information necessary for the safety of exchanges.

Non-inclusion of religion beliefs and other personal data in identity cards

The most important and controversial decision of the Hellenic Data Protection Authority, referred to the non-inclusion of a number of personal data in citizens' identity cards in Greece. This decision included data referring to religion beliefs and based on the following reasons:

1. The identity cards constitute public documents containing personal data. These data are registered in relevant public authorities' filing systems and are subject to processing, the aim of the said processing being the verification of the subject's identity.

2. According to article 4 § 1 section b of the Greek Data Protection Act 2472/1997, in order that personal data be lawfully processed they "must be relevant, appropriate and not exceeding what may be required in any particular case in the context of said purposes". The principle of the purpose of processing as well as those of necessity and appropriateness of the data with regard to the purpose of processing are thus established as a fundamental condition for the lawful operation of any filing system whatsoever. Any processing of personal data which exceeds the pursued purpose or which is neither appropriate nor necessary for the achievement of such purpose is considered to be unlawful.

3. In this instance, in view of the purpose of processing being the verification of the identity of the data subject, the following data provided for in Decree 127/1969 regarding identity cards issued by police authorities exceed the purpose of processing for the following reasons:

   a. Fingerprint of the data subject: It is not necessary for the verification of the identity of the data subject since this is, in principle, evident from the photograph. In addition, according to the common perception, the fingerprint ("record") is associated with the suspicion or the ascertainment of criminal activity ("branded criminals"). Attributing such a feature to the entire Greek population, even in the potentiality of it, exceeds the necessary measure and offends human dignity that is protected by the Constitution.

   b. Full name of spouse: Since 1983 marriage does not bring about the change of the spouses' surname. Moreover, its entry does not serve the purpose for which the identity card is issued.

   c. Profession: It does not constitute an element of one's physical identity, it is subject to change and does not necessarily reflect reality at a time other than that of the issuance of the card. Moreover, it is socially discriminating, a feature which should not necessarily be subject to processing.

   d. Citizenship / nationality: According to the legislation in force, only Greek citizens bear identity cards.

   e. Residence: It is neither necessary nor appropriate (for it is subject to change) in order to prove one's identity.

   f. Religion: It refers to the inner world of the individual and it is therefore neither appropriate nor necessary in order to prove one's identity.

4. The processing of the aforementioned data is unlawful even if the data subject has given his/her explicit consent according to Act 2472/1997, Articles 5 §1 and 7 §2 section a, since the data subject's consent does not allow for any form of processing when unlawful or contrary to the principles of purpose and necessity. The content and the exercise of the right to determine oneself within an informational framework, expressed, among other ways, by the consent of the data subject with regard to the processing of his/her personal data are not determined in abstract. They are determined within the context of and in close relation to the purpose of the filing system or processing in the sense that the said right may not lead to the registration of data which are irrelevant to the purpose of each and every filing system / processing.

The Council of State examined an appeal against the aforementioned decision. The Council's judgement is anticipated at the end of February 2001.

Decision on fingerprints

The Data Protection Authority is responsible for examining the lawfulness of the processing of these personal data, since said processing, which consists in the collection, comparison and filing of biometric characteristics, constitutes an automated processing to the extent that the recognition of physical persons is allowed, in the terms of Law 2472/97.

The Authority draws the attention of Controllers to the fact that, in the event that data are collected by the aforementioned means, said collection and processing exceeds the limits set by the principle of proportionality, according to article 4 paragraph 1b of Law 2472/97, since the pursued purpose, i.e. monitoring the presence of workers, may be achieved by more moderate means. The identification of the data subject by means of taking fingerprints has served, and still does, anti-criminal politics. Therefore, the filing of fingerprints with view to monitoring the presence of workers, apart from the data subjects' reasonable reaction, cannot be assumed to weigh more than the need of protection of the right to privacy and there is no reason for exemption from the general principle that such information is collected and recorded only by authorities which are bound to keep relevant files by virtue of law. Such an exemption could be accepted only in special cases, e.g. for the purpose of monitoring the access to areas where confidential files are kept or to access-restricted installations.

Therefore, the Authority considers the specific means of collection and processing of personal data to be unlawful.

Finally, it must be noted that, since the collection of data is deemed unlawful, as it exceeds its purpose, any eventual consent of data subjects does not legitimize the processing.

Therefore, according to article 21 paragraph 1 of Law 2472/97, the Data Protection Authority considers that Controllers must be obligated, within a period of a month upon notification of these presents, to interrupt the processing (in the event that it has already started) and to destroy all relevant data (the fingerprint files). The Controllers are obliged to select more moderate and more effective monitoring means, prioritizing administrative monitoring means that are valid and provided for by law.

IRELAND

A. Legislative measures adopted in Ireland under the first pillar of the EU (excluding Directives 95/46/EC and 97/66/EC)

None

B. Changes made in Ireland under the second and third pillar of the EU

None

C. Major case law

None in this sphere

D. Specific issues

Recent Developments
Article 29 WG 4th Annual Report (EC)

No major problems arose apart from the question of the use of reverse directories by telecommunications, which was the subject of later discussions at the Art. 29 meeting which led to the opinion 7/2000.

E. Website

www.dataprivacy.ie

ITALY

A. Legislative measures adopted in Italy under the first pillar (excluding Directives 95/46/EC and 97/66/EC)

Reference can be made to:

- Decree no. 250 of 22.06.99 by the President of the Italian Republic regulating the use of devices for monitoring the access of vehicles to city centres and recording images in connection with road traffic (road traffic control, punishment of road traffic offences). Use of said devices is also regulated with regard to the arrangements applying to collection and keeping of the data; Decree no. 437 of 22.10.99, laying down requirements and arrangements for issuing electronic identity cards and electronic identity documents;

- Decree of 08.02.99, including technical rules for creating, transmitting, duplicating [etc.] electronic documents;

- Act no. 422 of 19.10.99, ratifying the Convention on the service in Member States of the European Union of judicial and extra-judicial documents in civil or commercial matters;

- Decree of 18.02.99, for the approval of the National Statistics Plan, in which greater attention is paid by statisticians to data subjects and their personal data;

- Legislative decree no. 261 of 22.07.99, transposing Directive 97/67/EC on common rules for the development of the internal market of Community postal services and the improvement of quality of service, where confidentiality of correspondence and protection of personal data are included among the fundamental requirements;

- Decree no. 14 of 16.03.99 by the President of the Italian Republic including the implementing regulations for Directives 95/18/EC and 95/19/EC on the licensing of railway undertakings and the allocation of railway infrastructure capacity, respectively. Under Article 7 of said decree, managers are required to comply with the data protection provisions laid down in Act no. 675/1996;

- the Prime Minister's Guidelines on computerised management of the information flow among public administrative agencies.

B. Changes made in Italy under the second and third pillar of the EU
None

C. Major case law

The focus of case law in 1999 was on the assessment of the scope of application of the provisions for access to administrative records (Act no. 241 of 07.08.90) as related to those laid down in the DPA. Various decisions were taken by the courts during 1999; reference can be made in particular to two decisions by the 6 th Division of the State Council (no. 59 of 26.01.99 and no. 65 of 27.01.99).

The arrangements for lodging a complaint with the Garante – as per Article 29 in the DPA - were put into practice starting in 1999. They represent an alternative approach to legal action in court and allow data subjects to obtain expeditious decisions. This type of complaint can only be lodged in case of partial or total failure to exercise the rights granted to data subjects by Article 13 of the DPA (rights of access, rectification, information, erasure, etc.). 150 complaints were lodged with the Garante in 1999; in only three cases was the decision by the authority challenged before an ordinary court.

In all the three cases, the Garante appeared in court in order to defend its decision. Reference should be made in this regard to a case concerning the possibility to apply the DPA – and therefore, to allow a data subject to object – even with regard to processing operations unrelated to the existence a data bank. The issue at stake had to do with the performance of journalistic activities and the role played by the code of conduct for journalists which was drafted in cooperation with the relevant sectoral associations - as a tool supplementing the principles laid down in the DPA.

D. Specific issues

In order to thoroughly regulate data protection issues in Italy and to ensure the full transposition into national law of the principles laid down in Directives 95/46/EC and 97/66/EC, legislative measures are required with regard to such sectors as direct marketing, social security, employment, information flows on electronic networks.

Considerable importance is also to be attached to the definition of mechanisms and safeguards applying specifically to processing operations for judicial and law enforcement purposes – which are currently regulated by the DPA only in part. From a general standpoint, the above processing operations are not covered by either Directive since they fall outside the scope of application of Community law. However, it was the Parliament's intention not to exempt these operations from the relevant data protection provisions, which would be laid down subsequently by means of ad-hoc measures.

The following issues were especially addressed in 1999 both in order to ensure the actual implementation of data protection provisions and with a view to establishing mechanisms for the effective exchange of opinions and information with the Garante in connection with the decision-making of either Parliament or administrative agencies – as also related to computer science and technological development:

- Need to establish effective consultation mechanisms in respect of the Garante pursuant to Article 28(2) of Directive 95/46/EC
- Assessment and regulation of video surveillance activities
- Processing of genetic data
- Provision of simplified information to data subjects in respect of banking activities
- Rules applying to consent for processing operations in the medical sector
- Access to personal data as included, for instance, in employee evaluation records, medical expert opinions etc.
- Itemised billing
- Follow-up at Community level of the discussion on the directives concerning digital signature and e-commerce
- Provisions applying to the processing of data within the framework of so-called Third Pillar activities

E. Website

www.garanteprivacy.it

PORTUGAL

B. Changes made in Portugal under the second and third pillar

The ratification of the CIS Convention, by the Decree of the President of the Republic 129/99, and by the Resolution of the Parliament nr. 32/99, both of 21 April.

C. Major case law

Proc. 41025, 1st Section of the Administrative Supreme Court - Sentence of 15 April 1999
Proc. 41022, 1st section of the Administrative Supreme Court - Sentence of 15 April 1999
Decisions of appeals presented by data controllers against deliberations of the Portuguese Data Protection Authority. Both decisions were favorable to the understanding of the Portuguese DPA.

4. Website

http://www.cnpd.pt
We have also available a summary report in English.

SPAIN

A. Legislative measures adopted in Spain under the first pillar of the EU (excluding Directives 95/46/EC and 97/66/EC)

Royal Decree No. 994/1999 of 11 June 1999 approved the regulation on the security measures for automatic filing systems containing personal data.

B. Changes made in Spain under the second and third pillar of the EU

In 1999, the **French Data Protection Commission** (**CNIL**) made five requests for cooperation to the Agency under Article 114.2 of the Schengen Convention in relation to requests for access to the files of the Schengen Information System (SIS) and for cancellation if possible, in respect of individuals listed in the SIS as not to be admitted to Schengen territory, whose data were entered by the Spanish authorities.

Action was therefore taken to establish whether those individuals' data had been correctly registered under current legislation. In every case, it was established that the individuals had been deported from national territory following expulsion proceedings pursuant to the Immigration Law and the issue of a ban on entering the country. In every case investigated, the CNIL was informed of the action taken and of the grounds for entering these individuals on the SIS.

Where public files relating to activities contained in the third pillar are concerned, 46 referring to judicial proceedings and 45 relating to the actions of Security Forces were registered in 1999.

Most of the nine data inspections concerning the State Security Forces undertaken by the Agency in 1999 were proactive.

Although it predates 1999, **Organic Law No. 4/1997** regulating the use of video cameras by the Security Forces in public places deserves mention.

C. Major case law

1. Jurisprudence of the Constitutional Court relating to Article 18.4 of the Constitution:

In 1999, the Constitutional Court issued three judgements, No. 30/1999 of 8 March, No. 44/1999 and No. 45/1999 of 23 March directly concerning the protection of personal data. In these, the Constitutional Court reasserted the precept observed throughout 1998, specifically on the basis of Judgement No. 11/1998 of 13 January, recognising what is called information self-determination or, according to German jurisprudence, "informationelle Selbstbestimmung".

The three judgements refer to a single event, involving an employer's use of data on trade union membership to deduct sums of money in connection with workers' exercise of the right to strike.

The complainants, members of a specific trade union, were providing their services in a company in which the Works' Council, with the support of the trade unions, called a strike.

Although they did not take part in the strike, the company deducted sums from all employees who were on record as being members of a specific trade union – one of those which supported the strike. The company took this course because it could obtain data on trade union membership thanks to certain electronic keys used to denote membership of each union.

While the company reimbursed the sums on request, the workers appealed to the Constitutional Court alleging that their right to freedom in trade union matters under Article 28 of the Spanish Constitution had been breached on the terms of Article 18.4, which provides for legal limits set on the use of information technology to uphold the right to honour and to personal and family privacy.

The complaint was admitted on the grounds that data concerning trade union membership, an ideological choice protected by Article 16 of the Constitution, are afforded special protection by Spanish law, but were used for purposes other than those providing the grounds for their collection and that the corresponding electronic key had been improperly used since care should be taken to avoid the computerisation of personal data favouring discriminatory behaviour.

The judgement held that both the right to freedom in trade union matters and the right to privacy had been infringed.

2. Most significant judgements delivered by the administrative courts in 1999 in their role of overseeing the activity of the Data Protection Agency:
In 1999, the higher Courts of Justice delivered 29 judgements in administrative appeals lodged against DPA rulings, a considerable increase on the 13 judgements delivered by the same courts during the previous year.

Of the 29 judgements delivered this year, 27 were in punitive proceedings and two in proceedings to protect rights. None deserves any particular comment because they entailed no substantive innovation.

D. Specific issues
Applications to the General Data Protection Register in 1999 increased by 50% on 1998. The applications for international transfer authorisations processed were 25% up on the preceeding year. No setbacks were encountered in managing any of file registrations.

On 31 December 1999, a total of 1,081 files had been entered on the register for international data transfers, 1,028 of which were in private ownership and 53 in public ownership.

Of the 39 applications submitted for authorisation of international personal data transfers in 1999, 36 were granted, two were shelved or discontinued by the controller, and one remains outstanding by 31 December 1999. Data inspection activities could be classed in two large groups. One was dealing with complaints of breach of the principles laid down in the law then in force, LORTAD, and the other was developing Proactive Sectoral Inspection Plans to check the level of compliance with the rules on the protection of personal data in both the public and the private sectors.

Action taken in response to complaints concerned the right of access to clinical records and questions such as the registration of files used by medical and healthcare staff in public hospitals when these were transferred to private management.

As part of the sectoral plans in the public sector, inspections were carried out in bodies such as the State Tax Administration Agency, the Directorate-General of Traffic, the National AIDS Register and two publicly-owned hospitals, following all of which the Director of the Agency issued a series of recommendations. In the private sector, a series of inspections focused on the main fixed telephone operators: Telefónica de España, S.A.; Retevisión S.A.; Lince Telecomunicaciones S.A. (UNI 2) and Euskaltel, S.A.

The following three cases are prime examples of the Data Protection Agency's supervisory work.

The first concerned TAIR, a project carried out by the Spanish health authorities, one of the aims of which was to set up flexible management of the invoicing and processing of pharmaceutical prescriptions. For these purposes, during the consultation, the doctor treating the patient issues an adhesive label carrying the data identifying the patient in text and a bar code to facilitate subsequent reading, which is stuck to the pharmacological prescription. Subsequently, under an agreement between the health authorities (which finance part of the cost of the medications) and the Colleges of Pharmacists (which invoice the health authorities for the part of the costs these bear), all the information contained on the prescription is computerised by the College of Pharmacists to create a personalised file which is sent to the health authorities for subsequent processing on the terms laid down by the healthcare legislation. After careful inspection of the entire process, the Agency found that both, the legal guarantees and the security measures adopted, ensured that this processing did not breach Spanish law. In view of the particular implications for personal privacy, the Agency has continued and will continue, in conjunction with the health authorities, to supervise the development of the project to ensure that it complies at all times with the rules on data protection and affords adequate guarantees.

Another investigation looked at a file located in Spain which was registered by the Spanish subsidiary of a North-American company. The investigation was begun because the file included data on the names, surnames, postal and electronic addresses and professional background of some 130,000 individuals, most of whom were resident in Spain. These data were reported to have been obtained from a database located in the North-American parent company, on which persons resident anywhere in the world who were interested in receiving information on the company's products could voluntarily register via the firm's Web pages.

To analyse whether this processing complied with Spanish data protection rules, it was necessary to consider the circumstances in relation to the principles of information and consent obtaining when the data were collected at origin, on Web pages located in the USA.

The Data Protection Agency ruled that, in view of the lack of adequate information, for the purposes of Spanish data protection rules, concerning the transfer of data to the Spanish subsidiary and subsequent processing thereof by the subsidiary, the consent provided by the user, in the absence of fundamental information, was not sufficient for the subsidiary legitimately to process these data and, accordingly, sanctions were applied against the Spanish company.

In the third case, inspections were carried out in relation to so-called "scoring procedures". A telecommunications operator refers a report on its own or potential clients to another body specialising in information on solvency and credit rating. This report is subsequently returned with a new classification containing information on the creditworthiness of each of these clients to support the operator's decisions to accept or reject service applications. This may constitute the transfer and processing without consent of personal data in terms of Spanish legislation on the protection of personal data, for which reason sanctions proceedings were begun against several operators.

At the **Spring Conference of Control Authorities**, held in Helsinki in April 1999, the delegations from the Spanish and Netherlands Control Authorities presented the results of a joint project to develop common - or harmonised - methodologies and procedures for privacy inspections or audits. Two teams of inspectors from both authorities had exchanged ideas and experiences at a seminar held in Madrid in April 1999. The two delegations sketched out the broad outlines to be followed, and invited other delegations to join the project.

The first inspection using common methods, as agreed at the Madrid seminar, was planned and carried out. Internet service providers - ISPs - were chosen as these companies provide identical services anywhere in the world. Both delegations decided to continue to use the model because it yielded the expected results, and two further audits have been carried out on another two ISPs.

Similarly, the latest edition of the catalogue of **Recommendations to Internet users** compiled by the Data Protection Agency in 1997 was published in May 1999. It is intended to inform users on secure access to the Web.

On similar lines, it should be emphasised that Spain has led the European Union in drawing up and registering a data protection code for the Internet which is promoted by the Spanish Electronic Commerce Association.

Another event which deserves mention is the drafting of the **Data Protection Agency Recommendations to data controllers in companies providing solvency and credit rating information** with the aim of bringing the operation of this kind of company further into line with the provisions of LORTAD.

The recommendations are in three groups. The first two refer to the two broad kinds of file devoted to providing services on solvency and credit ratings. The first group refers to files containing data concerning breaches of monetary obligations provided by creditors or parties acting on their behalf and in their interests. The second group concerns files processing data obtained from sources which are accessible to the public. The third group of recommendations concerns the implementation of measures covered by the Regulation on Security Measures.

By law, the Data Protection Agency has a duty to inform citizens, and it therefore deals with enquiries and complaints, and informs citizens on their rights in relation to the automatic processing of personal data. In 1999, the Agency mounted publicity campaigns in the media, published brochures, manuals and CD-ROMs and posted information on its own Web page, which registered 506,362 visitors over the year, 43% more than in 1998.

The Agency provides personal advice in its offices, by telephone and via ordinary or electronic mail. The 15,000 enquiries handled in 1999 represented a 20% increase on the written enquiries received in 1998, largely due to the mail link provided on the Web page.

The greatest numbers of enquiries concerned those sectors of greatest interest to citizens: the right to obtain information from the Agency, solvency and credit records, publicity files and the exercise of the rights of access, rectification and cancellation vis-à-vis data controllers.

The sectors giving rise to most enquiries were: the scope of the data protection law, its security regulation, telecommunications, health data, electoral census data, statistical data, data transfers, professional colleges, insurance and labour relations. This last is coming increasingly to the fore by virtue of issues such as employers' access to employees' electronic mail, the recording of employees' images and access to these via company Web pages.

One of the duties assigned the Data Protection Agency by Article 37h of Organic Law No. 15/1999 on the protection of personal data is "to provide consultative opinions on general provisions which it is planned to develop pursuant to this law". Over the year, the Data Protection Agency was consulted on a total of 35 provisions, 59% more than in 1998. These included the following, in particular:

- the preliminary draft law on measures to control chemical substances liable to be diverted for the manufacture of chemical weapons pursuant to the Convention on the prohibition of the development, production, stockpiling and use of chemical weapons and on their destruction, signed in Paris on 13 January 1993;
- the proposed law for updating the regulation governing the Banco de España's risk assessment centre, the *Central de Riesgos del Banco de España* – CIRBE;
- the preliminary draft law creating the Catalan Data Protection Agency;
- the preliminary draft law on electronic signature, subsequently approved by Royal Decree-Law No. 14/1999 of 17 September 1999 on electronic signature;
- the preliminary draft law on fiscal, administrative and social measures, accompanying the Budget Law 2000;

Lastly, the Agency's efforts throughout 1999 to provide information and clarification and to publicise the principles, criteria, obligations and other issues concerned by the Security Regulation before this came into effect deserve particular mention.

E. Website

Part of the Agency's Annual Report can be found at: https:// www.agenciaprotecciondatos.org/ It is planned to include the latest annual report of the Spanish Authority on these pages.

SWEDEN

A. Legislative measures in Sweden under the first pillar of the EU (excluding Directives 95/46/EC and Directive 97/66/EC)

None

B. Changes made in Sweden under the second and third pillar of the EU

Several new laws relating to processing of personal data were adopted in Sweden in 1999, e.g. the Act (1999:90) relating to processing of personal data by tax authorities when assisting criminal investigations and the Act (1999:163) relating to money laundering records.

The Police Data Act, which was adopted in 1998, was supplemented by the Police Data Ordinance (1999:81) in 1999.

The above mentioned statutes contain specific provisions regarding processing of personal data within these sectors. The Personal Data Act, which is generally applicable, shall apply to the extent that the processing has not been specifically regulated in these or other provisions.

C. Major case law

In April, the City Court of Stockholm sentenced a businessman for violation of the old Data Act. The businessman had published disparaging opinions and assessments about a great number of persons on his Website. He had claimed, i.a., that the right to freedom of expression should allow him to publish such information on the Internet. The city court's decision was appealed to the Svea Court of Appeal in Stockholm, which was of the opinion that the publishing instead constituted a violation of the new Personal Data Act. The Svea Court of Appeal did not approve of the businessman's objection that he had published information *solely* for journalistic purposes and that the Personal Data Act therefore should not apply. The Svea Court of Appeal's decision has been appealed to the Supreme Court where it is still pending.

D. Specific issues

In 1999, the Data Inspection Board investigated a Website where a list of hospital staff that had been reproved by a disciplinary board had been published. The Data Inspection Board found, however, that the information on the Website was published by an editorial body of a periodical publication and that the publishing thus fell under the Fundamental Law on Freedom of Expression. The Personal Data Act was consequently not applicable.

In another supervision case that concerned the Internet, a Swedish municipal authority had published a list of names on its Website of all the inhabitants in the municipality without first obtaining the individuals' consent. The municipal authority claimed that the list was to be seen as an artistic expression and that it was therefore exempted from the prerequisite to obtain consent according to a provision in the Personal Data Act. The Data Inspection Board considered however that, even though the term "artistic expression" is difficult to define, the legislator cannot have meant to exempt processing of data such as the publishing in question. The municipal authority subsequently deleted the information from the Website and the supervision case was closed.

Processing of personal data on the Internet was the subject of a vivid discussion in Sweden in 1999. In the end of 1998, the Data Inspection Board had been commissioned by the Swedish Government to investigate the need for supplementary provisions in order to exempt, from the prohibition in section 33 of the Personal Data Act, certain third country transfers that could be considered harmless, especially in connection with processing of personal data in international communication networks such as the Internet. The Data Inspection Board proposed a rapid amendment of the Personal Data Ordinance (1998:1191) to the Government and the proposal was essentially favourably received. However, there were major arguments for amending the Personal Data Act instead. The Government thus proposed an amendment of section 33 of the Personal Data Act. The proposal was adopted by the Swedish

Parliament and the amendment (as described under point 2.1.1.) came into force on 1 January 2000.

E. Website

Recent Developments
Article 29 WG 4th Annual Report (EC)

The Data Inspection Board's annual report referring to the year 1999 is available in English on the Website: www.datainspektionen.se/in_english/

THE NETHERLANDS

A. Legislative measures adopted in the Netherlands under the first pillar of the EU (excluding Directives 95/46/EC and 97/66/EC)

None

B. Changes made in the Netherlands under the second and third pillar of the EU

None

C. Major case law

None

D. Specific issues

In 1999, the Registratiekamer dedicated special attention to three issues:

1. The position of consumers on the electronic highway.

The combined breakthrough of Internet and mobile communications means many new capabilities and opportunities for consumers. Obviously because of the Internet, the consumer has more choices in buying goods, making use of services, etc., but it also means a threat, because it is difficult for a consumer to trust an electronic store. If you order something from a Website, you cannot be sure if the goods you ordered would be the right ones and if the right person will receive your money. The Registratiekamer concludes that almost everything the 'digital consumer' does is recorded while the consumer is not aware of this. Therefore, the consumer has to be informed and protected. Because of this, a lot of attention was being payed to the privacy of consumers and an investigation was started by the Registratiekamer of the use of personal data by Internet service providers. The results of this were published in June 2000.

2. The preparation of the entry into force of the 'Wet Bescherming Persoonsgegevens'.

In February 1998, the Draft Bill of the 'Wet Bescherming Persoonsgegevens' (WBP or Personal Data Protection Act) was presented to the Second Chamber. Since then it has been a hot issue. This Act will implement the Directive 95/46 on the Protection of Individuals with regard to the Processing of Personal Data. The Registratiekamer advised the Permanent Parliament Committee of Justice on the consequences of this Act. The Second Chamber unanimously accepted the WBP in November 1999. The WBP will take effect in 2001.

3. The screening of people and companies, which has developed strongly during 1999

Screening involves determining whether someone, for instance an applicant or business partner, is reliable or thrustworthy. To do this, several sources are consulted. Not only the effectiveness of screening is overstated, but it also involves drastic invasion on an individual's privacy. Screening should only take place if there is no less drastic alternative. It should take place according to clear, predetermined criteria and on the basis of lawfully aquired information. In order to achieve the best picture possible of the existing integrity instruments, the Registratiekamer organised during the year a round table conference on screening in the Netherlands.

Most important publications

All publications are fully available in Dutch on the Website of the Registratiekamer. In most of the cases, an English summary of each publicable is also available on-line.

-*'Informatieverstrekking door de fiscus – ontheffing van de fiscale geheimhoudingsplicht in het licht van privacywetgeving' (information provision by tax authorties – exemption from the obligation to fiscal secrecy in the context of data protection legislation)*. This report was offered to State Secretary of Finance and to the Second Chamber. In this report, the Registratiekamer explains why the statutory regulations for the granting of personal data by the tax authorities is no longer up-to-date. The tax law has therefore to be revised.

-*'Werken met gegevens' (working with Information'*. This publication deals with 'CWIs': Centres for Work and Income. Public and private institutions for work and income are combining forces even more often. Because of this, executive bodies, social services and employment agencies are offering their services in these Centres. The Registratiekamer listed and analysed the possibilities and limits of the CWIs and offered a number of rules for dealing with this kind of cooperation in practice.

-*'Koning Klant' (King Client)*. In this report, the Registratiekamer indicated how the standards and rules of the WBP apply to the processing of consumer information and how organisations' economic interests should be measured against clients' privacy interests when processing them.

-*'Intelligent Software Agents and Privacy' (set up in cooperation with the Canadian privacy supervisory authority in Ontario) and 'At face value: on biometrical identification and privacy'*. These two reports deal with new technological developments that might have consequences for citizens' privacy.

- Another publication dealt with a research on the set-up and explotation of the population register (GBA) in three municipalities. This report shows that citizens' information saved in the GBA is insufficiently protected. It is, of course, likely that this will also be the case in other municipalities.

E. Websites

Recent Developments
Article 29 WG 4th Annual Report (EC)

The Website of the Dutch data protection authority is: http://www.registratiekamer.nl In addition to the full Dutch version of the annual report, an English summary is also published on-line.

THE UNITED KINGDOM

A. Legislative measures adopted in the United Kingdom under the first pillar of the EU (excluding Directives 95/46/EC and 97/66/EC)

No other legislative measures were adopted.

B. Changes made in the United Kingdom under the second and third pillar of the EU

No substantial changes were made in 1999 in the area of data protection and privacy under the second and third pillar.

C. Major case law

Midlands Electricity plc appealed to the Data Protection Tribunal on 7 May 1999 against an Enforcement Notice issued by the Data Protection Registrar on 1December 1998, pursuant to Section 10 of the Data Protection Act 1984. The Enforcement Notice resulted from the use of personal data for direct marketing purposes, where the data were obtained for the purpose of the provision of energy supply. The direct marketing in question related to goods and services provided by third parties which did not relate to the supply of electricity or electrical products, sent to customers via a magazine insert with their billing details. The Tribunal upheld the Enforcement Notice, which came into effect on 1 January 2001 and requires Midlands Electricity plc to obtain the consent of customers to continue distributing the magazine.

D. Specific issues

Implementation of the EU Data Protection Directive 95/46/EC and the remaining provisions of the EU Telecommunications Directive 97/66/EC were top priorities in 1999.

E. Website

www.dataprotection.gov.uk

2.5 Community activities

2.5.1 Draft Regulation on Data Protection in Community Institutions and bodies

Institutions and Community bodies, and the Commission in particular, deal usually with personal data within the framework of their activities. The Commission exchanges personal data with Member States within the framework of the common agricultural policy, for the management of the customs procedure, of the Structural Funds and within the framework of other Community policies. In order that this exchange is not called into question by Member

States for reasons of data protection, the Commission declared in 1990 too that it would observe the principles contained in the draft Directive that it proposed then.

At the time of the adoption of Directive 95/46/EC, which aims at establishing a Community framework to harmonise the provisions of Member States, the Commission and the Council undertook, in a public declaration, to comply with it and called upon the other Community institutions and bodies organisms to do likewise.

At the time of the Intergovernmental Conference on the review of the Treaties, the question of the application of the rules on data protection to the Community Institutions was raised. At the end of the negotiations, the Treaty signed in Amsterdam inserted, in the Treaty establishing the European Community, a provision specific to this effect.

The new Article 286 provides therefore that as from 1 January 1999, Community institutions and bodies have to apply the Community rules on data protection, laid down for the most part by Directives 95/46/EC and 97/66/EC. It also stipulates that the application of the aforesaid rules will have to be supervised by an independent supervisory body.

The Commission answered this call by submitting on 14 July 1999 its proposal for a Regulation of the European Parliament and of the Council on the protection of individuals with regard to the processing of personal data by the institutions and bodies of the Community and on the free movement of such data. From the beginning of the legislative procedure, the European Parliament and the Council announced that they shared the objective of the Commission of arriving at a rapid agreement which would make it possible to adopt this Regulation on a first reading, a new way introduced by the Treaty of Amsterdam into the codecision procedure.

2.5.2 *Electronic Signatures Directive*

As follow-up to the Commission Communication "Ensuring Trust and Confidence in Electronic Communication – Towards a European Framework for digital signatures and encryption" of October 1997, the European Commission proposed in May 1998 a proposal for a directive establishing a legal framework for electronic signatures. The directive was adopted on 13 December 1999 [37]. It aims at guaranteeing EU-wide recognition of electronic signatures. Electronic signatures allow someone receiving data over electronic networks, via the Internet for example, to determine the origin of the data and to check that this data has not been altered. The Directive is not designed to regulate everything in detail but defines the

---

[37] Directive 1999/93/EC of the European Parliament and of the Council on a Community framework for Electronic signatures, OJ L 13 of 19.01.2000, p. 12. http://europa.eu.int/comm/internal_market/en/sign/index.htm

requirements for electronic signature certificates and certification services so as to ensure minimum levels of security and allow their free movement throughout the Internal Market.

Its main elements are:

- Legal recognition: The Directive stipulates that an electronic signature cannot be legally discriminated against solely on the grounds that it is in electronic form.
- Free circulation of products and services related to electronic signatures
- Liability of service providers
- A technology-neutral framework
- Data Protection

Given that electronic signatures may also serve as a means of identification and authentification, service providers have to verify the identify of their clients and are liable for the indications they make in the certificate. It was, therefore, considered necessary to further develop the general principles regarding the collection of personal data and purpose limitation (Article 8 of the directive). Since most of commercial transactions do not legally require the identity of the customer, it is essential to be able to use pseudonyms in the certificate. Where no legal identification requirements prevail, the user thus has the choice of indicating his name or pseudonyms in the certificates. This is an indispensable element to combine the need for authentication with privacy and data protection requirements in electronic commerce.

2.5.3 *Electronic Commerce Directive*

As announced in the Commission Communication of May 1997 on Electronic Commerce, the European Commission proposed in November 1998 a Directive to establish a coherent legal framework for electronic commerce throughout the Internal Market. Political agreement was reached in Council in December 1999 [38] .

The directive does not contain specific data protection and privacy rules for electronic commerce. The Working Party invited Commission services at its meetings of March and May 1999 on the basis of the Commission proposal that the relationship between this directive and the data protection directives should be clarified. Recitals 14, 15 and 30 explain that the existing framework for the protection of individuals with regard to the processing of their personal data fully applies to the processing of personal data in the context of electronic commerce. It is also stated that the implementation of the e-commerce directive has to be in full compliance with the data protection rules. The text of the article excluding certain matters from its scope has also been clarified.

---

[38] Directive 2000/31/EC of 8 June of the European Parliament and of the Council on certain legal aspects of information society services, in particular electronic commerce, in the Internal Market (Directive on electronic commerce), OJ L 178 of 17 July 2000, p. 1. Available at: see footnote 39.

Economic actors who intend to process personal data thus have to comply also with the obligations following from Directives 95/46/EC and 97/66/EC. Individuals have the same rights as off-line. This is of particular importance with regard to the information of the consumer about intended processing, purpose specification and limitation, need for a legitimate basis for the processing and more specifically the rules concerning commercial communications, whether prior consent is needed or not.

2.5.4 Transparency Directive 98/34/EC

This Directive extends the scope of Directive 83/189 (which covers national rules affecting the free movement of goods) to include rules on Information Society services. The instrument requires that, before they are definitively adopted, all draft national rules directly affecting these services must be notified to the Commission and reviewed with the other Member States to ensure that they are compatible with the free movement of services and the country of origin control principle (i.e. the one stop regulatory shop whereby, once a service offered in a Member State, respects the laws of that Member State it can benefit from the legal certainty of circulating freely throughout the European Union irrespective of the laws of the other Member States). According to the case law of the Court of Justice (ruling of 30.4.96 in case C-194/94), if a Member State failed to notify such a national rule, the rule would not be binding on economic operators.

Such a system of structured dialogue between national administrations and the Commission, founded on Single Market rules, has the advantage of making it possible to anticipate any problems arising from the development of on-line services and to provide immediate solutions.

During the year 1999, technical texts with an impact on the provision of these services as well as the free flow of personal data such as interception, access to traffic data systems, electronic signatures were notified [39].

2.5.5 Telecom review 1999

The Commission had to review the implementation and needs for adaptation of the legal instruments to the technological development in the telecommunications sector. The Commission focused in particular on the convergence of communication means. It proposed to create a simplified, clear and technology neutral legal framework. All necessary provisions should be contained in a framework directive which should be complemented by a few more specific directives, one of them on data protection. To this end, the Commission proposed to modify Directive 97/66/EC on privacy in the telecommunications sector. The Commission Communication launched a public consultation.

---

[39] http://europa.eu.int/comm/enterprise/tris/

2.5.6 Standardisation

As follow-up to preparatory meetings with European standardisation bodies, industry, data protection authorities, privacy experts and Member States as well as the discussions at various international conferences, the European Commission issued in 1999 a mandate to the EU standardisation bodies. The purpose of the mandate is to support the implementation of Directive 95/46/EC, both within the EU as at international level.

The first step is to provide an analysis and evaluation of the potential role of the European Standardization Organisations in support of Directive 95/46/EC. In particular, European consensus platforms may contribute to a smooth implementation of the Directive in the Member States and to improve the level of protection of individuals with regard to the processing of their personal data in third countries. Such activity could cover both substantive (data protection principles, enforcement and redress) and procedural aspects (open procedure, create "win-win" situations, enhance competition). It could include the development of codes of conduct and foster the development of privacy-enhancing technologies while responding to the need for a coherent system providing an adequate level of interoperability. With respect to international initiatives, the need arises to co-ordinate the European position in order to avoid frictions with the legal requirements as laid down by the Directive.

2.5.7 Privacy Enhancing Technologies

The European Commission promotes the concept of privacy enhancing technologies: for example by organising the Workshop on Data Protection and Technology on 20 October 1999 with speakers also from data protection authorities. Also during the preparation of the Information Society Technologies Work Programme 2000, it was proposed to include a specific action line on PETs and to use horizontal measures to accompany projects with impact on privacy.

2.5.8 Europol

The Council of the European Union adopted on 12 March 1999 rules governing the transmission of personal data by Europol to third States and third bodies.

3. THE COUNCIL OF EUROPE

The Council of Europe continued the work that it regularly carries out on the issue of data protection.

The Convention's Consultative Committee (T-PD) finalised its work on an amendment to Convention ETS No 108 allowing the European Communities to accede to Convention ETS No 108. This amendment was adopted by the Committee of Ministers on 15 June 1999 and opened for acceptance by all parties. The Committee further continued its work on a Draft Additional Protocol to Convention ETS No 108 regarding supervisory authorities and transborder data flows. The project group on data protection (CJ-PD) adopted on 15 October 1999 a Draft Recommendation on the protection of personal data collected and processed for insurance purposes, while the drafting of its Explanatory Memorandum was to be finished in 2000. Recommendation No. R (99) 5 for the protection of privacy on the Internet was adopted by the Committee of Ministers on 23 February 1999. The Group delivered its opinions regarding the Parliamentary Assembly's Recommendation 1402 (1999) on the Control of Security Services, the draft Convention on Cybercrime, and prepared a Draft Opinion on the second Additional Protocol to the European Convention on Mutual Assistance on Criminal Matters.

The Community, represented by the Commission, intervenes within both the CJ-PD and the Consultative Committee when the items under discussion fall within the external competencies resulting from Directives 95/46/EC and 97/66/EC. This was the case for the texts referred to above. This co-operation with the Council of Europe aims to ensure full compatibility with Community directives.

4. PRINCIPAL DEVELOPMENTS IN THIRD COUNTRIES

4.1 European Economic Area

The EEA Joint Committee adopted two Decisions incorporating Directive 95/46/CE and 97/66/CE to the Agreement on the European Economic Area40. They impose the obligation on the EFTA/EEA countries to transpose the Directives and they extend the free movement of personal data provided for in Article 1 of the Directive 95/46/EC to the whole of the European Economic Area.[40] The decisions further lay down a special procedure for the implementation by the EFTA/EEA countries of the Commission decisions on third country adequacy. However, the Joint Committee Decisions did not entered into force immediately, since Norway, Iceland and Liechtenstein had indicated the need for national procedures according to Article 103 of the EEA Agreement. Only when all three countries have notified the completion of their national procedure the EEA Joint Committee Decisions can enter into force and the Directives apply throughout the EEA.

4.1.1 Iceland

A. Legislative measures adopted in 1999 in your country under the first pillar of the EU

No legislative measures were adopted in Iceland in 1999 which had a specific impact on privacy and data protection.

---

[40] Decision No 83/1999 of 25 June 1999 amending Protocol 37 and Annex XI (Telecommunication services) to the EEA Agreement and Decision No 84/1999 of 25 June 1999 amending Annex XI (Telecommunication services) to the EEA Agreement

B. Changes made in Iceland under the second and third pillar of the EU

Iceland is not a member of the EU and does not therefore, under the EEA agreement, adopt measures under the second pillar of the EU. Further, Iceland adopts only those measures under the third pillar of the EU that have been accepted as a part of the EEA agreement. No changes were made in 1999 in Iceland in the area of data protection and privacy under the third pillar of the EU.

C. Major case law (national courts) /jurisprudence

Very few judicial cases in Iceland in 1999 dealt with issues of privacy and data protection, and none can be said to have had a cross border perspective. One of a few cases with a privacy protection perspective is the decision of the Supreme Court of Iceland in case no. 252/1998, which was rendered on 25 February, 1999. In the decision it was affirmed that the publication, in a book, of information regarding the private affairs of a patient constituded a punishable offence under section 230 of the General Penal Code.

D. Specific issues

There were no other specific issues.

E. Website

www.personuvernd.is

4.1.2 Norway

A. Legislative measures adopted in 1999 in your country under the first pillar of the EU

The Directive 95/46/EC was not yet implemented in national legislation. The Ministry of Justice was, at this stage, preparing the legislation for handling in the Parliament. The Directive 97/66/EC was partly implemented in the Telecommunication Act of 1995, though not the regulation concerning data protection and privacy. The Data Inspectorate worked on developing a regulation for the telecommunication sector. The objective of this work was to implement the Directive's regulation on data protection and privacy.

Other data protection legislation in 1999 under the first pillar in the EU.
The Act on the Schengen Information System (SIS) was passed through the Parliament in 1999. This Act regulates the processing of personal data in the SIS. Apart from this, there were not passed any legislation through Parliament with major impact on data protection and privacy.

B. Changes made in Iceland under the second and third pillar of the EU

Other data protection legislation in 1999 under the second and third pillar of the EU.

The Schengen Information system as mentioned above is also included in the third pillar of the EU. The Act on the Schengen Information System also includes regulation of data protection issues under the third pillar.

Apart from this, there were not passed any legislation through Parliament with major impact on data protection and privacy.

C. Major case law (national courts) /jurisprudence

In 1999, Cases concerning data protection issues were primarily decided by the Data Inspectorate with the Ministry of Justice as appeal body. The cases in 1999 have mostly been related to the fact whether or not the data subject's consent is required, and if so, what form the consent should have. The most important cases are:

- National Public Road Administration - The Data Inspectorate denied the transfer of data on smoking habits from the company health service to a hospital for research purposes without the acquiring the data subject's active consent prior to the transfer. The case was appealed to the Ministry of Justice which allowed the transfer with a presumed consent.
- American Express – The Data Inspectorate decided that an active written consent from the data subject is required in order to transfer transaction data from American Express to their cooperating partners. The Ministry of Justice affirmed the decision.
- Telenor Media AS – The Data Inspectorate decided that an active consent from the data subject was necessary in order to publish catalog data on the Internet. The Ministry of Justice affirmed the decision. These decisions were made applying the Norwegian Data Protection Act of 1978.

D. Specific issues

One important issue in 1999 was a case that was handled by the Supreme Court, concerning the Police access to IP-number data about customers of the telecommunication company Telenor. The issue was whether or not the Police need to acquire a warrant from a court of law before these data can be accessed. The Supreme Court concluded that a warrant was not necessary for the data in question. The decision was made applying the Telecommunication Act of 1995.

E. Website

Our Website can be found on the following address www.datatilsynet.no. It contains some basic information in English and English translation of the current legislation on data protection.

4.2 Acceeding Countries

For all the applicant countries, the reinforced pre-accession strategy aims at allowing integration of the Community 'acquis'. In this spirit, the accent is put both on the adoption of legislation as well as on the administrative structures necessary for its effective implementation, such as independent supervisory authorities. In most of the applicant countries legislative projects were under way in order to bring data protection legislation in line with the Community directives, either through adoption of new data protection acts or through amendments to existing legal texts. Slovenia adopted its Personal Data Protection Act on 8 July 1999. In Slovakia, the Personal Data Protection Inspection was established on 6 October 1999. On 21.4.1999, Poland signed the Council of Europe Convention for the protection of individuals with regard to automatic processing of personal data ETS No. 108.

4.3 United States of America

Safe Harbor (see in detail chapter 2.3.1.1)

4.4 Other third countries

4.4.1 Australia

The Commission has kept the Working Party fully informed of developments in Australia. During the first months of 1999, its services contributed with comments to the National Principles for the Fair Handling of Personal Information (NPFHPI), issued by the Federal Privacy Commissioner. The working party received copy of the Commission's services submission.

On the Working Party's 15 th meeting held on 30 March, the Commission informed the Working Party of having held a meeting on 3 rd March 1999 with Mr Norman Reaburn, Deputy Attorney General, whose office is presently working on draft legislation to cover the private sector.

In August, the Australian government released an information paper on the proposed legislation to back up self-regulatory schemes for the private sector to public comment. The Commission services contributed informally, and copied comments to the Working Party.

On 16 December 1999, the Federal Government announced that it would legislate to support and strengthen self-regulation. The proposed legislation is based on the Privacy Commissioner's "National Principles for the Fair Handling of information". This concept covers "*à la carte*" arrangements of codes plus default legislation for cases not covered by the codes. This would ensure a minimum uniform standard throughout Australia. Codes would have to be approved by the Privacy Commissioner.

4.4.2 Canada

Canada is in the process of adopting the "Personal Information Protection and Electronic Documents Act". The Bill establishes a right to the protection of personal information collected, used or disclosed in the course of commercial activities and lays down the principles governing the processing of data. Furthermore, it provides for the Privacy Commissioner to receive complaints which - if unresolved - can be taken to the Federal Court. On 16 February 1999, the Commission's services forwarded its comments to Industry Canada, copy to the Working Party.

4.4.3 Japan

The Commission's services have been involved since 1998 in a high level dialogue with MITI representatives ("Ministry for international Trade and Industry") on the contents of the "MITI guidelines on the protection of computer processed personal data in the private sector". Meetings took place in March, July and September 1999. The working party was kept informed of progress in the discussions.

4.4.4 Hungary

see chapter 2.3.1.2.

4.4.5 Switzerland

see chapter 2.3.1.3.

5. OTHER DEVELOPMENTS AT INTERNATIONAL LEVEL

5.1 Organisation for Economic Co-operation and Development (OECD) Conference on electronic commerce

The OECD organized a Forum on Electronic Commerce in Paris on 12-13 October 1999. The main goal of this Conference was to assess progress on the three action plans decided in the Ottawa Ministerial Conference (October 1998). Therefore, the objectives of the meeting were threefold: a) to promote and strengthen the broadly based dialogue among the stakeholders in the digital economy which had begun in Ottawa; b) to take stock of progress in meeting commitments implementing the work described in the action plans developed in Ottawa (this took up the four themes that formed the "blueprint" of the Ottawa Ministerial Conference: "building trust", "enhancing the infrastructure", establishing the ground rules", and "maximising the benefits"; c) to assess priorities and share views on what remains to be accomplished in the light of the expanding global electronic marketplace. It was highlighted that the respect of privacy is one of the most important step for "building trust" of consumers and consequently to develop the Electronic commerce. The Report of the Forum is available at the following address: http://www.oecd.org//dsti/sti/it/ec/act/Paris_ec/pdf/forum_report.pdf

Contractual clauses for international transfers of personal data
After a first study by Mr Dix (Data Protection Commissioner, Brandenburg, Germany), the OECD commissioned to an expert (Elisabeth Longworth from New Zealand) a report on the use of *contractual solutions for transborder data flows* (TDBF); this report was discussed for the first time in the December' meeting of the Working Party on Information Security and Privacy (WPISP). The report was finally adopted in May 2000.

Privacy Wizard

In order to increase awareness among visitors about the privacy practices of Websites which they browse, the OECD, in co-operation with industry, privacy experts and consumer groups, decided to build an "html" Privacy Policy Statement Generator, called Wizard, based on the OECD Privacy Guidelines. The Wizard, fulfilling certain requirements, allow the Webmasters to develop a privacy policy and generate a privacy statement that informs visitors to a Website of an organisation's privacy policy. This Generator, finally adopted in 2000, is not a labelling procedure but only an educational tool which reflects solely the organisations' data protection practices.

5.2 World Trade Organisation (WTO)

In its work programme on electronic commerce, WTO also included data protection.

5.3 Word Intellectual Property Organisation (WIPO)

In the context of the development of the Internet Domain Name System, Commission services made comments to ICANN ((Internet Corporation for Assigned Numbers and Names) on the new registration process for the Internet Domain Name allocation, in particular on the ICANN model agreement between Registrars and Second level Domain Name applicants. Commission services also commented to WIPO on its proposals on trade mark protection and the allocation of domain names. Commission services started preparing a draft communication on the whole issue including the data protection aspects and a proposal for an EU top level domain [41] .

6. ANNEXES

I   Members of the Article 29 Data Protection Working Party
II   List of documents adopted by the Art. 29 Data Protection Working Party
         until 1999
III   Websites of national data protection authorities

Done at Brussels, 17 May 2001
For the Working Party
The Chairman
Stefano RODOTA

---

[41] COM(2000) 202 final; adopted on 11 April 2000.

Selected Bibliography

Books

Philip E. Agre and Marc Rotenberg, eds., *Technology and Privacy: the New Landscape* (Cambridge: MIT Press, 1997)

Ellen Alderman and Caroline Kennedy, *The Right to Privacy* (New York: Knopf, 1995)

Anita L. Allen, *Uneasy Access: Privacy for Women in a Free Society* (Totowa: Rowman and Littlefield, 1988)

David Banisar and Simon Davies, *Privacy and Human Rights: An International Survey of Privacy Laws and Developments* (Washington, DC: Global Internet Liberty Campaign 1998)

Colin J. Bennett, *Regulating Privacy: Data Protection and Public Policy in Europe and the United States* (Ithica: Cornell University Press, 1992)

Colin J. Bennet and Rebecca Grant, eds., *Visions of privacy: Policy Choices for the Digital Age* (Toronto: University of Toronto Press, 1999)

David Burnham, *The Rise of the Computer State* (New York: Random House, 1983)

Fred H. Cate, *Privacy in the Information Age* (Washington, DC: Brookings Institution Press, 1997)

Judith W. Decew, *In Pursuit of Privacy: Law, Ethics, and the Rise of Technology* (Ithaca and London: Cornell University Press, 1997)

Amitai Etzioni, *The Limits of Privacy* (New York: Basic Books, 1999)

David H. Flaherty, *Protecting Privacy in Surveillance Societies: the Federal Republic of Germany, Sweden, France, Canada, and the United States* (Chapel Hill: University of North Caroline Press, 1989)

Oscar H. Gandy, Jr., *The Panoptic Sort: A Political Economy of Personal Information* (Boulder: Westview Press, 1993)

Privacy Resources
Selected Bibliography

Simson Garfinkel. *Database Nation: The Death of Privacy in the 21st Century* (Cambridge: O'Reilly, 2000)

Jerry Kang, *Communications Law and Policy* (Aspen 2001)

David Lyon, *The Electronic Eye: The Rise of Surveillance Society* (Minneapolis: University of Minnesota Press, 1994)

Wayne Madsen, *Handbook of Personal Data Protection* (New York: Stockton Press, 1991)

James Michael, *Privacy and Human Rights* (UNESCO Publishing 1994)

Arthur Miller, *The Assault on Privacy: Computers, Data Banks and Dossiers* (Ann Arbor: University of Michigan Press, 1970)

A.C.M. Nugter, *Transborder Flow of Personal Data within the EC* (Deventer: Kluwer, 1990)

Vance Packard, *The Naked Society* (New York: McKay, 1964)

Priscilla M. Regan, *Legislating Privacy: Technology, Social Values, and Public Policy* (Chapel Hill: University of North Caroline Press, 1995)

Jeffrey Rosen, *The Unwanted Gaze: The Destruction of Privacy in America* (New York: Random House, 2000)

James B. Rule, *Private Lives and Public Surveillance: Social Control in the Computer Age* (London: Allen Lane, 1973)

Ferdinand D. Schoeman, ed., *Philosophical Dimensions of Privacy* (Cambridge: Cambridge University Press, 1984)

Paul M. Schwartz and Joel R. Reidenberg, *Data Privacy Law* (Charlottesville: Michie, 1996)

Robert Ellis Smith, Ben Franklin's Web Site: Privacy and Curiosity from Plymouth Rock to the Internet (Providence: Privacy Journal, 2000)

Philippa Strum, *Privacy: The Debate in the United States Since 1945* (Fort Worth: Harcourt Brace 1998)

Peter P. Swire and Robert E. Litan, *None of Your Business: World Data Flows, Electronic Commerce, & the European Privacy Directive* (Washington, DC: Brookings Institution 1998)

Richard Turkington and Anita L. Allen, *Privacy Law: Cases and Materials* (St. Paul: West Group, 1999)

Alan F. Westin, *Privacy and Freedom* (New York: Atheneum, 1967)

Reg Whitaker, *The End of Privacy: How Total Surveillance is Becoming a Reality* (New York: The New Press, 1999)

Law Review Symposia

Annual Survey of American Law, *Privacy Rights in Personal Information Issue* (1986)

Case Western Reserve Law Review, *Symposium: The Right to Privacy One Hundred Years Later* (1991)

Iowa Law Review, *Symposium: Data Protection Law and the European Union's Directive: The Challenge in the United States* (March 1995)

Stanford Law Review, *Cyberspace and Privacy: A New Legal Paradigm?* (June 2000) [http://www.stanford.edu/group/lawreview/symposium/index.html]

Privacy Resources

AGENCIES

Australia

Office of the Federal Privacy
Commissioner
Level 8
Piccadilly Tower
133 Castlereagh Street
Sydney NSW 2000
Australia
Tel 00 61 2 9284 9600
http://www.privacy.gov.au/

Austria

Büro der Datenschutzkommission und des
Datenshutzrates Bundeskanzleramt
Ballhausplatz, 1
A - 1014 WIEN
Tel 43 1 531 15 25 28

Belgium

Ministère de la Justice
Commission de la protection de la vie
privée
Avenu de la Porte de Hal 5-8
1060 BRUXELLES
Tel 32 2 542 72 00
http://www.privacy.fgov.be/

Canada

Privacy Commissioner of Canada
112 Kent Street, Ottawa Ontario
K1A 1H3
Tel 613 995 2410 or 1 800 267 0441
http://www.privcom.gc.ca/

Czech Republic

Urad pro Ochranu Osobnich Udaju
Havelkova 22
130, 00 Prague 3
Tel 420 2 21 00 84 42
http://www.uoou.cz/

Denmark

Registertilsynet
Christians Brygge, 28 - 4
DK - 1559 KOEBENHAVN V
Tel 45 33 14 38 44
http://www.datatilsynet.dk/

Estonia

Siseministeeriumi Andmekaitse Osakond
Vaike-Ameerika 19
10129 Tallinn
Tel 0 6 274 135
http://www.dp.gov.ee/

Finland

Office of the Data Protection
Ombudsman
P.O. Box 315
FIN-00181 Helsinki
Tel 358 9 18251
http://www.tietosuoja.fi/

France

Commission Nationale de l'Informatique
et des Libertés
Rue Saint Guillaume, 21
F - 75340 PARIS CEDEX 7
Tel 33 1 53 73 22 22
http://www.cnil.fr/

Germany

Der Bundesbeauftragte für den Datenschutz
Friedrich-Ebert-Straße 1,
53173 BONN
Tel (0228) 819 95 0
Fax (0228) 819 95 550
poststelle@bfd.bund400.de
http://www.bfd.bund.de/

Greece

Greek Data Protection Authority
8 Omirou Street
106 54 ATHENS
Tel 30 1 33 52 600
Fax 30 1 33 52 617
http://www.dpa.gr/ (in Greek)

Hong Kong

Privacy Commissioner's Office
Unit 2001, 20/F
Office Tower
Convention Plaza
1 Harbour Road
Wanchai
Tel 2827 2827
http://www.pco.org.hk/

Hungary

Parliamentary Commissioner for Data
Protection and Freedom of Information
1054 Budapest, Tüköry u. 3.
Tel 36 1 2693537
http://www.obh.hu/adatved/indexek/index.
htm

Iceland

Ministry of Justice Data Protection
Commission
Persónuvernd
Rau_arárstígur 10
105 Reykjavik
Tel 354 510 96 00
Rau_arárstígur 10
www.personuvernd.is

Ireland

Data Protection Commissioner
Irish Life Centre, Block 4
Talbot Street, 40
IRL - DUBLIN 1 Tel
Tel 353 1 874 85 44
http://www.dataprivacy.ie/

Privacy Resources
Agencies

Israel

Registrar of Databases
Ministry of Justice
29 Salah A-Din St.
91010 Jerusalem
Tel 972 26 24 5101
http://www.itpolicy.gov.il/laws/privacy.ht
m (in Hebrew)

Italy

Garante per la protezione dei dati personali
Piazza Monte Citorio
I - 00186 ROMA
Tel 00 39 6 696 77763
http://www.dataprotection.org/garante/

Japan

Management and Coordination Agency
3-1-1 Kasumigaseki, Chiyoda-ku
TOKYO 100 - 8905
Tel 81 3 3581 2128
Fax 81 3 3580 0760

Luxembourg

Commission à la Protection des Données
Nominatives
Ministère de la Justice
Boulevard Royal, 15
L - 2934
Tel 352 478 45 46

Lithuania

State Data Security Inspection
Gedimino pr. 27/2 Vilnius
Tel 8 22 22 75 32

Monaco

Commission de Contrôle des Informations
Nominatives
le "Gildo Pastor Center"
7, rue du Gabian - Bloc B
Bureau 409
98000 Monaco
Tel: 377 97 70 22 44

Netherlands

Registratiekamer
Prins Clauslaan 20
Postbus 93374
NL - 2509 AJ `s-GRAVENHAGE
Tel 31 70 381 13 00
http://www.registratiekamer.nl/

New Zealand

Office of the Privacy Commissioner
PO Box 466
Auckland
Tel 09 302 8680
http://www.knowledge-
basket.co.nz/privacy

Norway

Datatilsynet
The Data Inspectorate
P.B. 8177 Dep
N - 0034 OSLO
Tel 47 22 42 19 10
http://www.datatilsynet.no/

Poland

Office of the Inspector General for the
Protection of Personal Information
PL. Polstancow A-LY 1,
WARSAW
Tel 48 22 827 88 10
Fax 48 22 827 88 11
http://www.giodo.gov.pl/ (in Polish)

Portugal

Commissào Nacional de Protecçao de
Dados Pessoais Informatizados
R. de S. Bento, 148-3°
P - 1200-821 LISBOA
Tel 351 1 392 84 00
http://www.cnpd.pt/

Slovak Republic

Commissioner for the Protection of
Personal Data in Information Services
Statistical Office of the Slovak Republic
Dúbravská cesta 3
842 21 BRATISLAVA
Tel 421 7 59379 253
http://www.statistics.sk

Spain

Agencia de Protección de Datos
C/Sagasta, 22
28004 MADRID
Tel 91 399 62 00
http://www.ag-protecciondatos.es/

Sweden

Datainspektionen
Fleminggatan, 14
9th Floor
Box 8114
S - 104 20 STOCKHOLM
Tel 46/8/657.61.00
http://www.datainspektionen.se/in_english

Switzerlandd

Federal Data Protection Commissioner
Eidgenössischer Datenschutzbeauftragter
Feldeggweg 1
CH - 3003 Berne
Tel 41 31 322 4395
http://www.edsb.ch/

Taiwan

The Ministry of Justice
130 Sec 1 Chung Ching
South Road
TAIPEI 100 ROC 100
Tel 886 2 381 39 39

United Kingdom

The Office of the Data Protection
Registrar
Water Lane
Wycliffe House
WILMSLOW - CHESHIRE
SK9 5AF
Tel 44 1625 53 57 11
http://www.dataprotection.gov.uk/

NATIONAL LEGISLATION

Privacy Resources
National Legislation

References

Europa, "Data Protection, Implementation of Directive 95/46"
http://europa.eu.int/comm/internal_market/en/dataprot/law/impl.htm

EPIC and Privacy International, *Privacy and Human Rights: An International Survey of Privacy Laws and Developments*

PrivacyExchange, Index of National Law
http://www.privacyexchange.org/legal/nat/omni/

Privacy International, "Country Reports"
http://www.privacyinternational.org/countries/index.html

Albania
Law No. 8517/1999, on the Protection of Personal Data.

Argentina
Personal Data Protection Act of 2000
http://www.ulpiano.com/Dataprotection_argentina.htm

Australia
Privacy Act 1988
http://www.austlii.edu.au/au/legis/cth/consol_act/pa1988108/

Austria
Datenschutzgesetz (1978)
http://www.ad.or.at/office/recht/dsg.htm (in German)

Belgium
Belgium Data Protection Act of 1992
http://www.privacy.fgov.be/

Brazil

Habeas Data Act of 1997
http://www.ulpiano.com/Recusos_Privacidad_Ley%20brasilera.html (in Portuguese)

Canada
The Personal Information Protection and Electronic Documents Act (2000)
http://www.privcom.gc.ca/legislation/index_e.asp

Chile

Law for the Protection of Private Life of 1999

Cyprus

1999 Law on the Protection of Personal Data.

Czech Republic

Act of 6 June 2000 on the Protection of Personal Data

http://www.uoou.cz/eng/101_2000.php3

Act of 29 April 1992 on Protection of Personal Data in Information Systems

http://www.psp.cz/ (in Czech)

Denmark

The Act on Processing of Personal Data (2000)

http://www.datatilsynet.dk/eng/index.html

The Public Authorities' Registers Act (1991)

http://www.registertilsynet.dk/lovgivning/maina.html (in Danish)

The Private Registers Act (1987)

http://www.registertilsynet.dk/lovgivning/main1.html (in Danish)

Finland

Personal Data File Act (1999)

http://www.om.fi/1077.htm (in Finnish)

http://www.om.fi/1227.htm (English summary)

France

Law N° 78-17 Relating to Data Processing, Files and Freedoms (1978)

http://www.cnil.fr/textes/ttext.htm (in French)

Germany

Federal Data Protection Act (1977)

http://www.datenschutz-berlin.de/gesetze/bdsg/bdsgeng.htm

Greece

Law on the Protection of Individuals with regard to the Processing of Personal Data 1997

http://www.dpa.gr/2472.htm (in Greek)

Privacy Resources
National Legislation

Hungary

Data Protection and Freedom of Information Law (1992)
 http://www.obh.hu/adatved/indexek/index.htm

Iceland
Act Concerning the Registration and Handling of Personal Data (1989)
http://www.althingi.is/lagasofn/nuna/1989121.html (in Icelandic)

Ireland
Data Protection Act (1988)
http://www.dataprivacy.ie/6ai.htm

Israel
Protection of Privacy Law (1981)
http://www.law.co.il/computer-law/privacy_law_english.htm

Italy
Data Protection Act (1996)
http://www.privacy.it/indice675/indicealfa.html (in Italian)

Japan
Law for the Protection of Computer Processed Personal Data Held by Administrative Organs (1988)\

Lithuania
Data Protection Law of 1996
http://www.lrs.lt/cgi-bin/preps2?Condition1=38025&Condition2

Luxembourg
Act Regulating the Use of Nominal Data in Computer Processing (1979)

Macedonia
Data Protection Law of 1994

Monaco
Law No. 1165 of 1993 on Personally Identifiable Data.

Netherlands
Data Registration Act (1988)
http://www.unimaas.nl/~privacy/wpr.htm (in Dutch)

New Zealand

Privacy Act (1993)

 http://rangi.knowledge-basket.co.nz/gpacts/public/text/1993/an/028.html

Norway

Act No. 48 of 9 June 1978 Relating to Personal Data Filing Systems (1978)

http://www.datatilsynet.no/arkiv/engelsk/LOV-ENG.html

Paraguay

Law for the Protection of Personal Data in the Private Sector (2000)

http://www.ulpiano.com/habeasdaata_paraguay_Ley.htm (in Spanish)

Poland

Law on the Protection of Personal Data, 1997.

http://www.giodo.gov.pl/English/english.htm

Portugal

Act on the Protection of Personal Data (1998)

http://www.cnpd.pt (in Portuguese)

Russia

Federal Law on Information, Informatization, and Information Protection (1995)

http://www.datenschutz-berlin.de/gesetze/internat/fen.htm (excerpts)

Slovenia

Law on the Protection of Personal Data (1999)

http://www.statistics.sk/webdata/english/acts/act5298/act5298.htm

South Africa

Promotion of Access to Information Act of 2000

South Korea

Law on the Protection of Personal Data of 1994

Spain

Law 5/1992 of 29 October Relating to the Automated Processing of Personal Data (1992)

http://www.ag-protecciondatos.es/datd1.htm (in Spanish)

Sweden

Personal Data Ordinance (1998)

Privacy Resources
National Legislation

http://www.datainspektionen.se/in_english/
Personal Data Act (1998)
http://www.din.se/PDF-filer/ovrigt/pul-eng.pdf

Switzerland

Federal Act on Data Protection (1992)
http://edsb.ch/pdf/dsge.pdf

Taiwan

Computer-Processed Personal Data Protection Law of 11 August 1995 (1995)
Available at http://wjirs.judicial.gov.tw:8000/ (in Chinese)

Thailand

Thailand Official Information Act
http://www.krisdika.go.th/law/text/lawpub/e02092540/text.h)

United Kingdom

The Data Protection Act (1998)
http://www.hmso.gov.uk/acts/acts1998/19980029.htm

ORGANIZATIONS

US Organizations

American Civil Liberties Union
125 Broad Street, 18th Floor
New York, New York 10004-2400
Tel 1 212 549 2500
http://www/aclu.org

The American Civil Liberties Union is the United States foremost advocate of individual rights -- litigating, lobbying, and educating the public on a broad array of issues affecting individual freedom in the United States.

Americans for Computer Privacy
http://www.computerprivacy.org/

Americans for Computer Privacy (ACP) is a coalition working to ensure that the privacy of all Americans' confidential files and communications is preserved and protected in the information age. ACP opposes new federal restrictions on the use of encryption products in the U.S. and supports the sale of strong U.S. encryption products to customers around the world.

Better Business Bureau Online
BBB Online Privacy Program
4200 Wilson Boulevard, 8th Floor
Arlington, VA 2220
Tel 1 703 247 9336 (Privacy Seal Program)
Tel 1 888 679 3353 (Online Privacy Dispute Resolution Intake Center
Fax 1 703 276 8112
http://www.bbbonline.org/businesses/privacy/index.html

The BBBOnLine Privacy program will feature verification, monitoring and review, consumer dispute resolution, a compliance seal, enforcement mechanisms and an educational component.

Center for Democracy and Technology
1634 Eye Street NW, Suite 1100
Washington, DC 20006
Tel 1 202 637 9800
Fax 1 202.637 0968
http://www.cdt.org/

The Center for Democracy and Technology works to promote democratic values and constitutional liberties in the digital age.

Center for Media Education
2120 L Street, NW Suite 200
Washington, DC 20037
Tel 1 202 331 7833
Fax 1 202 331 7841
cme@cme.org
http://www.cme.org
http://kidsprivacy.org/ (Children's privacy)

The Center for Media Education is a nonprofit research and advocacy organization founded in 1991 to educate the public and policymakers about critical media policy issues.

Consumers Against Supermarket Privacy Invasion and Numbering
http://www.nocards.org

Privacy Resources
Organizations

C.A.S.P.I.A.N. seeks to raise awareness of the privacy implications of supermarket "value cards" which collect information on consumers' habits, while providing them with discounts on food items.

Consumer Project on Technology
P.O. Box 19367
Washington, DC 20036
Tel 1 202.387.8030
Fax 1 202.234.5176
http://www.cptech.org/

CPT is involved with issues of intellectual property rights with respect to public health, antitrust enforcement, telecommunications policy, privacy, and electronic commerce.

Electronic Privacy Information Center
1718 Connecticut Ave., NW Suite 200
Washington, DC 20009
Tel 1 202 483 1140 (tel)
Fax 1 202 483 1248 (fax)
info@epic.org
http://www.epic.org/

EPIC is a public interest research center in Washington, D.C. It was established in 1994 to focus public attention on emerging civil liberties issues and to protect privacy, the First Amendment, and constitutional values.

Harvard Information Infrastructure Project
John F. Kennedy School of Government
79 John F. Kennedy Street
Cambridge, Massachusetts 02138
Tel 1 617 495 1960
Fax 1 617 495 5776
http://www.ksg.harvard.edu/iip

The HIIP provides a neutral, interdisciplinary forum for addressing a wide range of emerging policy issues relating to information infrastructure, its development, use, and growth. The HIIP convenes experts from government, industry, and academia and draws on the perspectives and insights of policy-makers, managers, economists, lawyers, political scientists, and technologists in pursuit of its mission to advance the understanding of emerging issues related to the development of information infrastructure.

Health Privacy Project
Institute for Health Care Research and Policy
Georgetown University
2233 Wisconsin Ave., NW, Suite 525
Washington, DC 20007
Tel 1 202 687 0880
Fax 1 202 687 3110
http://www.healthprivacy.org

The Health Privacy Project is dedicated to raising public awareness of the importance of ensuring health privacy in order to improve health care access and quality, both on an individual and a community level.

Junkbusters
http://www.junkbusters.com/
ideas@junkbusters.com

Junkbusters Corp. helps consumers defend themselves against intrusive marketing and protect their privacy online. The company provides resources for stopping telemarketing calls, unwanted physical mail, junk email, and commercial invasions of privacy on the Internet. Its privacy-enhancing software, the Internet Junkbuster Proxy (TM), blocks unwanted cookies and banner ads.

Model State Public Health Privacy Project
Georgetown University Law Center
Washington, DC
http://www.critpath.org/msphpa/privacy.htm

The purpose of the Model State Public Health Privacy Project is to develop a model state law addressing privacy and confidentiality issues arising from the collection, use, and dissemination of health information by public health departments at the state and local levels. A principal goal is to develop of a model privacy law that facilitates national HIV reporting by protecting the confidential, identifiable information held by public health departments against unauthorized publication and uses without significantly limiting the ability of departments to use such information for legitimate public health objectives at present and in the future.

Privacy Resources
Organizations

National Coalition for Patients Rights
c/o Maine Civil Liberties Union
401 Cumberland Avenue, Portland, ME 04101
Tel 1 207 774 8800
Fax 1 207 774 1103
ncpr@nationalcpr.org
http://www.nationalcpr.org/

National CPR is a non-profit organization dedicated to the premise that patients have the right to privacy when they consult a health-care professional. CPR believes that the interests of employers, insurers, government agencies, police and others should not be allowed to supersede that basic right.

Online Privacy Alliance
http://www.privacyalliance.org/

The Online Privacy Alliance is a group of corporations and associations who have come together to introduce and promote business-wide actions that create an environment of trust and foster the protection of individuals' privacy online.

Privacy Foundation
Mary Reed Building
2199 S. University Blvd.
Denver, CO 80208
Tel 303 871 4971
Fax 303 871 7971
http://www.privacyfoundation.org/

The Privacy Foundation exists to educate the public, in part by conducting research into communications technologies and services that may pose a threat to personal privacy. The foundation will attempt to be fair and objective in its research projects and public reports.

Privacy Rights Clearinghouse
3100 - 5th Ave., Suite B
San Diego CA 92103
Tel 1 619 298 3396
Fax 1 619 298 5681
prc@privacyrights.org
http://www.privacyrights.org/

The Privacy Rights Clearinghouse is a nonprofit consumer information and advocacy program. It offers consumers an opportunity to learn how to protect their personal privacy and publications that provide information on a variety of informational privacy issues, as well as practical tips on safeguarding personal privacy.

Privacy Forum
lauren@vortex.com
Tel 1 818 225 2800
http://www.vortex.com/privacy.htm

The Privacy Forum includes a moderated e-mail digest for the discussion and analysis of issues relating to the general topic of privacy in the information age of the 1990's and beyond.

Truste
10080 N. Wolfe Road, SW3-160
Cupertino, CA 95014
Tel 1 408 342 1940
Fax 1 408 3421950
info@truste.org
http://www.truste.org/

Online privacy seal program. Web site offers advice and information about online privacy. Trustmark program awards seals to Web sites that meet privacy policy requirements and enforcement criteria. Licensed Web sites are required to post privacy statements.

International Organizations

BEUC
The European Consumer Organisation
Avenue de Tervueren, 36/
B-1040 Brussels
BELGIUM
Tel 32 2 743 15 90
Fax 32 2 735 74 55
consumers@beuc.org
http://www/beuc.org

BEUC, the European Consumers' Organisation, is the Brussels based federation of independent national consumer organisations from all the Member States of the EU and from other

Privacy Resources
Organizations

European countries. BEUC's job is to try to influence, in the consumer interest, the development of EU policy and to promote and defend the interests of all European consumers.

Consumers International
Head Office
24 Highbury Crescent
London
N5 1RX
UNITED KINGDOM
Tel 44 171 226 6663
Fax 44 171 354 0607
consint@consint.org
http://www.consumersinternational.org/

A worldwide non-profit federation of consumer organisations, dedicated to the protection and promotion of consumer interests.

Cyber-Rights & Cyber-Liberties
http://www.cyber-rights.org/

Cyber-Rights & Cyber-Liberties (UK) is a non-profit civil liberties organisation founded in 1997. Its main purpose is to promote free speech and privacy on the Internet and raise public awareness of these important issues. Includes extensive materials on Internet-related civil liberties issues, encryption, and police surveillance.

Global Internet Liberty Campaign
http://www.gilc.org

International coalition of NGOs involved with privacy, free speech, encryption and other Internet related issues.

International Helsinki Federation for Human Rights
Wickenburgg. 14/7,
A-1080 Vienna, AUSTRIA
Tel. 43 1 408 88 22
Fax 43 1 408 88 22-50
office@ihf-hr.org
http://www.ihf-hr.org/

The International Helsinki Federation for Human Rights is a self-governing group of non-governmental, not-for-profit organizations that act to protect human rights throughout Europe,

North America, and the Central Asian republics formed from the territories of the former Soviet Union.

Human Rights Watch
350 Fifth Ave
34th Floor
New York, N.Y. 10118
http://www.hrw.org/

Human Rights Watch is dedicated to protecting the human rights of people around the world. Web sites includes comprehensive information about human rights campaigns around the globe.

Internet Privacy Coalition
http://www.privacy.org/ipc/

The mission of the Internet Privacy Coalition is to promote privacy and security on the Internet through widespread public availability of strong encryption and the relaxation of export controls on cryptography.

Privacy International
London, UK
pi@privacy.org
http://www.privacyinternational.org/

Privacy International is a human rights group formed in 1990 as a watchdog on surveillance by governments and corporations. PI is based in London, UK and has an office in Washington, D.C. PI has conducted campaigns in Europe, Asia and North America to counter abuses of privacy by way of information technology such as telephone tapping, ID card systems, video surveillance, data matching, police information systems, and medical records.

PUBLICATIONS

Privacy Resources
Publications

US Publications

Access Reports
1624 Dogwood Lane
Lychnburg, VA 24503
Tel 1 804 384 5334
Fax 1 804 384 8272
hhammitt@accessreports.com
http://www.accessreports.com/

Electronic Commerce & Law Report
Bureau of National Affairs
1231 25th St., NW
Washington, DC 20037-1197
Tel 1 202 4524200
http://www.bna.com/e-law/

PX Newsflash
Privacy and American Business
Two University Plaza, Suite 414
Hackensack, NJ 07601.
Tel 1 201 996 1154
http://www.privacyexchange.org/

Privacy Journal
P.O. Box 28577
Providence, RI 02908
Tel 1 401 274 7861
5101719@mcimail.com.
http://www.townonline.com/privacyjourna
l/

Privacy Newsletter
PO Box 8206
Philadelphia PA 19101-8206
privacy@mindspring.com

Privacy Times
P.O. Box 21501

Washington, DC 21501
Tel 1 202 829-3660
http://www.privacytimes.com/

International Publications

Computer Law & Security Report
Elsevier Advanced Technology
PO Box 150
Kidlington, Oxford OX5, 1AS
UNITED KINGDOM
Tel 44 1865 843848/843000
Fax 44 1865 843971
s.j.saxby@soton.ac.uk
http://www.elsevier.nl/locate/complaw

ISPI Clips
Institute for the Study of Privacy Issues
Victoria, British Columbia
CANADA
ISPI4Privacy@ama-gi
ISPI4Privacy@earthlink.net

Privacy Files
Progesta Publishing Inc
1788 d'Argenson, Ste-Julie
Quebec
CANADA J3E 1E3
privacy.files@progesta.com
Tel 1 514 922 9151
Fax 1 514 922 9152

Privacy Laws and Business
Roxeth House, Shaftesbury Avenue,
Harrow, Middlesex
HA2 0PZ, United Kindgom.
Tel 44181 4231300
Fax 44181 423 4536
Info@privacylaws.co.uk
http://www.privacylaws.co.uk

Privacy Law and Policy Reporter
Level 11, Carlton Centre
55-63 Elizabeth Street
Sydney, NSW 2000, Australia
Tel 61 2 221 6199
http://www.austlii.edu.au/au/other/plpr/

Reports

15th Annual Report of the Data Protection
Registrar, United Kingdom
http://wood.ccta.gov.uk/dpr/dpdoc.nsf

Report of the Dutch Data Protection
Commission
http://www.registratiekamer.nl/bis/top_2_
11.html

Privacy Online: Fair Information Practices
in the Electronic Marketplace
Federal Trade Commission Report to
Congress (May 2000)
http://www.ftc.gov/os/2000/05/index.htm
#22

WEB SITES

General Interest

Anonymity and Privacy on the Internet
http://www.stack.nl/~galactus/remailers/

This site gives you information on how to be anonymous, and how to secure your communications and files from third parties, as well as several other important security aspects that may arise when you are on the Internet.

Anti-Telemarketer.Com
http://www.antitelemarketer.com

If you've had your dinner interrupted one too many times, this website dedicated to eradicating telemarketers' hold over your time may be for you. The site explores a number of ways to reduce the calls you get, as well as providing forums in which you may express your grievances against the corporate establishment.

Bacard's Privacy Page
http://www.andrebacard.com/privacy.html

Privacy Resources
Web Sites

Bacard's Privacy Page offers practical links to maintaining private e-mail, private computer files, and private finances.

Roger Clarke's Dataveillance and Information Privacy Pages
http://www.anu.edu.au/people/Roger.Clarke/DV/

Data Surveillance (Dataveillance) is the systematic use of personal data systems in the investigation or monitoring of the actions or communications of one or more persons. This Page discusses "Current Hot Topics" on Dataveillance, provides links to major electronic resources and e-lists, e-newsletters, and e-zines.

Computers, Freedom, and Privacy Conference 2000
http://www.cfp2000.org/program/full-program.html

The CFP Page provides information on past and upcoming conferences on "Computers, Freedom, and Privacy." It also contains links to conference newsletters, reports, and papers.

The Dutch Privacy Page
http://home.planet.nl/~privacy1/

This site is dedicated to Privacy Law. The Privacy Page has links to international treaties concerning privacy, Dutch (privacy) law, various national Privacy Commissioners and links to other privacy sites on the Web.

Echelon Watch
http://www.aclu.org/echelonwatch/index.html

Run by the American Civil Liberties Union, this website is dedicated to providing information on Echelon, the controversial communications surveillance system run by the United States in concert with Canada and several European countries. Gives good general information on Echelon, as well as providing updates on government measures dealing with Echelon around the world.

EPIC Online Guide to Privacy Resources
http://www.epic.org/privacy/privacy_resources_faq.html

This site contains links to printed publications, US and international privacy sites, and electronic mailing lists and newsgroups. It also contains information about upcoming privacy related conference and events.

EPIC Bookstore
http://www.epic.org/bookstore/

At EPIC Bookstore you will find all of EPIC's past and present publications on issues such as privacy, cryptography, free speech and consumer protection. You will also find links to a wide range of other books recommended by EPIC.

Law of Information Privacy
http://www.epic.org/misc/gulc/

This site contains a description of the Law of Information Privacy course taught at Georgetown University. It contains links to recent privacy cases, privacy articles, and a bibliography of books on privacy and related topics.

Politics of Information
http://sitka.dcf.uvic.ca/poli/bennett/courses/456/

Politics of Information contains a Privacy Archive of over 230 unique links and serves as a valuable resource for privacy related research.

Privacy Exchange
http://www.privacyexchange.org

Privacy Exchange is an online global resource for consumer privacy and data protection. It contains a library of privacy laws, practices, publications, websites and other resources concerning consumer privacy and data protection developments worldwide.

Privacy International
Country Reports
http://www.privacy.org/pi/countries/

The Privacy International website provides the latest news on privacy issues. It contains a list of country reports concerning privacy laws and online reports. The site also provides information about past conferences and activities.

The Privacy Journal
http://www.townonline.com/privacyjournal/

Privacy Journal is a monthly newsletter reporting on new technology and its impact on personal privacy. The site gives tips on how to protect privacy and provides an outline of Model Privacy Policies.

Privacy Resources
Web Sites

The Privacy Page
http://www.privacy.org/

Privacy.org provides the latest news on privacy related issues. It contains links to other privacy sites. It also provides access to previous articles concerning privacy.

Privacy Scan Reports
http://www.retrace.com

www.privacy.it

A project of Polytecna, an independent group of Italian technology professionals, www.privacy.it operates as a clearinghouse site on global internet privacy and security law. Its links section gives a rundown of most of the national legislation on privacy, as well as links to the homepages of various national data protection authorities. The site is in Italian.

Protect Personal Privacy in Korea
http://kpd.sing-kr.org/idcard/main-e.html

Ulpiano.com
http://www.ulpiano.com

Searchable Spanish-language database on cyberlaw issues. Especially useful for researching cyberlaw in South America, but the listings are global. Strong attention paid to privacy issues.

Stop Carnivore
http://www.stopcarnivore.org

Site urging action against the FBI's Carnivore program. Contains useful information on how Carnivore functions, what it can accomplish, and on privacy tools in general.

The Virtual Law Firm
http://vlf.juridicum.su.se

The Virtual Law Firm is a project of the University of Stockholm. It aims to be a clearinghouse site on global cyberlaw issues. Makes available papers and law review articles on national data protection legislation, as well as other privacy initiatives. This site is in English.

Yahoo! Full Coverage "Internet Privacy"
http://headlines.yahoo.com/Full_Coverage/Tech/Internet_Privacy/

This site provides extensive coverage of current news pertaining to privacy issues. It also provides access to other privacy related sites.

Yahoo's Privacy Resources
http://www.yahoo.com/Government/Law/privacy/

A general links-clearinghouse site with links to major privacy websites and government information. Evenhanded coverage of different points of view, plus links to Usenet discussion groups.

Government

The 23rd International Conference on Privacy and Data Protection (Paris)
http://www.paris-conference-2001.org/

The 22nd International Conference on Privacy and Data Protection (Venice)
http://www.dataprotection.org/

The 21st International Conference on Privacy and Personal Data Protection (Hong Kong)
http://www.pco.org.hk/english/infocentre/conference.html

Information regarding the 21st International Conference on Privacy and Personal Data Protection is available through the pco.org website. The site includes links to reports presented at the conference and other information about privacy in Hong Kong.

The 19th International Conference on Privacy and Personal Data Protection (Brussels)
http://www.privacy.fgov.be/conference/

Information regarding the 19th International Conference on Privacy and Personal Data Protection is available here. The site includes links to papers, reports, and subjects of the conference.

The European Commission
"Media, Information Society, and Date Protection"
http://europa.eu.int/comm/internal_market/en/media/index.htm

Privacy Resources
Web Sites

This website offers information about and links to issues relating to information society, electronic commerce, electronic signatures, data protection, commercial communications, and infringements.

The European Parliament
Temporary committee on the Echelon interception system
http://www.europarl.eu.int/committees/echelon_home.htm
Final Draft Report on Echelon
http://www.europarl.eu.int/tempcom/echelon/prechelon_en.htm

Includes the materials on the mission, studies, calendar of meetings and agenda, meeting documents, working documents, members, and the final draft report on Echelon.

Federal Trade Commission
Privacy Initiatives
http://www.ftc.gov/privacy/index.html

The FTC Privacy Initiatives page educates consumers and businesses about the importance of personal information privacy. It talks about FTC efforts, what they've learned, and what consumers can do to protect the privacy of their personal information. The site also contains news releases and online privacy reports to Congress.

Organization for Economic Cooperation and Development
Information and Communication Policy
http://www.oecd.org/dsti/sti/it/

The OECD's Information and Communication Policy site offers extensive list of reports released by the OECD about workshops, conferences and activities regarding e-commerce and internet communications.

Organization for Economic Cooperation and Development
Information Security and Privacy
http://www.oecd.org/dsti/sti/it/secur/

The OECD's Information Security and Privacy site provides reports and information about OECD workshops, conferences and activities concerning internet security.

Legal

Australasian Legal Information Institute
World: Subject Index: Privacy
http://www.austlii.edu.au/links/World/Subject_Index/Privacy/

Key features of this site include links to organizations, businesses, agencies that work in the area of privacy. It also offers information about individuals, decisions, and conferences pertaining to privacy.

EUR-Lex
European Union Law
http://www.europa.eu.int/eur-lex/en/index.html

This site provides links to European treaties, legislation, case law, and documents of interest.

Legal Information Institute
Cornell Law School
http://www.law.cornell.edu/

The Legal Information Institute provides access to constitutions and codes, court opinions, and law directories.

Library of Congress
"THOMAS "
http://thomas.loc.gov/

THOMAS provides extensive information about legislative activities. It contains Library of Congress Web links and information about the legislative process.

Organizations

American Civil Liberties Union
Freedom Network
Privacy
http://www.aclu.org/issues/privacy/hmprivacy.html

The ACLU website features privacy articles, news updates, privacy resources, privacy legislation under the 107th Congress.

Privacy Resources
Web Sites

Center for Media Education
"A Parents' Guide to Online Privacy"
http://kidsprivacy.org/

Key features of this site include information about COPPA and tips for guiding children online.

Computer Professionals for Social Responsibility
Privacy and Civil Liberties
http://www.cpsr.org/program/privacy/privacy.html

This site contains links to other privacy sites, CPSR's privacy archives and reports as well as information about CPSR's campaigns on privacy.

Electronic Frontiers Australia
"Campaign for Fair Privacy Laws"
http://efa.org.au/Issues/Privacy/

The EFA site contains information about and links to privacy laws, privacy campaign documents and general privacy reference materials.

Electronic Frontier Foundation
"Privacy, Security, Crypto, & Surveillance"
http://www.eff.org/pub/Privacy/

An extensive Privacy, Security, Cryptography and Surveillance archive

EPIC
Privacy Archive
http://www.epic.org/privacy/

EPIC's Privacy Archive contains an A to Z list of topics relating to privacy, general privacy information, and hot topics as well as new resources relating to privacy.

Foundation for Information Policy Research
http://www.fipr.org/

FIPR is an independent body that studies the interaction between information technology and society. The site contains news releases relating to privacy issues, information about conferences and presentations, research links, and a policy archive.

Privacy Rights Clearinghouse
Fact Sheets
http://www.privacyrights.org/fs/#English (in English)
http://www.privacyrights.org/FS/spanfs.htm (in Spanish)

The site contains fact sheets about workplace privacy, overcoming the emotional impact of identity theft, privacy in Cyberspace, online shopping tips, protecting financial privacy, and much more.

Statewatch
http://www.statewatch.org/

Statewatch monitors the state and civil liberties in the European Union. The site provides links to Statewatch online news and publications, information about openness and secrecy in the EU, information about the EU-FBI telecommunications surveillance plan, and a link to the Statewatch search database.

World Wide Web Consortium
Platform for Privacy Preference
P3P Project
http://www.w3.org/P3P/

This site contains information about P3P, current working drafts and notes relating to P3P, as well as papers, presentations, critiques, and media coverage concerning P3P.

INDEX OF PRIVACY RESOURCES

19th International Conference on Privacy and Personal Data Protection, 619

21st International Conference on Privacy and Personal Data Protection, 619

22nd International Conference on Privacy and Data Protection, 619

23rd International Conference on Privacy and Data Protection, 619

Access Reports, 614

Albania, 602

American Civil Liberties Union, 606, 621

Americans for Computer Privacy, 606

Anonymity and Privacy on the Internet, 615

Argentina, 602

Australasian Legal Information Institute, 621

Australia, 592, 598, 602

Austria, 538, 542, 560, 598, 602

Bacard's Privacy Page, 615

Belgium, 539, 543, 562, 598, 602

Better Business Bureau Online, 607

BEUC, 611

Brazil, 602

Canada, 593, 598, 602

Center for Democracy and Technology, 607

Center for Media Education, 607, 622

Chile, 603

Computer Law & Security Report, 614

Computer Professionals for Social Responsibility, 622

Computers, Freedom, and Privacy: The Global Internet, 616

Consumer Project on Technology, 608

Consumers Against Supermarket Privacy Invasion and Numbering, 607

Consumers International, 612

Cyber-Rights & Cyber-Liberties, 612

Cyprus, 603

Czech Republic, 598, 603

Denmark, 539, 543, 563, 598, 603

Dutch Privacy Page, 616

Echelon, 620

Electronic Commerce & Law Report, 614

Electronic Frontier Foundation, 622

Electronic Frontiers Australia, 622

Electronic Privacy Information Center, 608, 622

EPIC Bookstore, 617

EPIC Online Guide to Privacy Resources, 616

Estonia, 598

European Commission, 619

European Union Law, 621

Europol, 588

Federal Trade Commission, 615, 620

FEDMA, 558

Finland, 539, 543, 564, 599, 603

Foundation for Information Policy Research, 622

France, 539, 543, 567, 599, 603

Germany, 539, 543, 568, 599, 603

Global Internet Liberty Campaign, 612

Greece, 572, 599, 603

Harvard Information Infrastructure Project, 608

Health Privacy Project, 609

Hong Kong, 599

Human Rights Watch, 613

Hungary, 550, 599, 604

IATA, 558

Iceland, 590, 599, 604

International Helsinki Federation for Human Rights, 612

International Labour Office, 364

Internet Privacy Coalition, 613

Ireland, 541, 543, 599, 604

ISPI Clips, 614

Israel, 600, 604

Italy, 540, 543, 574, 600, 604

Japan, 593, 600, 604

Junkbusters, 609

Law of Information Privacy, 617

Legal Information Institute, 621

Library of Congress, 621

Lithuania, 600, 604

Luxembourg, 541, 543, 600, 604

Macedonia, 604

Model State Public Health Privacy
  Project, 609
Monaco, 600, 604
National Coalition for Patients Rights,
  610
Netherlands, 541, 544, 584, 600, 604, 615
New Zealand, 600, 605
Norway, 591, 600, 605
Online Privacy Alliance, 610
Organization for Economic Cooperation
  and Development, 594, 620
P3P, 555
Paraguay, 605
Poland, 601, 605
Politics of Information, 617
Portugal, 541, 543, 574, 601, 605
Privacy Enhancing Technologies, 588
Privacy Exchange, 617
Privacy Files, 614
Privacy Forum, 611
Privacy Foundation, 610
Privacy International, 613, 617
Privacy Journal, 614
Privacy Law and Policy Reporter, 615
Privacy Laws and Business, 615
Privacy Newsletter, 614
Privacy Page, 618
Privacy Rights Clearinghouse, 610, 623
Privacy Scan Reports, 618
Privacy Times, 614

Protect Personal Privacy in Korea, 618
PX Newsflash, 614
Roger Clarke's Dataveillance and
  Information Privacy Pages, 616
Russia, 605
Safe Harbor, 548
Slovak Republic, 601
Slovenia, 605
South Africa, 605
South Korea, 605
Spain, 541, 543, 580, 601, 605
Statewatch, 623
Stop Carnivore, 618
Sweden, 541, 544, 582, 601, 605
Switzerland, 549, 601, 606
Taiwan, 601, 606
Thailand, 606
The Privacy Journal, 617
The Virtual Law Firm, 618
Truste, 611
Ulpiano.com, 618
United Kingdom, 541, 544, 584, 601, 606,
  615
Word Intellectual Property Organisation
  (WIPO), 594
World Trade Organisation (WTO), 594
World Trade Organization (WTO), 362
World Wide Web Consortium, 623
Yahoo! Full Coverage "Internet Privacy",
  619